WORLD AT RISK

A Global Issues Sourcebook

CQ PRESS

A Division of Congressional Quarterly Inc.
Washington, D.C.

CQ Press
1255 22nd Street, N.W., Suite 400
Washington, DC 20037

202-822-1475; 800-638-1710

www.cqpress.com

♾ The paper used in this publication meets the minimum requirements of the American National Standard for Information Sciences—Permanence of Paper for Printed Library Materials, ANSI Z39.48-1992.

Editorial development by The Moschovitis Group, Inc., New York, New York

Interior design by Debra Naylor, Naylor Design Inc.
Typeset by Sheridan Books, Ann Arbor, Michigan
Cover design by Nadine Johnson

Printed and bound in the United States of America

06 05 04 03 02   5 4 3 2 1

Library of Congress Cataloging-in-Publication Data

World at risk : a global issues sourcebook.
p. cm.
Includes bibliographical references and index.
ISBN 1-56802-707-9 (hardcover : alk. paper)
1. International relations. 2. World politics—1989
3. Environmental policy. 4. Social history—21st century. I. CQ Press.
JZ1242 .W67 2002
300—dc21

2001008737

CONTENTS

TABLES, MAPS, AND FIGURE

TABLES

MAPS

FIGURE

CONTRIBUTORS

Tim Allman, Freelance Writer, Nottingham, United Kingdom

Suresh C. Babu, Senior Research Fellow, International Food Policy Research Institute

David E. Bloom, Clarence James Gamble Professor of Economics and Demography, Harvard School of Public Health

Daan Bronkhorst, Staff Writer, Amnesty International, Netherlands

David Canning, Professor of Economics, Queen's University, Belfast

Bruce Cronin, Assistant Professor of Political Science, University of Wisconsin, Madison

James Heintz, Professor, Political Economy Research Institute, University of Massachusetts, Amherst

Anya Hogoboom, Graduate Student, Department of Linguistics, University of California, Santa Cruz

Edward Kissi, Visiting Assistant Professor, Department of History and Center for Holocaust and Genocide Studies, Clark University

Ulla Larsen, Associate Professor of Demography, Harvard School of Public Health

David Leheny, Assistant Professor of Political Science, University of Wisconsin, Madison

Stephen C. Lubkemann, Assistant Professor of Anthropology, George Washington University

Scott B. Martin, Consultant and Lecturer on International Affairs, Columbia University

Erin McCandless, Co-Executive Editor, *Journal of Peacebuilding and Development*

Timothy L. H. McCormack, Australian Red Cross Professor of International Humanitarian Law, University of Melbourne

Richard B. Norgaard, Professor of Energy and Resources, University of California, Berkeley

Henry J. Rutz, Professor of Anthropology, Hamilton College

Tamara Schuyler, Freelance Writer, Santa Cruz, California

Mary Hope Schwoebel, Adjunct Faculty, Justice and Peace Program, Georgetown University

J. Peter Scoblic, Editor, *Arms Control Today*

Murat Somer, Mellon-Sawyer Fellow, Henry M. Jackson School of International Studies, University of Washington

Eric Stover, Director, Human Rights Center, University of California, Berkeley

Aili Tripp, Associate Professor of Political Science and Women's Studies, and Director, Women's Studies Research Center, University of Wisconsin, Madison

Catherine Weaver, Research Fellow, Foreign Policy Studies, Brookings Institution

Kar-yiu Wong, Professor of Economics, University of Washington

Chris Woodford, Co-founder, UK Rivers Network, and Freelance Writer, Staffordshire, United Kingdom

PREFACE

As economic and cultural connections bring countries closer every day and make their relations more complex, the issues that affect one region of the world quickly become the concerns of everyone everywhere. *World at Risk: A Global Issues Sourcebook* provides introductory analysis and reference material on thirty key issues facing the world today, including those in the fields of economics, the environment, human development, law, politics, and security.

The structure of each chapter allows readers to compare the different issues and their components. The discussions move from general analysis to detailed assessments on regional and national levels. Each topic lends itself to a cross-disciplinary approach. For example, human development issues, such as health, also relate to topics in economics, such as income inequality and development aid. Cross-references help readers navigate these cross-disciplinary pathways.

Because of the interconnectedness of today's world, some overlap among the issues featured here is necessary. For instance, the chapter "Pollution" discusses air, water, and terrestrial pollution, while "Global Warming" explores one particularly troublesome aspect of pollution on a global scale. Such is also the case with "AIDS," "Epidemics," and "Health." Some of the issues covered in "Health"—which offers an overview of the range of concerns arising from health conditions throughout the world—overlap with those in "AIDS" and "Epidemics," two topics that warrant more focused discussion because of their seriousness.

Each chapter opens with a summary describing the importance of that particular issue to the world community. Historical Background and Development follows this introduction, providing readers with an understanding of the historical context in which the contemporary issue has developed. Next, in Current Status, authors review the state of research on the issue and discuss how it defines the topic; they also address the policies and programs being undertaken in response to the issue's impact. These discussions explore a wide range of thoughts and practices, some of which are controversial.

The next section, Regional Summaries, which includes a map to supplement the analysis presented, ranges from general assessments to specific examples of how the issue plays out in different areas of the world. Regional categories differ between chapters because of variations in how researchers approach their subjects. For example, researchers studying environmental issues divide the world into regions that differ from those devised by researchers analyzing economic issues or arms control.

Next, the Data section provides tabulated information to further illustrate the topic under discussion. In most cases, the statistics and other material in this section derive from generally accepted sources; the nomenclature and presentation have been standardized throughout. Sources are provided for each table should readers want to refer to the data sets in their entirety. In a few instances, however, the data presented are complete, having been researched and compiled by the author.

The Case Study section brings the issue into sharper focus. Here the authors illustrate how the general research and policy parameters being discussed have manifested in specific situations and countries, instructing the reader through example.

Helpful reference sections follow the case studies: short biographies of researchers, policymakers, and political leaders and activists who have had an impact on current research and policymaking; a directory of government agencies, nongovernmental and multinational organizations, and research institutions that includes a mission statement and contact information for each group; and a bibliography of books, articles and reports, and Web sites to guide the reader to the sources used and to augment further investigation. Each chapter closes with extracts from treaties, conventions, and reports crucial to the development of the international community's understanding of and response to the issue at hand. Sources for accessing the full texts are provided in this section or, occasionally, in the bibliography.

A detailed index concludes the volume, offering various points of entry to the issues since researchers come to them from assorted angles and with different questions in mind. For instance, in researching AIDS, a reader might go directly to the chapter on AIDS or, alternatively, might approach the topic through index entries on specific regions or countries, manifestations of the disease, or the economic or social consequences of the pandemic.

The statistical sources are incorporated in the text, and citations for these sources, if written reports, articles, or books, appear in the bibliography. In-text sources for widely accepted data and those that are considered part of the historical record have not been included. Occasionally, authors cite statistics from the tables in the Data section; in these cases, they omit in-text citations. The authors have made every effort to present the most up-to-date information and analysis possible. It is expected that updated editions will be published periodically.

For the Moschovitis Group, executive editor Valerie Tomaselli supervised editorial development of *World at Risk*, and Sonja Matanovic served as editorial coordinator and Rashida Allen as production assistant. Illustrator Richard Garratt drafted the maps. For CQ Press, acquisitions editor Adrian Forman and assistant editor Grace Hill worked with the Moschovitis Group to finalize the content and format of the book. Project editor Robin Surratt copyedited the manuscript, and production editor Belinda Josey coordinated proofreading and indexing.

AIDS

Tamara Schuyler

According to recent estimates by the National Institutes of Health, every day fourteen thousand people become infected with HIV (human immunodeficiency virus), which causes AIDS (acquired immunodeficiency syndrome). More than 21 million people have died of AIDS since the first cases were reported in 1981 (see Table 1), and according to the Joint United Nations Programme on HIV/AIDS (UNAIDS), 40 million people were estimated to be living with HIV at the end of 2001.

HIV attacks the immune system and makes those people carrying it susceptible to diseases they would ordinarily ward off. People living with AIDS suffer immensely. AIDS-related deaths leave behind thousands of orphans every year, and the epidemic threatens the economic development of many nations. AIDS is more prevalent in some areas of the world than others, but no one is immune to HIV infection. Without international cooperation to stem rising infection rates and develop a vaccine, AIDS will continue to spread its devastation globally.

Historical Background and Development

The origins of HIV are unclear. Because of the remarkably high rates of HIV infection in sub-Saharan African countries relative to the rates in other regions, HIV is thought by most scientists to have originated in Africa. There are two widely accepted theories regarding the source of the epidemic. One is that HIV has existed for the past one hundred years in small, isolated human populations and that it was introduced into the broader population in the 1970s as these isolated communities came into more frequent contact with outsiders. A second theory is that HIV originated in animals and crossed into the human population sometime during the last forty or fifty years, perhaps through contact with animal blood while hunting or slaughtering. The virus is believed to have spread to other continents through infected tourists, migratory workers, and military personnel.

On 5 June 1981, the Centers for Disease Control and Prevention (CDC) reported the deaths of five young men due to *Pneumocystis carinii* pneumonia, a disease that is rarely fatal. In July 1981, the CDC reported a similarly unusual incident: twenty-six young men had been diagnosed with Kaposi's sarcoma, a cancer normally found among older men. It was later assumed that these two groups of men died of the disease that became known as AIDS. Earlier, in December 1977, a Danish physician who had worked in Zaire died of *Pneumocystis carinii* pneumonia. She is assumed to have been infected with HIV and to have died of AIDS.

In 1982 the newly recognized disease was officially designated AIDS, and it was discovered that the disease-causing virus could be transmitted through infected blood and blood products, through sexual intercourse, and from mother to child (MTCT). By 1983 it was clear to health care officials that an AIDS epidemic had erupted in Africa, fueled almost exclusively by heterosexual transmission; by 1984 every region in the world had reported cases of AIDS. Epidemic proportions were not reached in other parts of the world until later in the decade. In the United States, despite an exponentially increasing number of AIDS deaths in the early 1980s, it was not until 1986, when Surgeon General C. Everett Koop issued a report on the epidemic, that the public became widely aware of it. By the late 1980s, around the globe, the epidemic was raging in high-risk populations—intravenous drug users, men who have sex with men, and commercial sex workers—and was beginning to take hold among other populations.

In January 1983 a team of researchers led by Luc Montagnier of the Pasteur Institute in Paris isolated the virus presumed to be responsible for suppressing the immune system of AIDS patients. They named the virus lymphoadenopathy-associated virus (LAV), because they had isolated it in a patient with lymphoadenopathy, or swollen lymph glands. In 1984 Robert Gallo of the National Cancer Institute in the United States and a team of scientists also isolated a virus associated with AIDS, which they named third human T-cell lymphotropic virus (HTLV III). By 1985 the scientific community had agreed on the name human immunodeficiency virus for the virus that causes AIDS.

AIDS is not a single disease, but a condition consisting of a compromised immune system weakened by HIV plus the illnesses and diseases resulting from it. Once inside the body, HIV multiplies and attacks the immune system's T-cells, also known as CD4. The onset of opportunistic illnesses usually takes years. Early in the epidemic, the characteristics of the disease made it difficult to define, and several distinct definitions were adopted through the 1980s. This affected the early surveillance and treatment of patients as well as incidence reporting. In 1993, when the current definition of AIDS was adopted—infection with HIV plus a CD4 count below 200 or the presence of one or more opportunistic infections or both—the reported incidence went up worldwide due to the increased number of people whose condition fit the new definition. The Harvard Global AIDS Policy Coalition estimated in 1992 that the global incidence of the disease had been about a hundred thousand in 1981 and that by 1992 it had reached 12.9 million. At the end of 2000 authorities estimated that 36.1 million people were living with AIDS (see Table 2 and map, p. 8).

In March 1985 the first test was introduced in the United States for detecting HIV. Infection was confirmed by the presence of HIV antibodies in the blood; antibodies are made by the immune system to help protect the body from foreign invaders, such as viruses. The new test enabled scientists to check frozen blood samples from people who had died prior to 1981 from conditions similar to those of recognized AIDS patients. Researchers also detected antibodies to HIV in blood samples that had been collected in 1959 in Central Africa and in the blood of an American man who had died in 1969. Hospital records indicated a possible AIDS death in the United States in 1952 and one in 1959 based on symptoms of the disease.

Two major events in the history of AIDS occurred in 1987. The first was the formation of numerous organizations to address the accelerating epidemic: the World Health Organization's Special Programme on AIDS (later the Global Programme on AIDS), the International Council of AIDS Service Organizations, and the Global Network of People Living with AIDS. The second event was the approval by the U.S. Food and Drug Administration of the first drug for combating AIDS, Zidovudine (AZT). Two years later, doctors and scientists reported that strains of HIV had become resistant to AZT.

By the late 1980s it was clear that the AIDS epidemic in Africa was unprecedented in its rate of spread; it was also evident that its effects were likely going to be worse than earlier anticipated in terms of people's health and well-being and in economic terms. As AIDS cases continued to climb everywhere, observers recognized that the epidemic had become a global crisis (see Table 3). Strategies for education, prevention, care, treatment, and counseling were initiated in many regions of the world, but most developing nations—where the epidemic hit the hardest—did not have the resources to implement far-reaching policies. UNAIDS reported one unexpected success, in Uganda, where the number of HIV-infected pregnant women decreased between 1991 and 1993 (see Case Study—Uganda).

In 1994 AZT was first used in the United States to reduce the risk of transmission of HIV from mother to infant. Triple antiretroviral drug therapy, which keeps HIV in check, was approved in 1996 in the United States. The drugs are so expensive that they are effectively unavailable to most people in developing nations and even some people in developed countries as well. The prohibitive cost led activists around the world to begin demanding that pharmaceutical companies lower the cost of the drugs in poor countries. In 1997 South Africa altered its patent laws to allow the importation and manufacture of generic forms of patented drugs. This move started an on-going battle between leading pharmaceutical companies, which sought to prevent the copying of their patented products, and governments of some developing nations (as well as activists), which sought to provide affordable treatment to their AIDS-ravaged populations. Even though some headway was made in providing drugs at a reduced cost to poorer countries, the goal of providing cheap or free AIDS drugs to people in sub-Saharan Africa and other poor regions is most likely far off, as the legal and logistical requirements remain complicated and daunting. Even if drugs were made easily available to poor countries, in many cases their health care systems would not be capable of effectively distributing them.

Current Status

There is no cure or vaccination for AIDS. The HIV virus can be present in the blood, semen, vaginal secretions, and breast milk of an infected person and can therefore be transmitted through sexual contact, through direct contact with blood (for example, through blood transfusions or pricks from needles containing contaminated blood or the reuse or sharing of needles), and through childbirth and breast-feeding. There are drug regimens that fight the effects of HIV and prolong the lives of HIV-positive people for years, but as noted above the drugs are expensive and consequently available primarily to people in developed countries. Many people believe that the only hope for a global solution to the AIDS pandemic is a vaccine against HIV. Numerous researchers are currently working to develop one.

Research

There are currently four main avenues of research related to the global AIDS epidemic: vaccines and other therapeutic forms of prevention, drug treatment, transmission reduction from mother to infant, and sociological studies related to behavioral prevention of the disease, care of victims and survivors, and the economic impact of the epidemic. A variety of groups are involved in this research: national and international government-sponsored research institutions, private research agencies, and nonprofit organizations.

The effort to develop a vaccine against HIV is guided by the International AIDS Vaccine Initiative (IAVI), a nonprofit scientific organization. At a press conference on 26 June 2001, Seth Berkley, IAVI president and chief executive officer, called for officials in all nations to put more resources toward the AIDS-vaccine effort. He asserted that the project is considerably underfunded and called for authorities in all nations to put further resources into the AIDS vaccine effort.

One of the challenges faced by scientists working toward a vaccine is the absence of an appropriate animal model on which to experiment. Since HIV does not affect animals in the same way that it affects humans, most of the work has to be done on humans, which raises difficult ethical questions, such as experimenting on people without knowing the potential risks. Another challenge is that there are various strains of HIV, so scientists are fairly certain that a vaccine that is effective against the predominant strain in one region of the world will not necessarily be effective in other regions. Another difficulty is that scientists do not know what type of vaccine is the most likely to be successful. A vaccine that would completely prevent infection is the most desirable option, but less desirable possibilities include vaccines for people who are already infected, for example, vaccines that reduce the chance of transmission or that stop or delay progression of the disease. The latter type of vaccine might turn out to be more easily and quickly developed. Scientists and health care officials are conflicted about how best to distribute research resources among the various vaccine-development ideas.

Even if an effective vaccine is developed, delivery of it will be difficult. In addition to the challenges related to the enormous cost of manufacture and delivery, there are potential roadblocks, such as whom to target for vaccination first and how to reach high-risk groups. IAVI released a report on 21 June 2001 with recommendations for addressing these problems in advance of the development of a vaccine. By mid-2001 one vaccine had entered phase III clinical trials, the final stage of testing before a drug can be approved for distribution. The vaccine, AIDSVAX, was developed by VaxGen, a California-based firm, and is being tested in Europe, North America, and Thailand for complete preventive efficacy. Worldwide there are at least thirty other vaccine candidates in phase I or phase II trials, the early stages of clinical trials.

Another important area of research involves microbicides, substances that can be applied to the body in the form of a cream or gel to prevent infections. In the case of HIV, researchers hope to develop a microbicide that can be applied vaginally to help prevent infection with HIV and other sexually transmitted microorganisms. Some microbicides being studied have blocked HIV infection in the laboratory, and others have prevented disease-causing organisms from sticking to the outer layer of the reproductive tract (thus preventing infection). About sixty candidate microbicides have been tested on animals, proven safe, and are currently being tested on humans. Microbicides have been hailed as a potential HIV-prevention breakthrough because they might offer a way for women to protect themselves against infection. Many women in developing countries—where, according to National Institutes of Health statistics, 95 percent of new HIV infections occur—are not in control of decisions concerning abstinence, monogamy, and condom use. For these women, microbicides might offer a method of protection against HIV infection.

Numerous research universities and other institutions are researching more effective drug treatments and drug combinations to combat HIV. The treatment that is currently accepted as the most effective is called highly active antiretroviral therapy (HAART), which involves taking daily doses of a combination of drugs. The precise combination differs from patient to patient, depending on which drugs he or she has taken in the past and which have proven effective. The drugs work by inhibiting the ability of HIV to attack the immune system. This combination therapy has been shown to be effective at all stages of infection. Some people, however, cannot tolerate the side effects of HAART, such as redistributed body fat, increased cholesterol, and altered metabolisms. Other people show no benefit, for reasons not yet understood.

According to the 2000 spring–summer *Harvard AIDS Review,* approximately six hundred thousand infants were infected with HIV through mother-to-child transmission in 1999. MTCT can occur before, during, or after birth. Research has shown that the risk of MTCT can be significantly reduced by improved postpartum care, HIV testing and counseling, antiretroviral drug treatment, and avoidance of breast-feeding. One current large-scale investigation on preventing MTCT is being sponsored by the New York–based Population Council, a private research organization, in collaboration with the governments of Kenya and Zambia. The research attempts to determine which services most effectively prevent MTCT while meeting the needs of HIV-positive pregnant women in sub-Saharan Africa.

Sociological investigations related to HIV/AIDS span a broad range of topics. The disease affects individuals, families, communities, and entire countries, in various manners and with varying urgencies. Numerous organizations have researched the most promising responses that groups and governments can undertake in the face of the AIDS crisis. One major finding across a range of studies concerns the substantial material needs of people infected with HIV and their families and communities. Recommended responses to these needs include providing resources for children orphaned by AIDS; providing economic relief to families and communities affected by AIDS; increasing access to health care services; and increasing literacy and educational access (thus increasing potential access to more lucrative employment). Research has also revealed the need for improved and increased counseling services within communities affected by HIV.

Policies and Programs

International efforts to combat HIV/AIDS are focused on implementing expanded prevention, care, and counseling services, increasing drug availability, gathering more extensive surveillance data, and research into vaccines and other biomedical vehicles to fight the disease.

The illness and death caused by AIDS threatens the gains in socioeconomic development made by third world nations over the past few decades, especially nations in sub-Saharan Africa. Authorities have recorded negative trends in infant mortality rates, life expectancy, literacy, poverty levels, gross national product, and gender inequity. HIV/AIDS has also increased the incidence of other infectious disease, such as tuberculosis, which places a double burden on already fragile health care systems (see EPIDEMICS). Increasingly, policies are addressing the developmental burden that HIV/AIDS places on national economies and ultimately on the global economy. The United Nations Development Programme (UNDP) provides guidance and development services to developing countries to combat the harmful effects of HIV/AIDS on their economies. This policy has resulted in practical gains that can, for example, be seen in a UNDP-supported study, *Botswana: Human Development Report, 2000.* The report, which discusses how AIDS is increasing poverty in that country, led the Botswanan government to allocate funding so that the nation's AIDS patients—17 percent of the population—could receive free antiretroviral drugs. The UNDP also sponsors surveys and studies that help businesses decrease their HIV/AIDS-related losses. An anonymous HIV-testing project conducted at six firms in Tanzania indicated that HIV/AIDS is to blame for the companies' increasing loss of income due to worker illness. The companies were encouraged to develop prevention programs and to plan for their future health care needs.

In 2001 UN secretary-general Kofi Annan began a campaign to mobilize worldwide political commitment to fighting HIV/AIDS. Annan set forth five priorities: preventing the further spread of HIV/AIDS; reducing transmission of HIV from mother to child; providing care and treatment to all; pursuing scientific breakthroughs; and protecting those people made most vulnerable by the disease's impact, such as orphans. Annan also identified the factors crucial for meeting these goals: leadership and commitment, particularly from national officials; engagement of local communities; empowerment of women; strengthening of public health care systems; and commitment of more money. The need for more money led Annan to propose the formation of a $7 billion to $10 billion global fund to fight HIV/AIDS. He called on all sectors—governments, nongovernmental organizations, corporations, foundations, and the United Nations—to rise to the challenges posed by HIV/AIDS.

Annan's mobilization campaign culminated in a UN General Assembly Special Session on HIV/AIDS held 25–27 June 2001, in New York. At the meeting, Peter Piot, executive director of the Joint United Nations Programme on HIV/AIDS, called on all nations to create a path toward defeating the epidemic. Topics covered at the session included advances made and lessons learned during the past twenty years; human rights; women and children; urban and rural strategies for fighting the epidemic; HIV and tuberculosis; the current status and trends of the epidemic; prevention and care; hunger and poverty; orphans; mobile and migrant populations; microbicides; the socioeconomic impact of the epidemic; and HIV/AIDS education. The session resulted in the adoption of a formal Declaration of Commitment on HIV/AIDS by the heads of participating governments. The declaration touches on all of the topics covered during the session and emphasizes the particular importance of leadership in combating AIDS (see Document 1).

At the special session, some disagreement was voiced about the various approaches to fighting the epidemic. For example, some delegates from Islamic countries disapproved of the mention of gays and prostitutes in official reports, while others stressed the importance of speaking openly about high-risk groups. Participants also disagreed about the amount of industrialized nations' contributions and how a global fund should be distributed. Another issue of contention related to religious bans on condoms. After the session, on 31 July 2001, Roman Catholic bishops in southern Africa declared their refusal to relax the ban on the use of condoms, even for married couples. The declaration came at the end of a conference that had been called because of various organizations growing vocalization that condom use can significantly reduce the risk of HIV infection in epidemic-torn sub-Saharan Africa.

Regional Summaries

Every country has citizens and residents living with HIV/AIDS, but the face of the epidemic varies from region to region. Its variables include the primary mode of transmission, the availability of drug treatments and care, and the effects on the community and economy.

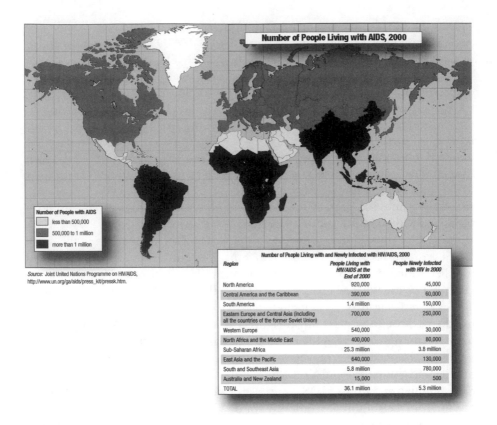

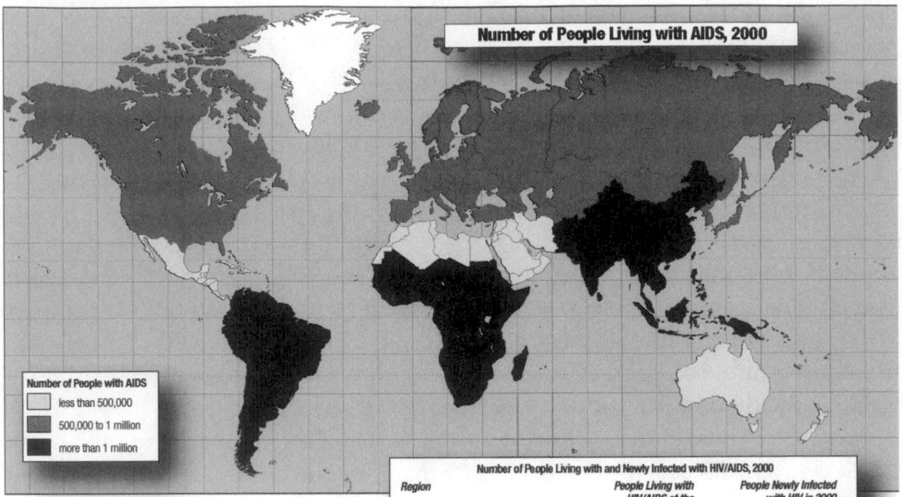

Source: Joint United Nations Programme on HIV/AIDS, http://www.un.org/ga/aids/press_kit/pressk.htm.

Number of People Living with and Newly Infected with HIV/AIDS, 2000

Region	People Living with HIV/AIDS at the End of 2000	People Newly Infected with HIV in 2000
North America	920,000	45,000
Central America and the Caribbean	390,000	60,000
South America	1.4 million	150,000
Eastern Europe and Central Asia (including all the countries of the former Soviet Union)	700,000	250,000
Western Europe	540,000	30,000
North Africa and the Middle East	400,000	80,000
Sub-Saharan Africa	25.3 million	3.8 million
East Asia and the Pacific	640,000	130,000
South and Southeast Asia	5.8 million	780,000
Australia and New Zealand	15,000	500
TOTAL	36.1 million	5.3 million

North America

The AIDS epidemic in North America has thus far taken its largest toll on gay men and intravenous drug users. The disease spread rapidly through these populations in the 1980s, leading their communities to initiate prevention strategies, including safe-sex education and needle-exchange programs. In some areas of North America, notably those with large numbers of gay men, such as New York and San Francisco, high-profile education campaigns had been launched by the mid-1980s. The reported level of unprotected sex among gay men fell during the decade, and although the number of HIV-infected members of this population rose during that time, health officials estimate that the infection rate would have been much worse without concerted prevention efforts. The number of gay men in North America with AIDS eventually leveled off in the early 1990s. It began to climb again in 1996, coinciding with reports of increasing incidents of unprotected sex among young gay men in the United States.

Prevention strategies aimed at intravenous drug users, such as needle-exchange programs and non-injected alternative drug maintenance, are expensive and controversial, and their implementation has been difficult for supporters to maintain. Education in prevention is less successful among drug users than among the general population, because users are difficult to locate and educate openly and because it is difficult for most addicts to simply stop taking drugs. HIV infection rates among intravenous drug users in North America have risen steadily since the beginning of the epidemic, and in 2000 a large percentage of new infections occurred in this population. In Canada, almost one-fourth of new infections during the first half of 2000 were in this group; their percentage had been steadily rising during the 1990s, according to *HIV and AIDS in Canada: Surveillance Report to June 30, 2000.*

Because North America is a high-income region, AIDS drugs are relatively accessible. Consequently, AIDS patients there tend to live longer and remain healthier than those in the rest of the world. It is thought that a stall in the effectiveness of prevention efforts in the late 1990s was due mainly to the success of medical breakthroughs. With new treatments, AIDS patients were not dying as quickly or in the same numbers as they had been at the beginning of the epidemic, thus reducing fears among people in high-risk groups about contracting the disease.

Heterosexual transmission of HIV was also on the rise in the late 1990s in North America, where women were particularly at risk. According to *HIV and AIDS in Canada,* in 1999 heterosexuals who were diagnosed with AIDS contracted through sexual contact with high-risk individuals, made up 10.7 percent of newly diagnosed cases, compared to 4.8 percent in 1991. In the United States, according to UNAIDS' "Epidemic Update, December 2001," women constituted nearly one-third of all new HIV-positive diagnoses in 2000; among these women, intravenous drug use and heterosexual intercourse were the primary modes of transmission. In the United States, the African American population has been hit disproportionately hard: blacks constitute 47 percent of AIDS cases but make up only 12 percent of the population.

Latin America

In Latin America, the AIDS epidemic varies greatly from country to country. Relative to other countries in the region, the Caribbean island states—where the majority of HIV transmissions are heterosexual—have been hit the hardest by the epidemic, as judged by the percentage of the population that is HIV-positive. According to a 12 July 2000 report in the *Chicago Tribune,* Haiti faces the worst AIDS epidemic in the Western Hemisphere. "HIV/AIDS Profile: Haiti," a report by the U.S. Census, estimates that in 2000 in Port-au-Prince 10 percent of pregnant women were living with HIV, and more than 5 percent of adults in all of Haiti were living with the virus. The 12 July *Chicago Tribune* report estimates that by July 2000, some 190,000 Haitian children had lost their mothers to AIDS. "HIV/AIDS Profile: Dominican Republic," by the U.S. Census, reports that in Santo Domingo nearly 1.5 percent of pregnant women tested positive in 1998, and 4 percent of sex workers were HIV-positive. It is believed that the Caribbean epidemic is fueled by the fact that sexual activity typically begins at relatively younger ages, and young people frequently change sex partners. This fact, coupled with the poverty endemic to much of the region, makes the epidemic difficult to manage. In 2000 several high-level meetings among Caribbean government officials took place to discuss the region's response to the HIV/AIDS epidemic. The leaders pledged new commitments and cooperation in fighting the disease.

In Central and South America, AIDS is most prevalent in the countries bordering the Caribbean and in Brazil. According to UNAIDS epidemiological fact sheet reports, in 1997 close to 4 percent of pregnant women in urban Guyana were HIV-positive, and in the capital of Georgetown and other urban areas 44 percent of female sex workers were living with HIV. Belize, Guatemala, and Honduras have adult AIDS-prevalence rates of between 1 percent and 2 percent, and nearly 5 percent in some urban areas. The epidemic is mostly the result of heterosexual transmission in these countries. Brazil faces a growing AIDS epidemic among heterosexuals in addition to already experiencing high rates of infection among men who have sex with men and intravenous drug users. More than half a million adults—nearly 6 percent of the population—are HIV-positive. The Brazilian government mandates that antiretroviral drug treatment be provided to all people with HIV. The government has also funded significant education and prevention efforts, which likely were largely responsible for the adoption of safer sex practices by young people in the late 1990s. According to a 7 December 1999 World Bank report, part of the Development News series on World Bank–supported HIV/AIDS projects, Brazil's campaign for safe sex is thought to have contributed to a drop in AIDS cases over the five years. In particular, there has been a 30 percent decline in deaths attributed to AIDS among leading risk groups. UNAIDS epidemiological fact sheet reports state that in Bolivia, Colombia, Mexico, and Peru, the highest prevalence rates are among men who have sex with men. Overall adult prevalence in these countries is relatively low for the region.

Europe and the Former Soviet Union

The pictures of HIV/AIDS in Western Europe and in the countries of the former Soviet Union are very different. Many AIDS patients in Western Europe, as in North America, have access to antiretroviral drugs, and many countries of Western Europe launched education, prevention, and surveillance programs early in the epidemic. EuroHIV was formed in 1984 to collect, analyze, and distribute information on the size, location, and nature of the epidemic in participating countries. Currently, fifty of the fifty-one countries in the World Health Organization European Region report data to EuroHIV that are then used to guide prevention and treatment policies.

Similar to the situation in North America, in the late 1990s in Western Europe HIV transmissions rates began to rise after a few years of being stable. Authorities believe this trend might have been due to complacency with respect to prevention. In the late 1990s Western Europeans (as well as North Americans) in high-risk groups, such as men who have sex with men, were more isolated from the direct effects of the epidemic than had been members of these groups in the 1980s, when gay communities lost so many people to AIDS that HIV infection seemed always a very present threat. The same was not necessarily the case for young people in high-risk groups in these regions in the late 1990s. Since current drug therapies keep many patients alive and healthy for long periods of time, HIV/AIDS may no longer appear to be life-threatening, thus leading young people in high-risk groups to let down their guard.

The situation is different in Eastern Europe and the republics of the former Soviet Union. In these countries the AIDS epidemic has taken its heaviest toll among intravenous drug users, a trend that has recently accelerated drastically. Experts suspect that social and economic instability is fueling drug use and commercial sex, both of which create communities in which HIV infection has the potential to spread rapidly. According to UNAIDS' "Epidemic Update, December 2001," in the Ukraine, the country most affected in the region, the use of intravenous drugs is responsible for three-fourths of HIV infections. In the Russian Federation, hardly any cases were registered in 1987, as compared to 130,000 total as of June 2001.

North Africa and the Middle East

There is not enough accessible data for an accurate report on the prevalence of HIV or organized prevention and care initiatives in North Africa and the Middle East. Workers at locations where surveillance is taking place indicate that HIV infection is spreading in the general population. UNAIDS estimates that there were about 80,000 new infections in the region in 2001, according to "Epidemic Update, December 2001." Studies have shown that HIV prevalence among pregnant women visiting neonatal clinics is close to 1 percent in southern Algeria. The region as a whole had an estimated 440,000 people living with HIV/AIDS patients at the end of 2000.

Sub-Saharan Africa

The countries of sub-Saharan Africa have suffered the most from the global AIDS epidemic. According to UNAIDS' "Epidemic Update, December 2001," in 2001 3.4 million people in the region became infected with HIV, and 28.1 million people were living with HIV/AIDS by the year's end. The AIDS epidemic presents countries south of the Sahara with enormous challenges. Besides the loss of life, perhaps the most important concern is the long-range effect on their economies. Many countries of the region face a tremendous loss of economic viability, along with correlative damage to social infrastructure and safety nets, as the epidemic ravages vast portions of their populations. One out of five adults is HIV-positive in several countries in southern Africa, and at least five countries in western Africa face an HIV prevalence rate of more than 5 percent.

There are at least three issues in need of immediate and ongoing attention. First, growing populations of HIV-infected patients and their families need better access to health care and financial support. Second, the rate of new infections needs to be stemmed, by undertaking wide-scale prevention education. Third, mechanisms need to be provided to help communities cope with the effects of AIDS deaths, including an increasing number of orphans and other survivors and damage to economic development.

The epidemic in sub-Saharan Africa has spread primarily through heterosexual transmission. In most of the region, infection rates among young women are higher than in young men. A UNAIDS study examined this trend and reported its findings in a 14 September 1999 report, "Differences in HIV Spread in Four Sub-Saharan African Cities." It found greatly diverging HIV prevalence rates between the two sexes, particularly in the 15- to 19-year-old category. The highest divergence in the four towns it studied was in Kisumu, Kenya, where more than 3 percent of male teenagers tested positive, whereas 23 percent of female teenagers did so. The September 2000 issue of *Populi,* published by the United Nations Population Fund (UNFPA), reports that in the eight African countries with an HIV prevalence rate of 15 percent or higher among adults aged 15 to 49, AIDS will eventually claim the lives of about one-third of 15 year olds. The eight countries are Botswana, Lesotho, Malawi, Namibia, South Africa, Swaziland, Zambia, and Zimbabwe.

A few statistics for 2000 from UNAIDS country fact sheets underscore the shocking toll of the epidemic: In Botswana, 35.8 percent of adults were living with HIV/AIDS. In South Africa, the country with the largest number of HIV-infected people in the world—4.1 million—19.9 percent of adults were infected. More than 19 percent of all adults in Zambia were living with HIV/AIDS.

Estimates from the UNFPA's *Preventing HIV Infection, Protecting Reproductive Health* show, however, that the overall incidence of HIV in sub-Saharan Africa was stabilizing in 2001. The infection rate dropped in 2000 to 3.8 million new cases from 4 million in the previous year. Experts suspect that this was due to two factors: the epidemic has already reached a large number of people whose behavior puts them at high risk of infection, and many countries' prevention efforts are yielding successes.

Also according to *Preventing HIV Infection, Protecting Reproductive Health,* more people died of AIDS in sub-Saharan Africa in 2000 than in 1999. Because the antiretroviral drugs that can prolong the lives of AIDS patients are too expensive for most Africans, this trend is likely to continue for several years. Efforts by some drug companies to give countries discounts have not made the drugs affordable to the majority of African AIDS sufferers.

The HIV/AIDS epidemic in sub-Saharan Africa is so acute that it affects every level of society. Households have to cope financially and emotionally with the sickness and death of family members. Communities and surviving family members, who are often poor, are faced with the responsibility of caring for the thousands of children orphaned by AIDS every year, and national economies are becoming burdened by the toll that HIV/AIDS takes on business and economic and social development. Policies to address these problems are beginning to take shape as the epidemic places increasing pressures on already strained economic and social infrastructures.

Asia and the Pacific

Asia has a fairly low prevalence of HIV/AIDS in most areas, but in some cases the numbers belie the extent of the epidemic, because the total population is so large. Cambodia, Myanmar, and Thailand have the highest prevalence of

HIV among 15 to 49 year olds in the region. In these countries, according to *Preventing HIV Infection, Protecting Reproductive Health,* the prevalence is higher than 1 percent, and the epidemic is fueled by heterosexual transmission. Although Thailand has been successful at slowing the rate of heterosexual transmission through prevention measures, this progress has been countered by increasing rates of transmission through drug use and among men who have sex with men.

In areas of China, Nepal, Malaysia, and Vietnam where there is a widespread epidemic, the primary mode of transmission appears to be intravenous drug use, according to UNAIDS' "Epidemic Update, December 2001." In the seven provinces of China that have a problem with AIDS and HIV, more than 70 percent of intravenous drug users are infected. Given that there are estimated to be about 3 million such people in China, an explosion of new infections may be on the horizon. China is also experiencing mass population movements, which offer opportunities for the rampant spread of HIV.

In India, the source of transmission varies from region to region, and the number of people infected is high. Although HIV/AIDS prevalence among adults is only 7 out of 1,000, the UNAIDS "Epidemic Update" estimates that 3.7 million people had been infected by the end of 2000. The only country in the world with a worse epidemic in terms of raw numbers was South Africa.

The Pacific region has relatively low levels of HIV/AIDS. In the largest countries in the region—Australia and New Zealand—HIV prevalence rates are .13 percent, according to the "Epidemic Update." The number of adults living with the disease at the end of 2000 was fifteen thousand, a minor fraction of the numbers in sub-Saharan Africa and Latin America. Nevertheless, some evidence exists that rates of infection are on the rise in Australia, where unsafe sex and intravenous drug use are the primary causes of the upsurge.

Data

Table 1 AIDS Deaths Worldwide

AIDS deaths in 2000	
Adults	2,500,000
Women	1,300,000
Children <15 years	500,000
Total	3,000,000
AIDS deaths from the beginning of the epidemic to the end of 2000	
Adults	17,500,000
Women	9,000,000
Children <15 years	4,300,000
Total	21,800,000

Source: Joint United Nations Programme on HIV/AIDS (UNAIDS) and World Health Organization, *AIDS Epidemic Update, December 2000* (Geneva: UNAIDS and WHO, 2000).

Table 2 Regional HIV/AIDS Statistics and Features, 2000

Region	Start of Epidemic	Main Modes of Transmission for Adults[a]	People Living with HIV/AIDS	People Newly Infected with HIV in 2000	Adult Prevalence Rate[b] (%)	Adult Females with HIV (%)
Sub-Saharan Africa	late 1970s–early 1980s	H	25,300,000	3,800,000	8.80	55
North Africa and the Middle East	early 1980s	H, IDU	400,000	80,000	0.20	40
South and Southeast Asia	early 1980s	H, IDU	5,800,000	780,000	0.56	35
East Asia and the Pacific	early 1980s	IDU, H, MSM	640,000	130,000	0.07	13
South America	late 1970s–early 1980s	MSM, H, IDU	1,400,000	150,000	0.50	25
Latin America	late 1970s–early 1980s	H, MSM	390,000	60,000	2.30	35
Eastern Europe and Central Asia	early 1980s	IDU	700,000	250,000	0.35	25
Western Europe	late 1970s–early 1980s	IDU, MSM	540,000	30,000	0.24	25
North America	late 1970s–early 1980s	H, IDU, MSM	920,000	45,000	0.60	20
Australia and New Zealand	late 1970s–early 1980s	MSM	15,000	500	0.13	10
Total			36,100,000	5,300,000	1.10	47

Source: Joint United Nations Programme on HIV/AIDS (UNAIDS) and World Health Organization, *AIDS Epidemic Update, December 2000* (Geneva: UNAIDS and WHO, 2000).

[a]H, heterosexual transmission; IDU, transmission through injecting drug use; MSM, sexual transmission among men who have sex with men.

[b]Proportion of adults, 15 to 49 years of age, living with HIV/AIDS in 2000, using 2000 population numbers.

Table 3 Estimated Adults and Children Living with HIV/AIDS and Female and Male HIV Prevalence Rates for Selected Countries, 1999

Country	Adults Living with HIV/AIDS[a]	Children Living with HIV/AIDS[b]	Prevalence among Young Females (low) (%)	Prevalence among Young Females (high) (%)	Prevalence among Young Males (low) (%)	Prevalence among Young Males (high) (%)
Algeria	11,000*	—	—	—	—	—
Argentina	120,000	4,400	0.23	0.34	0.68	1.04
Australia	14,000	140	0.01	0.02	0.07	0.21
Brazil	530,000	9,900	0.23	0.33	0.55	0.84
Canada	49,000	500	0.05	0.09	0.15	0.44
China	500,000	4,800	0.02	0.03	0.07	0.18
Congo, Republic of	1,100,000	53,000	4.31	5.84	1.66	3.32
Egypt	8,100*	—	—	—	—	—
France	130,000	1,000	0.15	0.30	0.16	0.49
Georgia	<500	<100	—	—	—	—
Germany	37,000	500	0.03	0.05	0.05	0.14
Guatemala	71,000	1,600	0.81	1.03	0.93	1.38
India	3,500,000	160,000	0.40	0.82	0.14	0.58
Indonesia	52,000	680	0.02	0.04	0.01	0.04
Israel	2,400	<100	0.05	0.06	0.05	0.07
Japan	10,000	<100	0.01	0.01	0.02	0.04
Russian Federation	130,000	1,800	0.09	0.15	0.19	0.32
Saudi Arabia	1,100*	—	—	—	—	—
Spain	120,000	<100	0.15	0.30	0.24	0.71
Sweden	3,000	<100	0.03	0.05	0.03	0.09
Switzerland	17,000	<100	0.22	0.43	0.18	0.55
Tajikistan	<100	<100	—	—	—	—
Thailand	740,000	13,900	1.53	3.11	0.47	1.89
Turkey	2,500	—	—	—	—	—
Uganda	770,000	53,000	6.65	8.99	2.56	5.12
United Kingdom	30,000	500	0.03	0.06	0.05	0.14
United States	840,000	10,000	0.16	0.30	0.25	0.75

Source: UNAIDS, "Report on the Global HIV/AIDS Epidemic, June 2000," http://www.unaids.org/epidemic_update/report/index.html.

Note: An asterisk indicates figures derived from a 1994 prevalence rate adjusted for a 1999 adult population due to a lack of data for 1999.

[a]Ages 15 to 24.

[b]Ages 0 to 14.

Case Study—Uganda

Uganda is representative of sub-Saharan African countries in that a large number of its people are HIV-positive. According to UNAIDS epidemiological fact sheet reports, at the end of 1999 an estimated 8.3 percent of Ugandan adults were living with HIV/AIDS. Uganda, however, is unique in having successfully taken steps to lower HIV-infection rates throughout the 1990s. Uganda's policies serve as a model for countries prepared to aggressively address the AIDS epidemic within their borders.

Uganda was among the first countries to experience an alarming spread of HIV during the early 1980s, and late in the decade it had one of the highest rates of infection in the world. The U.S. Agency for International Development estimated that some 14 percent of the adult Ugandan population in the early 1990s were HIV-positive, and in urban centers the incidence was higher and climbing.

In the late 1980s and early 1990s, the Ugandan government organized an AIDS prevention campaign involving governmental institutions and non-governmental organizations. Officials invited leaders from traditional, religious, and educational communities to raise awareness of the threat of AIDS and to carry out prevention initiatives. As in the rest of Africa, the primary mode of HIV transmission in Uganda is (and has always been) unprotected sexual intercourse between men and women. Therefore, programs to reduce infection rates focused largely on educating people about safer sexual behavior, such as delaying the onset of sexual activity, using condoms, and having fewer partners. Information was disseminated via newspapers, radio, posters, and theater. Counselors were trained to help families who were living with HIV/AIDS, and HIV-testing services became more widely available.

The numbers suggest that these policies were crucial factors in reducing the incidence of HIV/AIDS in Uganda during the 1990s. Because Uganda's AIDS epidemic has been among the most systematically documented in Africa, statistics are readily available. Also, in 1989 and 1995, Ugandan government officials carried out surveys in the large cities of Kampala and Jinja, asking people to report anonymously on various aspects of their sexual behavior. According to a report of the survey's results published in *AIDS 1997,* Okiror Asiimwe and a team of analysts found that during the six-year period covered, among people aged 15 to 24 a two-year delay in the start of sexual activity had evolved, and the frequency of men indulging in casual sex dropped by 9 percent. Additionally, officials reported that men used condoms 40 percent more often in 1995 than in 1989 and that women experienced the use of condoms 30 percent more often.

Pregnant women attending health clinics provided the most reliable data regarding rates of HIV infection over time (because pregnant women were consistently tested, while other sectors of the population were not). According to HIV InSite, the number of HIV-positive pregnant women in urban areas has fallen markedly since the early 1990s, most significantly those aged 15 to 19. The incidence of HIV infection among adults continued to decline in urban and rural areas of Uganda in the late 1990s. Additionally, the national blood supply of Uganda has been screened for HIV since the late 1980s. The BBC on 15 May 2000 reported that as a result, in 2000 contaminated blood transfusions accounted for only 1 percent of new HIV infections, compared to 1990, when 8 percent of new HIV infections were caused by contaminated blood.

In 1997 Uganda was among four countries to participate in a pilot drug-access initiative sponsored by the United Nations that involved negotiating with pharmaceutical companies for discounted AIDS drugs. The program has reduced an individual's cost for antiretroviral drug therapy by more than half. In 2000 Uganda became the first African country to begin a trial of candidate HIV vaccines. Additionally, Uganda is taking part in a task force organized among several African nations to investigate the effectiveness of traditional remedies, such as herbal treatments, in fighting HIV and relieving symptoms of AIDS.

Authorities caution against celebrating too soon, as there are still serious challenges to be faced before the AIDS epidemic in Uganda can be considered under control. A study targeted at the Mbale district and published in the March 2000 issue of *Studies in Family Planning* suggests that although most adolescents knew that unprotected sex could result in HIV infection, they were not willing, for a variety reasons, to act on this knowledge. The study indicated that large numbers of males and females find condom use and abstinence from sex "unacceptable" practices, and that most young people reported that engaging in early sex was encouraged by their communities as an important rite of passage.

Other problems typical of underdeveloped sub-Saharan countries—including women's limited access to contraception and low funding for health services and education—exacerbate the AIDS-related problems these countries face. Additionally, poverty, illiteracy, and poor overall health are rampant, particularly among women and especially in rural areas, where HIV-infection rates are still high.

AIDS in Uganda is taking a toll on the country's socioeconomic status and prospects. The U.S. Census Bureau estimates that the average Ugandan's life expectancy will be forty-eight years in 2010, but that in the absence of AIDS it would have been sixty years. Reports indicate that the financial hardship exacted by the death of a spouse, by treatment and care giving, and by funerals has caused people to begin selling property and to give up their businesses. By 1995 AIDS deaths had decreased the country's urban work force by 20 percent, according to a 1999 POLICY Project report. Labor shortages have left agricultural land uncultivated, and land still in use is being used increasingly for subsistence crops rather than cash crops. The economic injuries that AIDS has inflicted on Uganda exemplify the effect of AIDS on all sub-Saharan African countries with a high incidence of the disease.

Biographical Sketches

Harley Henriques do Nascimento is an influential AIDS activist working to prevent the advance of AIDS in low-income areas of Brazil. In the late 1980s do Nascimento founded the Support Group for the Prevention of AIDS in Bahia, or GAPA-

BA, a nonprofit organization that works with community volunteers to provide AIDS prevention and care-giving services, public policy guidance, and education programs aimed at reducing human rights violations and discrimination against people with HIV. Do Nascimento's work has served as a model for volunteer recruitment strategies, and he has received humanitarian awards for his role in jump-starting Brazil's response to the AIDS epidemic.

Robert Gallo is the director of the Institute of Human Virology and professor of medicine, microbiology, and immunology in the School of Medicine at the University of Maryland, Baltimore. Gallo, a pioneer in the study of human retroviruses, and his team of researchers in 1983 isolated the virus that would become known as HIV. Gallo also led the team that developed the first HIV antibody test, which was approved in 1985, and performed crucial research that led to the development of drugs to fight HIV and treat AIDS.

David Ho is scientific director and chief executive director of the Aaron Diamond AIDS Research Center in New York and professor at Rockefeller University. Working on the front lines of HIV/AIDS research, Ho was instrumental in the development of the life-saving triple antiretroviral drug therapy, the so-called AIDS cocktail, introduced in the United States in 1996.

Luc Montagnier is Distinguished Professor and director of the Center for Molecular and Cellular Biology at Queens College, City University of New York. He led the first team to isolate and describe the virus that would later be called HIV. At the time of this discovery, he worked at the Pasteur Institute in Paris. Montagnier's earlier work had been instrumental in revealing the mode by which RNA viruses replicate themselves. His contributions in this field enabled further research into the causes and treatments of some tumor-causing viruses. In 1993 Montagnier co-founded the World Foundation for AIDS Research and Prevention, a global network of HIV/AIDS research institutions. His work today focuses on the design of an HIV vaccine and making drug treatments available to AIDS sufferers without sufficient funds to purchase them.

Peter Piot is executive director of the Joint United Nations Programme on HIV/AIDS (UNAIDS). He heads a staff of 129 people and yearly distributes $60 million in the effort to reduce the burden and threat of HIV/AIDS to the global community and economy. Before joining UNAIDS in 1994, Piot worked as a scientific researcher and professor at various institutes in Africa, Europe, and the United States. He is credited as a co-discoverer of the Ebola virus.

Directory

Centers for Disease Control and Prevention, c/o Public Inquiries/MASO, Mailstop F07, 1600 Clifton Road, Atlanta, GA 30333. Telephone: (800) 311-3435, Email: go to http://www.cdc.gov/netinfo.htm, Web: http://www.cdc.gov
U.S. government agency for protecting public health and safety

European Centre for the Epidemiological Monitoring of AIDS, 12 Rue de Val d'Osne, 94415 Saint-Maurice, France. Telephone: (33) 0 1 41 79 67 00, Email: f.hamers@invs.sante.fr, Web: http://www.ceses.org
Organization performing HIV/AIDS surveillance in Europe

Family Health International, HIV/AIDS Department, 2101 Wilson Boulevard, Suite 700, Arlington, VA 22201. Telephone: (703) 516-9779, Email: services@fhi.org, Web: http://www.fhi.org
Organization aimed at providing health prevention and care services globally

Global Network of People Living with HIV/AIDS (GNP+), P.O. Box 11726, 1001 GS Amsterdam, Netherlands. Telephone: (31) 20 689 8218, Email: gnp@gn.apc.org, Web: http://www.xs4all.nl/~gnp
Organization working to improve the quality of life of people living with HIV/AIDS

International AIDS Society, P.O. Box 4249, Folkungagatan 49, 102 65 Stockholm, Sweden. Telephone: (46) 8 556 970 50, Email: secretariat@ias.se, Web: http://www.ias.se
Professional society of scientists and health care workers engaged in HIV/AIDS prevention, control, and care

International AIDS Vaccine Initiative, 110 William Street, New York, NY 10038-3901. Telephone: (212) 847-1111, Email: info@iavi.org, Web: http://www.iavi.org
Organization working to speed the development and distribution of AIDS vaccines

International Council of AIDS Service Organizations, 399 Church Street, 4th Floor, Toronto, ONT MB5 2J6, Canada. Telephone: (416) 340-2437, Email: richardb@icaso.org, Web: http://www.icaso.org
Network of community-based AIDS organizations

National Pediatric and Family HIV Resource Center, University of Medicine and Dentistry of New Jersey, 30 Bergen Street, ADMC 4, Newark, NJ 07103. Telephone: (973) 972-0410 or (800) 362-0071, Email: ortegaes@umdnj.edu, Web: http://www.pedhivaids.org/education/children_living.html
Organization offering training of health and social service HIV/AIDS professionals through education, consultation, and technical assistance

UNAIDS, The Joint United Nations Programme on HIV/AIDS, 20 Avenue Appia, 1211 Geneva 27, Switzerland. Telephone: (41) 22 791 3666, Email: unaids@unaids.org, Web: http://www.unaids.org
Agency advocating worldwide action against HIV/AIDS

United Kingdom National AIDS Trust, New City Cloisters, 188/196 Old Street, London EC 1V 9FR, England. Telephone: (41) 22 791 3666, Email: info@nat.org.uk, Web: http://www.nat.org.uk
Organization promoting HIV/AIDS education, prevention, and patient treatment and care

World Health Organization, 20 Avenue Appia, 1211 Geneva 27, Switzerland. Telephone: (41) 22 791 2111, Email: info@who.int, Web: http://www.who.int
UN agency advocating health for all people

Further Research

Books

Bastos, Cristiana. *Global Responses to AIDS: Science in Emergency.* Bloomington: Indiana University Press, 1999.

Buchanan, David, and George Cernada, eds. *Progress in Preventing AIDS? Dogma, Dissent, and Innovation: Global Perspectives.* Amityville, N.Y.: Baywood Publishing Company, 1998.

Cohen, Jon. *Shots in the Dark: The Wayward Search for the AIDS Vaccine.* New York: W. W. Norton, 2001.

Feldman, Douglas A., ed. *Global AIDS Policy.* Westport, Conn.: Bergin and Garvey, 1994.

Global AIDS Policy Coalition. Edited by Jonathan M. Mann and Daniel J. M. Tarantola. *AIDS in the World II: Global Dimensions, Social Roots, and Responses.* New York: Oxford University Press, 1996.

Grmek, Mirko. *History of AIDS: Emergence and Origin of a Modern Pandemic.* Princeton, N.J.: Princeton University Press, 1990.

Hope, Kempe Ronald, ed. *AIDS and Development in Africa: A Social Science Perspective.* New York: Haworth Press, 1999.

Levy, Jay. *HIV and the Pathogenesis of AIDS.* Washington, D.C.: ASM Press, 1995.

Rauh, Elizabeth, and Bethel Boston, eds. *AIDS: Readings on a Global Crisis.* Boston: Allyn and Bacon, 1995.

Reid, Elizabeth, ed. *HIV and AIDS: The Global Inter-Connection.* West Hartford, Conn.: Kumarian Press, 1995.

Shilts, Randy. *And the Band Played On: Politics, People, and the AIDS Epidemic.* New York: St. Martin's Press, 1987.

Söderholm, Peter. *Global Governance of AIDS: Partnerships with Civil Society.* Lund, Sweden: Lund University Press, 1997.

Stine, Gerald J. *Acquired Immune Deficiency Syndrome: Biological, Medical, Social, and Legal Issues.* 3d ed. Upper Saddle River, N.J.: Prentice-Hall, 1998.

Articles and Reports

Asiimwe-Okiror, G., et al. "Change in Sexual Behaviour and Decline in HIV Infection among Young Pregnant Women in Urban Uganda." Draft document, Geneva, UNAIDS, 1997.

Booker, Salih, and William Minter. "Global Apartheid." *Nation,* 9 July 2001, 11.

Borzello, Anna. "AIDS in Uganda: Investigating the Causes of High-Risk Sexual Behaviour," http://www.idrc.ca/books/reports/1997/20-01e.html.

Brandt, Richard. "Gates Gives Booster Shot to AIDS Vaccines." *Science,* 2 February 2001, 809.

Burr, Chandler. "The AIDS Exception: Privacy vs. Public Health." *Atlantic Monthly,* June 1997, 57.

Caldwell, John, and Pat Caldwell. "The African AIDS Epidemic." *Scientific American,* March 1996, 62.

Centers for Disease Control. "Pneumocystis Pneumonia—Los Angeles." *Morbidity and Mortality Weekly Report,* vol. 30 (1981), 250.

Coghlan, Andy. "Time Stands Still." *New Scientist,* 14 July 2001, 17.

Cohen, Jon. "Merck Reemerges with a Bold AIDS Vaccine Effort." *Science,* 6 April 2001, 24.

———. "Disputed AIDS Theory Dies Its Final Death." *Science,* 27 April 2001, 615.

Day, Michael. "Hopes Dashed." *New Scientist,* 23 December 2000, 20.

DeCarlo, Pamela, with contributions by Ann Menting. "Protecting Mothers and Children." *Harvard AIDS Review* (spring–summer 2000).

Garbus, Lisa. "Uganda: Context of the Epidemic," http://hivinsite.ucsf.edu/InSite.jsp?page=cr-02-01&doc=2098.41a6.
HIV and AIDS in Canada: Surveillance Report to June 30, 2000, http://www.hc-sc.gc.ca/hpb/lcdc/publicat/aids/hiv-aic11-00/index.html.
Holmes, Bob. "Fatal Flaw." *New Scientist,* 28 October 2000, 34.
Hulton, Louise, Rachel Cullen, and Symons Wamala Khalokho. "Perceptions of the Risks of Sexual Activity and Their Consequences among Ugandan Adolescents." *Studies in Family Planning,* March 2000.
National Institute of Allergy and Infectious Diseases. *The Relationship between the Human Immunodeficiency Virus and the Acquired Immune Deficiency Syndrome.* Bethesda, MD. National Institutes of Health, 1995.
Schwartländer, Bernhard, Geoff Garnett, Neff Walker, and Roy Anderson. "AIDS in a New Millennium." *Science,* 7 July 2000, 64.
UNAIDS. "Differences in HIV Spread in Four Sub-Saharan African Cities," 14 September 1999, http://www.unaids.org/publications/documents/epidemiology/determinants/lusaka99.html.
———. "Epidemic Update, December 2001," http://www.unaids.org/epidemic_update/report_dec01.
———. Epidemiological Fact Sheets by Country, http://www.unaids.org/hivaidsinfo/statistics/fact_sheets/index_en.htm.
United Nations Development Programme. *Botswana: Human Development Report, 2000,* http://www.bw.undp.org/publications.html#botswana.
United Nations Population Fund. *Preventing HIV Infection, Protecting Reproductive Health: The UNFPA Response to HIV/AIDS,* http://www.unfpa.org/aids.
U.S. Census Bureau. *Country Reports on HIV/AIDS,* http://www.census.gov/ipc/hiv.
U.S. Congress. House. Committee on International Relations. *The Spread of AIDS in the Developing World: Hearing before the Committee on International Relations.* 105th Cong., 2d sess., 16 September 1998.

Web Sites

ACT UP (AIDS Coalition to Unleash Power)
http://www.actupny.org

AIDS in Africa
http://www.aidsandafrica.com

AIDS Prevention and Vaccine Research Site (*Science*)
http://AIDScience.com

AIDS Vaccine Advocacy Coalition
http://www.avac.org

allAfrica.com: Uganda, Top News
http://allafrica.com/uganda

Family Health International
http://www.fhi.org/en/aids/naids.html

Harvard AIDS Review
http://www.aids.harvard.edu/publications/har/index.html

HIV/AIDS Fact Sheets, Centers for Disease Control and Prevention
http://www.cdc.gov/hiv/pubs/facts.htm

HIV Insight
http://hivinsite.ucsf.edu/InSite

International AIDS Economic Network
http://www.iaen.org

International AIDS Vaccine Initiative News and Events
http://www.iavi.org/load_section.asp?lnav=news_lnav.asp&body=sections/news_home.asp

JAMA HIV/AIDS Information Center (*Journal of the American Medical Association*)
http://www.ama-assn.org/special/hiv/hivhome.htm

Population Council, AIDS Brochure
http://www.popcouncil.org/hivaids/aidsbrochure.html

Uganda AIDS Commission
http://www.aidsuganda.org/hiv-aids.htm

Uganda Family Planning Promotion Project
http://www.jhuccp.org/pubs/field_reports/fr7/contents.html

UNAIDS, links
http://www.unaids.org/links/national.asp

UN General Assembly Special Session on HIV/AIDS
http://www.un.org/ga/aids/coverage

World Health Organization
http://www.who.int/m/topics/hiv_aids/en/index.html

Document

1. Declaration of Commitment on HIV/AIDS: Global Crisis-Global Action

Joint United Nations Programme on HIV/AIDS, Special Session on HIV/AIDS, New York, 2001

The full text is available at http://www.unaids.org/whatsnew/others/un_special/Declaration 2706_en.htm.

Extracts

1. We, Heads of State and Government and Representatives of States and Governments, assembled at the United Nations, from 25 to 27 June 2001, for the twenty-sixth special session of the General Assembly convened in accordance with resolution 55/13, as a matter of urgency, to review and address the problem of HIV/AIDS in all its aspects as well as to secure a global commitment to enhancing coordination and intensification of national, regional and international efforts to combat it in a comprehensive manner;

2. Deeply concerned that the global HIV/AIDS epidemic, through its devastating scale and impact, constitutes a global emergency and one of the most formidable challenges to human life and dignity, as well as to the effective enjoyment of human rights, which undermines social and economic development throughout the world and affects all levels of society—national, community, family and individual;
3. Noting with profound concern, that by the end of the year 2000, 36.1 million people worldwide were living with HIV/AIDS, 90 percent in developing countries and 75 percent in sub-Saharan Africa;
4. Noting with grave concern that all people, rich and poor, without distinction of age, gender or race are affected by the HIV/AIDS epidemic, further noting that people in developing countries are the most affected and that women, young adults and children, in particular girls, are the most vulnerable;
5. Concerned also that the continuing spread of HIV/AIDS will constitute a serious obstacle to the realization of the global development goals we adopted at the Millennium Summit; . . .
36. Solemnly declare our commitment to address the HIV/AIDS crisis by taking action as follows, taking into account the diverse situations and circumstances in different regions and countries throughout the world;

Leadership

Strong leadership at all levels of society is essential for the effective response to the epidemic

Leadership by Governments in combating HIV/AIDS is essential and their efforts should be complemented by the full and active participation of civil society, the business community and the private sector

Leadership involves personal commitment and concrete actions

37. By 2003, ensure the development and implementation of multisectoral national strategies and financing plans for combating HIV/AIDS that address the epidemic in forthright terms; confront stigma, silence and denial; address gender and age-based dimensions of the epidemic; eliminate discrimination and marginalization; involve partnerships with civil society and the business sector and the full participation of people living with HIV/AIDS, those in vulnerable groups and people mostly at risk, particularly women and young people; are resourced to the extent possible from national budgets without excluding other sources, inter alia international cooperation; fully promote and protect all human rights and fundamental freedoms, including the right to the highest attainable standard of physical and mental health; integrate a gender perspective; and address risk, vulnerability, prevention, care, treatment and support and reduction of the impact of the epidemic; and strengthen health, education and legal system capacity. . . .

Prevention must be the mainstay of our response

47. By 2003, establish time-bound national targets to achieve the internationally agreed prevention goal to reduce by 2005 HIV prevalence among young men and women aged 15 to 24 in the most affected countries by 25 percent and by 25 percent globally by 2010, and to intensify efforts to achieve these targets as well as to challenge gender stereotypes and attitudes, and gender inequalities in relation to HIV/AIDS, encouraging the active involvement of men and boys.

ARMS CONTROL

J. Peter Scoblic

Although the threat of a nuclear war has greatly diminished since the end of the cold war, weapons of mass destruction (WMD) remain one of the chief security concerns of the international community. Most of the established nuclear powers have significantly reduced their nuclear arsenals, but despite increasingly tight diplomatic constraints, a number of countries persist in trying to develop chemical, biological, and nuclear weapons and the missiles to deliver them. The 11 September 2001 attacks on the United States and subsequent cases of anthrax have also heightened concern about the possibility of terrorists acquiring and using weapons of mass destruction. International diplomacy has proven effective in reversing the superpower arms race and slowing the proliferation of these weapons, but significant challenges remain if the world is to avoid the devastating loss of life and property that the use of these weapons can cause.

Historical Background and Development

In 1945 the United States conducted the first test of a nuclear weapon and a few months later dropped two atomic bombs on Japan, killing a hundred thousand people and changing the nature of warfare forever. The Soviet Union tested its first atomic weapon in 1949, and as the U.S.-Soviet geopolitical rivalry grew, an arms race ensued. Over the next two decades both superpowers built weapons far more powerful than those used against Japan and developed ballistic missiles that could strike each other's homeland despite the thousands of miles between them. Indeed, the United States and the Soviet Union built enough weapons to ensure that a major nuclear conflict would destroy both sides, regardless of who struck first. This uncomfortable but perversely stable relationship became known as mutual assured destruction, or MAD; it deterred each superpower, given their massive destructive capacity, from a first strike against the other.

By the mid-1960s, Britain, China, and France had also conducted nuclear tests, and international concern about the uncontrolled spread of nuclear weapons led to the negotiation of the Treaty on the Non-Proliferation of

Nuclear Weapons, commonly referred to as the Non-Proliferation Treaty (NPT) (see Document 1). The treaty, signed by fifty-eight countries in 1968 and by more later, allowed the five states that had already conducted nuclear tests to retain their weapons (though it committed them to eventual disarmament), but prohibited all others from developing them.

In the late 1960s, the United States and the Soviet Union began to discuss ways to stabilize their nuclear competition. In 1972 they signed the Anti-Ballistic Missile (ABM) Treaty, prohibiting most defenses against strategic ballistic missiles (see Document 2). The rationale behind the treaty was that if either side developed a defense that could counter its enemy's offensive missiles, its opponent would simply be spurred to expand its offensive capacity, which in turn would call for better defenses, and so on. The pace of the arms race, already proceeding at a frightening clip, would increase.

The United States and the Soviet Union were also working diplomatically to cap the number of weapons that each could deploy, but although two agreements—SALT I and II, from the Strategic Arms Limitation Talks—were signed in the 1970s, it was not until the mid-1980s that real progress was made. In 1987 the United States and the Soviet Union banned intermediate-range missiles through the Intermediate-Range Nuclear Forces (INF) Treaty. In 1991, with the cold war winding down and the Soviet Union disintegrating, the two nations signed the Strategic Arms Reduction Treaty (START I), obligating each side to reduce its strategic arsenal to six thousand deployed nuclear warheads—nearly a 50 percent reduction for the United States and the Soviet Union. Two years later, they signed START II, obligating each side to further reduce its arsenal to thirty-five hundred warheads.

The atmosphere of cooperation that followed the end of the cold war also allowed the international community to redouble its nonproliferation efforts and negotiate the Comprehensive Test Ban Treaty. The agreement bans all nuclear testing with the objective of prohibiting states without nuclear weapons from getting them and stopping nations with nuclear weapons from developing new, more dangerous ones. A number of key countries, including the United States, have yet to ratify the treaty, so it has not yet taken effect.

The international community first acted to restrict chemical and biological weapons years before the detonation of a nuclear weapon. In 1925, after the devastation of World War I and the protracted international talks that followed it, the Geneva protocol that outlawed the use of chemical and biological weapons was signed. This ban was reinforced in 1972 by the Biological Weapons Convention, which prohibited the development, production, or possession of germ weapons, and in 1993 by the Chemical Weapons Convention, which did the same for chemical weapons. No international treaty regulates the proliferation of ballistic missiles, but in 1989 several industrialized nations with advanced missile capabilities agreed to restrict their export of missiles and missile technology. This arrangement, the Missile Technology Control Regime (MTCR), has grown to include thirty-three members, and it remains the primary political barrier against the spread of ballistic missiles to new nations.

Current Status

Arms control refers to the use of diplomatic and legal instruments to reduce military threats and is intended to complement the security provided by traditional military defenses. Though arms control measures have been applied to conventional weapons, such as tanks and ships, the term more frequently refers to the use of diplomacy to contain the threat from weapons of mass destruction, which is the focus here.

Since the advent of the nuclear age in 1945, the international community has used arms control for a variety of purposes: to stabilize, slow, and eventually reverse the nuclear arms race between the United States and the Soviet Union; to prevent the spread of nuclear weapons; to outlaw biological and chemical weapons; and to disarm nations of particular concern to global security. In the twenty-first century arms control remains a useful tool for combating the remaining problems posed by nuclear, chemical, and biological weapons and missiles, but several efforts to expand the arms control regime have stalled, in part because of a lack of support from the administration of U.S. president George W. Bush, which has argued that traditional arms control is an ineffective guarantor of U.S. security.

Research

Understanding which countries have what weapons of mass destruction and missiles is a difficult task because of the secrecy with which governments guard such programs. The most accessible data tends to come from U.S. intelligence sources, but the information they provide is often vague and must be treated with some skepticism.

Nuclear Weapons. The 1968 nuclear Non-Proliferation Treaty, which has been signed by nearly every country in the world, gave only five states—Britain, China, France, the Soviet Union, and the United States—the legal right to possess nuclear weapons and required all others to refrain from developing them. The United States and Russia each have nearly six thousand strategic nuclear warheads deployed, and Britain, China, and France have a combined total of less than a thousand strategic warheads deployed? (see map, p. 31). It is important to note that these warheads are "strategic" only—that is, warheads with high explosive yields intended to be delivered against the homeland of an adversary. "Tactical" weapons, on the other hand, generally have smaller yields and are intended for use on the battlefield, as if they were simply powerful conventional explosives. It is difficult to estimate how many of these each nuclear state has. To further blur matters, certain states have indicated they might use strategic weapons in a tactical role. "Deployed" warheads refer to those actually mounted on missiles or on bombers and ready for use. The United States and Russia also maintain warheads in an inactive stockpile, which can be put on weapons if needed.

India, Israel, and Pakistan also have nuclear weapons, but they are not members of the NPT and are not legally recognized as nuclear weapon states. Based on the amount of fissile material each of these countries is thought to have,

Pakistan is believed capable of building 30 to 50 warheads, and India is thought to be capable of building 45 to 95 warheads. Israel, which has never publicly acknowledged its possession of nuclear weapons, is believed to have enough fissile material for 75 to 125 warheads. It is not, however, well understood how far these nations have progressed in "weaponizing" their nuclear material, such as mounting warheads on missiles. Cuba is the only other country that is not a member of the NPT, but it is not suspected of having a nuclear weapons program.

Another set of nations—Iran, Iraq, and North Korea—are members of the NPT but are of concern because they may have nuclear weapons or nuclear weapons programs. Though Iran is a member in good standing of the NPT, the United States believes that it has a nuclear weapons program supported by its civilian nuclear power projects, which are being aided by Russia. Iraq had a large nuclear weapons program that was discovered after its defeat in the 1991 Persian Gulf War, at which time the United Nations required and verified that Iraq destroy its weapons program. It is thought, however, that Iraq still has nuclear ambitions. North Korea was suspected of having a nuclear weapons program in the early 1990s, but it agreed to halt its nuclear activities in 1994 in exchange for international assistance in developing a civilian nuclear energy program. Nevertheless, North Korea may have enough fissile material to build one or two weapons (see Case Study—North Korea).

Biological and Chemical Weapons. The 1972 Biological Weapons Convention, which now has 144 signatories, outlaws weapons that use microbial agents or toxins to cause harm, but the Bush administration believes that there are 13 nations pursuing biological weapons. A January 2001 Defense Department report, "Proliferation: Threat and Response," asserts that North Korea may have biological weapons ready for use and that Iran, Libya, and Syria are pursuing offensive biological weapons programs. The same report notes that Iraq, which had a germ warfare program prior to its disarmament after the Persian Gulf War, may be trying to reconstitute its efforts. The report also expresses concern that China and Russia may still maintain elements of biological weapons programs that they ostensibly dismantled years ago.

The 1993 Chemical Weapons Convention banned weapons that use poisonous compounds to incapacitate or kill. Though chemical weapons are considered weapons of mass destruction, it is far more difficult to kill large numbers of people with them than with nuclear or biological weapons. India, Russia, South Korea, and the United States, as per their obligations under the convention, have formally admitted possessing chemical weapons and are in the process of destroying them. A number of other countries have declared facilities for producing chemical weapons and are either destroying them or converting them to peaceful uses.

Despite the prohibition on chemical weapons, a number of countries are believed to still be pursuing them. According to the U.S. Defense Department, North Korea has a "large stockpile" of chemical weapons. In 1998 Iran admitted once having had a chemical weapons program, and the United States believes that Iran still has chemical weapons and continues to develop them.

Though most of Iraq's chemical weapons were destroyed after the Persian Gulf War, Baghdad may be trying to rebuild its chemical weapons arsenal. Syria and Libya are also thought to have or be in pursuit of chemical weapons.

Ballistic Missiles. Ballistic missiles are guided rockets that can deliver conventional, nuclear, chemical, or biological warheads to great distances. The type of warhead that can be delivered depends on the size of the missile and the weight of the warhead. Ballistic missiles themselves are not considered weapons of mass destruction, but their proliferation is considered almost as important because they allow countries to deliver such weapons at a great range and with little possibility that the country being attacked will be able to defend itself. The United States has developed an advanced version of the Patriot anti-missile system (used during the Persian Gulf War) that is capable of shooting down short-range missiles. Neither the United States nor any other nation, however, has the ability to defend against intercontinental ballistic missiles (ICBMs), which have ranges of more than 5,500 kilometers (3,300 miles) and travel much faster than short-range missiles.

Only a handful of nations have missiles that can reach the United States. Approximately thirty-three nations have ballistic missiles that can travel farther than 100 kilometers (60 miles)—and twenty-seven of these countries have ballistic missiles that can travel 300 kilometers (180 miles) or more (see Table 1)—but most of these countries have only short-range Scud missiles, low-grade weapons bought or inherited from the Soviet Union. (Iraq used these missiles during the Persian Gulf War). Each of the five nuclear weapon states deploys land-based ICBMs or submarine-launched ballistic missiles (SLBMs) or both. India, Iran, Israel, Pakistan, and North Korea have either produced or flight-tested a missile with a range greater than 1,000 kilometers (620 miles). Because of their nuclear arsenals and history of conflict, the Indian and Pakistani programs are of particular concern. Both countries are aggressively developing ballistic missiles, with Russia providing assistance to India and with China providing assistance to Pakistan. Iran has tested a 1,300-kilometer ballistic missile but is actively pursuing longer-range missiles with the help of China, North Korea, and Russia. Currently, the chief focus of U.S. anxiety is North Korea, which shocked the world in 1998 by test firing an intermediate-range missile over Japan. Though it has not conducted a flight-test since, North Korea's missile capability is advanced for a developing nation and has become the chief rationale for U.S. development of a national missile defense.

Policies and Programs

Despite arms control's success in containing the superpower arms race and limiting the spread of biological, chemical, and nuclear weapons, significant challenges and threats remain: the United States and Russia still deploy thousands of strategic warheads; China is upgrading its nuclear arsenal; India and Pakistan have begun an arms race; and the so-called rogue states, Iraq and North Korea, continue their pursuit of weapons outlawed or restricted by international treaties.

A number of international efforts have been underway in recent years to address these problems by strengthening existing arms control agreements, forging new ones, and negotiating directly with countries of concern. For example, the Comprehensive Test Ban Treaty (CTBT), opened for signing in 1996 but not yet in effect, would outlaw all nuclear tests. Another nuclear nonproliferation measure that has yet to be negotiated is the fissile material cutoff treaty, intended to cap the existing supply of uranium and plutonium suitable for use in weapons by making it illegal for countries to produce more.

Unfortunately, many of these arms control efforts have stalled, in no small part because of Washington's refusal to participate. For example, in 1999 the U.S. Senate rejected the CTBT, arguing that the treaty would threaten the United States' ability to maintain its nuclear stockpile. The Bush administration argues that its approach is one of "a la carte multilateralism," whereby it picks and chooses agreements that are most suitable, but to date it appears to have found no arms control agreements appetizing. Rather than acting with other developed nations to address outstanding threats through multilateral action, the United States is increasingly opting for unilateral military solutions to protect itself from weapons of mass destruction.

The most salient example of the administration's approach to arms control and international security is its December 2001 decision to withdraw from the ABM Treaty and deploy a national missile defense, which would theoretically give the United States the capability to shoot down incoming enemy missiles. Such a system, however, is years, if not decades, away from deployment. Intuitively, the ability to defend oneself from missiles sounds like an important and worthwhile policy goal, but the United States and the Soviet Union signed the ABM Treaty because they feared that the capability would precipitate a dangerous arms race in which, during a crisis, each might think it was to its advantage to launch first.

According to the Bush administration, however, the ABM Treaty is a relic of the cold war designed to codify the concept of mutually assured destruction. Furthermore, missile defense advocates argue, rogue states' ballistic missile programs could soon give unstable countries like North Korea the ability to strike the United States directly. President Bush has argued that the United States must forge a "new strategic framework" for the post–cold war world that incorporates missile defenses, as well as unilateral cuts in the U.S. nuclear arsenal. His administration, however, has not explained how its new strategic framework changes the realities of nuclear deterrence. Because nuclear weapons are of such great military significance, no nuclear nation wants to run the risk that it might be vulnerable to attack while its opponent is not—in other words, that assured destruction would no longer be mutual. For this reason, U.S. missile defense plans have raised serious international concern. For example, in 2001 Russia said it would withdraw from all bilateral arms control agreements with the United States, such as the START agreements, if Washington pulled out of the ABM Treaty. China also strongly opposed a U.S. missile defense because even a limited system would be able to counter Beijing's small nuclear force, leaving it unable to deter a U.S. attack. Although the initial international reaction was muted to the U.S. announcement of its withdrawal from the ABM Treaty, Russia's and China's fundamental security concerns remain unresolved. It is not clear how U.S. plans will affect the global strategic balance.

Another agreement affected by the Bush administration's attitude toward arms control is the Biological Weapons Convention. Although the convention outlawed biological weapons, it did not include enforcement provisions, that is, it provided no way for member states to ascertain if others were abiding by or cheating on the treaty. Since 1994 an international negotiating body, the Ad Hoc Group, has been meeting to draft an addition, or protocol, to the treaty for verifying each state's compliance. It released a preliminary text in 2000. The United States, however, quickly rejected the proposal, arguing that it was not strong enough and would merely offer a false sense of security. Washington subsequently put forward its own suggestions for improving the treaty but indicated that it would like nations to take voluntary, rather than legally binding, steps to strengthen the convention. In November 2001 the United States infuriated the international community by moving to disband the Ad Hoc Group and permanently scuttle its work.

The Chemical Weapons Convention is one treaty whose implementation has not been threatened by the Bush administration. Four nations, including the United States and Russia, have declared their chemical weapons stockpiles and are currently working to get rid of them. There are, however, problems with implementing the treaty. Several key nations have not signed the treaty, and some that have are still suspected of developing chemical weapons. Though the treaty includes enforcement provisions, no state has chosen to use them to pursue suspected violators.

Regional Summaries

United States–Russia

Though separated by thousands of miles, the United States and the Soviet Union constituted the single most important "region" for arms control during the cold war. Today the U.S.-Russian axis remains critical because of the large number of nuclear weapons these nations still possess and the international influence they continue to wield.

Despite rapid progress in the late 1980s and early 1990s with the INF Treaty and START I and START II, the future of coordinated reductions in U.S. and Russian nuclear weapons is uncertain. In 1997 Presidents Bill Clinton and Boris Yeltsin agreed to pursue a START III agreement that would further reduce the number of deployed nuclear weapons to 2,500 warheads each, but those talks accomplished little after the Clinton administration linked progress in the discussion to Russia allowing limited missile defenses. The potential for progress was further diminished when the Russian legislation ratifying START II, which was not passed until April 2000, mandated that the treaty not legally take effect until the United States had approved a package of ABM Treaty–related agreements signed in 1997.

The strategic reductions process received a welcome push in November 2001, when President Bush announced that the United States would cut its deployed strategic arsenal to between 1,700 and 2,200 warheads. The following month Russian president Vladimir Putin reciprocated, saying Russia wanted to cut the number of its deployed strategic warheads to between 1,500

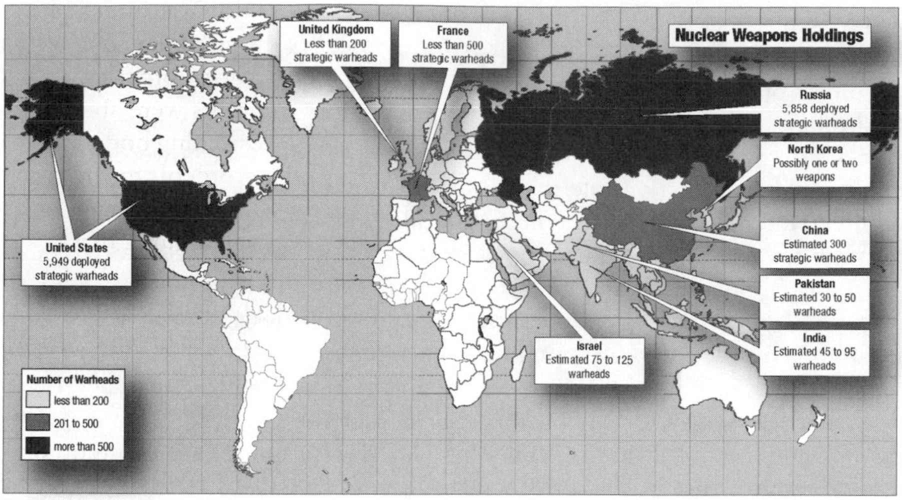

Source: Arms Control Association, Washington, D.C.

and 2,200. Unfortunately, the two countries disagreed over how to implement the cuts, with the Russians favoring a legally binding START-like treaty and the Americans pushing for informal unilateral (but reciprocal) reductions. These differences have been made more salient by the U.S. intention to withdraw from the ABM Treaty and establishment of a "new strategic framework" that is to include national defenses against strategic ballistic missiles. Despite these problems, U.S.-Russian arms control initiatives in other areas have continued. Through a set of programs collectively known as cooperative threat reduction, the United States is helping Russia downsize its vast nuclear weapons complex and secure its nuclear materials to prevent their theft by terrorists. The United States and Russia are also working to ensure that one country's mistaken belief that it is under nuclear attack does not cause it to retaliate before realizing its error. The two nations currently have accords requiring them to notify each other before launching rockets or testing missiles. They also have an agreement to build a center in Moscow to share early warning information, and the United States is considering, according to Bush, taking its missiles off high alert in the hope that Russia will reciprocate.

The United States and Russia are also working to destroy their stockpiles of chemical weapons, which were outlawed by the Chemical Weapons Convention. At the time the convention was signed, the United States declared that it had approximately thirty thousand tons of chemical agent, and Russia asserted that it had forty thousand tons. Neither country is expected to finish the destruction of their stockpiles until after 2010. Russia, in particular, has had difficulties fulfilling its convention requirements because of its economic troubles, though the United States has offered some assistance.

The United States and the Soviet Union both pledged to give up biological weapons when they signed the Biological Weapons Convention in 1972, but the Soviets continued operating a clandestine germ warfare program. Currently, the United States has several cooperative programs in place to help employ former Soviet bioweapons scientists and secure former bioweapons facilities.

Europe

Although Britain and France are de jure nuclear weapon states and permanent members of the UN Security Council, Europe's role in proliferation and arms control was long subordinate to the superpower rivalry between the United States and the Soviet Union. Since the end of the cold war, however, Europe has taken a more active role in arms control, particularly in areas where the United States does not seem willing to lead. After the START process stalled, a group of eight European nations formed the New Agenda Coalition to push for quicker nuclear disarmament. It also appears that Europe will play an important role in the dispute between the United States and Russia over U.S. plans for a missile defense. Though Europe is diplomatically much closer to the United States than it is to Russia, it is geographically closer to Russia and eager for good relations with Moscow. As U.S. plans for a missile defense system have become more serious, Europe has played a cautionary role, questioning the severity of the threat from rogue states and urging the United States to consider the strategic ramifications of deployment.

European nations have also played a central role in trying to control the spread of biological weapons, taking the lead in international negotiations to strengthen the Biological Weapons Convention. European nations have also been key participants in the Australia Group, an organization that seeks to regulate the export of chemical and biological agents, as well as dual-use equipment, in order to reduce the risks of proliferation.

North Africa and the Middle East

The Middle East is one of the most problematic areas for arms control and nonproliferation efforts, because Iran and Iraq (as well as Libya and Syria) are states of concern to the United States and because Israel is a nuclear weapon power that refuses to acknowledge its capability and complicates efforts to prevent Arab states from acquiring weapons of mass destruction. Israel is thought to have developed a nuclear weapons capability several decades ago, with French assistance and U.S. consent. Israel has never officially acknowledged having nuclear weapons, however, saying only that it would not be the first to introduce nuclear weapons into the region.

According to the International Atomic Energy Agency (IAEA), the organization responsible for seeing that states comply with the NPT, Iran is an NPT member in good standing, but the United States believes that Tehran is working on a secret nuclear weapons project supported by its nuclear energy program. With significant Russian aid, Iran is building a 1,000-megawatt nuclear reactor in Bushehr, scheduled for completion in 2003. Although the United States has tried to persuade Russia to halt its assistance, because Iran's nuclear facilities remain under IAEA safeguards there is no legal recourse for U.S. concerns.

The United States also believes that Iran has a substantial stockpile of chemical weapons, as well as the means to deliver them short distances. Because Iran is a member of the Chemical Weapons Convention, other signatories have the right to request an international inspection of Iran's facilities. The United

States, despite its repeated accusations of Iran's gross violation of the treaty, has never demanded an inspection.

Iraq is the other chief state of concern to the United States in the Middle East. As a result of Iraq's 1990 invasion of Kuwait and its subsequent defeat, the UN Security Council placed Iraq under strict economic sanctions and mandated that it destroy its nuclear, chemical, and biological weapons, as well as all missiles with a range greater than 150 kilometers. Unfortunately, UN weapons inspectors were forced to leave Iraq in 1998, and efforts to have them return have failed as the Security Council's resolve has faltered.

Although Iraq is allowed to sell oil and import food and humanitarian supplies to feed and care for its citizens, President Saddam Hussein has diverted Iraqi income and used the pathetic condition of Iraq's economy and people to leverage international support for lifting the sanctions. In early 2001 the United States and Great Britain tried to revamp the sanctions regime with a plan that would have permitted most commercial transactions while prohibiting weapons-related imports, but their efforts were blocked by Moscow. Without UN inspectors in the country, little is known about Iraq's weapons programs, but many analysts fear that the government has spent the past several years trying to reconstitute its ability to produce weapons of mass destruction.

Northeast Asia

China first tested a nuclear weapon in 1964 and proceeded to develop a small nuclear arsenal as a way of putting itself on more equal footing with the United States and the Soviet Union during the cold war. Today its arsenal remains small—the U.S. Defense Department estimates that China has only twenty or so nuclear-armed missiles capable of hitting the United States—but Beijing is modernizing its nuclear forces and developing more advanced missiles.

For decades China refused to participate in international arms control efforts. For example, even though the NPT allowed China to retain nuclear weapons, it was not until 1992 that China acceded to the treaty. In the past ten years, however, China has increased its participation, signing the Chemical Weapons Convention and the Comprehensive Test Ban Treaty. It has not, however, joined the MTCR, and although the government has agreed not to export missiles capable of delivering nuclear weapons, the United States maintains that China continues to ship missiles and missile components to Pakistan.

China strongly opposes development of a U.S. missile defense because even a limited system would negate Beijing's minimal deterrent. There is disagreement in the United States about how its missile defense plans could affect China's arsenal, with some arguing that China is going to upgrade its nuclear weaponry regardless, while others argue that a missile defense would prompt quantitative, as well as qualitative, improvements to China's nuclear armory. Some U.S. policymakers and analysts have also expressed concern that a Chinese nuclear buildup could encourage Japan and Taiwan to develop nuclear weapons of their own.

The other significant player in Northeast Asia is North Korea, an impoverished, communist dictatorship that is considered a "rogue state" by the United

States. Despite its horrible economic situation, North Korea has persisted in devoting significant resources to developing weapons of mass destruction and the means for delivering them. Its nuclear weapons program was halted by a 1994 agreement with the United States (see Case Study—North Korea), but it continues work on a ballistic missile program. In 1998 it raised international (particularly U.S.) concern by test firing an intermediate-range ballistic missile over Japan. North Korean missiles are of particular concern because North Korea has chemical weapons and because it may have biological weapons, although it is a member of the Biological Weapons Convention.

North Korea's relatively advanced missile program has publicly served as the chief rationale for U.S. missile defense plans, but the North Korean leadership has exhibited a willingness to give up its missile program in exchange for compensation from the United States. The Clinton administration was reportedly close to such a deal near the end of its second term, but President Bush declined to follow up after entering office. At present, although the United States has indicated an interest in resuming talks with North Korea, it has linked further negotiations on the country's missile program with talks on its nuclear and conventional weapons, a linkage North Korea opposes.

South Asia

India exploded what it called a "peaceful nuclear device" in 1974. Although India never acknowledged having a nuclear weapons program, it was thereafter assumed that India could build at least primitive nuclear arms. India's rival Pakistan is thought to have acquired a nuclear weapons capability in the mid-1980s, but it too kept quiet about its capabilities. The programs of these states remained below board until May 1998, when India conducted several nuclear tests to demonstrate its weapons capability. Days later, Pakistan reciprocated, and the South Asian nations' nuclear weapons capabilities came fully out of the closet. Immediately after the 1998 tests, India and Pakistan both announced a moratorium on further tests. Both have also indicated an interest in signing the Comprehensive Test Ban Treaty, but they have not yet done so, and their weapons programs continue apace. According to the U.S. Defense Department, India and Pakistan are at an advanced stage of nuclear and missile development.

An Indo-Pakistani nuclear arms race has been of particular concern because unresolved tensions between the two nations have led to three wars in the past fifty years. Pakistan's nuclear weapons have recently generated even greater concern because of the domestic unrest caused by President Pervez Musharraf's support of U.S. military action against the Taliban in Afghanistan. Some analysts fear that Musharraf, who took power in a military coup in 1999, could lose power and that Pakistan's nuclear weapons would fall into the hands of rebels or Islamists.

The United States imposed economic and military sanctions on India and Pakistan in 1998 in an attempt to roll back their nuclear programs, but the sanctions had little impact. Following the 11 September 2001 attacks on the United States, Washington quickly lifted most sanctions on both countries to secure their cooperation in the campaign against Afghanistan. A reversal of the nuclear arms buildup on the subcontinent in the near future appears unlikely.

Data

Table 1 Distribution of Ballistic Missiles with Ranges of 300 Kilometers or More

Country	System	Status	Range/Payload	Source
Afghanistan	Scud-B	Operational	300 km/1,000 kg	Soviet Union
Armenia	Scud-B	Operational	300 km/1,000 kg	Russia
Azerbaijan	Scud-B	Operational	300 km/1,000 kg	Soviet Union
Belarus	Scud-B	Operational	300 km/1,000 kg	Soviet Union
Bulgaria	Scud-B	Operational	300 km/1,000 kg	Soviet Union
	SS-23	Operational	500 km/450 kg	Soviet Union
China	DF-11	Operational	300 km/800 kg	Domestic
	DF-15	Operational	600 km/500 kg	Domestic
	Julang 1 (SLBM)	Operational	1,000 km/600 kg	Domestic
	DF-21	Operational	2,500 km/600 kg	Domestic
	DF-21A	Operational	1,800 km/2,000 kg	Domestic
	DF-3A	Operational	2,800 km/2,150 kg	Domestic
	DF-4	Operational	5,500 km/2,200 kg	Domestic
	DF-31	Tested/Development	8,000 km/700 kg	Domestic
	Julang 2 (SLBM)	Tested/Development	8,000 km/700 kg	Domestic
	DF-5A	Operational	13,000 km/3,200 kg	Domestic
Egypt	Scud-B	Operational	300 km/1,000 kg	Soviet Union
	Project-T	Operational	450 km/985 kg	Domestic/North Korea
	Scud-C	Operational	550 km/600 kg	North Korea
	Vector	Development	685 km/450 kg	Domestic/North Korea
France	M4A/B (SLBM)	Operational	6,000 km/1,200 kg	Domestic
	M45 (SLBM)	Operational	6,000 km/1,200 kg	Domestic
Georgia	Scud-B	Operational	300 km/1,000 kg	Soviet Union
India	Dhanush	Tested/Development	350 km/1,000 kg	Domestic
	Sagarika (SLCM?)	Development	350 km/500 kg	Domestic/Russia
	Agni-1	Prototype Only	1,500 km/1,000 kg	Domestic
	Agni-2	Serial Production?	2,000 km/1,000 kg	Domestic
	Agni-3	Development	3,000–5,500 km/N.A.	Domestic
	Surya	Development	5,500+ km/2,000 kg	Domestic/Russia
Iran	Scud-B	Operational	300 km/1,000 kg	Libya/North Korea
	Scud-C	Operational	550 km/600 kg	North Korea
	Shahab-3	Tested/Development	1,300 km/700 kg	Domestic/North Korea/Russia
	Shahab-4	Development	2,000 km/1,000 kg	Domestic/North Korea/Russia
	Shahab-5	Concept Stage	3,000–5,500 km/1,000 kg	Domestic/Russia
Israel	Jericho-1	Operational	500 km/500 kg	Domestic/France
	Jericho-2	Operational	1,500 km/1,000 kg	Domestic/France
	Jericho-3	Development	2,500 km/1,000 kg	Domestic
Libya	Scud-B	Operational	300 km/1,000 kg	Soviet Union
	Scud-C	Potential Acquisition	550 km/600 kg	North Korea
	Nodong-1	Potential Acquisition	1,300 km/750 kg	North Korea

Table 1 Distribution of Ballistic Missiles with Ranges of 300 Kilometers or More (*continued*)

Country	System	Status	Range/Payload	Source
North Korea	Scud-B	Operational	300 km/1,000 kg	Domestic
	Scud-C variant	Operational	550 km/700 kg	Domestic
	Nodong-1	Operational	1,300 km/750 kg	Domestic
	Nodong-2	Development	1,500 km/770 kg	Domestic
	Taepo Dong-1	Tested/Development	2,000 km/1,000 kg	Domestic
	Taepo Dong-2	Development	5,000–6,000 km/ 1,000 kg	Domestic
Pakistan	Hatf-2	Program Canceled?	300 km/500 kg	Domestic/China
	Hatf-3	Development	300 km/500 kg	Domestic/China
	Tarmuk	Development	300 km/800 kg	Domestic/China
	Shaheen-1	Tested/Development	750 km/500 kg	Domestic/China
	Ghauri-1	Tested/Development	1,300+ km/700 kg	Domestic/North Korea
	Shaheen-2	Development	2,000 km/?	Domestic/North Korea
	Ghaznavi	Development |	2,000 km/?	Domestic
	Ghauri-2	Tested/Development	2,300 km/700 kg	Domestic/North Korea
Russian Federation	Scud B	Operational	300 km/1,000 kg	Domestic
	SS-X-26	Development	300 km/N.A.	Domestic
	SS-18	Operational	11,500 km/8,800 kg	Domestic
	SS-19	Operational	10,000 km/4,350 kg	Domestic
	SS-24 (silo, rail)	Operational	10,000 km/4,050 kg	Domestic
	SS-25	Operational	11,200 km/1,200 kg	Domestic
	SS-27 (silo)	Operational	10,000 km/1,000 kg	Domestic
	SS-N-8 (SLBM)	Operational	8,000 km/1,100 kg	Domestic
	SS-N-18 (SLBM)	Operational	5,600 km/1,650 kg	Domestic
	SS-N-20 (SLBM)	Operational	8,800 km/2,550 kg	Domestic
	SS-N-23 (SLBM)	Operational	8,000 km/2,800 kg	Domestic
Saudi Arabia	DF-3A	Operational	2,800 km/2,150 kg	China
Slovak Republic	Scud-B	Operational	300 km/1,000 kg	Soviet Union
Syria	Scud-B	Operational	300 km/1,000 kg	Domestic/Soviet Union
	Scud-C	Operational	500 km/600 kg	Domestic/North Korea
	Scud-D	Tested/Development	750 km/200 kg	Domestic/North Korea
Taiwan	Tien Chi	Development	300 km/500 kg	Domestic
Turkmenistan	Scud-B	Operational	300 km/1,000 kg	Soviet Union
Ukraine		Operational		Soviet Union
United Arab Emirates	Scud-B	Operational	300 km/1,000 kg	Soviet Union
United Kingdom	D-5 Trident II (SLBM)	Operational	7,400 km/2,800 kg	United States

Table 1 Distribution of Ballistic Missiles with Ranges of 300 Kilometers or More (*continued*)

Country	System	Status	Range/Payload	Source
United States	MX/Peacekeeper	Operational	11,000 km/3,950 kg	Domestic
	Minuteman III	Operational	13,000 km/1,150 kg	Domestic
	C-4 Trident I (SLBM)	Operational	7,400 km/1,500 kg	Domestic
	D-5 Trident II (SLBM)	Operational	7,400 km/2,800 kg	Domestic
Vietnam	Scud-B	Operational	300 km/1,000 kg	Soviet Union
Yemen	Scud-B	Operational	300 km/1,000 kg	Soviet Union

Source: Arms Control Association.

Note: Iraq's missiles with ranges in excess of 150 kilometers were to be destroyed after the 1991 Persian Gulf War. In December 1992 the United Nations Special Commission (UNSCOM) claimed to have destroyed all of Iraq's proscribed ballistic missiles as well as items related to their production and development. In October 1996, however, UNSCOM admitted that Iraq had not provided a complete accounting of all weapons and other capabilities in the missile area.

N.A. Data not available.

? Data uncertain.

Case Study—North Korea

In December 1985 North Korea acceded to the nuclear Non-Proliferation Treaty, which required it to forego nuclear weapons but allowed it to maintain nuclear facilities for peaceful purposes, such as energy production. To ensure that supposedly benign nuclear programs are not used to advance weapons programs, the NPT requires the placement of all nuclear facilities under safeguards administered by the International Atomic Energy Agency, but for six years after joining the treaty North Korea refused to submit to IAEA safeguards. At the same time, it began operating and expanding a nuclear complex at Yongbyon, which Western authorities feared was being used to produce weapons-grade plutonium.

U.S. concern over North Korea's apparent ambition to build nuclear weapons grew in the late 1980s and early 1990s, but in 1992 North Korea finally signed a safeguards agreement with the IAEA, submitting a declaration of its nuclear activities and allowing international inspections of its nuclear program. Inspectors quickly discovered inconsistencies in North Korea's declarations and suspected that it had produced more plutonium than it had admitted. In February 1993 the IAEA demanded special inspections of two undeclared nuclear sites that it thought might house nuclear waste, essentially accusing Pyongyang of cheating on its NPT commitments. North Korea refused, and on March 13 it announced its intention to withdraw from the treaty. Washington began high-level talks with Pyongyang almost immediately, but although North Korea agreed to suspend its withdrawal from the NPT, it would allow only limited IAEA activities in the country. By the end of 1993 little progress had been made, and in December U.S. intelligence estimated that North Korea probably had separated enough plutonium for one or two weapons.

In April 1994 North Korea inflamed growing international tensions over the state of its nuclear program by shutting down the five-megawatt nuclear reactor it had been operating at Yongbyon in order to refuel it. The used fuel from the reactor contained enough plutonium for several nuclear bombs, and the IAEA was also concerned that if the fuel from the reactor was unloaded without supervision the agency would not be able to resolve the inconsistencies in North Korea's declarations about its nuclear program. When North Korea began to remove the spent fuel from the reactors, the United States redoubled its efforts to persuade the international community to impose sanctions against Pyongyang for its refusal to cooperate with the IAEA. The United States also began preparing for war.

As tensions escalated, former U.S. president Jimmy Carter traveled to Pyongyang to discuss the situation with North Korean officials. Carter, whose trip was unofficial, persuaded the North Koreans to freeze their nuclear program in exchange for high-level talks with the United States. The Clinton administration agreed, and talks began that summer. On 21 October 1994, the United States and North Korea signed the Agreed Framework, which calls for North Korea to freeze operation and construction of (and eventually dismantle) its nuclear reactors. Pyongyang also agreed to allow special IAEA inspections to verify its compliance. In return, an international consortium would be established to build North Korea two light-water reactors, which are nuclear reactors from which it is difficult to derive weapons-usable fissile material. Until the light-water reactors are complete, North Korea will receive shipments of heavy-fuel oil to meet its energy needs.

Implementation of the Agreed Framework has encountered a number of obstacles, namely, delays in construction of the light-water reactors, but it appears that North Korea is abiding by the terms of the agreement. For example, when the United States developed concerns in 1998 that North Korea was operating a secret underground nuclear facility in Kumchang-ni, Pyongyang permitted an inspection in 1999 and a follow-up inspection in 2000, both of which yielded no evidence of illicit activity.

Some analysts have criticized the Agreed Framework because it seems to reward North Korea for violating its international commitments and because it provided North Korea with nuclear technology (albeit proliferation-resistant technology) in the form of the light-water reactors. Nevertheless, the Agreed Framework is widely considered one of the more successful arms control actions in the post–cold war era because it persuaded a reluctant state to give up its nuclear weapons program. Of course, it must not be forgotten that some of North Korea's plutonium remains unaccounted for, and U.S. intelligence still believes that North Korea has enough plutonium for at least one, and maybe two, nuclear weapons.

Biographical Sketches

Hans Blix is a longtime Swedish diplomat who headed the International Atomic Energy Agency from 1991 to 1997, during which time he oversaw the nuclear disarmament of Iraq, the dismantling of South Africa's nuclear weapons program, and the halt of North Korea's nuclear weapons program. In 2000 he was appointed executive director of the United Nations Monitoring, Verification and Inspection Commission (UNMOVIC), the organization created to replace the United Nations Special Commission (UNSCOM) and oversee Iraq's compliance with its disarmament obligations.

George Bush served as the United States' first post–cold war president. He took advantage of thawed relations with Moscow to conclude a number of major arms control agreements, including START I and II, the strategic arms reduction treaties that drastically reduced the U.S. and Soviet arsenals. In 1991 Bush unilaterally withdrew all naval tactical nuclear weapons from aboard U.S. ships and submarines, and in 1992 he declared a moratorium on U.S. nuclear testing.

Mikhail Gorbachev was Soviet head of state from 1985 to 1991. His assumption of power marked the beginning of improvements in the U.S.-Soviet relationship and allowed for nuclear tensions to be eased. Faced with President Ronald Reagan's plans for a U.S. missile defense shield, often referred to as Star Wars, Gorbachev countered with a proposal for total nuclear disarmament. Although Reagan and Gorbachev never settled the issue, in 1987 they were able to conclude the Intermediate-Range Nuclear Forces Treaty, the first accord to eliminate a class of weapons, and begin negotiations for the Strategic Arms Reduction Treaty.

Robert McNamara was U.S. secretary of defense from 1961 to 1968. A key figure in the Kennedy and Johnson administrations, McNamara was one of the first U.S. policymakers to articulate the concept of mutual assured destruction, or MAD, which maintained that the strategic situation between the United States and the Soviet Union would remain stable as long as each had the ability to inflict unacceptable damage on the other in a nuclear conflict, regardless of who struck first.

Ronald Reagan was president of the United States from 1981 to 1989 and initiated a buildup of U.S. strategic forces. In 1983 he shocked U.S. defense planners by calling on U.S. scientists to construct a missile shield that would render nuclear weapons "impotent and obsolete." Dubbed Star Wars by critics, Reagan's missile defense program produced no results during his administration, but his second term saw significant progress in arms control, including the signing of the Intermediate-Range Nuclear Forces Treaty and the beginning of negotiations for the Strategic Arms Reduction Treaty.

Directory

Arms Control Association, 1726 M Street NW, Suite 201, Washington, DC 20036. Telephone: (202) 463-8270, Email: aca@armscontrol.org, Web: http://www.armscontrol.org
Nonpartisan organization that works to promote public understanding and support for effective arms control policies, publishes Arms Control Today

Ballistic Missile Defense Organization, U.S. Department of Defense, The Pentagon, Arlington, VA 20301-1400. Telephone: (703) 697-8855, Email: birc@bmdo.osd.mil, Web: http://www.acq.osd.mil/bmdo/bmdolink/html/bmdolink.html
Central manager of the Defense Department's efforts to develop weapons systems to protect the United States, as well as deployed U.S. forces, from attack by ballistic missiles

Bureau of Arms Control, U.S. State Department, 2201 C Street NW, Washington, DC 20520. Telephone: (202) 647-4000, Web: http://www.state.gov/t/ac
Section of the State Department responsible for negotiating and implementing arms control agreements to which the United States is party

Center for Nonproliferation Studies, Monterey Institute for International Studies, 425 Van Buren Street, Monterey, CA 93940. Telephone: (831) 647-4154, Email: cns@miis.edu, Web: http://www.cns.miis.edu
Largest U.S. nongovernmental organization devoted to researching weapons of mass destruction and training new specialists in nonproliferation, publishes the Nonproliferation Review

Federation of American Scientists, 1717 K Street NW, Suite 209, Washington, DC 20036. Telephone: (202) 546-3300, Email: fas@fas.org, Web: http://www.fas.org
Research and advocacy group focusing on issues at the intersection of science and public policy, including nuclear and biological weapons

Henry L. Stimson Center, 11 Dupont Circle NW, 9th Floor, Washington, DC 20036. Telephone: (202) 223-5956, Email: webmaster@stimson.org, Web: http://www.stimson.org
Think tank devoted to international security issues

International Atomic Energy Agency, P.O. Box 100, 5 Wagramer Strasse, 1400 Vienna, Austria. Telephone: (43) 1 2600 0, Email: Official.Mail@iaea.org, Web: http://www.iaea.org/worldatom
UN-based agency supporting the peaceful use of nuclear technology, responsible for ensuring that states comply with the Nuclear Non-Proliferation Treaty

Natural Resources Defense Council, 40 West 20th Street, New York, NY 10011. Telephone: (212) 727-2700, Email: nrdcinfo@nrdc.org, Web: http://www.nrdc.org
Environmental advocacy and research organization that seeks to reduce the threat from nuclear weapons

Non-Proliferation Project, Carnegie Endowment for International Peace, 1779 Massachusetts Avenue NW, Washington, DC 20036. Telephone: (202) 483-7600, Email: npp@ceip.org, Web: http://www.ceip.org/npp
Project that produces a variety of materials addressing weapons of mass destruction

Nuclear Threat Initiative, 1747 Pennsylvania Avenue NW, 7th Floor, Washington, DC 20006. Telephone: (202) 296-4810, Email: gwinnti@aol.com, Web: http://www.nti.org
Foundation founded by media mogul Ted Turner and former U.S. senator Sam Nunn to support activities designed to reduce the threat from weapons of mass destruction

Organization for the Prohibition of Chemical Weapons, 32 Johan de Wittlaan, 2517 The Hague, Netherlands. Telephone: (31) 70 416 3300, Email: inquiries@opcw.org, Web: http://www.opcw.org
International body responsible for ensuring the implementation of the Chemical Weapons Convention

Stockholm International Peace Research Institute, 9 Signalistgatan, 169 70 Solna, Sweden. Telephone: (46) 8 655 9700, Email: sipri@sipri.org, Web: http://www.sipri.org
Think tank addressing issues related to international peace and security

Union of Concerned Scientists, 2 Brattle Square, Cambridge, MA 02238-9105. Telephone: (617) 547-5552, Email: ucs@ucsusa.org, Web: http://www.ucsusa.org
Organization that promotes environmental issues and addresses such nuclear weapons–related issues as missile defense and nuclear testing through its Global Security Program

United Nations Department for Disarmament Affairs, Monitoring, Database and Information, DDA, S-3151 United Nations, 1st Avenue at 46th Street, New York, NY 10017. Email: ddaweb@un.org, Web: http://www.un.org/Depts/dda/dda.htm
Agency that analyzes global developments concerning disarmament, observes the implementation of existing arms control agreements, and assists with the negotiation of new ones

Further Research

Books

Albright, David, and Kevin O'Neil, eds. *Solving the North Korean Nuclear Puzzle.* Washington, D.C.: ISIS Press 2000.

Arms Control Association. *Arms Control and International Security: An Introduction.* Washington, D.C.: Arms Control Association, 1989.

Barton, John H., and Lawrence D. Weiler, eds. *International Arms Control: Issues and Agreements.* Stanford: Stanford University Press, 1976.

Baucom, Donald R. *The Origins of SDI, 1944–1983.* Lawrence: University Press of Kansas, 1992.

Bundy, McGeorge. *Danger and Survival: Choices about the Bomb in the First Fifty Years.* New York: Random House, 1988.

Butler, Richard. *The Greatest Threat: Iraq, Weapons of Mass Destruction, and the Growing Crisis in Global Security.* New York: Public Affairs, 2000.

Cochran, Thomas B., William M. Arkin, Robert S. Norris, and Milton M. Hoenig. *Nuclear Weapons Databook.* Vol. 1, *U.S. Nuclear Forces and Capabilities.* New York: National Resources Defense Council, 1984.

Cohen, Avner. *Israel and the Bomb.* New York: Columbia University Press, 1998.

FitzGerald, Frances. *Way Out There in the Blue: Reagan, Star Wars, and the End of the Cold War.* New York: Simon and Schuster, 2000.

Freedman, Lawrence. *The Evolution of Nuclear Strategy.* New York: St. Martin's Press, 1981.

Holloway, David. *Stalin and the Bomb: The Soviet Union and Atomic Energy, 1939–1956.* New Haven: Yale University Press, 1994.

International Institute for Strategic Studies. *The Military Balance, 2000–2001.* London: Oxford University Press, 2000.

Jones, Rodney W., and Mark McDonough. *Tracking Nuclear Proliferation: A Guide in Maps and Charts, 1998.* Washington, D.C.: Carnegie Endowment for International Peace, 1998.

Kaplan, Fred. *The Wizards of Armageddon.* New York: Simon and Schuster, 1983.

Miller, Judith, Stephen Engelberg, and William Broad. *Germs: Biological Weapons and America's Secret War.* New York: Simon and Schuster, 2001.

National Academy of Sciences. *Nuclear Arms Control: Background and Issues.* Washington, D.C.: National Academy Press, 1985.

Norris, Robert S., Andrew S. Burrows, and Richard W. Fieldhouse. *Nuclear Weapons Databook.* Vol. 5, *British, French, and Chinese Nuclear Weapons.* Boulder: Westview Press, 1994.

Perkovich, George, *India's Nuclear Bomb: The Impact on Global Proliferation*. Berkeley: University of California Press, 1999.

Reiss, Mitchell. *Bridled Ambitions: Why Countries Constrain Their Nuclear Capabilities.* Washington, D.C.: Woodrow Wilson Center Press, 1995.

Rhodes, Richard. *The Making of the Atomic Bomb.* New York: Simon and Schuster, 1986.

Sagan, Scott D., and Kenneth N. Waltz. *The Spread of Nuclear Weapons: A Debate.* New York: W. W. Norton, 1997.

Schwartz, Stephen, ed. *Atomic Audit: The Costs and Consequences of Nuclear Weapons since 1940.* Washington, D.C.: Brookings Institution Press, 1998.

Sigal, Leon V. *Disarming Strangers.* Princeton, N.J.: Princeton University Press, 1997.

Smith, Gerald. *Doubletalk: The Story of SALT I.* Garden City, N.Y.: Doubleday and Company, 1980.

Stockholm International Peace Research Institute. *SIPRI Yearbook, 2000: Armaments, Disarmament, and International Security.* New York: Oxford University Press, 2000.

Talbott, Strobe. *Deadly Gambits: The Reagan Administration and the Stalemate in Nuclear Arms Control.* New York: Knopf, 1984.

Tucker, Jonathan B., ed. *Toxic Terror: Assessing Terrorist Use of Chemical and Biological Weapons.* Cambridge, Mass.: MIT Press, 1999.

Articles and Reports

Central Intelligence Agency. "Unclassified Report to Congress on the Acquisition of Technology Relating to Weapons of Mass Destruction and Advanced Conventional Munitions, 1 July through 31 December 2000," September 2001, http://www.cia.gov/cia/publications/bian/bian_sep_2001.htm.

National Intelligence Council. "Foreign Missile Developments and the Ballistic Missile Threat to the United States through 2015," September 1999, http://www.cia.gov/cia/publications/nie/nie99msl.html.

Office of the Secretary of Defense. "Proliferation: Threat and Response," January 2001, http://www.cia.gov/cia/publications/nie/nie99msl.html.

Operational Test and Evaluation, Department of Defense. "Report in Support of National Missile Defense Deployment Readiness Review," 10 August 2000 (made public 26 June 2001), http://www.fas.org/spp/starwars/program/nmdcoylerep.pdf.

Perry, William J. "Review of United States Policy toward North Korea: Findings and Recommendations," 12 October 1999, http://www.state.gov/www/regions/eap/991012_northkorea_rpt.html.

"Report of the Commission to Assess the Ballistic Missile Threat to the United States" (The Rumsfeld Report), 15 July 1998, http://www.house.gov/hasc/testimony/105thcongress/BMThreat.htm.

Web Sites

Arms Control Today
http://www.armscontrol.org/act/

Bulletin of the Atomic Scientists
http://www.bullatomsci.org

Disarmament Diplomacy
http://www.acronym.org.uk/dddesc.htm

Nonproliferation Review
http://www.rienner.com/npr.htm

Documents

1. Treaty on the Non-Proliferation of Nuclear Weapons (Nuclear Non-Proliferation Treaty), 1 July 1968

The full text is available at http://www.state.gov/www/global/arms/treaties/npt1.html.

Extract

The States concluding this Treaty, hereinafter referred to as the "Parties to the Treaty,"

Considering the devastation that would be visited upon all mankind by a nuclear war and the consequent need to make every effort to avert the danger of such a war and to take measures to safeguard the security of peoples,

Believing that the proliferation of nuclear weapons would seriously enhance the danger of nuclear war,

In conformity with resolutions of the United Nations General Assembly calling for the conclusion of an agreement on the prevention of wider dissemination of nuclear weapons,

Undertaking to cooperate in facilitating the application of International Atomic Energy Agency safeguards on peaceful nuclear activities, . . .

Have agreed as follows:

Article I

Each nuclear-weapon State Party to the Treaty undertakes not to transfer to any recipient whatsoever nuclear weapons or other nuclear explosive devices or control over such weapons or explosive devices directly, or indirectly; and not in any way to assist, encourage, or induce any non-nuclear weapon State to manufacture or otherwise acquire nuclear weapons or other nuclear explosive devices, or control over such weapons or explosive devices.

Article II

Each non-nuclear-weapon States Party to the Treaty undertakes not to receive the transfer from any transferor whatsoever of nuclear weapons or other nuclear explosive devices or of control over such weapons or explosive devices directly, or indirectly; not to manufacture or otherwise acquire nuclear weapons or other nuclear explosive devices; and not to seek or receive any assistance in the manufacture of nuclear weapons or other nuclear explosive devices.

Article III

1. Each non-nuclear-weapon State Party to the Treaty undertakes to accept safeguards, as set forth in an agreement to be negotiated and concluded with the International Atomic Energy Agency in accordance with the Statute of the International Atomic Energy Agency and the Agency's safeguards system, for the exclusive purpose of verification of the fulfillment of its obligations assumed under this Treaty with a view to

preventing diversion of nuclear energy from peaceful uses to nuclear weapons or other nuclear explosive devices. Procedures for the safeguards required by this article shall be followed with respect to source or special fissionable material whether it is being produced, processed or used in any principal nuclear facility or is outside any such facility. The safeguards required by this article shall be applied to all source or special fissionable material in all peaceful nuclear activities within the territory of such State, under its jurisdiction, or carried out under its control anywhere.

2. Each State Party to the Treaty undertakes not to provide: (a) source or special fissionable material, or (b) equipment or material especially designed or prepared for the processing, use or production of special fissionable material, to any non-nuclear-weapon State for peaceful purposes, unless the source or special fissionable material shall be subject to the safeguards required by this article.

3. The safeguards required by this article shall be implemented in a manner designed to comply with article IV of this Treaty, and to avoid hampering the economic or technological development of the Parties or international cooperation in the field of peaceful nuclear activities, including the international exchange of nuclear material and equipment for the processing, use or production of nuclear material for peaceful purposes in accordance with the provisions of this article and the principle of safeguarding set forth in the Preamble of the Treaty.

4. Non-nuclear-weapon States Party to the Treaty shall conclude agreements with the International Atomic Energy Agency to meet the requirements of this article either individually or together with other States in accordance with the Statute of the International Atomic Energy Agency. Negotiation of such agreements shall commence within 180 days from the original entry into force of this Treaty. For States depositing their instruments of ratification or accession after the 180-day period, negotiation of such agreements shall commence not later than the date of such deposit. Such agreements shall enter into force not later than eighteen months after the date of initiation of negotiations.

2. Treaty between the United States and the Union of Soviet Socialist Republics on the Limitation of Anti-Ballistic Missile Systems (ABM Treaty), 26 May 1972

The full text is available at http://www.state.gov/www/global/arms/treaties/abm/abm2.html.

Extracts

The United States of America and the Union of Soviet Socialist Republics, hereinafter referred to as the Parties,

Proceeding from the premise that nuclear war would have devastating consequences for all mankind,

Considering that effective measures to limit anti-ballistic missile systems would be a substantial factor in curbing the race in strategic offensive arms and would lead to a decrease in the risk of outbreak of war involving nuclear weapons,

Proceeding from the premise that the limitation of anti-ballistic missile systems, as well as certain agreed measures with respect to the limitation of strategic offensive arms, would contribute to the creation of more favorable conditions for further negotiations on limiting strategic arms,

Mindful of their obligations under Article VI of the Treaty on the Non-Proliferation of Nuclear Weapons,

Declaring their intention to achieve at the earliest possible date the cessation of the nuclear arms race and to take effective measures toward reductions in strategic arms, nuclear disarmament, and general and complete disarmament,

Desiring to contribute to the relaxation of international tension and the strengthening of trust between States,

Have agreed as follows:

Article I

1. Each Party undertakes to limit anti-ballistic missile (ABM) systems and to adopt other measures in accordance with the provisions of this Treaty.

2. Each Party undertakes not to deploy ABM systems for a defense of the territory of its country and not to provide a base for such a defense, and not to deploy ABM systems for defense of an individual region except as provided for in Article III of this Treaty.

Article II

1. For the purpose of this Treaty an ABM system is a system to counter strategic ballistic missiles or their elements in flight trajectory, currently consisting of:

(a) ABM interceptor missiles, which are interceptor missiles constructed and deployed for an ABM role, or of a type tested in an ABM mode;

(b) ABM launchers, which are launchers constructed and deployed for launching ABM interceptor missiles; and

(c) ABM radars, which are radars constructed and deployed for an ABM role, or of a type tested in an ABM mode.

2. The ABM system components listed in paragraph 1 of this Article include those which are:

(a) operational;

(b) under construction;

(c) undergoing testing;

(d) undergoing overhaul, repair or conversion; or

(e) mothballed.

Article III

Each Party undertakes not to deploy ABM systems or their components except that:

(a) within one ABM system deployment area having a radius of one hundred and fifty kilometers and centered on the Party's national capital, a Party may deploy: (1) no more than one hundred ABM launchers and no more than one hundred ABM interceptor missiles at launch sites, and (2) ABM radars within no more than six ABM radar complexes, the area of each complex being circular and having a diameter of no more than three kilometers; and

(b) within one ABM system deployment area having a radius of one hundred and fifty kilometers and containing ICBM silo launchers, a Party may deploy: (1) no more than one hundred ABM launchers and no more than one hundred ABM interceptor missiles at launch sites, (2) two large phased-array ABM radars comparable in potential to corresponding ABM radars operational or under construction on the date of signature of the Treaty in an ABM system deployment area containing ICBM silo launchers, and (3) no more than eighteen ABM radars each having a potential less than the potential of the smaller of the above-mentioned two large phased-array ABM radars.

Article IV

The limitations provided for in Article III shall not apply to ABM systems or their components used for development or testing, and located within current or additionally agreed test ranges. Each Party may have no more than a total of fifteen ABM launchers at test ranges.

BIODIVERSITY

Tim Allman

Biodiversity, a contraction of the term *biological diversity,* refers to the variety observed within the biosphere, or living world. This richness and variety of life is perhaps Earth's greatest wonder and one of its most important resources, since human survival depends on the effective functioning of global biological systems. Most of Earth's diversity remains undiscovered, as science has classified only a small proportion of the large number of species estimated to exist.

The study of biodiversity has been divided into three categories—genetic, species, and ecosystem. Genetic diversity is the inheritable variation that derives ultimately from variations in DNA sequence; species diversity characterizes the variety of different species observed in an area; and ecosystem diversity refers to the patterns of variation seen in ecosystems. Biodiversity in all these categories is declining ever more rapidly because of human activities. As the rate of decline increases, the struggle to conserve it becomes all the more urgent.

Historical Background and Development

Given that many early societies exhibited an interest and affinity with nature and its diversity, it seems quite probable that human societies have always sought to classify to some degree the species that they have encountered. Such cultural analyses of diversity are invariably related to the importance of the various species to the society. For example, the indigenous inhabitants of the remote Arfak mountains of New Guinea have names for at least 136 species of birds, which, interestingly, correspond almost exactly to the species recognized by Western taxonomy, the science of the classification of organisms. New Guineans, however, do not distinguish between any of the numerous species of ants by which they are surrounded. This is because the Arfak depend on birds for food, but have little interest in ants.

Recorded attempts at taxonomic classification began with the ancient civilizations of Europe and Asia, with philosophers from Greece, Rome, and Arabia proposing basic schemes. Classification and compilation of species inventories have been a theme of various scientific inquiries ever since, but studies of biological diversity really began in earnest in eighteenth-century Europe, as scientific exploration, specimen collection, and classification came into vogue. The work of Carolus Linnaeus advanced taxonomy greatly. A century later, studies of the natural world were advanced sufficiently for Charles Darwin to develop his theory of evolution. This theory revolutionized the biological sciences by providing a coherent mechanism for explaining the staggering variety of life on Earth and provided the theoretical foundation for modern studies of the living world.

Since Darwin, the biological sciences have developed greatly, examining the biosphere from DNA to communities. Biodiversity, however, is a relatively new field of study, the term itself being coined in 1985. The concept of biodiversity began gaining currency against a background of increasing concern about the environment in many parts of the world two decades before the term was coined. This concern was reflected by the signing of such important agreements as the 1963 Convention on International Trade in Endangered Species (CITES), the 1972 World Heritage Convention, the 1983 Convention on Migratory Species, and the 1971 Ramsar Convention on Wetlands.

Research and policy focused specifically on biodiversity and its conservation only came to the fore in the 1990s. Such initiatives were given great impetus by the "Earth Summit" held in Rio de Janeiro in 1992 and the resulting Convention on Biological Diversity, which came into force in December 1993. Recognition of the threats to global biodiversity and the possible repercussions helped create general consensus about the urgency of the problem. The critical question for the future is whether sufficient time, financial support, and political will exist to fight the decline in biodiversity at local, national, and international levels in the face of the factors driving the decline.

Current Status

There is no single, universally applicable unit of measure for biodiversity, only the requirement that the parameters used are appropriate to the situation. Biodiversity, however, is most often studied and described by scientists and policymakers at the species level. In particular, species richness—the number of species in an area or community, ideally relative to the total number of individuals of each species present—is a widely used measure of diversity.

Research

However biodiversity is characterized and despite differing estimates of its degree, it is clear that human activity threatens and reduces biodiversity in numerous ways. Today habitat destruction is the primary factor contributing to the decline in biodiversity in almost every area of the world. Future trends in biodiversity, however, will increasingly be influenced by climate change resulting from global warming, which is expected to have dramatic effects on species and ecosystems (see GLOBAL WARMING).

The depletion of biodiversity has reached an alarming rate. The California Academy of Sciences estimates that more than 10,000 species of plant and animal become extinct every year and that one-fourth of Earth's biodiversity will be threatened with extinction within the first twenty or thirty years of the twenty-first century. In 1988 biologist Robert May, writing for *Science,* memorably dubbed conservation biology a "science with a time limit."

While the need for ongoing, accurate biodiversity research is urgent, the field is complex and broad. It tends to rely on three scientific disciplines: genetics, taxonomy, and ecology. Each approaches the analysis of diversity at a different level of organization but are intimately related. For example, the geneticist studying DNA variation in a population of organisms might provide the taxonomist with knowledge that enables a revised classification of organisms to be made; this in turn could improve the ecologist's understanding of the ecosystem of which the organisms are a part. Most research focuses on the estimation of the diversity that exists in an area or community, and the scientific assessment of which components of this diversity are of most significance to overall biodiversity, especially with regard to the prioritization of conservation efforts. Tackling these questions for even a small wildlife reserve is a considerable task. The work required on a global scale is daunting.

That there is no single measure of biodiversity means that whatever criteria are used will involve simplification. The choice of measure is crucial, however, and a body of research has concentrated on evaluating different measures in different situations. For example, comparing the biodiversity value of an area containing a large number of nationally common plant species with another area displaying a much smaller number of rarer plants would force a scientist to make value judgments about the contribution of each to overall biodiversity. In this case, the first assessment would be between the measures of species richness and species rarity. Further assessments would likely be made on the basis of genetic diversity within populations, the diversity of types of organism within the ecosystem, and other factors.

Scientists frequently discuss the "importance" or "significance" of a species or habitat or some other component of biodiversity. This type of valuation attempts to convey the contribution a particular component makes to biodiversity as a whole and must be made with reference to some type of geographical scale. Thus, a globally important species is one considered significant for biodiversity on a worldwide scale; one example is the Asiatic Lion, which once roamed throughout southeastern Europe, southwestern Asia, and northern India but is now only found in one Indian forest reserve. Conservation biologists define the geographical scale of threat to species in a similar way and would therefore describe the Asiatic Lion as globally threatened.

The decline of biodiversity is a serious problem, so it is imperative to estimate its current global extent. This can be done by extrapolating from samples of smaller areas. Given the complexity of the project, species richness is the best measure of diversity because it is relatively simple to measure in most situations and easily compared between ecosystems (see Table 1). It is no surprise that estimates of the number of species differ greatly, varying from 5 million to more than 50 million according to the assumptions made. Most reasonable working assessments fall between 10 million and 20 million. The United Nations Environment Programme's (UNEP) 1995 estimate, published in its Global Biodiversity Assessment report, was 14 million species. According to the report, only about 1.75 million species are currently known, and the ecology of only about 1 percent of these has been studied, and of known species, the majority—900,000—are insects. Higher plants, seed plants and ferns—around 250,000—constitute the next largest group.

Research has also focused on how specific changes in biodiversity affect the functioning of ecosystems. For instance, it is generally accepted that more diverse communities are more productive. That is, they produce more organic matter, such as plant growth, in a given time and are more robust than less diverse ones, being better able to withstand disturbance. This principle is illustrated in a study by researchers at the Universities of Minnesota and Toronto who planted a patchwork of small experimental grassland plots with a controlled number of species. As reported in a May 1996 *Scientific American* article, "The More Species the Merrier," the plant cover of the plots increased from 33 to 49 percent as the number of species planted increased from one to six. Other research has attempted to explain the various interrelationships between geographical patterns and biodiversity, the best known of which is the general increase in diversity as latitudes approach the equator. Such scientific examinations of biodiversity and subsequent predictions of the effects of biodiversity loss are of great value to policymakers.

It is certain that the discovery and classification of the majority of species will not keep pace with extinction rates. The scale of the task is too immense, and there are not enough taxonomic researchers, especially those specializing in poorly understood groups of organisms. Efforts are being made, however, to assist and coordinate taxonomic research. The most notable of these projects is Species 2000, which was established by the International Union of Biological Sciences in 1994 with support from other groups. This project aims to establish a standardized index of all currently identified species. Taxonomic organizations worldwide are collaborating to catalog information in an Internet-accessible index that is updated annually. Species 2000 also hopes to aid in the establishment of new databases for identifying gaps in knowledge. It is estimated that only 40 percent of all known species are cataloged in existing databases.

Policies and Programs

The decline in biodiversity was one of the issues that dominated the 1992 "Earth Summit," formally known as the United Nations Conference on Environment and Development. At the conference, 168 countries signed the Convention on Biological Diversity, the first global agreement on biodiversity conservation (see Document 1). The convention has three objectives: conservation of biodiversity, sustainable use of biodiversity's components, and the equitable sharing of genetic resources. A key challenge for signatories is achieving a balance between the first two objectives. This means conserving biodiversity and all its components—such biological resources as species and habitats—while allowing sustainable human exploitation of these resources. The third objective also applies to human use of a component of diversity—genetic variation. In this respect the convention aims to ensure that genetic resources—for example, wild plants whose genes may be of use to biotechnologists in the development of new drugs—provide as wide a benefit to humanity as possible.

Conservation is perhaps the most important aim of the convention and the focus of much of the policymaking efforts flowing from it. There are two broad approaches through which each country can conserve its biodiversity: in situ and ex situ. In situ, or on site, conservation aims to conserve biodiversity in its natural environment. This is the preferred approach and involves programs for the establishment of protected areas such as wildlife reserves and the legal protection of endangered species (see Table 2, map, p. 53, and Document 2). "Ex situ," or off site, conservation measures focus on individual species and include the use of zoos, seed banks, and DNA storage facilities to preserve species. Because of the expense and effort required for ex situ conservation, especially for animals, such measures are generally limited to particularly rare, valued, or threatened species (see Table 3).

Policy approaches to biodiversity conservation tend to be utilitarian. That is, they seek to protect diversity because of its actual and potential value to humanity and the biosphere and, therefore, aim primarily to protect the most "valuable" elements of biodiversity. Although this pragmatic, resource value" approach is necessary because of the scale of the problem and limits on time and resources, many groups involved in conservation programs argue that biodiversity should deserve protection in its own right, and they point out that placing value on diversity will always be subjective. For example, the London-based Friends of the Earth states on its Web site home page, "Every form of life is unique and warrants respect regardless of its worth to human beings." Furthermore, because of the sheer complexity of the living world, even the most utilitarian-minded analysts agree that any loss to biodiversity might have serious and possibly irreversible effects.

The Convention on Biological Diversity has provided the policy framework for numerous projects relating to the full scope of its purposes, not just conservation, by national governments and international organizations. The convention is legally binding, and countries that ratify it are obliged to implement it. Although the convention has a scientific advisory body and a permanent secretariat, its ultimate authority derives from decisions made at the Conference of the Parties (COP) sessions, which are meetings of signatory states.

COP sessions have approved important initiatives for achieving the objectives of the convention. Some of these initiatives are classed as thematic programs, such as studying inland waters, forests, drylands, and agricultural lands to measure the biodiversity of specific ecosystem types. Other initiatives are much broader; for example, the UNEP Global Biodiversity Assessment provided an appraisal of the status and trends of biodiversity resources and outlined possible approaches to tackle its decline. This latter initiative was launched in 1995, by COP2, which also called for the periodic production of *Global Biodiversity Outlook* (GBO), regular reports that build on this first assessment. In effect, the GBO is a status report on the progress made in achieving the aims of the biodiversity convention. The first edition was published in November 2001.

One of the most important policy developments of the Convention on Biological Diversity has been in the field of biotechnology. Recent advances in the biotech industry have led to the increasing introduction of living modified organisms (LMOs), also called genetically modified organisms (GMOs), as foodstuffs, pharmaceuticals, and other products. There are concerns about LMOs, because the creation of organisms with entirely novel genetic combinations may pose unknown risks to the genetic diversity of wild populations of similar organisms. Such concerns led to the negotiation of the Cartagena Protocol on Biosafety, a subsidiary agreement to the convention that was adopted in January 2000. This allows countries to restrict imports of agricultural products that contain LMOs and requires commodities containing LMOs to be labeled or declared as such before export.

Because the general awareness and understanding of biodiversity issues in many countries is poor, COP5 proposed the launch of a worldwide educational and training initiative. The aim of this program is to integrate education into all programs of the convention wherever possible. Furthermore, a coalition of international scientific bodies, with the endorsement of COP5, used the turn of the millennium to promote awareness of biodiversity research through International Biodiversity Observation Year 2001–2002.

As with all international agreements, the success of the Convention on Biological Diversity depends mainly on actions taken by signatory countries. Among the commitments under the convention, governments are required to draft national biodiversity action plans and to integrate these into broader national plans for the environment and development. These plans vary but tend to be based on surveys of existing biodiversity resources coupled with evaluations of their importance and vulnerability. This permits governments to set targets for the conservation and sustainable use of local biodiversity and to craft strategies for meeting them. Other governmental obligations under the convention include the prevention of the spread of invasive species, restoration of degraded ecosystems, and the promotion of public participation in conservation measures. Each government is required to submit a report at COP meetings describing what it has done in fulfillment of its treaty obligations. These reports are one of the key means by which the success of the convention can be judged.

Regional Summaries

North America

The United States and Canada have per capita consumption rates of energy and resources that are among the highest in the world, creating enormous pressure on natural resources across the region (and, indeed, contributing disproportionately to pressures globally). According to a Canadian report, *Learning from Nature,* a wide and important range of species is nonetheless found across this vast area, with Canada possessing one-fourth of the world's wetlands. That said, biodiversity is generally higher in the warmer, southern part of the region but is in decline throughout North America, with rates of habitat depletion increasing during the last century. *Wild Species 2000: The General Status of Species in Canada* reports that twenty-five mammal species in Canada are considered extinct or threatened, and the U.S. Fish and Wildlife Service's Threatened and Endangered Species System estimated in November 2000 that

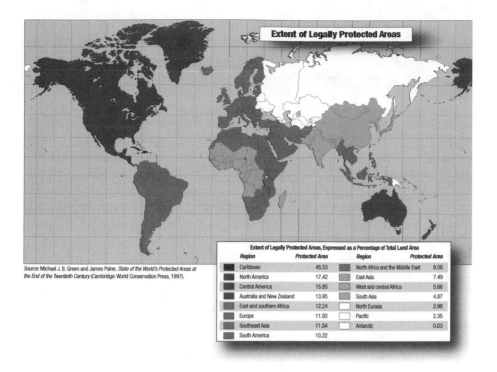

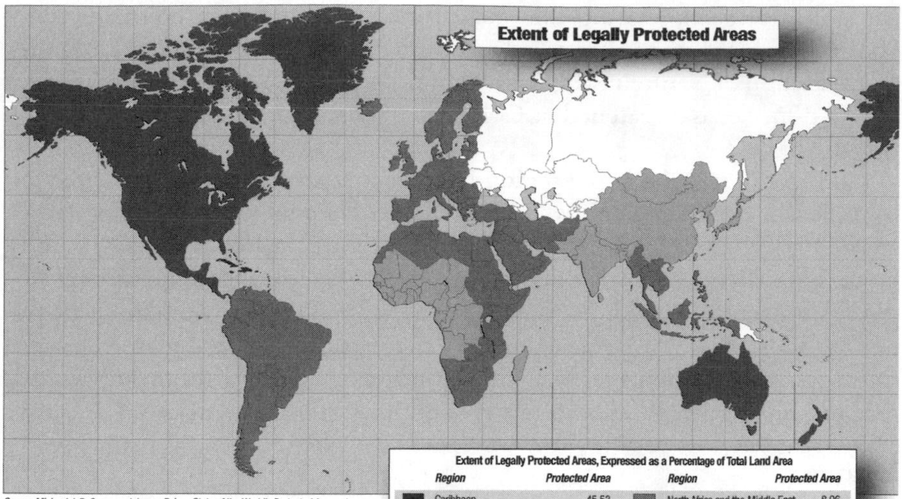

Source: Michael J. B. Green and James Paine, *State of the World's Protected Areas at the End of the Twentieth Century* (Cambridge: World Conservation Press, 1997).

Extent of Legally Protected Areas, Expressed as a Percentage of Total Land Area

Region	*Protected Area*	*Region*	*Protected Area*
Caribbean	45.53	North Africa and the Middle East	8.06
North America	17.42	East Asia	7.49
Central America	15.85	West and central Africa	5.66
Australia and New Zealand	13.95	South Asia	4.87
East and southern Africa	12.24	North Eurasia	2.98
Europe	11.93	Pacific	2.35
Southeast Asia	11.54	Antarctic	0.03
South America	10.22		

more than seventy mammal species are endangered or threatened in the United States. The Nature Conservancy contends that one-third of plant and animal species in the United States are at some risk of extinction. The main causes are intensive agriculture, development, resource extraction, and clearance of old growth forest. The introduction of exotic species has also affected biodiversity. The U.S. Congress estimated in 1993 that there were at least forty-five hundred species of foreign origin across the United States, with approximately 15 percent of these causing economic and ecological problems.

Policy initiatives to conserve biodiversity are generally well developed in Canada and the United States, with some 17 percent of the North American land area legally protected. The number and area of protected sites, however, is growing slowly. The United States is one of the few signatory nations not to have taken steps toward ratifying the Convention on Biological Diversity. Its reluctance to commit to action casts a shadow over the prospects for long-term biodiversity conservation in the region.

Latin America

Latin America is exceptionally biodiverse, possessing 40 percent of the world's animal and plant species and 68 percent of its tropical rain forests. This region is also thought to have the highest diversity of plants anywhere on Earth—with an estimated eighty thousand species in the Amazon rain forest alone, according to National Geographic's "Ethnobotony: Medicinal Amazon Plants"—and yet it is still relatively poorly studied, especially its tropical zones. Habitat destruction across the region is the primary threat to biodiversity, with agricultural conversion, logging, and infrastructure construction the main causes. Species across the region are at risk. For instance, the International Union for Conservation of Nature's Red List of Threatened Species cites more than three hundred species as threatened in Colombia and in Ecuador, and 608 species in Brazil.

Countries throughout the region have responded to biodiversity depletion by establishing protected areas. One of the best-known networks of protected areas can be found in Costa Rica, which has thirty national parks. There is, however, evidence that such designated areas have not in practice always provided sufficient protection in many countries, even in such well-run park systems as those in Costa Rica. Moreover, the expanding population and widespread poverty that characterize the majority of Latin America suggest that pressures for further development will continue.

Europe

Europe—the region with the longest history of industrialization and a relatively high population density—has suffered a lengthy decline in biodiversity, which accelerated to its greatest extent during the last century. Biodiversity is under strain from infrastructure development, forestry, agriculture, air and water pollution, the overexploitation of natural resources, and the impact of introduced species. It is estimated that half of vertebrate species in many European countries are threatened—for example, 10.5 percent of Germany's mammals are threatened, according to Animal Info statistics—and the European Union's "Wildlife in the EU" estimates that one quarter of the region's bird species have suffered a significant decline in the last twenty years. Protected areas have been increasing in size and number since the middle of the twentieth century. Eleven national parks have been designated in England and Wales since 1949, for instance, with two more currently in the process of being created.

Europe has a relatively strong and popular Green movement, and awareness of Europe's declining biodiversity is well established among the public and policymakers. Nonetheless, biodiversity seems likely to continue to decline across the region, with perhaps the strongest test being the ability of conservation measures to protect the relatively undeveloped habitats of Eastern Europe from the pressures of rapid economic expansion.

North Africa and the Middle East

This predominantly arid or sub-arid region is home to a variety of wildlife, including many rare species. The coastal and freshwater zones are especially important, with more than twelve hundred species of fish and two hundred species of crab in the Arabian and Red Seas. Biodiversity is declining due to overgrazing, desertification, deforestation, drainage, water pollution and soil salinization, unsustainable hunting and fishing, and industrial and urban development. The Arabian Oryx became extinct in the wild in 1972 because of overhunting across the Middle East; it was reintroduced to Oman (from captive stock) in 1982, but it still suffers from poaching and remains among the most threatened of animals in the world. Degradation due to the above factors seems likely to grow as the population increases and development spreads. The protected areas that have been established in the region seem insufficient to reverse these trends.

Sub-Saharan Africa

Sub-Saharan Africa possesses a vast richness of species, with notable concentrations of biodiversity in the equatorial zone, on the southern cape, and on the island of Madagascar. The most extensive habitat type in Africa is savannah grassland, which occurs in a belt to the south of the Sahara Desert and dominates the eastern part of the continent. The savannah supports the world's largest concentration of large mammals and a host of other species from other groups. Decline in biodiversity can be attributed mainly to deforestation, wetland drainage, and water scarcity. Political conflicts, urban expansion and resettlement, and agricultural activities also threaten biodiversity. For example, around 10 percent of the plants of Mozambique, South Africa, and Zimbabwe are classed as threatened. Although there are around three thousand protected areas across the continent, intense competition for land use outside (and sometimes within) such areas means that the rates of species decline are likely to increase. As the population grows rapidly and the vast majority remains poor, it is difficult to see how pressures on biodiversity can fail to increase dramatically.

Asia

Asia contains an enormous variety of habitat types and climate zones, ranging from equatorial to subarctic, and concentrations of extremely high biodiversity. China alone is the third most biodiverse nation; according to *China: Biodiversity Conservation Action Plan* it possesses more than 12 percent of all known mammal species and more than 13 percent of all known bird species. The region is also the world's most densely populated and most rapidly developing, so biodiversity is under ever-increasing stress. Deforestation, urbanization, agricultural expansion, and pollution have all taken their toll. Wildlife also suffers directly from uncontrolled harvesting, hunting, and fishing. A large number of species are endangered, including such high-profile animals as the Siberian tiger, giant panda, snow leopard, and orangutan. The generally poor status of data collection in many parts of Asia means that the true extent of the decline in most species remains uncertain. The genetic diversity of crop plants is also in decline, with Indonesia losing around fifteen hundred rice varieties from 1975 to 1990. These problems are compounded by the patchy effectiveness of the protected areas across the region, with many of them suffering from a lack of resources and weak policy enforcement. For example, the Tanjung Puting reserve in Indonesia suffers from illegal logging and poaching, and associated allegations of corruption have been made against ranger staff. Biodiversity conservation is likely to be a low priority in this poor region as its population and economies continue to grow and increase pressure to use scarce land (see Case Study—Biodiversity and Its Protection in India).

The Pacific

The main feature of Australian biodiversity is the high level of endemism, the occurrence of species unique to an area. Some 90 percent of Australia's plants are endemic, according to Plant-Talk, as are more than 80 percent of its mammals, according the Australian Museum. Many of the other islands in this region feature similarly high endemism. The last 200 years have seen dramatic declines in many aspects of Australian biodiversity. The *Australia State of the Environment Report, 1996,* estimates that during this period 10 out of 144 marsupial species disappeared—the world's worst mammal extinction. The Australian Wildlife Conservancy reports that Australia has suffered significant ecological damage caused by the artificial introduction of many species—rabbits from Europe number 200 million—as have New Zealand and many of the Pacific islands. Meanwhile, rich marine life in all parts of Oceania, including valuable coral reef systems, is being depleted by commercial fishing and pollution. Protected areas are reasonably common in the developed nations of Australia and New Zealand but rarer on most of the Pacific islands.

Data

Table 1 Species Richness of Three Vertebrate Groups for Selected Countries

Country	Mammals	Birds	Reptiles
Algeria	92	375	—
Argentina	320	976	220
Australia	252	751	748
Brazil	394	1,635	468
Canada	193	578	41
China	394	1,244	340
Colombia	359	1,695	584
Congo, Republic of	200	569	—
Egypt	102	439	83
France	93	506	32
Georgia	—	—	46
Germany	76	503	12
Guatemala	250	669	231
India	316	1,219	389
Indonesia	436	1,531	511
Israel	92	500	—
Japan	132	583	66
Russia	—	—	58
Saudi Arabia	77	413	84
Spain	82	506	53
Sweden	60	463	6
Switzerland	75	400	14
Tajikistan	—	—	38
Thailand	265	915	298
Turkey	116	418	102
Uganda	338	992	149
United Kingdom	50	590	8
United States	428	768	280

Source: Brian Groombridge, ed., *Biodiversity Data Sourcebook* (Cambridge: World Conservation Press, 1994).

Table 2 Extent of the Protection of Major Biomes

Biome	Area (km²)	Protected Areas: Number	Extent (km²)	Percentage of Biome
Mixed island systems	3,252,563	1,980	530,676	16.32
Subtropical / temperate rain forests / woodland	3,930,979	977	404,497	10.29
Mixed mountain systems	10,633,145	2,766	967,130	9.10
Tropical humid forests	10,513,210	1,030	922,453	8.77
Tundra communities	22,017,390	171	1,845,188	8.38
Tropical grasslands / savannahs	4,264, 832	100	316,465	7.42
Tropical dry forests / woodlands	17,312,538	1,290	1,224,566	7.07
Cold winter deserts	9,250,252	290	546,168	5.90
Temperate needle-leaf forests / woodlands	15,682,817	1,492	897,375	5.72
Warm deserts / semi-deserts	24,279,843	605	1,173,025	4.83
Evergreen sclerophyllous forests	3,757,144	1,469	164,883	4.39
Temperate broad-leaf forests	11,216,659	3,905	403,298	3.60
Lake systems	517,695	66	5,814	1.12
Temperate grasslands	8,976,591	495	88,127	0.98
Total	145,605,658	16,636	9,489,665	6.52

Source: Michael J. B. Green and James Paine, *State of the World's Protected Areas at the End of the Twentieth Century* (Cambridge: World Conservation Press, 1997).

Table 3 Threatened Species in Selected Animal Groups

Class	Threatened Status: EX	EW	CR	EN	VU	Totals
Vertebrates						
Mammals	83	4	180	340	610	1,217
Birds	128	3	182	321	680	1,314
Reptiles	21	1	56	79	161	318
Amphibians	5	0	25	38	83	151
Invertebrates						
Crustaceans	8	1	56	72	280	417
Insects	72	1	45	118	392	628

Source: International Union for the Conservation of Nature, *2000 IUCN Red List of Threatened Species* (Cambridge: IUCN, 2000).

Note: EX, extinct, EW, extinct in the wild (known only in captivity), CR, critically endangered (extremely high risk of extinction in the wild in the immediate future); EN, endangered (very high risk of extinction in the wild in the near future); and VU, vulnerable (high risk of extinction in the wild in the medium-term future).

Case Study—Biodiversity and Its Protection in India

India is the second largest country in Asia and the seventh largest in the world, with a population of some 850 million people and growing. It encompasses a range of landforms, from the Himalaya Mountains to the extensive river plains of the Ganges and Brahmaputra and the central Deccan Plateau. According to the World Conservation Monitoring Center's "Biodiversity Profile of India," the country features habitat zones ranging from tropical to temperate and a wealth of biodiversity. India has at least twelve hundred species of birds—more than 12 percent of the global total—and fifteen thousand species of higher plants—6 percent of the global total. Some 33 percent of plant species are endemic, with reptiles and amphibians also at high levels of endemism. In contrast, endemism is low among mammals and birds. India's living resources are such that it is considered one of the twelve "megadiversity" countries.

India has a greater number of scientific resources for the study of biodiversity than many Asian nations, so the general state of knowledge about its biological resources is relatively good. Scientists have identified various elements of Indian biodiversity that are in danger. The "Biodiversity Profile of India" estimates that as many as four thousand plant species are considered to be under some degree of threat, and 172 animal species are categorized as globally threatened. India is home to globally important populations of some of Asia's rarest mammals, such as the Asiatic lion (found only in the Gir forest in Gujarat), the Indian rhinoceros, and the marbled cat.

As is the situation in many other Asian countries, India's biodiversity is under severe strain from demands on its resources and land created by an expanding economy and a large and growing population. There is, however, a fairly well developed policy framework, primarily focused on the legal protection of important areas to combat declining biodiversity. The first modern protected areas were established in the years shortly after independence in 1947, and the number and extent of areas grew rapidly in the 1970s and 1980s, following the adoption of the National Policy for Wildlife Conservation (1970) and the Wildlife Act (1972). In 1990 there were sixty-nine national parks and four hundred ten other reserves; together these encompassed 4.52 percent of the country's total land area, which is low compared to the global proportion of nearly 9 percent. Nonetheless, India's protected areas are generally well managed and often well funded, and many have proved successful in conserving biodiversity within their boundaries. As with all countries, the extent of protection varies greatly between reserves; for example, commercial plantation forestry and resource extraction are permitted in the Parambikulam wildlife sanctuary in Kerala State.

India ratified the Convention on Biological Diversity in February 1994 and is also party to most of the other international conventions relating to biodiversity, commitments that have assisted its developing a framework for conservation policy. There is, however, a major weakness in India's biodiversity protection strategy: enforcement problems in protected areas, due mainly to conflict with local populations. For example, the Great Himalayan National Park in the northwestern state of Himachal Pradesh is sparsely populated, but the floral diversity of the park is threatened by the collection of plants for use as food and medicines. People from the area surrounding the park have low incomes; for them the food and medicines derived from the plants are an important source of revenue. The number of rural poor in India is large, and their legitimate desire to improve their circumstance brings them into conflict with conservation laws. This is perhaps the greatest challenge facing India's well-established conservation policies.

Biographical Sketches

Gonzalo Castro is a Peruvian biologist and former assistant professor of biology at Universidad Peruana Cayetano Heredia in Lima. He leads the biodiversity team of the World Bank's environment department, which has funded in full or in part numerous biodiversity projects in a variety of countries.

Tom E. Lovejoy is chief biodiversity adviser for the World Bank and its lead specialist for Latin America and the Caribbean. A former member of the White House Science Council, Lovejoy is an expert on South American birds and currently works at the Smithsonian Institution. He founded the popular PBS series *Nature.*

Sue Mainka is a veterinarian who has worked extensively on captive wildlife conservation. She is best known for her work on the giant panda captive breeding program. Mainka has worked in this capacity on China's Wolong reserve since 1987 and is now the coordinator of the Species Program for the International Union for the Conservation of Nature /World Conservation Union. Mainka's role there includes supporting the organization's Species Survival Commission.

Jeffrey A. McNeely is chief scientist of the International Union for the Conservation of Nature/World Conservation Union, heading its biodiversity policy co-ordination division. McNeely has done important work on the effectiveness of protected areas, notably in his capacity as the secretary-general of the 1992 World Congress on National Parks and Protected Areas.

Vandana Shiva is a writer, activist, and policy advocate and director of the Research Foundation for Science, Technology, and Natural Resource Policy. Shiva is well known for her work on biodiversity in relation to agriculture, and she is a fierce critic of the role of the biotech industry in agriculture.

Hamdallah Zedan is executive director of the Secretariat of the Convention on Biological Diversity, which is responsible for organizing meetings (especially Conference of the Parties sessions), drafting reports, and various other roles important to the implementation of the convention. Zedan is an Egyptian scientist who previously worked for the United Nations Environment Programme's biodiversity unit.

Directory

Association for Biodiversity Information, 1101 Wilson Boulevard, 15th Floor Arlington, VA 22209. Telephone: (703) 908-1800, Web: http://www.infonatura.org/Labinhn.htm
Conservation research body

California Academy of Sciences Biodiversity Resource Center, Golden Gate Park, San Francisco, CA 94118. Telephone: (415) 750-7361, Email: library@calacademy.org, Web: http://www.calacademy.org/research/library/biodiv.htm
Research institute and resource base

Friends of the Earth International, P.O. Box 19199, 1000 Amsterdam, Netherlands. Telephone (31) 20 622 1369, Email: foei@foei.org, Web: http://www.foei.org
World's largest federation of environmental groups, campaigns include biodiversity

International Union for the Conservation of Nature / World Conservation Union (IUCN), 28 Rue Mauverney, 1196 Gland, Switzerland. Telephone: (41) 22 999-0001, Email: info@lucn.org, Web: http://www.iucn.org
Partnership of government agencies and scientists aiming to conserve the diversity of nature

International Union of Biological Sciences, 51 Boulevard de Montmorency, 75016 Paris, France. Telephone (33) 14 525 0009, Email: iubs@paris7.jussieu.fr. Web: http://www.iubs.org
Organization promoting and facilitating the study of biological sciences

Species 2000, Center for Plant Diversity and Systematics, School of Plant Sciences, University of Reading, Reading RG6 6AS, United Kingdom. Telephone: (44) 118 931 6466, Email: sp2000@sp2000.org, Web: http://www.sp2000.org
Collaborative project to create an index of species by coordinating taxonomic databases

United Nations Environment Programme (UNEP), United Nations Avenue, Gigiri, P.O. Box 30552, Nairobi, Kenya. Telephone: (254) 262 1234, Email: eisinfo@unep.org, Web: http://www.unep/org
Agency tackling a range of environmental issues on an international basis

World Conservation Monitoring Centre, 219 Huntingdon Road, Cambridge CB3 0DL, United Kingdom. Telephone: (44) 1223 277314, Email: info@unep-wcmc.org, Web: http://www.unep-wcmc.org
UNEP body concerned with providing information for conservation policy and action

World Resources Institute, 10 G Street NE, Suite 800, Washington, DC 20002. Telephone: (202) 729-7600, Email: front@wri.org, Web: http://www.wri.org/biodiv/
Environmental organization with a focus on biodiversity, aiming to inspire public action through public education

World Wildlife Fund, 1250 24th Street NW, Washington, DC 20037-1175. Telephone: (202) 293-4800, Web: http://www.worldwildlife.org
U.S. office of the world's largest privately supported conservation body

Further Research

Books

Dobson, Andrew P. *Conservation and Biodiversity.* New York: Scientific American Library, 1996.

Eldredge, Niles. *Life in the Balance: Humanity and the Biodiversity Crisis.* Princeton, N.J.: Princeton University Press, 1998.

Gaston, K. J., ed. *Biodiversity: A Biology of Numbers and Difference.* Oxford: Blackwell Science, 1996.

Gaston, K. J., and Spicer, J. I. *Biodiversity: An Introduction.* Oxford: Blackwell Science, 1998.

Hawksworth, D. L., ed. *Biodiversity: Measurement and Estimation.* London: Chapman and Hall, 1995.

Heywood, V. H., ed. *Global Biodiversity Assessment.* New York and Cambridge: Cambridge University Press, 1995.

Howes, Chris. *The Spice of Life: Biodiversity and the Extinction Crisis.* London: Blandford, 1997.

Kim, K. C, and Weaver, R. D. *Biodiversity and Landscapes.* New York and Cambridge: Cambridge University Press, 1994.

Kushwar, Ram Bir Singh, and Vijay Kumar. *Economics of Protected Areas and Its Effects on Biodiversity.* New Delhi: APH, 2001.

Lawton, J. H, and May, R. M., eds. *Extinction Rates.* New York and Oxford: Oxford University Press, 1995.

Leakey, Richard, and Lewin, Roger. *The Sixth Extinction: Biodiversity and Its Survival.* New York: Doubleday, 1995.

Shiva, Vandana, et al. *Biodiversity: Social and Ecological Perspectives.* London: Zed Books, 1991.

Wilson, Edward O. *The Diversity of Life.* New York and London: Penguin, 1992.

Articles and Reports

China: Biodiversity Conservation Action Plan, http://www.bpsp-neca.brim.ac.cn/books/actpln_cn/Ecosystem%20Diversity.

"Ethnobotany: Medicinal Amazon Plants," http://pulseplanet.nationalgeographic.com/ax/archives/01_naturetemplate.cfm?programnumber=2009.

Food and Agricultural Organization. *Planning a Wildlife Protected Area Network in India.* Rome: FAO, 1988.

Green, Michael J. B., and James Paine. *State of the World's Protected Areas at the End of the Twentieth Century.* Cambridge: World Conservation Press, 1997.

Groombridge, Brian, ed. *Global Biodiversity: Status of the Earth's Living Resources.* London: Chapman and Hall, 1992.

———. *Biodiversity Data Sourcebook.* Cambridge: World Conservation Press, 1994.

Hearn, Josephine. "Unfair Game." *Scientific American,* June 2001.

Indira Gandhi Conservation Monitoring Center and World Conservation Monitoring Center. *Biodiversity Profile of India,* 1994, http://www.unep-wcmc.org/igmc/main.html.

International Union for the Conservation of Nature / World Conservation Union. *Review of the Protected Areas System in the Indo-Malayan Realm.* Gland, Switzerland, and Cambridge: IUCN, 1986.

———. *1997 United Nations List of National Parks and Protected Areas.* Gland, Switzerland, and Cambridge: IUCN, 1998.

———. *2000 Red List of Threatened Species.* Gland, Switzerland, and Cambridge: IUCN, 2000.

Learning from Nature: Canada—The Ecosystem Approach and Integrated Land Management. Canada's contribution to the Eighth Session of the United Nations Commission on Sustainable Development, 24 April–25 May 2000, http://www.ec.gc.ca/agenda21/2000/landnat.htm.

Macdonald, David. "Eight Years from Rio." *BBC Wildlife,* November 2000.

MacKenzie, Deborah. "Sick to Death." *New Scientist,* 27 January 2001.
May, Robert M. "How Many Species Are There on Earth?" *Science,* 16 September 1988.
Myers, Norman, et al. "Biodiversity Hotspots for Conservation Priorities." *Nature,* no. 403 (2000): 853.
Oldfield, S., C. Lusty, and A. MacKinven. *The World List of Threatened Trees.* Cambridge: World Conservation Press, 1998.
Purvis, Andy, and Andy Hector. "Getting the Measure of Biodiversity." *Nature,* no. 405 (2000): 212.
Stork, N. E. "How Many Species Are There?" *Biodiversity and Conservation* 2 (1993): 215.
U.K. Steering Group. *Biodiversity: The UK Steering Group Report.* London: Her Majesty's Stationery Office, 1995.
Vane-Wright, R. L., C. J. Humphries, and P. H. Williams. "What To Protect—Systematics and the Agony of Choice." *Biological Conservation* 55 (1991): 235.
Wild Species 2000: The General Status of Species in Canada, http://www.wildspecies.ca/en/Home_E.html
"Wildlife in the EU," http://eur-op.eu.int/opnews/200/en/t0605.htm
World Resources Institute and International Union for the Conservation of Nature/World Conservation Union. *Climate, Biodiversity, and Forests: Issues and Opportunities Emerging from the Kyoto Protocol.* Washington, D.C.: World Resources Institute, 1998.
World Resources Institute et al. *World Resources, 2000–2001.* Washington, D.C.: WRI, 2000.

Web Sites

Animal Info
http://www.animalinfo.org

Australian Museum Online, Fact Sheet
http://www.amonline.net.au/factsheets/mammals.htm

Biodiversity and Biological Diversity Web Server
http://biodiversity.uno.edu

Biodiversity Counts, American Museum of Natural History
http://www.amnh.org/learn/biodiversity_counts

Biodiversity Is Life, World Conservation Union
http://iucn.org/bil

Convention on Biological Diversity
http://www.biodiv.org

Convention on International Trade in Endangered Species of Wild Fauna and Flora
http://www.cites.org

Convention on Migratory Species of Wild Animals
http://www.wcmc.org.uk/cms

Databases in Biodiversity
http://biodiversity.soton.ac.uk/database

DIVERSITAS
http://icsu.org/diversitas

Endangered Species
http://jparadise.virtualave.net/endangered.html

Global Biodiversity Information Facility
http://www.gbif.org

Global Change and Terrestrial Ecosystem
http://www.gcte.org

International Biodiversity Observation Year
http://www.nrel.colostate.edu/iboy

NatureServe
http://natureserve.org

Plant Talk
http://www.plant-talk.org

2000 IUCN Red List of Threatened Species
http://redlist.org

UK Agricultural Biodiversity Coalition
http://ukabc.org

UK Biodiversity Action Plan
http://www.ukbap.org.uk

Virtual School of Biodiversity
http://ibis.nott.ac.uk/vsb

"Worldmap," Natural History Museum (U.K.)
http://www.nhm.ac.uk/science/projects/worldmap

Documents

1. Convention on Biological Diversity

United Nations, Conference on Environment and Development, Rio de Janeiro, June 1992

The full text is available at http://www.biodiv.org/convention/articles.asp.

Extracts

Article 1. Objectives
The objectives of this Convention, to be pursued in accordance with its relevant provisions, are the conservation of biological diversity, the sustainable use of its components and the fair and equitable sharing of the benefits arising out of the utilization of genetic resources, including by appropriate access to genetic resources and by appropriate transfer of relevant technologies, taking into account all rights over those resources and to technologies, and by appropriate funding. . . .

Article 6. General Measures for Conservation and Sustainable Use
Each Contracting Party shall, in accordance with its particular conditions and capabilities:

(a) Develop national strategies, plans or programmes for the conservation and sustainable use of biological diversity or adapt for this purpose existing strategies, plans or programmes which shall reflect, inter alia, the measures set out in this Convention relevant to the Contracting Party concerned; and

(b) Integrate, as far as possible and as appropriate, the conservation and sustainable use of biological diversity into relevant sectoral or cross-sectoral plans, programmes and policies.

Article 7. Identification and Monitoring
Each Contracting Party shall, as far as possible and as appropriate, in particular for the purposes of Articles 8 to 10:

(a) Identify components of biological diversity important for its conservation and sustainable use having regard to the indicative list of categories set down in Annex I;

(b) Monitor, through sampling and other techniques, the components of biological diversity identified pursuant to subparagraph (a) above, paying particular attention to those requiring urgent conservation measures and those which offer the greatest potential for sustainable use;

(c) Identify processes and categories of activities which have or are likely to have significant adverse impacts on the conservation and sustainable use of biological diversity, and monitor their effects through sampling and other techniques; and

(d) Maintain and organize, by any mechanism data, derived from identification and monitoring activities pursuant to subparagraphs (a), (b) and (c) above.

Article 8. In-situ Conservation
Each Contracting Party shall, as far as possible and as appropriate:

(a) Establish a system of protected areas or areas where special measures need to be taken to conserve biological diversity;

(b) Develop, where necessary, guidelines for the selection, establishment and management of protected areas or areas where special measures need to be taken to conserve biological diversity;

(c) Regulate or manage biological resources important for the conservation of biological diversity whether within or outside protected areas, with a view to ensuring their conservation and sustainable use;

(d) Promote the protection of ecosystems, natural habitats and the maintenance of viable populations of species in natural surroundings;

(e) Promote environmentally sound and sustainable development in areas adjacent to protected areas with a view to furthering protection of these areas;

(f) Rehabilitate and restore degraded ecosystems and promote the recovery of threatened species, inter alia, through the development and implementation of plans or other management strategies;

(g) Establish or maintain means to regulate, manage or control the risks associated with the use and release of living modified organisms resulting from biotechnology which are likely to have adverse environmental impacts that could affect the conservation and sustainable use of biological diversity, taking also into account the risks to human health;

(h) Prevent the introduction of, control or eradicate those alien species which threaten ecosystems, habitats or species;

(i) Endeavour to provide the conditions needed for compatibility between present uses and the conservation of biological diversity and the sustainable use of its components;

(j) Subject to its national legislation, respect, preserve and maintain knowledge, innovations and practices of indigenous and local communities embodying traditional lifestyles relevant for the conservation and sustainable use of biological diversity and promote their wider application with the approval and involvement of the holders of such knowledge, innovations and practices and encourage the equitable sharing of the benefits arising from the utilization of such knowledge, innovations and practices;

(k) Develop or maintain necessary legislation and/or other regulatory provisions for the protection of threatened species and populations;

(l) Where a significant adverse effect on biological diversity has been determined pursuant to Article 7, regulate or manage the relevant processes and categories of activities; and

(m) Cooperate in providing financial and other support for in-situ conservation outlined in subparagraphs (a) to (l) above, particularly to developing countries.

Article 9. Ex-situ Conservation
Each Contracting Party shall, as far as possible and as appropriate, and predominantly for the purpose of complementing in-situ measures:

(a) Adopt measures for the ex-situ conservation of components of biological diversity, preferably in the country of origin of such components;

(b) Establish and maintain facilities for ex-situ conservation of and research on plants, animals and micro-organisms, preferably in the country of origin of genetic resources;

(c) Adopt measures for the recovery and rehabilitation of threatened species and for their reintroduction into their natural habitats under appropriate conditions;

(d) Regulate and manage collection of biological resources from natural habitats for ex-situ conservation purposes so as not to threaten ecosystems and in-situ populations of species, except where special temporary ex-situ measures are required under subparagraph (c) above; and

(e) Cooperate in providing financial and other support for ex-situ conservation outlined in subparagraphs (a) to (d) above and in the establishment and maintenance of ex-situ conservation facilities in developing countries.

Article 10. Sustainable Use of Components of Biological Diversity
Each Contracting Party shall, as far as possible and as appropriate:

(a) Integrate consideration of the conservation and sustainable use of biological resources into national decision-making;

(b) Adopt measures relating to the use of biological resources to avoid or minimize adverse impacts on biological diversity;

(c) Protect and encourage customary use of biological resources in accordance with traditional cultural practices that are compatible with conservation or sustainable use requirements;

(d) Support local populations to develop and implement remedial action in degraded areas where biological diversity has been reduced; and

(e) Encourage cooperation between its governmental authorities and its private sector in developing methods for sustainable use of biological resources.

2. State of the World's Protected Areas at the End of the Twentieth Century

Michael J. B. Green and James Paine, World Conservation Monitoring Centre

The full text is available at http://www.unep-wcmc.org/protected_areas/albany.pdf.

Extract

1. Introduction

Protected areas are widely held to be among the most effective means of conserving biological diversity *in situ*. A considerable amount of resources has been invested in their establishment over the last century or more, with the result that most countries have established or, at least, planned national systems of protected areas. The purpose of this paper is to examine the extent of the world's protected areas globally and regionally and to consider other options for its further strengthening and development during the twenty-first century.

1.1 What is a protected area?

A protected area is defined by the IUCN [International Union for the Conservation of Nature] World Commission on Protected Areas (IUCN, 1994) as:

An area of land and/or sea especially dedicated to the protection and maintenance of biological diversity, and of natural and associated cultural resources, and managed through legal or other effective means.

In practice, protected areas are managed for a wide variety of purposes which may include:

- scientific research
- wilderness protection
- preservation of species and ecosystems
- maintenance of environmental services
- protection of specific natural and cultural feature
- tourism and recreation
- education
- sustainable use of resources from natural ecosystems, and
- maintenance of cultural and traditional attributes.

The IUCN definition is rather more precise with respect to what is protected than that used in the Convention on Biological Diversity:

A geographically defined area which is designated or regulated and managed to achieve specific conservation objectives.

1.2 How are the different types of protected area classified?

Over 1,388 different terms are known to be used around the world to designate protected areas, each of which is defined within respective national legislation with respect to its objectives and legal protection. There may be only marginal differences between countries for essentially the same type of protected area. For example, there are *managed nature reserves* in the Bahamas, *strict nature reserves* in Bhutan, *nature reserves* in Ontario, Canada, *national nature reserves* in Czech Republic, *nature reserves* and *marine nature reserves* in Indonesia, *nature conservation areas* in Japan and *strict natural reserves* in Sri Lanka, all of which are strictly protected and accessible primarily for scientific research. Conversely, the same term may imply very different characteristics and management objectives in different countries. The classic example is the widely used term *national park,* the world's first being Yellowstone National Park, established in 1872 as a "public park or pleasuring ground for the benefit and enjoyment of the people." While national parks in many parts of the world (Americas, Africa, South and South-East Asia, Australia and New Zealand) tend to be large, natural areas, some national parks in Europe are distinctive landscapes that have evolved over many hundreds of years as a result of traditional interactions between people and nature. Examples of the latter include all 11 national parks in England and Wales, most national parks in Germany, Cevennes National Park in France and Danube-Drava National Park in Hungary.

CULTURAL PRESERVATION

Henry J. Rutz

The greater economic interdependence of nation-states today, signaled by rapid increases in global flows of capital, information, goods, people, and cultural exchange, has increased and heightened awareness of cultural diversity the world over. Immigration during the last few decades has increased the density of cultures beyond homeland borders while at the same time isolating people who maintain communities and identities separate from those around them. The nation-state is faced with the challenge of responding to demands for cultural rights, including partial political autonomy. The issues of what constitutes acceptable cultural diversity, and who decides what is acceptable and with what consequences for the protection of cultural rights and prospect of economic enfranchisement, are crucial to understanding cultural conflict and cultural pluralism in the era of globalization. Policies and programs for sustainable cultural pluralism, while still in their infancy, have made progress in the last few years.

Historical Background and Development

Economic globalization is the latest phase in the historical development of capitalism, which began in the sixteenth century. Modern nation-states, from their origin in the American and French revolutions at the end of the eighteenth century, progressively replaced empires as the form of political community that would shape the identity of culturally diverse people within sovereign territories. The end of the cold war in 1989, the disintegration of the Soviet Union in 1991, and the expansion of globalization after 1980 resulted in the disintegration of several nation-states and new cultural conflicts in which ethnic affiliation became the basis for claims to nationhood (see ETHNIC AND REGIONAL CONFLICT). From its inception, the Western nation-state was imagined as a bounded sovereign territory representing the unity of one people, one culture, and one language. Cultural diversity was acceptable as long as it did not interfere with national unification and loyalty to the nation. The most acceptable type of cultural diversity was the kind that did not lay claims to cultural rights, partial autonomy, or economic enfranchisement that could threaten national unity.

Within practically every sovereign territory there were groups of people whose cultures were "minoritized" or devalued as "folk" in order for the dominant ethnic group to represent itself as the national culture. To take several examples, Celtic culture and language in Great Britain and France were marginalized by the state, indigenous cultures and languages of Latin American states were marginalized by Spanish cultural and linguistic heritage, and a dominant Anglo-Saxon culture subordinated cultures of successive waves of European immigrants to U.S. shores. In each case, the state set out to create a normative national culture to homogenize historical diversity by establishing the boundaries of acceptable cultural differences. A paradox of Western nation-state making, one that was later transplanted in many newer nation-states through colonialism, is that a patently new form of political community—the nation-state—was imagined as having its origin in a "folk" culture or "ancient" civilization. Practically every nation-state, whatever its political ideology—from the Chinese government's recognition of fifty-six official "minorities" to Australian and American struggles to define and give official meaning to "multiculturalism"—has had to wrestle with the problem of acceptable difference within some normative conception of national culture and unification of the nation. Some of the most recent fratricidal conflicts over cultural rights, as well as the complementary issues of partial autonomy and economic enfranchisement, are in Africa—in Burundi, the Congo, and Rwanda—where ethnic, tribal, and indigenous arrangements continue to command greater loyalty among most people than does an appeal to national pride.

The worldwide flow of immigrants during the last few decades is the largest such migration since the beginning of the twentieth century (see Table 1). The movement has been primarily from the lesser developed countries to the more economically developed countries. Unlike the earlier immigrants, for whom political ideologies played a role in shaping national policies of cultural assimilation, many new Asian and Latin American immigrants identify culturally with more than one place. Many nation-states have already embraced the concept of "multiculturalism," a form of cultural pluralism that recognizes cultural rights as a basis for collective identity as well as for claims to such resources as jobs, education, and access to grants for development. In New York City during the 1990s, the federal government created "empowerment zones" based on large community development grants to "multicultural" neighborhoods, such as those in Williamsburg with large numbers of African American, Jewish, and Spanish residents. Empowering minorities is a recognition of cultural values and the right to protect them in the context of urban development. Australia, Canada, many European nations, and the United States began to recognize indigenous claims, native-born minority claims, and new immigrant claims to cultural rights along with a promise of economic enfranchisement. The immigrants of an earlier era of capitalism and national pride neither enjoyed such recognition or tolerance nor the promise of economic enfranchisement anchored by cultural rights. In some cases, these rights have extended to recognition of partial political autonomy.

The nation-state remains important in any global order that would define or regulate what constitutes acceptable cultural pluralism, but globalization has weakened the power of nation-states to regulate the meaning of cultural diversity. Several factors have taken on increased significance in analyzing diversity issues: the rapid increase of global cultural exchange through increased wealth; the use of evolving technologies and new media (see map, p. 77); the contraction of cultural distance between groups of immigrants and their host countries; and the ambiguity of cultural classification and blurred identities. Cultural preservation in its political form—acceptable diversity—has become a global as well as a national issue.

Current Status

The global debate about preservation of cultural diversity involves several different arenas, including the marketplace, citizenship, and religion. The first arena concerns the creation and management of a regulatory culture in an environment of global free trade and how this regulatory culture comes into conflict with the sovereign right of every state to protect and preserve its national culture, including its minorities. The second arena involves the creation of transnational identities resulting from international immigration and how these new identities create problems of citizenship and sense of place. The third arena concerns religious identities that reach across millennia and borders to create political conflicts that can destabilize globalization.

Research

Renato Ruggiero, director-general of the World Trade Organization (WTO) in 1997, is quoted as saying, "Managing a world of converging economies, peoples and civilizations, each one preserving its own identity and culture, represents the great challenge and the great promise of our age." The connections among globalization, preservation of national cultures, and cultural rights, and the potential conflicts arising from these movements are pressing realities and can be illustrated by the debate over so-called cultural industries.

One group of nations, led by the United States, argues that cultural industries—film, radio, television, book publishing, magazines, and sound recordings—merely represent "entertainment" and should be treated like any other commodity. Another group of nations, led by France and Canada, defines products of national culture as trade goods that convey values, ideas, and meaning integral to a national identity. Economics, politics, and culture merge in heated debates about "cultural exceptions" in global trade agreements. For example, debate framed by "protectionism versus preservation" is enjoined in a Canadian law that requires that 60 percent of the programming on Canadian television channels be of Canadian origin. U.S. television producers argue that the Canadian law is a protectionist measure contrary to the spirit and rules of the World Trade Organization, the aim of which is to reduce all barriers to trade across national borders. Canadians invoke cultural rights, arguing that the state has an interest in preserving and protecting the "authenticity" of national culture and ensuring its dissemination. The premise of a cultural exception is that family life, freedom of speech, or sexual mores as portrayed by Canadian producers and received by Canadian viewers, for example, convey different values and meanings from their American television counterparts.

The expansion of global trade in the past several decades has brought economic value and cultural value closer, blurring the boundaries that once separated them and helping to create and define conflicts such as the cultural industries debate. Arguing that cultural goods traded on the world market are different from other commodities, nation-states that want to protect their cultural industries have demanded a "cultural exception" for a range of goods that fit their definition and image of their national identity. William Merkin, a trade consultant, argues that it is unreasonable for governments to assume that they can determine for themselves which cultural industries should receive a cultural exception. It is also unreasonable, however, to think that cultural products are the same as other commercial products, such as refrigerators or cars. From a different perspective, David Throsby, in *Economics and Culture,* wonders whether the debate would be altered if the tables were turned—that is, if it were a given that cultural products were not open to free trade and that corporations were required to seek an "exception" from nation-states for treating national culture and heritage as goods to be sold on international markets. He believes that the use of the word *exception* to describe the treatment of cultural goods conveys the negative meaning that a nation's struggle to preserve and protect its cultural values is less worthy than the market's attempt to profit from them.

The definition of citizenship, and corresponding issues of cultural preservation, has also become more complex as globalization has progressed. Greatly increased immigration over the past several decades, in part because of increased global competition and pressure to import labor, has resulted in a new world of "guest workers" and "partial citizens." For example, there are Turkish guest workers who have lived in Germany since the 1960s but by law are prohibited from becoming German citizens. As a result, they and their children have access to education, but because they are not citizens they do not have access to pensions. For two centuries this same legal system has made several hundred thousand "Germans" living in Russia eligible for immediate German citizenship even when the duration of their settlement in Russia extends to the second generation and, in some cases, the third generation. Meanwhile, similar terms are not offered German Turkish youth who have attended German schools, speak German, and identify with Germany as their home. Recent changes in German law that will make it easier for Turkish residents to obtain citizenship illustrate how economic globalization has affected the way in which states view acceptable cultural diversity. In this example, Germany is becoming more inclusive of cultural differences in its ideas about citizenship and belonging, a phenomenon that is happening in many other parts of the world.

Accepting a world of cultural pluralism means rethinking the relationship between a people and their place in at least two dimensions. One dimension is the separation of a people within a nation-state and state recognition of partial legal and political autonomy of that people within its national territory. The Soviet Union used this model, and China has granted partial autonomy to selected official minorities but withheld it from others. Canada created an autonomous nation within a nation, Nunavut, to satisfy the aspirations of the Native American Inuits, as did the United States when it recognized its treaty with the Native American Oneida nation. In these cases, the autonomous people retain individual rights of citizenship within the larger nation and territory but also possess additional cultural, political, and economic rights as a collective.

The other dimension involves the dispersion of people who share a national culture but who live in the sovereign territories of other states and become part of another national culture or cultures. In the era of globalization, these diasporas, or dispersed people with a shared culture living in different countries, have led to a sense of belonging in both or to several places while retaining strong ties to their community of national origin. Chinese, Dominican, Indian, Iranian, Lebanese, Mexican, and many other diasporic communities that exist around the globe have emerged with greater social solidarity and cultural cohesiveness during the era of globalization than at any previous period. Their elites have played a prominent role in creating a global middle class that is simultaneously cosmopolitan, multinational, and local in their cultural identities.

Cultural anthropologist Arjun Appadurai and Katerina Stenou, director of the Sector for Culture for the United Nations Educational, Scientific and Cultural Organization (UNESCO), point out in their article "Sustainable Pluralism and the Future of Belonging" that nation-states will continue to be the parties responsible for sustaining cultural pluralism within national borders. The challenge, however, is to manage acceptable cultural diversity in their increasingly complex political environments, where tensions can arise between new and established ethnic communities as well as between such communities abroad. The politics of identity has affected how governments think about governing in many parts of the world. Increasingly, there is a call for partnerships among official government agencies, nongovernmental organizations, and corporations with respect to issues of cultural recognition and economic redistribution.

Over the past several decades, new immigrants as cultural minorities—be they refugees or guest workers—have been able to articulate cultural rights in their new homes as human rights to the point where there is a right to cultural difference in such areas as clothing, prayer, diet, housing, marriage, language, health, and social welfare (see HUMAN RIGHTS). In debates about citizenship and belonging, xenophobia can be the counterpart to increased recognition of cultural rights as well as cultural pluralism. The debates over prayer in public schools and offices in the United States and Muslim women wearing headscarves in France are emblematic of conflicts over cultural rights and emerging cultural pluralism in an era of increasing global economic integration and the changing relationship of nation-states to people who reside within their borders. The scarf or its variant is an intricate part of the way in which Muslim women make a statement about their modesty, an essential quality of being Muslim, being a woman, and belonging to a community. To many non-Muslims the scarf is a statement of oppression, subservience to men, and a sign of backwardness. The prayer debate in the United States, and elsewhere also, is the symbolic equivalent of the scarf debate in Muslim countries. Both are emblematic of the significance of the politics of cultural identity in the era of globalization.

The politics of national identity and citizenship are not the only forms of identity conflict that have increased with globalization. Expanded global influence of cultures also plays out in the religious arena. Conflicts frequently arise from these influences and are often rooted in economic issues. In fact, there is growing agreement among people of many nations that globalization is cultural imperialism dressed as free trade. More specifically, Thomas Friedman, in *The Lexus and the Olive Tree,* asserts that globalization is perceived as Americanization in many parts of the world. Access to the best jobs in the global economy often requires knowing English; people around the world want the economic benefits that flow from globalization, but they resist the idea that one culture fits all. Resentment of the predominance of the U.S. economy and American culture often outweighs the perceived benefits of American enterprise. The 2001 attacks on the World Trade Center towers—buildings symbolic of the increasing global reach of U.S. power and wealth over the past several decades—can be interpreted as an expression of that resentment, as a clash between two civilizations, one Western, the other Eastern, one predominantly Christian, the other predominantly Muslim. Differences between civilizations, perceived or otherwise, frame the issue of cultural identity as one not merely of citizenship and national affiliation, but also one relating to the fundamental question "What are you?" One can change citizenship, and even class, more easily than one can change religious beliefs, that is, faith about the nature of humanity, the universe, and the place of one's own civilization in the scheme of ultimate purpose.

Policies and Programs

Although specific policies and programs concerning acceptable cultural diversity are not in place, a consensus has emerged concerning the desirability of a world of nation-states that recognizes the value of cultural pluralism in an era of globalization. In 1995 UNESCO assembled the Scientific Committee and charged it with the task of fact-finding and framing issues for the purpose of developing policies and programs for promoting pluralism and preserving diversity. In the preliminary stages, the committee's priorities included establishing principles, finding the right language, plotting a direction, and collecting data and fact-finding. The conclusions they reached can be found in three documents: *World Culture Report, 2000; World Heritage Sites; and Culture, Trade and Globalization.*

The proposed direction of future policies and programs can be gleaned from five principles detailed in *World Culture Report, 2000.* First, whether the content of cultural diversity is trade goods, material heritage, or daily social rituals, emphasis should be placed on preservation of the underlying diversity of experiment, invention, and interpretation that occurs in ways humans live together and give meaning to their lives. Second, following on this view, preservation is an active and ongoing process of selection, interpretation, and retention of cultural production in a changing world. Third, globalization should be viewed as a set of related processes that have increased the realm of opportunity and possibility for cultural diversity. Fourth, diversity is not a "good" in and of itself. Rather, according to co-authors Lourdes Arizpe and Ann-Belinda Preis in their general introduction to the report, governments and civil societies must assist diversity by finding "ways of channeling exchanges through democratic practices that respect human rights, gender equity and sustainability." Fifth, nation-states will have to take the lead in determining acceptable cultural diversity, but organizations such as UNESCO should continue to take a leadership role in setting guidelines that move the world toward cultural pluralism. In addition, *World Culture Report, 2000* calls for partnerships among nation-states and corporations, international organizations, nongovernmental organizations, research firms and institutions and, especially, local communities.

State recognition and support of cultural pluralism, as enshrined in the above principles, must extend to the empowerment of minorities through economic enfranchisement if cultural diversity is to be sustained. In "Sustainable Pluralism and the Future of Belonging," Appadurai and Stenou argue that cultural pluralism and cultural rights are not sustainable without economic enfranchisement. Political scientist and social philosopher Nancy Fraser, in "Redistribution, Recognition and Participation," calls for nation-states to adopt policies based on social justice that include the redistribution of resources and recognition of cultural rights as one problem in an approach aimed at sustainable cultural pluralism. In "The Social Investment State," sociologist Anthony Giddens suggests that social democracy is the best political and economic framework within which to achieve the goal of a fair and just distribution of resources in a society that embraces cultural pluralism. This may in some cases require that national governments grant partial autonomy to ethnic communities that share a collective cultural identity different from the dominant national culture.

Globalization has shortened the distance between economic values and cultural values and in the process has raised national tensions and identity issues. Cultural production has always been exchanged, but increasingly it is becoming the property of global media and communications corporations and sold on world markets. This has raised fears among some nations and their subcultures that local control over meaning and interpretation in the creation and maintenance of collective identities will be lost. Economist Elie Cohen, in "Globalization and Cultural Diversity," departs somewhat from the general policy direction taken by most authors in *World Culture Report, 2000* when he makes several policy recommendations for reducing the tension between globalization and local identity claims. More in line with the thinking in *Culture, Trade and Globalization,* Cohen recommends that nation-states influence public opinion in favor of globalization and give the responsibility for resolving trade disputes to international organizations. He also recommends, however, that a body like UNESCO should define what qualifies as a cultural exception, "the only problem that market forces can't resolve."

A knotty problem, addressed only indirectly here, is the conservation of the world's cultural heritage. Questions about how to define cultural heritage and who should pay for it were taken up by UNESCO when it established the World Heritage List, which now contains 630 sites; UN member states submit candidates to a panel that then selects the sites to be added to the list. A mix of economic and cultural value frames questions about what criteria to use in selecting sites for the list and who will pay for their preservation. All *World Culture Report, 2000* authors conclude that economic analysis alone cannot and should not determine cultural value, but they caution that selection on the basis of cultural value without economic consideration is a formula for disaster. Preservation projects often run into the tens of millions of dollars and require cooperation among international foundations, states, private donors, and corporations.

Data collection on cultural diversity remains in its infancy. The *World Culture Report, 2000* includes findings from two comparative surveys designed with policy considerations in mind. In the survey concerning international public opinion and perceptions of national identity, researchers found that more than half the citizens of countries surveyed opposed the arrival of more immigrants. The native populations stigmatized them as criminals and perceived them as unemployed masses who contribute little or nothing to the national economy. The second survey measured national and international practices regarding cultural diversity by analyzing such indicators as newspapers, libraries, radio and television, cinema, and heritage practices. One conclusion that can be drawn from this data is that the globalization of the print and electronic media has encountered problems in the significantly uneven development in national economies, which limits mass participation in national culture. A valuable aspect of this data collection project is that it will be administered repeatedly for future reports so performance can be measured over time.

UNESCO's *World Culture Report, 2000* makes clear that not all forms of cultural diversity are considered acceptable (see Document 1). In the first chapter, "Cultural Diversity, Conflict and Pluralism," Lourdes Arizpe and her co-authors raise the question, "Who decides what qualifies for admission to a world order premised on cultural pluralism?" Beyond the shared understanding that each nation-state will continue to play an important role in deciding what diversity in cultural expression is acceptable within its borders, the UNESCO Universal Declaration on Cultural Diversity outlines the final stages of a process begun in 1995 to establish guidelines and an action plan for member states (see Document 2). This document calls for movement on such proposals as establishing an international legal instrument on cultural diversity, ensuring the inclusion and participation of persons and groups from varied cultural backgrounds in the formulation of what constitutes acceptable cultural diversity, clarifying the content of cultural rights as an integral part of human rights, incorporating traditional pedagogies into the education process as a way to preserve cultural knowledge, and encouraging the production, protection, and dissemination of diversified content in media and global information networks. More specific social policies and action plans for every member state would deal with public debate over such issues as acceptable forms of marriage, sexuality, redress for wrongs, the treatment of women and children, sacrifice of humans and animals, medical and other practices having to do with the body (such as male and female genital mutilation), fundamental beliefs in the value of human life, attitudes toward nature, relations between religion and the state, censorship and freedom of speech, and the proper relationship between a government and its people.

Regional Summaries

The issue of acceptable cultural diversity and its preservation enjoins issues of cultural rights and partial autonomy. It appears that, with the exception of Europe, for now at least these issues are left to each nation-state to decide. States in all regions of the world have felt the effects of globalization on cultural diversity but they have experienced them in different ways and to varying degrees. In considering regional differences the reader should keep in mind that each region consists of heterogeneous cultures and political communities, only a few of which are represented here.

North America

Canada and the United States have two of the world's richest economies and are the most popular destinations for immigrants. Although these immigrants come from practically every country, large numbers are from Southeast Asia, South Asia, and East Asia. In a 1996 study of immigration and ethnic recruitment to labor markets, Roger Waldinger found that the "ethnicization" of labor recruitment and retention meant that social mobility had become a matter of ethnic queuing, that is, one group replaces another in the queue as long as an economy continues to grow. This process proceeded with relatively low levels of ethnic conflict during the sharp upturn in the Canadian and U.S. economies during the latter part of the 1990s. Even though Canada's unemployment rate was high, the relative lack of conflict was a marked difference from the period of labor unrest during downsizing and layoffs that took place in the 1980s.

In terms of cultural rights, the most remarkable recent development has been the creation of transnational identities for immigrants referred to as "global nations," indicating the separation of national loyalty from territorial sovereignty. For example through bilateral agreements between the United States and the Dominican Republic and Mexico, Dominicans and Mexicans living in the United States were encouraged by their respective governments to participate fully in the national life of their host country and to become good citizens. At the same time, however, they were also to maintain a sense of belonging to their community back home. Intergovernmental agreements about remittances, travel back and forth, involvement in community affairs, and holding office

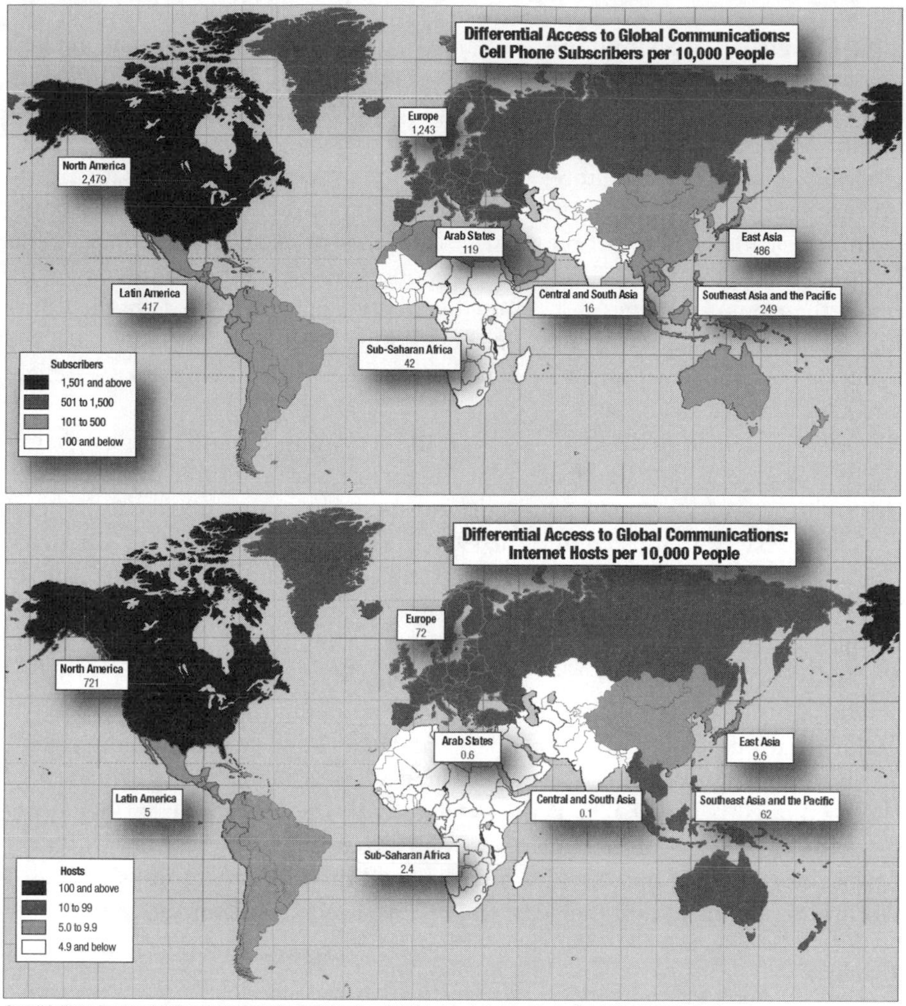

Source: United Nations Educational, Scientific and Cultural Organization, *World Culture Report, 2000: Cultural Diversity, Conflict and Pluralism* (Paris: UNESCO, 2001), 371, table 20.
Note: All data are for 1997–1998. Regional values are based on samples of countries for each region. Israel is classified as part of Europe.

in their country of origin while voting and participating in the host country reinforced a sense not only of dual citizenship but also of belonging to more than one country. As a result, the second generation has developed a sense of identity that is, for example, neither American nor Mexican but "transnational" in ways not experienced by most previous waves of immigrants.

Latin America

The main lines of cultural cleavage and conflict in the nation-states of Latin America derive from a colonial legacy that places descendants of Spanish and Portuguese conquerors at the top of a social hierarchy characterized by class, race, language, and ethnicity. The social hierarchy varies by country but most have two tiers. The first tier is composed of Spanish and Portuguese descendants born in the New World. They are referred to as *mestizos* or *ladinos* and constitute the political, economic, and social elite. They are the interpreters of the national culture and communicate with the larger world through the global languages of Spanish or Portuguese. At the bottom of the social hierarchy are marginalized indigenous kinship communities. The diverse languages and cultures of these people are often lumped together in national media and public discourse, where they are referred to as *indios.* They are poorly integrated into the national culture, marginal to the economy, and associate mostly within their own relatively small linguistic communities. Some of these communities of indigenous peoples and descendants of African slaves have been integrated into the national culture and economy as peasant communities who retain their own languages and culture but also participate in those of the dominant class of mestizos. Among the best known and largest of these are the Quechua of Peru, the Quiche of Ecuador, and the Maya of Guatemala, Belize, and southern Mexican states.

Class and language diversity has been the spawning ground for a language-rights movement that is part of a global effort to have nation-states recognize the right of every cultural community to sustain its own language as integral to the preservation of its culture. In 1996 the World Conference on Language Rights took place in Barcelona, Spain. One of the main goals of the conference was to approve a universal declaration of language rights as a complement to the United Nations Universal Declaration of Human Rights (see HUMAN RIGHTS). Rigoberta Menchu, a well-known Maya-Quiche intellectual and activist from Guatemala, presided over the conference. Walter Mignolo, in "Globalization, Civilization Processes, and the Relocation of Languages", attributes great significance to the declaration as "a radical transformation of those colonial beliefs that linked languages with the boundaries of humanity from the early stages of modernity and globalization." Globalization, by weakening the powers of the state, has strengthened marginalized groups' claims to cultural rights, including the right to preserve their own language.

Europe

Europe, through the integration of its nation-states into the European Union, is the exception to the reality elsewhere that cultural rights and issues of partial autonomy are left almost completely to the policies of nation-states. The European Union recognizes the cultural value of protecting minority languages and cultures within its borders, for instance, Welsh and Breton. It provides funds for education, research, and cultural production. The union's image of itself is not only of an economic community but also of a community with its own culture. The creation of a supranational culture premised on the belief that all Europeans share a common identity leads to a search for what it means to be "European." The appearance of common passports and the construction of EU universities are a further step in the direction of shaping the cultural policies of member nations. "What is a European?" is a question that has revived a centuries-old belief in this region that there is a shared civilization.

Immigrant workers, called guest workers, a designation that conveys intentional barriers to citizenship, have in the past decade become more vocal in their demands for cultural rights. Many of them are now second- and third-generation "guests," with only residency and work rights but no promise of citizenship at all. These ethnic minorities think of themselves as German or French or Swiss or Austrian, instead of identifying with the land of their origin or ancestry. The stakes are high for these would-be Europeans: along with citizenship comes economic enfranchisement not only through their "host" country but also through access to other EU states. Demands for full rights that would bring greater access to education and social welfare benefits continue to shape the issue of sustainable cultural pluralism in Europe. Joseph Becker, in a descriptive study on international public opinion and national identity for *World Culture Report, 2000,* found that two-thirds to three-quarters of citizens in the twenty-three nations that receive the highest numbers of immigrants wanted to restrict immigration. Among them were those of Austria, Great Britain, Italy, the Netherlands, and Spain.

North Africa and the Middle East

Most nation-states in North Africa and the Middle East are characterized by Islamic, Arab, and indigenous influences on cultural diversity. How these influences intersect to shape the issue of cultural rights varies from state to state. For example, Saudi Arabia and Kuwait are both Islamic and Arab states that have adopted the European model of "guest workers" as part of their policy of national economic development. Workers from Egypt, Palestine, and other Islamic and Arab countries in the region face most of the same restrictions on types of employment, eligibility for citizenship, duration of stays, legal rights, and ethnic prejudices as those faced by guest workers in Europe. In Saudi Arabia, the cultural rights of guest workers are further curtailed by strict moral codes for public behavior. Egypt, although also Muslim and Arab, is more secular than Saudi Arabia, and its moral codes are more "westernized." Ironically, minority nomadic Bedouin tribes that the Egyptian government relocated into settlements consider their culture to be superior on the grounds that it represents authentic Arab culture.

Turkey is the most secular country in this region. The Turkish state has been engaged in a struggle against Kurdish nationalists in the southeastern part of the country for more than sixty years and has, in the recent past, outlawed not only the teaching of the Kurdish language but also the use of the appellation *Kurds,* assigning them instead the official name "Mountain Turks." Small numbers of Greeks, Armenians, and Jews have been able to maintain a presence as "communities" under the international Treaty of Lausanne, which recognized Turkey as a sovereign state in 1923. This agreement guarantees cultural rights to maintain ethnic schools, to teach minority languages, and to retain property. In Israel, the most culturally different of the nation-states in this region, there are a million Arab Israeli citizens who constitute a minority and have limited cultural and political rights relative to the Jewish majority. Palestinians in Jewish-occupied territories are denied basic political, legal, and cultural rights of electoral participation, equal access to education, and judicial fairness, equal employment opportunities, land for housing, and economic enfranchisement generally.

Sub-Saharan Africa

The major issues concerning cultural rights in this region are the disenfranchisement of ethnic groups and the ethnic basis of the unequal distribution of national wealth. In one-party states, such as Kenya, Nigeria, and the Republic of Congo, a dominant ethnic group controls the state and protects its own interests, marginalizing all other ethnic groups in the process. In these countries, civil society is weak, and uncensored cultural pluralism is not possible; diversity does exist, however, below the purview of the state, where large ethnic communities with tribal organizations wage battles over control of the state for exploitable resources. Ethnic wars have broken out in Burundi, Rwanda, and Sudan over competition for power and privilege. South Africa is an exception and continues its struggle to create a multicultural civil society in the post-apartheid era.

Central and South Asia

Two very different recent histories frame issues of cultural rights in this region. The first involves the breakup of the Soviet Union in 1991, and the second concerns the postcolonial history of nation making in South Asia in the late 1940s, particularly in India and Pakistan. The breakup of the Soviet Union led to the creation of new states, among them the Central Asian republics and the Ukraine. Minority communities of Russians who settled in these countries during the Soviet era enjoyed privileges as political and economic elites. After the Soviet breakup, they became the targets of ethnic hatred and were encouraged to resettle in Russia. Within Russia the government used force to suppress self-determination movements by Chechens and South Ossetians in the Caucasus region. The Caucasus is an area of cultural conflict that has simmered for centuries, in part defined by clashes between Russian Orthodox and Muslim communities.

A clash of religious civilizations fueled by nationalist sentiment also characterizes the conflict between Indian and Pakistan over Kashmir, where a Hindu state controls a region with a Muslim majority. When India became independent after 1948, a civil war broke out between Hindus and Muslims that ended in shifts in population and the separation of predominantly Muslim Pakistan from predominantly Hindu India. Mutual claims to Kashmir are a residuum of the war. This conflict over Kashmir periodically erupts, threatening the entire region, particularly now that both countries have a nuclear weapons capability. In addition to cross-border cultural conflict, each state has its own internal cultural conflicts—in Pakistan between several million ethnic Pashtuns in the northwest and Pakistani nationalists, and in India between Sikhs and Hindu nationalists. Strong nationalist and equally strong religious sentiments are intertwined and lead to shows of force rather than tolerance of cultural differences. Minority cultural rights continue to be a sensitive issue in the political stability of both countries.

The war in Afghanistan following the 11 September 2001 attack on the World Trade Center towers and the Pentagon involved Islamists from a number of countries—among them, Pakistan, Tajikistan, and Uzbekistan—fighting alongside the Taliban, the Islamist group that took control of most of Afghanistan in 1994. The Taliban's suppression of women's and minorities' rights received global attention. Prior to Taliban control of the country, women were crucial to the functioning of civil society in their capacity as teachers, lawyers, doctors, and administrators. The right to work, but also the right to move freely in public and to have a strong voice, was greatly diminished. The restricted movements and privileges accorded to women in many societies are touchstones to issues of cultural rights in general, how to think about acceptable cultural diversity, and how to sustain cultural pluralism in the world today.

East Asia and the Pacific

Australia and New Zealand embrace different forms of multiculturalism that have as their goal cultural pluralism and economic enfranchisement, but both countries' policies have encountered a degree of popular resistance; according to Joseph Becker's descriptive study on international public opinion and national identity, two-thirds of Australians and New Zealanders favor restrictions on further immigration, about the same percentage as those in Canada and the United States. Australia and New Zealand also face ethnic discontent among their indigenous populations: Australian Aborigines and New Zealand Maori both suffer economic disenfranchisement and marginalization from national culture and society. Both communities seek greater recognition of their existence and want partial autonomy from the state to run their own affairs. At the same time, they also seek greater economic enfranchisement in the form of development projects and welfare benefits, including better health and educational opportunities.

Language rights are viewed as crucial to the sustainability of the Aborigine and Maori ways of life. Ayres Rock in Central Australia, a destination of tourists from around the world, illustrates the complexities surrounding claims of cultural autonomy. In addition to being a tourist attraction, this outcrop is also a sacred site for Aboriginal ancestor rituals. The Australian government and Aboriginal leaders recognize the claims of the other in terms of the area's economic and cultural value, so tourist movements at the site are restricted in deference to cultural rights, which include the right to perform rituals. Aborigines are employed by the national park service as guides and park rangers, creating a dual meaning for the rock as well as a path to economic enfranchisement.

Pacific island states are comparative newcomers to nationhood, most of them having achieved independence only since 1970. Some, like Papua New Guinea, consist of hundreds of tribal peoples who speak hundreds of different languages, which makes it extremely difficult to imagine and implement a national culture that can command the loyalty normally given to small kinship communities. Hence cultural pluralism in Papua New Guinea can be characterized as cultural anarchy. In contrast, Fiji, Samoa, and Tonga have well-established bureaucratic and administrative institutions and national cultures that are imagined as modern chiefdoms. Acceptable diversity and cultural pluralism are conceived mainly through what it means to be Fijian, Samoan, or Tongan. Only in Fiji, where half the population is Indian (from the subcontinent) do questions about citizenship and belonging shape issues of cultural rights and economic enfranchisement. Fijian political culture dominates the issue of recognition (denied Indians), and Indian commercial interests dominate the issue of economic enfranchisement (denied Fijians).

Data

Table 1 International Migration, 1999

Country of Settlement	Inflow	Main Country of Origin
United States	796,000	Mexico
Germany	615,000	Poland
Russian Federation	583,000	Kazakhstan
Mexico	480,000	United States
Japan	275,000	China
United Kingdom	237,000	United States
Canada	216,000	Hong Kong
Ukraine	130,000	Russian Federation
France	102,000	Algeria
Australia	86,000	New Zealand
Netherlands	77,000	Turkey
Switzerland	73,000	Yugoslavia
Austria	53,000	Turkey
Croatia	52,000	Bosnia-Herzegovina
Belgium	49,000	France
Denmark	49,000	Somalia
Kazakhstan	38,000	Russian Federation
Sweden	33,000	Yugoslavia
Belarus	31,000	Russian Federation
Norway	22,000	Sweden

Source: United Nations Educational, Scientific and Cultural Organization, *World Culture Report, 2000: Cultural Diversity, Conflict and Pluralism* (Paris: UNESCO, 2001).

Note: Listed in descending order of total number of immigrants.

Case Study—The Transnational Identity of Tibetan Exile Communities in Nepal

Following the Chinese takeover of Tibet in 1959, Tibetan Buddhist exiles fled to Butan, India, and Nepal, where they settled in small communities. Poor, landless, and stateless, these communities survived in their adopted homelands largely without cultural rights or economic enfranchisement, but they soon became the objects of interest to international groups wishing to preserve the Tibetan Buddhist way of life. The relationship between international assistance organizations and the cultural identity of Tibetan exile communities is complex, raising questions about what it means to be Tibetan and who decides issues of cultural authenticity.

Cultural anthropologist Ann Frechette, in *We Are Like Bats: Identity, Community, and Entitlement among Tibetan Exiles in Nepal,* isolates two elements common to international "friends of Tibet": they all support Tibetan exile communities because "Tibet is important to their own personal lives, goals, and visions for the future of humanity," and they all promote "beliefs that emphasize the individual as the most basic social unit, with the right to live a life of his or her own choosing." These values are expressed variously as Western ideas about human rights, Western Buddhism, or multiculturalism. Tibetan exile communities have incorporated these values, which are not necessarily part of the core belief of Tibetan Buddhism, and added them to their cultural identity in order to be recognized globally and to gain cultural rights in Nepal and other countries. By making their culture attractive to Western aid organizations and thereby encouraging contributions, their collective identity has been sustained for more than four decades; but the process has raised questions about authenticity and the meaning of cultural preservation.

What cultural accommodations have Tibetans made to international aid associations that might compromise their core cultural values? Most of the accommodations have been in the schools, where Tibetans have adopted a Western curriculum that includes the teaching of English. In keeping with the liberal humanist values of their friends, the schools, Frechette notes, portray "a unique way of life not only for Tibetans, but for anyone who wants to participate, for the benefit of all humanity." When potential donors visit, children dressed in British school uniforms perform rituals taught them by their Tibetan teachers as part of "traditional" Tibetan culture. Visitors are treated to a performance that incorporates the Scottish Highland tradition of fife and drum, British Indian forms of assembly, and the use of national flags, anthems, and emblems of various nation-states to illustrate how Tibetan "traditional" culture is open to individuals and adaptable to all nations. Frechette notes that the Tibetan exiles had wanted to use schools to create social cohesion but had no established norms to guide them. The result was similar to what the historian Eric Hobsbawm calls "invented traditions," which he defines as a set of practices that develops in the present context yet implies continuity with the ancient and historic past due to its ritual repetition. In the Tibetan schools, children come to learn that the past of everyone else is their own "tradition."

The Tibetan monasteries in exile faced a different challenge to their cultural authenticity. Because the monasteries were the aspect of Tibetan Buddhist culture and society that was most threatened with extinction by Chinese authorities when they seized control, Tibetan exiles made the reestablishment of monasteries a priority. The exile monastic system retained its traditions of Buddhist texts and ritual practices. As a result, within the monasteries there was much less willingness to make accommodations to the values of Western individualism and freedom in order to win over potential international donors. There were, however, accommodations that had implications for cultural preservation. A number of monks from the exile communities migrated to the United States and other countries. Americans, and many others of foreign lands, began to reinterpret Tibetan Buddhist texts and ritual practices in terms of the cultural values of freedom and individualism, creating a distinct American Buddhism that has led to a transnational debate about which Buddhism is the authentic Buddhism. Tibetan exile communities staunchly maintain that Tibetan Buddhism is an essential part of their culture and that only Tibetans have the right to decide the issue of authenticity of belief and practice. Their assertion of cultural rights clashes with Western Buddhist assertions that acquiring knowledge of the texts and rituals entitles them to decide for themselves how to practice Buddhism. Tibetan exiles need the language of freedom and the language of cultural preservation to sustain their transnational identity in an increasingly complex world.

Biographical Sketches

Arjun Appadurai is Barbara E. and Richard J. Franke Professor in the Departments of South Asian Languages and Anthropology at the University of Chicago. He has been influential in developing the field of cultural studies known as transnational identity and public culture. Along with several colleagues, he helped to organize the Society for Transnational Cultural Studies and establish its journal, *Public Culture,* at the forefront of the critical understanding of global cultural flows and how these emerge as public phenomena. Appadurai currently heads the Globalization Project at the University of Chicago to advance the study of global cultural pluralism.

Anthony Giddens is a sociologist and director of the London School of Economics and Political Science. He has been at the forefront of a group of scholars who seek a so-called third way, between capitalism and socialism, of framing issues of inequality created by globalization. His proposal for a social investment state, a partnership among corporations, states, and citizens that combines cultural pluralism with economic enfranchisement, appears in UNESCO's *World Culture Report, 2000* and in his *Runaway World: How Globalization Is Reshaping Our Lives* (2000).

Ulf Hannerz is professor of social anthropology at Stockholm University and was among the first to recognize that globalization was changing the relationship between cultural identity and territory, and creating transnational identities. In *Exploring the City: Inquiries toward an Urban Anthropology* (1980) and *Transnational Connections: Culture, People, Places,* (1996), Hannerz defines cultural globalization as increasing connectedness over greater distances and revives the concept of "cosmopolitanism" to explore the interrelationship of the global and the local in world cities.

David Maybury-Lewis is a professor of anthropology at Harvard University and a founder of Cultural Survival, a not-for-profit organization dedicated to the perpetuation of indigenous peoples whose lives and cultures are threatened by pollution, encroachment, disease, poverty, prejudice, and violence. Among Maybury-Lewis's many publications are *Peoples of the World: Their Cultures, Traditions, and Ways of Life* (2001), *Indigenous Peoples, Ethnic Groups, and the State* (1996), and *Millennium: Tribal Wisdom and the Modern World* (1992).

Roland Robertson is a professor of sociology at the University of Pittsburgh and was among the first to articulate the importance of a cultural perspective on globalization, which he did in *Globalization: Social Theory and Global Culture* (1992). As a member of the editorial board of a monograph series on global culture for the influential journal *Theory, Culture, and Society,* Robertson has for more than a decade been at the heart of the debates on culture and the need for a global perspective.

Directory

Cultural Survival, 215 Prospect Street, Cambridge, MA 02139. Telephone: (617) 441-5147, Email: csinc@cs.org, Web: http://www.cs.org
Organization that promotes local projects aimed at the survival of endangered cultures and endangered lives

Culture and Development Co-ordination Office, UNESCO, Place de Fontenoy, 75007 Paris, France. Telephone: (33) 3 45 68 14 07, Email: wccd@unesco.org, Web: http://www.unesco.org/culture_and_development/ocd/intro.html
UN office that sponsored the World Commission on Culture and Development and follow-up efforts relating to the relationship between development and culture

From Diversity to Pluralism, UNESCO Sector for Culture, 2 UN Plaza, New York, NY 10017. Telephone: (212) 963-5981, Email: newyork@unesco.org, Web: http://www.unesco.org/culture/pluralism
UN office that prepared the UNESCO Universal Declaration on Cultural Diversity

United Nations High Commissioner for Refugees (UNHCR), 2500 Case Postale, 1211 Geneva 2, Switzerland. Telephone: (41) 22 739 8111, Email: go to http://www.unhcr.ch/cgi-bin/texis/vtx/contact?hq=y, Web: http://www.unhcr.ch/cgi-bin/texis/vtx/home
UN agency that promotes the welfare of displaced persons

Women and Gender Equality, UNESCO Sector for Culture, 2 UN Plaza, New York, NY 10017. Telephone: (212) 963-5981, Email: newyork@unesco.org, Web: http://www.unesco.org/culture/women.
Education mission aimed at HIV/AIDS prevention and care, policies toward women in science and technology, and policies for economic independence

Further Research

Books

Anderson, Benedict. *Imagined Communities.* London: Verso, 1983.
Appadurai, Arjun. *Modernity at Large: Cultural Dimensions of Globalization.* Minneapolis: University of Minnesota Press, 1996.
Featherstone, Mike, ed. *Global Culture: Nationalism, Globalization and Modernity.* London: Sage Publications, 1990.
Frechette, Ann. *We Are Like Bats: Identity, Community, and Entitlement among Tibetan Exiles in Nepal.* New York: Berghahn Books, forthcoming 2002.
Friedman, Jonathan. *Cultural Identity and Global Process.* London: Sage Publications, 1994.
Friedman, Thomas L. *The Lexus and the Olive Tree.* New York: Anchor Books, 2000.
Gellner, Ernst. *Nations and Nationalism.* Oxford: Basil Blackwell, 1990.
Hannerz, Ulf. *Transnational Connections: Culture, People, Places.* New York: Routledge, 1996.

Hobsbawm, Eric, and Terence Ranger. *The Invention of Traditions.* Cambridge: Cambridge University Press, 1983.

Huntington, Samuel P. *The Clash of Civilizations and the Remaking of the Global Order.* New York: Simon and Schuster, 1996.

Jameson, Fredric, and Masao Miyoshi, eds. *The Cultures of Globalization.* Durham, N.C.: Duke University Press, 1999.

King, Anthony D., ed. *Culture, Globalization, and the World-System: Contemporary Conditions for the Representation of Identity.* Minneapolis: University of Minnesota Press, 1997.

Mazrui, A. A. *A World Federation of Cultures: An African Perspective.* New York: Free Press, 1980.

Robertson, Roland. *Globalization: Social Theory and Global Culture.* London: Sage Publications, 1992.

Throsby, David. *Economics and Culture.* Cambridge: Cambridge University Press, 2001.

Waldinger, Roger. *Still the Promised City.* Cambridge, Mass.: Harvard University Press, 1996.

Articles and Reports

Appadurai, Arjun, and Katerina Stenou. "Sustainable Pluralism and the Future of Belonging." In *World Culture Report, 2000: Cultural Diversity, Conflict and Pluralism.* Paris: UNESCO, 2001.

Arizpe, Lourdes, Elizabeth Jelin, J. Mohan Rao, and Paul Streeten. "Cultural Diversity, Conflict and Pluralism." In *World Culture Report, 2000: Cultural Diversity, Conflict and Pluralism.* Paris: UNESCO, 2001.

Arizpe, Lourdes, and Ann-Belinda S. Preis. General Introduction to *World Culture Report, 2000: Cultural Diversity, Conflict and Pluralism.* Paris: UNESCO, 2001.

Becker, Joseph W. "International Public Opinion and National Identity: A Descriptive Study of Existing Data." In *World Culture Report, 2000: Cultural Diversity, Conflict and Pluralism.* Paris: UNESCO, 2001.

Bernier, Ivan. "Cultural Diversity and International Trade Regulations." In *World Culture Report, 2000: Cultural Diversity, Conflict and Pluralism.* Paris: UNESCO, 2001.

Cohen, Elie. "Globalization and Cultural Diversity." In *World Culture Report, 2000: Cultural Diversity, Conflict and Pluralism.* Paris: UNESCO, 2001.

Fraser, Nancy. "Redistribution, Recognition, and Participation." In *World Culture Report, 2000: Cultural Diversity, Conflict and Pluralism.* Paris: UNESCO, 2001.

Friedman, Jonathan. "Cultural Logics of the Global System." *Theory, Culture, and Society* 5, nos. 2–3 (June 1988): 477–460.

Giddens, Anthony. "The Social Investment State." In *World Culture Report, 2000: Cultural Diversity, Conflict and Pluralism.* Paris: UNESCO, 2001.

Haeri, Shahla. "Obedience versus Autonomy: Women and Fundamentalism in Iran and Pakistan. In *The Globalization Reader,* edited by Frank J. Lechner and John Boli, 350–358. Malden, Mass.: Blackwell Publishers, 2000.

Hannerz, Ulf. "Notes on the Global Ecumene." *Public Culture* 1, no. 2 (1989): 66–75.

Hilton, Isabel. "The Pashtun Code: An Unruled Tribe and Afghanistan's Future." *New Yorker,* 3 December 2001, 58–71.

Jameson, Fredric. "Postmodernism, or the Cultural Logic of Late Capitalism." *New Left Review,* July–August 1984, 53–92.

Lechner, Frank J. "Ethnicity and Revitalization in the Modern World System." *Sociological Focus* 17, no. 3 (1984): 243–256.

Lewis, Bernard. "The Revolt of Islam." *New Yorker,* 19 November 2001, 50–63.

Mignolo, Walter D. "Globalization, Civilizational Processes, and the Relocation of Languages and Cultures." In *The Cultures of Globalization,* edited by Fredric Jameson and Masao Miyoshi, 32–53. Durham, N.C.: Duke University Press, 1999.

Robertson, Roland. "Globalization Theory and Civilization Analysis." *Comparative Civilizations Review* 17 (fall 1987): 20–30.

Robertson, Roland, and J. Chirico. "Humanity, Globalization, and Worldwide Religious Resurgence." *Sociological Analysis* 46, no. 3, (1985): 219–242.

Rushdie, Salman. "Summer of Solanka." *New Yorker,* 16 July 2001, 66–75.

Sullivan, Andrew. "This Is a Religious War." *New York Times Magazine,* 7 October 2001, 44–47.

United Nations Educational, Scientific and Cultural Organization. *Culture, Trade and Globalization.* Paris: UNESCO, 2000.

———. *World Culture Report, 2000: Cultural Diversity, Conflict and Pluralism.* Paris: UNESCO, 2001.

Documents

1. World Culture Report, 2000: Cultural Diversity, Conflict and Pluralism

United Nations Educational, Scientific and Cultural Organization, 2001

The full text is available at http://www.unesco.org/unesco publishers/.

Extracts

Preface, by Koichiro Matsuura, director-general of UNESCO

Unequal access to means of cultural expression . . . implies exclusion from the "knowledge society" . . . a knowledge-rich world has to be a culturally diverse world . . . a world of cultural pluralism will help us learn to live together.

General Introduction, by Lourdes Arizpe and Ann-Belinda S. Preis

If cultural diversity is an irrepressible manifestation of the inventiveness of the human spirit, the creation of difference is equally inexorable. No attempt should be made to stifle or repress it. Yet the manner in which such difference is defined and acted upon by governments and social custom determines whether it is to lead to greater overall social creativity or else to violence and exclusion.

"Cultural Diversity, Conflict and Pluralism," by Lourdes Arizpe, Elizabeth Jelin, J. Mohan Rao, and Paul Streeten

Cultural diversity has to be understood for what it is: conscious and deliberate choices that distinguish one culture from another. . . . There are three general modes for dealing with diversity. The first one is relativism. Relativism takes the universality of culture . . . to the extreme. If everything is culture, then there are no parameters to judge and compare traits and practices across cultures. . . . Relativism implies that the standards of one culture cannot be applied to others. . . . At the other extreme . . . is the premise that in any given society or country, there is a "majority" or "dominant" culture. Minorities, indigenous groups, migrants, in sum the "others," are expected to adopt (or adapt themselves to) the dominant patterns. . . . The perspective we are proposing here, that of creative pluralism, steers clear of both relativism and absolutism. Pluralism is not mere tolerance and indifference, which are the hallmarks of relativism. Nor is it a mere subterfuge for effectively assimilating or subordinating minority cultures into the "mainstream" culture. Creative pluralism involves an active and dynamic coexistence of diverse groups.

2. UNESCO Universal Declaration on Cultural Diversity

United Nations Educational, Scientific and Cultural Organization, 16 December 2001

The full text is available at http://www.unesco.org/culture/pluralism/.

The General Conference,

Reaffirming that culture should be regarded as the set of distinctive spiritual, material, intellectual and emotional features of society or a social group, and that it encompasses, in addition to art and literature, lifestyles, ways of living together, value systems, traditions and beliefs,

Noting that culture is at the heart of contemporary debates about identity, social cohesion, and the development of a knowledge-based economy,

Considering that the process of globalization, facilitated by the rapid development of new information and communication technologies, though representing a challenge for cultural diversity, creates the conditions for renewed dialog among cultures and civilizations,

Proclaims the following principles and adopts the present Declaration, . . .

IDENTITY, DIVERSITY AND PLURALISM

Article 2 From cultural diversity to cultural pluralism

[C]ultural pluralism gives policy expression to the reality of cultural diversity. Indissociable from a democratic framework, cultural pluralism is conducive to cultural exchange and to the flourishing of creative capacities that sustain public life. . . .

CULTURAL DIVERSITY AND HUMAN RIGHTS

Article 4 Human rights as guarantees of cultural diversity

The defense of cultural diversity is an ethical imperative, inseparable from respect for human dignity. It implies a commitment to human rights and fundamental freedoms, in particular the rights of persons belonging to minorities and those of indigenous peoples. No one may invoke cultural diversity to infringe upon human rights guaranteed by international law, nor to limit their scope. . . .

CULTURAL DIVERSITY AND INTERNATIONAL SOLIDARITY

Article 11 Building partnerships between the public sector, the private sector and civil society

Market forces alone cannot guarantee the preservation and promotion of cultural diversity, which is the key to sustainable human development. From this perspective, the pre-eminence of public policy, in partnership with the private sector and civil society, must be reaffirmed.

DEFORESTATION

Tim Allman

Forests are estimated to have covered 40 to 50 percent of Earth's land surface in the pre-agricultural period. Today, according to the Food and Agriculture Organization's Forest Resources Assessment (FRA) 2000, they cover about 30 percent of the land. Deforestation continues, mainly in the tropics, at alarmingly rapid rates, and the quality of forests in temperate regions is declining even as they slowly increase in extent. Reversing these trends to protect and restore the planet's forests is essential for the long-term survival of natural systems and human societies.

Historical Background and Development

Throughout history, humans have exploited forests for wood and other products or cleared them to use the land for farming or other purposes. The potentially disastrous effects of deforestation are not modern phenomena, as the collapse of Mayan civilization around A.D. 800 suggests. This complex society, centered in the forests of what is now Guatemala, had been established for centuries. Its decline in less than a century, thought to be due to overexploitation of the forests of the region, is often cited as an example of the consequences of rapid development outstripping the carrying capacity of the local environment.

Recognition of the importance of forests as a resource has been a theme of all human societies, although earlier measures to protect forests were generally intended to preserve them for specific uses rather than for the forests' sake. For example, the primary objective of the strict forest laws of the English medieval period was the preservation of hunting rights for the king and nobility.

Deforestation reached new highs during the twentieth century, but it was only in the latter part of the century that serious attention began to be drawn to the global scale of the problem. The general burst of concern about environmental issues that characterized the 1970s and 1980s in developed countries was expressed in Europe by interest in the damage done to forests by air pollution and acid rain (see POLLUTION). The plight of the world's tropical forests, however, seems to have made even more of an impact on public consciousness. Images from NASA's Landsat satellites first became available in the

1970s, providing striking illustrations of the scale of forest destruction. This revelation coincided with a surge of forest clearance in Latin America, mainly for cattle ranching and logging.

A consensus among the public, scientists, and policymakers about the urgency of rain forest conservation formed in developed nations during the 1980s and 1990s. The problem was, however, viewed differently in developing nations, many of which expressed resentment that developed countries—already having cleared the majority of their forests and reaping the development benefits from it—were placing pressure on poorer countries not to follow the same pattern. This polarization hampered efforts to tackle tropical deforestation.

In 1983 the first UN-sponsored International Tropical Timber Agreement (ITTA) attempted to regulate trade between producer and consumer nations. Two years later a collaboration between the World Resources Institute (WRI), the World Bank, the United Nations Development Programme, and the UN's Food and Agriculture Organization (FAO) produced the Tropical Forestry Action Plan (TFAP), a framework within which individual countries could adopt strategies, formulated as National Forestry Action Plans, to attract foreign aid and investment. The ITTA and TFAP attracted criticism and were judged to be of limited effectiveness. The TFAP, in particular, was condemned by nongovernmental organizations (NGOs), some claiming that tropical deforestation could actually increase in some countries as a result of its influence by, for example, funding new roads that would open new timber areas to harvesting. The 1980s in general were marked by controversies such as these, and little progress was made in tackling deforestation even as the issue reached its highest profile to date.

The 1992 United Nations Conference on Environment and Development—the "Earth Summit" in Rio de Janeiro—rejuvenated the debate, and a number of new initiatives followed, most of which aimed to address the polarization between developed and developing nations. The profile and activities of NGOs rose, with several undertaking joint projects with such intergovernmental bodies as the World Bank or FAO. There evolved a realization that solutions to deforestation were beyond the scope of simple forestry or conservation measures. Rather, it necessarily involved fundamental issues of political and economic organization.

Current Status

Although human activities have affected the composition and extent of forests throughout history, there is no doubt that forests have been damaged and cleared at ever-increasing rates as human societies have expanded and technology has advanced. Forest destruction has accelerated dramatically in the last two hundred years, mainly due to agricultural expansion, timber extraction, and economic development (see map, p. 95).

Research

Forests perform a number of important roles in the functioning of natural systems. They are vital reservoirs of biodiversity that play a key role in rainfall cycles, consolidate soils, and reduce erosion (see BIODIVERSITY). Their absorption of carbon dioxide from the atmosphere is a crucial aspect of the global carbon cycle, hence the loss of forests exacerbates the problem of global warming (see GLOBAL WARMING). According to the Intergovernmental Panel on Climate Change, forest clearance is estimated to add in the order of 2 billion metric tons (1.97 billion tons) of carbon to the atmosphere each year.

Humans rely heavily on forest timber for construction materials, fuel, and paper (which now demands a quarter of the world's timber harvest). Forests also supply such products as fruits and nuts, medicines and drugs, oils and resins, and various other natural chemicals. Non-wood forest products number at least 150 and are of significance to international trade, according to the International Tropical Timber Organization. Furthermore, forests represent direct shelter and subsistence and help people around the world maintain their cultural identity. The vast majority of these people live in developing countries, where deforestation is generally at its greatest. The drastic decline of Earth's forests, in quantity and quality, is therefore a serious global issue.

The starting point for an analysis of the extent of deforestation is the estimation of the forest cover of the studied area at a point in time and its subsequent change (see Table 1). This requires crafting definitions of what is meant by *forest* and *deforestation,* which is not as straightforward as might be expected. The FAO regards a forested area as one with a minimum tree canopy cover of 10 percent and without agricultural usage. This is one of the most widely used benchmarks. Other bodies have defined different categories of forest in more detail, with, for example, the International Union for the Conservation of Nature (IUCN) recognizing twenty-five types of forest.

Definitions of "deforestation" follow on from definitions of "forest." Thus, the FAO, whose quantification of global deforestation is the most widely used, considers deforestation the depletion of canopy cover to below 10 percent of the area in question. It also defines deforestation as involving the conversion of forest for other land uses, not including the felling of forests that are to be replanted or allowed to regenerate. The 10 percent criterion is convenient, but alone it offers only a partial analysis, as it neglects reductions in forest cover—for example, from 80 percent coverage to 20 percent coverage—that may greatly affect biodiversity or the carbon cycle and other systems.

However deforestation is defined, measuring it relies on a variety of methods. Data on deforestation is available from ecological field surveys, project reports from government departments and NGOs, and information from such corporate bodies as timber companies. This type of data tends to give only a patchy picture of deforestation and is usually restricted in its geographical scope. The FAO compiles information obtained from governments to help develop global deforestation statistics, but this process is problematic because of inconsistencies in the methods and definitions used by the various countries to gather the data.

Remote sensing—the scanning of Earth's surface from satellites or aircraft—has proved extremely valuable in studying deforestation. Aerial photography can provide adequate localized information, but satellite data is necessary for large-scale surveys. Various types of systems are used, employing a range of electromagnetic bands to suit the variety of information to be gathered. For example, the use of radar allows penetration through clouds and smoke. There are a number of satellite mapping projects underway, notably NASA's Pathfinder survey, the European Union's TREES project, and the FAO's global Forest Resources Assessment. Such projects tend to use Geographical Information System (GIS) computer technology to collate satellite data and draft maps.

Comparing satellite surveys to corresponding ground data gives the best overall estimate of forest cover and its changes. This is the approach used by the FAO in compiling its influential FRA reports, the most recent of which was produced in 2000. FRA 2000 estimates that global forests decreased by 2.2 percent in the 1990s. Although forest cover increased in almost all developed countries during this same period, the majority of developing countries displayed greater reductions in cover, particularly in tropical rain forests, than the overall global rate. Despite the simplifications and assumptions inherent in the FRA study (as in all estimates of deforestation), the general picture is clear—deforestation continues (see Table 2). It is especially drastic in the tropics.

Studying the causes of deforestation is vital to developing policies to address the problem. In this regard, researchers have identified two sets of factors. Proximate factors are those that immediately affect land use, such as agricultural clearance, fuelwood cutting, and logging. Behind these are underlying, driving factors, which include overconsumption of resources, population pressures, and poverty. For example, a major proximate cause of rain forest clearance in the tropics of central Africa and the Amazon Basin is the practice of uncontrolled shifting cultivation, in which farmers clear a small plot of forest to grow crops. After a few years the farmer moves on to clear new ground, leaving the old plot to regrow. This is a traditional and sustainable land use, provided the land is farmed for a few years only and is subsequently allowed to regenerate for a sufficient period. Large numbers of inexperienced farmers, however, exploit this system inappropriately and degrade the forest. In this example, the underlying factors are the displacement of the urban and rural poor onto "new" forest lands and the interplay of land uses. Here, commercial logging encourages encroachment by farmers on to forest land by providing road access. As with most environmental and social problems, attempting to analyze the causes of deforestation is a complex and politically charged exercise.

Policies and Programs

Although the scale of global deforestation began to trigger serious concern in the 1970s, with particular attention paid to the plight of tropical rain forests, it took some time for this concern to crystallize into international policy initiatives. Most current programs have built on the foundations laid at the Earth Summit in 1992. The conference launched a (nonbinding) statement, Forest Principles, outlining a model for sustainable management and conservation practices (see Document 1).

Since Rio, there have been a number of attempts to formulate international strategies and policies to tackle deforestation, but no binding mandatory agreement has been reached. A new International Tropical Timber Agreement was negotiated in 1994 (see Document 2). This aimed to introduce criteria for sustainable forestry into the tropical timber trade, with the particular goal that by 2000 all tropical timber being traded internationally would be produced in a sustainable manner. The ITTA has been useful in providing a framework for reform of the trade, but the goal of an entirely sustainable international timber trade remains unrealized (see Table 3).

International policy consensus on tackling deforestation thus remains elusive. The driving force behind the quest for consensus is the United Nations Intergovernmental Forum on Forests (IFF). The IFF is working toward a legally binding treaty on forests, but it faces the problem of conflicting interests among the parties involved. This is illustrated by tensions at the broadest level: developing countries are under great pressure to exploit their natural resources to fuel their development aspirations through agricultural expansion and infrastructure improvement, but developed countries are pressing for tropical forest conservation while not restricting their own high rate of use of such forest resources as timber and paper. The independent World Commission on Forests and Sustainable Development (WCFSD) has considered the potential for resolving such conflicts. The WCFSD, established by a group of world leaders in 1995, issued a summary report in 1999 linking forest degradation and poverty and proposing "global, national and local level arrangements to involve people in all decisions concerning their forests."

In the absence of global agreements, various bodies have established their own ambitious programs. These tend to involve partnerships among and between various local, national, or international bodies and sponsorship of local projects and case studies that illustrate and advance program objectives. The most high profile examples include the Forest Alliance of the World Bank and Worldwide Fund for Nature, the Forest Frontiers Initiative of the World Resources Institute, and the Forest Conservation Program of IUCN. Some interesting work is being done. For example, Conservation International, an NGO, has helped to establish a partnership of forest community leaders, governmental representatives, and multinational pharmaceutical companies in Suriname, in South America. This partnership harvests medicinal forest plants and searches for potential new pharmaceutical compounds while ensuring that local communities receive a share of any resulting financial benefits. The forest is thus conserved. The long-term success of the partnership will depend largely on the control that each of the participants has over the project.

Another notable program that takes a novel approach is the Forest Stewardship Council (FSC), perhaps the most successful effort at influencing the commercial timber industry to adopt sustainable practices. The FSC is an assembly of NGOs, indigenous groups, and scientific and industry groups that has developed rigorous procedures by which timber can be traced from forest to shop and certified as being produced according to FSC principles of sustainable forestry. Twenty-eight countries had FSC-certified forests in 1999, and the scheme is expanding. Some environmentalists, however, have expressed doubts about the ability of the FSC to take on deforestation, arguing that because only a tiny proportion of the world's tropical forests are certified, certification may actually increase deforestation by making tropical timber a more attractive and acceptable product, thus generating increased demand for timber that must be satisfied from uncertified stocks.

The long-term success of any program aimed at tackling deforestation will depend mainly on how well it confronts the underlying causes of forest loss. Since many of these causes are rooted in complex social and political issues and often involve conflicts of interest between various parties, successful programs need to be ambitious and to look beyond the forest at the broader picture. Unfortunately, there are few signs of a global consensus on measures to address such underlying factors as inequality of resource consumption and of income.

Regional Summaries

Deforestation has occurred in all regions of the world, but to different extents and at different rates. Various types of human activity—industrial development, commercial exploitation, and use of wood for fuel—are the primary causes of deforestation worldwide.

North America

According to the United Nations Environment Programme's *Global Environment Outlook, 2000,* or GEO-2000, around one-fourth of Canada and the United States is forested, representing the world's second largest expanse of natural forest and 13 percent of the world's total forest cover. This area of forest has remained fairly constant in recent years, displaying a slight increase since 1990 as planting and regrowth have outstripped removal. This positive trend seems set to continue. The ecological quality of North America's forests, however, is declining, largely due to overexploitation and inappropriate management by the forestry industry. In the west, the felling of old-growth stands—considered of extremely high wildlife value—has been particularly controversial. Industrial pollution has also damaged forests in some areas, such as in the mountains of the northeastern United States. The forestry industry is technologically advanced, and Canada and the United States are both important producers and consumers of forest products, notably paper and timber. The pressure on North America's forests is likely to continue due to rising demand for forest products and increasing recreational and other social demands.

Latin America

Around one-fourth of the world's forests is found in the Caribbean and Central and South America. GEO-2000 reports that Amazonia is the largest stretch of intact forest in the world and that almost half the land of Central and South America—which here includes Mexico—is forested. Nearly all of this forest is in the tropical zone. This impressive and important forest area is declining; 6 percent of it was lost between 1980 and 1990, the largest area of forest loss anywhere during the decade. More recently the rate of deforestation has slowed, but agricultural expansion, development (especially new roads), logging, fires, and extraction of oil and minerals continue to fragment and reduce forest cover.

The tropical forests of Latin America are of global significance as a carbon sink for removing carbon dioxide from the atmosphere and as one of the most ecologically diverse ecosystems on Earth. There is thus a policy impetus to protect Latin America's forests, a desire partly driven by more developed

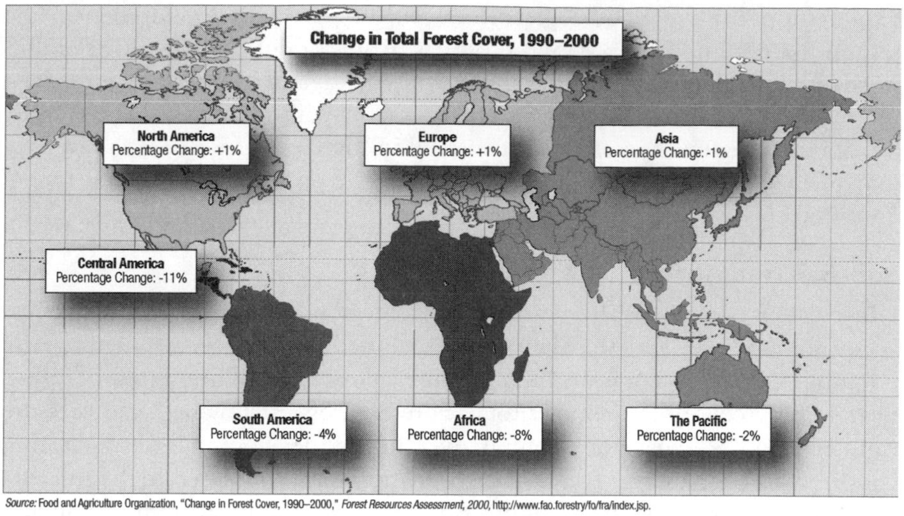

Source: Food and Agriculture Organization, "Change in Forest Cover, 1990–2000," *Forest Resources Assessment, 2000*, http://www.fao.forestry/fo/fra/index.jsp.

countries outside the region (see Case Study—Extractive Reserves in the Brazilian Amazon).

Europe

Much of Europe's original forest cover was cleared centuries ago, particularly in the west. According to GEO-2000 only about 1 percent of Western Europe's natural temperate forests survives. Some larger blocks of indigenous forest persist in the east and the far north, but the forests of Europe have generally been significantly altered by human activity. They cover about 42 percent of the region and the extent of forest cover is growing steadily in almost every European country as a result of plantation and regeneration schemes. Some impressive increases have been achieved; for example, Ukraine has increased its forest cover by 21 percent in thirty years. The general trend toward increased forest cover seems likely to continue throughout Europe, although in many cases new plantings are of low wildlife value. Forest quality has declined in recent decades due mainly to pollution; 60 percent of the forests of Western and Central Europe are believed damaged to some degree. The Chernobyl nuclear disaster of 1986 was also significant, contaminating some 7 million hectares (17.3 million acres) of forested land with radioactivity. As air pollution is reduced and mitigation measures develop, the health of Europe's forests should improve, although this will be a slow process.

North Africa and the Middle East

The Middle East and North Africa have a long history of deforestation, and their climatic and soil conditions are generally not ideal for tree regrowth. They are the most sparsely forested of the world's regions. According to the Food and Agriculture Organization's Food for All project, Morocco has a forest cover of less than 7 percent, but it still boasts the largest proportion of land area under forest of any country in the area. Natural forest is extremely limited in extent in most countries. Continuing pressures on forests include overgrazing, fire, exploitation for fuelwood, agricultural expansion, and development. The region is a net importer of wood products. Rates of deforestation are stabilizing over much of the Middle East and North Africa, and forest extent is increasing in some countries. Forestation schemes in various countries, for example, Syria and Lebanon, have proved successful in increasing forest areas, but they may be inadequate to compensate for losses as the pressures on land and forests continue.

Sub-Saharan Africa

Close to 17 percent of the world's forests are found in sub-Saharan Africa, according to GEO-2000. They are distributed unevenly; the Democratic Republic of Congo alone has 135 million hectares (333 million acres) of forest, nearly 20 percent of the region's total. Forests across Africa are under pressure from agricultural expansion, logging, overgrazing, development, drought, fire, and firewood harvesting. Rates of deforestation have thus been high, and forest cover continues to decline in most sub-Saharan countries at an overall rate faster than in any other region. For example, a UNEP report, "EIS in Environment Management," estimates Ethiopia's forest cover to once have been 35 percent, but by 1999 it had declined to 3 percent. Plantations and agroforestry schemes have been established in parts of the region, but they are proceeding at a rate slower than the pace of deforestation. The future for Africa's forests seems bleak, as growing populations, increasing poverty, rapid urbanization, and political unrest seem certain to continue to exert severe pressure on the land.

Central, South, and East Asia

Central, South, and East Asia contain large tracts of forests, according to the United Nations Economic and Social Commission for Asia and the Pacific, including the world's second largest rain forest system—most of which is found in Malaysia, Indonesia, and other parts of southeast Asia—but many countries have suffered extensive deforestation in recent decades. Deforestation rates have generally increased in recent decades, with, according to GEO-2000, rates in the countries of the Mekong Delta region losing forests at 1.6 percent per year. The primary causes of this loss are agricultural expansion and commercial logging. Asia currently dominates the international market in tropical timber, although it is estimated that reserves will last less than 40 years if current extraction rates continue. Forest loss can also be attributed to development and infrastructure expansion, mining, fuelwood collection, and fire. Mongolia lost around one-fourth of its forests, that is, 3 million hectares (7.4 million acres) to uncontrolled fires in 1996, and 1 million hectares (2.5 million acres) of Indonesia's forests burnt in 1997. Asia is the most populous and rapidly developing part of the world, so its deforestation rates seem likely to rise in general. The region has a good record of reforestation, which has compensated (in terms of area, but not in terms of biodiversity) for forest loss in some countries. China, for instance, has increased its forest cover from 12 percent in the 1980s to almost 14 percent by 1996, and the figure is expected to reach 17 percent by 2010. Restrictions on commercial logging have been introduced by some countries in an attempt to reduce the rate of deforestation (see Case Study—Deforestation and Floods in China).

The Pacific

In the Pacific region, forests have generally declined in extent and continue to do so. According to GEO-2000, Australia, the largest country in the area, has lost about 40 percent of its original forest, and many of the smaller islands have suffered significant losses. Deforestation rates in Samoa, an island group in the southwestern Pacific, for example, have recently climbed to close to 2 percent per year. Commercial logging, agriculture, and development are some of the main pressures on the forests of Oceania. Coastal mangrove forests have been cleared for aquaculture, such as shrimp farming, in many areas. Plantation schemes in New Zealand and Australia have increased forest cover there in the last decade, but elsewhere the picture is one of net loss.

Data

Table 1 Total Forest Cover in Selected Countries, 2000

Country	Forest Area (1,000 ha)	Land Area (%)	Forest Area per Capita (ha)
Algeria	2,145	0.9	0.1
Argentina	34,648	12.7	0.9
Australia	154,539	20.1	8.3
Brazil	543,905	64.3	3.2
Canada	244,571	26.5	7.9
China	163,480	17.5	0.1
Colombia	49,601	47.8	1.2
Congo, Republic of	22,060	64.6	7.7
Egypt	72	0.1	N.S.
France	15,341	27.9	0.3
Georgia	2,988	43.7	0.6
Germany	10,740	30.7	0.1
Guatemala	2,850	26.3	0.3
India	64,113	21.6	0.1
Indonesia	104,986	58.0	0.5
Israel	132	6.4	N.S.
Japan	24,081	64.0	0.2
Russian Federation	851,392	50.4	5.8
Saudi Arabia	1,504	0.7	0.1
Spain	14,370	28.8	0.4
Sweden	27,134	65.9	3.1
Switzerland	1,199	30.3	0.2
Tajikistan	400	2.8	0.1
Thailand	14,762	28.9	0.2
Turkey	10,225	13.3	0.2
Uganda	4,190	21.0	0.2
United Kingdom	2,794	11.6	N.S.
United States	225,993	24.7	0.8
World Total	3,869,455	29.6	0.65

Source: "Forest Cover, 2000," *Forest Resources Assessment, 2000,* http://www.fao.org/forestry/fo/fra/main/index.jsp.

Note: N.S. indicates not significant.

Table 2 Total Area of Original, Current, and Frontier Forest

Region	Original Forest (1,000 km²)	Remaining Forest (Frontier and Non-Frontier Forest)[a] (1,000 km²)	Remaining as a Percentage of Original Forest	Frontier Forest (1,000 km²)	Frontier Forest as a Percentage of Original Forest	Frontier Forest as a Percentage of Remaining Forest
Africa	6,799	2,302	34	527	8	23
Asia	15,132	4,275	28	844	6	20
Central America	1,779	970	55	172	10	18
Europe[b]	16,449	9,604	58	3,462	21	36
North America	10,877	8,483	78	3,737	34	44
Pacific[c]	1,431	929	65	319	22	34
South America	9,736	6,800	70	4,439	46	65
Total	62,203	33,363	54	13,501	22	40

Source: Dirk Bryant et al., *The Last Frontier Forests: Ecosystems and Economies on the Edge* (Washington, D.C.: World Resources Institute, 1997).

[a]Frontier forest refers to large tracts of relatively undisturbed forest.

[b]Includes Russia.

[c]Oceania here consists of Australia, New Zealand, and Papua New Guinea.

Table 3 Value of Trade in Tropical Timber by International Tropical Timber Organization Producer Regions

		Imports				Exports			
		Value (thousands of dollars)		Unit Value (dollars per m³)		Value (thousands of dollars)		Unit Value (dollars per m³)	
Region	Product	1997	1998	1997	1998	1997	1998	1997	1998
Africa	Logs	77	366	61	251	768,289	559,355	144	127
	Sawn	404	1,067	67	534	479,031	453,127	395	353
	Veneer	242	797	—	1,110	117,431	141,725	380	400
	Ply	788	1,411	394	470	51,432	43,971	440	550
Asia and the Pacific	Logs	559,249	199,075	215	104	1,327,783	786,350	130	98
	Sawn	508,964	244,509	272	170	1,259,620	1,262,370	337	330
	Veneer	54,566	47,067	650	590	348,274	234,776	356	249
	Ply	15,891	12,282	370	236	4,185,701	2,441,341	337	220
Latin America	Logs	2,529	517	170	89	31,019	14,877	131	64
	Sawn	27,521	10,453	65	40	374,918	249,322	340	264
	Veneer	15,165	10,091	473	1,473	11,741	55,166	777	3,364
	Ply	14,437	1,172	491	51	315,789	199,240	448	342
Producers Total	Logs	561,855	199,958	215	104	2,127,091	1,360,582	135	108
	Sawn	536,889	256,029	234	150	2,113,569	1,964,819	349	324
	Veneer	69,972	57,955	603	663	477,447	431,667	367	329
	Ply	31,116	14,865	418	191	4,552,921	2,684,552	344	228
World Total		1,199,832	528,808	235	139	9,271,027	6,441,620	255	203

Source: International Tropical Timber Organization, *Annual Review and Assessment of the World Timber Situation, 1999*, http://www.itto.or.jp/inside/review1999/index.html.

Case Study—Deforestation and Floods in China

China has a long history of deforestation, which reached a peak in the twentieth century. According to the World Resources Institute's country profiles, China's estimated original cover was 52 percent. GEO-2000 reports that less than 7 percent of its land area remained under forest by the middle of the twentieth century. The pace of deforestation then quickened, with timber harvests increasing from 20 million cubic meters (706 million cubic feet) per year in the 1950s to 63 million cubic meters (2,225 million cubic feet) per year in the 1990s. Large-scale replanting has since succeeded in increasing the area of forest, with more than 17 percent of the country now under forest cover. This restoration, however, masks a serious decline in the country's natural forests, as the plantation schemes have used fast-growing species, often not native to the area, while the remaining natural forests suffer from continued logging for their valuable timber.

This change in the composition of China's forests has had serious consequences for biodiversity, and the logging of natural forests has caused massive soil erosion in many areas. China's remaining natural forests tend to be located on mountainous terrain unsuitable for agriculture. This type of terrain is particularly vulnerable to erosion after the removal of the trees, whose roots bind the soil, and of the vegetation, which shelters the soil from direct rain.

In 1998 the Yangtze, the fifth longest river in the world, flooded spectacularly (see FRESHWATER). Combined with inundations elsewhere in the country, China suffered its worst flooding in fifty years. More than 3,500 people died, 10 million lost their homes, and at least $30 billion in damage resulted, according to UNEP ReliefWeb figures. The Yangzte has always been prone to flooding, and development on flood plains (especially for agriculture), wetland drainage, and climate change may all have contributed to the 1998 floods. The Chinese government, however, attributed the catastrophic scale of the flooding to deforestation. Large amounts of eroded soil from clear-felled areas were washed into river systems, silting up their lower reaches and raising water levels dramatically.

To combat the problem, the government introduced various measures, which were consolidated into the Natural Forest Conservation Program (NFCP). This program covers more than two-thirds of China's land area, including the higher reaches of the Yangtze and Yellow Rivers, both of which have been heavily deforested during the last fifty years. The NFCP aims to protect and restore natural forests and expand forest cover in degraded or sensitive areas. It includes such measures as land management planning, education, mandatory conversion of some farmland to plantations, and resettlement and retraining of local populations. The scale of the NFCP is vast. From 1997 to 2000, timber production was cut from 26.7 million cubic meters to 14.34 million cubic meters, and another reduction of 3.64 million cubic meters is expected by 2010, according to the Chinese Academy of Forestry's Kelin Ye, Jianxiong Lu, and Kazumasa Shimzu, writing in "Sustainable Utilization of Plantation Timber in China."

Although the scale of China's reforestation effort is impressive, the program has been criticized, not least because of the degree of compulsion imposed on people in forested areas. The people facing compulsory resettlement and retraining are culturally diverse, and their antipathy to the project, and the inevitable accompanying controversy, may be a serious handicap to its success. There are also fears that as China protects its own forests while consuming ever more timber, forests in other countries will suffer to meet the demand. Indeed, in "Campaigns and Reports: Forests," the Environmental Investigation Agency reports that China's timber imports rose from 5 million cubic meters to 15 million cubic meters between 1997 and 2000.

Case Study—Extractive Reserves in the Brazilian Amazon

A distinctive strategy for forest management can be seen in the Amazon of Brazil, where the destruction of tropical rain forest is perhaps at its highest profile. An area the size of France—that is, more than 13 percent of the Amazon—has already been cleared, and the rate of deforestation continues to increase.

There is a long history in the Amazon of latex extraction from the rubber tree *Hevea brasiliensis,* which grows naturally in parts of the area. Rubber tapping has been a commercial endeavor in the Amazon for around 130 years, often combined with other extractive practices, such as the gathering of Brazil nuts and small-scale, subsistence-level shifting cultivation. Generally, these uses have been considered a sustainable use of forest reserves.

In the 1980s the rising global demand for tropical timber, coupled with increasing local land values, led to the purchase of large areas of the Amazon by logging companies, cattle ranchers, and speculators. Logging and ranching are destructive to the rain forest and incompatible with rubber tapping. By disrupting the ecology of an area, they impinge on the livelihood of rubber-tappers even when they do not directly displace such people. There was, therefore, resistance from the tappers, expressed as a social movement demanding land rights. This movement faced violent retribution from ranchers and loggers, with the 1989 murder of prominent movement activist Chico Mendez—only one of many such murders—bringing international attention to the struggle. Awareness of the issue outside Brazil, coupled with the continuing organization of the tappers, forced the Brazilian government finally to agree to designate more "extractive reserves," on a model proposed by the tappers and provisionally agreed to by the government in 1987. The establishment of each reserve is initiated by the tappers, who must form a legally registered association and ask the government to create the reserve. If the reserve fulfills various social, economic, and ecological criteria, a utilization plan is negotiated. The residents' association then grants permits for residence and for extraction to individual households.

This system has been extended to other parts of Brazil and to other extractive practices, such as palm collection. It is a model of community involvement in forest conservation geared to low-impact exploitation of the forest and conservation of forest-based ways of life, in contrast to the general perception that human exploitation of rain forests is always highly damaging. The partnership between government (which establishes the broad principles of forest use) and local communities (which actually manage the forest) tends to be effective, because both have an interest in the long-term protection and sustainable management of the forest. Indeed, extractive reserves have generally preserved most of the ecological value of the forest.

The major test of the Brazilian system will be its long-term robustness in the face of economic pressures. This seems likely to become an issue considering the precarious economics of the Brazilian rubber industry, which competes poorly with the rubber plantation industry of Southeast Asia. Also, most extractor communities remain poor. The majority of the profits realized by their commodities are intercepted by powerful intermediaries during the various stages of trading and transportation. This is especially the case when products are exported. Such persistent poverty can only threaten the future of the extractive reserves in the long term.

Biographical Sketches

Daniel Botkin is a professor of biology at George Mason University, Fairfax, Virginia, a research professor at the University of California, Santa Barbara, and president of the Center for the Study of the Environment, Santa Barbara. Botkin is best known for his development of the first successful ecological computer simulation, a model of forest growth known as the forest gap model. This type of modeling has become a subdiscipline of ecology.

Jeff Burley is director of the Oxford Forestry Institute, United Kingdom. His field of expertise is forest genetics. He is formerly president of the International Union of Forestry Research Organizations, with whom he established a task force on sustainable forest management.

Hosny El-Lakany is head of the forestry department at the Food and Agriculture Organization. He is well known for his work on the Casuarina tree, a native of Australia that has proved well suited for creating windbreaks in desert areas of the Middle East. His development of Casuarina as a tree crop in Egypt has been valuable in combating the spread of desertification to agricultural land.

Norman Myers is an ecologist whose work has been among the most influential in tropical deforestation. His 1979 *Sinking Ark* brought attention to the alarming extent of forest loss in the tropics, claiming that 44 percent of Earth's original tropical forest cover had been lost. Myers also drew attention to the potentially disastrous effects of such loss on biodiversity. Although there has subsequently been debate about the validity of Myers' estimates, he remains one of the foremost authorities on tropical deforestation rates, and his work has been pivotal in attempting to understand the scale of global deforestation.

Mauricio Castro Schmitz is a Colombian conservationist and working forestry coordinator for the World Wildlife Fund in Colombia. He is also the chair of the Forestry Stewardship Council and has a research interest in the conservation of protected areas.

Directory

Food and Agriculture Organization (FAO), Viale delle Terme di Caracalla, 00100 Rome, Italy. Telephone: (39) 06 57051, Email: fao-hq@fao.org, Web: http://www.fao.org
Lead UN agency for forestry, agriculture, fisheries, and rural development

Forestry Stewardship Council, 502 Avenida Hidalgo, 68000 Oaxaca, Mexico. Telephone: (52) 951 46905, Email: fscoax@fscoax.org, Web: http://www.fscoax.org
Organization advocating the sustainable use of forests for commercial purposes through marketplace-based incentives

Friends of the Earth International, P.O. Box 19199, 1000 Amsterdam, Netherlands. Telephone: (31) 20 622 1369, Email: foei@foei.org, Web: http://www.foei.org
World's largest federation of environmental groups, campaigns include deforestation

International Tropical Timber Organization, International Organizations Center, 5th Floor, Pacifico-Yokohama 1-1-1, Minato-Mirai, Nishi-ku, Yokohama 220-0012, Japan. Telephone: (81) 45 223 1110, Email: itto@itto.or.jp, Web: http://www.itto.or.jp
Organization providing a platform for policy cooperation on the tropical timber economy

Natural Resources Defense Council, 40 West 20th Street, New York, NY 10011. Telephone: (212) 727-2700, Email: nrdcinfo@nrdc.org, Web: http://www.nrdc.org
Organization campaigning for the protection of wild places

Rainforest Action Network, 221 Pine Street, Suite 500, San Francisco, CA 94104. Telephone: (415) 398-4404, Email: rainforest@ran.org, Web: http://www.ran.org
Group campaigning and lobbying to preserve tropical rain forests and protect the human rights of people living in and near them

Society of American Foresters, 5400 Grosvenor Lane, Bethesda, MD 20814-2198. Telephone: (301) 897-8720, Email: safweb@safnet.org, Web: http://www.safnet.org
Professional forestry organization in the United States

Taiga Rescue Network, P.O. Box 116, 96223 Jokmokk, Sweden. Telephone: (46) 971 17039, Email: info@taigarescue.org, Web: http://www.taigarescue.org
Network of groups campaigning for the protection of boreal (northern) forests

Temperate Forest Foundation, 14780 SW Osprey Drive, Suite 355, Beaverton, OR 97007-8070. Telephone: (503) 579-6762, Email: office@forestinfo.org, Web: http://www.forestinfo.org
Scientific charity for increasing public awareness and education about temperate forests

United Nations Environment Programme (UNEP), United Nations Avenue, Gigiri, P.O. Box 30552, Nairobi, Kenya. Telephone: (254) 262 1234, Email: eisinfo@unep.org, Web: http://www.unep.org
Agency tackling a range of environmental issues on an international basis

U.S. Forest Service, P.O. Box 96090, Washington, DC 20090-6090. Telephone: (202) 205-1760, Email: mailroom_wo@fs.fed.us, Web: http://www.fs.fed.us
U.S. government agency responsible for forestry in the United States

World Bank, 1818 H Street NW, Washington, DC 20433. Telephone: (202) 473 1053, Email: feedback@worldbank.org, Web: http://www.worldbank.org
International economic development institution that also supports environmental projects

World Conservation Monitoring Centre, 219 Huntingdon Road, Cambridge, CB3 0DL, United Kingdom. Telephone: (44) 1223 277314, Email: info@unep-wcmc.org, Web: http://www.unep-wcmc.org
UNEP body concerned with providing information for conservation policy and action

World Rainforest Movement, 1858 Maldonado, Montevideo 11200, Uruguay. Email: wrm@wrm-org.uy, Web: http://www.wrm-org.uy
International network of citizens groups involved in defending rain forests

World Resources Institute, 10 G Street NE, Suite 800, Washington, DC 20002. Telephone: (202) 729-7600, Email: front@wri.org, Web: http://www.wri.org/forests
Environmental organization disseminating knowledge about environmental research and issues to encourage public action

World Wildlife Fund, 1250 24th Street NW, Washington, DC 20037-1175. Telephone: (202) 293-4800, Web: http://www.worldwildlife.org
U.S. office of the world's largest privately supported conservation body

Further Research

Books

Anderson, A. B., ed. *Alternatives to Deforestation: Steps towards Sustainable Use of the Amazon Rain Forest.* New York: Columbia University Press, 1990.

Aplet, Gregory H., et al. *Defining Sustainable Forestry.* Washington, D.C.: Island Press, 1993.

Barraclough, Solon, and Krishna B. Ghimire. *Agricultural Expansion and Tropical Deforestation.* London: Earthscan, 2000.

Carrere, R., and L. Lohmann. *Pulping the South: Industrial Tree Plantations and the World Paper Economy.* London: Zed Books, 1996.

Colchester, M., and L. Lohmann, eds. *The Struggle for Land and the Fate of the Forest.* London: Zed Books, 1993.

Dudley, N., J. P. Jeanrenaud, and F. Sullivan. *Bad Harvest? The Timber Trade and the Degradation of the World's Forests.* London: Earthscan, 1995.

Fairhead, James, and Melissa Leach. *Reframing Deforestation: Global Analysis and Local Realities: Studies in West Africa.* London: Routledge, 1998.

Hecht, Susanna, and Alexander Cockburn. *The Fate of the Forest: Developers, Destroyers and Defenders of the Amazon.* New York and London: Penguin, 1989.

Grainger, Alan. *Controlling Tropical Deforestation.* London: Earthscan, 1993.

Jepma, Catrinus J. *Tropical Deforestation: A Socio-Economic Approach.* London: Earthscan, 1995.

Küchli, Christian. *Stories of Regeneration.* London: Earthscan, 1997.

Sargent, Caroline, and Stephen Bass, eds. *Plantation Politics: Forest Plantations in Development.* London: Earthscan, 1992.

Whitmore, Timothy. *An Introduction to Tropical Rain Forests.* Oxford: Oxford University Press, 1998.

Articles and Reports

Bowles, Ian A., et al. "Logging and Tropical Forest Conservation." *Science,* 19 June 1998.

Bryant, Dirk, et al. *The Last Frontier Forests: Ecosystems and Economies on the Edge.* Washington, D.C.: World Resources Institute, 1997.

Environmental Investigation Agency. *Corporate Power, Corruption and the Destruction of the World's Forests: The Case for a New Global Forest Agreement.* Washington, D.C.: EIA, 1995.

Fearnside, P. M. "Extractive Reserves in Brazilian Amazonia." *Bioscience* 39 (1989): 387.

Food and Agriculture Organization. *The State of the World's Forests.* Rome: FAO, 1999.

Hellier, Chris. "Stemming the Tide." *Geographical,* June 1999, 42.

Johnston, Nels, and Bruce Cabarle. *Surviving the Cut: Natural Forest Management in the Humid Tropics.* Washington, D.C.: World Resources Institute, 1993.

Krishnaswarmy, Ajit, and Arthur Hanson, eds. *Our Forest, Our Future: Summary Report.* Winnipeg: World Commission on Forests and Sustainable Development, 1999.

Laschefski, Klemens, and Nicole Freris. "Saving the Wood from the Trees." *Ecologist,* July/August 2001, 40.

Menotti, Victor. "Forest Destruction and Globalisation." *Ecologist,* May/June 1999, 180.

Monastersky, R. "The Deforestation Debate." *Science News,* 10 July 1993, 26.

O'Neill, Thomas. "New Sensors Eye the Rain Forest." *National Geographic,* September 1993, 118.

Understanding Global Issues. *The Disappearing Forests.* Cheltenham: UGI, 1999.

Web Sites

Agroforestry Research Trust
http://www.agroforestry.co.uk

Food for All
http://www.foodforall.org

Forest Monitor
http://www.gn.apc.org/fmonitor

Forest Resources Assessment, 2000
http://www.fao.org/forestry/fo/fra/main/index.jsp

Forests.org
http://forests.org

Global Forest Watch
http://www.globalforestwatch.org

New Forests Project
http://www.newforestsproject.com

Rainforest Net
http://www.rain.org/~jinj/rainforest.html

ReliefWeb
http://www.reliefweb.int/w/rwb.nsf

Timber Trade Federation
http://www.ttf.co.uk/index1.htm

Trees for Life
http://www.treesforlife.org.uk

Tropical Forests Conservation Archive
http://forests.lic.wisc.edu/forests/rainforest.html

Virtual Library of Forestry
http://www.metla.fi/info/vlib/Forestry

Documents

1. Forest Principles

United Nations Conference on Environment and Development, Rio de Janeiro, 1992

The full text is available at http://www.un.org/documents/ga/conf151/aconf15126-3annex3.htm.

Extracts

Non-legally binding authoritative statement of principles for a global consensus on the management, conservation and sustainable development of all types of forests

Principles/Elements

1. (a) States have, in accordance with the charter of the United Nations and the principles of international law, the sovereign right to exploit their own resources pursuant to their own environmental policies and have the responsibility to ensure that activities within their jurisdiction or control do not cause damage to the environment of other states or of areas beyond the limits of national jurisdiction.
   (b) The agreed full incremental cost of achieving benefits associated with forest conservation and sustainable development requires increased international cooperation and should be equitably shared by the international community.
2. (a) States have the sovereign and inalienable right to utilize, manage and develop their forests in accordance with their development needs and level of socioeconomic development and on the basis of national policies consistent with sustainable development and legislation, including the conversion of such areas for other uses within the overall socioeconomic development plan and based on rational land-use policies.
   (b) Forest resources and forest lands should be sustainably managed to meet the social, economic, ecological, cultural and spiritual needs of present and future generations. These needs are for forest products and services, such as wood and wood products, water, food, fodder, medicine, fuel, shelter, employment, recreation, habitats for wildlife, landscape diversity, carbon sinks and reservoirs, and for other forest products. Appropriate measures should be taken to protect forests against harmful effects of pollution, including airborne pollution, fires, pests and diseases, in order to maintain their full multiple value.
   (c) The provision of timely, reliable and accurate information on forests and forest ecosystems is essential for public understanding and informed decision making and should be ensured.

(d) Governments should promote and provide opportunities for the participation of interested parties, including local communities and indigenous people, industries, labour, nongovernmental organizations and individuals, forest dwellers and women, in the development, implementation and planning of national forest policies. . . .

5. (a) National forest policies should recognize and duly support the identity, culture and the rights of indigenous people, their communities and other communities and forest dwellers. Appropriate conditions should be promoted for these groups to enable them to have an economic stake in forest use, perform economic activities, and achieve and maintain cultural identity and social organization, as well as adequate levels of livelihood and well-being, through, inter alia, those land tenure arrangements which serve as incentives for the sustainable management of forests.
   (b) The full participation of women in all aspects of the management, conservation and sustainable development of forests should be actively promoted.

6. (a) All types of forests play an important role in meeting energy requirements through the provision of a renewable source of bio-energy, particularly in developing countries, and the demands for fuelwood for household and industrial needs should be met through sustainable forest management, afforestation and reforestation. To this end, the potential contribution of plantations of both indigenous and introduced species for the provision of both fuel and industrial wood should be recognized.
   (b) National policies and programmes should take into account the relationship, where it exists, between the conservation, management and sustainable development of forests and all aspects related to the production, consumption, recycling and/or final disposal of forest products.
   (c) Decisions taken on the management, conservation and sustainable development of forest resources should benefit, to the extent practicable, from a comprehensive assessment of economic and non-economic values of forest goods and services and of the environmental costs and benefits. The development and improvement of methodologies for such evaluations should be promoted.
   (d) The role of planted forests and permanent agricultural crops as sustainable and environmentally sound sources of renewable energy and industrial raw material should be recognized, enhanced and promoted. Their contribution to the maintenance of ecological processes, to offsetting pressure on primary/old-growth forest and to providing regional employment and development with the adequate involvement of local inhabitants should be recognized and enhanced.
   (e) Natural forests also constitute a source of goods and services, and their conservation, sustainable management and use should be promoted. . . .

8. (a) Efforts should be undertaken towards the greening of the world. All countries, notably developed countries, should take positive and transparent action towards reforestation, afforestation and forest conservation, as appropriate.
   (b) Efforts to maintain and increase forest cover and forest productivity should be undertaken in ecologically, economically and socially sound ways through the rehabilitation, reforestation and reestablishment of trees and forests on unproductive, degraded and deforested lands, as well as through the management of existing forest resources.

(c) The implementation of national policies and programmes aimed at forest management, conservation and sustainable development, particularly in developing countries, should be supported by international financial and technical cooperation, including through the private sector, where appropriate.
(d) Sustainable forest management and use should be carried out in accordance with national development policies and priorities and on the basis of environmentally sound national guidelines. In the formulation of such guidelines, account should be taken, as appropriate and if applicable, of relevant internationally agreed methodologies and criteria.
(e) Forest management should be integrated with management of adjacent areas so as to maintain ecological balance and sustainable productivity.
(f) National policies and/or legislation aimed at management, conservation and sustainable development of forests should include the protection of ecologically viable representative or unique examples of forests, including primary/old-growth forests, cultural, spiritual, historical, religious and other unique and valued forests of national importance.
(g) Access to biological resources, including genetic material, shall be with due regard to the sovereign rights of the countries where the forests are located and to the sharing on mutually agreed terms of technology and profits from biotechnology products that are derived from these resources.
(h) National policies should ensure that environmental impact assessments should be carried out where actions are likely to have significant adverse impacts on important forest resources, and where such actions are subject to a decision of a competent national authority.

9. (a) The efforts of developing countries to strengthen the management, conservation and sustainable development of their forest resources should be supported by the international community, taking into account the importance of redressing external indebtedness, particularly where aggravated by the net transfer of resources to developed countries, as well as the problem of achieving at least the replacement value of forests through improved market access for forest products, especially processed products. In this respect, special attention should also be given to the countries undergoing the process of transition to market economies.
(b) The problems that hinder efforts to attain the conservation and sustainable use of forest resources and that stem from the lack of alternative options available to local communities, in particular the urban poor and poor rural populations who are economically and socially dependent on forests and forest resources, should be addressed by governments and the international community.

10. New and additional financial resources should be provided to developing countries to enable them to sustainably manage, conserve and develop their forest resources, including through afforestation, reforestation and combating deforestation and forest and land degradation.

11. In order to enable, in particular, developing countries to enhance their endogenous capacity and to better manage, conserve and develop their forest resources, the access to and transfer of environmentally sound technologies and corresponding know-how on favourable terms, including on concessional and preferential terms, as mutually agreed, in accordance with the relevant provisions of Agenda 21, should be promoted, facilitated and financed, as appropriate. . . .

14. Unilateral measures, incompatible with international obligations or agreements, to restrict and/or ban international trade in timber or other forest products should be removed or avoided, in order to attain long-term sustainable forest management.
15. Pollutants, particularly airborne pollutants, including those responsible for acidic deposition, that are harmful to the health of forest ecosystems at the local, national, regional and global levels should be controlled.

2. International Tropical Timber Agreement

International Tropical Timber Organization, Yokohama, Japan, 1994

The full text is available at http://www.itto.or.jp/inside/agreement.html.

Extract

Article 1

Objectives

Recognizing the sovereignty of members over their natural resources, as defined in Principle 1 (a) of the Non-Legally Binding Authoritative Statement of Principles for a Global Consensus on the Management, Conservation and Sustainable Development of all Types of Forests, the objectives of the International Tropical Timber Agreement, 1994 (hereinafter referred to as "this Agreement") are:

(a) To provide an effective framework for consultation, international cooperation and policy development among all members with regard to all relevant aspects of the world timber economy;

(b) To provide a forum for consultation to promote non-discriminatory timber trade practices;

(c) To contribute to the process of sustainable development;

(d) To enhance the capacity of members to implement a strategy for achieving exports of tropical timber and timber products from sustainably managed sources by the year 2000;

(e) To promote the expansion and diversification of international trade in tropical timber from sustainable sources by improving the structural conditions in international markets, by taking into account, on the one hand, a long term increase in consumption and continuity of supplies, and, on the other, prices which reflect the costs of sustainable forest management and which are remunerative and equitable for members, and the improvement of market access;

(f) To promote and support research and development with a view to improving forest management and efficiency of wood utilization as well as increasing the capacity to conserve and enhance other forest values in timber-producing tropical forests;

(g) To develop and contribute towards mechanisms for the provision of new and additional financial resources and expertise needed to enhance the capacity of producing members to attain the objectives of this Agreement;

(h) To improve market intelligence with a view to ensuring greater transparency in the international timber market, including the gathering, compilation and dissemination of trade-related data, including data related to species being traded;

(i) To promote increased and further processing of tropical timber from sustainable sources in producing member countries with a view to promoting their industrialization and thereby increasing their employment opportunities and export earnings;

(j) To encourage members to support and develop industrial tropical timber reforestation and forest management activities as well as rehabilitation of degraded forest land, with due regard for the interests of local communities dependent on forest resources;

(k) To improve marketing and distribution of tropical timber exports from sustainably managed sources;

(l) To encourage members to develop national policies aimed at sustainable utilization and conservation of timber-producing forests and their genetic resources and at maintaining the ecological balance in the regions concerned, in the context of tropical timber trade;

(m) To promote the access to, and transfer of, technologies and technical cooperation to implement the objectives of this Agreement, including on concessional and preferential terms and conditions, as mutually agreed; and

(n) To encourage information sharing on the international timber market.

DEVELOPMENT AID

Catherine Weaver

Behind the facade of the globalized, integrated world economy lays the stark reality of growing disparities between the wealthier countries of the North and the struggling nations of the South. According to *Human Development Report, 2001* issued by the United Nations Development Programme (UNDP), more than 1 billion people in the developing world live on less than the equivalent of $1 per day, and nearly 3 billion live on less than $2 per day. More than 850 million people are illiterate, nearly 1 billion do not have access to improved water sources, and the absence of adequate health care and education has contributed to the rapid spread of HIV/AIDS, leaving nearly 34 million people in the developing world with the disease in 2000. Despite the substantial progress made in development over the last sixty years, the demands and challenges of international development aid are still great.

Historical Background and Development

International development aid began after World War II. Viewing economic instability in the 1930s as one of the main causes of the war, U.S. secretary of state George C. Marshall called in June 1947 for massive U.S. assistance to help rebuild European economies through the European Recovery Program. The Marshall Plan, as it soon became known, was supported by an earlier declaration by President Harry S. Truman in a speech to a joint session of Congress in March 1947. The Truman Doctrine called for U.S. development aid to be a key component in the U.S. strategy of containment, with the belief that economically stable countries would be able to "choose freedom" over communism. U.S. foreign aid soon spilled over to the developing world; as European countries recovered, they too became donors, providing assistance to developing regions. Most often, the direction of aid was dictated by political motives, as much of European official development assistance targeted the economic recovery of the former colonies, and U.S. aid focused on regions deemed susceptible to Soviet influence. In 1961 President John F. Kennedy made a plea to the United Nations General Assembly for a "decade of development," sweeping in a golden age of international development aid and witnessing the peak of U.S. development aid in 1964, when the United States contributed nearly two-thirds of all official development assistance.

The 1970s saw a gradual transformation in emphasis from development aid based on economic growth to a broader theory incorporating social and human development. This was triggered by a 1974 World Bank report, *Redistribution with Growth,* which argued that traditional development strategies were leading to a "development gap" in the third world. Although economic growth projects funding industrial infrastructure and promoting foreign investment did lead to higher economic growth rates in terms of gross domestic product (GDP), growing national incomes were not being distributed equally within and between developing countries (see INCOME INEQUALITY). The report further showed that nearly half of the population in the developing world was living in a state of absolute poverty, defined in 1979 to the World Bank Group by former bank president Robert McNamara as "a condition of life so limited by malnutrition, illiteracy, disease, high infant mortality, and low life-expectancy as to be below any rational definition of human decency."

The recognition and definition of absolute poverty quickly led to the basic human needs approach to development assistance. Although this new strategy by no means replaced the economic growth strategy, it shifted considerable attention to the provision of basic social services and the necessities of life, including increased numbers of grants and loans for improvements in agriculture, rural employment, education, sanitation, and health. During the 1980s the World Bank became the preeminent international development aid institution. Under McNamara's leadership, the bank quadrupled in size, and its lending for development projects increased by six times. Nearly sixty years after its inception, the World Bank continues in this role, disbursing an average of $20 billion per year for development aid projects and programs, producing the most widely read research on development, and publishing the most influential and cited reports and statistical resources, including the annual *World Development Report* and *World Development Indicators.*

In the 1980s, however, the World Bank and its sister institution, the International Monetary Fund (IMF), came under attack. As a result of oil crises in the 1970s and deterioration in the international prices of export commodities, developing countries ran out of the currency reserves necessary to make payments on their international loans. As a result, the developing world suffered a series of severe debt crises, beginning with Mexico's default on commercial bank and development aid loans in 1982. The World Bank and IMF response was to initiate structural adjustment lending, issuing loans designed to bail out countries suffering from unsustainable balance of payment deficits caused by the value of imports exceeding the revenues derived from exports. These loans, however, came with strict conditions obligating recipient countries to institute massive macroeconomic reforms, including wide-scale deregulation, removal of state-controlled pricing, decentralization, and privatization of the economy. Later called the Washington consensus, this set of orthodox economic reforms did improve economic growth rates, but at a high social cost, as developing country governments were forced to cut back on social spending on welfare, health care, and education. The tension between the economic growth strategies and the basic human needs approach did not go unnoticed by critics.

As the adverse effects of structural adjustment were realized in the late 1980s and 1990s, the ideologies informing development aid began to shift away from poverty alleviation through economic growth to older notions of basic human needs, finding new life within the framework of sustainable development, good governance, and empowerment. Development aid now also faces the daunting challenges of stemming the spread of HIV/AIDS, assisting populations suffering from an increasing number of natural disasters related to changing global climate patterns, and protecting refugees and rebuilding societies recovering from ethnic conflict and civil war (see AIDS, GLOBAL WARMING, ETHNIC AND REGIONAL CONFLICT). Although development aid has changed much in its sixty-year history, it is clear that the learning experience is far from over.

Current Status

Development seeks to improve the welfare of people living in conditions of economic and social poverty (see Table 1). How the alleviation of poverty is achieved, however, is contentiously debated. Nonetheless, there is today a widely held consensus in international development discourse that the focus should be on the role of women, ecologically friendly and sustainable economic growth, and the link between the political problems of corruption and conflict in relation to social and economic development. These new focal points do not necessarily replace older approaches to development, rather they amend and add to them. The result is a greatly enriched understanding that drives a diverse, expanding field of research. Yet at the same time, this growth in theory has in practice contributed to increasingly unwieldy agendas of international aid organizations, which now face the complex task of translating these new views of development into manageable policies and programs.

Research

Development aid research is devoted to understanding the causes and consequences of poverty in the third world. As noted purely economic conditions are no longer the primary variables in discussions of underdevelopment. The experience of the past century reveals that social, environmental, and political variables are equally if not more important. Economic growth gauged through increases in gross national product and per capita incomes does not result in real and equitable development absent human progress, which is measured in terms of the ability of individuals to meet their most basic needs in health and personal safety and to acquire the skills and education necessary to improve the lives of themselves and their children. Likewise, increases in the productive industrial and agriculture capacity of developing nations can actually pose a catch-22 if economic advancement is won at the price of the environment, thereby sacrificing the long-term supply of natural resources and endangering health through pollution, deforestation, and man-made disasters caused by, for example, oil spills, soil erosion, and excessive irrigation. Finally, globalization has incited controversial discussions concerning the relationships between development and widespread corruption, ethnic conflict, civil war, and terrorism, thus adding a fourth dimension to development (see TERRORISM).

Three topics stand out as illustrative of current trends in development research. The first concerns the link between socioeconomic development and the environment. The relationship is symbiotic: changes in the environment, such as global warming, rising pollution levels, and increasing occurrences of droughts or floods, can affect the health, livelihood, and security of populations. Likewise, economic growth associated with industrialization, urbanization, and growing populations can place enormous stresses on the environment by increasing the demand for finite natural resources, causing deterioration of land, contamination of water sources, and threats to biodiversity. In 1987 the UN-sponsored World Commission on Environment and Development, or the Brundtland Commission, published a report that articulates this relationship using the concept of sustainable development, which is defined as the ability to meet "the needs of the present without compromising the ability of future generations to meet their own needs" (see Document 1). The report asserts that environmental degradation constitutes a cause and consequence of perpetual poverty, so to achieve development for future generations environmental considerations must be fully integrated into development aid.

The second dimension of development research focuses on the twin notions of participatory development and empowerment of the poor. As embodied in *World Development Report, 2000–2001* and the *Voices of the Poor* series, both produced by the World Bank in 2000, the key to poverty alleviation is to target opportunities directly to the most impoverished, thereby allowing those most in need to identify the priorities of development and the chance to lift themselves out of poverty. Likewise, participatory development builds on this bottom-up approach by asserting that the people toward whom development assistance is aimed should participate fully in the decision-making process surrounding development, and as many people as possible should enjoy the benefits of economic growth. Both concepts point to the need to include groups previously neglected in development discourses or groups that have not received their fair share of development aid benefits under past development strategies.

Central in this debate is the role of women in development, which has been spurred by concern that women have traditionally benefited far less from economic growth than men. In the past decade the UNDP *Human Development Report* has included statistics derived from a gender empowerment measure (GEM) and a gender-related development index (GDI). Each composite index is designed to gauge levels of equality between men and women along economic and political lines, such as access to economic resources and political participation, as well as social and human lines, such as life expectancy, literacy rates, and access to health care and higher levels of education. There is now a consensus among researchers that progress in women's development feeds into the broader goals of development: Decreased fertility rates contribute to lower population growth rates, increased participation of women in the workforce raises overall levels of economic growth, and an awareness of health issues decreases levels of malnutrition and helps stem the spread of infectious diseases, such as HIV/AIDS. Moreover, research indicates that the development and empowerment of women also has a powerful and direct effect on the welfare of children. Women who have greater access to employment and health care can take better care of their children, and those who enjoy a higher level of education tend to encourage their children to pursue the same.

The third dimension of research is the political nature of development in the third world, a topic that has risen in response to the failure of past development aid policies and programs. This research agenda recognizes that progress in social and economic development has been repeatedly set back, and sometimes reversed, by state failures, rampant corruption, ethnic conflict, and civil war. This has prompted research in part to address public administration infrastructures of developing nations and their institutional capacity—as evident in the public accessibility, transparency, and predictability of the legal, financial, and regulatory systems—to successfully implement and sustain development programs. The underlying logic of research on the role of "good governance" reflects the belief that strong, stable democracies, the rule of law, and vibrant market economies are the springboards for sustainable and participatory development.

Policies and Programs

As research continues to explore the multiple dimensions of poverty, aid policies and programs struggle daily to address the growing demands of development. The resulting agendas are often a laundry list of vaguely defined and sometimes contradictory goals, creating gaps between the goals of development theory and what can be realistically accomplished in practice.

Development aid can be funded through governments, private voluntary organizations and charities, private commercial agencies, and nongovernmental organizations. The focus here is on official development assistance, or ODA, defined as the funds provided by governments for the purpose of promoting economic growth and human welfare in the developing world. Such assistance can take the form of grants, project loans, financial credits, and technical assistance offered through bilateral agencies of individual donor countries, for example, the U.S. Agency for International Development (USAID), and multilateral governmental organizations, such as the World Bank, the IMF, the various regional development banks, and the specialized agencies of the United Nations. The amount, direction, content, and effectiveness of official development assistance is carefully tracked each year by the Development Assistance Committee (DAC) of the Organization for Economic Cooperation and Development (OECD). The committee is composed of the European Commission and the twenty-two industrialized countries that constitute the major donors in international development aid (see Table 2 and map, p. 118). A majority of the nearly $53 billion in official development assistance is devoted to social development, such as education, although a large proportion of it is still targeted at the economic infrastructure of developing nations, including loans disbursed for road building, telecommunication networks, and large-scale agricultural reform (see Table 3). Although such issues as debt relief and emergency aid, including humanitarian relief and food aid, do not show up in numerical terms as major objectives of official development assistance, both issues have also recently received considerable attention.

The three areas of development research discussed above have had an important effect on aid policies and programs. The articulation of the notion of sustainable development by the Brundtland Commission in 1987 was firmly embraced by a large number of nongovernmental organizations and other watchdog institutions calling for greater monitoring of the environmental effects of projects sponsored by international aid agencies, especially the World Bank. In 1992 the United Nations Conference on Environment and Development resulted in the creation of the UN Sustainable Development Commission and the Global Environmental Facility of the World Bank to conduct research, including critical data sources, related to the environment. Environmental assessment reports are now required parts of project appraisals and evaluations by multilateral development agencies. Protection of the environment has drawn attention in large part because of the devastating ecological effects of previous aid projects aimed at building economic infrastructure. A case in point is the Three Gorges Dam in central China (see FRESHWATER). This multibillion-dollar project, co-sponsored initially by the World Bank, intends to build a dam to produce energy, open seaways, and prevent seasonal flooding in one of the poorest regions of China. The construction of the dam was also expected to create a 370-mile reservoir, requiring the involuntary resettlement of nearly 2 million people and causing irreparable harm to local wildlife. The outcry eventually led the World Bank to withdraw funding from the project. The debate over the economic versus social and environmental costs and benefits of this project illustrates well the impact of the sustainable development concept and the tensions between dimensions of development that complicate current aid policy.

The role of women in development has likewise earned a place on policy agendas and in major publications of international development agencies. In 1976 the United Nations created the Development Fund for Women (UNIFEM), which is devoted to promoting the economic equality and empowerment of women. It has sponsored several global conferences, including the 1995 World Conference on Women held in Beijing, that have brought worldwide attention to this issue. Each year, a greater number of aid projects specifically target women, focusing on education opportunities and improvements in health facilities and training that advocate family planning practices, aim to decrease maternal and child mortality rates, and address HIV/AIDS. Yet perhaps the most popular development aid strategy aimed at women is the global phenomenon of grassroots microlending institutions, that grant credit for small business ventures to the most impoverished sections of society, which normally do not qualify for loans from traditional commercial banks. Although microlending institutions do not solely target women, women have been by far the primary recipients of the programs, since they are the segment of society in developing nations most unlikely to have the legal right or opportunity to borrow money under traditional banking systems. Evaluations have shown that microlending institutions not only enhance the economic opportunities and education of women, but have a direct effect on the well-being of children and contribute significantly to the economic growth of developing nations as a whole (see Case Study—Women in Development: Microlending in Bangladesh).

Finally, the political face of development is expressed in the good governance agendas of major donor organizations. These target the underlying institutional structure of the political economy, including the modernization of banking and financial systems and public sector administration. Most noticeable is the amount of aid devoted in the 1990s to building the rule of law in developing countries as a means of empowering the poor through greater access to the judicial system and creating an environment favorable for foreign investment and free market economies through stable laws and efficient courts. Bilateral agencies, such as USAID, have devoted considerable resources toward legal and judicial reforms as part of a broader democracy-building agenda since the 1970s. Yet the rule of law agenda took off in the early 1990s, when the World Bank, which previously viewed legal reform as incompatible with its apolitical mandates, justified it as critical to the successful economic transition of post-authoritarian systems in Latin America, Eastern Europe, and the former Soviet Union. The World Bank is now the largest donor in the area of legal and judicial reform, lending nearly $500 million dollars for projects since 1992.

An understanding of recent trends in development aid must note two other phenomena. The first is the increasing number of actors involved in international development assistance. In addition to bilateral and multilateral governmental agencies, there are thousands of nongovernmental organizations, grassroots associations, and civil society groups that are directly involved in the creation, implementation, and monitoring of official and nonofficial development aid projects and policies. Their involvement enhances the participatory framework for development agendas, but it also has become a source of redundancy, conflict, and lack of coordination in the delivery of aid. A second and more disturbing trend is the decline in the overall amount of official development assistance since the end of the cold war (see Table 2). The most noticeable decline is from the United States, which was once the largest development aid donor but now contributes the lowest level of assistance in terms of its gross national product (GNP), the total amount of goods and services produced within a country's jurisdiction. The reasons for "aid fatigue" are complex, but in part it can be attributed to the collapse of the Soviet Union and the subsequent loss of justification for development aid as a strategic tool for the containment of communism. This has created a serious dilemma in international development aid circles, which must cope with diminishing funds as demands and challenges in the third world grow.

Recent events may, however, reverse this trend. As a result of the 11 September 2001 attacks on the United States, food aid, debt relief, and a myriad of other aid packages are being offered to Pakistan, the states of Central Asia, and the Middle East in an effort to build support for an international coalition against terrorism. In addition, widespread media coverage of famine and repression under the Taliban regime in Afghanistan noticeably increased public awareness and support for humanitarian relief, and the eminent security threat has enabled development agencies to argue that poverty alleviation is key to preventing an increase in terrorism. These are both critical factors in convincing wealthy donor states to allocate increased funding for official development assistance. This renewed emphasis on geopolitics, however, raises concerns that aid will become heavily burdened with conditions not directly related to development goals. Moreover, as during the cold war, such aid might target areas of the world that may be politically important but that do not necessarily have the greatest need for such assistance, leaving the most impoverished areas, such as sub-Saharan Africa, neglected.

Regional Summaries

OECD Countries

The countries of the Organization for Economic Cooperation and Development represent the twenty-two major states offering official development aid: Australia, Austria, Belgium, Canada, Denmark, Finland, France, Germany, Greece, Ireland, Italy, Japan, Luxembourg, Netherlands, New Zealand, Norway, Portugal, Spain, Sweden, Switzerland, United Kingdom, and the United States. Since 1990 the top contributors in terms of total dollars have been Japan, followed by the United States, Germany, the United Kingdom, France, and the Netherlands (see Table 2). These numbers do not, however, accurately represent each country's devotion to development aid. The largest donors in absolute terms are among the lowest contributors in terms of aid expenditures as a percentage of gross national product. The United States, surpassed by Japan in 1993 in total dollars contributed, is now the lowest donor in terms of GNP, a remarkable drop since the country's initiation of development aid in the 1940s. Only four countries—Denmark, the Netherlands, Norway, and Sweden—actually meet the assistance target of 0.7 percent of GNP established by the United Nations.

A large portion of development assistance is given to the multilateral development agencies—the World Bank, IMF, and specialized UN agencies—as well as the regional development banks—the African Development Bank, Asian Development Bank, European Bank for Reconstruction and Development, and the Inter-American Development Bank. Member states' influence over the policies and programs of these organizations varies and is often a matter of great debate. Political control over the majority of official development assistance is exercised through bilateral aid, coordinated through domestic organizations, such as USAID. Bilateral development assistance is often considered a key part of foreign policy, and as such the content and direction of aid is largely shaped by prevailing national interests. European countries, for example, tend to direct aid to former colonies in Africa, Latin America, and South Asia, while the United States expends nearly 10 percent of its aid on

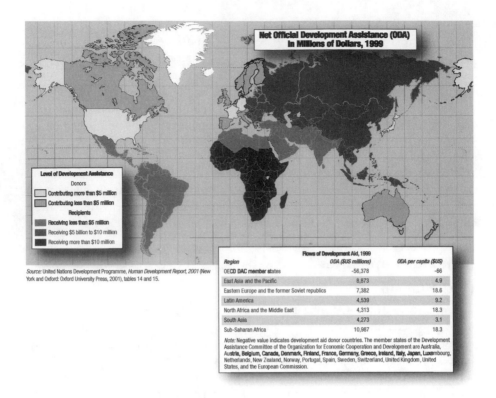

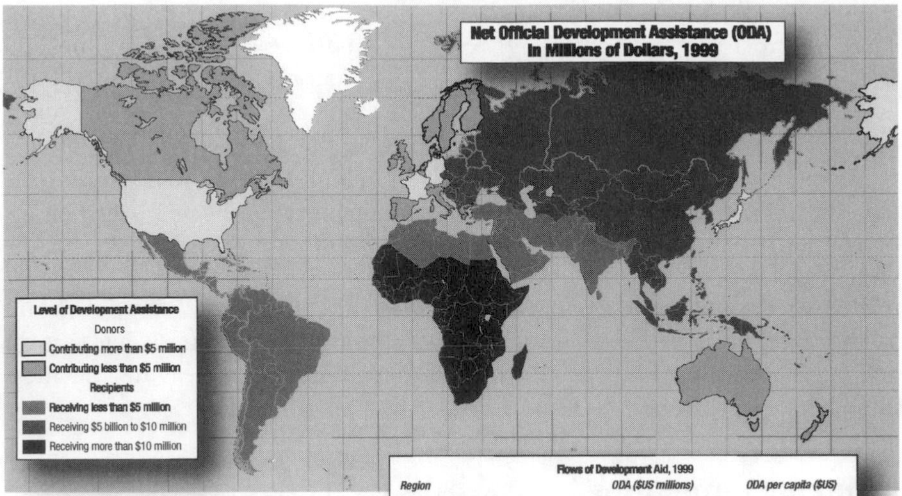

Source: United Nations Development Programme, *Human Development Report, 2001* (New York and Oxford: Oxford University Press, 2001), tables 14 and 15.

Flows of Development Aid, 1999

Region	*ODA ($US millions)*	*ODA per capita ($US)*
OECD DAC member states	-56,378	-66
East Asia and the Pacific	8,873	4.9
Eastern Europe and the former Soviet republics	7,382	18.6
Latin America	4,539	9.2
North Africa and the Middle East	4,313	18.3
South Asia	4,273	3.1
Sub-Saharan Africa	10,987	18.3

Note: Negative value indicates development aid donor countries. The member states of the Development Assistance Committee of the Organization for Economic Cooperation and Development are Australia, Austria, Belgium, Canada, Denmark, Finland, France, Germany, Greece, Ireland, Italy, Japan, Luxembourg, Netherlands, New Zealand, Norway, Portugal, Spain, Sweden, Switzerland, United Kingdom, United States, and the European Commission.

Israel, despite that country's relatively high level of socioeconomic development. Similarly, funds are usually allocated for specific purposes, with certain amounts earmarked by borrowing countries to purchase equipment or hire consultants from donor countries. The prevalence of such "tied aid" undermines the altruistic image of development aid.

Latin America

Although the countries of Latin America and the Caribbean have on average made considerable progress in a few areas of human development, stagnating economic growth from 1999 to 2001 has contributed to an increasing income distribution inequality. For example, according to UNDP's *Human Development Report, 2001,* in Paraguay the poorest 10 percent of the population earn less than 1 percent of the national income, while the richest 10 percent earn less than 44 percent.

Nearly 40 percent of the region's people live on less than $2 per day, and 74.9 percent live in densely populated urban areas, increasing the risk of infectious disease through overcrowding, a lack of clean water, and other unsanitary conditions. Moreover, in many countries the transition is ongoing from authoritarian government to consolidated democracy. The fear of political instability leading to economic instability has steered development aid toward rule of law, governance, anti-corruption efforts, and civil society–building projects. Sustainable development is also a concern in relation to increasing deforestation in the Amazon, soil erosion due to poor agricultural practices, and industrial pollution in the major cities. Recent hurricanes in Central America and the Caribbean as a result of El Niño events and two earthquakes in El Salvador in early 2001 made the region one of the largest recipients of development assistance in the form of disaster relief and reconstruction aid.

Eastern Europe and the Former Soviet Union

The flow of development assistance to Eastern Europe and the former republics of the Soviet Union has increased, according to *World Development Indicators, 2001,* from around 1 percent of total ODA in the 1960s through the 1980s to nearly 20 percent of total ODA in the 1990s. This is directly attributed to the collapse of communism in 1989 in Eastern Europe and in 1991 in the Soviet Union, after which the countries of the region went from being net aid donors to being net recipients of aid. Russia, due to its sheer size and political importance, has been one of the largest recipients of development aid, receiving nearly $2 billion in 1999 alone. Although the region enjoys levels of social development on par with OECD countries, including highly educated societies with an average literacy rate of close to 99 percent, development aid continues to address the slow and often painful transition to market capitalism and democracy. The European Bank for Reconstruction and Development was created in 1991 specifically for this purpose. Aid strategies have focused on privatization of the economy, deregulation of state sectors, public policy reform, institutional development, civil society, good governance and elimination of corruption, and introduction of the rule of law. Development aid is also being used to clean up environmental pollution resulting from years of industrial mismanagement under the centrally planned economies. Aid has further been allocated to political and economic programs in the Balkan Peninsula to help that area recover from ethnic conflict and war in the former Yugoslavia and Macedonia.

North Africa and the Middle East

The countries of North Africa and the Middle East have on average higher rates of GNP per capita and lower levels of poverty than other developing regions, yet the geopolitical importance of the region ensures that it receives a disproportionate share of development assistance. As previously mentioned, Israel is the top recipient of U.S. assistance. Egypt is the third largest recipient of U.S. development aid, and the fourth largest recipient of total assistance from OECD member states.

The social and environmental dimensions of development remain the primary areas of concern for international development agencies involved in the region. Inequality in the development status of men and women remains a significant challenge, with a literacy rate for women of only 49 percent. The region also exhibits high birth rates and subsequent population growth. Stress on the environment is felt most in the strain on scarce water resources. Several billion dollars in development aid from multiple organizations is devoted each year to agricultural and infrastructure projects addressing overirrigation and improper treatment of waste water.

Sub-Saharan Africa

Sub-Saharan Africa has made the least progress in socioeconomic development. The region has suffered from declining economic growth rates for more than a decade, 46 percent of the population lives on less than $1 per day, and many countries, such as Tanzania, suffer from severe and unsustainable external debt burdens that detract from critical social and human welfare expenditures. Population growth remains a serious problem, due to a high fertility rate of nearly six children per woman, compared to an average of less than two children per women in the high-income OECD countries. This high population growth threatens scarce environmental resources in a region that is not endowed with fertile soil or adequate water supplies.

Although sub-Saharan Africa remains the largest recipient of official development assistance, with 25.6 percent of total ODA, the effectiveness of development aid programs has been hindered by constant political instability and widespread corruption that contributes to the misuse of funds. Yet the most serious development challenge in sub-Saharan Africa today is the spread of HIV/AIDS. According to "AIDS Epidemic Update, 2000," a product of the Joint United Nations Programme on HIV/AIDS (UNAIDS), nearly 9 percent of the region's adult population lives with AIDS, compared to less than 1 percent of the adult populations in all other developing regions, with the exception of Latin America, where 2.3 percent of adults are infected with HIV. In Botswana, the most seriously affected country, 35.5 percent of the adult population has HIV/AIDS. Life expectancy as of 1999 had rapidly declined to only forty-six years and forty-eight years for men and women, respectively, according to *World Development Indicators, 2001* figures. The World Bank reports that the spread of AIDS has actually reversed progress in development. As a result, alleviation of the AIDS crisis in this region is the number one objective of international development aid as asserted at the G-8 summit in Genoa, Italy, in July 2001.

South Asia

South Asia has experienced strong economic growth compared to the rest of the developing world. This growth, however, has not translated into poverty reduction. South Asia is home to 40 percent of the world's poor, according to USAID's fiscal year 2001 budget justification report. More than 500 million South Asians live on less than $1 per day. In India, more than 44 percent of people live on less than $1 per day, according to the UNDP's *Human Development Report, 2001*; the adult illiteracy rate is 43.5 percent.

Widespread malnutrition, maternal and infant mortality rates, and the spread of HIV/AIDS in the region top the list of development aid concerns. Family planning, the building of health care facilities, and provisioning of health education are popular aid programs. Women's development is also at risk, with females having a much higher illiteracy rate than men—59 percent as opposed to 35 percent. Many leading aid loans are dedicated to educational opportunities for young girls. Microlending programs, modeled on the Grameen Bank in Bangladesh, have made some progress in creating economic opportunities for the poor, especially women. Moreover, environmental degradation due to rapid population growth, industrialization, and urbanization has threatened sustainable development. Several natural disasters in the past few years, including an earthquake in India in 2001 that left 20,000 people dead and 800,000 homeless, have increased demand for disaster relief. Finally, political instability, particularly in Indonesia and East Timor, has disrupted economic growth and increased the need for foreign aid in the form of refugee assistance.

East Asia and the Pacific

The countries of East Asia and the Pacific are relatively well off compared to the rest of the developing world. Led by the "four tigers"—Hong Kong, South Korea, Taiwan, and Singapore—the region experienced tremendous economic growth for nearly two decades, leading the World Bank to call it in the early 1990s the East Asian Miracle. The Asian financial crisis of 1997 reversed this trend, but many countries in the region have begun to see positive economic growth rates only after three years of recovery. According to *World Development Indicators, 2001,* the economic boom of the early 1990s was so great that even in the wake of the 1997 crisis, South Korea and Singapore enjoyed an average GDP per capita growth rate of 9.7 and 4.6 percent, respectively, between 1998 and 1999; the United States' growth rate during this same period was 2.4 percent. Since the initial bailouts in 1997 totaling several billion dollars, development aid has concentrated on the perceived causes and consequences of the crisis. Aid has been directed toward restructuring banks and corporations to restore their financial viability and ensure sound management of the increasing public sector debt. Concern over increasing unemployment and decreased public expenditures on health care have also drawn aid toward rebuilding the social safety net.

Data

Table 1 Key Indicators of Social and Economic Development for Selected Countries in Relation to Development Aid, 1999

	GDP per Capita, PPP (current international $US)[a]	Adult Illiteracy Rate, Aged 15 and Above (%)	Life Expectancy (years)	Infant Mortality Rate (per 1,000 live births)	Official Development Assistance and Official Aid (current $US million)[b]	Aid per Capita ($US)[b]
Algeria	5,063	33	71	34	89	3
Argentina	12,277	3	74	18	91	2
Australia	24,574	—	79	5	–982	–50
Brazil	7,037	15	67	32	184	1
Canada	26,251	—	79	5	–1,699	–55
China	3,617	17	70	30	2,324	2
Colombia	5,749	9	70	23	301	7

Table 1 Key Indicators of Social and Economic Development for Selected Countries in Relation to Development Aid, 1999 (*continued*)

	GDP per Capita, PPP (current international $US)[a]	Adult Illiteracy Rate, Aged 15 and Above (%)	Life Expectancy (years)	Infant Mortality Rate (per 1,000 live births)	Official Development Assistance and Official Aid (current $US million)[b]	Aid per Capita ($US)[b]
Congo, Republic of	—	40	46	85	132	3
Egypt	3,420	45	67	47	1,579	25
France	22,897	—	79	5	–5,637	–99
Georgia	2,431	—	73	15	239	44
Germany	23,742	—	77	5	–5,515	–69
Guatemala	3,674	32	65	40	293	26
India	2,248	44	63	71	1,484	1
Indonesia	2,857	14	66	42	2,206	11
Israel	18,440	4	78	6	906	148
Japan	24,898	—	81	4	–15,323	–106
Russian Federation	7,473	1	66	16	1,816	12
Saudi Arabia	10,815	24	72	19	29	1
Spain	18,079	2	78	5	–1,363	–35
Sweden	22,636	—	79	4	–1,630	–190
Switzerland	27,171	—	80	5	–969	–140
Tajikistan	—	1	69	20	122	20
Thailand	6,132	5	69	28	1,003	17
Turkey	6,380	15	69	36	–10	0
Uganda	1,167	34	42	88	590	27
United Kingdom	22,093	—	77	6	–3,401	–57
United States	31,872	—	77	7	–9,145	–33
East Asia and the Pacific	3,824	15	69	35	9,811	5
Europe and Central Asia	6,170	3	69	21	10,878	23
Latin America	6,817	12	70	30	5,856	12
Middle East and North Africa	5,109	36	68	44	5,128	18
South Asia	2,115	46	63	74	4,254	3
Sub-Saharan Africa	1,600	39	47	92	12,546	20
World	6,941	—	66	54	59,125	10

Source: World Bank, *World Development Indicators, 2001* (Washington, D.C.: World Bank, 2001); Organization for Economic Cooperation and Development, Development Assistance Committee, *Development Cooperation Report, 2000*, http://www.oecd.org/dac.

[a]GDP per capita is calculated according to the purchasing price parity (PPP) model.

[b]Negative value indicates a net outflow of official development assistance.

Table 2 Aid Fatigue: Declining Development Aid Contributions of OECD DAC Member Countries since 1990

Official Development Assistance ($US billions)

	France	Germany	Japan	Netherlands	United Kingdom	United States	Other Member States	Total
1990	7.2	6.3	9.1	2.5	2.6	11.4	13.9	53.0
1991	7.4	6.9	11.0	2.5	3.2	11.3	13.8	56.7
1992	8.3	7.6	11.2	2.8	3.2	11.7	16.1	60.9
1993	7.9	7.0	11.3	2.5	2.9	10.1	14.8	56.5
1994	8.5	6.8	13.2	2.5	3.2	9.9	15.0	59.2
1995	8.4	7.5	14.5	3.2	3.2	7.4	14.6	58.9
1996	7.4	7.5	9.4	3.2	3.2	9.1	15.3	55.1
1997	6.3	5.9	9.4	2.9	3.4	6.9	13.4	48.3
1998	5.7	5.6	10.6	3.0	3.9	8.8	14.4	52.1
1999	5.6	5.5	15.3	3.1	3.4	9.1	14.3	56.4
2000	4.2	5.0	13.1	3.1	4.5	9.6	13.7	53.1

Official Development Assistance as a Percentage of Gross National Product

	France	Germany	Japan	Netherlands	United Kingdom	United States	Other Member States	Total
1990	0.60	0.42	0.31	0.92	0.27	0.21	0.49	0.33
1991	0.62	0.40	0.32	0.88	0.32	0.20	0.49	0.33
1992	0.63	0.39	0.30	0.86	0.31	0.20	0.47	0.33
1993	0.63	0.37	0.26	0.82	0.31	0.15	0.49	0.30
1994	0.64	0.33	0.29	0.76	0.31	0.14	0.48	0.30
1995	0.55	0.31	0.28	0.81	0.29	0.10	0.44	0.27
1996	0.48	0.32	0.20	0.81	0.27	0.12	0.44	0.25
1997	0.45	0.28	0.22	0.81	0.26	0.09	0.44	0.22
1998	0.40	0.26	0.28	0.80	0.27	0.10	0.44	0.23
1999	0.38	0.26	0.35	0.79	0.23	0.10	0.45	0.24
2000	0.33	0.27	0.27	0.82	0.31	0.10	N.A.	0.22

Source: Organization for Economic Cooperation and Development, Development Assistance Committee, *International Development Statistics, 2001,* http://www.oecd.org/dac; World Bank, *World Development Indicators, 2001* (Washington, D.C.: World Bank, 2001).

Note: The members of the Development Assistance Committee of the Organization for Economic Cooperation and Development are Australia, Austria, Belgium, Canada, Denmark, Finland, France, Germany, Greece, Ireland, Italy, Japan, Luxembourg, Netherlands, New Zealand, Norway, Portugal, Spain, Sweden, Switzerland, United Kingdom, United States, and the European Commission.

Table 3 Aid by Sector and Purpose, 1999

	Total Bilateral Aid (%)	Total Multilateral Aid (%)	Total Aid from Regional Development Banks (%)	Total Aid (%)
Social and administrative infrastructure	29.9	34.5	49.1	40.1
Education	10.7	6.3	2.4	4.8
Health	4.2	2.1	1.0	1.7
Population	1.8	1.0	—	0.6
Water supply and sanitation	4.1	2.4	7.3	4.3
Government and civil society	4.2	12.4	16.6	14.1
Other social infrastructure/services	4.9	10.3	21.7	14.7
Economic Infrastructure	17.2	30.2	16.0	24.7
Transport and communications	8.7	13.6	8.5	11.6
Energy	4.6	1.9	6.4	3.6
Other	3.9	14.7	1.1	9.4
Production	8.1	12.4	23.5	16.7
Agriculture	5.5	9.4	2.7	6.8
Industry, mining, and construction	2.2	2.6	20.6	9.6
Trade and tourism	0.4	0.4	0.2	0.3
Multisector	7.4	4.5	7.2	5.5
Programme assistance	6.9	1.8	—	1.1
Debt relief	7.4	—	—	—
Emergency aid	11.1	4.3	—	2.6
Administrative expenses	5.9	—	—	—
Unspecified	6.1	12.4	4.3	9.2

Source: Organization for Economic Cooperation and Development, Development Assistance Committee, *Development Cooperation Report, 2000,* http://www.oecd.org/dac.

Case Study—Debt Forgiveness in Tanzania

Tanzania is one the poorest countries in sub-Saharan Africa. More than 50 percent of the country's 30 million people live in a condition of extreme poverty, with 19.9 percent of its population living on less than $1 per day, according to *World Development Indicators, 2001.* Its average fertility rate of 5.5 children per woman has caused a high population growth rate with dire consequences for the environment, scarce resources, and an underfunded and overextended health care and educational system already distressed by political and economic instability. Today the average adult has a life expectancy of only 45 years, the infant mortality rate is nearly 10 percent, and the mortality rate for children under five is more than 15 percent. Perhaps the most disturbing effect of poverty in Tanzania has been the spread of infectious diseases. As of 1999, 8.1 percent of the adult Tanzanian population was infected with AIDS.

The ability of Tanzania to address the causes and consequences of poverty is hindered by its growing debt burden, including annual payments on the principal and interest of loans provided by bilateral and multilateral development agencies. In 1998, according to the *Human Development Report, 2000,* Tanzania's total external debt equaled 94.5 percent of its gross national product. The real impact of the debt situation is felt in opportunity costs, meaning that money is more often spent on repaying loans than on critically needed social services. A report by Oxfam International argues that more than one-third of the budgetary expenditures of the government are allocated to external debt servicing, that is, paying the interest on the debt it holds from other countries. On a per capita basis, Tanzania is spending four times as much on debt servicing as on primary education and nine times as much on debt as on basic health services. In simplest terms, this means that Tanzania's growing debt burden is diverting scarce resources from areas critical for social and human development, ultimately undermining the country's ability to lift itself out of poverty.

Tanzania has recently qualified to participate in the Highly Indebted Poor Countries Initiative (HIPC), a program jointly established by the World Bank and the IMF in 1996. The purpose of the HIPC is to provide debt relief to the poorest of the developing countries that can no longer sustain their debt obligations without severe costs to development programs. Under the initiative, approximately half of Tanzania's overall external debt will be forgiven. In exchange, Tanzania must establish a "satisfactory track record" in the use of World Bank and IMF loans and prepare and implement a wide-reaching poverty reduction program. Ultimately, the debt relief initiative is intended to create room for public expenditures in such areas as health care and education, as well as capacity-building and sustainable development projects, which will enhance the country's ability to achieve long-term economic growth and poverty reduction. This, in turn, will reduce the need for future additional development aid and its accompanying risk of further debt.

Debt relief has become an increasingly important component of official development assistance. Currently thirty-three countries qualify to participate in the HIPC initiative. The program is not without controversy. As witnessed by the protests at the Group of Eight summit in July 2001 in Genoa, Italy, nongovernmental organizations and other developing country advocacy groups, such as Jubilee Plus and the Drop the Debt campaign, generally welcome the HIPC initiative. Yet, they also argue that the program does not go far enough and comes with too many strings attached. The eligibility requirements are strict and based upon inflexible economic criteria, which often disqualify countries for which debt burdens appear unsustainable in almost every aspect. The staunchest critics further assert that bilateral and multilateral aid agencies should be obligated to grant more extensive debt relief. They view the cause of the growing debt burden in the developing world as a result of excessive lending by international donor agencies, which disbursed billions of dollars to the poorest countries in the third world without achieving any real success in development aid goals. In fact, 40 percent of Tanzania's external debt payments go to the IMF and World Bank. Aid donors respond by arguing that the past failure of aid policies was due to corrupt governments, the misuse of aid funds, and external shocks in the international economy. Although this debate is unlikely to be resolved in the near future, it is clear that the causes of severe debt and the need for debt relief will remain central to debates surrounding development aid.

Case Study—Women in Development: Microlending in Bangladesh

According to the *Human Development Report, 2001,* Bangladesh is one of the most densely populated and impoverished countries in South Asia. Nearly 30 percent of the population lives on less than $1 per day, only 53 percent has access to adequate sanitation facilities, and 38 percent is considered undernourished, including 56 percent of children under five who are underweight. The extreme poverty of Bangladesh has affected women and children the most. Child and maternal mortality rates are high, only 14 percent of births are attended by skilled health staff, and 29.3 percent of women over the age of fifteen are literate, as opposed to 51.7 percent of men. Official development assistance to Bangladesh has focused on the most basic needs, including aid directed at education, health care, sanitation, and agriculture. Floods and famines have also created demand for disaster relief funds. Overall, however, poverty alleviation through traditional means of official development assistance has made only modest progress.

In 1976 economics professor Muhammad Yunus from the University of Chittagong conducted a research project to explore the possibilities of a program that would provide small loans to the rural poor without the need for the assets normally required for bank lending. The goal was to enable the poorest sections of the society—most often women and the illiterate, who have difficulty qualifying for commercial bank loans—to gain access to credit and create opportunities for self-employment. The underlying belief was that the poor can lift themselves out of poverty if provided with the education and financial means to do so.

After the resounding success of the pilot project in the small village of Jobra, the program was extended to several other villages. In 1983 the Grameen Bank project, as it was later called, was turned into an independent bank, and today 90 percent of its shares are owned by the rural poor who are the bank's borrowers. Small amounts of money are lent on a weekly basis to groups of five people who, through peer pressure and commitment to the Grameen Bank's sixteen "decisions" (see Document 2), ensure that the loans are repaid and profits are reinvested. Women make up more than 90 percent of the borrowers; most use their funds for small entrepreneurial ventures, such as pottery, weaving, and other retail services.

The program also has an educational purpose in teaching the participants not only how to handle money but also how to take care of their families and how to build and maintain safe housing and sanitary conditions. Among the sixteen decisions are pledges by borrowers to become more self-sufficient in food production, become more involved in the education of their children, and practice family planning. The Grameen Bank has expanded rapidly in the last twenty-five years and now has more than a thousand branch offices throughout Bangladesh, more than 2 million members in nearly forty thousand villages, and an astonishing repayment rate of 97 percent—far above that of conventional commercial banks.

The Grameen Bank, a private commercial organization, has been heralded as a model for multilateral and bilateral development aid strategies targeting grassroots assistance and the empowerment of women. There are now more than two hundred private Grameen Bank–type programs in fifty-eight countries, and the microlending model has been integrated into the development agendas of major institutions, including the World Bank. More important, the Grameen Bank's emphasis on enabling the poor to improve their own condition through financial and educational opportunities reflects a shift in development aid thinking based on poverty alleviation through simple macroeconomic growth to a more equitable, participatory and grassroots approach capturing the social and human aspects of development.

Biographical Sketches

Robert S. McNamara is a former U.S. secretary of defense under Presidents John F. Kennedy and Lyndon B. Johnson. He was president of the World Bank from 1968 to 1981. During his tenure at the bank, McNamara fundamentally changed the focus of international development aid by defining the concept of absolute poverty. In doing so, he shifted the focus of the bank from building basic economic infrastructure to broader development goals based on the fulfillment of basic human needs, including the alleviation of malnutrition, illiteracy, disease, infant mortality, and low life expectancy. During McNamara's presidency, the World Bank became the premier global development aid institution.

Jeffrey Sachs is an economics professor and director of the Center for International Development at Harvard University. He is one of the most widely recognized economists of the 1980s and 1990s, having served as an adviser to governments in Eastern Europe, Latin America, and the former Soviet Union. Sachs was the primary author of the shock therapy method of transition from command to market economies in Poland and Russia. More recently, Sachs has served on the U.S. Advisory Commission on the International Financial Institutions and has become a vocal critic of the International Monetary Fund and the World Bank.

Amartya Sen won the 1998 Nobel Prize in Economics and has promoted a theory of development based upon the empowerment of the poor through opportunities in education and work. He argues that improvement in per capita income is not enough absent real progress in the social aspects of development. In 1990 Sen was one of the authors of the first *Human Development Report,* in which he formulated a new measure of development, the human development index, based on the three variables of life expectancy, adult literacy, and income.

George Soros is a Hungarian investment banker and philanthropist and one of the leading individuals in development aid. During the past two decades, he established a network of Open Society Institutions in Eastern Europe, Guatemala, Haiti, southern

Africa, the nations of the former Soviet Union, and the United States dedicated to building the infrastructure and institutions of a free market economy and democracy.

Joseph Stiglitz is a prize-winning economist and former senior vice president and chief economist of the World Bank. As an academic, Stiglitz helped to create the new and influential theory of the economics of information. As a policymaker, Stiglitz has become well known for his opposition to the Washington consensus, the set of policies favoring free market principles that have informed the development agendas of the World Bank and the International Monetary Fund since the 1980s. Stiglitz was pushed out of the World Bank after publicly criticizing the International Monetary Fund's response to the Asian financial crisis in 1997. In October 2001 Stiglitz received the Nobel Prize in Economics.

Directory

African Development Bank, Rue Joseph Anoma, 01 BP 1387 Abidjan 01, Côte d'Ivoire. Telephone: (225) 20 20 44 44, Email: afdb@afdb.org, Web: http://www.afdb.org
Institution that targets social and economic development in Africa by facilitating partnerships between African and non-African countries

Asian Development Bank, 6 ADB Avenue, Mandaluyong, 0401 Metro Manila, Philippines. Telephone: (632) 632 4444, Email: www@mail.asiandevbank.org, Web: http://www.asiandevbank.org
Institution that promotes economic and social development in the Asia-Pacific region

CARE International, 151 Ellis Street NE, Atlanta, GA 30303-2439. Telephone: (800) 521-CARE, ext. 999, Email: info@care.org, Web: http://www.care.org
One of the largest private international relief and development organizations

Development Assistance Committee, 2 Rue Andre Pascal, 75775 Paris, France. Telephone: (33) 1 4524 8200, Email: doc.contact@oecd.org, Web: http://www.oecd.org/dac
Specialized committee of the Organization for Economic Cooperation and Development that provides a forum for consultation, development research, and aid coordination among the organization's major donor countries and the European Commission

European Bank for Reconstruction and Development, 1 Exchange Square, London EC2A 2EH, England. Telephone: (44) 171 338 6000, Email: harrisob@ebrd.com, Web: http://www.ebrd.org
Institution promoting economic reform and the emergence of democracies in the former Soviet Union and Eastern Europe

50 Years Is Enough: U.S. Network for Global Justice, 3628 12th Street NE, Washington, DC 20017. Telephone: (202) 463-2265, Email: 50years@50years.org, Web: http://www.50years.org
Coalition of more than two hundred U.S.-based nongovernmental organizations advocating the radical reform or elimination of the World Bank and International Monetary Fund

Food and Agricultural Organization, Viale delle Terme di Caracalla, 00100 Rome, Italy. Telephone: (39) 06 5705 1, Email: fao-hq@fao.org, Web: http://www.fao.org
UN agency devoted to alleviating poverty and hunger through food security

Grameen Bank, Mirpur Two, Dhaka 1216, Bangladesh. Telephone: (88) 02 9005257 68, Email: grameen.bank@grameen.net, Web: http://www.grameen.org
Microlending institution established in Bangladesh in 1977

Inter-American Development Bank, 1300 New York Avenue NW, Washington, DC 20577. Telephone: (202) 623-1000, Email: webmaster@iadb.org, Web: http://www.iadb.org
Institution providing development assistance to Latin American and Caribbean countries through the provision of low-interest loans and technical assistance

International Monetary Fund, 700 19th Street NW, Washington, DC 20431. Telephone: (202) 623-7000, Email: webmaster@imf.org, Web: http://www.imf.org
Institution promoting international monetary cooperation and the growth of world trade by stabilizing foreign exchange rates, promoting an open trading system by deterring protectionist policies, and serving as a lender of last resort

Oxfam International, Oxfam House, 274 Banbury Road, Oxford OX2 7DZ, United Kingdom. Telephone: (44) 186 531 1311, Email: Oxfam@oxfam.org.uk, Web: http://www.oxfam.org
Coalition of international nongovernmental organizations devoted to development issues, advocacy, and relief

UNAIDS, Joint United Nations Programme on HIV/AIDS, 20 Avenue Appia, 1211 Geneva 27, Switzerland. Telephone: (41) 22 791 3666, Email: unaids@unaids.org, Web: http://www.unaids.org
Agency advocating worldwide action against HIV/AIDS

United Nations Children's Fund (UNICEF), 3 United Nations Plaza, New York, NY 10017. Telephone: (212) 326-7000, Email: netmaster@unicef.org, Web: http://www.unicef.org
Agency working to resolve problems related to the poverty and rights of children around the world

United Nations Conference on Trade and Development (UNCTAD), Palais des Nations, 8-14 Avenue de la Paix, 1211 Geneva 10, Switzerland. Telephone: (41) 22 907 1234, Email: webmaster@unctad.org, Web: http://www.unctad.org
Agency responsible for trade and development issues

United Nations Development Fund for Women (UNIFEM), 304 East 45th Street, 15th Floor, New York, NY 10017. Telephone: (212) 906-6400, Email: unifem@undp.org, Web: http://www.unifem.undp.org
Agency devoted to promoting women's empowerment and gender equality

United Nations Development Programme (UNDP), 1 United Nations Plaza, New York, NY 10017. Telephone: (212) 906-5034, Email: aboutundp@undp.org, Web: http://www.undp.org
Agency addressing the causes of poverty and promoting development, the protection of human rights, and the empowerment of women, publishes the Human Development Report

United Nations Environment Programme (UNEP), United Nations Avenue, Gigiri, P.O. Box 30552, Nairobi, Kenya. Telephone: (254) 262 1234, Email: eisinfo@unep.org, Web: http://www.unep.org
Agency tackling a range of environmental issues on an international basis, including the study and promotion of sustainable development

U.S. Agency for International Development (USAID), 1300 Pennsylvania Avenue NW, Washington, DC 20523-1000. Telephone: (202) 712-4810, Email: pinquiries@usaid.gov, Web: http://www.usaid.gov
Primary U.S. government agency through which U.S. development assistance is channeled

World Bank, 1818 H Street NW, Washington, DC 20433. Telephone: (202) 477-1234, Email: comments@www.worldbank.org, Web: http://www.worldbank.org
World's largest and most influential multilateral development bank

World Health Organization, 20 Avenue Appia, 1211 Geneva 27, Switzerland. Telephone: (41) 22 791 2111, Email: info@who.int, Web: http://www.who.ch
UN agency advocating health for all people

Further Research

Books

Akira, Nishigaki, and Shimomura Yasutami. *The Economics of Development Assistance: Japan's ODA in a Symbiotic World.* Tokyo: LTCB International Library Foundation, 1998.

Brohman, J. *Popular Development: Rethinking the Theory and Practice of Development.* London: Blackwell, 1996.

Cassen, Robert, et al. *Does Aid Work? Report to an Intergovernmental Task Force.* Oxford: Clarendon Press, 1986.

Chenery H. B., ed. *Redistribution with Growth.* London: Oxford University Press for the World Bank, 1974.

Counts, Alex. *Give Us Credit: How Muhammas Yunus's Micro Lending Revolution Is Empowering Women from Bangladesh to Chicago.* New York: Random House, 1996.

Crump, Andy. *The A to Z of World Development.* Oxford: New International Publications, 1998.

Gibbons, S. David. *The Grameen Reader.* Dhaka: Grameen Bank, 1994.

Holcombe, Susan. *Managing to Empower: The Grameen Bank's Experience of Poverty Alleviation.* Atlantic Highlands, N.J.: Zed Books, 1995.

Independent Commission on International Development Issues (Brandt Commission). *North-South: A Programme for Survival. Report of the Independent Commission on International Development Issues.* Cambridge, Mass.: MIT Press, 1980.

McNamara, Robert. *The McNamara Years at the World Bank: Major Policy Addresses of Robert S. McNamara, 1968–1981.* Baltimore: John Hopkins University Press for the World Bank, 1981.

Narayan, Deepa, et al. *Crying Out for Change: Voices of the Poor.* Washington, D.C.: World Bank, 2000.

Rapley, John. *Understanding Development: Theory and Practice in the Third World.* London: UCL Press, 1996.

Rich, Bruce. *Mortgaging the Earth: The World Bank, Environmental Impoverishment, and the Crisis of Development.* Boston: Beacon Press, 1994.

Tarp, Finn, ed. *Foreign Aid and Development: Lessons Learnt and Directions for the Future.* New York: Routledge, 2000.

Tisch, Sarah J., and Michael B. Wallace. *Dilemmas of Development Assistance: The What, Why, and Who of Foreign Aid.* Boulder: Westview, 1994.

Todd, Helen. *Women at the Centre: Grameen Bank Borrowers after One Decade.* Boulder: Westview Press, 1996.

World Bank. *Making Development Sustainable.* Washington, D.C.: World Bank, 1994.

———. *Assessing Aid: What Works, What Doesn't, and Why.* Washington, D.C.: World Bank, 1998.

World Commission on Environment and Development. *Our Common Future.* Oxford and New York: Oxford University Press, 1987.

Articles and Reports

Development Assistance Committee of the Organization for Economic Cooperation and Development. *Development Cooperation Report.* Paris: OECD, various years.

European Network on Debt and Development (Eurodad). "Overview of the HIPC Initiative," http://www.eurodad.org/1debts/analyses/general/hipcdiagram.pdf.

Faber, Mike. "Evaluating Development Aid: Issues, Problems, and Solutions." *Journal of Development Studies* 37, no. 4 (April 2000): 181.

Hashemi, Syed M, Sidney Schuler, and Ann Riley. "Rural Credit Programs and Women's Empowerment in Bangladesh." *World Development,* April 1996.

Oxfam International. "Debt Relief for Tanzania: An Opportunity for a Better Future." Position Paper, April 1998, http://www.oxfam.org.uk/policy/papers/tanzdebt/index.htm.

———. "Oxfam International Submission to the Heavily Indebted Poor Country (HIPC) Debt Review." 1998, http://www.oxfam.org.uk/policy/papers/hipc/hipcreview.htm.

Sachs, Jeffrey. "What's Good for the Poor Is Good for America." *Economist,* 14 July 2001, 32.

Schuurman, Frans J. "Paradigms Lost, Paradigms Regained? Development Studies in the Twenty-First Century." *Third World Quarterly* 21, no. 1 (February 2000): 7.

Speth, James G. "The Plight of the Poor: The United States Must Increase Development Aid." *Foreign Affairs* 78, no. 3 (May–June 1999): 13.

United Nations Development Programme. *Human Development Report.* New York and Oxford: Oxford University Press for the UNDP, various years.

U.S. Agency for International Development. "Asia and the Near East Overview," Fiscal Year 2001 Congressional Budget Justification, http://www.usaid.gov/pubs/bj2001/ane/.

———. "Bangladesh Country Report, 2001: Budget Justification," http://www.usaid.gov/regions/ane/newpages/one_pagers/ban01a.htm.

———. "Tanzania Country Report, 2001: Budget Justification," http://www.usaid.gov/regions/afr/tanzania.html.

World Bank. *Global Development Finance.* Washington, D.C.: World Bank, various years. Also available on CD-ROM.

———. *World Development Indicators.* Washington, D.C.: World Bank, various years. Also available on CD-ROM.

———. *World Development Report.* Washington, D.C.: World Bank, various years.

Web Sites

Bellanet—Global Development Connection
http://www.bellanet.org

Drop the Debt Campaign
http://www.dropthedebt.org/index.html

Electronic Development and Environment Information System (ELDIS)
http://www.ids.ac.uk/eldis

Global Development Network, World Bank
http://www.gdnet.org/index.htm

Highly Indebted Poor Countries Initiative, World Bank
http://www.worldbank.org/hipc

International Development Goals
http://www.developmentgoals.org

International Development Network
http://www.idn.org

One World Online
http://www.oneworld.org

ReliefNet
http://www.reliefnet.org

United Nations Development Watch
http://www.undp.org/devwatch

USAID Development Links
http://www.usaid.gov/about/resources

Virtual Library on International Development
http://w3.acdi-cida.gc.ca/virtual.nsf

Women Watch
http://www.un.org/womenwatch

World Directory of Development Organizations and Programs
http://www.energ.polimi.it/development

Documents

1. Our Common Future (The Brundtland Report)

World Commission on Environment and Development, 1987

Extract

Sustainable Development

Humanity has the ability to make development sustainable—to ensure that it meets the needs of the present without compromising the ability of future generations to meet their own needs. The concept of sustainable development does imply limits—not absolute limits but limitations imposed by the present state of technology and social organization on environmental resources and by the ability of the biosphere to absorb the effects of human activities. But technology and social organization can be both managed and improved to make way for a new era of economic growth. The Commission believes that widespread poverty is no longer inevitable. Poverty is not only an evil in itself, but sustainable development requires meeting the basic needs of all and extending to all the opportunity to fulfill their aspirations for a better life. A world in which poverty is endemic will always be prone to ecological and other catastrophes.

2. The Sixteen Decisions of the Grameen Bank

Available at http://www.grameen-info.org/bank/the16.html.

1. We shall follow and advance the four principles of Grameen Bank—discipline, unity, courage and hard work—in all walks of our lives.
2. Prosperity we shall bring to our families.
3. We shall not live in dilapidated houses. We shall repair our houses and work towards constructing new houses at the earliest.
4. We shall grow vegetables all the year round. We shall eat plenty of them and sell the surplus.
5. During the plantation seasons, we shall plant as many seedlings as possible.
6. We shall plan to keep our families small. We shall minimize our expenditures. We shall look after our health.
7. We shall educate our children and ensure that they can earn to pay for their education.
8. We shall always keep our children and the environment clean.
9. We shall build and use pit-latrines.
10. We shall drink water from tubewells. If it is not available, we shall boil water or use alum.
11. We shall not take any dowry at our sons' weddings, neither shall we give any dowry at our daughter's wedding. We shall keep our centre free from the curse of dowry. We shall not practice child marriage.
12. We shall not inflict any injustice on anyone, neither shall we allow anyone to do so.
13. We shall collectively undertake bigger investments for higher incomes.
14. We shall always be ready to help each other. If anyone is in difficulty, we shall all help him or her.
15. If we come to know of any breach of discipline in any centre, we shall all go there and help restore discipline.
16. We shall introduce physical exercise in all our centres. We shall take part in all social activities collectively.

ENERGY

Richard B. Norgaard

Energy is integral to human well-being, but it is also central to global political and environmental problems. Energy heats and lights dwellings, fuels the transportation of people and products, and powers industry and modern agriculture. Problems exist, however, concerning the ways in which societies produce this vital resource. Many nations depend on the Middle East, a politically unstable region, for their oil. The mining and transport of fossil fuels causes water pollution and limits other uses of the land. Fossil fuel conversion and combustion cause air pollution and drive the long-term problem of global warming. While many people equate ever-increasing energy use with the progress of humankind and conquering nature, others are actively seeking ways to continue improving human well-being, especially that of the poor, while using less energy and more environmentally sensitive sources of energy.

Historical Background and Development

Life evolved on Earth some 3 billion years ago. As plants captured energy from the sun through photosynthesis, life flourished, building organic matter from carbon in the atmosphere and increasing the air's oxygen content, making the globe suitable for animal life. Through various geological processes, some carbon became fossil fuels—coal, oil, and natural gas.

People evolved on Earth some 3 million years ago. For most of human history, people have used energy from the sun. Plants photosynthesize the sun's energy to combine carbon from the air and other matter from the soil, and humans exploited this process by turning the plants into food for eating, fuel for cooking, and fodder for livestock used for plowing and transport. The wind, generated by the differential warming of Earth's surface by the sun, powered sailboats and mills for grinding grain. Water wheels tapped into the hydrologic cycle, which is also driven by the sun.

Beginning only about two centuries ago, people began to switch from the renewable energy sources produced by the sun's energy and to exploit past flows of the sun's energy stored in the form of fossil hydrocarbons. Europeans, starting with the British, tapped into coal after their forests were too depleted to provide adequate fuel. Later, Americans developed petroleum resources. Initially, fossil fuels were inconvenient, but they eventually proved superior to other forms of energy because of the far higher amount of energy they produced per kilogram compared to wood. This recent transition vastly accelerated and transformed economic activity, redefined the nature of power, improved food supplies through the mechanization of agriculture and the application of synthetic fertilizers, facilitated population growth in the developing world, and improved material well-being overall. Tapping into fossil fuels, however, has also produced, or is closely associated with, many if not most of the environmental problems of today: air, soil, and water pollution; congestion, long commutes, and urban sprawl; and the expansion of human activity into fragile ecosystems and the related loss of biodiversity. Burning fossil fuels is also rapidly reversing the earth's biogeochemical development by releasing carbon accumulated in fossil fuels back into the atmosphere, causing global warming, and threatening human well-being and all life over the long term (see Document 1 and BIODIVERSITY, FRAGILE ECOSYSTEMS, GLOBAL WARMING, and POLLUTION).

Current Status

Current research, policies, and programs in the energy field are aimed at increasing access to energy sources, ensuring the availability of supplies in the future, and reducing harmful environmental impacts, including the emission of the greenhouse gases that drive global warming. These research and policy efforts are being undertaken by a variety of entities, including private enterprise, governments, and international governmental organizations. Some endeavors have been more productive than others, and much work remains to be done.

Research

Toward the end of the 1990s energy use worldwide approached the equivalent of 10 billion metric tons of oil, or about 1.6 tons per capita, according to the *World Energy Assessment, 2000.* Fossil fuels, which are used mostly in the industrialized world, accounted for nearly 80 percent of all energy consumed; hydropower, nuclear power, and modern technologies for utilizing geothermal, wind, and biomass energy were also important, amounting to slightly more than 10 percent of all energy consumed; wood and other forms of biomass played a critical role for cooking and heating in the nonindustrialized world and provided nearly 10 percent of the total energy used (see Table 1). Supplies of coal are fairly well distributed geographically, but most of the world's oil reserves are concentrated in the Middle East. Because most oil is consumed in Europe, Japan, and the United States but is concentrated in the Middle East, oil is the most important item in world trade (see WORLD TRADE).

As dependence on fossil fuels increased during the twentieth century, many observers became concerned that available supplies might be rapidly depleted. Numerous studies comparing existing reserves to consumption levels indicate that coal is relatively abundant, but oil and gas supplies are limited to a few decades. Because reserves are defined as deposits with an existing mine or well, a more realistic picture is provided by comparing resources that are thought to exist—rather than known reserves—to projected increases in demand. Such a comparison suggests that about a century of oil supplies exists, two centuries of natural gas, and ten centuries of coal (see Table 1). Burning all of this fossil fuel using current technology, however, would release vast amounts of carbon dioxide into the atmosphere and cause excessive global warming, which is a real concern among researchers and policymakers.

Access to energy, which is highly unequal between rich countries and poor countries, is another serious issue that raises economic, social, and political concerns. According to *World Resources, 2000–2001,* published by the World Resources Institute, the United States consumes the equivalent of nearly 9 tons of energy per capita, while Vietnam consumes less than 0.2 tons per capita. Greater access to energy is seen as essential to economic growth in the less developed world.

Policies and Programs

Augmenting the supply of energy has been a key theme of developing countries and development agencies (see DEVELOPMENT AID). The World Bank, other multilateral development agencies, and private banks from the industrialized countries dedicate a significant portion of their loan portfolio to financing the construction of large dams for hydropower production, the construction of electricity transmission systems, and development of other aspects of the energy sectors of developing countries. Nongovernmental organizations have taken the lead in the development and transfer of technologies utilizing renewable resources of energy, including improved stoves to reduce indoor pollution and the use of small hydro facilities, photovoltaic panels, and wind turbines for generating electricity for villages beyond transmission grids.

Access to energy in developing countries has historically been facilitated by subsidy policies and programs that made energy available at below market prices. Energy subsidies, which reduce the costs of purchasing energy, were seen as a way to promote development of industry and commerce as well as a way to assist the poorest households. Low prices promoted greater use, but not necessarily more rapid development, and the low prices could only be maintained by collecting taxes elsewhere in the economy to offset the subsidies. For countries with petroleum resources, revenues from the export of oil have played an important role in economic development, though greater exports have sometimes reduced the local availability of energy.

Since the 1990s international financial and development agencies have encouraged developing countries to restructure their energy sectors to raise prices to world levels. State-owned electricity companies that historically charged low rates are being privatized in many developing countries, driving electricity prices up and leading to consumer protests. Gasoline is now being sold at world market prices rather than those reflecting the local cost of production. Thus energy is now being priced as an exportable product, rather than as a means to promote energy-intensive development or to help the poor. For countries with active energy industries, petroleum exports, although an important source of development revenues, have also provided an important source of economic power to political elites that in some cases have distorted development.

Like developing countries, the United States has long subsidized the availability of fossil fuels through tax advantages provided largely at the mining phase. Some of these subsidies were phased out after the energy crises of the 1970s, but others remain. European nations, in contrast, tax fossil fuels and subsidize renewable sources of energy to a greater extent than in the United States. Denmark and Germany are aggressively investing in wind and other renewable energy technologies for producing electricity and intend to produce a significant portion of their electricity through renewable energy sources over the next decade. Other European nations are also moving in this direction. While France is highly dependent on nuclear power and content with how it is managing the risks associated with it, many European nations now prohibit the building of additional nuclear power plants and plan to phase out existing ones. Western Europe is also actively assisting Eastern European nations to replace or improve their aging Soviet-era nuclear power plants and is pressuring the United States to move away from fossil fuels and toward renewable sources of energy to ameliorate climate change.

The developed nations are taking the lead in efforts to assure the availability of energy for the future, although it must be kept in mind that the developed nations are also consuming the vast majority of energy resources. Research to reduce the cost of drilling for oil and gas and mining for coal, as well as to reduce the environmental damage of these activities, is largely being undertaken by private firms based in the industrialized countries. Such research does help lower the cost of developing fossil fuel from existing and new resources for future use. It can also facilitate access to lower-quality petroleum resources beyond the Middle East and thereby limit the economic vulnerability of oil-importing nations to the political instabilities of that region.

The promise of reducing the environmental impact of fossil energy use is being realized through research on pollution control technologies and through pollution control policies. Sulfur and soot emissions from the burning of coal are being reduced through better power plant design and, in some cases, through processes that clean the coal before it is burned. Research is also under way to develop technologies to decarbonize fossil fuels. Decarbonization reduces the proportion of carbon to hydrogen, making petroleum more like natural gas and reducing natural gas to hydrogen, thereby reducing the local environmental impact of combustion. The real interest, however, is in the next step: the sequestration of the carbon in natural gas or petroleum fields or the deep ocean so that the carbon is not released into the atmosphere as carbon dioxide, further contributing to global warming. This technological path is likely to play some role in ameliorating global warming and at the same time support the continued use of fossil fuels and associated technologies. It will also sustain the economic structure and political power of the energy industry.

Some energy companies and automobile manufacturers are actively exploring the potential of fuel cell technologies. Fuel cells combine hydrogen with oxygen in a process that results in electricity and water as the only waste products. They have provided electricity for spacecraft and are now being used to supply backup electricity for hospitals. Fuel cells can be scaled down, albeit currently at some cost, to generate electricity to power electric motors for vehicles and to do so with no pollution from the vehicle. This, however, requires the development of technologies to safely store highly compressed hydrogen on board vehicles. Hydrogen is more flammable than gasoline, so a hydrogen tank must be able to withstand severe crashes. Another concern about fuel cell technology is that energy in the form of electricity is needed to convert water to hydrogen, or to decarbonize natural gas to create hydrogen, for use in the fuel cell. To the extent that the energy sources used to produce this hydrogen are a source of pollution themselves, the advantages of fuel cells are diminished. For this reason, many renewable energy advocates argue that electricity from solar and wind energy should be used to produce hydrogen, thereby resulting in little pollution. Producing hydrogen for storage in fuel cells also offers a form of energy storage that offsets the periodic nature of the availability of sun and wind. There is also interest in technologies for producing hydrogen from gasoline on board vehicles. On-board hydrogen production from fossil fuels would still increase the efficiency of fossil fuel use and produce less pollution than conventional internal combustion engines, though not so much as larger scale, more centralized methods of producing hydrogen.

Public expenditures on energy research have complemented private research on technologies for fossil fuel development. Public funding is aimed at increasing energy efficiency, developing nuclear energy, and reducing the costs of renewable technologies. According to the 1997 report of the President's Committee of Advisors on Science and Technology, the U.S. Department of Energy spent $1.3 billion on energy research during 1997, with about 28 percent going to fossil fuel technologies, 29 percent to increasing energy efficiency, 21 percent to nuclear power, and 21 percent to renewable sources of energy. The report also reveals, however, that public expenditures for energy research overall in the United States had declined substantially during the last quarter of the twentieth century.

The production of electricity from nuclear energy has been plagued by high costs, safety concerns, and problems associated with the long-term management of radioactive waste. Nuclear energy's future remains cloudy. On the one hand, nuclear power advocates argue that the production of electricity through nuclear energy does not directly produce greenhouse gases, though there are some produced indirectly in plant construction and the mining, processing, and management of nuclear fuels. Advocates also argue that the new generation of nuclear technologies is less expensive and safer. Detractors, on the other hand, argue that the problem of long-term waste storage—finding safe and convenient ways and acceptable places to store the dangerous byproducts of nuclear power processes—must be resolved before new plants are constructed. Many are also concerned that a well-planned terrorist attack on a nuclear plant might result in the release of radioactive materials that could cause large numbers of deaths and contaminate wide areas for years.

Market approaches to reaching environmental goals are increasingly being advocated. Sulfur emissions from electricity generated from coal are being controlled in the United States through least-cost policies that fix the amount of sulfur that can be emitted from all power plants but allow emissions permits to be traded. Power plants that can reduce sulfur emissions for the least cost therefore are able to sell permits to those plants that would otherwise have to reduce their emissions at considerably higher costs. It is likely that global greenhouse gas emissions will be limited at least cost through a system whereby carbon emission permits are assigned to each nation. States that can control their emissions relatively cheaply will be able to sell some of their permits to nations that can control emissions only at excessively higher cost.

To reach specified goals of electricity production from renewable resources at least cost, many U.S. states have adopted tradable obligation programs known as renewables, which are portfolio standards comparable to tradable permit programs. Producers of electricity from renewable sources sell electricity to the power grid—the high-voltage, long-distance transmission lines that deliver electricity from power plants to local distribution systems—and renewable energy "credits" to wholesale or retail distributors of electricity. Distributors of electricity compete to purchase credits, and each distributor must hold a number of credits in proportion to its total electricity sales.

Because energy is so important, energy systems have long been a target of terrorists (see TERRORISM). Electricity grids in developing countries have been shut down by explosives detonated at the base of transmission towers. Nuclear power plants and petroleum refineries in the industrialized world are considered likely targets. The future of fossil fuel decarbonization and centralized hydrogen production for fuel cells is also darkened by concern over terrorism. The more cost-effective facilities will probably be large, and therefore inviting targets. Hence the threat of terrorism complements other arguments for the decentralization of energy facilities. Decentralization favors renewable energy technologies that tend to be comprised of large numbers of relatively small units, even small units on consumers' sites. Electricity can also be produced using small-scale natural gas–fired generators located close to their markets.

Regional Summaries

Energy use varies widely across regions (and among countries within regions) due to differences in levels of economic development and the availability of particular forms of energy (see map, p. 140). Asia and the Pacific islands, Europe, and North America are energy-importing regions, while the others are energy exporting regions, with the Middle East and North Africa being the most significant. Although income inequalities between nations are increasing slowly,

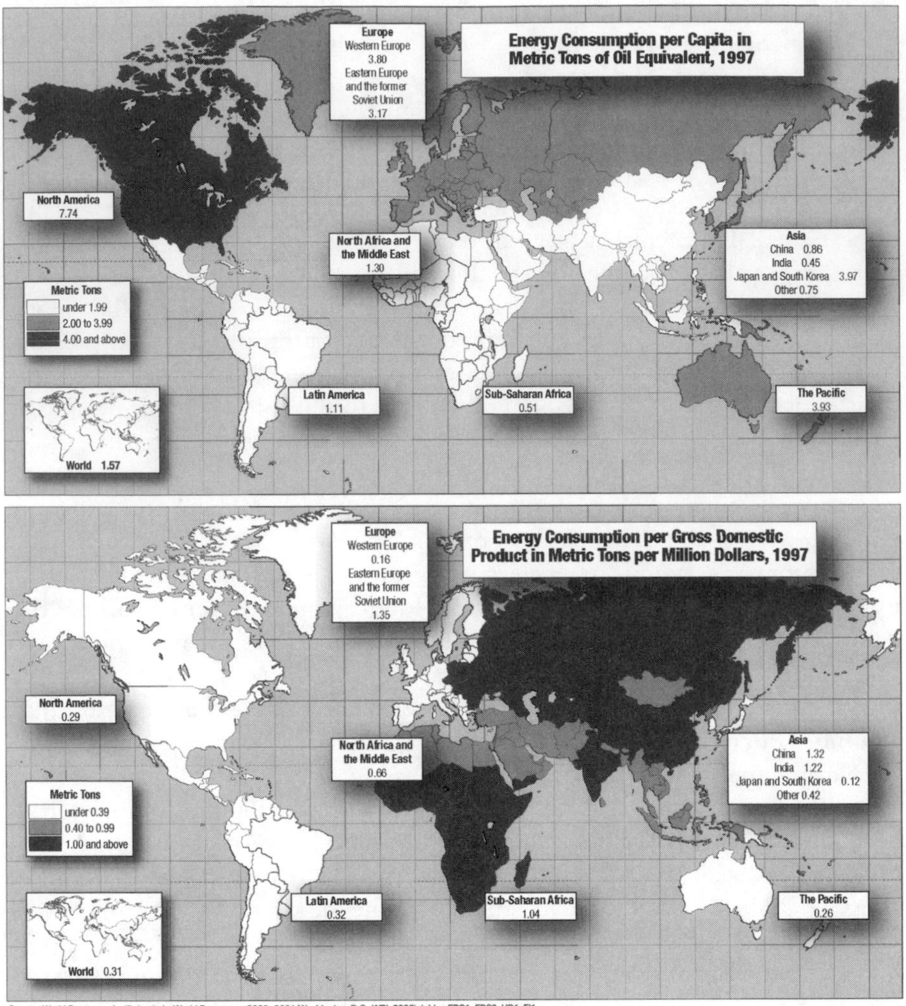

Source: World Resources Institute et al., *World Resources, 2000–2001* (Washington, D.C.: WRI, 2000), tables ERC1, ERC2, HD1, EI1.
Note: For some countries (Afghanistan, Cuba, Iran, Iraq, Libya, Myanmar, etc.), the gross domestic product data are missing from the original source; in these cases, the GDP was approximated by the author.
GDP per capita is exchange rate–based, 1995 U.S. dollars. If purchasing power parity were used, GDP per capita for Japan and South Korea would be about 40% less, while the former Soviet Union's would be about twice as high and China's about three times as high.

disparities between the rich and poor within nations has widened the gap in energy use between the richest people and the poorest people overall (see INCOME INEQUALITY). See Table 2 and its sources for the information presented below.

North America

North America was a net exporter of energy for the first half of the twentieth century, but became a net importer in the second half of the century, as its reserves were depleted. The region now imports about 7 percent of its total energy needs, including more than 60 percent of the petroleum it uses. What additional petroleum resources remain in North America are largely in the Arctic regions of the continent and offshore. Further petroleum extraction and development of abundant coal resources are advocated to increase energy independence, but at the same time these measures are strongly opposed by environmentalists. Energy use based on gross domestic product is higher than in Western Europe due to policies that have subsidized energy consumption and facilitated the use of cars rather than public transit and due to the greater distances between cities. Not only is the number of automobiles per thousand people notably higher in North America, but the cars are notably larger and fuel efficiency lower. For these reasons, emissions of carbon dioxide per capita are extremely high in the region.

Latin America

Latin America is a net exporter of energy, with nearly all of it traded to North America. The number of energy-exporting countries, however, is small: Ecuador, Mexico, and Venezuela. Venezuela, a major exporter since the 1950s, lived off its oil earnings rather than investing it in educational, agricultural, and industrial development. All Latin American countries have some hydropower and wood energy resources, but those without significant quantities of oil have sacrificed trade earnings to import additional energy to promote development. By the late 1960s and early 1970s, development was quite rapid. High oil prices during the 1970s and early 1980s, however, drove these countries deep into debt, drastically slowing and at times reversing development during the 1980s and into the 1990s. Periodic economic crises since the 1990s have been confounded with energy problems.

Europe

The eastern and western parts of Europe differ widely in economic output and energy use. Western Europe, which imports most of the fossil fuels it uses, has long sought energy efficiency through high taxes. (Charging elevated taxes on the purchase of energy creates incentives for consumers to conserve energy.) According to a 1998 LTI Research Group report, several key European countries are moving aggressively toward renewable energy for electricity production. For these reasons, per capita fossil fuel use and emissions of carbon dioxide are considerably less than half that of North Americans, who have a comparable standard of living. The Soviet Union's economy was run on extremely inefficient energy technologies, and the new economies of the former republics have still not attained the same levels of production as under the old economy, making it difficult to invest in energy-efficient technologies. Taken together, the former Soviet republics are net exporters of energy, that is, they export more than they import. Russia has tremendous amounts of coal and natural gas, as well as considerable quantities of petroleum. Its per capita energy use, however, is comparable to that of Western Europe even though per capita income is about one-tenth as high.

North Africa and the Middle East

The nations with the greatest reserves of petroleum are in the Middle East and North Africa. Much of these nations' income, accumulated wealth, and hence distribution of political power is directly related to oil. Multinational oil companies, many of them based in the West, and oil-consuming nations have collaborated in the establishment and maintenance of authoritarian governments in this region. The oil-producing countries founded the Organization of Petroleum Exporting Countries (OPEC) in the 1950s, and by the late 1960s had begun to limit the amount of oil exported in order to raise prices. Some governments have broken from and are hostile to Western development and policy in the region. The states that have not broken with the West are in some instances balancing their dependence on the West against popular animosity toward the ideas, attitudes, and lifestyles of Western nations and of the authoritarian regimes themselves. Indeed, financial resources derived indirectly from petroleum exports are in some instances financing activities against the West.

Sub-Saharan Africa

Sub-Saharan Africa includes many of the poorest countries of the world and has the lowest energy consumption of any region. The exception is South Africa, parts of which are very well developed and have relatively high rates of energy consumption. Sub-Saharan Africa's population density is relatively low, which, when combined with the low level of development, means that only those people who live in major cities have access to electricity from a grid. The reliability of the grids, however, is notoriously low. Transportation infrastructures in the region are also poorly developed. One contradictory outcome of the poor energy and transportation infrastructures and greater distances that need to be traveled is that high-tech solar photovoltaic panels and air travel play a relatively greater role in the region than in many other developing areas, though only the relatively rich can afford to take advantage of them.

Asia and the Pacific

Asia is home to more than half the world's population and some of the richest and poorest nations. Asia is a net importer of energy, but energy policies vary widely across countries. India, which has a very low per capita income, consumes less than half a ton of energy, measured in oil equivalent per capita. It imports 12 percent of its total energy, but considerably more than half of its petroleum. Japan and South Korea, with very high per capita incomes, consume about four tons of oil equivalent per capita and import more than 80 percent of their energy. Energy consumption per capita in the very poor countries of Bangladesh and Vietnam is approximately one one-hundredth of Japan's. Controversies have arisen over the Three Gorges Dam project in China (see FRESHWATER) and over the Narmada project in India, because in each case the reservoirs of the hydropower dams will flood areas in which millions of people live.

Australia and New Zealand are two well-developed economies with small populations. They use large quantities of fossil fuels per capita and have proportionately high carbon dioxide emissions. Australia is a significant producer of coal, most of which it exports. Although New Zealand has well-developed hydropower resources, neither it nor Australia has made much effort to shift from fossil fuels and toward renewable resources. In addition, neither country has nuclear power.

Data

Table 1 Worldwide Primary Energy Consumption, Developed Reserves, and Estimated Resources, 1998

Resource	Primary Energy (billion tons of oil equivalent)	Portion of World Resources (%)	Years of Existing Reserves at Current Consumption Levels	Years of Estimated Resources at Current Consumption Levels	Years of Estimated Resources with Exponential Growth in Consumption
Fossil Fuels	7.63	79.6			
Oil	3.39	35.3	45	~200	95
Natural gas	2.02	21.1	69	~400	230
Coal	2.22	23.1	452	~1,500	1,000
Renewables	1.33	13.9	Renewable		
Large hydro	0.21	2.2	Renewable		
Traditional biomass	0.91	9.5	Renewable		
"New" renewables[a]	0.21	2.2	Renewable		
Nuclear[b]	0.62	6.5	50	>300[c]	
Total	9.58	100.0			

Source: Adapted from United Nations Development Programme, United Nations Department of Economic and Social Affairs, and World Energy Council, *World Energy Assessment, 2000: Energy and the Challenge of Sustainability* (New York: UNDP, 2000).

[a] Includes modern biomass, small hydropower, geothermal energy, wind energy, solar energy, and marine energy.

[b] Converted from electricity produced to fuels consumed assuming 33% thermal efficiency of power plants.

[c] Based on a once-through uranium fuel cycle, excluding thorium and low concentration uranium from seawater. The uranium resource base is effectively 60 times larger if fast breeder reactors are used.

Table 2 Energy and Economic Statistics by Major Regions, 1997 (except where noted otherwise)

Region	Energy Consumption (millions of metric tons of oil equivalent)	Energy Production (millions of metric tons of oil equivalent)	Energy Consumption per Capita (metric tons of oil equivalent per capita)	Energy Consumption per GDP (metric tons per million dollars)[a]	Auto-mobiles per 1,000 People, 1996	Carbon Dioxide Emissions per Capita (metric tons per capita)
Asia[b]	2,959	2,321	0.87	0.33	23	2.3
China	1,099	1,097	0.86	1.32	3	2.7
India	461	405	0.45	1.22	4	1.1
Japan and South Korea	691	131	3.97	0.12	313	9.2
Other	708	688	0.75	0.42	17	1.8

Table 2 Energy and Economic Statistics by Major Regions, 1997 (except where noted otherwise) (*continued*)

Region	Energy Consumption (millions of metric tons of oil equivalent)	Energy Production (millions of metric tons of oil equivalent)	Energy Consumption per Capita (metric tons of oil equivalent per capita)	Energy Consumption per GDP (metric tons per million dollars)[a]	Auto-mobiles per 1,000 People, 1996	Carbon Dioxide Emissions per Capita (metric tons per capita)
Europe	2,554	2,222	3.51	0.25	289	8.4
Western Europe	1,471	991	3.80	0.16	444	8.3
Eastern Europe and the former Soviet Union	1,083	1,231	3.17	1.35	113	8.5
Middle East and North Africa	526	1,497	1.30	0.66	43	3.8
Sub-Saharan Africa	326	573	0.51	1.04	14	0.9
North America[c]	2,400	2,047	7.74	0.29	484	19.1
Latin America	578	789	1.11	0.32	44	2.6
Pacific[d]	118	213	3.93	0.26	364	11.8
World	95,223	966,533	1.57	0.31	84	4.2

Source: World Resources Institute et al., *World Resources, 2000–2001* (Washington, D.C.: WRI, 2000), tables ERC1, ERC2, HD1, EI1.

Note: The differences between total production and consumption are due to net changes in storage, energy used during transport, and accounting discrepancies.

[a] GDP is exchange rate–based, 1995 U.S. dollars. If purchasing power parity were used, GDP per capita for Japan and South Korea would be about 40% less while the former Soviet Union's would be about twice as high and China's about three times as high.

[b] Excludes the former Soviet Union, and the Middle East and includes the Indonesian archipelago.

[c] Excludes Mexico.

[d] Includes Australia, Fiji, New Zealand, Papua New Guinea, and the Solomon Islands.

Case Study—Nigeria

Petroleum was discovered in Nigeria, the most populated country in Africa, in 1958. During the 1960s numerous multinational oil companies began to develop Nigeria's offshore and onshore oil fields. By the 1970s Nigeria had become a significant exporter of oil. According to Jedrzej Georg Frynas, Nigeria was exporting 2 million barrels a day, making it the sixth largest exporter. By the late 1990s, Frynas reports, approximately half of Nigeria's gross domestic product came from oil and natural gas, and more than 95 percent of its foreign exchange earnings came from petroleum.

Beyond petroleum extraction, however, there has been little development in Nigeria's oil industry. The government has not maintained the refineries and therefore has had to import refined petroleum products. The national oil company, which works with multinational firms, provided gasoline and kerosene to Nigerians for below world market prices. This, however, promoted as much waste as development. Most of the wealth generated by oil revenues became concentrated among a few people at the top of the authoritarian government, and additional revenues were allocated to support the strongest military force in Africa.

Most Nigerians are poor, but the Ogoni people, the ethnic group who live in the oil-producing region, are especially so. Air and water pollution, combined with the fact that the Ogoni benefit little from petroleum extraction, led to a series of protests and sabotage operations in the early 1990s. Nine rebels and activists were executed in 1995. The national and multinational oil companies were accused of assisting the government in putting down these local insurrections. The international community protested and has put considerable pressure on the government to reform Nigeria's political system.

Poverty in Nigeria has created other problems as well. Pipelines delivering refined products are frequently "tapped" by poor people, who then sell the gasoline and kerosene they collect locally. In 1998 some seven hundred Nigerians were burned to death when products spilled from tapped pipelines ignited. In 1999 a constitution was adopted, democracy established, and efforts were initiated to correct decades of limited or nonexistent social and economic development efforts. The oil companies have been spending a share of their earnings on community development. The national oil company has been privatized, raising local prices and causing some protest, but overall the situation has begun to improve.

Biographical Sketches

Sir John Browne was appointed chief executive officer of British Petroleum, one of the foremost international oil companies in the world, in 1994. In May 1997 he broke ranks with the rest of the petroleum industry and argued that climate change is real and serious and that switching toward renewable energy is the solution to reversing, or at least slowing, the effects of global warming.

Jose Goldemberg is a physicist and former rector of the University of São Paulo. He served as Brazilian secretary of science and technology from 1992 to 1996. He has campaigned against nuclear power and for the development of renewable energy sources and participated in numerous international energy and climate change assessments.

Amory Lovins is an activist inventor and the author of numerous books on energy. He has worked to promote the development of a super-energy-efficient "hyper-car." Lovins is also the co-founder of the Rocky Mountain Institute, an organization that researches energy efficiency, renewable energy, and corporate incentives to be environmentally responsible.

Ralph Nader is a lawyer who helped develop the consumer advocacy movement in the United States. Using various platforms, including a run for the U.S. presidency in

2000, Nader has brought many issues to the forefront of U.S. political discourse. He has argued that energy conservation and the development of renewable energy resources could help the United States disentangle itself from authoritarian governments in the Middle East.

Ahmed Zaki Yamani is a lawyer, politician, and Harvard-educated economist who served as Saudi minister of petroleum and mineral resources from 1962 to 1986. During his tenure as minister, he helped moderate the policies of the Organization of Petroleum Exporting Countries toward the United States while also reducing Saudi oil production to keep oil prices from plummeting.

Directory

American Petroleum Institute, 1220 L Street NW, Washington, DC 20005-4070. Email: pr@api.org, Web: http://www.api.org
Organization that collects information for the petroleum industry and represents its interests to the U.S. government

Greenpeace International, 176 Keizersgracht, 1016 Amsterdam, Netherlands. Telephone: (31) 20 523 6222, Email: greenpeace.usa@wdc.greenpeace.org, Web: http://www.greenpeace.org
Membership organization that aims to raise awareness of environmental degradation

Institute for Energy and Environmental Research, 6935 Laurel Avenue, Suite 204, Takoma Park, MD 20912. Telephone: (301) 270-5500, Email: ieer@ieer.org, Web: http://www.ieer.org
Nongovernmental research institute promoting the democratization of science with a strong research program on nuclear waste

International Association of Oil and Gas Producers, 25/28 Old Burlington Street, London W1S 3AN, United Kingdom. Telephone: (44) 20 7292 0600. Email: llewellyn@ogp.org.uk., Web: http://www.ogp.org.uk
Organization that represents the perspective of producers of oil and gas to international agencies

World Coal Institute, Cambridge House, 180 Upper Richmond Road, Putney, London SW15 2SH, United Kingdom. Telephone: (44) 20 8246 6611, Email: info@wci-coal.com, Web: http://www.wci-coal.com
Organization that represents the perspective of the coal industry at international venues

World Resources Institute, 10 G Street NE, Suite 800, Washington, DC 20002. Telephone: (202) 729-7600, Email: front@wri.org, Web: http://www.wri.org
Nongovernmental organization that researches and disseminates information on resources and the environment

Further Research

Books

Frynas, Jedrzej Georg. *Oil in Nigeria: Conflict and Litigation between Oil Companies and Village Communities.* Piscataway, N.J.: Transaction Publishers, 1999.

Nakienovi, Nebojŝa, Arnulf Grübler, and Alan McDonald, eds. *Global Energy Perspectives.* Cambridge: Cambridge University Press, 1998.

Schneider, Stephen H., and Randi Londer. *The Coevolution of Climate and Life.* San Francisco: Sierra Club Books, 1984.

United Nations Development Programme, United Nations Department of Economic and Social Affairs, and World Energy Council. *World Energy Assessment, 2000: Energy and the Challenge of Sustainability.* New York: UNDP, 2000.

World Resources Institute et al. *World Resources, 2000–2001.* Washington, D.C., 2000.

Reports

LTI Research Group, ed. *Long-Term Integration of Renewable Energy Sources into the European Energy System.* Heidelberg: Physica-Verlag, 1998.

President's Committee of Advisors on Science and Technology, Energy Research and Development Panel. *Federal Energy Research and Development Challenges for the Twenty-first Century.* Washington, D.C.: Executive Office of the President, 1997.

U.S. Environmental Protection Agency. *The United States Experience with Economic Incentives for Protecting the Environment.* Washington, D.C.: EPA, Office of Policy, Economics, and Innovation, 2001.

Web Sites

Energy Information Administration, U.S. Department of Energy
http://www.eia.doe.gov

International Energy Agency
http://www.iea.org

World Energy Assessment
http://www.undp.org/seed/eap/activities/wea

World Energy Council
http://www.worldenergy.org

Document

1. Climate Change

Sir John Browne, Group Chief Executive Officer, British Petroleum
(BP America), Commencement Speech, Stanford University, 19 May 1997

The full text is available at http://www.wbcsd.ch/newscenter/speeches/archives/ARCClimate.

Extracts

A new age demands a fresh perspective of the nature of society and responsibility.

The passing of some of the old divisions reminds us we are all citizens of one world, and we must take shared responsibility for its future, and for its sustainable development. . . .

I believe we've now come to an important moment in our consideration of the environment. It is a moment when because of the shared interest I talked about, we need to go beyond analysis to seek solutions and to take action. It is a moment for change and for a rethinking of corporate responsibility.

A year ago, the Second Report of the Inter-Governmental Panel on Climate Change was published. That report and the discussion which has continued since its publication, shows that there is mounting concern about two stark facts.

The concentration of carbon dioxide in the atmosphere is rising, and the temperature of the earth's surface is increasing. . . .

The prediction of the IPCC is that over the next century temperatures might rise by a further 1 to 3.5 degrees centigrade, and that sea levels might rise by between 15 and 95 centimetres. Some of that impact is probably unavoidable, because it results from current emissions.

Those are wide margins of error, and there remain large elements of uncertainty—about cause and effect . . and even more importantly about the consequences.

But it would be unwise and potentially dangerous to ignore the mounting concern.

The time to consider the policy dimensions of climate change is not when the link between greenhouse gases and climate change is conclusively proven . . . but when the possibility cannot be discounted and is taken seriously by the society of which we are part.

We in BP have reached that point.

It is an important moment for us. A moment when analysis demonstrates the need for action and solutions.

To be absolutely clear—we must now focus on what can and what should be done, not because we can be certain climate change is happening, but because the possibility can't be ignored. . . .

How should we respond to this mixture of concern and uncertainty? . . .

As I see it, there are two kinds of actions that can be taken in response to the challenge of climate change.

The first kind of action would be dramatic, sudden and surely wrong. Actions which sought, at a stroke, drastically to restrict carbon emissions or even to ban the use of fossil fuels would be unsustainable because they would crash into the realities of economic growth. They would also be seen as discriminatory—above all in the developing world.

The second kind of action is that of a journey taken in partnership by all those involved. A step by step process involving both action to develop solutions and continuing research that will build knowledge through experience.

BP is committed to this second approach, which matches the agreement reached at Rio based on a balance between the needs of development and environmental protection. The Rio agreements recognise the need for economic development in the developing world. We believe we can contribute to achievement of the right balance by ensuring that we apply the technical innovations we're making on a common basis—everywhere in the world. . . .

Of the world's total carbon dioxide emissions only a small fraction comes from the activities of human beings, but it is that small fraction which might threaten the equilibrium between the much greater flows.

You could think of it as the impact of placing even a small weight on a weighscale which is precisely balanced.

But in preserving the balance we have to be clear where the problem actually lies.

Of the total carbon dioxide emissions caused by burning fossil fuels only 20 percent comes from transportation.

Eighty percent comes from static uses of energy—the energy used in our homes, in industry and in power generation. Of the total 43 percent comes from petroleum. . . .

We have a responsibility to act, and I hope that through our actions we can contribute to the much wider process which is desirable and necessary.

BP accepts that responsibility and we're therefore taking some specific steps:

To control our own emissions
To fund continuing scientific research
To take initiatives for joint implementation
To develop alternative fuels for the long term
And to contribute to the public policy debate in search of the wider global answers to the problem. . . .

More research is needed—on the detail of cause and effect; on the consequences of what appears to be happening, and on the effectiveness of the various actions which can be taken. . . .

We believe that policy debate is important. We support that debate, and we're engaged in it, through the World Business Council on Sustainable Development . . . through the president's own Council here in the United States . . . and in the UK where the government is committed to making significant progress on the subject.

Knowledge in this area is not proprietary, and we will share our expertise openly and freely.

Our instinct is that once clear objectives have been agreed, market-based solutions are more likely to produce innovative and creative responses than an approach based on regulation alone.

Those market-based solutions need to be as wide ranging in scope as possible because this is a global problem which has to be resolved without discrimination and without denying the peoples of the developing world the right to improve their living standards. . . .

To be sustainable, companies need a sustainable world. That means a world where the environmental equilibrium is maintained but also a world whose population can all enjoy the heat, light and mobility which we take for granted and which the oil industry helps to provide. . . .

Nowhere is the need for that sort of social order—at the global level—more important than in this area. The achievement of that has to be our common goal.

EPIDEMICS

Tamara Schuyler

As recently as the late 1960s, health care authorities in the Western Hemisphere were confidently announcing the end of the era of human epidemics, the occurrence of infectious disease in a large number of people in a given community. At the beginning of the twenty-first century, however, it is clear that the end of epidemics is still far off. The last thirty years of the twentieth century witnessed the emergence of newly identified infectious diseases and the reemergence of diseases once thought to be nearly eradicated. Outbreaks of deadly diseases occurred on every continent in the 1990s and at the turn of the century, and drug resistance is becoming an alarming problem worldwide. Halting the spread of epidemics will require altering human behaviors that contribute to disease and cooperating internationally to develop and deliver vaccines and treatments.

Historical Background and Development

Epidemics have been a part of human society throughout history, but their record is likely incomplete. Ancient writers describe events that were probably major epidemics, but in many cases they did not record the information necessary for historians to identify the specific diseases.

One ancient disease that experts have identified with relative certainty is smallpox. Egyptian mummies from 1570 to 1085 B.C. have skin disfigurements that match those caused by smallpox. Analysis of texts written in the thirteenth century B.C. in the Hittite Empire—today's Turkey and northern Syria—indicates that smallpox was widespread in that region. Chinese texts describe a vast epidemic that struck the empire in 243 B.C. Historians believe from the descriptions that the disease was smallpox. A disease that also sounds like smallpox appears in Indian medical texts written before A.D. 400. Historians are confident that smallpox has afflicted communities in many parts of the world throughout human history. In the eighteenth century it became a major cause of death worldwide. In 1798, after two years of experimentation, British physician Edward Jenner introduced an effective smallpox vaccine. After two centuries of worldwide immunization efforts, smallpox was declared eradicated in 1980. Few other diseases have followed a course to complete eradication.

Another epidemic that appears in historical texts is the plague, a tick-borne disease caused by infection with the *Yersinia pestis* bacterium and resulting in massive internal organ destruction and dementia. The plague swept through Europe from the fourteenth to the seventeenth century, killing about 25 million people—one-third of the population—in what became known as the Black Death. In 1894 between 80,000 and 100,000 people in Canton and Hong Kong were killed by the plague before it spread to other countries and killed an estimated 10 million people worldwide.

European conquest of the Americas starting in the fifteenth century led to devastating epidemics among indigenous populations. Explorers and invaders brought smallpox, measles, and other deadly infectious diseases, leaving communities crippled. For instance, in the first fifty years following the arrival of the Spanish in Mexico, the Aztec population decreased from 30 million people to 1.5 million. A major portion of this loss was due to the introduction of new infectious diseases.

Several proposals that infectious disease is caused by microscopic particles or organisms were put forth in the sixteenth and seventeenth centuries, but this "germ theory" of disease was not widely adopted until the second half of the nineteenth century in Europe. Major discoveries that led to the acceptance of germ theory were made by German pathologist Friedrich Henle, French scientist Louis Pasteur, and German physician Robert Koch. In 1885 British physician John Snow performed the first scientific studies of epidemics. Suspecting that cholera in London that year was being transmitted by the handle of a public water pump, he removed the handle and consequently stopped the epidemic. He also showed that a cholera outbreak downstream from London was caused by drinking water from the Thames River that was contaminated with sewage.

In the middle of the nineteenth century transnational cooperation began in the area of epidemics. In 1851 the first International Sanitary Conference was held in Paris to discuss the prevention of infectious diseases spreading from one country to another. In 1902 delegates from across the Americas met in Washington, D.C., to develop strategies for the prevention of yellow fever, plague, cholera, and smallpox. This meeting led to the precursor of the Pan American Health Organization, created in 1949.

When an outbreak of infectious disease afflicts a number of countries at once, health scientists call it a pandemic. Five cholera pandemics occurred in the nineteenth century, starting in India and spreading to many other countries. A cholera pandemic beginning in Indonesia in 1961 spread throughout Asia and the Pacific before moving on to Africa in 1970. Cholera hit Peru in 1991 and spread to several other South and Central American countries, infecting more than 1.2 million people through 1997.

In 1918 a worldwide influenza epidemic killed more than 20 million people, more than twice the number killed during World War I. In 1997 a sudden outbreak in Hong Kong of the "chicken flu" or "bird flu" caused widespread alarm, but it was quickly contained and killed relatively few people. Another modern pandemic is infection by the Ebola virus. Ebola spread through parts of Africa from 1976 into the 1990s, causing a usually deadly hemorrhagic fever, which is associated with the massive destruction of organs and heavy internal bleeding. An outbreak of what became known as Legionnaires' disease struck in Philadelphia in 1977. It was caused by a previously unidentified parasite. Perhaps the most famous modern pandemic is acquired immunodeficiency syndrome (AIDS), caused by the human immunodeficiency virus (HIV), which began with force in 1981 (see AIDS).

Current Status

Infectious diseases are caused by viruses, bacteria, or larger parasites, such as worms or funguses. Transmission can occur in various ways, including by the breath, blood, or other bodily fluids or by a vector, such as a mosquito or tick. According to *Emerging Infectious Diseases from the Global to the Local Perspective,* a publication of the U.S. National Academy of Sciences, there are six illnesses that represent 90 percent of infectious disease deaths worldwide: acute respiratory infection (for example, pneumonia), 3.5 million; AIDS, 2.3 million; diarrheal diseases (caused by a variety of organisms), 2.2 million; tuberculosis (TB), 1.5 million; malaria, 1.1 million; and measles, 0.9 million. Of these six, a preventive vaccine is available only for measles. The organisms that cause tuberculosis and malaria have evolved to include a number of disease-causing strains that are resistant to the most common antibiotics available.

Although the development of vaccines has decreased the number of deaths caused by infectious disease, the World Health Organization (WHO) estimates that in 2001 close to 3 million people could have been spared a host of illnesses had they been immunized. The figures for individual diseases range widely, including estimates as high as 900,000 for hepatitis B and 888,000 for measles. Other estimates include *Hemophilus influenza b* (Hib), 400,000; pertussis (whooping cough), 346,000; neonatal tetanus, 215,000; tetanus, 195,000; yellow fever, 30,000; diphtheria, 5,000; and poliomyelitis, 720.

Research

International research efforts to combat epidemics of infectious diseases are focused on overcoming antibiotic resistance and developing vaccines and pharmaceutical treatments for those diseases that take the largest toll on human life and national economies. Antibiotics combat diseases caused by bacteria, such as malaria and tuberculosis. Antibiotic resistance refers to microbes' ability to change in response to drug treatments. Strains of a disease-causing microbe can evolve to survive in the body even when an infected person is treated with a particular antibiotic. Antibiotic resistance is an increasing threat worldwide, because once a strain of a microbe resistant to drugs spreads, chances of eradicating the disease dwindle (see Table 1).

Although antibiotic resistance is a natural process, certain human behaviors speed its progress. In particular, taking less than the prescribed dose of an antibiotic regimen allows a few microbes to survive and possibly become resistant to the drug. Other problems include prescriptions of insufficient amounts of antibiotics and, conversely, prescription of antibiotics when they are not necessary. These issues are being addressed by education programs at various levels, but there is still a need for new drug development (see Document 1).

The primary difficulty facing drug research efforts is underfunding. The Pharmaceutical Research and Manufacturers of America report in "Pharmaceutical Industry Profile, 2001" that it costs a company about $500 million to develop a drug and bring it to market; in 2000 combined private funding for research and development of treatments for acute respiratory infection, diarrheal diseases, tuberculosis, and malaria was less than this amount. Experts estimate that it takes ten to twenty years to develop a completely new class of antibiotic, and at the beginning of the twenty-first century no drug companies were reporting development of a new class (although development of drugs related to those already on the market was ongoing).

By serving as grant provider and consultant, WHO actively encourages governments and private organizations to fund drug research. WHO's aim is to reduce development costs so that financial risk is minimized and pharmaceutical companies have the incentive to produce and market new drugs. In 1997 WHO, the U.S.-based National Institute of Allergy and Infectious Diseases, and other organizations around the world launched the Multilateral Initiative on Malaria (MIM) to expand research on the disease. MIM's efforts include increasing understanding of the biology of the malaria-causing microbe and its interaction with the mosquitoes that carry it, increasing understanding of the way the microbe causes disease in the body, and developing new methods of preventing and treating the disease.

Another infectious disease demanding research funding is tuberculosis, which is caused by an airborne bacterium and infects about 8 million people annually, killing some 2 million of them. The HIV/AIDS epidemic is increasing the number of TB cases, because TB more easily infects and kills people whose immune systems are weakened. About 15 percent of AIDS-related deaths are due to TB infection (see Table 2). There is at least one strain of TB that is resistant to a TB drug in every country, and there are several strains that are resistant to all the major TB drugs. These multidrug-resistant strains, called MDR-TB, threaten the global effort to eradicate TB. To be cured, people infected with multidrug-resistant TB must be treated with intensive chemotherapy, which is expensive and far more toxic to the patient than antibiotic treatment.

To manage MDR-TB, WHO and other international health organizations formed the DOTS-Plus Working Group in 2000. DOTS—directly observed treatment short-course—is the TB detection and treatment strategy recommended by WHO that involves the following elements: political commitment, microscopy services for detection, continually sufficient drug supplies, surveillance and monitoring systems, and standardized (six- to eight-month) drug regimens with direct treatment observation by a health care professional. The main goal of DOTS is to prevent the development and spread of MDR-TB strains.

Studies have proven its effectiveness in Bangladesh, China, Peru, Vietnam, and various countries of West Africa. By the end of 1998 the twenty-two countries that were identified as having the highest TB rates, together hosting 80 percent of all TB cases, had adopted DOTS. Most of these countries are in sub-Saharan Africa, Southeast Asia, and the former Soviet Union. Still, however, only about 25 percent of TB cases were being treated under DOTS in 2000. WHO was pursuing education campaigns to increase this percentage.

The main targets of infectious disease research include the biology of the disease-causing organism (see Table 3), the physiology of the disease in the body, and the production of drugs and vaccines. Epidemiological studies are also important. These include research into the most effective methods of disease detection, reporting, and response and creation of mathematical models of how diseases spread to aid in the formulation of policies and programs. Epidemic diseases being researched around the world in addition to acute respiratory infection, AIDS, diarrheal diseases, tuberculosis, and malaria include the following (among others): Chagas' disease, cholera, diphtheria, Ebola, gonorrhea, guinea worm disease, hantavirus, influenza, leishmaniasis, leprosy, lymphatic filariasis, poliomyelitis (polio), viral hepatitis, and variant Creutzfeldt-Jakob disease.

Policies and Programs

Policies and programs related to global epidemics are concerned primarily with preventing antibiotic resistance, disseminating disease-management recommendations, delivering vaccines to affected regions, monitoring closely and reporting carefully disease outbreaks (see map, p. 157), and correcting the environments and human behaviors that contribute to disease spread. Programs increasingly involve collaborations between public and private sectors.

Antibiotic resistance is fueled partly by misinformation. Patients in many areas believe that antibiotics are the cure for almost anything, due to advertisements and articles in the mass media. Many health care practitioners are likewise misinformed, due to insufficient education, and have overprescribed antibiotics, particularly when they feel pressured by their patients. In 1999 WHO analyzed studies carried out at hospitals around the world and found that between 40 percent and 90 percent of antibiotics prescribed were unnecessary or inappropriate. Programs run by advisory and funding bodies to prevent antibiotic resistance therefore include education. For instance, WHO's DOTS-Plus Working Group cooperates with health care providers in countries with heavy TB burdens to distribute information about avoiding the misuse of antibiotics.

WHO recommends a host of standardized intervention strategies, but few low-income nations have been able to fully implement them because of such factors as lack of funding, political instability, and inadequate health care infrastructure. WHO's recommendations include Integrated Management of Childhood Illnesses, which outlines effective tools for the control of acute respiratory infection, diarrheal diseases, and malaria across large populations. WHO also promotes its Global Strategy for the Containment of Antimicrobial Resistance, outlining methods of preventing antibiotic resistance (see Document 1). In

1948 WHO initiated the Influenza Program, aimed at curtailing the spread of influenza. At the end of the century, the program was running strong, maintaining 110 National Influenza Centers in eighty-three countries and four Collaborating Centers for Virus Reference and Research (in Atlanta, London, Melbourne, and Tokyo). These centers perform research on strains of influenza circulating the globe and make recommendations each season on the composition of vaccines to be offered. The centers are linked electronically by the Influenza Surveillance Network so that they can share information and keep on top of outbreaks.

An important international collaboration to distribute vaccines was the Global Polio Eradication Initiative, launched in 1988 by delegates to the forty-first World Health Assembly. Poliomyelitis is a highly infectious virus-caused disease that can lead to complete, irreversible paralysis within hours of infection, although most infections typically result in partial immobility. In 1988 the disease affected an estimated 350,000 people, mostly children. Vaccination against polio protects a person for life. The Global Polio Eradication Initiative involved large-scale immunization campaigns around the world, with the aim of eradicating poliomyelitis by the year 2000. Although that goal was not reached, the program was widely successful. In 2000 there were only 3,500 reported cases of polio, which according to WHO were concentrated mostly in Afghanistan, Angola, Bangladesh, the Democratic Republic of Congo, Ethiopia, India, Nigeria, Pakistan, Somalia, and Sudan. Authorities expect that polio will be completely eradicated by 2005.

A noteworthy private initiative for vaccine distribution, as well as research, was launched at the beginning of 2000 by the Bill and Melinda Gates Foundation, which is a major source of funding in the area of infectious disease. The foundation contributed $100 million for malaria, tuberculosis, and HIV vaccine research, $750 million for the Global Alliance for Vaccines and Immunization to distribute vaccines to children in low-income regions, and an additional $50 million for the Medicines for Malaria Venture, a Swiss-based nonprofit organization coordinating the efforts of private and public institutions to fight drug resistance in malaria strains.

The Global Public Health Intelligence Network (GPHIN) is an enormous, informal, and heavily relied upon outlet for reporting potential disease outbreaks. The GPHIN, based in Canada, surveys the World Wide Web for reports of diseases; it informs WHO of an average of five potential outbreaks a week. An example of how powerful the network is occurred in 1999, when it reported the spread of a lethal respiratory disease in rural Afghanistan. Authorities at GPHIN suspected that the quickly spreading disease was anthrax. Investigators dispatched by WHO to the scene reported within two weeks that the disease was influenza and that it was occurring in a population that had not seen influenza for thirty years. Another surveillance system is WHO's International Health Regulations, which reports on outbreaks of cholera, plague, and yellow fever.

As outlined in the 1992 *Emerging Infections: Microbial Threats to Health in the United States,* a widely read report by the Institute of Medicine, an advisory body to the U.S. National Academy of Sciences, factors that contribute to the emergence and spread of infectious diseases include the following: travel and commerce; human demographics (population growth and migration); human behaviors (such as civil conflict, sexual behavior, intravenous drug use); technology and industry (such as biological advances applied to agriculture and livestock, changes in food preparation and packaging, organ transplantation); ecological change; microbial adaptation and antibiotic resistance; breakdown of public health infrastructure; and biological terrorism (see Document 2). During the mid- to late 1990s these factors were incorporated in the development of policies and recommendations primarily focused on improving surveillance and reporting strategies. For instance, the National Academy of Sciences began collaborating in 1996 with scientists at biological warfare facilities in the former Soviet Union to coordinate public health efforts. One such effort is to turn a former biological research facility in Kazakhstan into a national tuberculosis reference center. Mexico instituted a refined disease-surveillance program after Hurricane Mitch, which hit parts of Honduras and Nicaragua in 1998, increased the number of people migrating from Central America into Mexico. These events precipitated new infectious diseases and worsened conditions, such as overcrowding, that contribute to high rates of infection.

Due to increases in travel and global commerce and the potential threat these activities carry in the realm of public health, many responses to emerging infectious diseases have been transnational. An ongoing joint effort of the African Regional Office of WHO, the U.S. Centers for Disease Control and Prevention, and the U.S. Agency for International Development (USAID) aims to improve disease surveillance and epidemic preparedness in the forty-seven member states of the African Regional Office of WHO. In June 1995 the Pan American Health Organization, which covers health issues in all of the Americas, held a meeting of international health experts to discuss plans for the prevention of emerging infectious diseases at the regional and subregional levels. The European Union also allocated funds for epidemic prevention strategies for all member states in the late 1990s.

Regional Summaries

Every region of the world suffers from human epidemics. Most infectious diseases, however, hit hardest in regions where the population is overwhelmingly poor and where health care systems are underdeveloped (see HEALTH and POVERTY).

North America

Infectious disease generally declined in the United States and Canada during the twentieth century, with the exception of AIDS, the rate of which have risen since the beginning of the epidemic in 1981. There have been isolated and short-lived outbreaks of other deadly diseases in the region since the 1970s. Preventing the emergence of new and foreign diseases constitutes a major concern of many people in this area.

In 1900 the three leading causes of death in the United States were pneumonia, tuberculosis, and diarrheal diseases, all caused by infectious agents and

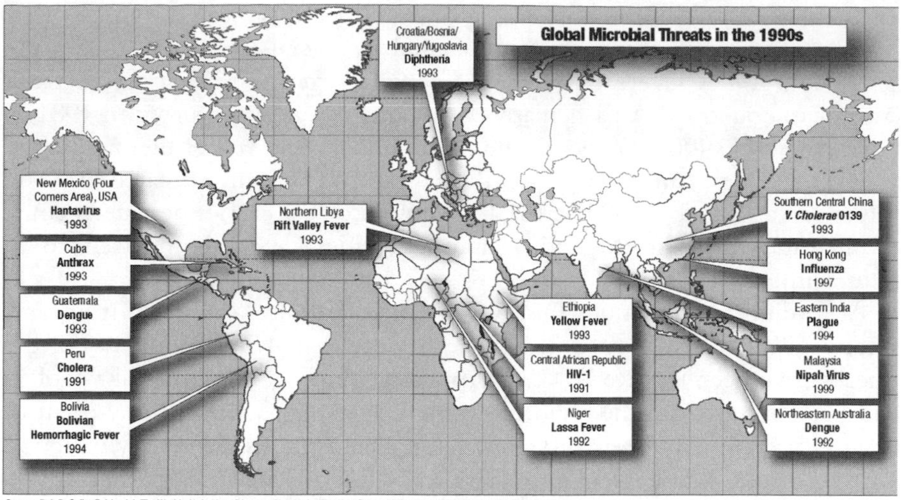

Source: Rob DeSalle, *Epidemic! The World of Infectious Diseases* (New York: The New Press, 1999), 56, and AP and Reuters news services.

part of worldwide pandemics. During the twentieth century, these epidemics were brought under control in North America by standardized policies of health care made possible by the high income of the region and its highly developed scientific and medical industries. Effective programs of urban sanitation, immunization, and treatment with antibiotics and other drugs were carried out. In 2000 the leading causes of death were heart disease, cancer, and stroke, all noninfectious illnesses. Canada has a similar infectious disease profile as the United States.

Epidemic outbreaks in the 1990s in the region included the parasite *Cryptosporidium parvum,* which infected more than 400,000 people in Milwaukee, Wisconsin, in 1993 and killed more than 50 of them, most of whom likely had compromised immune systems. The large number of people infected sent a warning signal to U.S. citizens that they were not—despite what many people had come to believe—safe from large-scale epidemics. In New Mexico in 1993, a previously unidentified hantavirus infected twenty-four people and claimed twelve lives. Hantaviruses, carried by rodents, cause fevers, kidney failure, fatigue, and in the New Mexico case, respiratory distress. This episode also shocked the nation, as hantaviruses were popularly considered problematic in Asia and Eastern Europe. It was surprising that they showed up suddenly in a landlocked area of North America.

Latin America

The toll of epidemics in Latin America was reduced in the second half of the twentieth century, due to immunization programs and improving health care systems. HIV/AIDS, cholera, leptospirosis, and dengue, however, still pose serious threats. The incidence of dengue—a disease characterized in its less severe form by a flu-like set of symptoms and in its most severe form by massive internal bleeding and organ destruction—had been reduced in most countries of Latin America during the 1950s and 1960s with the partial elimination of infestations of the mosquito that transmits disease-causing dengue viruses. These control methods were not sustained in several areas, and during the 1970s and 1980s severe outbreaks of dengue occurred in almost all Latin American countries. A particularly devastating outbreak occurred in 1981 in Cuba, affecting 400,000 people and killing more than 150 of them. Dengue activity rose again in 1995, when the region suffered an estimated 200,000 infections and almost 100 deaths. The mosquito that carries dengue is common from Mexico to Argentina, and authorities have redoubled efforts to reduce infestations.

According to "Infectious Diseases in Latin America and the Caribbean," since a 1991 outbreak of cholera in Peru more than 1.2 million cases of the disease have been reported in Latin America. Prior to this outbreak, cholera had been absent from the region for ninety years. Peru was also the point of origin for a 1995 outbreak of yellow fever. Leptospirosis, caused by infection with leptospira parasites and characterized by internal bleeding, particularly in the lungs, infected more than 2,400 people in Nicaragua in 1995, leaving 250 hospitalized and about 15 dead. The disease is an ongoing problem that has received little international attention.

The reemergence of dengue, cholera, and yellow fever in Latin America is due in part, authorities theorize, to economic recession. Funds have been diverted from health care to more immediate concerns, and urban centers have become crowded, with more people living in unsanitary conditions. In 1995 the Pan American Health Organization expressed its commitment to improved infectious disease surveillance and response, the latter by increasing the region's capacity for laboratory research.

Europe and the Former Soviet Union

In Europe, including the former Soviet republics, a number of infectious diseases that had been absent from the region for decades reemerged in the 1990s. New diseases and antimicrobial resistance were also spreading. These problems were confined mainly to Central and Eastern Europe and the former Soviet Union.

Since 1990 an epidemic of diphtheria—a bacteria-caused disease resulting in inflammation of the heart, nervous system, and respiratory tract—has been sweeping through the former Soviet Union, infecting about 158,000 people and killing about 4,000, according to WHO's "Diphtheria Control." Cases of diphtheria were also reported in some northern European countries in the 1990s.

Europe was nearly rid of malaria in the 1980s, but the number of reported cases in the region rose drastically in the early 1990s. Most cases were in Eastern Europe and the former Soviet Union. Government implementation of the Roll Back Malaria strategies devised by the United Nations Children's Fund, the United Nations Development Programme, WHO, and the World Bank in 1998 helped get the disease under control in the latter part of the decade. Also in the eastern part of the region, tuberculosis made a comeback in the 1990s, including strains resistant to major antibiotics.

Sexually transmitted infections, for example, syphilis, were on the rise in the region at the close of the twentieth century. Health care officials suspect that the increase was due to unsafe sex practices and underfunding of medical services for sexually transmitted diseases.

Experts blame the social, political, and economic upheaval since 1989 for surges in infectious disease in the region. National governments set up coalitions in the 1990s to address these problems, and the numbers for diphtheria, malaria, and tuberculosis cases were reported to be slowly declining. By 1997 polio immunization programs had reached 95 percent of people in the Mediterranean and Caucasus areas. Immunization also had led to an enormous reduction in death from measles by late in the decade.

North Africa and the Middle East

With respect to infectious disease prevalence, North Africa and the Middle East are split between higher-income nations and lower-income nations. The former include Israel and the oil-rich countries of the Arabian Peninsula, where infectious diseases are controlled by high rates of government spending on health care, immunization, and sanitation. The latter include the remaining countries of the region, where poorer health care systems and fewer institutionalized health programs allow some epidemics to flourish. A common thread throughout most of the region, however, is the likelihood that infectious diseases are underreported.

Tuberculosis, including strains resistant to multiple drugs, is a problem, particularly in Iran, Iraq, Libya, and Yemen. It caused an estimated 57,000 deaths in those countries in 1999, according to country profiles by WHO's Regional Office for the Eastern Mediterranean. Malaria is of major significance only in Iran, Iraq, and Yemen; the climate of other parts of the region is not favorable for the malaria-carrying mosquito. Diarrheal diseases caused an estimated 500,000 deaths in the entire region in 1998. Other diseases that cause significant numbers of infections and deaths include hepatitis (all types, but particularly B and C), brucellosis, leishmaniasis, and sandfly fever. Egypt suffers the world's highest prevalence of hepatitis C. War-related population movements in the region have led to overcrowding in some areas, which in turn has lead to unsanitary living conditions that contribute to disease spread.

Sub-Saharan Africa

Sub-Saharan Africa is the region hardest hit by epidemics. More than 90 percent of the world's malaria cases occur in the sub-Sahara, according to WHO's "Malaria" fact sheet, as do more than 95 percent of the cases of onchercerciasis (river blindness). Every child in the region suffers on average from five bouts of diarrhea (caused by infectious agents) per year, and about 1.5 million children die of pneumonia each year.

A number of other infectious diseases severely affect the region as well. In 1998 121 out of 100,000 people in the region suffered from tuberculosis, the highest prevalence rate in the world, according to the United Nations Development Programme's *Human Development Report, 2001.* Outbreaks of cholera, hepatitis B, measles, human schistosomiasis (a disease caused by infection with water-borne parasitic worms), and polio are also typical. The region's raging HIV/AIDS epidemic exacerbates other epidemics, particularly the number of tuberculosis cases.

WHO's "Malaria" fact sheet reports that malaria kills more than 1 million people throughout the world each year and that the overwhelming majority of these deaths are suffered by children in rural sub-Saharan Africa. Illness and death due to malaria (and other diseases) have taken an economic toll on the region. According to research published in 2000 by WHO, Harvard University, and the London School of Hygiene and Tropical Medicine, malaria shaves 1.3 percent off the region's potential economic growth each year. The researchers calculated that without malaria, the region's gross domestic product would have been some 32 percent greater in 2000. In 2001 projects to control malaria were reported to be making progress. In particular, the global Roll Back Malaria program had been adopted in thirty African countries. Participating nations receive funds for improving health delivery systems and are advised on early detection and treatment techniques. New facilities were opened for the development of antimalarial drugs.

Other improvements in the region's response to epidemics were reported in 2001. Forty countries had adopted the WHO-recommended DOTS tuberculosis treatment strategy, and thirty-two counties were implementing WHO's Integrated Management of Childhood Illnesses. The prevalence of guinea worm disease—caused by infection with a parasitic worm that infests and damages the skin and sometimes deeper tissues—and leprosy were down, and the region had drafted a strategy for the control of schistosomiasis. A regional network of laboratories had been established to research ways to control epidemics. The project involved seventeen countries across the region.

Asia and the Pacific

WHO views Asia as divided into two regions: Southeast Asia (Bangladesh, Bhutan, India, Indonesia, Maldives, Nepal, Sri Lanka, and Thailand) and the Western Pacific (Australia, Cambodia, China, Japan, Hong Kong, Korea, Malaysia, New Zealand, Papua New Guinea, the Pacific islands, Philippines, Samoa, Singapore, and Vietnam). The nature and rates of infectious disease in the two regions are reported separately.

In Southeast Asia, infectious disease kills nearly 7 million people each year. Malaria is among the biggest killers, and although rates of the disease declined in the 1960s and early 1970s they have since been increasing. This trend is partly due to the development of pesticide resistance in strains of the mosquito that transmits the malaria-causing microbe and to the evolution of antibiotic-resistant strains as well. WHO's *Global Tuberculosis Control, 2000* reports that there were more than 1,300,000 cases of tuberculosis in the region in 1998. This disease kills more adults per year—750,000—than any other epidemic. The region's tuberculosis cases currently account for 39 percent of all TB cases, while the region holds only 25 percent of the world's population. In the mid-1990s, all WHO member states adopted the organization's DOTS treatment program for TB, which has reduced the number of TB deaths.

Although leprosy had long been a critical problem in the region, by 2000 most governments had drastically reduced their commitment to controlling the disease. According to *Southeast Asia Progress towards Health for All, 1977–2000,* dengue fever is of major concern, threatening 1.3 billion people in areas where it currently exists. In 1998 dengue afflicted 400,000 people and killed 8,000 of them. A vaccine against dengue was developed in Thailand at the end of the decade and was in the human trials stage in 2000. Polio and guinea worm disease were nearly eradicated from the region by 2000, although the former was threatening to make a comeback.

The Western Pacific was declared free of polio in 2000. Diarrheal diseases and acute respiratory infection affect about 1 million children each year, according to WHO's "Regional Statistics: Basic Health Information in the Western Pacific Region." Major strategies for coping with and controlling childhood illnesses are taking hold. WHO's "Regional Statistics: Disease Specific Indicators of the Western Pacific Region" reports that Hepatitis B affected an estimated 150 million people considered chronic carriers, and cases of dengue fever numbered more than 45,000 in 2000. Malaria, though still a problematic epidemic in the region, has been losing ground since the mid-1980s. Tuberculosis, on the other hand, is climbing. There were more than 823,000 cases reported in 1999. In that same year, according to *Tuberculosis Control in WHO Western Pacific Region,* DOTS treatment was reportedly reaching 68 percent of TB cases, up from 58 percent in the previous year.

Data

Table 1 Antibiotic-Resistant Disease-Causing Bacteria

Disease	Microbe	Antibiotic Resistance
Dysentery	*Shigella dysenteriae*	Multidrug resistant
Gonorrhea	*Neisseria gonorrhoeae*	Penicillin and tetracycline resistant
Nosocomial infections[a]	Enterococcus species	Vancomycin resistant
	Klebsiella species	Multidrug resistant
	Pseudomonas species	Multidrug resistant
	Staphylococcus aureus	Methicillin resistant
Pneumonia	*Streptococcus pneumoniae*	Multidrug resistant
Typhoid	*Salmonella enterica*	Multidrug resistant

Source: Jonathan R. Davis and Joshua Lederberg, eds., *Emerging Infectious Diseases from the Global to the Local Perspective: A Summary of a Workshop of the Forum on Emerging Infections* (Washington, D.C.: National Academy Press, 2001).

[a]Infections that are acquired within health care settings.

Table 2 HIV/AIDS Prevalence in Adult Populations and Malaria and Tuberculosis Cases in Selected Countries

Country	People Living with HIV/AIDS, 1999[a] (%)	Malaria Cases, 1997 (per 100,000 people)	Tuberculosis Cases, 1998 (per 100,000 people)
Algeria	0.07	1	51
Argentina	0.69	2	34
Australia	0.15	—	5
Brazil	0.57	240	51
Canada	0.30	—	6
China	0.07	2	36
Colombia	0.31	452	22
Congo, Republic of	6.43	350	139
Egypt	0.02	<0.5	19
France	0.44	—	12
Georgia	<0.01	—	96
Germany	0.10	—	13
Guatemala	1.38	305	26
India	0.70	275	115
Indonesia	0.05	79	20
Israel	0.08	—	10
Japan	0.02	—	35
Russian Federation	0.18	—	82
Saudi Arabia	0.01	106	16
Spain	0.58	—	23
Sweden	0.08	—	5
Switzerland	0.46	—	10
Tajikistan	<0.01	507	41
Thailand	2.15	163	26
Turkey	0.01	56	35
Uganda	8.30	—	142
United Kingdom	0.11	—	10
United States	0.61	—	7

Source: United Nations Development Programme, *Human Development Report, 2001,* http://www.undp.org/hdr2001/indicator.

[a]Aged 15 to 49.

Table 3 Examples of Disease-Causing Microbes Identified since 1973

Year	Microbe	Disease
1973	Rotavirus	Major cause of infantile diarrhea globally
1976	*Cryptosporidium parvum*	Acute and chronic diarrhea
1977	*Campylobacter jejuni*	Enteric diseases distributed globally[a]
	Ebola virus	Ebola hemorrhagic fever
	Hantaan virus	Hemorrhagic fever with renal syndrome
	Legionella pneumophila	Legionnaires' disease
1979	Ross River virus	Ross River fever, arthritis
1980	Human T-lymphotropic virus 1 (HTLV-1)	T-cell lymphoma leukemia
1981	Toxin-producing strains of *Staphylococcus aureus*	Toxic shock syndrome
1982	*Escherichia coli* O157:H7	Hemorrhagic colitis, hemolytic uremic syndrome
	HTLV-II	Hairy cell leukemia
	Borrelia burgdorferi	Lyme disease
1983	*Helicobacter pylori*	Peptic ulcer disease
	Human immunodeficiency virus (HIV)	Acquired immunodeficiency syndrome (AIDS)
1988	Hepatitis E	Enterically transmitted non-A, non-B hepatitis
1989	Hepatitis C virus	Hepatitis C
1990	Guanarito virus	Venezuelan hemorrhagic fever
1991	*Ehrlichia chaffeensis*	Human ehrlichiosis
	Encephalitozzon hellem	Conjunctivitis, disseminated disease
1992	*Bartonella henselae*	Cat-scratch disease, bacillary angiomatosis
	Vibrio cholerae O139	New strain associated with epidemic cholera
1993	*Cyclospora cayestanensis*	Epidemics of diarrhea
	Sin Nombre hantavirus	Hantavirus pulmonary syndrome
1994	Sabia virus	Brazilian hemorrhagic fever
1995	Hepatitis G virus	Parenterally transmitted non-A, non-B hepatitis
	Human herpes virus-8	Associated with Kaposi sarcoma in AIDS patients
1996	Prion of bovine spongiform encephalopathy (BSE)	Variant Creutzfeldt-Jakob disease (vCJD)
1997	H5N1 influenza virus	Influenza (chicken or bird flu)
1999	Nipah virus	Febrile viral encephalitis

Source: Jason Eberhart-Phillips, *Outbreak Alert: Responding to the Increasing Threat of Infectious Diseases* (Oakland: New Harbinger Publications, 2000); World Health Organization, "Emerging and Re-Emerging Infectious Diseases," fact sheet no. 97, http://www.who.int/inf-fs/en/fact097.html.

[a] Most common bacterial cause of food poisoning.

Case Study—Peru

Peru has suffered under the shadow of several major epidemics during the twentieth century, and its residents are still threatened by bubonic plague, cholera, malaria, and tuberculosis. Poverty and unsanitary conditions in many parts of the country create an environment that allows infectious diseases to spread. Political instability has produced a vacuum in which effective health care systems would ordinarily exist. Experts believe that Peru will not be able to extinguish infectious diseases until the government organizes a strong, unified program of public health.

Bubonic plague was the first epidemic to hit Peru in the 1900s. The epidemic lasted from 1903 until 1930, affecting more than 20,000 people, according to Marcos Cueto, in *The Return of Epidemics.* Bubonic plague is transmitted in the bites of fleas that have lived on rats infected with the plague microbe. The excessive population and overcrowded living conditions in Peruvian cities at the turn of the century, along with unsanitary dwellings and untreated refuse and sewage, gave rise to large rat populations. Outbreaks of bubonic plague—moving from port cities to rural areas to low-altitude highland areas—simultaneously caused panic and led to the creation of three new official institutions of public health and hygiene. These organizations slowly cleaned up the country, but the final decline of the plague was due also to efforts by the Pan American Sanitation Bureau (later the executive arm of the Pan American Health Organization) to eliminate rat populations.

Yellow fever struck Peru in 1919, and by 1921 it had infected an estimated 15,000 people, according to *The Return of Epidemics,* and killed an estimated 1,000. The most effective control strategy, discovered by visiting American physician and public health expert Henry Hanson, was to introduce a number of freshwater fish to the basins that people used for drinking and bathing. The fish eat the larvae of mosquitoes that transmit yellow fever.

Typhus and smallpox were common in the Andes Mountains of Peru from early in the twentieth century until mid-century. Vast vaccination and sanitation campaigns aimed at both diseases and carried out in large part by self-appointed health brigades brought both epidemics under control.

Malaria is a recurring burden, as the mosquito that transmits the disease-causing microbe thrives in Peru's coastal and rain forest areas. The Peruvian government waged campaigns against malaria throughout the 1900s. From early in the century until 1940, it focused on controlling mosquito larvae and treating sick patients with quinine. From 1940 to 1970, its focus shifted to establishing specialized services for malaria, including the building of malaria hospitals and the initiation of programs committed to fighting the disease. During this time Peru also received assistance from foreign countries in battling and preventing the disease. In the 1950s, after spraying the pesticide DDT as part of an international campaign to eliminate the disease, malaria rates fell. In 1946 malaria had been the leading cause of death in Peru, but by 1955 it had dropped to number ten.

By 1968 malaria was believed to be a vanishing threat in Peru, but by the mid-1970s it was clear that the mosquitoes were developing resistance to DDT and that the malaria microbe was becoming immune to quinine treatment. Also, in 1974 the price of DDT skyrocketed, making it less readily available to low-income countries like Peru. During the 1980s no standardized control methods were undertaken, and by the 1990s malaria again existed throughout the country. Current antimalaria strategies are focused on treating patients and interrupting transmission; little is being done to alter the ecological factors that allow malaria-carrying mosquitoes to thrive.

In 1991 a cholera outbreak struck Peru. According to "Medical Geography and Cholera in Peru," within days of the outbreak all of Peru's coastal regions had been affected. In all, more than 300,000 people became sick that year and nearly 3,000 of them died. Living conditions at the time were extremely bad; the sanitation and refuse systems in the cities were limited, with people regularly drinking contaminated water and raw sewage draining into coastal waters that harbored the cities' seafood. Because cholera had not visited Peru for decades, there was no natural immunity in the population. Other countries banned the import of Peruvian seafood, and tourism in Peru suffered. The country is estimated to have lost at least $770 million during the first year of the epidemic.

According to a report issued by USAID at the outset of the cholera epidemic, Peru would have to increase its spending on water and drainage by ten times during the following ten years, an investment that would cost at least $100 million. The Peruvian government could not afford such an operation, so cholera has since taken hold as a potentially long-term epidemic among the population. Some historians believe that the legacy of the cholera epidemic in Peru has been and will be to motivate individuals, faced with a political system that has ignored their health needs, to take it upon themselves to improve the sanitation and hygiene of their communities.

Biographical Sketches

Gro Harlem Brundtland is a former prime minister of Norway and leader of that country's Ministry of Environment. Brundtland is currently the director-general of the World Health Organization and serves as the chair of the Global Alliance for Vaccines and Immunization, a worldwide partnership of foundations, nongovernmental organizations, and corporate interests that have joined forces to extend access to comprehensive and effective immunization programs for all children. Brundtland was instrumental in developing and promoting an understanding of the link between the environment and health.

Anthony S. Fauci has been the director of the National Institutes of Health's National Institute of Allergy and Infectious Diseases (NIAID) since 1984. He has been at the center of numerous research efforts for the study and understanding of infectious disease, including the mechanisms of the human immune system, and has been at the forefront on public health questions relating to immunization and epidemics, including AIDS.

Stuart Levy is a physician who has committed his professional life to curbing the development and spread of antibiotic resistance among disease-causing organisms. In

1979 he discovered how some bacteria are able to survive tetracycline, a commonly prescribed antibiotic. In 1992 Levy published *The Antibiotic Paradox: How Miracle Drugs Are Destroying the Miracle,* which warns of the dangers of antibiotic misuse and calls for international cooperation to battle drug resistance.

Francine Ntoumi is a molecular biologist who has devoted her professional life to malaria research. She is a senior scientist at the Medical Parasitology Unit of the Centre International de Recherches Médicales de Franceville (CIRMF) in Gabon. Ntoumi holds several awards and grants for her outstanding leadership in the field of infectious disease research and her commitment to improving public health in Africa.

Palmira Ventosilla is a microbiologist who developed an innovative and ecologically friendly way of controlling malaria. In the 1970s researchers showed that a strain of the bacterium *Bacillus thuringiensis* (Bti), which is harmless to humans and other animals, feeds on and destroys infestations of mosquito larvae. In the 1990s Ventosilla and her research team developed an inexpensive method of producing Bti involving the injection of the bacterium into coconuts and sealing them. Bti had previously been too expensive for low-income countries to make. By the late 1990s experiments showed that two to three coconuts could provide a forty-five-day larvae-killing dose of Bti.

Directory

American Society for Microbiology, 1752 N Street NW, Washington, DC 20036. Telephone: (202) 737-3600, Email: EducationResources@asmusa.org, Web: http://www.asmusa.org
Private organization that conducts and supports research in microbiology, including infectious disease

Centers for Disease Control and Prevention, c/o Public Inquiries/MASO, Mailstop F07, 1600 Clifton Road, Atlanta, GA 30333. Telephone: (800) 311-3435, Email: go to http://www.cdc.gov/netinfo.htm, Web: http://www.cdc.gov
U.S. government agency for protecting citizens' health and safety

Family Health International, 2101 Wilson Boulevard, Suite 700, Arlington, VA 22201. Telephone: (703) 516-9779, Email: services@fhi.org, Web: http://www.fhi.org
Organization providing health prevention and care services globally

Global Alliance for Vaccines and Immunization, c/o UNICEF, Palais des Nations, 1211 Geneva 10, Switzerland. Telephone: (41) 22 909 5019, Email: Gavi@unicef.org, Web: http://www.vaccinealliance.org
International partnership dedicated to equal access to vaccination and immunization for children around the world

National Institute of Allergy and Infectious Disease, 200 Independence Avenue SW, Washington, DC 20201. Telephone: (202) 619-0257 or (877) 696-6775, Email: hhsmail@os.dhhs.gov, Web: http://www.niaid.nih.gov/default.htm
Division of the National Institutes of Health supporting allergy and infectious disease research

Pharmaceutical Research and Manufacturers of America, 1100 15th Street NW, Washington, DC 20005. Telephone: (202) 835-3400, Email: go to http://www.phrma.org/who/contact.phtml, Web: http://www.phrma.org
Pharmaceutical industry advocacy and support association informing policymakers and the public about issues and accomplishments of the industry and its member companies

Save the Children Fund, UK, 17 Grove Lane, London SE5 8RD, United Kingdom. Telephone: (44) 020 7703 5400, Email: go to http://www.savethechildren.org.uk/functions/indx_contact.html, Web: http://www.savethechildren.org.uk
International organization that supports children's rights and welfare, including health-related issues

Special Programme for Research and Training in Tropical Diseases, c/o World Health Organization, 20 Avenue Appia, 1211 Geneva 27, Switzerland. Telephone: (41) 22 791 3725, Email: tdr@who.int, Web: http://www.who.int/tdr/index.html
UN organization supporting research into diseases that afflict low-income regions

World Health Organization, 20 Avenue Appia, 1211 Geneva 27, Switzerland. Telephone: (41) 22 791 2111, Email: info@who.int, Web: http://www.who.int
UN agency advocating health for all people

Further Research

Books

Cueto, Marcos. *The Return of Epidemics: Health and Society in Peru during the Twentieth Century.* Aldershot, England: Ashgate Publishing, 2001.

DeSalle, Rob. *Epidemic! The World of Infectious Diseases.* New York: The New Press, 1999.

Eberhart-Phillips, Jason. *Outbreak Alert.* Oakland: New Harbinger Publications, 2000.

Garrett, Laurie. *The Coming Plague: Newly Emerging Diseases in a World Out of Balance.* New York: Penguin Books, 1994.

———. *Betrayal of Trust: The Collapse of Global Public Health.* New York: Hyperion, 2000.

Koop, C. Everett, Clarence E. Pearson, and M. Roy Schwarz, eds. *Critical Issues in Global Health.* San Francisco: Jossey-Bass, 2001.

Morse, S. S. *Emerging Viruses.* New York: Oxford University Press, 1993.

Whitman, Jim, ed. *The Politics of Emerging and Resurgent Infectious Diseases.* New York: St. Martin's Press, 2000.

Articles and Reports

Arbona, Sonia, and Shannon Crum, "Medical Geography and Cholera in Peru." The Geographer's Craft Project, Department of Geography, University of Colorado, Boulder, http://www.colorado.edu/geography/gcraft/warmup/cholera/cholera.html.

Brandling-Bennett, A. David, and Francisco Pinheiro. "Infectious Diseases in Latin America and the Caribbean: Are They Really Emerging and Increasing?" *Emerging Infectious Diseases* 2, no. 1 (1996).

Brown, P. "Parasites Move In When Forests Are Cleared." *New Scientist,* 5 October 1992.

Cohen, J. "Is an Old Virus Up To New Tricks?" *Science,* 18 July 1997, 312.

Colwell, R. R. "Global Climate and Infectious Disease: The Cholera Paradigm." *Science,* 20 December 1996, 2025.

Davis, Jonathan R., and Joshua Lederberg, eds. *Emerging Infectious Diseases from the Global to the Local Perspective: A Summary of a Workshop of the Forum on Emerging Infections.* Washington, D.C.: National Academy Press, 2001.

Gibbs, W. W. "Trailing a Virus." *Scientific American,* August 1999, 65.

Gladwell, M. "The Dead Zone." *New Yorker,* 29 September 1997, 52.

Groopman, J. "The Shadow Epidemic." *New Yorker,* 11 May 1998, 48.

Homewood, B. "Pneumonia Runs Riot in Brazil's Creches." *New Scientist,* 26 October 1996, 7.

Lanchester, J. "A New Kind of Contagion." *New Yorker,* 2 December 1996, 70.

Laver, W. G., N. Bischofberger, and R. G. Webster. "Disarming Flu Viruses." *Scientific American,* January 1999, 56.

Lederberg, J., R. E. Shopes, and S. C. Oaks, Jr., eds. *Emerging Infections: Microbial Threats to Health in the United States.* Washington, D.C.: National Academy Press, 1992.

Levy, S. B. "The Challenge of Antibiotic Resistance." *Scientific American,* March 1998, 46.

Pharmaceutical Research and Manufacturers of America. "Pharmaceutical Industry Profile, 2001," http://www.phrma.org/publications/publications/profile01/intro_toc.pdf.

Saul, H. "Year of the Rat." *New Scientist,* 5 October 1996, 32.

Shell, E. R. "Resurgence of a Deadly Disease." *Atlantic Monthly,* August 1997, 45.

United Nations Development Programme. *Human Development Report, 2001.* New York and Oxford: Oxford University Press, 2001.

Winslow, C. E. A. *The Conquest of Epidemic Disease.* Princeton, N.J.: Princeton University Press, 1943.

World Health Organization. "Cholera in the Americas." *Weekly Epidemiological Record,* no. 67 (1992): 33.

———. "Diphtheria Control: Current Situation in Europe and Epidemiological Trends," http://www.euro.who.int/eprise/main/WHO/Progs/DCP/Home.

———. "Eastern Mediterranean Region Country Profiles," http://www.emro.who.int/index.asp.

———. "Global Alliance for Vaccines and Immunization (GAVI)." Fact Sheet no. 169, http://www.who.int/inf-fs/en/fact169.html.

———. *Global Tuberculosis Control, 2000,* http://www.who.int/gtb/publications/globrep00/download.html.

———. "Malaria." Fact Sheet no. 94, http://www.who.int/inf-fs/en/fact094.html.

———. "Regional Statistics: Basic Health Information in the Western Pacific Region," http://www.wpro.who.int/public/Regstatistics/reg_info.asp#diarrhoeal.

———. "Regional Statistics: Disease Specific Indicators of the Western Pacific Region," http://www.wpro.who.int/public/Regstatistics/reg_spec.asp.

———. *Southeast Asia Progress towards Health for All, 1977–2000,* http://w3.whosea.org/progress/index.htm.

———. *Tuberculosis Control in WHO Western Pacific Region, 2000 Report.* Manila: WHO Regional Office for the Western Pacific, 2001. Also available at http://www.wpro.who.int/pdf/tbcontrol_final.pdf.

Web Sites

Alliance for the Prudent Use of Antibiotics
http://healthsci.tufts.edu.apua

American Public Health Association
http://www.apha.org

Emerging Infections Information Network, Yale University
http://info.med.yale.edu/EIINet

Global Health Network
http://www.pitt.edu/HOME/GHNet

Infectious Diseases Society of America
http://www.idsociety.org

Institute of Medicine
http://www.iom.edu

Johns Hopkins Infectious Diseases
http://hopkins-id.edu

Outbreak
http://www.outbreak.org

Peru—Health Promotion and Care
http://www.undp.org/seed/water/PIP/latinAmerica_caribbean/PER-h.htm

Program for Monitoring Emerging Infectious Diseases (ProMED)
http://www.healthnet.org/programs/promed.html#archives

WHO Communicable Disease Surveillance and Response
http://www.who.int/emc

WHO Disease Outbreak News
http://www.who.int/emc/outbreak_news/index.html

WHO Information Office, Fact Sheets
http://www.who.int/inf-fs/en/index.html

WHO Weekly Epidemiological Record
http://www.who.int/wer

Documents

1. Overcoming Antimicrobial Resistance

World Health Organization Report on Infectious Diseases, 2000

The full text is available at http://www.who.int/infectious-disease-report/index.html.

Extract

Preface: Our Window of Opportunity Is Closing

We are the first generation ever to have the means of protecting itself from the most deadly and common infectious diseases. Today, we possess the knowledge to prevent or cure diseases such as malaria, tuberculosis, HIV, diarrhoeal diseases, pneumonia and measles.

Smallpox eradication and a reduction of deaths due to measles [have] been made possible by the introduction of widespread immunization campaigns. And while there are still no effective vaccines to prevent infection from other leading killers (tuberculosis, malaria, HIV, diarrhoeal diseases and pneumonia), control and containment using existing interventions is well within our reach. Within the past two decades, the scientific community has developed successful strategies and products to counter threats posed by infectious diseases in both wealthy and poorer nations.

In all countries, these diseases can be prevented or treated with tools and medicines that usually cost a few dollars—often mere cents. Because of advances in the use of anti-malarials and insecticide-treated bednets, malaria deaths are no longer common in Viet Nam. Mexico has achieved a five-fold reduction in diarrhoeal deaths through the use of oral rehydration. Increased condom use and health education have enabled Thailand and Uganda to reduce the spread of HIV. The effective use of antibiotics in parts of India has resulted in a seven-fold decrease in tuberculosis deaths.

Previous generations once prayed for these lifesaving drugs, interventions and control strategies. But now that they are available, the world has been slow to put them to wide use. In disease endemic countries, global efforts have remained embarrassingly modest. Only 3% of Africa's children have bednets. Effective anti-TB medicines and treatment strategies reach only 25% of the world's TB cases and only half of developing countries have adopted the effective Integrated Management of Childhood Illnesses (IMCI) package.

The underuse and misuse of recent health breakthroughs has been catastrophic for people living and working in developing countries. Two out of every three deaths among young people in the poorest countries of Africa and Asia continue to result from just a handful of illnesses. Each year worldwide, more than 11 million people die from these preventable or curable afflictions. Most deaths are among young parents and children.

The Threat of Antimicrobial Resistance Is Growing

We are now beginning to pay for our neglect—a price over and above the tragedy and suffering infectious diseases inflict on millions of people annually. Our failure to make full use of recently discovered medicines and products means that many will slip through our grasp.

This is evident in wealthy countries which have exclusively focused efforts on fighting disease within their own borders, while failing to help eliminate them globally. Proliferating elsewhere, many bacteria, viruses and parasites mutate, become drug resistant and venture back to wealthy countries via modern transportation.

Resistance is also seen where health workers have exclusively focused on providing drugs for their patients while inadvertently failing to take time to ensure proper diagnosis, prescription and adherence to treatment.

Antimicrobial resistance is a natural biological phenomenon. But it becomes a significant public health problem where it is amplified many-fold owing to human misuse and neglect. Drug resistance is the most telling sign that we have failed to take the threat of infectious diseases seriously. It suggests that we have mishandled our precious arsenal of disease-fighting drugs, both by overusing them in developed nations and, paradoxically, both misusing and underusing them in developing nations. In all cases, half-hearted use of powerful antibiotics now will eventually result in less-effective drugs later.

This report describes the growing threat of antimicrobial resistance. It documents how once lifesaving medicines are increasingly having as little effect as a sugar pill. Microbial resistance to treatment could bring the world back to a pre-antibiotic age.

The Window of Opportunity Is Closing

Before long, we may have forever missed our opportunity to control and eventually eliminate the most dangerous infectious diseases. Indeed, if we fail to make rapid progress during this decade, it may become very difficult and expensive—if not impossible—to do so later. We need to make effective use of the tools we have now.

The eradication of smallpox in 1980, for example, happened not a moment too soon. Just a few years' delay and the unforeseen emergence of HIV would have undermined safe smallpox vaccination in populations severely affected by HIV.

While many exciting research efforts are currently underway, there is no guarantee that they will yield new drugs or vaccines in the near future. Since 1970, no new classes of antibacterials have been developed to combat infectious diseases. On average, research and development of anti-infective drugs [take] 10 to 20 years. Currently, there are no new drugs or vaccines ready to emerge from the research and development pipeline.

Moreover, for the major infectious killers, research and development funding continues to be woefully inadequate. A very small percentage of all global health research and development funding is currently devoted to finding new drugs or vaccines to stop AIDS, acute respiratory infections (ARI), diarrhoeal diseases, malaria and TB. The pharmaceutical industry reports that it costs them a minimum of U.S. $500 million just to bring one drug to market. Combined funding for research and development into ARI, diarrhoeal diseases, malaria and TB last year was under that amount.

A Massive Effort Is Required

Although prevention through vaccination continues to be the ultimate weapon against infection and drug resistance, no vaccines are available to prevent five of the six major infectious killers. Yet it is a needless tragedy that 11 million people perish each year awaiting the advent of newer miracle drugs and vaccines. Prevention and treatment strategies using tools available now can be provided to populations throughout the world to help eliminate high-burden diseases of poverty.

We need not stand by helplessly watching antimicrobial resistance increase and drug effectiveness decrease. As this report shows, resistance can be contained. When an infection is addressed in a comprehensive and timely manner, resistance rarely becomes a public health problem. The most effective strategy against antimicrobial resistance is to get the job done right the first time—to unequivocally destroy microbes—thereby defeating resistance before it starts.

Today—despite advances in science and technology—infectious disease poses a more deadly threat to human life than war. This year—at the onset of a new millennium—the international community is beginning to show its intent to turn back these microbial invaders through massive efforts against diseases of poverty—diseases which must be defeated now, before they become resistant. When diseases are fought wisely and widely, drug resistance can be controlled and lives saved.

2. Emerging Infections: Microbial Threats to Health in the United States

Institute of Medicine, National Academy of Sciences, 1992

The full text is available at http://www.nap.edu/openbook/0309047412/html/index.html.

Extract

Executive Summary

Disease-causing microbes have threatened human health for centuries. The Institute of Medicine's Committee on Emerging Microbial Threats to Health believes that this threat will continue and may even intensify in the coming years. The committee's report, which is summarized here, describes key elements responsible for the emergence of infectious diseases; it also presents recommendations that, if appropriately implemented, should allow the United States to be better prepared to recognize and respond rapidly to these public health threats.

What are these factors, operating both singly and in combination, that are contributing to the emergence of such pathogens? Like other living organisms, infectious agents are subject to genetic change and evolution. This quality is manifested by their ability to infect new hosts, by alterations in their susceptibility to antimicrobial drugs, and by changes in their response to host immunity. Alterations can also occur in geographic ranges; in some cases, modern transport has led to rapid movement of agents throughout the world. The human host has changed as well. We have adopted new types of personal behavior and new food-processing methods that may enhance transmission of some microbes. New diseases and modern medical treatments may result in immunosuppression and thus increase susceptibility to pathogenic microorganisms. Moreover, in recent years, the human population has experienced rapid growth and increased mobility resulting in intrusion into new ecological settings. These changes in infectious agents and human populations favor exposure to new pathogens and more efficient transmission of recognized microbes.

Other changes are also affecting disease emergence. For example, some infectious agents exist in vertebrate reservoirs such as wild animals. These agents, in some instances, have migrated and increased in number. Some microbes that are transmitted by insects or other vectors exhibit these characteristics as well; in addition, they may have become resistant to pesticides, which impedes efforts at control. Finally, the environment has changed and will continue to change. Humanity has altered the world's ecology through deforestation, urbanization, and industrialization, which some believe may lead to global climate change. Moreover, the world periodically experiences civil unrest and war, which can lead to regional breakdowns in sanitation, allowing microbes to flourish. Individually and collectively, these and other factors lead to the emergence and reemergence of microbial pathogens.

Infectious diseases remain the major cause of death worldwide (World Health Organization, 1992) and will not be conquered during our lifetimes. With the application of new scientific knowledge, well-planned intervention strategies, adequate resources, and political will, many of these diseases may be prevented by immunization, contained by the use of drugs or vector-control methods, and, in a very few cases, even eradicated—but the majority are likely to persevere. We can also be confident that new diseases will emerge, although it is impossible to predict their individual emergence in time and place. The committee believes that there are steps that can and must be taken to prepare for these eventualities. Its recommendations address both the recognition of and intervention against emerging infectious diseases.

ETHNIC AND REGIONAL CONFLICT

Murat Somer

Ethnic and regional conflict threatens the stability of nations and nation-states, which continue to be the key players in the global economy and politics. Globalization, which depends on the cooperation of nation-states to thrive, affects ethnic and regional conflict in competing ways. On the one hand, it lessens the likelihood of such conflicts, first, by enabling people to interact and perhaps identify with people outside of their ethnic group and regions and, second, by helping countries prosper and democratize through the international movement of ideas, commodities, capital, and labor. On the other hand, globalization may act as a catalyst for ethnic and regional conflict to some extent, first, by making politically or economically disadvantaged groups more aware of the world's inequalities and, second, by possibly weakening states (which often resolve or suppress ethnic and regional conflicts) before alternative international, supranational, and nongovernmental institutions have sufficiently developed to provide for security and stability.

Historical Background and Development

Before nation-states first emerged in Western Europe in the seventeenth and eighteenth centuries, most of the world was a kaleidoscope of ethnic, religious, and linguistic communities loosely connected to each other by monarchies and empires. Ruling establishments cared little about their subjects' identities and concerned themselves only with military loyalty and taxation. The borders between empires were not well defined because states had neither the resources nor sufficient interest to effectively control movements across borders.

The emergence of territorially defined nation-states led to the homogenization of national cultures and to the forging of strong and cohesive nations in which citizens were expected to be more loyal to their nation than they were to their ethnic group, region, or religion. This facilitated the transfer of power from monarchies to popular sovereignty by creating a national identity and justification for groups to obtain self-rule. Nationalism also helped many societies' economic development by fostering common legal and linguistic standards and trade between people of different ethnic and regional backgrounds. The process, however, was not smooth and painless.

All ethnic and regional groups and cultures did not participate in the nation-building process on equal terms. Usually one group dominated the process and took the lion's share in controlling economic and political resources and in the determination of the national culture. Thus the price of nation building was often that certain groups fell behind economically, and their cultures and languages came to be overshadowed by the dominant group—Anglo-Saxon Protestants in the United States, for example, and the French in France—whose culture and language became the mainstream. It is illustrative that in 1789, long before nation building homogenized France culturally and linguistically, French was only spoken by half of the "Frenchmen." The rest of the population spoke dozens of languages and dialects.

Today, the damage that nationalism has wrought on cultural diversity is regretted similarly to industrialization's effects on the environment. Assimilation into mainstream culture has often been achieved through pressure and manipulation (see CULTURAL PRESERVATION). Members of some minorities, such as Native Americans in the United States, were practically barred from assimilation into the mainstream culture, ultimately leading their cultures into oblivion. Such groups as the indigenous peoples in areas colonized by the Europeans and the Jewish and Roma minorities in pre–World War II Europe suffered extermination at the hands of the dominant groups where nationalism coalesced with colonialism or fascism. Such "ethnic cleansing" was intended to effect ethnic homogenization.

From the eighteenth through the twentieth centuries, nationalism spread from Western Europe to Africa, Asia, the Americas, Central and Eastern Europe, and the Middle East. The creation of nation-states was especially painful in the areas of multiethnic and multicultural empires, such as those controlled by the Austro-Hungarians and the Ottomans, who had for centuries respected the ethnic and regional autonomies of their subjects and had encouraged interethnic coexistence and mixing. The "unmixing" of these people in the early twentieth century in pursuit of homogeneous nation-states led to numerous fratricidal wars, suffering, and conflicts between ethnic and regional groups and the emerging states.

Another major wave of ethnic and regional conflict erupted in the aftermath of World War II, when numerous colonies in Africa and Asia gained their independence. Many of these new nations were subsequently divided into smaller entities. In 1947, for instance, British India's Muslims seceded to form Pakistan, and Bangladesh seceded from the latter in 1971. For a variety of reasons in many of these new nations, ethnic and regional groups and tribes failed to achieve economic and political integration. Many of the inequalities created by colonialist powers carried over into the postindependence period, thus creating a foundation for ethnic and regional conflicts.

A rash of ethnic and regional conflicts broke out in formerly socialist states following the end of the cold war. The former Yugoslavia disintegrated through a tragic war. Numerous ethnically heterogeneous new states were founded as a result of the Soviet Union's disintegration, and ethnic and regional groups suddenly found that they had become minorities within the borders of the newly independent countries. These groups mobilized to secure their position or to settle old accounts. Economic decline and political chaos generated popular frustration and created opportunities for ethnic and regional nationalists. All of these factors contributed to conflict, such as religious and civil conflict in Tajikistan, which has been suspended since 1997, and the ongoing conflict between the Russian government and Chechen separatists in Chechnya.

Globally, some ethnic and regional movements that seek autonomy or independence can be viewed in part as reactions to past injustices in nation building. At the same time, the resentment created by past injustices is one reason why fewer people in Western societies see their societies as melting pots into which minorities and newcomers are expected to assimilate. Instead, increasing numbers imagine their nations as multicultural salad bowls in which the diversity of ethnic communities and cultures is protected, and sometimes promoted, by national institutions.

New social norms and policies echo this trend. For instance, the term *melting pot* is no longer considered politically correct, especially if articulated in the presence of minority group members. Meanwhile, terms such as *kaleidoscope* and *rainbow coalition* are gaining increasing currency in descriptions of the ethnic composition of Western nations. Another trend is the growing interest in heritage, in retrieving old ways and reinventing ostensible traditions. These movements contrast sharply with the attitude that prevailed among nineteenth-century liberals as well as Marxists, who underscored the importance of social cohesion based on modernization and cultural homogenization.

The changing attitudes and political trends in Western democracies affect the way people view and express themselves in the rest of the world and vice versa. Wherever people are troubled by ethnic divisions, they use to differing degrees such concepts as multiculturalism, diversity, and self-determination (all initially developed in the West) to conceptualize, justify, and promote their cause. Conversely, the pervasiveness of violent ethnic conflict in the developing world lures some Western observers into complacency about the relative peacefulness of ethnic relations in their own countries. Others, however, doubt that Western democracies are immune to ethnic disintegration.

Current Status

Along with the steadily increasing number of states, the frequency of violent ethnic and regional conflict has been increasing steadily since the 1950s, but with a declining trend since the early 1990s (see Table 1). Nevertheless, since the cold war ended and the Soviet Union disintegrated in 1991, such conflicts have become the most conspicuous threats to global peace (see map, p. 182). Religiously or otherwise inspired global terrorism is a related phenomenon. Terrorist groups flourish in regions where ethnic, regional, and religious conflicts have generated either oppressive states and popular resentment, as in the case of many Middle Eastern and North African countries, or weak states, chaos, and widespread poverty as in Sudan and Afghanistan.

Research

Current research on ethnic and regional conflict deals with questions of prevention, management, and reconstruction. In order to examine how to prevent conflicts, researchers analyze the nature of ethnic and regional identities and the causes of conflict. They also examine the relationships between ethnic and regional conflict and economic and political development. Researchers investigate conflict management and postconflict restructuring by examining social and political institutions that can help reconcile ethnic and regional grievances and render the recurrence of conflict less likely. Hence, researchers and practitioners of conflict resolution are trying to develop blueprints and guidelines for policymakers (see PEACEMAKING AND PEACEBUILDING). A major area of investigation is the proper role of foreign intervention and of international and supranational organizations in preventing, managing, and rehabilitating conflicts.

Cross-country studies conducted by researchers at the World Bank and by others reveal that ethnic and linguistic heterogeneity—measured in terms of ethnolinguistic fractionalization indices—are significantly correlated with low economic and political development. This is not to say that ethnic and linguistic fractionalization automatically create conflict and underdevelopment, and vice versa. On the contrary, there are many successful examples, such as Switzerland and the United States, that have prospered and have developed successful democracies despite their considerable ethnic, cultural, and linguistic diversity. In particular, a country's ability to establish a working democracy seems to improve its ability to overcome the challenges of heterogeneity. Success stories are not limited to wealthy developed countries. India, a low-income developing country, has been able to manage existing interethnic and interregional conflicts relatively peacefully and has been able to sustain a working democracy despite its tremendous diversity and economic challenges.

Successful examples of stable ethnic and linguistic heterogeneity also show that there is no single way of managing and utilizing diversity. Switzerland recognized and institutionalized ethnic and linguistic differences by organizing the country administratively into cantons, each representing one of the constituent groups. The United States achieved intergroup coexistence and cooperation by cultivating the strong public consciousness of a common identity and by supporting a common language, English, although ethnic group members' cultural and linguistic needs are respected and accommodated whenever it is economically and politically feasible to do so. In turn, examples of failures, most notably many sub-Saharan African countries, demonstrate that ethnic and regional conflict are associated with ineffective and corrupt regimes that are unable to spur economic growth and that lack a power base crosscutting ethnic and regional divisions (see Table 2).

Any inquiry into conflict prevention should start with identifying the nature of ethnic and regional identities and the causes of intergroup conflict. This is not easy. Across time and in different parts of the world, ethnic and regional identities have taken different forms, and interethnic and interregional grievances have had different sources. Consequently, ethnic identities are by no means well-defined categories. Max Weber, the renowned German sociologist and political economist, defined ethnicity as a subjective belief in common descent; no objective blood relationship is necessary. Ethnic group members may form their belief in common descent on the basis of a different combination of shared characteristics, such as race, religion, language or dialect, custom, occupation, or social class. Often, the dominant markers of group membership are the characteristics that visibly distinguish group members from neighboring groups. Similarly, outsiders may ethnically label a group of people for a variety of reasons. The outsiders' and insiders' categorizations need not coincide. In the United States, for instance, outsiders may view all Spanish-speaking Americans as Hispanics, although many people in this group may prefer to call themselves, say, Mexican American or Guatemalan American, or simply American.

Although ethnic and cultural diversity has been part of society throughout history, it has not always caused conflict. Ethnic or regional activists tend to base their claims for resources in ancient disputes and enduring traditions, but most current conflicts are actually rooted in modern disagreements. Many neighboring groups have long histories of coexistence, intermingling, and cooperation. Often, national or religious identities override ethnic or regional identities. In some cases, intergroup grievances have been created by invaders or outside rulers who used ethnic classification as an easy means of categorizing and controlling people. Many times, colonial powers favored one group over the other and used the former as intermediaries to rule over the latter. Rwanda, where a cycle of violence since the 1960s has cost the lives of more than a million people, including those who died in the genocide of 1994, offers a good example. Relations between the Hutu and Tutsi, the country's two main ethnic groups, were relatively stable and peaceful, and interethnic mixing was common until the Belgians colonized the country after World War I. The Belgian administration sowed the seeds of future interethnic conflict by choosing to rule through the Tutsi elite in exchange for economic and educational favors for the members of that group. This turned majority Hutus and minority Tutsis against each other by creating a highly unequal relationship between them. Over time, group boundaries were solidified and intergroup animosities were cultivated, demonstrating how the nature of ethnic and regional group relations can change in response to economic and political circumstances.

The core of ethnic and regional group identity can also prove quite resilient to changing circumstances, and memories of past conflicts can resurface during contemporary conflicts even after long years of peace and cooperation. The primordialist perspective of conflict prevention focuses on the psychological and historical aspects of ethnic and regional conflicts. Primordialists highlight that ethnic identities are determined by birth and are rooted in the human cognitive and psychological tendency to favor one's own group members. They assert that the "family resemblance" of ethnic group membership, that is, the blood tie that is purported to exist among group members, makes intergroup relations more inflammatory and compromise less likely. Primordialists generally are skeptical of nation-building practices that underestimate the zeal of ethnic group members for cultural and political autonomy in multicultural societies. They are also generally against outside involvement in peacemaking in ethnic conflicts, because they believe that foreign intervention has little to contribute to the resolution of age-old conflicts that are inherently of a complex nature.

Another perspective, instrumentalism, highlights the fact that current ethnic and regional identities are more products of modern situations than circumstances of the distant past. Instrumentalists observe that previously insignificant ethnic categories become important when ethnic groups mobilize in pursuit of economic and political interests and in competition over scarce natural resources. Sometimes the geographical distribution of ethnic groups creates disadvantages for some groups, which then mobilize politically to improve their lot. In other situations, governments encourage ethnic interest groups to become politically active by tying government benefits to group membership or by failing to create equal opportunities for individuals regardless of ethnic descent. Thus, ethnic groups become vehicles for promoting economic and political ends, whether in the form of interest groups, political parties, or armed organizations or rebel groups. Accordingly, the key to preventing conflict is to remedy region- or ethnic-based advantages, or disadvantages, and to create equal opportunities for all individuals. Another point that instrumentalists emphasize is the role that elite interests and elite manipulation play in the creation of ethnic and regional conflict. For instance, in the former Yugoslavia formerly communist political elites incited interregional grievances and ethnonationalist sentiments in order to remain in power following the decline of socialism.

The constructivism perspective emphasizes the social processes that underlie the creation of ethnic, regional, and national identities. It points to the discourse of ethnic and national politics and maintains that competition over the use of names, images, and historical myths in the construction of identities is a source of conflict. For instance, Greeks initially objected to Macedonians' naming their country Macedonia, because they considered it part of the Greek national heritage (see Case Study—Macedonia). Constructivists encourage people to recognize the biases in their own ethnic and national self-images and to use inoffensive and conciliatory language to prevent conflict. At the same time, constructivists usually maintain that political and cultural institutions should explicitly recognize the multiethnic and multicultural composition of societies, enable people to express their ethnic and cultural identities, and accommodate identity needs in educational and cultural policies. In other words, they advocate multiculturalism as opposed to the homogenization of societies through forced or voluntary assimilation into a common cultural identity.

Policies and Programs

The issue of whether particular ethnic identities are modern holds important policy implications. For example, insofar as Macedonian identity is ancient and nations are based in ethnic identities, the territory of ancient Macedonia becomes a contested area divided between three contemporary nation-states: Bulgaria, Greece, and Macedonia. Insofar as Macedonian identity today is a modern phenomenon that emerged as a consequence of Macedonia's status as a constituent republic within the former Yugoslavia, those parts of ancient Macedonia that are now part of Greece and Bulgaria become irrelevant to those interested in state building.

The way in which researchers address such issues affects international public opinion and the actions that the international community takes regarding ethnic and regional conflicts. The fate of nation-states is largely an internationally determined phenomenon. Bosnia is held together by an international coalition because the members of the coalition concluded that Bosnia's partition would destabilize the Balkans. The coalition's concern about regional stability led it to disregard assertions that such a country could never be viable in the face of the interethnic divisions and grievances created during the preceding war. By contrast, Kurds, a large ethnic group in the Middle East whose members mostly live in Iran, Iraq, and Turkey, do not have a state in which they form the core, or titular, ethnic group. One of the primary reasons is that such an idea has been opposed by states in the region. They view a Kurdish state as counter to their national interests and also argue that it would destabilize the region. Nevertheless, the claims of Kurdish activists that they constitute an ancient ethnic group entitled to a nation-state have garnered some support within the larger international community.

In terms of policy, the best prospects for conflict prevention and postconflict rehabilitation lie in the proliferation and strengthening of such international organizations as the United Nations, whose body of covenants and declarations include important instruments of international law relating to the protection of ethnic groups (see Documents 1 and 2). Other international and supranational organizations include the Association of Southeast Asian Nations (ASEAN), the European Union (EU), the Organization for Security and Cooperation in Europe (OSCE), and the Southern Cone Common Market (MERCOSUR). These organizations help resolve ethnic and regional conflicts in two major ways. First, they induce economic and political integration among the participating countries. This has the effect of taking the edge off many ethnic and regional conflicts. Take for example the conflict in Cyprus, a strategically important eastern Mediterranean island that is de facto divided between a Turkish Cypriot state in the north and a Greek Cypriot state in the south. Unification efforts have not borne fruit so far largely because the parties have not been able to find ways to reconcile minority ethnic Turks' fears of domination by ethnic Greeks, which the former associate with mainland Greece. Ethnic Greeks respond that their counterparts in the north seek dominance through unification with mainland Turkey. Presumably, however, these concerns could lessen if all parties to the conflict became members of a much larger entity, such as the European Union, within which neither group had dominant status. The economic cooperation opportunities within an organization like the European Union would also create a reason to seek political stability and avoid conflict.

Second, international and supranational organizations have effective conflict resolution mechanisms and are active in peacekeeping and postconflict missions. Over time, these organizations have learned from past missions and mistakes. Along with the advancement of practical and scholarly knowledge on ethnic and regional conflict, these organizations' contributions have become more sophisticated and constructive. In the past, international involvement in such conflicts began only after confrontations had erupted and was limited to peacekeeping missions. International involvement is now more focused on conflict prevention, which entails intervention at an early stage. International and supranational organizations have a large array of early warning systems in place. In Kosovo and Macedonia, for instance, intervention occurred at a much earlier stage and to a more significant extent than in Rwanda or Bosnia, for which the international community was widely criticized for improper and delayed action.

In 1999 UN secretary-general Kofi Annan called for increased international involvement in conflict prevention under the mandate of the United Nations. In response to criticisms that the North Atlantic Treaty Organization (NATO) had intervened in Kosovo without seeking the authority of the United Nations Security Council, Annan responded that although such authority is desirable, action without approval to prevent an imminent human tragedy is preferable to inaction brought on by indecision, which could cause the loss of hundreds of thousands of lives. Annan also invited states to redefine their national interests to recognize their common interest in an international system in which human rights and the protection of individual sovereignty take precedence over the sovereignty and protection of those who abuse human rights. To minimize human tragedies during ethnic and regional conflict, advance knowledge and early intervention are crucial. Hence the development of early warning systems is a major focus of current research and policy. The Conflict Early Warning Systems Project (CEWSP) sponsored by the International Social Science Council is a promising example.

Another focus is on postconflict reconstruction. In the aftermath of conflict, priority should be given to measures that will help prevent the recurrence of conflict. These include check-and-balance mechanisms, legal and effective guarantees for the protection of human rights, and confidence-building measures to reestablish trust between ethnic or regional groups (see INTERNATIONAL CRIMINAL JUSTICE). International monitoring of and assistance in the implementation of peace accords and reconstruction efforts are crucial. Prominent examples of ongoing missions and projects in this respect include the following:

- the OSCE mission to Bosnia to promote democratic values, monitor and further the development of human rights, organize and supervise elections, and implement arms control and security-building measures;
- the UN-mandated International Force in East Timor (INTERFET) to monitor elections, report human rights abuses, and build and maintain peace after East Timor voted for independence in 1999, rejecting continued Indonesian control;
- the NATO-led international force in Kosovo (KFOR) to maintain law and order until the UN Mission in Kosovo can assume peacekeeping responsibility;

- the OSCE Spillover Monitor Mission in Macedonia to monitor the border with Yugoslavia and promote communication between ethnic Albanian and Slavic Macedonians.

Regional Summaries

An imperfect yet often reliable predictor of the level of ethnic and regional conflict in a country is the region of the world in which the country is situated. Generally, the ability to manage such conflicts increases with economic and democratic development, and countries in general are clustered with others that have similar levels of democracy and prosperity. Another element indicating the location of conflict is contagion: peace as well as conflict tends to spread among neighboring countries for various reasons. The result is that the level of conflict in a country correlates to that country's region. Presently, for instance, none of the prosperous democracies in Western Europe face major armed insurgencies. Although there are significant conflicts in France, Spain, and Northern Ireland, the level of violence is incomparably less than in Central and Southeast Asia. Similarly, the level of armed conflict in Latin America and the Caribbean significantly subsided during the 1990s alongside a general trend toward democratization in the region. By contrast, the former republics of the Soviet Union and sub-Saharan African nations are much more likely to suffer from ethnic and regional conflicts.

North America

The most important sources of ethnic and religious conflict in the Americas have traditionally been the treatment of indigenous peoples and racial minorities and related regional inequalities. The exception is the separatist movement in Canada's Quebec province, where the majority of French speakers voted for secession in 1995. (The proposal was defeated largely by the votes of indigenous people and other minorities, who feared that their rights would not be respected in an independent Quebec.) Québécois separatist sentiment is not thought likely to lead to violence because Canada, as a prosperous democracy, is committed to multiculturalism and multilingualism. Although the United States has had numerous ethnic and regional conflicts, and current interethnic and interracial relations are far from perfect, the country retains a high capacity to resolve group conflict before it becomes violent.

Latin America

The overall trend concerning ethnic and regional conflict in Latin America has been positive in the 1990s, largely thanks to democratization. The case of Mexico is illustrative. The government of Vicente Fox devoted considerable efforts to accommodate the Zapatistas, who had begun an armed uprising on 1 January 1994, the day the North American Free Trade Agreement (NAFTA) came into effect. The Zapatistas seek more autonomy and economic and cultural rights for the indigenous people living in the Chiapas

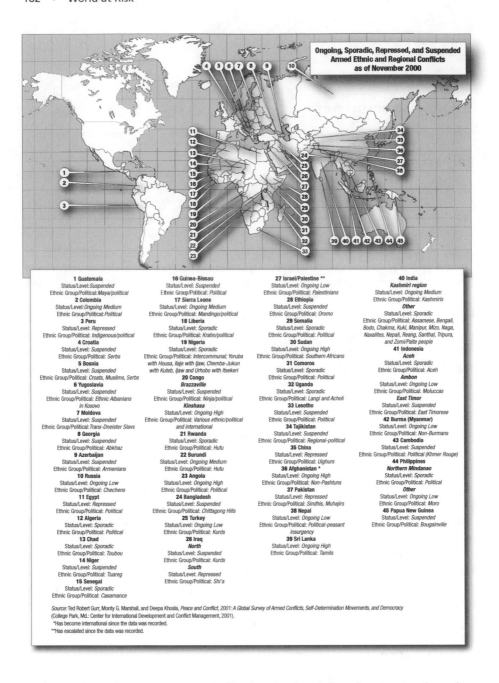

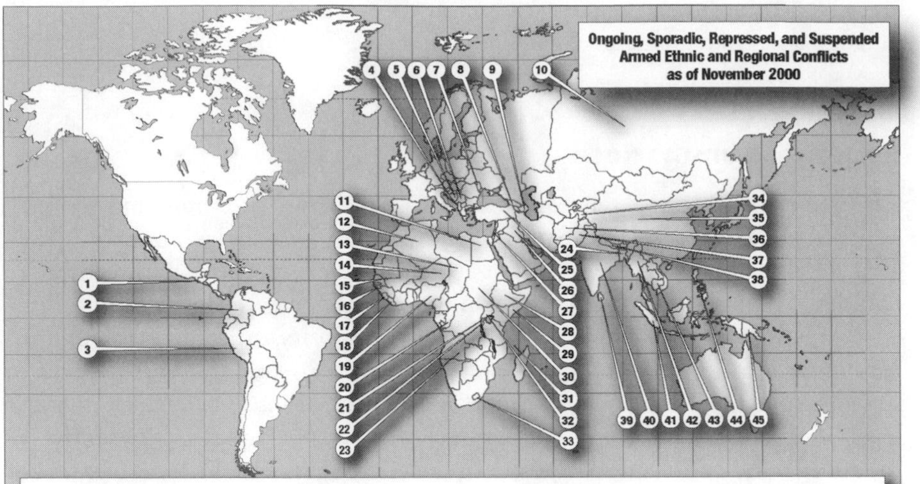

1 Guatemala
Status/Level: *Suspended*
Ethnic Group/Political: *Maya/political*
2 Colombia
Status/Level: *Ongoing Medium*
Ethnic Group/Political: *Political*
3 Peru
Status/Level: *Repressed*
Ethnic Group/Political: *Indigenous/political*
4 Croatia
Status/Level: *Suspended*
Ethnic Group/Political: *Serbs*
5 Bosnia
Status/Level: *Suspended*
Ethnic Group/Political: *Croats, Muslims, Serbs*
6 Yugoslavia
Status/Level: *Suspended*
Ethnic Group/Political: *Ethnic Albanians in Kosovo*
7 Moldova
Status/Level: *Suspended*
Ethnic Group/Political: *Trans-Dneister Slavs*
8 Georgia
Status/Level: *Suspended*
Ethnic Group/Political: *Abkhaz*
9 Azerbaijan
Status/Level: *Suspended*
Ethnic Group/Political: *Armenians*
10 Russia
Status/Level: *Ongoing Low*
Ethnic Group/Political: *Chechens*
11 Egypt
Status/Level: *Repressed*
Ethnic Group/Political: *Political*
12 Algeria
Status/Level: *Sporadic*
Ethnic Group/Political: *Political*
13 Chad
Status/Level: *Sporadic*
Ethnic Group/Political: *Toubou*
14 Niger
Status/Level: *Suspended*
Ethnic Group/Political: *Tuareg*
15 Senegal
Status/Level: *Sporadic*
Ethnic Group/Political: *Casamance*
16 Guinea-Bissau
Status/Level: *Suspended*
Ethnic Group/Political: *Political*
17 Sierra Leone
Status/Level: *Ongoing Medium*
Ethnic Group/Political: *Mandingo/political*
18 Liberia
Status/Level: *Sporadic*
Ethnic Group/Political: *Krahn/political*
19 Nigeria
Status/Level: *Sporadic*
Ethnic Group/Political: *Intercommunal; Yoruba with Housa, Ilaje with Ijaw, Chemba-Jukun with Kuteb, Ijaw and Urhobo with Itsekeri*
20 Congo
Brazzaville
Status/Level: *Suspended*
Ethnic Group/Political: *Ninja/political*
Kinshasa
Status/Level: *Ongoing High*
Ethnic Group/Political: *Various ethnic/political and international*
21 Rwanda
Status/Level: *Sporadic*
Ethnic Group/Political: *Hutu*
22 Burundi
Status/Level: *Ongoing Medium*
Ethnic Group/Political: *Hutu*
23 Angola
Status/Level: *Ongoing High*
Ethnic Group/Political: *Political*
24 Bangladesh
Status/Level: *Suspended*
Ethnic Group/Political: *Chittagong Hills*
25 Turkey
Status/Level: *Ongoing Low*
Ethnic Group/Political: *Kurds*
26 Iraq
North
Status/Level: *Suspended*
Ethnic Group/Political: *Kurds*
South
Status/Level: *Repressed*
Ethnic Group/Political: *Shi'a*
27 Israel/Palestine **
Status/Level: *Ongoing Low*
Ethnic Group/Political: *Palestinians*
28 Ethiopia
Status/Level: *Suspended*
Ethnic Group/Political: *Oromo*
29 Somalia
Status/Level: *Sporadic*
Ethnic Group/Political: *Political*
30 Sudan
Status/Level: *Ongoing High*
Ethnic Group/Political: *Southern Africans*
31 Comoros
Status/Level: *Sporadic*
Ethnic Group/Political: *Political*
32 Uganda
Status/Level: *Sporadic*
Ethnic Group/Political: *Langi and Acholi*
33 Lesotho
Status/Level: *Suspended*
Ethnic Group/Political: *Political*
34 Tajikistan
Status/Level: *Suspended*
Ethnic Group/Political: *Regional-political*
35 China
Status/Level: *Repressed*
Ethnic Group/Political: *Uighurs*
36 Afghanistan *
Status/Level: *Ongoing High*
Ethnic Group/Political: *Non-Pashtuns*
37 Pakistan
Status/Level: *Repressed*
Ethnic Group/Political: *Sindhis, Muhajirs*
38 Nepal
Status/Level: *Ongoing Low*
Ethnic Group/Political: *Political-peasant insurgency*
39 Sri Lanka
Status/Level: *Ongoing High*
Ethnic Group/Political: *Tamils*
40 India
Kashmiri region
Status/Level: *Ongoing Medium*
Ethnic Group/Political: *Kashmiris*
Other
Status/Level: *Sporadic*
Ethnic Group/Political: *Assamese, Bengali, Bodo, Chakma, Kuki, Manipur, Mizo, Naga, Naxalites, Nepali, Reang, Santhal, Tripura, and Zomi/Paite people*
41 Indonesia
Aceh
Status/Level: *Sporadic*
Ethnic Group/Political: *Aceh*
Ambon
Status/Level: *Ongoing Low*
Ethnic Group/Political: *Moluccas*
East Timor
Status/Level: *Suspended*
Ethnic Group/Political: *East Timorese*
42 Burma (Myanmar)
Status/Level: *Ongoing Low*
Ethnic Group/Political: *Non-Burmans*
43 Cambodia
Status/Level: *Suspended*
Ethnic Group/Political: *Political (Khmer Rouge)*
44 Philippines
Northern Mindanao
Status/Level: *Sporadic*
Ethnic Group/Political: *Political*
Other
Status/Level: *Ongoing Low*
Ethnic Group/Political: *Moro*
45 Papua New Guinea
Status/Level: *Suspended*
Ethnic Group/Political: *Bougainville*

Source: Ted Robert Gurr, Monty G. Marshall, and Deepa Khosla, *Peace and Conflict, 2001: A Global Survey of Armed Conflicts, Self-Determination Movements, and Democracy* (College Park, Md.: Center for International Development and Conflict Management, 2001).
*Has become international since the data was recorded.
**Has escalated since the data was recorded.

region, where they are economically deprived and fear domination by other ethnic groups as well as by powerful landowners. The Zapatista rebels' denouncement of armed struggle in favor of an international media campaign had helped the Fox government gain power through promises of democratization. The Fox government returned the favor by letting the guerrillas address the national legislature at the end of a well-publicized two-week-long Zapatour trip to Mexico City. Although a much-expected Indian Rights Bill was watered down in the Mexican assembly, its passage was nevertheless a positive sign. In the long run, the course of this problem will be determined by the level of economic progress in Chiapas.

In an ongoing conflict in Colombia, the United Self-Defense Forces of Colombia, a pro-government paramilitary group, the Revolutionary Armed Forces of Colombia (FARC), and the National Liberation Army continue to fight over control of the country's hinterland and profits from the lucrative drug trade. In Peru, a revolutionary movement of indigenous people has been weakened and repressed since 1997. In Guatemala, an armed conflict pitting the Maya against government forces ended with a negotiated settlement in 1996. Other conflicts, notably those involving the indigenous people of Brazil and Chile, Tobagonians in Trinidad and Tobago, and Nevisians in St. Kitts-Nevis, continue as low-level strife that mostly play out within the context of conventional politics.

Europe

Europe has been home to numerous movements of militant nationalism and ethnic and regional conflict in the past. Western Europe, however, has mostly been able to manage such conflicts and to prevent related violence since World War II thanks largely to economic prosperity, democracy, and economic and political integration under the umbrella of the European Union and its predecessors. This is not to say that there are no significant ethnic or regional conflicts, but that they are largely managed through negotiation and within the confines of democratic politics. In Belgium there are tensions between the Flemish and the Walloon and in Northern Ireland between the Catholics and Protestants and between the pro-British and those opposed to the British. Other conflicts in Western Europe include those in France involving the Corsicans, in Spain involving the Basques, and in Italy involving the Germans of South Tyrol.

Violent conflict in Europe has occurred most recently in Eastern Europe and Eurasia, where communist rule and Soviet domination ended in the late 1980s and 1990s. The most flagrant of these conflicts occurred in the Balkans among the heirs of the former Yugoslavia. The containment of these conflicts in the 1990s benefited from two factors that are lacking in such places as Africa: intense international involvement in conflict prevention and peacekeeping and the positive influence of the prospects of integration with Europe. The most notable exception to this rule is the Chechen conflict in Russia.

Political chaos and conflict largely ended in Albania in 1997, when the country began to focus on integration with the rest of Europe. In Bosnia, the future of a fragile peace and multiethnic government, which were achieved with the 1996 Dayton accords, depends on continuing international involvement and economic and political development in neighboring countries. Peace has largely been established in Croatia's Krajina region. The Kosovo conflict in Yugoslavia is benefiting from overall democratization in Yugoslavia following the ouster of President Slobodan Milosevic in 2000 and his subsequent trial for war crimes and crimes against humanity (see INTERNATIONAL

CRIMINAL JUSTICE). Relations between the ethnic Albanians and Serbs in Kosovo remain extremely fragile. A lasting peace is yet to be achieved between ethnic Georgians and the secessionist Abkhaz in Georgia although a cease-fire is holding. The Trans-Dneister region in Moldova and the Armenian-inhabited Nagorno-Karabakh region in Azerbaijan enjoy de facto autonomy but no permanent peace. Warfare between Russian forces and Chechen rebels in Chechnya continues. In Turkey, armed conflict between security forces and Kurdish nationalists has all but ceased since the capture and trial of the Kurdish rebels' leader, but the conflict has the potential to escalate in the future.

North Africa and the Middle East

Since the end of World War II, the Middle East and North Africa have been a hotbed of ethnic and regional conflict. For centuries ethnic communities in this region have historically lived side by side relatively peacefully. To find the origins of ethnic and regional conflict here, one must look elsewhere: to insecure and oppressive states, ill-fated foreign interventions lured by the region's vast oil reserves, and economic straits that make the young unemployed turn to militant political and religious groups. Even the most important conflict in the region, the one between Israelis and Palestinians, was imported. The founding of Israel resulted when masses of Jews who were persecuted in Europe poured into Palestine in search of safe haven and displaced the Palestinian Arabs. Arguably, one reason that the United Nations recognized Israel, despite fierce opposition from the Arab world, was the sympathy for the victims of the Holocaust, which took place in Europe, where anti-Semitism was much stronger than in the Middle East.

As in other regions of the world, ethnic and regional conflicts in North Africa and the Middle East have been decreasing since the early 1990s. In Algeria, which was the scene of a murderous civil war between the government and Islamist forces, large numbers of rebels have accepted the military regime's offer of a general amnesty, and violence has been waning. In Egypt, Islamists, most notably the Gamaat-i Islamiyya, appear to have been repressed and forced underground. In northern Iraq, Kurds who were formerly persecuted by President Saddam Hussein enjoy de facto autonomy and relative peace made possible by Western enforcement of a "no-fly" zone. The Kurds' situation, however, remains precarious since the future of Hussein's regime in Baghdad is uncertain. Kurdish nationalist ambitions continue to be a potential source of instability in the region, along with the conflict between Israelis and Palestinians and the influence of radical Islam. Conflicts in the Middle East have a very high potential to damage economic growth and political stability on a global scale because of the importance of the region's energy resources and its cultural linkages to the rest of the world.

Sub-Saharan Africa

Sub-Saharan Africa is the epitome of ethnic and regional conflict. Economic and democratic development have not been successful in most countries in this part of the world; the relationship between underdevelopment and ethnic and regional conflict runs two ways. There are, however, some sub-Saharan success stories. In 1994 South Africa was able to terminate the age-old National Party regime based on racial separation, apartheid, and since has taken major steps in facing its past and establishing interracial trust and peace. South Africa's positive steps appear to have influenced its neighbors. Botswana, Madagascar, and Namibia have been able to avoid conflict and spur economic and political development. Nigeria, if it is successful in its transition to democracy, could trigger positive effects in neighboring West African states. This large and resourceful country is beset by numerous ethnic rivalries as well as regional and religious rifts between the north and the south.

Ethnic and regional conflicts with high potential for violence are ongoing in several countries, including Angola, Burundi, the Democratic Republic of Congo, Liberia, Sierra Leone, Somalia, and Sudan. Evidence in Africa as well as elsewhere in the world indicates that three factors can lead to improvements in ethnic and regional conflict: the establishment of stable and effective states and advancement toward democracy and economic growth; international involvement in conflict prevention and management; and economic and political cooperation among states and the emergence of new countries as positive role models. Because of sub-Saharan Africa's relatively insignificant role in the world economy, and because of its relative isolation from the rest of the world, conflicts here have lower potential to affect conflicts in other parts of the world. At the same time, as the example of once-ignored Afghanistan has shown, it would be a grave mistake to think that ethnic and regional conflict in sub-Saharan Africa can forever be contained on the continent and therefore ignored.

Central and South Asia

Central and South Asia are prime candidates for international crises with the potential to cause major damage to global security and cooperation. The region is home to a host of countries that are unable to control flourishing ethnic and religious movements as well as drug trafficking and corruption within their territory. Afghanistan, ridden with interethnic rivalries, is a country currently in chaos and a major source of international terrorism and instability in the region. Pakistan has ethnic and cultural bonds with Afghanistan, so developments in the latter could destabilize Pakistan. If this happens, it would be difficult to shield India, Iran, Tajikistan, and Uzbekistan from the fallout. They all have significant economic and ideological interests in and ethnic and religious ties with Pakistan and Afghanistan.

Pakistan and India have nuclear arms, and relations between them are already volatile, largely because of their conflict over Kashmir. This disputed area has been divided between the two countries by a "line of control" since 1972, and Kashmiri insurgents and their Pakistani supporters fight India for secession in the southern and southeastern parts of the area. India also has significant interests in neighboring Sri Lanka, where a violent conflict is ongoing between the majority Sinhala and minority Tamil communities. Similarly, instability in Central Asia would immediately invite Russian involvement, and thus affect democratic development there. Russia views this region as its periphery, and substantial numbers of ethnic Russians continue to live in Central Asian states. The United States also has significant interests in the region and its relationship with Russia is still evolving.

As in the case of the Middle East and sub-Saharan Africa, the best prospects for the prevention of ethnic and regional conflict in this region lie in economic and political development and in foreign assistance. For example, most countries in Central Asia are ruled by authoritarian-yet-insecure states that possess important natural resources but are unable to exploit them because they do not have adequate access to Western markets. External assistance could focus on providing such access and in supporting democratic development. Regional cooperation among the Central Asian states would also contribute to stability, but would require overcoming old rivalries and animosities, such as between Uzbekistan and Tajikistan. Almost all of the regimes in Central Asia fear radical Islamic movements but also use them as an excuse to oppress all opposition.

East Asia and the Pacific

The Pacific Rim is a mixture of relatively ethnically homogenous countries—China, Japan, and South Korea—and enormously heterogeneous countries—Indonesia and Papua New Guinea. It also combines prosperous countries that have little prospect of ethnic and regional conflict, such as Japan, with countries that have a high potential for conflict, such as Indonesia. Since the region is evolving as an economic powerhouse, its stability is important. An armed regional conflict between China and Taiwan would be a threat to world peace. Especially during the cold war, the region experienced severe wars, such as in Vietnam and Cambodia, especially during the cold war but ethnic and regional conflicts have been declining since 1991. The Philippine government, for instance, has been able to contain a thirty-year rebellion by leftist insurgents. There is, however, the likelihood of renewed conflict in the region. In particular, conflicts in South Asia could spread to the Pacific Rim especially if they destabilized India. Indonesia's territorial integrity and stability are vulnerable to Muslim-Christian conflicts and separatist movements in Aceh and East Timor.

With the exception of Australia, Japan, and New Zealand, the states in this region are developing nations. Some of them, such as South Korea, are already prosperous, but the rest are mostly middle- and low-income countries. Democratic development in this region has not, however, matched the level of economic development. Burgeoning regional and international organizations, such as the Asia-Pacific Economic Cooperation forum and the Association of Southeast Asian Nations tend to focus on economic cooperation but avoid political and security issues. To manage ethnic and regional conflicts the way Europe has, the countries of the Pacific Rim might be advised to expand their economic cooperation to democracy and human rights issues. Finally, the greatest unknown in this region is China. If China manages to develop economically and democratize at the same time, it will generate very positive effects in the whole region.

Data

Table 1 Armed Conflicts for Self-Determination and Their Outcomes, Pre-1956–2000

Period	New Armed Conflicts	Ongoing Conflicts at End of Period	Conflicts Contained	Conflicts Settled or Won
Pre-1956		4		
1956–60	4	8		
1961–65	5	12		1
1966–70	5	15	2	
1971–75	11	23		3
1976–80	10	30	2	1
1981–85	5	34		1
1986–90	10	40	2	2
1991–95	16	38	7	11
1996–2000	2	26	7	6
Total	68	230	20	25

Source: Ted Robert Gurr, Monty G. Marshall, and Deepa Khosla, *Peace and Conflict, 2001: A Global Survey of Armed Conflicts, Self-Determination Movements, and Democracy* (College Park, Md.: Center for International Development and Conflict Management, 2001).

Table 2 Armed Self-Determination Conflicts between 1955 and 2000 by Region and Regime Type

Region	Conflicts	Democracies	Countries in Transition from Autocracy to Democracy	Autocracies
East, South, and Central Asia	32	12	8	3
Latin America	1	21	1	1
North Africa and the Middle East	5	3	11	6
Socialist bloc and successor states	11	13	4	10
Sub-Saharan Africa	15	9	6	30
Western democracies and Japan	3	23	0	0
Total	67	81	30	50

Source: Ted Robert Gurr, Monty G. Marshall, and Deepa Khosla, *Peace and Conflict, 2001: A Global Survey of Armed Conflicts, Self-Determination Movements, and Democracy* (College Park, Md.: Center for International Development and Conflict Management, 2001).

Case Study—Macedonia

In many ways, events in Macedonia exemplify ethnic and regional conflict in the age of globalization. First, Macedonian identity is contested by Macedonians themselves as well as by the people, politicians, and academics of neighboring countries, all of whom ardently defend their version of Macedonian identity as the historical "truth." Varying conceptions of Macedonian identity not only reflect different readings of the historical record, but they are also products of the competing economic and geopolitical interests of the actors involved. Second, the independent state of Macedonia is the product of changing global circumstances, that is, the end of the cold war, which temporarily reduced the geopolitical importance of the former Yugoslavia and thus led to the disintegration of the country and to Macedonian statehood. Third, ethnic conflict in Macedonia is of a transnational nature and cannot be viewed as a domestic or isolated phenomenon. It has the potential to spill over and destabilize the Balkans and possibly Eastern Europe or the Middle East. Fourth, the international community has been heavily involved in state building and conflict prevention in Macedonia from the start. Fifth, Macedonia exhibits the difficulties of democratization and economic development in multiethnic and multicultural societies.

The first historical identity of Macedonia stems from the ancient kingdom of Macedonia, which is believed to have been created in the sixth century B.C. and enlarged by Alexander the Great in the fourth century B.C. The geographical area that came to be called Macedonia thereafter consists of a southern section now in Greece, a northern part that comprises the present Macedonian state, and an eastern portion now in Bulgaria. This area was subsequently invaded and controlled by the Romans, Slavs, Bulgars, Byzantines, and Ottoman Turks. Macedonia remained under Ottoman rule from the fourteenth century until the end of the Balkan Wars (1912–1913), when it was partitioned between Bulgaria, Greece, and Serbia. After World War I, the area covering present-day Macedonia was placed under the Kingdom of Croats, Serbs, and Slovenes and was called South Serbia. During World War II, the Germans gave control of Macedonia to Bulgaria.

After the war, Macedonia became an autonomous republic within the new socialist Federal Republic of Yugoslavia. Part of the reason Josif Tito, the leader of Yugoslavia from 1945 until his death in 1981, chose to give Macedonia autonomous status instead of making it part of Serbia was to curtail Serb power within Yugoslavia. Over time, Macedonia acquired significant economic and political autonomy within Yugoslavia, like the other Yugoslav republics: Bosnia-Herzegovina, Croatia, Montenegro, Serbia, and Slovenia. Economically, it was one of the poorest regions in Yugoslavia, along with Kosovo and Bosnia.

Most Macedonians appear to have been pro-Yugoslav at the time of the country's disintegration. As a low-income republic, Macedonia was at the receiving end of most Yugoslav federal funds. Ethnic Albanians were also wary of independence because it would make majority Slavs, about 64 percent of the population, the dominant group in the nation, and they knew that Slavic

Macedonians viewed them as potential separatists who would rather unite with neighboring Albania. When the other republics seceded from Yugoslavia in 1991, however, Macedonians decided to secede, leaving Serbia and Montenegro alone in the federation. Macedonia's independence was quickly recognized internationally. From the start, however, nation building in Macedonia faced external and internal hurdles.

The most important external hurdle were relations with Yugoslavia, which is dominated by Serbs. Although ethnic Serbs make up a minuscule portion of the Macedonian population, many Serbs continued to refer to Macedonia as South Serbia. As late as 2000, when Yugoslavia began to democratize, there was a real threat of Serbian aggression against Macedonia. Serbs were also suspicious of ethnic Albanian Macedonians' intentions to create a "Greater Albania," along with their ethnic brethren in Kosovo (a Serbian province) and Albania. Furthermore, neighboring Greece objected to the establishment of a country with the name "Macedonia," since they considered this the name of the region in northern Greece. Threatened by the possibility of a separatist movement in its northern territory, Greece imposed an economic embargo on Macedonia, which ended in 1995 with a compromise on the name of the country, which officially became the Former Yugoslav Republic of Macedonia.

Internally, the hurdles included maintaining the country's territorial integrity and inter-ethnic peace, especially between the majority Slavs and ethnic Albanians, the latter of whom constitute a quarter to a third of the population; other ethnic groups include Croats, Roma, Serbs, Turks, and Vlachs. Croatia and Bosnia were not able to meet this challenge without bloodshed after seceding from Yugoslavia. Compared to these states, Macedonia was considered a relative success story, until 1997–1998. Macedonia established a multiethnic democracy in which ethnic Albanians were represented. The international community was involved from the beginning. To monitor the border with Serbia, the Committee for Security and Cooperation in Europe (now the OSCE) stationed observers in Macedonia. In 1995 a 1,050-person UN Preventive Deployment Force (UNPREDEP) was sent to Macedonia. NATO troops took over in 1998, when China vetoed the renewal of UNPREDEP because Macedonia had recognized Taiwan in return for foreign aid.

Macedonia's economic performance proved moderate at best. Many ethnic Albanians complained that they were unable to find jobs, housing, and schooling. They also complained that they were unable to teach Albanian beyond secondary school and that they were underrepresented in the police force. Albanian nationalists who wanted to create a binational Macedonia—or a Greater Albania—began to gain strength, as did their Macedonian nationalist (Slavic) opponents, who wanted to curtail Albanian autonomy. Relations between the two communities deteriorated in 1997–1998, when ethnic Albanian nationalists escalated their demands for more autonomy and clashed with security forces. These developments were certainly also influenced by the 1998–1999 escalation of the conflict between the ethnic Albanians and Serbs in Kosovo; when NATO bombings of Serbian positions in Kosovo and Serbian aggression created thousands of ethnic Albanian refugees, many found refuge in

Macedonia. The National Liberation Army of ethnic Albanians in Macedonia increasingly armed itself, and the Macedonian government increased its pressure on ethnic Albanians.

In early 2001 bloodshed seemed almost inevitable. In order to prevent the mistakes that were made in Bosnia, however, the United States and the European Union went to great lengths to prevent a war. A Western-brokered peace accord was reached in Ohrid in August 2001. Ethnic Albanians achieved greater cultural rights and a greater role in the police in return for disarming. Hostilities ceased to a large extent. Lasting peace, however, will hinge upon continuing economic and political development and international support.

Biographical Sketches

Frederik Willem de Klerk was South African president from 1989 to 1994 and led his country from an apartheid state, and growing social unrest and international isolation, to official acceptance of racial integration, inclusive democracy, and international acceptance. With Nelson Mandela, whom de Klerk released from prison, he was awarded the Nobel Prize for Peace in 1993.

Ted Robert Gurr is Distinguished University Professor at the University of Maryland, College Park, and a leading expert on ethnic and regional conflict. He is best known for his empirical work on ethnopolitical conflict and for his policy-related work on conflict prevention and early warning systems. He co-founded the Minorities at Risk project, which is a major source of data for researchers, and his 1993 book by the same name has become an authoritative text for advanced students in peace studies. Gurr has been a senior consultant on the White House State Failure Task Force since 1994 and on the steering committee of the Conflict Early Warning Systems Research Program of UNESCO's International Social Science Council.

Donald Horowitz is a professor of law and political science at Duke University and a leading expert on ethnic conflict in general and on constitutional engineering in divided societies in particular. His 1985 *Ethnic Groups in Conflict* has become a must read for researchers with an interest in the subject. Horowitz's proposals have contributed to institution building in divided societies, including in Fiji, Nigeria, Northern Ireland, and Russia. In *The Deadly Ethnic Riot* (2001), he investigates the group dynamics of ethnic group violence.

Nelson Mandela is a political activist for black rights, statesman, and former president of South Africa (1994–1999). Mandela, who was jailed between 1964 and 1990, played a key role in the relatively peaceful death of apartheid in South Africa. Although he earlier preached violent resistance, his relatively moderate stance and lack of vindictiveness contributed to the fact that the ruling South African whites agreed to share power with the blacks without a decisive and bloody military battle. As president, Mandela established the Truth and Reconciliation Commission to investigate past human rights abuses and help the society to come to terms with its past. Together with Frederik Willem de Klerk, he was awarded the Nobel Prize for Peace in 1993.

Jose Ramos Horta is a political activist for peace and independence in East Timor, which has been under Indonesian rule since 1975 but is scheduled to attain independence in 2002. He is best known for speaking out against human rights violations in East Timor by pro-Indonesian militias and for promoting a peace plan to end the violence in his country. With Bishop Carlos F. X. Belo, Horta received the Nobel Prize for Peace in 1975.

Directory

Amnesty International, 322 8th Avenue, New York, NY 10001. Telephone: (212) 807-8400, Email: aimember@aiusa.org, Web: http://www.aiusa.org
Nongovernmental organization that campaigns against human rights abuses and pressures governments and others to refrain from such activities

Doctors Without Borders, 6 East 39th Street, 8th Floor, New York, NY 10016. Telephone: (212) 679-6800, Email: doctors@newyork.msf.org, Web: http://www.doctorswithoutborders.org
Grassroots humanitarian aid organization that provides assistance to people caught in ethnic and regional conflicts

Human Rights Watch, 350 Fifth Avenue, 34th Floor, New York, NY 10118-3299. Telephone: (212) 290-4700, Email: go to http://www.hrw.org/contact.html, Web: http://www.hrw.org
Watchdog organization that reports and condemns human rights abuses, pressures governments and others to refrain from such abuses

Organization for Security and Cooperation in Europe (OSCE), OSCE Secretariat, Kärntner Ring 5-7, 4th Floor, 1010 Vienna, Austria. Telephone: (43) 1 14-36 180, Email: info@osce.org, Web: http://www.osce.org
Regional security organization heavily involved in postconflict reconstruction and in preventing and managing ethnic and regional conflicts in Europe and Eurasia

United Nations, First Avenue at 46th Street, New York, NY 10017. Telephone: (212) 963-4475, Email: inquiries@un.org, Web (for peacekeeping operations): http://www.un.org/Depts/dpko/dpko/home_bottom.htm
International organization that attempts to prevent ethnic and regional conflicts through negotiation and multilateral sanctions and maintain peace through multilateral operations

United States Institute of Peace, 1200 17th Street NW, Suite 200, Washington, DC, 20036-3011. Telephone: (202) 457-1700, Email: usip_requests@usip.org, Web: http://www.usip.org
An independent, nonpartisan federal institution that tries to strengthen the United States' capacity to promote the peaceful resolution of international conflict, mainly through research and educational activities

Further Research

Books

Cashmore, Ellis, with Michael Banton, James Jennings, Barry Troyna, and Pierre L. Van Den Berghe. *Dictionary of Race and Ethnic Relations.* New York: Routledge Books, 1996.

Cowan, Jane K., ed. *Macedonia: The Politics of Identity and Difference.* London: Pluto Press, 2000.

Glenny, Misha. *The Fall of Yugoslavia: The Third Balkan War.* New York: Penguin Books, 1993.

Gurr, Ted Robert. *Minorities at Risk: A Global View of Ethnopolitical Conflicts.* Washington, D.C.: United States Institute of Peace Press, 1993.

Gurr, Ted Robert, and Barbara Harff, eds. *Ethnic Conflict in World Politics.* Boulder: Westview Press, 1994.

Horowitz, Donald L. *The Deadly Ethnic Riot.* Berkeley: University of California Press, 2001.

———. *Ethnic Groups in Conflict.* Berkeley: University of California Press, 1985.

Human Rights Watch. *Slaughter among Neighbors: Political Origins of Communal Violence.* New Haven: Yale University Press, 1995.

Hutchinson, John, and Anthony D. Smith, eds. *Ethnicity.* New York: Oxford University Press, 1996.

Keating, Michael, and John McGarry, eds. *Minority Nationalism and the Changing International Order.* Oxford: Oxford University Press, 2001.

Lake, David A., and Donald Rothchild, eds. *The International Spread of Ethnic Conflict: Fear, Diffusion, and Escalation.* Princeton, N.J.: Princeton University Press, 1998.

Levinson, David. *Ethnic Groups Worldwide: A Ready Reference Book.* Phoenix: Oryx Press, 1998.

Malcolm, Noel. *Kosovo: A Short History.* New York: New York University Press, 1998.

Minority Rights Group, ed. *World Directory of Minorities.* London: Minority Rights Group International, 1997.

Rubin, Barnett R., and Jack Snyder. *Post-Soviet Political Order: Conflict and State-Building.* New York: Routledge, 1998.

Tellis, Ashley J., Thomas S. Szayna, and James A. Winnefeld. *Anticipating Ethnic Conflict.* Santa Monica: RAND, 1997.

Wippman, David, ed. *International Law and Ethnic Conflict.* Ithaca: Cornell University Press, 1998.

Articles and Reports

Annan, Kofi. "Two Concepts of Sovereignty." *Economist,* 16 September 1999.

Easterly, William. "Polarized People." In *The Elusive Quest for Growth: Economists' Adventures and Misadventures in the Tropics.* Cambridge, Mass.: MIT Press, 2001.

Gurr, Ted Robert, Monty G. Marshall, and Deepa Khosla. *Peace and Conflict 2001: A Global Survey of Armed Conflicts, Self-Determination Movements, and Democracy.* College Park, Md.: Center for International Development and Conflict Management, 2001.

"The Nation-State Is Dead. Long Live the Nation-State." *Economist,* 23 December 1996.

United States Institute of Peace. *The Future of Macedonia: A Balkan Survivor Needs Reform.* Washington, D.C.: USIP, 2001.

Web Sites

Balkans Today, European Internet
http://www.europeaninternet.com/balkans

Conflict Early Warning Systems Database
http://www.usc.edu/dept/LAS/ir/cis/cews

Conflict, Security and Development
http://csdg.kcl.ac.uk/Publications/html/journal.htm

Ethnic and Racial Studies
http://www.tandf.co.uk/journals/routledge/01419870.html

Ethnic Conflict Research Digest
http://www.incore.ulst.ac.uk/ecrd/index.html

Ethnologue.com
http://www.ethnologue.com

Immigrants and Minorities
http://www.frankcass.com/jnls/im.htm

Journal of Conflict Resolution
http://www.sagepub.co.uk/journals/details/j0058.html

Minorities at Risk
http://www.bsos.umd.edu/cidcm/mar

Project on Peacekeeping and the United Nations
http://www.clw.org/pub/clw/un/index.html

United Institute of Peace Library, Peacekeeping Web Links
http://www.usip.org/library/topics/peacekeeping.html

United Nations High Commissioner for Human Rights
http://www.unhchr.ch/html/racism/01-minoritiesguide.html

World Conference Against Racism, United Nations Guide for Indigenous Peoples
http://www.unhchr.ch/html/racism

Documents

1. Declaration on the Rights of Persons Belonging to National or Ethnic, Religious and Linguistic Minorities

United Nations General Assembly, Resolution 47/135, 18 December 1992

The full text is available at http://www.unhchr.ch/html/racism/minorpart1-1.doc.

Extracts

Article 1

1. States shall protect the existence and the national or ethnic, cultural, religious and linguistic identity of minorities within their respective territories and shall encourage conditions for the promotion of that identity.
2. States shall adopt appropriate legislative and other measures to achieve those ends.

Article 2

1. Persons belonging to national or ethnic, religious and linguistic minorities (hereinafter referred to as persons belonging to minorities) have the right to enjoy their own

culture, to profess and practice their own religion, and to use their own language, in private and in public, freely and without interference or any form of discrimination.
2. Persons belonging to minorities have the right to participate effectively in cultural, religious, social, economic, and public life.
3. Persons belonging to minorities have the right to participate effectively in decisions on the national and, where appropriate, regional level concerning the minority to which they belong or the regions in which they live, in a manner not incompatible with national legislation.
4. Persons belonging to minorities have the right to establish and maintain their own associations.
5. Persons belonging to minorities have the right to establish and maintain, without any discrimination, free and peaceful contacts with other members of their group and with persons belonging to other minorities, as well as contacts across frontiers with citizens of other States to whom they are related by national or ethnic, religious or linguistic ties.

Article 3

1. Persons belonging to minorities may exercise their rights, including those set forth in the present Declaration, individually as well as in community with other members of their group, without any discrimination.
2. No disadvantage shall result for any person belonging to a minority as the consequence of the exercise or non-exercise of the rights set forth in the present Declaration.

Article 4

1. States shall take measures where required to ensure that persons belonging to minorities may exercise fully and effectively all their human rights and fundamental freedoms without any discrimination and in full equality before the law.
2. States shall take measures to create favourable conditions to enable persons belonging to minorities to express their characteristics and to develop their culture, language, religion, traditions and customs, except where specific practices are in violation of national law and contrary to international standards.
3. States should take appropriate measures so that, wherever possible, persons belonging to minorities may have adequate opportunities to learn their mother tongue or to have instruction in their mother tongue.
4. States should, where appropriate, take measures in the field of education, in order to encourage knowledge of the history, traditions, language and culture of the minorities existing within their territory. Persons belonging to minorities should have adequate opportunities to gain knowledge of the society as a whole.
5. States should consider appropriate measures so that persons belonging to minorities may participate fully in the economic progress and development in their country.

2. International Convention on the Elimination of All Forms of Racial Discrimination

United Nations General Assembly, Resolution 2106 (XX), 21 December 1965, entry into force 4 January 1969

The full text is available at http://www.unhchr.ch/html/menu3/b/d_icerd.htm.

Extracts

The States Parties to this Convention,

Considering that the Charter of the United Nations is based on the principles of the dignity and equality inherent in all human beings, and that all Member States have pledged themselves to take joint and separate action, in co-operation with the Organization, for the achievement of one of the purposes of the United Nations which is to promote and encourage universal respect for and observance of human rights and fundamental freedoms for all, without distinction as to race, sex, language or religion,

Considering that the Universal Declaration of Human Rights proclaims that all human beings are born free and equal in dignity and rights and that everyone is entitled to all the rights and freedoms set out therein, without distinction of any kind, in particular as to race, colour or national origin,

Considering that all human beings are equal before the law and are entitled to equal protection of the law against any discrimination and against any incitement to discrimination,

Considering that the United Nations has condemned colonialism and all practices of segregation and discrimination associated therewith, in whatever form and wherever they exist, and that the Declaration on the Granting of Independence to Colonial Countries and Peoples of 14 December 1960 (General Assembly resolution 1514 (XV)) has affirmed and solemnly proclaimed the necessity of bringing them to a speedy and unconditional end,

Considering that the United Nations Declaration on the Elimination of All Forms of Racial Discrimination of 20 November 1963 (General Assembly resolution 1904 (XVIII)) solemnly affirms the necessity of speedily eliminating racial discrimination throughout the world in all its forms and manifestations and of securing understanding of and respect for the dignity of the human person,

Convinced that any doctrine of superiority based on racial differentiation is scientifically false, morally condemnable, socially unjust and dangerous, and that there is no justification for racial discrimination, in theory or in practice, anywhere,

Reaffirming that discrimination between human beings on the grounds of race, colour or ethnic origin is an obstacle to friendly and peaceful relations among nations and is capable of disturbing peace and security among peoples and the harmony of persons living side by side even within one and the same State,

Convinced that the existence of racial barriers is repugnant to the ideals of any human society,

Alarmed by manifestations of racial discrimination still in evidence in some areas of the world and by governmental policies based on racial superiority or hatred, such as policies of apartheid, segregation or separation,

Resolved to adopt all necessary measures for speedily eliminating racial discrimination in all its forms and manifestations, and to prevent and combat racist doctrines and practices in order to promote understanding between races and to build an international community free from all forms of racial segregation and racial discrimination,

Bearing in mind the Convention concerning Discrimination in Respect of Employment and Occupation adopted by the International Labour Organization in 1958, and the Convention against Discrimination in Education adopted by the United Nations Educational, Scientific and Cultural Organization in 1960,

Desiring to implement the principles embodied in the United Nations Declaration on the Elimination of All Forms of Racial Discrimination and to secure the earliest adoption of practical measures to that end.

FRAGILE ECOSYSTEMS

Chris Woodford

Ecosystems—complex, interdependent webs of life—are being threatened by severe disturbances around the globe. These events range from human intervention, such as overharvesting of trees, to environmental changes, such as drought. Some areas are more vulnerable to sudden change than are others, and this inherent fragility can cause problems when the interconnectedness of an areas' components—land, flora, fauna, and human life—is unknown, misunderstood, or neglected by the human communities they host. While scientists struggle to understand the nature and effects of this interdependency, the rate of destruction of fragile ecosystems continues to increase and the quality of life for humans that depend on them grows more threatened.

Historical Background and Development

Conservation and protection of fragile ecosystems may appear to be a particularly modern concern, but they also preoccupied ancient civilizations. The Incas, for example, developed terraced agriculture to prevent soil erosion on hillsides. Although modern society has constructed concepts such as biodiversity, ecosystems, and sustainable development to understand and address the problems facing threatened areas, it is generally believed that earlier civilizations instinctively lived more in tune with the carrying capacity of their immediate environment.

The foundations of the modern conservation movement were laid toward the end of the nineteenth century, when industrialization began taking its toll on natural resources. Wildlife artist John James Audobon aroused popular interest in nature conservation, while writers Ralph Waldo Emerson and Henry David Thoreau argued strongly for the conservation of wildlife and wilderness. Positive steps toward conservation included the establishment of the world's first national parks, including Italy's Gran Paradiso in 1856, Yellowstone in 1872, Canada's Hot Springs Reservation in 1885, and South Africa's Kruger National Reservation in 1898.

Some of the world's first conservation organizations were also established around this time, notably the Sierra Club (1892), Britain's National Trust

(1895), and the National Audobon Society (1905). Other important nineteenth-century initiatives included a petition by the American Association for the Advancement of Science to Congress in 1873 to promote wiser use of natural resources and the formation in 1891 of the federal forest reserves. These efforts toward conservation continued into the early decades of the twentieth century. President Woodrow Wilson formed the National Park Service in 1916, and the creation of several other federal organizations soon followed, including the Natural Resources Commission in 1934 (which surveyed the country's natural resources) and the Fish and Wildlife Service in 1940 (which was charged with protecting wildlife).

By the middle of the twentieth century, a number of international projects were being launched. Not long after the United Nations was established in 1945, the Food and Agriculture Organization (FAO) and the United Nations Educational, Scientific, and Cultural Organization (UNESCO) launched wildlife conservation programs. In 1948 UNESCO helped found the International Union for the Conservation of Nature/World Conservation Union (IUCN), which began systematic studies of threatened species. British naturalist Max Nicholson, who had run Britain's Nature Conservancy Council and had also been involved in the formation of the IUCN, coordinated the establishment of another international conservation body in 1961, the World Wildlife Fund (WWF).

With the publication of Rachel Carson's *Silent Spring* in 1962, protection of the environment suddenly figured more highly on the political agenda. Carson is often referred to as "the mother of the modern environmental movement," which was really born as a confluence of late 1960s political radicalism and growing environmental consciousness. The first Earth Day was held in 1970. This idealistic global celebration of environmentalism has been held annually ever since. In 1972 the United Nations Conference on Environment and Development was held, launching the United Nations Environment Programme (UNEP) and the study "Man and the Biosphere." Just as the end of the nineteenth century witnessed the birth of solid, traditional conservation organizations, such as the National Audobon Society and the Sierra Club, the closing decades of the twentieth century gave birth to a new generation of more radical green groups, including Survival International (1969), Friends of the Earth (1970), and Greenpeace (1971). An even more radical environmental group, Earth First!, was launched in 1979. Its supporters use direct action—such as chaining themselves to bulldozers or vandalizing construction machines—to make their point, which is borne out in their motto: "No compromise in defense of Mother Earth!"

The 1980s and 1990s saw a number of global initiatives to tackle threats to Earth's fragile ecosystems. In 1980 IUCN, UNEP, and WWF produced the World Conservation Strategy, which was launched in thirty-four world capitals. The United Nations adopted its World Charter for Nature two years later. In 1987 the World Commission on Environment and Development published *Our Common Future,* also known as the Brundtland Report, coining the term *sustainable development* and arguing that humankind did not have to choose between economic development and environmental protection: "species and their genetic materials promise to play an expanding role in development, and a powerful economic rationale is emerging to bolster the ethical, aesthetic, and scientific cases for preserving them" (see Document 1).

During the 1980s, conserving fragile ecosystems became more firmly grounded in the new concept of biodiversity, popularized by Edward O. Wilson and others (see BIODIVERSITY). The idea of maximizing biodiversity has informed most recent efforts to save ecosystems, including the UN-sponsored Convention on Biological Diversity, which entered into force in 1983, the 1992 UN Conference on Environment and Development's Agenda 21, and UNEP's 1995 Global Biodiversity Assessment. It also underpins one of the most recent and more ambitious efforts to save Earth's ecosystems: the Millennium Ecosystem Assessment, launched in 2001 (see Case Study—The Millennium Ecosystem Assessment).

Current Status

According to Stanford biologist Peter Vitousek and his colleagues, writing in *Science* in 1997, "Many ecosystems are dominated directly by humanity and no ecosystem on Earth's surface is free of pervasive human influence." A decade earlier, writing in *Bioscience,* Vitousek and others had estimated that nearly 40 percent of Earth's terrestrial productivity had been used directly, indirectly, or lost because of human activities. Drawing a clear picture of what is happening to Earth's ecosystems and using it to devise effective policies and programs has, however, proved remarkably difficult.

Research

Regular measurements of the carbon dioxide in Earth's atmosphere have prompted massive international efforts to understand the science of global warming. These efforts, in turn, have led to national and international policy initiatives to limit or reverse the damage caused by climate change (see GLOBAL WARMING). There are, however, no similarly compelling indicators for the damage caused to ecosystems by human activities, other than crude estimates of the rate at which habitat is being destroyed. Such measurements, however, reveal little about the quality of the ecosystem remaining.

How, then, should the fragility of ecosystems be measured? In 1995 three hundred scientists from fifty countries contributed to the UNEP Global Biodiversity Assessment. Conceived as a statement of what scientists wanted to say, rather than what policymakers needed to be told in order to act decisively, the $3 million, 1,140-page tome proved indigestible and largely ineffective as a prod for protecting the world's ecosystems. Undeterred, some of the report's authors continued to press for a comprehensive study of the state of the planet. In their 1999 "International Ecosystem Assessment" in *Science,* they argue, "The scientific community must mobilize its knowledge of these biological systems in a manner that can heighten awareness, provide information, build local and national capacity, and inform policy changes that will help communities, businesses, nations, and international institutions better manage Earth's living systems." The result of their efforts was the announcement by the United

Nations on 5 June 2001, World Environment Day, of the four-year Millennium Ecosystem Assessment, which will involve fifteen hundred of the world's scientists in the most extensive assessment of the global environment.

One difficulty in assessing the health of ecosystems lies in understanding the relationship between ecosystem function and biodiversity. As scientists and policymakers continue to debate ongoing reductions in global biodiversity, it is not always clear what this trend implies for specific ecosystems. Given the complexity of some ecosystems, are some species effectively "redundant"? Can ecosystems be maintained with a reduction in biodiversity? In "Biodiversity and Ecosystem Function: The Debate Continues," British ecologist J. P. Grime contends that high biodiversity is important in some ecosystems but not in others, yet "neither evolutionary theory nor empirical studies have presented convincing evidence that species diversity and ecosystem function are consistently and causally connected."

Another problem lies in understanding what makes an ecosystem "fragile." Fragility is a broad concept that needs to cover everything from natural but relatively infrequent threats, such as the fires and ice storms that in 1998 damaged millions of hectares of forest, to human-driven and sustained threats, such as the use of explosives for fishing and the progressive expansion of agricultural land. Ecosystems may be surprisingly resilient to large disturbances, yet there is a threshold beyond which they cannot adapt, and changes of a sufficient magnitude will tip the balance and transform them into completely different ecosystems. For instance, a highly destructive forest fire might change a rain forest ecosystem into a grassland ecosystem.

Different kinds of ecosystems are susceptible to different kinds of changes. The Global Biodiversity Assessment grouped human influences on ecosystems under five main headings:

- agriculture, fisheries, and the overharvesting of resources;
- habitat destruction, conversion, fragmentation, and degradation;
- introduction of exotic or invasive organisms and diseases;
- pollution of soil, water, and atmosphere; and
- global (environmental) change.

In the comprehensive biodiversity projections for the year 2100 that were published in *Science* in March 2000, Osvaldo Sala and his colleagues considered how the world's terrestrial biomes—large regions defined by their common vegetation and climate—would be affected by the five most important types of human-influenced changes, or "drivers," as the authors call them: land use; climate change; nitrogen deposition (such as fertilizer additions or sewage discharges); biotic exchange (such as the introduction of invasive organisms); and atmospheric carbon dioxide concentration (which will have direct effects on plant growth as well as indirect effects through climate change). They predicted the following:

- arctic and alpine ecosystems would be most affected by climate change;
- tropical and southern temperate forests would be greatly affected by land use changes (such as forest clearance for agriculture);

- freshwater ecosystems would be affected by land use, biotic exchange, and climate change;
- Mediterranean ecosystems and grassland (including savannah) would be most affected by land use changes, but also affected by most other drivers;
- northern temperate forests would be most changed by nitrogen deposition and acid rain;
- boreal ecosystems (coniferous forests) would be affected by land use, climate change, and nitrogen deposition; and
- deserts would be affected by all drivers other than nitrogen deposition.

Although all ecosystems are vulnerable to change, some ecosystems are more fragile than others. Coral reefs, for instance, are susceptible to a wide range of changes, from such relatively localized human activities as the use of cyanide and crowbars to capture reef fish for the aquarium trade to major fluctuations in climate. Such changes have resulted in extensive damage to many coral habitats throughout the world. According to the Global Coral Reef Monitoring Network's *Status of Coral Reefs of the World, 2000,* "Assessments to late 2000 are that 27% of the world's reefs have been effectively lost, with the largest single cause being the massive climate-related [El Niño–La Niña] coral bleaching event of 1998." The World Resources Institute's *Reefs at Risk* reports that 27 percent of reefs are at immediate risk of significant damage, and an additional 31 percent are under medium risk. Yet global statistics suggesting that all coral reef ecosystems are fragile may be misleading. Thus, *Status of Coral Reefs of the World, 2000* states, "The world's largest areas of coral reefs with the highest biodiversity [in Southeast and East Asia] are probably under the greatest threats from human activities . . . with many losses of 30-60%, and some as high as 80-90% with localized extinctions of prominent corals," whereas "the extensive reefs in the Pacific and off Australia are in reasonably good health with a positive outlook." Generally, reefs surrounded by deep water and far from land pollution are the least fragile and most likely to be pristine.

Coral reefs may be among the most "glamorous" of fragile ecosystems. They are almost certainly one of the most biodiverse, but they are not the only type of ecosystem under threat. Human activities have drastically reduced wetland cover. For instance, according to the U.S. Environmental Protection Agency's Office of Wetlands, Oceans, and Watersheds, more than 50 percent of the wetlands that once covered the United States have been lost, with marshes and mangroves filled in for agriculture or urban development. The World Resources Institute estimates that half of the world's mangrove ecosystems—environments dominated by mangrove trees in coastal regions and estuaries—have been damaged or destroyed by human activities.

At desert margins, land use changes such as deforestation and overgrazing have transformed large areas of grassland ecosystems into desert. At the UN-sponsored "Earth Summit" in 1992 in Rio de Janeiro, participants noted that desertification has wide-ranging consequences, affecting one-sixth of the world's population and 70 percent of the world's drylands, which amounts to one-fourth of the world's land area. Mountains and uplands have attracted increasing attention as sensitive ecosystems since the Earth Summit's Agenda

21 devoted an entire chapter to sustainable mountain development. According to mountain ecologist Martin Beniston, in *Environmental Change in Mountains and Uplands,* "Mountains are often perceived to be austere, isolated and inhospitable; in reality they are fragile regions whose welfare is closely related to that of the neighboring lowlands. . . . Mountain ecosystems and biodiversity have deteriorated and the resources upon which these populations depend have dwindled." Also, tundra—arctic and alpine ecosystems—are particularly threatened by climate change.

Policies and Programs

Because different types of human-induced changes affect different types of ecosystems, policies and programs have typically been proposed on a case by case basis. For example, at the Earth Summit chapters of Agenda 21 were devoted to saving forests (chapter 11), halting desertification and drought (chapter 12), protecting mountains (chapter 13), and conserving biodiversity (chapter 15). Sometimes policy studies consider the problems of fragile ecosystems and dwindling biodiversity together. In 1987, for example, a chapter of the Brundtland Report was titled "Species and Ecosystems: Resources for Development." Initiatives designed to conserve or increase biodiversity, such as the Convention on Biological Diversity, necessarily also benefit fragile ecosystems.

The traditional approach to protecting ecosystems has been to establish national parks and other wilderness areas. According to statistics from the World Conservation Monitoring Center and others, Earth has more than twenty-eight thousand protected areas covering some 6.4 percent of the planet's total land area (see Table 1 and map, p. 205). Almost every country in the world has some protected areas. Australia has more than thirty-seven hundred, for example, and the United States and Canada have more than three thousand. Although protected areas make a substantial contribution to conservation, according to the 1984 World Congress on National Parks, the area they cover must be tripled at least if global ecosystems are to be properly protected. Although protected areas are necessary for conservation, by themselves they are not sufficient. One difficulty is the way in which they implicitly seem to make it acceptable to damage and destroy natural areas that are not so highly protected, even when these too are of great conservation value.

Conserving a relatively small percentage of habitats and species in protected areas is an inadequate response to the current pace of ecosystem destruction. If predictions concerning climate change are correct, Earth needs a greater area of growing forest to offset carbon dioxide emissions than would be achieved solely through the preservation of trees in national parks on the grounds of biodiversity. The world's ever-increasing need for freshwater will require a much greater effort at conserving wetlands than would be achieved by simply protecting the most ecologically important sites because of their interest as areas of plant or bird conservation.

This situation implies that the world must not only conserve a minority of important ecosystems in protected areas, but must also prevent the destruction of a majority of perhaps somewhat less important ecosystems. With the decimation of the world's forests prompting considerable media coverage, public concern, and campaigns by nongovernmental organizations, initiatives to save forests have arguably been more concerted than for any other type of ecosystem (see DEFORESTATION). Yet efforts to save forests by managing them sustainably have had little effect (see Table 2). According to the Forestry Stewardship Council (FSC), which certifies and promotes wood products from sustainable forests, only 328,207 hectares (821,000 acres) of the world's 1.7 billion hectares (4.25 billion acres) of forests—or 0.02 percent—are managed in this way.

Some threatened ecosystems, such as mountains, will benefit only from systematic international attention. The world's coral reefs, for example, gained a higher profile through the International Year of the Reef in 1997; it was the oceans' turn for similar treatment in 1998; mountain ecosystems are expected to garner much more attention through the International Year of Mountains in 2002. This initiative, prompted by the United Nations General Assembly, aims to promote efforts to conserve mountains areas and develop these regions in sustainable ways in order to protect both the communities in the mountains as well as in the surrounding lowland.

Better scientific information is a key feature of programs to halt the destruction of most kinds of ecosystems. In one example, widely reported horror stories about the decimation of the world's coral reefs in the early 1990s were supplanted with a more relaxed attitude by the mid-1990s. In a 1997 issue of *Science,* the article "Brighter Prospects for the World's Coral Reefs" suggests that "some coral reef scientists are beginning to think that reefs may not be quite as widely imperiled as they once thought." That optimism was premature, for in 1998 massive coral bleaching killed substantial areas of reef around the world (see Table 3). By 2000 reef scientists were once again issuing a gloomy prognosis. Whether the optimists or the pessimists are correct remains to be seen, but monitoring the overall health of coral reefs—and all of Earth's other fragile ecosystems—is clearly an important part of preventing their destruction. Science has a vital role to play in this. Zoologist Jane Lubchenco, in her 1997 presidential address to the American Association for the Advancement of Science, stated, "Scientific understanding can help frame the questions to be posed, provide assessments about current conditions, evaluate the likely consequences of different policy or management options, provide knowledge about the world, and develop new technologies."

Scientific research into fragile ecosystems has traditionally considered the natural environment in isolation from the human environment. The degradation of habitats is considered quite separately from such issues as land rights, poverty, population growth, or cultural traditions, which may drive native or nonnative peoples to destroy ecosystems. Yet, as the 1995 Global Biodiversity Assessment report recognizes, "An understanding of the many aspects of human influences on biodiversity, and their underlying driving forces, is of crucial importance for setting priorities and directing conservation and sustainable use measures." Lubchenco further suggests, "National security, social justice, the economy, and human health are appropriately considered to be environmental issues because each is dependent to some degree on the structure, functioning, and resiliency of ecological systems." Future policies and programs will increasingly recognize the importance of integrating social, cultural, economic, and environmental issues in protecting fragile ecosystems. As Vitousek and others argue in the 1997 article "Human Domination of Earth's Ecosystems," "The challenge of understanding a human-dominated planet further requires that the human dimensions of global change—the social, economic, cultural, and other drives of human actions—be included within our analyses."

Regional Summaries

Because Earth's climate varies markedly across the planet, different types of ecosystems predominate in particular regions. As a result, conservation challenges differ from region to region. In the Pacific, for example, defense of coral reefs is of major importance, while in Europe and North America the conservation of wetlands is a pressing matter.

North America

Drastic changes in land use during the twentieth century have radically changed the balance of North America's ecosystems. Around half of all wetlands in the United States and many more in Canada have been destroyed or degraded, largely through drainage for agricultural production and urbanization. Coastal development and tourism have put increasing pressure on coastal wetlands in areas such as the Gulf of Mexico and the Florida Keys. In the Keys, agricultural pollution, tourism, and overfishing also place coral reefs under threat. According to a 1997 report by the World Wildlife Fund, other ecosystems at particular risk in the United States and southern Canada include temperate broadleaf and mixed forests, temperate grasslands, savannahs, and shrublands. An estimated 11 percent of total land area in North America is, however, protected in national parks and wilderness areas. In Canada, protected areas have increased by 15 percent since 1990. Future threats to U.S. lands include proposals by the administration of George W. Bush to allow oil exploration and development in the Arctic National Wildlife Refuge where, according to the World Wildlife Fund, the displacement of dozens of species could be threatened.

Latin America

With abundant tropical forests and coral reefs, Latin America and the Caribbean contain some of the most complex ecosystems in the world. Colombia, which occupies less than 1 percent of the world's total area, contains approximately 10 percent of the planet's plant and animal species, because its ecosystems have such a high degree of biodiversity, creating a rich web of biological interdependency. Much attention has been focused on preventing the destruction of the region's tropical forests for agricultural expansion and urbanization, but other types of forests are also threatened, including high-mountain habitats, cloud forests (high-altitude forests), and mangroves. Mexico is estimated to have lost 65 percent of its mangroves.

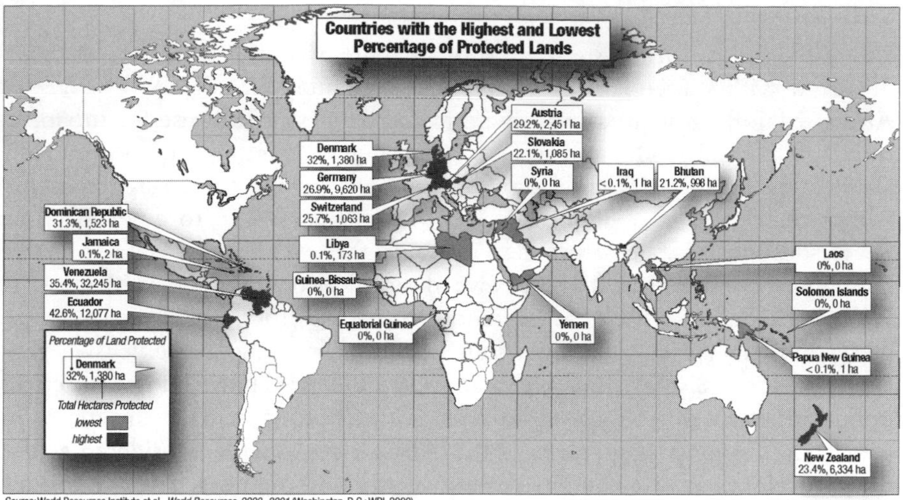

Source: World Resources Institute et al., *World Resources, 2000–2001* (Washington, D.C.: WRI, 2000).

Other ecosystems in Latin America and the Caribbean are also under grave threat. According to a 1991 UNEP estimate, almost 73 percent of South America's agriculturally used drylands were experiencing moderate to extreme degradation. In the *Global Biodiversity Assessment,* UNEP describes the region's savannah grasslands as "under continuous threat." The mountainous regions of Latin America, considered to have very high biodiversity, are also under considerable threat from mining, agricultural expansion, and other development pressures. In the northern Andes, population growth is putting tremendous pressure on cloud forests. Coral reefs surrounding many of the islands in the Caribbean are also under threat due, in part, to expanding tourism. One of the region's most important conservation initiatives is the Mesoamerican Biological Corridor, a protected area comprising 30 percent of Central America, stretching across Belize, Costa Rica, El Salvador, Guatemala, Mexico, Nicaragua, and Panama.

Europe

Habitat loss and fragmentation have been a major concern in Western Europe, with such developments as major highways dividing habitats into areas too small to support key species within ecosystems. Protection of wetlands is a major problem. According to the World Wildlife Fund, more than 60 percent of European wetlands were destroyed during the twentieth century. In the poorer countries of Central and Eastern Europe, the concentration of industry in urbanized regions and relative underdevelopment elsewhere have proved important for the conservation of wildlife. The North Sea, with a huge diversity of animal and plant life, is under threat due to primarily overfishing, but other threats result from chemical and fertilizer discharges from the land and petroleum extraction. Important initiatives for preserving habitats include the European Union's 1992 Habitats Directive, which seeks to protect biodiversity by conserving a selection of important habitats and species across member states.

Sub-Saharan Africa

The predominant ecosystem in sub-Saharan Africa is savannah—tropical grassland with scattered trees—which covers almost half the land surface of Africa. Major threats to savannah are from changes in land use for urbanization, agricultural production to feed increasing populations, and overgrazing, all of which make desertification one of Africa's most pressing problems. Almost half of Africa's population live in drylands subject to desertification. Severe drought has been a problem in Kenya for several years, large-scale tree felling in Tanzania threatens massive desertification, and desertification in Nigeria has led to substantial migrations of people from rural to urban areas. Desertification notwithstanding, sub-Saharan Africa also has extensive wetlands, such as the Okavanga Delta and Lake Victoria, but dam construction, pollution, water abstraction, and overfishing are putting many freshwater habitats at risk. Almost 40 percent of the African coastline is considered at risk from development, threatening mangrove swamps and coral reefs. Although Africa as a whole has around three thousand protected areas (totaling some 240 million hectares), increasing competition for land suggests that there will be little or no further increase in this figure.

North Africa and the Middle East

Wetlands, including the Nile Delta, are under increasing threat in North Africa and the Middle East, whose freshwater resources have long been under great pressure (see FRESHWATER). Desertification is also a major problem in the Sahel of North Africa, where deforestation is exacerbated by drought. Expanding development along the coast of North Africa and the Red Sea also places coastal ecosystems under threat. Increasing oil industry activity, including shipping, makes pollution a particular problem. Around 110 million tons (100 million metric tons) of oil is annually transported through the Red Sea. Discharges from petrochemical and chemical plants in Algeria, Egypt, Libya, Morocco, and Tunisia are a major problem. For these and other reasons (such as global warming), many coral reefs in the northern Red Sea and about two-thirds of those in the Persian Gulf are considered at risk. In Lebanon and Syria, coastal ecosystems are threatened by saltwater incursion, partly because of the rise in sea level caused by climate change and partly because of aggregate mining for the construction industry.

Desertification is also a major problem, caused by overgrazing, increasing competition for limited water resources, and deforestation. With the exception of Oman, few countries in this region have substantial protected areas. In Iraq, less than 0.1 percent of the total land area is protected for conservation, compared to 6.2 percent in China, 26.9 percent in Germany, and 13.1 percent in the United States.

Asia and the Pacific

Asia and the Pacific have a greater length of coastline than any other region and possess three-fourths of the world's largest cities. Pollution, coastal development for tourism, dredging, aquaculture (fish farming), overfishing, and sewage discharges all make the conservation of coastal and marine ecosystems one of the region's most important environmental issues. "Conservation" has come too late for some areas, however. Between 1961 and 1996, Thailand lost 57 percent of its coastal mangrove forests, and Vietnam lost 37 percent of its mangroves between 1950 and 1983.

Coral reefs have perhaps raised the most concern in the region, with up to 95 percent of reefs in some areas destroyed by coral bleaching during the 1997–1998 El Niño. Although pollution, overfishing (with explosives or cyanide), insensitive tourism, and climate change threaten Pacific reefs, those far from land are generally in good shape. Optimists claim that much of Australia's Great Barrier Reef—the world's largest reef and a UNESCO World Heritage Site—is in good condition; pessimists believe it could be dead in fifty to a hundred years. Initiatives to protect the region's ecosystems include the promotion of environmentally sensitive "ecotourism" in the Great Barrier Reef, mangrove replanting projects in Bangladesh, and, more generally, the use of integrated coastal zone management, a technique to manage coastal zones holistically so that conflicting demands (such as coastal resort development and habitat protection) can be reconciled.

Data

Table 1 Areas Protected by Global Agreements in Selected Countries, 2000-2001

	Biosphere Reserves[a]		World Heritage Sites[b]		Wetlands of International Importance[c]	
Country	Number	Area (1000 ha)	Number	Area (1000 ha)	Number	Area (1000 ha)
Algeria	3	7,294	1	8,000	3	5
Argentina	7	2,235	3[d]	861	7	1,000
Australia	12	5,093	13	42,297	53	5,249
Brazil	2	29,699	3[d]	1,974	5	4,537
Canada	8	1,512	8[d]	10,664	36	13,051
China	16	2,645	7	352	7	588[d]
Colombia	3	2,514	1	72	1	400
Congo, Republic of	3	283	5	6,855	2	866
Egypt	2	2,456	0	0	2	106
France	8[d]	832	2[d]	23	15	579
Georgia	0	0	0	0	2	34
Germany	14[d]	1,559	1	<1	31	673
Guatemala	2	3,141	1	58	4	503
India	0	0	5	292	6	193
Indonesia	6	1,329	3	2,845	2	243
Israel	1	27	0	0	2	<1
Japan	4	117	2	28	11	84
Russian Federation	20	23,386	5	17,343	35	10,324

Table 1 Areas Protected by Global Agreements in Selected Countries, 2000-2001 (*continued*)

	Biosphere Reserves[a]		World Heritage Sites[b]		Wetlands of International Importance[c]	
Country	Number	Area (1000 ha)	Number	Area (1000 ha)	Number	Area (1000 ha)
Saudi Arabia	0	0	0	0	N.A.	N.A.
Spain	16	1,008	4[d]	110	38	158
Sweden	1	97	1	940	30	383
Switzerland	1	169	0	0	8	7
Tajikistan	0	0	0	0	N.A.	N.A.
Thailand	4	56	1	622	1	<1
Turkey	0	0	2	10	9	159
Uganda	1	220	2	132	1	15
United Kingdom	13	47	4	11	140	664
United States	44	20,838	12[d]	9,741	17	1,178
World Total	368	263,897	149	142,209	1,019	73,012

Source: World Resources Institute et al., *World Resources, 2000–2001* (Washington, D.C.: WRI, 2000).

[a]Biosphere reserves shared by several countries are counted only once in the national and world totals.

[b]Sites shared by several countries are counted only once in the national and world totals.

[c]Countries that have not signed the Convention on Wetlands of International Importance are designated by N.A.

[d]Includes sites shared by two or more neighboring countries.

Table 2 Change in Forest Area, 1980–1995

Area	Percentage Change
Europe	+4.1
North America	+2.6
Australia, Japan, and New Zealand	+1.0
Developed world	+2.7
Africa	−10.7
Latin America	−9.7
Asia and the Pacific	−6.4
Developing world	−9.1

Source: Food and Agriculture Organization, *State of the World's Forests, 1999* (Rome: FAO, 1999).

Note: Data exclude the countries of the former Soviet Union.

Table 3 Status of Coral Reefs, 2000

Region	Destroyed before 1998 (%)	Destroyed in 1998 (%)	Critical Stage Loss in 2 to 10 years (%)	Threatened Loss in 10 to 30 years (%)
Arabian Region	2	33	6	7
Wider Indian Ocean	13	46	12	11
Australia and Papua New Guinea	1	3	3	6
Southeast and East Asia	16	18	24	30
and the Pacific	4	5	9	14
Caribbean Atlantic	21	1	11	22
Global*	11	16	14	18

Source: Clive Wilkinson, ed., *Status of Coral Reefs of the World* (Townsville: Australian Institute of Marine Science, 2000).

*Mean values adjusted for the proportional area in each region of the global total of coral reefs.

Case Study—The Millennium Ecosystem Assessment

Protecting fragile habitats and the species they harbor is an almost impossible task without a proper appreciation of the state of the world's ecosystems and the threats facing them. This is the purpose of the Millennium Ecosystem Assessment.

Between 2001 and 2005, fifteen hundred ecologists and social scientists will analyze the health of the world's ecosystems, supplying data to international policymaking fora and putting forward scientific and economic cases for the preservation of threatened ecosystems. According to Walter V. Reid, acting science director for the assessment, the project involves a more integrated and holistic methodology than previous ecological assessments, such as UNEP's much-criticized Global Biodiversity Assessment. Instead of exploring threats to ecosystems in isolation, the assessment will consider the links between different environmental problems, such as climate change, food production, freshwater supply, biodiversity loss, and demand for forests products. According to the project's architects, this holistic approach will make the assessment valuable as a tool for the management of ecosystems.

Conceived by World Resources Institute (WRI) president Jonathan Lash and Walter Reid in May 1998, the ecosystem assessment has already gained substantial financial, scientific, and institutional support. WRI tested the key concept of collecting global information about ecosystem health in its Pilot Analysis of Global Ecosystems (PAGE), launched in June 1998. The same year, forty leading scientists led by the World Bank's environment director, Robert Watson, published *Protecting Our Planet, Securing Our Future: Linkages among Global Environmental Issues and Human Needs,* calling for "a more integrative assessment process for selected scientific issues, a process that can highlight the linkages between questions relevant to climate, biodiversity, desertification, and forest issues." In their 1999 "International Ecosystem Assessment" in *Science,* an exploratory steering committee comprising the Consultative Group on International Agricultural Research, the International Council for Science, the IUCN, four UN agencies, the World Bank, WRI, and the World Business Council for Sustainable Development backed the assessment: "We believe the time is right—at the turn of the millennium—to undertake the first global assessment of the condition and future prospects of global ecosystems."

Assessment sponsors are optimistic about its role in ecosystem protection. Speaking at the launch of the project on 5 June 2001, UN secretary-general Kofi Annan asserted that the Millennium Ecosystem Assessment, in mapping the health of the planet, will fill in important gaps in knowledge that are needed to preserve it. Critics remain concerned about the sheer scope of the project and whether a large-scale, scientifically rigorous study of this kind can truly prove effective at influencing international environmental policy. If the experience of the Global Biodiversity Assessment is suggestive, it will not be easy. Conversely, the work of the Intergovernmental Panel on Climate Change (IPCC) suggests that it will not be impossible (see GLOBAL WARMING).

Case Study—The Fall and Rise of the Mangroves

Mangrove forests are one of the most biodiverse ecosystems, yet in some regions they are disappearing more quickly than the tropical rain forests. While the plight of the telegenic rain forests arouses strong public passion, the mangroves slip into oblivion, largely unnoticed. Fortunately, their destruction is not always irreversible. A number of mangrove replacement projects are successfully reintroducing these fragile wetland ecosystems to tropical coasts around the world.

According to the Mangrove Action Project, mangroves cover less than half of the original area they once did—around three-fourths of the coastline in tropical and subtropical regions. (Mangroves grow only at latitudes between 38 degrees south and 32 degrees north). Although they still occupy an estimated 16 million hectares (40 million acres), coastal resorts, sewage discharges, mariculture (marine fish farming) ponds, pollution, coastal mining, and a variety of other human activities have placed mangroves under considerable threat. With one "foot" in the sea and the other on land, mangroves are an important buffer against coastal erosion, and they improve water quality by filtering out pollutants. Their removal, apart from being ecologically destructive in its own right, can lead to a variety of other problems. Today around half the world's mangrove forests have been destroyed, approximately half of the remaining mangrove habitat is considered to be degraded, and mangroves are disappearing at a rate of 2 percent to 8 percent a year.

The recognition that mangrove swamps are ecologically important habitats has brought new efforts to stem their destruction. The Mangrove Action Project (MAP), founded in 1992 and based in Port Angeles, Washington, now links around 400 nongovernmental organizations and 250 scientists from sixty nations. MAP, in its role as information clearinghouse, promotes mangrove restoration projects, works with schools and local communities to increase awareness of the need to protect mangroves, and plays an important part in publicizing the plight of this fragile habitat around the world. MAP considers it vital to ensure the participation of local citizens in its projects, a feature that makes its programs unique.

MAP is just one of the organizations supporting mangrove replanting projects around the world. Other schemes include the Mangrove Replenishment Initiative, which began as a project to replant mangroves along the Florida coast, from Cape Canaveral to Biscayne Bay, using an innovative technique called encasement planting, which involves sheathing the replanted trees in PVC to enable them to grow more quickly. In the developing world, Kenya's Marine and Fisheries Research Institute (KMFRI) replanted some 300,000 mangroves in a cleared area in the mid-1990s. Mangrove replanting programs have also been successful in India, Indonesia, Malaysia, the Philippines, and Thailand. With pressure to develop the world's coastlines continually increasing, it remains uncertain whether projects such as these can truly turn the tide of mangrove destruction. Without these initiatives, however, there may be no hope for the survival of the mangroves at all.

Biographical Sketches

Gretchen Daily is an award-winning researcher in the Department of Biological Sciences at Stanford University. Her work focuses on the scientific, political, and institutional challenges of managing Earth's ecosystems. She has published widely, notably with population expert Paul R. Ehrlich, and has worked with a number of international organizations, including the United Nations and the World Bank.

Jacques Diouf is an agricultural economist and politician and director-general of the Food and Agriculture Organization of the United Nations. He plays an important role in international efforts to protect fragile ecosystems. Diouf has received many honors and awards for his work on the challenges facing agricultural development in Africa.

Jane Lubchenco is professor of zoology at Oregon State University. As a marine biologist and environmental scientist, her goal has been to make scientific research on environmental issues more accessible and to make it more responsive to the concerns of policymakers. She has served as president of the Ecological Society of America and of the American Association for the Advancement of Science.

Harold Mooney is a professor of environmental biology at Stanford University who has researched many of Earth's diverse ecosystems, from grasslands to deserts and tropical forests to tundra. Mooney is currently researching the responses of different ecosystems to global changes, such as increases in atmospheric carbon dioxide, and the effects of biodiversity on ecosystem function.

Edward O. Wilson is a distinguished Harvard biologist and one of the co-founders of the concept of biodiversity. He has argued that Earth could lose up to 20 percent of its species by the year 2020. A recipient of the National Medal of Science, Wilson has won two Pulitzer Prizes for his best-selling books about biodiversity and has influenced a generation of biologists.

Directory

Conservation International, 1919 M Street NW, Suite 600, Washington, DC 20036. Telephone: (202) 912-1000, Email: info@conservation.org, Web:http://www.conservation.org
International organization working to preserve biodiversity through scientific programs, local awareness campaigns, and economic initiatives

Food and Agriculture Organization (FAO), Viale delle Terme di Caracalla 00100 Rome, Italy. Telephone: (39) 06 5705 1, Email: fao-hq@fao.org, Web: http://www.fao.org
UN organization devoted to alleviating poverty and hunger through food security, including a focus on conservation issues related to food and agricultural production

International Union for the Conservation of Nature/World Conservation Union (IUCN), 28 Rue Mauverney, 1196 Gland, Switzerland. Telephone: (41) 22 999 0001, Email: info@iucn.org, Web: http://www.iucn.org
Partnership of government agencies, nongovernmental organizations, and other bodies dedicated to nature conservation

National Audubon Society, 700 Broadway, New York, NY 10003. Telephone: (212) 979-3000, Email: education@audubon.org, Web: http://www.audubon.org
Organization dedicated to conserving and restoring natural ecosystems

Natural Resources Defense Council, 40 West 20th Street, New York, NY 10011. Telephone: (212) 727-2700, Email: nrdcinfo@nrdc.org, Web: http://www.nrdc.org
Organziation dedicated to protecting wildlife and wild places

Sierra Club, 85 Second Street, 2nd Floor, San Francisco, CA 94105-3441. Telephone: (415) 977-5500, Email: information@sierraclub.org, Web: http://www.sierraclub.org
Environmental organization working to protect ecosystems and wild places

United Nations Environment Programme (UNEP), United Nations Avenue, Gigiri, PO Box 30552, Nairobi, Kenya. Telephone: (254) 262 1234, Email: eisinfo@unep.org, Web: http://www.unep.org
Agency addressing environmental issues of international importance

U.S. Fish and Wildlife Service, 4401 N. Fairfax Drive, Arlington, VA 22203. Telephone: (703) 358-1700, Email: contact@fws.gov, Web: http://www.fws.gov
U.S. government agency responsible for conserving wildlife and habitats and managing the National Wildlife Refuge System

Wilderness Society, 1615 M Street NW, Washington, DC 20036. Telephone: 1-800-THE-WILD, Email: member@tws.org, Web: http://www.wilderness.org
Organization working to protect U.S. wilderness through public education, scientific analysis, and advocacy

World Wildlife Fund, 1250 24th Street NW, Washington, DC 20037-1175. Telephone: (202) 293 4800, Web: http://www.worldwildlife.org
U.S. office of the world's largest privately supported conservation body

Further Research

Books

Athanasiou, Tom. *Slow Reckoning: The Ecology of a Divided Planet.* London: Secker and Warburg, 1997.

Beniston, Martin. *Environmental Change in Mountains and Uplands.* London: Arnold; New York: Oxford University Press, 2000.

Nicholson, Max. *The New Environmental Age.* Cambridge: Cambridge University Press, 1987.

Articles and Reports

Ayensu, Edward, et al. "International Ecosystem Assessment." *Science,* 22 October 1999, 685.

Bowles, I., R. Rice, R. Mittermeier, and G. da Fonseca. "Logging and Tropical Forest Conservation." *Science,* 19 June 1998, 1899.

Chadwick, Douglas. "Coral in Peril." *National Geographic,* January 1999, 31.

Grime, J. P. "Biodiversity and Ecosystem Function: The Debate Continues." *Science,* 29 August 1997, 1260.

Food and Agriculture Organization. *State of the World's Forests, 1999.* Rome: FAO, 1999.

———. *International Year of Mountains, 2002: Concept Paper.* Rome: FAO, 2000.

Hellier, C. "The Mangrove Wastelands." *Ecologist* 18, no. 2 (1988).

Heywood, V., ed. *Global Biodiversity Assessment.* Cambridge and New York: Cambridge University Press, 1995.

Kaiser, Jocelyn. "New Survey to Collect Global News You Can Use." *Science,* 8 September 2000, 1676.

Lubchenco, Jane. "Entering the Century of the Environment: A New Social Contract for Science." *Science,* 23 January 1998, 491.

Pennisi, Elisabeth. "Brighter Prospects for the World's Coral Reefs." *Science,* 25 July 1997, 491.

Rützler, Klaus, and Ilka C. Feller. "Caribbean Mangrove Swamps." *Scientific American,* March 1996, 70.

Sala, Osvaldo, et al. "Global Biodiversity Scenarios for the Year 2100." *Science,* 10 March 2000, 1770.

Vitousek, Peter, Paul Ehrlich, Anne Ehrlich, and Pamela Matson. "Human Appropriation of the Products of Photosynthesis." *Bioscience* 36, no. 6 (1986): 368.

Vitousek, Peter, Harold Mooney, Jane Lubchenco, and Jerry Melillo. "Human Domination of Earth's Ecosystems." *Science,* 25 July 1997, 494.

Wilkinson, Clive, ed. *Status of Coral Reefs of the World, 2000.* Townsville: Australian Institute of Marine Science, 2000. Also available online at http://www.aims.gov.au/pages/research/coral-bleaching/scr2000/scr-00gcrmn-report.html.

World Commission on Environment and Development. *Our Common Future.* New York and Oxford: Oxford University Press, 1987.

Web Sites

International Year of Mountains, 2002
http://www.mountains2002.org

International Year of the Ocean, 1998
http://ioc.unesco.org/iyo

Mangrove Action Project
http://www.earthisland.org/map/index.htm

Mangrove Replenishment Initiative
http://mangrove.org

Millennium Ecosystem Assessment
http://www.ma-secretariat.org

ReefBase
http://www.reefbase.org

United Nations Environment Programme, Global Environmental Outlook 2000 (GEO-2000)
http://www.unep.org/Geo2000

United Nations Sustainable Development, Agenda 21
http://www.un.org/esa/sustdev/agenda21.htm

U.S. Environmental Protection Agency, Office of Wetlands, Oceans, and Watersheds
http://www.epa.gov/owow

World Resources Institute, Pilot Analysis of Global Ecosystems (PAGE)
http://www.wri.org/wr2000/page.html

Document

1. Our Common Future (The Brundtland Report)

World Commission on Environment and Development, 1987

Extract

Chapter 6: Species and Ecosystems: Resources for Development

Conservation of living natural resources—plants, animals, and microorganisms, and the nonliving elements of the environment on which they depend—is crucial for development. Today, the conservation of wild living resources is on the agenda of governments; nearly 4 percent of the Earth's land area is managed explicitly to conserve species and ecosystems, and all but a small handful of countries have national parks. The challenge facing nations today is no longer deciding whether conservation is a good idea, but rather how it can be implemented in the national interest and within the means available in each country.

Species and natural ecosystems make many important contributions to human welfare. Yet these very important resources are seldom being used in ways that will be able to meet the growing pressures of future high demands for both goods and services that depend upon these natural resources.

FRESHWATER

Chris Woodford

Water is what most distinguishes Earth from other planets, yet only 1 percent of the water that covers nearly three-fourths of Earth's surface is usable freshwater. Water may be the ultimate renewable resource, but in many parts of the world demand now exceeds supply. One-sixth of the planet's population lacks a clean and safe supply of water, and its number is expected to double in the next twenty-five years. According to *Global Environment Outlook, 2000* (GEO-2000), by the United Nations Environment Programme (UNEP), "The declining state of the world's freshwater resources in terms of quantity and quality may prove to be the dominant issue on the environment and development agenda of the coming century"—a century that according to development agencies may be remembered for its "water wars" and "water refugees."

Historical Background and Development

Disputes over the world's water resources may seem a recent phenomenon, but according to water expert Peter Gleick, they date back to at least the sixteenth century. In one of the earliest recorded conflicts involving water, Leonardo da Vinci and Machiavelli devised a plan to divert Italy's Arno River during a conflict between Pisa and Florence in 1503. Water has figured in many conflicts since, including the 1980–1988 Iran-Iraq War, the 1991 Persian Gulf War, and the 1999 Kosovo conflict.

Numerous initiatives have been launched to address water problems beyond the nation-state level. The 1971 Ramsar Convention on Wetlands has been an important instrument in protecting wetlands throughout the world. Another major initiative was the International Drinking Water Supply and Sanitation Decade, which began in 1980. Although the campaign successfully drew attention to water and sanitation problems, some 1.3 billion people were still without safe water, and 1.9 billion were without adequate sanitation by the decade's end. In 1992 freshwater resources featured prominently at the "Earth Summit" held in Rio de Janeiro. A chapter of the Agenda 21 agreement to curtail environmental damage was signed at the meeting; the agreement was based largely on the Dublin Statement on freshwater management that had been accepted at the groundbreaking International Conference on Water and the Environment earlier that year (see Document 1). In December 2000, the European Union signed the Water Framework Directive, an important piece of legislation heralding a new age of integrated water management.

Global efforts to secure water resources have sometimes taken their cue from local campaigns. The International Rivers Network (IRN), an influential San Francisco–based nongovernmental organization formed in 1985, has made its name by fighting destructive dams across the world. Long-running IRN campaigns have included supporting the local efforts of a group called the Narmada Bachao Andolan (NBA) in fighting the proposed Sardar Sarovar dam in India's Narmada Valley. The struggle of the NBA, which included mass protests by tens of thousands of people in the 1980s and a near-fatal twenty-two-day hunger strike by celebrated activist Medha Patkar in 1991, helped to highlight problems with dams across the world. It was campaigns such as NBA's that prompted the World Bank to reevaluate its role in controversial development projects; the bank withdrew entirely from the Sardar Sarovar project in 1993. The campaign also led, ultimately, to the major study by the World Commission on Dams on the impact of large dams, released in November 2000.

For all the progress the world has made toward safer and more secure water resources, difficulties remain. Many nations seem increasingly prone to floods, droughts, and other natural disasters. In 1998 Hurricane Mitch displaced at least 3 million people and caused major water supply and sanitation problems across Latin America. In 2000 major flooding in Mozambique put 800,000 people at increased risk of infectious diseases. That same year, Kenya experienced its worst flooding in forty years, but in 2001 East Africa experienced its worst drought in living memory, with Kenya, ironically, hardest hit. In March 2001 WHO called for the recognition of access to safe water and adequate sanitation as "basic human rights." With other global problems, such as climate change and increasingly regular El Niño events complicating the world's water crisis, it remains unclear when (or if) all the world's people could ever, realistically, gain these rights.

Current Status

A variety of problems are contributing to the world's water crisis, and numerous policies and programs have been proposed to address it. Regardless, predictions for the future remain bleak. In March 2001 Tearfund, a U.K.-based relief and development agency, predicted that two out of every three people would be facing water shortages by 2025 (see map, p. 222).

Research

Superficially the world's water problem is simple: In countries already classed as water scarce, human population is increasing at the same time as conflicting demands for limited water supplies. According to an internationally accepted system proposed in 1989 by Swedish hydrologist Malin Falkenmark, water resources are assessed by the amount available per capita per year: more than 1,700 cubic meters, limited local water availability problems; 1,000 to 1,700 cubic meters, water stressed; less than 1,000 cubic meters, water scarcity; and less than 500 cubic meters, absolute water scarcity. The World Commission on Water for the 21st Century (commonly referred to as the World Commission on Water) estimates that during the twentieth century the global population tripled while global water consumption rose at least sixfold.

Although there is no shortage of water, resources are unevenly distributed (see Table 1). In many developing countries, water for basic survival is unavailable. According to WaterAid, a development charity, fifty-five developing countries have a per capita daily water consumption far below 50 liters (13 gallons). In the United States, on average, consumption is up to ten times greater. WHO's minimum recommended daily consumption per person is 20 liters (5.2 gallons).

Technologies for moving water to human settlements and irrigating crops were pioneered by the ancient Sumerians and contributed to a key stage in the advancement of civilization. Six thousand years later, WHO reported on World Water Day 2001 that 1 billion of the world's people still did not have access to clean drinking water, 2.4 billion people did not have proper sanitation, and more than 3.4 million people (mostly children) were dying each year from preventable, water-related diseases. Cholera, diarrhea, and typhoid are still common in developing countries, because of problems ensuring safe water and adequate sanitation (see EPIDEMICS). The Institute of Child Health reports that, on average, in developing countries children experience ten attacks of diarrhea before the age of five. Ten percent of children die from diarrhea or dehydration. Pakistani development expert Akhtar Hameed Khan pithily sums up the situation in "The Sanitation Gap: Development's Deadly Menace": "Access to safe water and adequate sanitation is the foundation of development. For when you have a medieval level of sanitation, you have a medieval level of disease, and no country can advance without a healthy population."

The problem of an adequate and clean supply of water is compounded by a progressive decline in the quality of the world's freshwater through mismanagement and pollution. The World Wildlife Fund (WWF) reported that one-fourth of the world's freshwater ecosystems were degraded between 1970 and 1995. In November 1999 the World Commission on Water announced that more than half the world's five hundred major rivers are going dry or are polluted. Mismanagement of land and water resources in river basins is substantially to blame for the displacement of 25 million "environmental refugees," who in 1998 exceeded the world's 21 million war refugees for the first time.

Rising human populations and degraded freshwater are still only part of the problem. Irrigation accounts for about 70 percent of global water use, industrial use for 20 percent, and municipal use for only about 10 percent. Per capita demand for water continues to rise in many countries, mostly for irrigation and industrial uses. Forty percent of the world's food comes from irrigated lands; agriculture is by far the biggest user of water worldwide. According to the World Commission on Water, the freshwater crisis is a major impediment to achieving global food security. Tearfund predicts that the global agricultural demand for water will increase by 50 percent by 2025, forcing developing nations to make difficult choices between supplying water to human settlements or to crops—that is, between having enough food or having enough water. Industrialization is also driving huge increases in the demand for water. According to the Worldwatch Institute, at current rates of economic growth China alone will require a fivefold increase in water consumption between 1995 and 2025 solely for industrial use (see Table 2).

If every country had complete control over its own water, guaranteeing adequate and safe supplies would be easier. Some nations share their water supplies with others, so their fate is necessarily intertwined. In the Middle East, for example, considerable tension results from the way four major waterways—the Nile, the Tigris and Euphrates, and the Jordan Rivers—are shared between nations. While Egypt is 97 percent dependent on the Nile for its freshwater, Ethiopia controls 86 percent of the river's flow upstream (see Case Study—Sharing the Nile). Namibia's plans to divert flows from the Okavanga River for irrigation prompted an outcry in neighboring Botswana, whose wildlife-rich Okavanga Delta, a major source of tourist income, is fed from the same source. Diplomats, including World Commission on Water chairman Ismail Serageldin and former UN secretary-general Boutros Boutros-Ghali, have repeatedly highlighted the potential that wars might be fought over water in the twenty-first century, just as, according to many analysts, the 1991 Persian Gulf War was fought over oil in the twentieth century.

Attempts to engineer solutions to the water problem have been a mixed blessing. On one hand, without large-scale irrigation schemes, reservoirs, and dams, Earth could not support the population that it currently does, and many more people would be suffering the effects of water scarcity. Yet the very solutions to some of Earth's water problems are the direct cause of other, sometimes related, problems. The world's 45,000-plus large dams, for example, have provided economic benefits, flood control, and a means of storing water for times of need; they also generate approximately one-fifth of the world's total electricity. Yet large dams have also ravaged ecosystems, fragmented rivers, and displaced millions of people. According to the World Commission on Dams, 40 million to 80 million people have been displaced by dams and their reservoirs. The commission's groundbreaking *Dams and Development: A New Framework for Decision-Making* confirmed the positive and negative effects of constructing large dams and raised questions about the future of some of the 1000-plus dams currently being planned or under construction worldwide.

Water also plays a key role in gender and family issues in many developing nations. WaterAid reports that in some parts of Sierra Leone, nine-year-old girls spend as much as six hours a day on water-related activities, such as fetching and carrying it. In rural Kenya, fetching water is a job that falls 95 percent of the time on the women of the household, who are also overwhelmingly responsible for hygiene, sanitation, and child care activities. Health, gender, family, education, and poverty issues are inextricably intertwined with access to clean water and sanitation. As noted, the water crisis compounds other pressing issues and is compounded, in turn, by other global concerns. In another example of the latter, global warming is predicted to drastically change the pattern of precipitation over much of the planet, increasing the severity of droughts and floods, particularly in nations already facing water scarcity (see GLOBAL WARMING).

Policies and Programs

According to the World Commission on Water, the starting point for solving the water crisis is integrated water resource management, an internationally accepted methodology based on sustaining the global ecosystem on which all water resources depend and planning the use of water and land "holistically" across river basins, even where national borders divide them (see Document 2). This approach provides the foundation for Agenda 21 and the European Union's Water Framework Directive. It also underpins the promotion of international cooperation on sustainable water management through an initiative called the Global Water Partnership. There are encouraging signs that water scarce nations see cooperation of this kind as a more productive route to solving their problems than confrontation. The United Nations is currently using integrated water resource management to help eight African nations resolve conflicting needs concerning the Zambesi River and to help Angola, Botswana, and Namibia share the Okavanga. The countries that share the Nile are now working together under the umbrella of the Nile Basin Initiative.

Starting from the assumption that there is no shortage of freshwater on Earth, another solution to the water crisis is to conserve and make better use of the water that is available. What that means, however, varies from country to country. According to Peter Gleick, up to 30 percent of the municipal water supply in developed nations is lost through leakage or poorly maintained systems. In developing nations, where irrigation accounts for up to 90 percent of water use, hose pipes or sprinklers can waste up to 50 percent of the water that flows through them from evaporation and runoff. Low-tech drip irrigation systems that supply water underground directly to plant roots reduce water use by up to 70 percent and improve yields by up to 90 percent. The World Commission on Water's vision for 2025 is based on "more crop per drop," with a 40 percent increase in agricultural production achieved through only a 9 percent increase in irrigation.

The systematic degradation of freshwater habitats is less of a "water problem" than an issue that needs to be addressed as part of a more general approach to conserving and protecting the world's fragile ecosystems (see FRAGILE ECOSYSTEMS and POLLUTION). Unlike other types of habitat destruction—the loss of coral reefs or tropical rain forests—the loss of freshwater habitats affects human needs more immediately. Various international conventions exist to preserve the world's freshwater habitats, most importantly, the Ramsar Convention on Wetlands (1971) and, within Europe, the European Union Habitats Directive (1992). Fortunately, degradation is not an irreversible process. Community groups play an important role in river and wetland restoration around the world, notably in the United

States, where numerous alliances have been formed to protect and restore inland waters within state boundaries and, more appropriately, across entire river basins.

Protecting freshwater habitats also necessarily implies a rethinking of large-scale construction works, such as hydroelectric dams, whose reservoirs can destroy vast areas of valuable habitat (and create other problems, such as disrupting the transport of sediments or the flow of fish along rivers). Although large dams may bring social, economic, and environmental benefits—for example, improving water supplies for a community, providing reliable electricity, or reducing dependence on fossil fuels—they also carry social, economic, and environmental costs—for example, displacing many thousands of people, diverting money from low-tech development projects, or destroying freshwater habitats. By balancing the economic, social, and environmental benefits against the costs of dams, the World Commission on Dams, *Dams and Development* was widely regarded as a milestone in the promotion and development of less-destructive projects.

Good management, better conservation, and halting degradation of freshwater habitats are grounded in the principle of sustainable development. There are also other equally valid ways of viewing and attempting to solve the water crisis. Water is essential to life, and the lack of clean water and adequate sanitation is a key factor in high infant mortality rates. Gro Harlem Brundtland, director-general of WHO, argued in a broadcast message on World Water Day, 22 March 2001, "Access to safe water is a universal need and indeed considered a basic human right." Although not explicitly recognized in the 1948 Universal Declaration of Human Rights, the right to water is implicitly recognized in the right to life, health, food, and an adequate standard of living. A human rights approach to the water crisis views the provision of water and sanitation as an obligation, not a charitable act, that must be respected and protected by national governments. Although viewing water as a basic human right is an important step forward, the history of human rights suggests that it is far from enough to guarantee water safety for everyone.

Economists may view the problem in terms of supply, demand, and pricing issues. Thus, if demand exceeds supply over much of the planet, economists would argue that water is underpriced virtually everywhere. The Dublin Statement recognized that "water has an economic value in all its competing uses and should be recognized as an economic good." In principle, addressing the water crisis then becomes an economic matter of making users pay the full cost of the water they use, or so-called full-cost pricing. This was one of the World Commission on Water's strongest recommendations; Daniel C. Sikazwe and Maria Gemma reported the commission's reasoning in "World Water Forum Whets Interest," stating that "without full-cost pricing, the present vicious cycle of waste, inefficiency, and lack of service for the poor will continue." According to WaterAid, the cost of water in poor countries, where people have the least ability to pay for clean water and sanitation, is usually much greater than in rich countries. The World Commission on Water nevertheless believes that this problem should, and could, be addressed.

For agencies working directly with people in developing nations who lack access to clean water and sanitation, theoretical discussions of the water crisis are less immediately important than pragmatic, technological solutions: installing an efficient water pump in a village is often of more direct benefit than talking about water pricing, sustainable development, or human rights. From the early irrigation schemes of the Sumerians to the elaborate hydroelectric dams funded by the World Bank, technology has always played a key role in water management and supply.

Today there is a considerable emphasis on what *Small Is Beautiful* writer E. F. Schumacher calls intermediate technology—small-scale, affordable technologies appropriate to the lives of the people involved. These include efficient, solar-powered water pumps, fog collectors (huge plastic sheets draped like fences over hillsides that catch fog and turn it into drinking water), simple techniques for purifying rainwater supplies through chlorination, and drip-feed irrigation systems to reduce water loss by evaporation. The WHO March 2001 report *Water for Health—Taking Charge* urges a strong commitment to tackling health problems by addressing clean water and sanitation through simple measures such as these. In the words of WHO's Brundtland, as reported in the 22 March 2001 press release "Water—Intermediate Solutions for Persistent Problems," "Simple, inexpensive measures, both individual and collective, are available that will provide clean water for millions and millions of people in developing countries—now, not in 10 or 20 years." More elaborate technological solutions continue to be proposed—including desalination (turning saltwater into freshwater), dragging freshwater by sea in large plastic bags from areas of plenty to areas of need, and towing icebergs—but they currently provide only a tiny amount of the world's usable freshwater.

Regional Summaries

Stresses on the world's water vary dramatically from region to region. Water supplies are relatively plentiful in parts of Northern Europe, the former Soviet Union, Central America, and West Africa. Elsewhere, notably in North Africa, the Middle East, and the western states of the United States, stresses on water are considerable.

North America

Although North America has plentiful freshwater, it is very unequally divided, with Canada having access to ten times as much water per capita as the United States. Dramatic increases in irrigation, power generation, and industrialization in the United States have led to the highest annual per capita water usage in the world: 1,798 cubic meters (2,337 cubic yards) compared to a world average of 645 cubic meters (839 cubic yards), according to GEO-2000. Sandra Postel of the Global Water Policy Project estimates that the United States has an average annual water deficit—the rate at which consumption exceeds natural regeneration of supplies—of 13.6 billion cubic meters (17.7 cubic yards). The western

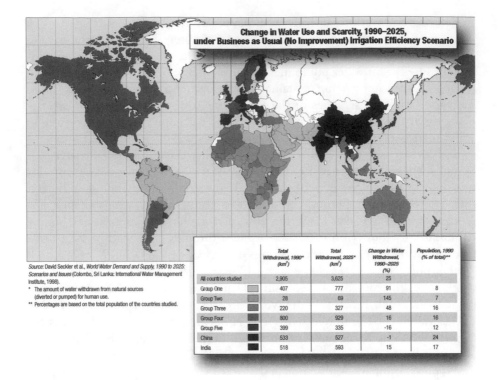

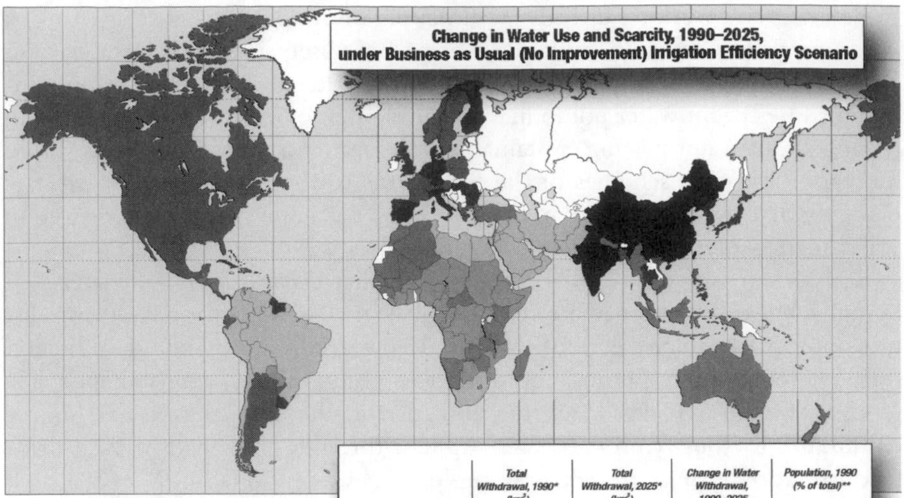

	Total Withdrawal, 1990* (km^3)	Total Withdrawal, 2025* (km^3)	Change in Water Withdrawal, 1990–2025 (%)	Population, 1990 (% of total)**
All countries studied	2,905	3,625	25	
Group One	407	777	91	8
Group Two	28	69	145	7
Group Three	220	327	48	16
Group Four	800	929	16	16
Group Five	399	335	-16	12
China	533	527	-1	24
India	518	593	15	17

Source: David Seckler et al., *World Water Demand and Supply, 1990 to 2025: Scenarios and Issues* (Colombo, Sri Lanka: International Water Management Institute, 1998).

* The amount of water withdrawn from natural sources (diverted or pumped) for human use.

** Percentages are based on the total population of the countries studied.

and midwestern states are the most water stressed and are among the regions of the world expected to become chronically short of water in the first few decades of the twenty-first century. In California, where more than 80 percent of agricultural land is irrigated, groundwater supplies are being overpumped by around 1.6 billion cubic meters (2.1 billion cubic yards) per year.

There have been some encouraging trends in the region's protection of freshwater resources, with some 500 dams removed from U.S. rivers in recent years. Canada, the second largest country in the world, has almost 20 percent of the world's total freshwater. With around one-ninth the population of the United States, Canada is under increasing pressure to export its water south of the border.

Latin America

With plentiful supplies of surface water from rivers, including the Amazon, Latin America is one of the least water stressed regions on Earth. Water availability, however, is quite different from access to clean water and adequate sanitation. A 1997 estimate from the World Bank suggests that as little as 2 percent of sewage in Latin America is properly treated, although 70 percent of Central Americans have access to piped water and therefore relatively good sanitation. Increases in irrigation, urbanization, and industrialization have sometimes led to localized water supply problems, because groundwater supplies are being pumped at rates exceeding their natural rate of regeneration or polluted through such activities as mining (see POLLUTION). According to the World Bank, upstream pollution has increased water treatment costs in Lima by 30 percent. Maintaining clean and affordable supplies of water to increasingly urban areas is one of the region's key challenges for the future. In the Caribbean, as the population increases, demand for housing does as well. New housing developments, in turn, put pressure on already fragile mountain and coastal ecosystems.

Europe and Central Asia

Although most Europeans enjoy adequate supplies of clean water, stress on river basins varies dramatically across the region. In northern countries and parts of the Russian Federation, water is relatively plentiful, though even in the United Kingdom, for example, hot summers produce restrictions on water use. In the hottest part of the region, the Mediterranean, water availability per capita is much more scarce due to the high degree of irrigated agriculture and the increasing demands of tourism. According to the European Environment Agency, since World War II water consumption in Western Europe has increased almost fivefold. GEO-2000 reports that in Eastern Europe economic restructuring has led to a temporary drop in water consumption during the 1990s, but that increasing standards of living and urbanization are expected to produce a doubling in water use by 2025. In Central Asia, where more than 90 percent of water is used for agriculture, inefficient irrigation wastes vast amounts of water in an area where it should be in abundance. Habitat protection remains a major problem throughout Europe. According to the World Wildlife Federation, more than 60 percent of the region's wetlands were destroyed in the twentieth century.

North Africa and the Middle East

This is the most water-stressed region in the world and, consequently, the region with the greatest potential for serious water disputes or water wars (see Case Study—Sharing the Nile). Agriculture uses a much greater proportion of water here than in other regions. In Iraq, according to GEO-2000, agriculture consumes 96.9 percent of available water resources, and the average agricultural consumption for the Mashriq is 95 percent. Mashriq countries are comparatively well supplied by the Tigris and Euphrates Rivers. On the Arabian Peninsula, agriculture accounts for 85 percent of water consumption. In North Africa and the Arabian Peninsula, water supplies come from so-called fossil aquifers, groundwater reserves from a once-wetter climate that receive very little resupply from the region's slight rainfall. Aquifer depletion is a serious problem in Libya, Morocco, Saudi Arabia, and other nations. North Africa has an annual average water deficit of around 10 billion cubic meters (13 billion cubic yards) per year, according to "Redesigning Irrigated Agriculture."

Sub-Saharan Africa

Sub-Saharan Africa has relatively abundant freshwater resources in numerous rivers and lakes and currently uses only about 4 percent of them. Forty-six percent of the region's people, however, lack access to clean water, according to the *Human Development Report, 2000,* and only around 52 percent have adequate sanitation. Wide variations in water availability across the region are complicated by poor management practices, frequent droughts, and the increasing effects of climate change. By 2025 twenty-five African nations and 16 percent of Africans (230 million people) will experience water scarcity, and another 32 percent (460 million people) will experience water stress, based on figures from *Solutions for a Water Short World.* Although agriculture is still by far the biggest user of water—accounting for 88 percent of consumption for Africa, including North Africa—industrialization, urbanization, increasing population, and pollution all present challenges for the future.

Asia and the Pacific

Agriculture dominates water use in Asia and the Pacific, according to GEO-2000, varying from around 50 percent of water consumption in industrialized nations to as much as 90 percent in the countries of South Asia. Annual per capita water availability also shows dramatic variations across the region: 172 cubic meters (224 cubic yards) in Singapore; 2,348 cubic meters (3,052 cubic yards) in China; and 174,000 cubic meters (226,000 cubic yards) in Papua New Guinea.

Per capita water availability for South Asia has fallen by half since 1950. Arid countries and developing countries in the region are experiencing increasing water shortages, through consumption, pollution, and mismanagement. The two biggest countries, India and China, are both expected to qualify as water stressed by 2025, though there are dramatic variations within each nation. Access to safe drinking water and sanitation is another major problem. Figures from 1997 by the Asian Development Bank show that a third of Asians lack access to a reliable water supply close to their homes, and half lack adequate sanitation. According to WHO, diarrhea caused by inadequate water and sanitation is the biggest threat to health for people in the region.

Data

Table 1 Freshwater Resources and Withdrawals in Selected Countries

	Average Annual Internal Renewable Water Resources		Annual River Flows		Annual Withdrawals			
Country	Total (km^3)	Per Capita, 2000 (m^3)	From Other Countries (km^3)	To Other Countries (km^3)	Year	Total (km^3)	Percentage of Internal Water Resources	Per Capita (m^3)
Algeria	13.9	442	0.4	0.4	1990	4.50	32	180
Argentina	360.0	9,721	623.0	X	1995	28.58	8	822
Australia	352.0	18,638	0.0	0.0	1995	15.06	4	839
Brazil	5,418.0	31,849	1,900.0	X	1992	54.87	1	359

Table 1 Freshwater Resources and Withdrawals in Selected Countries (*continued*)

	Average Annual Internal Renewable Water Resources		Annual River Flows		Annual Withdrawals			
Country	Total (km^3)	Per Capita, 2000 (m^3)	From Other Countries (km^3)	To Other Countries (km^3)	Year	Total (km^3)	Percentage of Internal Water Resources	Per Capita (m^3)
Canada	2,740.0	87,971	52.0	X	1990	45.10	2	1,623
China	2,812.4	2,201	17.2	719.0	1993	525.46	19	439
Colombia	2,133.0	50,400	0.0	X	1996	8.94	0	228
Congo, Republic of	935.0	18,101	313.0	X	1994	0.36	0	8
Egypt	1.8	26	66.7	0.0	1993	55.10	3,061	920
France	180.0	3,047	11.0	150.0[a]	1994	40.67	23	704
Georgia	58.1	11,702	8.4	X	1990	3.47	6	635
Germany	107.0	1,301	71.0	178.0[a]	1990	46.27	43	583
Guatemala	134.4	11,805	0.0	X	1992	1.16	1	126
India	1,260.6	1,244	647.2	1,307.0	1990	500.00	40	588
Indonesia	2,838.0	13,380	X	X	1990	74.35	3	407
Israel	1.9[b]	312	0.9	0.0	1997	1.71[c]	88	292
Japan	430.0	3,393	0.0	0.0	1992	91.40	21	735
Russian Federation	4,312.7	29,351	185.5	20.4	1994	77.10	2	520
Saudi Arabia	2.4	111	X	X	1992	17.00	708	1,002
Spain	111.8	2,821	0.3	29.0	1997	35.52	32	897
Sweden	178.0	19,977	12.2	178.0[a]	1995	2.73	2	310
Switzerland	40.0	5,416	13.0	54.0[a]	1995	2.60	6	363
Tajikistan	66.3	10,714	13.3	63.6[d]	1994	11.87	18	2,095
Thailand	210.0	3,420	199.9	X	1990	33.13	16	596
Turkey	196.0	2,943	7.6	60.4	1997	35.50	18	560
Uganda	39.0	1,791	27.0	X	1970	0.20	1	20
United Kingdom	145.0	2,465	2.0	X	1995	9.34	6	160
United States	2,460.0	8,838	18.0	X	1990	468.62	19	1,844
World Total	42,655.0	7,045	X	X	1995	3,760.00	9	664

Source: World Resources Institute et al., *World Resources, 2000–2001* (Washington, D.C.: WRI, 2000).

Note: "0" is zero or less than one-half the unit measure. "X" means not available. Total withdrawals may exceed 100 percent due to groundwater drawdowns, withdrawals from river inflows, and the operation of desalinization plants.

[a] Includes outflow to the sea.

[b] The Plan Bleu for the Mediterranean estimates 0.75 km^3 for 1995.

[c] The Plan Bleu for the Mediterranean estimates 2.05 km^3 for 1996, including recycled water.

[d] Figures for inflow from and outflow to other countries refer only to the quantity of water secured by treaties.

Table 2 Global Water Use in the Twentieth Century

Use	1900 (km^3)	1950 (km^3)	1995 (km^3)
Agriculture			
Withdrawal	500	1,100	2,500
Consumption	300	700	1,750
Industry			
Withdrawal	40	200	750
Consumption	5	20	80
Municipalities			
Withdrawal	20	90	350
Consumption	5	115	50
Reservoirs (evaporation)	0	10	200

Source: William J. Cosgrove and Frank R. Rijsberman, for the World Water Council, *World Water Vision: Making Water Everybody's Business* (London: Earthscan, 2000).

Note: All numbers are rounded. Withdrawal refers to water diverted or pumped for human use, consumption refers to withdrawn water that is actually used, and evaporation refers to water lost by natural evaporation from reservoirs.

Case Study—Sharing the Nile

The Nile is the world's longest waterway and also one of the most disputed. The Nile basin has long been forecast as the crucible of a future water war. The river is a key source of freshwater for a number of nations in North Africa and the Middle East, a region that contains around 5 percent of the world's population but less than 1 percent of its water. Water scarcity in the region has grown dramatically since 1955, when only three countries merited this designation. In 1990 eleven nations in the region were declared water scarce, according to *Solutions for a Water Short World,* and eighteen will be water scarce by 2025, including Egypt, Ethiopia, and Somalia, three countries in a long-term dispute over the Nile.

The river already suffers severely from human exploitation. In November 1999 the World Commission on Water described the Nile as one of the world's most polluted rivers. Once the Nile flowed largely uninterrupted from its source, the Kagera River in Burundi, to the Mediterranean, but more than 90 percent of the river's flow is now lost through irrigation or evaporation from reservoirs; the remainder is heavily polluted by fertilizers, irrigation drainage, and various forms of industrial waste. The situation is bound to worsen as demands on the Nile increase. Statistics from the Global Water Policy Project predict that the population of countries in and around the Nile River basin will increase by some 67 percent between 1999 and 2025.

Water is a constant source of tension in the Middle East and North Africa. Access to the Nile dominates relations between Egypt, Ethiopia, and Sudan. Egypt, by far the most powerful of the Nile-sharing nations, is 97 percent dependent on the river and has long recognized access to water as a matter of national security and a key element in its foreign policy. The construction of the enormous Aswan High Dam (forming Lake Nasser) in the 1960s merely postponed Egypt's water scarcity rather than eliminating it. Ethiopia, which controls 86 percent of the Nile's flow, has constructed dams on the river upstream of Egypt and wants to divert up to 39 percent of the waters of the Blue Nile—one of the three tributaries that forms the Nile, the others being the White Nile and the Atbara—to irrigate new settlements. According to water expert Sandra Postel, if Ethiopia irrigates only half of its irrigable land, the Nile's flow to Egypt would be reduced by as much as 16 percent. Sudan has also declared an interest in increasing its share of Nile waters. The Egyptian Toshka and Egyptian-Israeli Northern Sinai Agricultural Development Program (NSADP), both irrigation projects, have also caused tensions among the Nile-sharing nations by diverting waters to arid lands.

Former UN secretary-general Boutros Boutros-Ghali's infamous quote that "The next war in the Middle East will be fought over water, not politics" reflects his personal experience as Egypt's foreign minister. According to water authority Peter Gleick, water played a role in Middle Eastern conflicts on approximately twenty occasions during the twentieth century. Today, however, cooperation seems to be triumphing over confrontation where the Nile is concerned. Diplomatic efforts to share the river rest on overcoming the limitations of the 1959 Agreement for the Full Utilization of Nile Waters, a pact between Egypt and Sudan that made possible the Aswan High Dam downstream (Egypt's gain from the agreement) and allowed both nations increased water extraction and irrigation and hydroelectric schemes upstream (Sudan's compensation for having part of its land inundated by Lake Nasser). Remarkably, none of the other Nile nations were included or even consulted, including Ethiopia. Instead, the agreement simply split the Nile's waters between the two most downstream countries—87 percent to Egypt, 13 percent to Sudan—arguably allowing Egypt to claim historical rights to the Nile and to dominate the politics of the river.

A number of recent meetings of the Nile-sharing countries under the banner of the Nile Basin Initiative (formed in 1992) have led to agreements on irrigation, hydroelectricity, flooding, pollution, and soil erosion. Avoiding a future water war over the Nile, however, will involve the triumph of continued cooperation over the challenges of increasing population and demand and such stresses as climate change and increasing pollution.

Case Study—China's Water Crisis and the Three Gorges Dam

China is the classic example of a nation that can have too much and not enough water at the same time. Several times during the twentieth century, the Yangtze, China's most important river, flooded catastrophically. In 1931 more than 145,000 people were killed in floods, and severe flooding in 1991 and 1998 displaced millions. Yet China's water supplies are still under pressure. Its population is predicted to rise by 300 million by 2030, according to the United

Nations, and water consumption is expected to increase by 66 percent during the same period. According to Tearfund, two-thirds of China's cities are already facing severe water shortages. In Beijing the water table is falling by approximately 2 meters (6.5 feet) per year, as groundwater is pumped out to meet human needs. For more than seven months in 1997, China's Yellow River, crucial to the irrigation of the North China Plain, which supplies a high proportion of the nation's food, ran dry in its lower reaches, failing even to reach the sea. China needs water for agriculture to feed its growing population, and growing urbanization will also require a massive increase in water and energy consumption.

China's solution to some of these problems is probably the world's most ambitious civil engineering project ever: the construction of the world's largest hydroelectric dam on the Yangzte. The Three Gorges dam, expected to be completed in 2009, will be 2 kilometers (1.2 miles) long and 185 meters (607 feet) high. The reservoir it creates will be even more spectacular: some 663 kilometers (404 miles) long (approximately the length of Lake Superior), will inundate 13 cities, 140 towns, 1,352 villages, and 650 factories for a storage capacity of 39.3 billion cubic meters (51 billion cubic yards), which is roughly as much water as the city of Beijing would consume in seventeen years. The project is expected to cost $30 billion to $75 billion (and estimates are constantly being revised upward).

Supporters of the project point to its electricity-generating capacity, which will meet almost 10 percent of China's total energy needs, saving up to 50 million tons of coal and considerable greenhouse emissions each year. They claim that flood risk on the Yangtze will also be reduced. By raising the water level of the river some 10 to 100 meters (33 to 330 feet), it will allow massive container ships to transport goods to the city of Chongqing, 2,400 kilometers (1,500 miles) inland. Opponents, however, highlight the massive social and environmental cost of the dam. At least 2 million people will be displaced from their homes, some 80,000 hectares (200,000 acres) of much-needed, good quality agricultural land and forestry will be lost, and some of China's major tourist attractions (including archaeological sites more than 4,000 years old) will disappear beneath the water. Critics also argue that the river's heavy sediment load will block the dam's turbines and Chongqing harbor and, ironically, increase the risk of flooding upstream, in which case farmers will lose from the loss of sediment transport downstream, and fish stocks may be drastically reduced.

Since it was originally proposed in 1919, the dam has provoked enormous controversy inside and outside China. Under considerable pressure from environmentalists and human rights groups, the U.S. Export-Import Bank and the World Bank have refused to support the project. Construction of the dam proceeds, controversy notwithstanding, but it may be decades before the true impact of the project, for better or for worse, is fully appreciated.

Biographical Sketches

Mahmoud Abu Zeid, as president of the World Water Council, has played an important role in framing international solutions to the world's water crisis through such initiatives as the World Water Forum and the World Commission on Water for the 21st Century. As Egypt's minister of water resources and irrigation, Abu Zeid promoted integrated water resource management as a means of easing Egypt's water problems and tensions in the Middle East.

Asit K. Biswas has served as an adviser to seventeen governments and numerous international organizations, including UN agencies, the World Bank, and the Asian Development Bank. Biswas was in 1994 awarded the International Water Resources Association's prestigious Crystal Drop Award for "outstanding lifetime achievements in water management." He has published fifty-six books and more than 550 papers.

John Briscoe is chief of the World Bank's water and sanitation division. As the bank's senior adviser on water resources, he represents it on major international commissions and committees, including the World Commission on Dams and the Global Water Partnership. Formerly a professional water engineer, Briscoe has published numerous papers on the world's water crisis, notably from an economic perspective.

Malin Falkenmark is Emeritus Professor of Applied Hydrology at the Natural Science Research Council in Stockholm. As a hydrologist Falkenmark brought a new clarity to the world's water crisis in 1989 by comparing water availability in different nations using such defined terms as *water stress* and *water scarcity*. She is better known for developing the concept of green water, the water needed for plant growth, which is not generally accounted for in water statistics. Falkenmark has also made distinguished contributions to international water policy through the International Hydrological Programme, the 1992 International Conference on Water and the Environment in Dublin, and numerous other initiatives.

Peter H. Gleick is president of the Pacific Institute for Studies in Development, Environment, and Security in Oakland, California, and one of the world's leading experts on freshwater and the impact of climate change on the world's water resources. He is the author of many publications on the subject, including *The World's Water,* a biennial report on the state of the world's freshwater resources.

Sandra Postel is director of the Global Water Policy Project in Amherst, Massachusetts, a senior fellow of the Worldwatch Institute, and a leading international authority on global water problems. Author of numerous scholarly articles, she is perhaps best known for a number of popular books and articles championing the need for the more efficient use of water, particularly in regard to irrigation, including *The Last Oasis* (1992) and *Pillar of Sand: Can the Irrigation Miracle Last?* (1999).

Ismail Serageldin is a former vice president of the World Bank and has most recently served as chairman of the World Commission on Water in the 21st Century. He was instrumental in delivering its groundbreaking report, *A Water Secure World: Vision for Water, Life, and the Environment* (2000). Serageldin is also chairman of the Global Water Partnership.

Directory

Global Water Policy Project, 107 Larkspur, Amherst, MA 01002. Telephone: (413) 256-4808, Email (director): spostel@javanet.com.
Research and policy think tank specializing in global water strategy

Intermediate Technology Development Group, The Schumacher Centre for Technology and Development, Bourton Hall, Bourton-on-Dunsmore, Rugby CV23 9QZ, United Kingdom. Telephone: (44) 17 88 661100, Email: itdg@itdg.org.uk, Web: http://www.itdg.org
Organization working to assist developing countries using appropriate technologies

International Commission on Irrigation and Drainage, 48 Nyaya Marg, Chanakyapuri, New Delhi 110021, India. Telephone: (91) 11 6116837, Email: icid@icid.org, Web: http://www.icid.org
Organization dedicated to improving the world food supply through better water and land management

International Rivers Network, 1847 Berkeley Way, Berkeley, CA 94703. Telephone: (510) 848-1155, Email: irn@irn.org, Web: http://www.irn.org
Organization campaigning against the negative environmental and human rights impacts of dams

International Water Management Institute, P.O. Box 2075, Colombo, Sri Lanka. Telephone: (94) 1 867404, Email: iwmi@cgiar.org, Web: http://www.cgiar.org/iwmi
Organization that fosters and supports sustainable use of irrigation for agriculture

Pacific Institute for Studies in Development, Environment, and Security, 654 13th Street, Preservation Park, Oakland, CA 94612. Telephone: (510) 251-1600, Email: pistaff@pacinst.org, Web: http://www.pacinst.org
Academic institution researching a variety of global issues

Stockholm International Water Institute, 59 Sveavägen, 113 59 Stockholm, Sweden. Telephone: (46) 8 522 13960, Email: siwi@siwi.org, Web: http://www.siwi.org
International institution that promotes research and understanding into global water issues

Tearfund, 100 Church Road, Teddington, Middlesex TW11 8QE, United Kingdom. Telephone: (44) 208 977 9144, Email: enquiry@tearfund.org, Web: http://www.tearfund.org
Christian charity focusing on poverty relief in developing countries

United States Society on Dams, 1616 17th Street, Suite 483, Denver, CO 80202. Telephone: (303) 628-5430, Email: stephens@ussdams.org, Web: http://www2.privatei.com/~uscold
Organization concerned with dam issues

WaterAid, Prince Consort House, 27-29 Albert Embankment, London SE1 7UB, United Kingdom. Telephone: (44) 207 793 4500, Email: information@wateraid.org.uk, Web: http://www.wateraid.org.uk
Organization using water industry expertise to relieve water problems in developing countries

World Health Organization, 20 Avenue Appia, 1211 Geneva 27, Switzerland. Telephone (41) 227 912 111, Email: info@who.int, Web: http://www.who.int
UN organization advocating health for all people

World Bank, Water and Sanitation Division, 1818 H Street NW, Washington, DC 20433. Telephone: (202) 477-1234, Email: feedback@worldbank.org, Web: http://www.worldbank.org/html/fpd/water
International organization aiming to relieve poverty by financing development projects

World Commission on Dams, Hycastle House, 5th Floor, 58 Loop Street, P.O. Box 16002, Vlaeberg, Cape Town, South Africa. Telephone: (27) 21 426 4000, Email: info@dams.org, Web: http://www.dams.org
International commission that evaluates the economic, environmental, and social impacts of large dams

World Water Council, Les Docks de la Joliette, 13002 Marseille, France. Telephone: (33) 491 99 41 00, Email: wwc@worldwatercouncil.org, Web: http://www.worldwatercouncil.org and http://www.watervision.org/clients/wv/water.nsf
International think tank on global water policy responsible for the work of the World Commission on Water for the 21st Century

WWF Living Waters Campaign, c/o P.O. Box 7, 3700AA Zeist, Netherlands. Telephone: (31) 30 693 7803, Email: TDAwater@wwfnet.org, Web: http://www.panda.org/livingwaters
Organization campaigning for freshwater protection and restoration

Further Research

Books

De Villiers, Marq. *Water Wars: Is the World's Water Running Out?* London: Weidenfeld, 1999.

———. *Water: The Fate of Our Most Precious Resource.* New York: Mariner Books, 2001.

Gleick, Peter. *The World's Water, 2000–2001: The Biennial Report on Freshwater Resources.* Washington, D.C.: Island Press, 2000.

———, ed. *The World's Water.* Oxford and New York: Oxford University Press, 1993.

McCully, Patrick. *Silenced Rivers: The Ecology and Politics of Large Dams.* Berkeley: International Rivers Network, 1996.

Postel, Sandra. *Last Oasis: Facing Water Scarcity.* New York: W. W. Norton, 1992.

———. *Pillar of Sand: Can the Irrigation Miracle Last?* New York: W. W. Norton, 1999.

Articles and Reports

Berman, Ilan, and Paul Michael Wihbey. "The New Water Politics of the Middle East." *Strategic Review,* (summer 1999). Also available at http://www.iasps.org.il/strategic/water.htm.

Black, Maggie. "Mega-Slums: The Coming Sanitary Crisis," http://www.wateraid.org.uk/research/slums.html.

Cosgrove, William J., and Frank R. Rijsberman for the World Water Council. *Making Water Everybody's Business.* London: Earthscan, 2000. Also available at http://www.worldwatervision.org/reports.htm.

"Flood of Protest: Leave Our Rivers Alone." *New Internationalist,* no. 273, November 1995. A special issue devoted to river activism around the world. Also available at http://www.oneworld.org/ni/issue273/contnents.html.

Gleick, Peter. "Making Every Drop Count." *Scientific American,* February 2001. Also available at http://www.sciam.com/2001/0201issue/0201gleick.html.

Huus, Kari. "The Yangtze's Collision Course," MSNBC News, http://www.msnbc.com/news/307055.asp.

Khan, Akhtar Hameed. "The Sanitation Gap: Development's Deadly Menace," http://www.unicef.org/pon97/water1.htm.

Mufson, Steven. "Three Gorges. The Yangtze Dam: Feat or Folly," *Washington Post,* 9 November 1997. Also available at http://www.washingtonpost.com/wp-srv/inatl/longterm/yangtze/yangtze.htm.

Population Information Program, The Johns Hopkins School of Public Health. *Solutions for a Water-Short World: Population Reports* 26, no. 1 (September 1998).

Postel, Sandra. "Growing More Food with Less Water." *Scientific American,* February 2001. Also available at http://www.sciam.com/2001/0201issue/0201postel.html.

———. "Redesigning Irrigated Agriculture." In *State of the World, 2000.* London: Earthscan, 2000.

Postel, Sandra, Gretchen Daily, and Paul Ehrlich. "Human Appropriation of Renewable Fresh Water." *Science,* 9 February 1996, 785–788.

Robbins, Elaine. "Water, Water Everywhere: Innovation and Cooperation Are Helping Slake the World's Growing Thirst." *E Magazine,* September/October 1998, http://www.emagazine.com/september-october_1998/0998feat1.html.

Seckler, David, Upali Amarasinghe, David Molden, Radhika de Silva, and Randolph Barker. *World Water Demand and Supply, 1990 to 2025: Scenarios and Issues.* Colombo, Sri Lanka: International Water Management Institute, 1998. Also available at http://www.cgiar.org/iwmi/pubs/indexp.htm.

Shiklomanov, Igor. "Appraisal and Assessment of World Water Resources." *Water International,* 25, no. 1 (March 2000): 11–32.

Sikazwe, Daniel C., and Maria Gemma B. "World Water Forum Whets Interest." *New Agriculturalist Online,* http://www.new-agri.co.uk/00-3/develop/dev05.html.

Strategic Forecasting. "Nile River Politics: Who Receives Water?" http://www.stratfor.com/MEAF/commentary/0008100107.htm.

Tearfund. *Running on Empty: A Call for Action to Combat the Crisis of Global Water Shortages.* London: Tearfund, 2001.

United Nations Development Programme. *Human Development Report, 2000.* New York and Oxford: Oxford University Press, 2000.

United Nations Environment Programme. *Global Environmental Outlook, 2000.* London: Earthscan, 2000. Also available at http://www.grida.no/geo2000/english/0032.htm.

World Commission on Dams. *Dams and Development: A New Framework for Decision-Making.* London: Earthscan, 2001. Also available at http://www.dams.org.

World Commission on Water for the 21st Century. *A Water Secure World: Vision for Water, Life, and the Environment.* Cairo: World Water Council, 2000. Also available at http://www.worldwatervision.org/reports.htm.

Web Sites

Global Environmental Outlook, 2000 (GEO-2000)
http://www.grida.no/geo2000/english/0032.htm

Global Water Partnership
http://www.gwpforum.org

International Rivers Network, China Campaign, Three Gorges
http://www.irn.org/programs/threeg

Nile Basin Initiative
http://www.nilebasin.org

Nile River Dispute: Case Study
http://www.american.edu/projects/mandala/TED/ice/NILE.HTM

UK Rivers Network: Finding Out about Water
http://www.ukrivers.net/water/html

United Arab Republic and Sudan Agreement for the Full Utilization of Nile Waters, 1959
http://www.internationalwaterlaw.org/regionaldocs/UAR_Sudan.htm

WHO, Multimedia Page: World Water Day 2001
http://www.who.int/multimedia/wwd2001

World Commission on Water for the 21st Century
http://www.worldwatercommission.org

World Water Day
http://www.worldwaterday.org

The World's Water
http://www.worldwater.org

Documents

1. The Dublin Statement on Water and Sustainable Development

International Conference on Water and the Environment, 1992

The full text is available at http://www.wmo.ch/web/homs/icwedece.html.

Extracts

Guiding Principles

Concerted action is needed to reverse the present trends of overconsumption, pollution, and rising threats from drought and floods. The Conference Report sets out recommendations for action at local, national and international levels, based on four guiding principles.

Principle No. 1 Fresh water is a finite and vulnerable resource, essential to sustain life, development and the environment

Since water sustains life, effective management of water resources demands a holistic approach, linking social and economic development with protection of natural ecosystems. Effective management links land and water uses across the whole of a catchment area or groundwater aquifer.

Principle No. 2 Water development and management should be based on a participatory approach, involving users, planners and policy-makers at all levels

The participatory approach involves raising awareness of the importance of water among policy-makers and the general public. It means that decisions are taken at the lowest appropriate level, with full public consultation and involvement of users in the planning and implementation of water projects.

Principle No. 3 Women play a central part in the provision, management and safeguarding of water

This pivotal role of women as providers and users of water and guardians of the living environment has seldom been reflected in institutional arrangements for the development and management of water resources. Acceptance and implementation of this principle requires positive policies to address women's specific needs and to equip and empower women to participate at all levels in water resources programmes, including decision-making and implementation, in ways defined by them.

Principle No. 4 Water has an economic value in all its competing uses and should be recognized as an economic good

Within this principle, it is vital to recognize first the basic right of all human beings to have access to clean water and sanitation at an affordable price. Past failure to recognize the economic value of water has led to wasteful and environmentally damaging uses of the resource. Managing water as an economic good is an important way of achieving efficient and equitable use, and of encouraging conservation and protection of water resources.

2. A Water Secure World: Vision for Water, Life, and the Environment

World Commission on Water for the 21st Century, 2000

The full text is available at http://www.worldwatervision.org/reports.htm.

Extracts

Water is life. Every human being, now and in the future, should have access to safe water for drinking, appropriate sanitation, and enough food and energy at reasonable cost. Providing adequate water to meet these basic needs must be done in an equitable manner that works in harmony with nature. For water is the basis for all living ecosystems and habitats and part of an immutable hydrological cycle that must be respected if the development of human activity and well being is to be sustainable.

We are not achieving these goals today, and we are on a path leading to crisis and to future problems for a large part of humanity and many parts of the planet's ecosystems. Business as usual leads us on an unsustainable and inequitable path.

Achieving these goals requires drastic changes in the manner in which water is managed.

A holistic, systemic approach relying on integrated water resource management must replace the current fragmentation in managing water.

There are those who see water only by use: water for municipalities, for industry, for irrigation, for the environment, as if the last were a competing use, not an inherent part of maintaining the entire ecological system on which all water services depend. Or those who look at political and administrative boundaries as the basis of decision making when these seldom conform to the catchment and basin areas that nature prescribes as the management units for water. . . .

But it is as much by activities on land that we affect the quality and availability of useable freshwater as by the direct withdrawals that humans make. A holistic approach means taking these issues into account—and linking the quality and quantity aspects of water management. Water is affected by everything, and water affects everything and everyone. . . .

No more business as usual

Considerable progress has been made in many countries, and yet at a macro level the arithmetic of water still does not add up. In the next two decades it is estimated that water use by humans will increase by about 40%, and that 17% more water will be needed to grow food for a growing population. In addition, the water demands for industry and energy will increase rapidly. And we know that aquatic ecosystems throughout the world have been degraded and will need greater protection and that water quality is deteriorating in poor countries. In short, with current institutional arrangements and current technologies, the arithmetic of water simply does not add up. Rapid and imaginative institutional and technological innovation is required. "Business as usual" will not do. With the commitment of all, however, the problems can be overcome. A water-secure world is possible, but we must change the way we manage water, starting now!

GENOCIDE

Edward Kissi

Genocide is a twentieth-century term describing an ancient crime. In the minds of many people, it evokes images of mass murder by governments, but it is more complex than that. Genocide also includes the intentional killing of particular groups of people by non-state armed groups as well as killings that may not have been intended but were willfully neglected by those who could have stopped them. Significant efforts have been made by the United Nations, individual states, and scholars to define genocide as a crime against humanity punishable under international law. Yet genocide persists in many forms, and the perpetrators often escape the grasp of the law in their own countries and internationally.

Historical Background and Development

In Madrid in 1933, Raphael Lemkin, a Jewish lawyer from Poland, submitted a proposal at the Fifth International Conference for the Unification of Criminal Law asking the conferees to declare the destruction of "racial, religious or social collectivities" a crime under international law. Lemkin coined the word *genocide* from the Greek *genos* (race, nation, tribe) and the Latin *cide* (killing) to describe the destruction of groups. He, however, did not succeed in convincing the conference participants to adopt his proposal.

During World War II, the destruction of ethnic and political groups assumed new and frightening dimensions. Lemkin's *genocide* captured the horrors of the Holocaust—the destruction of the Gypsies (Roma), homosexuals, Jehovah's Witnesses, Jews, Poles, and other groups in Europe by Adolph Hitler's regime in Germany. After the war, with the images of the Holocaust still fresh, Lemkin got a second chance, when the post–World War II generation resolved to prevent and punish the type of genocide perpetrated by the Nazis.

Through Lemkin's lobbying, the newly established United Nations passed a unanimous resolution on genocide on 11 December 1946 that reflected the concept of genocide that Lemkin had had in mind since 1933. The resolution declared genocide a crime under international law, referring to the many instances in history in which racial, religious, political, and other groups had been partially or totally killed or exterminated. The resolution, however, was a nonbinding statement of the moment, aimed at condemning the crimes committed during World War II by the governments of Germany, Italy, and Japan and legitimizing the Nuremberg trials (see INTERNATIONAL CRIMINAL JUSTICE). Yet the resolution was important in another respect: It included political organizations in the list of groups whose partial or total destruction constitute genocide. The victorious Allied Powers—Britain, France, and the United States—wanted the reference to political groups to serve as a denunciation of the extermination of the communists and social democrats by the Nazi government. Political groups, however, were excluded from the UN convention on genocide adopted in December 1948. Politics was the primary reason.

During debate on the convention, delegates from Iran, Poland, and the Soviet Union had opposed the inclusion of political groups as protected groups. They argued that political organizations had no stable, natural, or permanent characteristics, as did racial and religious groups; people are born into races, religions, and nationalities. Although they can change their nationality and religion, such occurrences do not happen as frequently as people change their political beliefs. France and Haiti were the staunchest supporters of the inclusion and protection of political groups. The French delegation argued that past genocides had been committed on racial and religious grounds, and therefore it was likely that future genocides would be committed on political grounds. The Haitian delegation added that perpetrators of genocide could claim that they had annihilated a group for reasons of suppressing political rebellions or safeguarding national security and public order.

The U.S. delegation was less active than those from many other countries. The United States failed to press its argument that what bound religious and political groups was their belief in an idea and, therefore, the inclusion and protection of religious groups in a law on genocide made the inclusion and protection of a political group necessary and consistent. The U.S. delegation recoiled when the Soviets responded that religious groups had always been persecuted on grounds of the race and nationality of their members. Clearly, the Soviets wanted to limit the concept of genocide to the racial supremacy theories and imperialist ideologies that had characterized National Socialism in Germany. The U.S. delegation's lackluster participation in such an important debate highlighted their fear of Congress' reaction to an international treaty such as this. The Senate had previously rejected U.S. membership in the League of Nations after World War I, which represented Congress' distrust of internationally binding agreements that might restrict U.S. sovereignty.

On 9 December 1948, the United Nations General Assembly adopted the Convention on the Prevention and Punishment of the Crime of Genocide—the Genocide Convention—whose broad scope is consistent with Lemkin's view of genocide (see Document 1); as articulated in Lemkin's *Axis Rule in Occupied Europe,* genocide is "a coordinated plan of different actions" aimed at destroying the "essential foundations of the life of a nation or an ethnic group" as part of completely annihilating the group. Though a product of ideological compromise, the genocide convention is, today, the only internationally accepted document that defines genocide.

Current Status

Despite nearly universal condemnation of many acts of genocide, the lack of unanimity concerning genocide—legal instruments to adjudicate such atrocities, policies aimed at the prevention of them, and, indeed, the very definition of the word itself—continues to plague the international community.

Research

The Convention on the Prevention and Punishment of the Crime of Genocide sets standards for the determination of genocide. Article 1 declares that whether it is committed in a time of war or peace, genocide "is a crime under international law" which all members of the United Nations should pledge to "prevent and punish." According to Article 2, "genocide means any of the following acts committed with intent to destroy, in whole or in part, a national, ethnical, racial or religious group, as such": "killing members of the group"; "causing serious bodily or mental harm to members of the group"; "deliberately inflicting on the group conditions of life calculated to bring about its physical destruction in whole or in part"; "imposing measures intended to prevent births within the group"; "forcibly transferring children of the group to another group." The convention came into force on 12 January 1951. It took the United States thirty-five years to approve it, "with reservation," which was representative of the controversy surrounding the convention and, indeed, the concept of genocide itself.

The genocide convention continues to generate controversy. For example, the phrases "in whole" and "in part," the word *intent,*" and groups declared "racial," "religious," "ethnical," and "national" are not clearly defined. The convention also fails to resolve a number of questions: How many of the target group should be killed by the perpetrator for the group to be recognized in international law as a victim of genocide? Does the extermination of an ethnic group by members of the same group constitute genocide? What should be the standard of proof of intent to commit genocide? When is a group a group? These questions point to a key problem. If the success of prosecuting perpetrators of genocide depends upon proving the intent of the perpetrator to destroy a type of target group identified in the genocide convention, then genocide may be a hard crime to prosecute, as few perpetrators of genocide clearly explain or document their reasons for targeting a group for extermination. Historians, sociologists, anthropologists, and psychologists who study genocide have provided some answers to these questions. Many of them have called for a redefinition of the concept of genocide in light of recent mass murders.

Social scientists who study and write about genocide fall into two overlapping categories. The first group includes those who seek a narrow or restrictive concept or definition of genocide, out of concern that a broader concept might lead to the frivolous use of the word. Those who seek a restrictive definition of genocide, such as sociologist and legal scholar Leo Kuper, historian Frank Chalk, and sociologists Kurt Jonassohn and Helen Fein, argue that genocide should not be a cliche or a catchword to be used recklessly in political rhetoric and cultural discourse to describe every incident of massacre or communal violence. To make it so would distort the meaning of genocide and minimize the gravity of acts that are truly genocidal in nature. The second group comprises scholars who seek a broad definition of genocide that makes any killing of human beings on a substantial scale an act of genocide. This group includes psychologist Israel Charny and political scientist R. J. Rummel. They argue that every human life matters, and it would be morally absurd to exclude some instances of mass killing from recognition as genocide as if those lives were undeserving of protection.

For Kuper, the search for an appropriate definition of genocide is less important than the establishment of a strong genocide prevention mechanism in the form of an international court of justice to prosecute and punish perpetrators of genocide. In *Genocide: Its Political Uses in the Twentieth Century,* Kuper focuses on the social conditions that produce genocide, arguing that societies with rigid ethnic hierarchies and in which minority groups are always despised or viewed with suspicion have a greater capacity for mass violence (see ETHNIC AND REGIONAL CONFLICT). Under such social structures, the rise of minority groups to prominent economic, social, and political positions generates intense hatred of them by the majority and often-dominant ethnic group.

In the *History and Sociology of Genocide,* Frank Chalk and Kurt Jonassohn address the largest loopholes in the genocide convention, arguing that the United Nations made a mistake by excluding the protection of political groups—the key victims of state-organized genocide—from legal protection under the convention. Though Chalk and Jonassohn criticize the omission of these groups, they agree with the provision in the convention that for any killing to be considered a genocide, it must be part of a deliberate attempt by the perpetrator to destroy the group, an action that the United Nations labels "acts committed with intent."

Chalk and Jonassohn see the intent of a perpetrator to destroy a group as an essential identifier of genocide, so as to exclude cases in which genocide was the outcome of an action that was not originally intended to achieve that result. They criticize the failure of the framers of the genocide convention to draw a clear distinction (in the list of five actions that constitute genocide) between violence intended to destroy a group and nonviolent attacks on members of the group. Chalk and Jonassohn argue that violent acts intended to destroy a group, such as killing members of the group, should not be mixed with nonlethal or nonviolent acts, such as transporting members of the group to another group that could ultimately cause the destruction of the group when that result was not the primary intent behind the transportation. For example, Chalk and Jonassohn do not consider as genocide random acts of killing by individuals who do not aim to destroy a group. They call such acts murder, unless those individuals acted on behalf of a state or another state authority to carry out an extermination of the group. They also exclude from their conception of genocide civilian deaths resulting from military actions, such as aerial bombardments of enemy territory in times of war, no matter how morally objectionable those actions are, including, for example, the U.S. bombing of Japan in 1945 with nuclear weapons. They argue that in war civilians must be considered part of the group or nation that is at war, that, in effect, civilians become collateral targets of military actions.

Chalk and Jonassohn have, therefore, proposed a definition of genocide that classifies it according to the motives of the perpetrator: "a form of one-sided mass killing in which a state or other authority intends to destroy a group, as that group and membership in it are defined by the perpetrator." They argue that genocides have occurred throughout history, and in all cases the perpetrators have been states and governments, or agencies acting on their behalf, and they have acted on the basis of one or more of four motives: to eliminate a real or potential threat; to spread terror among real or potential enemies; to acquire economic wealth; or to implement a belief, a theory, or an ideology. In all four categories, the killing should be one-sided to constitute genocide. One-sided mass killings are killings in which the victims lack the means to defend themselves against annihilation or in which they possess the means but are still powerless to avert extermination because of the preponderant power of the perpetrator. Chalk and Jonassohn's definition of "mass killing" also includes killings in which all the members of a group are targeted for extermination even though the perpetrator does not succeed in eliminating the entire group.

A major contribution of Chalk and Jonassohn's definition is the view that it is the perpetrator of genocide who defines the characteristics of a target group. In situations of genocide, the perpetrator's ideology converts real ethnic, national, racial, and religious groups into political enemies to be destroyed. For example, it was the racist ideology of Nazi German that defined Jewishness in strict racial terms that provided no room for escape. In Cambodia in 1975, it was the Khmer Rouge's revolutionary ideology of racial and ideological purity that turned groups without immutable characteristics, such as educated people, traders, and urban dwellers, into "impure" Khmers to be destroyed. Intellectuals, traders, and Western-educated Cambodians that the Khmer Rouge killed in Cambodia from 1975 to 1979 became "groups" because they were defined as such by the Pol Pot regime. Their identity as a group was fabricated by the perpetrator, the Khmer Rouge, because the regime saw these Cambodians as posing a threat to their revolutionary ideology.

Helen Fein also takes up the issue of proving intent in her research on genocide. Fein suggests that the intent of a perpetrator to destroy a group can be proven by establishing an identifiable pattern that ultimately leads to the destruction of a significant number of the victim group. She cites three patterns of purposeful actions for identifying an ongoing genocide: sustained attacks on the group by an organized entity, such as a state, or a group of organized actors, such as armed political groups; victims who are selected because they belong to a group; and victims that are defenseless and persecuted on a sustained basis regardless of whether they resist or surrender. Based on these premises, Fein defines genocide, in *Genocide: A Sociological Perspective,* as "a sustained, purposeful action by a perpetrator to physically destroy a collectivity directly or indirectly through interdiction of the biological and social reproduction of group members, regardless of the surrender or lack of threat offered by the victim."

Political scientists Barbara Harff and Ted Robert Gurr have coined the term *politicide* to distinguish deliberate destruction of political groups from intentional racial killings, or genocide. As they admit in "Towards Empirical Theory of Genocides and Politicides," however, it is difficult to differentiate "genocide" from "politicide" because racial or ethnic victims of genocide are often politically active and, therefore, targeted on grounds of their political beliefs as well. Political scientist Robert Melson focuses his work on identifying contexts or situations that encourage genocide. To him, "revolution" and "war" provide such situations and contexts. Melson argues in *Revolution and Genocide* that it was extreme nationalist ideologies that led the Young Turks regime of the Ottoman Empire to kill 1.5 million Armenians during World War I and the Nazis to murder some 6 million Jews during World War II. In each of these cases, revolution and war provided the contexts for extreme ideologies to be turned into instruments of genocide. Melson is careful to note, however, that not every revolution leads to genocide, and not every genocide is the consequence of revolution or war.

In 1999 Israel Charny proposed a solution to the debate over definitions of genocide and groups to be protected under the genocide convention. In "Towards a Generic Definition of Genocide," he suggests that the sanctity of human life requires a broad definition of genocide that treats all cases of mass murder as genocide. Each instance of mass murder, however, should be assigned to one or more subcategories; over the course of time new categories of genocide could be created as the complexity of the human experience unfolds. Accordingly, Charny proposes the category "accomplices to genocide" to hold morally and legally accountable "those who assist, prepare, or furnish the mass murderers of the world with the means [such as weapons, tanks] to exterminate huge numbers of people."

R. J. Rummel sees an ethical solution to the debate on genocide in democide, a concept that he defines in *Death by Government* as "the murder of any person or people by a government." Rummel's approach to the study of genocide recognizes all systematic killings of human beings as worthy of sympathy and attention. Such a general definition of murder, however, overlooks the fact that genocide is a particular form of murder and should be recognized as such. Genocide risks losing its meaning if, for instance, it is subsumed under indiscriminate killings of students protesting high unemployment in a developing country, which may have nothing to do with government intentions to destroy particular ethnic and religious groups within the student population.

What is innovative about post-1990 research on genocide is the comparing of cases to detect similarities and differences. Consequently, scholars studying genocide have broadened their discussions beyond definitions of types and contexts of genocide to incorporate analyses of the indifference of bystanders, people or nations that look on while genocide occurs even though they could intervene to stop it. Two groups of bystanders have been identified: internal and external. Internal bystanders are often indifferent members of the perpetrator group or society but are not themselves perpetrators. Their lack of compassion for the victims often stems from a long tradition of enmity between the victims and the bystanders, cultures that bar interaction between them, and fear of authority or reprisals from the perpetrator. External bystanders are outside nations or groups who remain passive to the plight of the victims because the group is either geographically remote or racially different from the external bystander. Internal and external bystanders have one thing in common: They do not directly take part in the physical act of killing but participate, nonetheless, in the dehumanization of the victims by remaining aloof or by putting the group beyond their universe of moral obligations. For example, in 1994, while armed groups from the majority Hutu were slaughtering some eight hundred thousand Tutsi in Rwanda, with full U.S. awareness of what was happening, the Clinton administration found reasons not to use the word *genocide* to describe what was clearly a planned extermination campaign. As reported by Holly Burkhalter in "The Question of Genocide: The Clinton Administration and Rwanda," David Rawson, the U.S. ambassador to Rwanda at the time categorically stated, on 9 June 1994, "[A]s a responsible government, you don't just go around hollering 'genocide.' You say that acts of genocide may have occurred and they need to be investigated." This cautious statement arose from the U.S. concern that recognition of the Rwandan killings as "genocide" would impose a moral and legal obligation on the United States, under the UN genocide convention, to intervene. The Rwandan genocide occurred one year after eighteen American soldiers were killed in Somalia in a U.S. humanitarian intervention to make the country safer for international aid agencies to distribute food and medicine to Somalis affected by famine and war. After its experience in Somalia, the United States had no desire to intervene in another African country.

Policies and Programs

Since 1990 humanitarian interventions and international criminal tribunals have become the most popular genocide-prevention policies and programs. Intervening to stop genocide before it occurs and prosecuting perpetrators of genocides that could not be prevented affirm the readiness of the world's family of nations to do something about this persistent problem (see map, p. 245). The "humanitarian interventions" in Kosovo, in June 1999, do not offer a successful precedent. The armed intervention led by the North Atlantic Treaty Organization (NATO) to save ethnic Albanian Muslims in Kosovo—after more than a hundred thousand of them had been killed by the Serbian government in a clear case of genocide against a religious group—raises troubling questions. Intervening in a situation after massive killings have occurred might promote the use of extreme violence, such as air strikes, which is what happened in Kosovo. Analyzing existing areas of ethnic and political conflict for their potential to become genocidal situations, however, offers the possibility of using more benign methods to stop such conflicts. Barbara Harff and Ted Robert Gurr developed this policy of analysis and forecasting for the Clinton administration, but it remains to be tested.

In addition to intervention, trials on the international stage can help to prevent genocide (see INTERNATIONAL CRIMINAL JUSTICE and WAR CRIMES). The UN-sponsored International Criminal Tribunal for the Former Yugoslavia, established in April 1993 and based at The Hague, has indicted Bosnian Serb politicians Radovan Karadzic and Ratko Mladic for genocide against Bosnian Muslims. The tribunal has also defined rape and other dehumanizing sexual offenses against women, in wartime, as a crime of genocide. This designation is a new and important development in international policy on genocide prevention and one of the primary innovations of the tribunal. The International Criminal Tribunal for Rwanda, established by the United Nations in November 1994 and based in Arusha, Tanzania, has likewise set impressive precedents in the prosecution of genocide. As of October 2001, the tribunal had convicted six former Rwandan state officials of genocide, the first international tribunal since Nuremberg to do so. The convicted include former prime minister Jean Kambanda and Jean Paul Akayesu, a former prominent government official. There are other military and political figures in custody awaiting trial. The Rwanda tribunal is a testimony of the efficacy of international criminal tribunals as tools for combating genocide. Such tribunals offer victims the legal and moral satisfaction that justice has been served. Successful trials might also have a positive effect on social and political attitudes in postgenocide societies.

Progress in the institutionalization of international criminal tribunals occurred in June 1998. More than 160 countries met in Rome to discuss and adopt a treaty establishing the first permanent international criminal court for prosecuting perpetrators of genocide, war crimes, and other crimes against humanity. On 17 July 1998, 120 countries approved the treaty and 26 countries signed it the following day. The authority of the court, once it is established—60 nations must ratify the treaty for it to go into effect, and 37 countries had done so as of October 2001—is compromised by legal limitations. The court can only try cases of genocide that the Security Council refers to it, which means that Security Council members can use their veto to protect perpetrators of genocide in their own states or in states to which they are bound with a vital strategic interest. Furthermore, the court cannot try any perpetrator of genocide who is a citizen of a country that has not signed the treaty establishing the court. This is a serious flaw that allows some nations to put their citizens who perpetrate genocide beyond the jurisdiction of the court by their refusal to sign the treaty. Despite these limitations, the idea of a permanent international criminal court is important because it institutionalizes the principle of accountability.

Other, less direct and peaceful strategies have been considered to lessen the possibility of genocide or persuade those guilty of genocide to stop. These strategies include implementing democracy, human rights, and sanctions, but they assume, in a very simplistic way, that genocide is mainly the consequence of power struggles and denials of groups to their identity and basic rights to life (see HUMAN RIGHTS). In *Protection against Genocide: Mission Impossible?* advocates of democracy, human rights, and sanctions argue that if everyone lived under a democratic political system and had the right to vote in free elections and could speak and assemble freely, and if the states and governments that commit genocide could be denied the tools of murder through sanctions, the world would be a peaceful place.

Regional Summaries

R. J. Rummell has asserted that almost 170 million people were shot, beaten, tortured, murdered, burned, buried alive, bombed, starved, or worked to death by states, governments, and armed political movements during the first eighty-eight years of the twentieth century. He adds that struggles for power, absolute exercise of power, and ethnic conflicts led to the deaths of more than 203 million people in the twentieth century. Every region of the world has had its share of genocide.

Americas

It is difficult to know the exact number of indigenous populations—American Indians, or Native Americans—who have been systematically killed by governments in North, Central, and South America. With the settlement of Europeans in the Americas in the seventeenth century, and with the expansion of national borders and the pursuit of "development" by governments in Brazil, Canada, Chile, Colombia, Mexico, and the United States in the twentieth century, indigenous people have paid dearly with their lives. The process of destruction varied in time and place.

Intentional state-organized extermination of Native Americans has not occurred on a significant scale. A large number of the native populations died from infectious diseases carried by European settlers. In Mexico, for instance, more native people died from epidemics of infectious diseases than were killed in massacres. In the United States and Canada, however, local and federal authorities adopted policies that undermined what Lemkin would call the foundations of the livelihood of the native people. For example, according to some scholars, including Clinton Fink, during the California gold rush of the 1850s, entire groups of Native Americans were exterminated to gain access to their land. This is an example of what Chalk and Jonassohn call genocide committed for the purpose of acquiring economic wealth. Also, by destroying the buffalo, a key source of food and survival for native people, and by putting Native Americans on marginal agricultural lands (reserves), the governments of Brazil, Canada, and the United States exposed these groups to famine, starvation, and disease. To Chalk and Jonassohn, failure to mitigate the adverse conditions on the reserves that killed native people and lowered their birth rates constituted advertent omission, suggesting an intent to destroy them. In *Peace and Conflict, 2001,* Ted Robert Gurr, Monty Marshall, and Deepa Khosla identify the indigenous people of Brazil, Chile, Colombia, and Mexico as at risk of becoming victims of state-sponsored genocide in the twenty-first century.

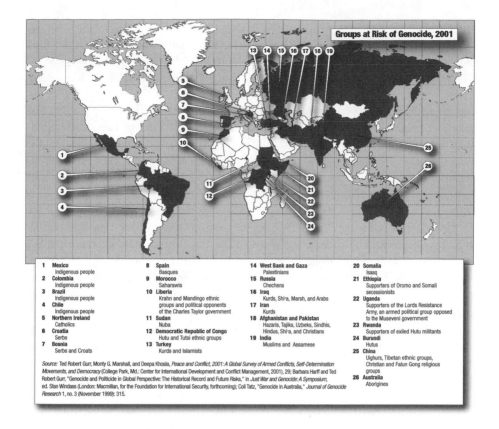

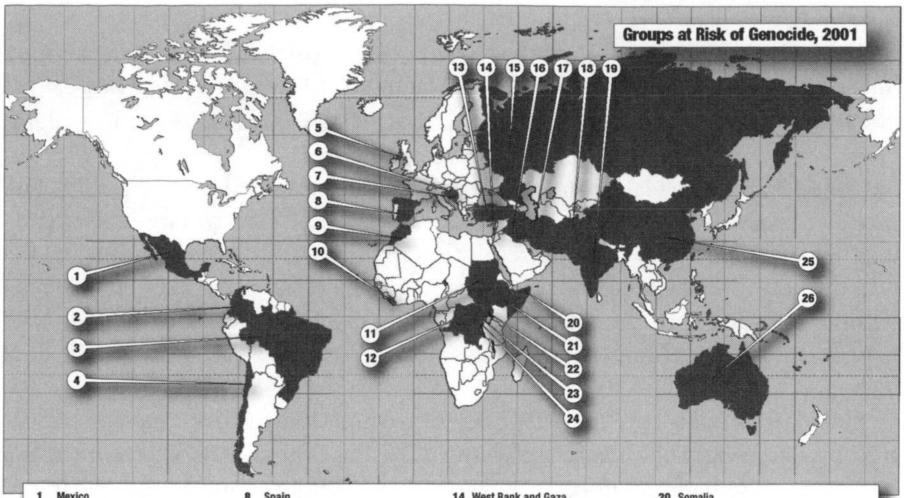

1 **Mexico**
Indigenous people
2 **Colombia**
Indigenous people
3 **Brazil**
Indigenous people
4 **Chile**
Indigenous people
5 **Northern Ireland**
Catholics
6 **Croatia**
Serbs
7 **Bosnia**
Serbs and Croats
8 **Spain**
Basques
9 **Morocco**
Saharawis
10 **Liberia**
Krahn and Mandingo ethnic groups and political opponents of the Charles Taylor government
11 **Sudan**
Nuba
12 **Democratic Republic of Congo**
Hutu and Tutsi ethnic groups
13 **Turkey**
Kurds and Islamists
14 **West Bank and Gaza**
Palestinians
15 **Russia**
Chechens
16 **Iraq**
Kurds, Shiʾa, Marsh, and Arabs
17 **Iran**
Kurds
18 **Afghanistan and Pakistan**
Hazaris, Tajiks, Uzbeks, Sindhis, Hindus, Shiʾa, and Christians
19 **India**
Muslims and Assamese
20 **Somalia**
Isaaq
21 **Ethiopia**
Supporters of Oromo and Somali secessionists
22 **Uganda**
Supporters of the Lords Resistance Army, an armed political group opposed to the Museveni government
23 **Rwanda**
Supporters of exiled Hutu militants
24 **Burundi**
Hutus
25 **China**
Uighurs, Tibetan ethnic groups, Christian and Falun Gong religious groups
26 **Australia**
Aborigines

Source: Ted Robert Gurr, Monty G. Marshall, and Deepa Khosla, *Peace and Conflict, 2001: A Global Survey of Armed Conflicts, Self-Determination Movements, and Democracy* (College Park, Md.: Center for International Development and Conflict Management, 2001), 29; Barbara Harff and Ted Robert Gurr, "Genocide and Politicide in Global Perspective: The Historical Record and Future Risks," in *Just War and Genocide: A Symposium*, ed. Stan Windass (London: Macmillan, for the Foundation for International Security, forthcoming); Coli Tatz, "Genocide in Australia," *Journal of Genocide Research* 1, no. 3 (November 1999): 315.

Europe

The major genocides of the twentieth century took place in Europe. Between 1915 and 1922, according to Richard Hovannisian's "Historical Dimensions of the Armenian Question, 1878–1930," about 1.5 million Armenians in the Ottoman Empire were killed by the Young Turks revolutionary government. These killings support Melson's view that war and revolution sometimes provide the conditions for genocide. From 1918 to 1921, some 100,000 to 250,000 Jews living in the Ukraine were killed by the Ukrainian government. In 1932 and 1933 Joseph Stalin used famine and starvation as weapons to kill about 38,000,000 Ukrainians. From 1939 to 1945 about 18,000,000 people were killed by the Nazi government of Germany in Europe alone. Approximately 5 million to 6 million of these people were Jews, 3.3 million were Soviet POW's, 2 million were Gypsies (Roma), 1 million were Serbs, and hundreds of thousands were Jehovah's Witnesses or handicapped people. In 1992, according to Thomas Cushman in his "Critical Theory and the War in Croatia and Bosnia," Croat and Serbian nationalists annihilated about 200,000 Muslims in Bosnia. According to Ted Robert Gurr, Monty Marshall, and Deepa Khosla in *Peace and Conflict, 2001,* the groups in Europe most seriously at risk of becoming victims of state-organized genocide and politicide include the Basques in Spain, Catholics in Northern Ireland, Chechens in Russia, Kurds and Islamists in Turkey, Serbs and Croats in Bosnia, and Serbs in Croatia.

North Africa and the Middle East

According to information in *Peace and Conflict, 2001,* the groups most seriously at risk of becoming victims of genocide in North Africa and the Middle East include the Kurds in Iran and Iraq, Palestinians in East Jerusalem, Gaza, and the West Bank, and Saharawis in Morocco. Since 1967 Israel has occupied Palestinian lands in East Jerusalem, Gaza, and the West Bank. The preponderant military power of Israel has often been used to target and eliminate Palestinians, who seek the resolution of issues relating to self-determination and the occupied territories. As Ted Gurr, Monty Marshall, and Deepa Khosla note, until all agreements between the Palestinian Authority and Israel have been implemented, conflict will progress and the Palestinians will be a vulnerable group in any hostility.

Since 1975 Morocco has stifled the determination of the Saharawi people to create an independent state in Western Sahara. Their leaders have been the targets of systematic Moroccan state-organized killings, and many Saharawis have been displaced. Kurds have been the targets of state repression, discrimination, and killing in Iran and Iraq since 1979. Their persecution results from their quest for more rights and privileges as a minority group.

UN actions in Iraq following the Persian Gulf War in 1991 have rekindled debate about the definition of genocide. According to some observers, the economic sanctions imposed on Iraq in the war's aftermath constitute actions that amount to genocide. According to this line of thinking, intent by the United Nations could be established by applying the standard of an act of omission, since UN Security Council members have been aware of the loss of life resulting from the continuing imposition of sanctions. On the other hand, as George Lopez argues in "Economic Sanctions and Genocide: Too Little, Too Late and Sometimes Too Much," "an international consensus exists about economic sanctions as a legitimate and effective instrument for deterring the potential for genocide."

Sub-Saharan Africa

Sub-Saharan Africa, home to numerous countries and thousands of ethnic groups, has experienced serious genocides in the twentieth century. In fact, scholars who study genocide agree that the first genocide of the twentieth century took place in Africa, when Gen. Lothar von Trotha led German troops against the defenseless Herero ethnic group in Germany's former colony of South-West Africa (now Namibia) in October 1904. Von Trotha's army wiped out 65,000 of the Herero population of 80,000. In Central Africa from 1965 to 1972, between 100,000 and 300,000 Hutus were killed by the Tutsi minority government in Burundi. More recently, within a hundred days, from April to July 1994, 800,000 Tutsis, or 10 percent of the total population, were slaughtered by extremist Hutu militia in Rwanda. According to Linda Melvern in *A People Betrayed: The Role of the West in Rwanda's Genocide,* the perpetrators of the genocide acted with impunity in part because they did not expect international intervention to stop them. Robert Melson has called the Rwandan genocide "Africa's version of the Holocaust."

According to Barbara Harff and Ted Robert Gurr in "Genocide and Politicide in Global Perspective," the groups most seriously at risk of becoming victims of genocide in sub-Saharan Africa include the Krahn and Mandingo ethnic groups as well as political opponents of the Charles Taylor government of Liberia; supporters of Oromo and Somali secessionists in Ethiopia; Isaaq ethnic groups in Somalia; Nuba ethnic groups in Sudan; supporters of the Lords Resistance Army, an armed political group opposed to the Museveni government in Uganda; Hutus in Burundi and supporters of exiled Hutu militants in Rwanda, and Hutu and Tutsi ethnic groups in the Democratic Republic of Congo.

Asia and the Pacific

There are deep historical memories of genocide in Asia, and the continent's numerous minority groups are still at risk of becoming victims of genocide in the twenty-first century. In 1975, Indonesia invaded East Timor and systematically targeted for annihilation ethnic, religious, and political groups who sought independence from Indonesian control. Between 1975 and 1978, about 200,000 of 800,000 East Timorese were massacred by Indonesian soldiers. According to Noam Chomsky in *Rogue States: The Rule of Force in World Affairs,* they did so "with U.S. diplomatic support and arms." Some sort of resolution of this crisis occurred on 30 August 1999, when the people of East Timor voted to become independent in an internationally observed referendum. From 1975 to 1979, about 2 million people in Cambodia were exterminated by the Khmer Rouge with diplomatic support and supplies of arms from China. The murdered included Vietnamese and Chinese ethnic groups, Cham Muslims, and educated and urban Khmer.

The groups most seriously at risk of becoming victims of state-organized genocide in the twenty-first century are mainly in East, Central, and South Asia. According to Barbara Harff and Ted Robert Gurr's "Genocide and Politicide in Global Perspective," in China groups at risk include Christian and Falun Gong religious groups, Tibetan ethnic groups, and Uighurs. In Afghanistan and Pakistan, the Christians, Hazaris, Hindus, Sindhis, Shi'a, Tajiks, and Uzbeks, are the groups at risk. Muslims and Assamese are greatly at risk of becoming victims of genocide in India. Aborigines, Australia's native people, are the victims of an ongoing genocide. Since 1788 they have been forcibly removed from their settlements, assimilated into the dominant white Australian population, and subjected to birth control injections for the purpose of preventing births within the group.

Case Study—Cambodia and Ethiopia

In the 1970s many Cambodians and Ethiopians thought that the political revolutions in their societies would improve their economic condition. Instead, the Ethiopian revolution claimed the lives of 1.2–2 million people out of a prerevolutionary population of 45 million, a death toll comparable to the 1.7–2 million Cambodians who died during the Khmer Rouge revolution of the same period. The estimated population of Cambodia before the revolution was 8 million. Some scholars and writers characterize these death tolls as genocide. Ethiopia and Cambodia ratified the UN genocide convention in 1951. Thus, their monarchies assumed legal and moral obligations to prevent and punish genocide. They failed to carry out this obligation.

Cambodia

Anthropologist Alexander Hinton, in "A Head for an Eye: Revenge, Culture, and the Cambodian Genocide," has argued that the determination of the Khmer Rouge to destroy whole families in Cambodia had some of its origin in "the Cambodian cultural model of disproportionate revenge." In Hinton's view, the object of revenge in Cambodian culture is "to completely defeat the enemy." Because Cambodians believe that "someone in the deceased foe's family [might] disproportionately avenge the death," people who kill are encouraged to obliterate the line of the deceased. According to Hinton, " the extreme violence of the Khmer Rouge period had deep roots in this 'cultural model' of killing, as the Pol Pot regime manipulated it in its exhortation of cadres to settle 'grudges' against their class enemies." There is, however, disagreement among scholars—for instance Ben Kiernan, David P. Chandler, and Michael Vickery—on whether what took place in Cambodia in the early 1970s constituted genocide or an unintended consequence of a social revolution. A case for genocide, as strictly defined in the genocide convention, can be made against the Khmer Rouge from the overwhelming evidence of its selective and systematic annihilation of large numbers of Chinese and Vietnamese racial groups, Cham Muslims, Khmer intellectuals, and people who lived in urban areas. The Khmer Rouge leadership was able to commit genocide of that magnitude because of the uncontested power and control it exercised during the revolution, from April 1975 to January 1979.

Ethiopia

Between 1974 and 1991 about 1.5 million people of all ethnic backgrounds and political affiliations were killed in Ethiopia in outright massacres and through deliberate starvation. The revolutionary military government headed by Mengistu Haile Mariam and the many armed political groups that opposed the regime share responsibility for these deaths. Ethiopian historian Merid Wolde Aregay sees national culture as the greatest constraint on the Ethiopian government's genocidal intentions. Merid argues that historically Ethiopians have accepted murder on political and ideological grounds, but that culturally, the extermination of people on the grounds of their race and ethnicity is a moral threshold that they have never crossed in their multiethnic society. Given these elements of national culture, it appears that the revolution and war that created the conditions for genocide in Cambodia would not have produced a similar situation in Ethiopia. More factors were at play in the Ethiopian situation than national culture.

Throughout its seventeen years of rule, from September 1974 to May 1991, Ethiopia's revolutionary military government faced determined armed opposition from numerous armed "liberation fronts," making the government's political opponents the target group. Thus, what happened during the Ethiopian revolution confirms Harff and Gurr's theory that opposition activity and the struggle for power between uncompromising armed groups create conditions for genocide. There are also lessons that can be drawn from Chalk's and Jonassohn's work on genocide. In Ethiopia, the revolutionary regime sought total power to implement its ideology of national unity. As a result, it alone defined the boundaries of the target groups it called "reactionary," "counterrevolutionary," and "anti-unity." Under these arbitrary definitions of target groups, one could find "reactionary" and "counterrevolutionary" Ethiopians who were Muslim or Christian or from particular economic and ethnic backgrounds. Here, the ethnic identity and religious beliefs of those labeled "reactionary" and targeted for annihilation were not the primary factors for their inclusion in the group to be destroyed. What mattered was the regime's perception of the political threat they posed to the ideology of the state.

Under the genocide convention, these crimes would not constitute genocide, but the Ethiopian experience raises an interesting issue in the definition and prosecution of genocide. According to the Ethiopian penal code, the killing of people on grounds of their political beliefs or opposition to the state—politicide—is a form of genocide (see Document 2). The leaders of the Mengistu regime are now on trial in Ethiopia for committing genocide. Under Ethiopian law, and the Chalk and Jonassohn definition of genocide, these leaders are perpetrators of genocide. The historical record also shows that those who opposed them are equally guilty of genocide under Ethiopian law.

Biographical Sketches

Frank Chalk is the president of the Association of Genocide Scholars and co-author, with Kurt Jonassohn, of the acclaimed *History and Sociology of Genocide: Analyses and Case Studies* (1990). The book presents a broad definition of genocide that protects political groups and identifies four types of genocide. Chalk has lectured and presented papers on genocide around the world, including before the prosecution staff of the International Criminal Tribunal for the Former Yugoslavia at The Hague.

Helen Fein is executive director of the Institute for the Study of Genocide, New York, and a research associate of the Belfer Center at the Kennedy School of Government, Harvard University. She coined the phrase "universe of moral obligation" to illustrate that perpetrators of genocide put their victims beyond their concept of moral obligation.

Barbara Harff is professor of political science at the U.S. Naval Academy in Annapolis, Maryland, and a senior consultant to the White House–sponsored State Failure Task Force. She has contributed to research on genocide by designing database analysis for the preconditions and accelerators of genocide and politicide for the U.S. Center for Early Warning Humanitarian Crisis. She has written extensively on the subject of genocide from a comparative perspective.

Kurt Jonassohn is a former professor of sociology and co-author, with Frank Chalk, of the *History and Sociology of Genocide: Analyses and Case Studies* (1990). He is also the co-director of the Montreal Institute for Genocide and Human Rights Studies at Concordia University in Montreal, Canada. Jonassohn's many articles and papers have influenced the study of genocide, especially in the growing field of comparative genocide. His sociological approach to the study of genocide has helped scholars determine intent from the extent of the actions of perpetrators.

Leo Kuper is a pioneer of the academic study of genocide. He was born in Johannesburg, South Africa, and practiced law there until the outbreak of World War II, in which he fought. In 1961 Kuper moved to the United States and taught sociology at the University of California, Los Angeles. He won international acclaim for *Genocide: Its Political Use in the Twentieth Century* (1981).

Robert Melson is a founder of the Association of Genocide Scholars. His work on the relationship between revolution and genocide is recognized as a groundbreaking approach to the study of genocide. It argues that during revolutions aimed at restructuring nations, identity and patriotism of inhabitants become contexts for defining who is a true member and patriot and should belong to the nation and who is expendable.

Directory

Cape Town Holocaust Center, Albow Centre, 88 Hatfield Street Gardens, Cape Town 8001, South Africa. Telephone: (21) 462-5553, Email: ctholocaust@mweb.co.za, Web: http://www.museums.org.za./ctholocaust
Organization that provides lectures, seminars, and films on the Holocaust and genocide

Center for Holocaust and Genocide Studies, Clark University, 950 Main Street, Worcester, MA 01610. Telephone: (508) 793-8897, Email: holocauststudies@clarku.edu, Web: http://www.clarku.edu/departments/holocaust
Leading teaching and research center providing undergraduate and graduate studies on the Holocaust and a broad range of interdisciplinary and comparative subjects relating to genocide in the non-Western world

Genocide Watch, P.O. Box 809, Washington, DC 20044. Telephone: (703) 448-0222, Email: info@genocidewatch.org, Web: http://www.genocidewatch.org
Organization coordinating an international campaign to end genocide

Institute for the Study of Genocide, John Jay College of Criminal Justice, 899 Tenth Avenue, 325 T, New York, NY 10019. Telephone: (617) 354-2785, Email: info@isg-iags.org, Web: http://www.isg-iags.org.
Organization that promotes and disseminates scholarship and analysis on the causes, consequences, and prevention of genocide

International Center for Human Rights and Democratic Development, 1001 de Maisonneuve Boulevard West, Suite 1100, Montreal, Quebec, Canada H2L 4P9. Telephone: (514) 283-6073, Email: ichrdd@ichrdd.ca, Web: http://www.ichrdd.ca
Organization that encourages and supports universal values of human rights and promotes democratic institutions and practices around the world

Montreal Institute for Genocide and Human Rights Studies, Concordia University, 1455 de Maisonneuve Boulevard West, Montreal, Quebec, Canada H3G 1M8. Telephone: (514) 848-2404, Email: go to http://migs.concordia.ca/feedback.html, Web: http://www.migs.org
Research institute for the comparative study of genocide and human rights

Tokyo Holocaust Education Resource Center, 28-105 Daikyo-cho, Shinjuku-ku, Tokyo 160-0015, Japan. Telephone (81) 3 5363 4808, Web: http://www.ne.jp/asahi/holocaust/Tokyo
Repository of important papers and videotapes on the Holocaust and genocide, offers seminars for teachers and students

Yad Vashem, The Holocaust Martyrs and Heroes' Remembrance Authority, P.O. Box 3477, Jerusalem, Israel 91034. Telephone: (972) 2 644 3400, Email: general.information@yadvashem.org.il, Web: http://www.yadvashem.org.il
Repository of archival materials on the Holocaust

Further Research

Books

Chalk, Frank, and Kurt Jonassohn. *The History and Sociology of Genocide: Analyses and Case Studies.* New Haven: Yale University Press, 1990.

Chandler, David P. *The Tragedy of Cambodian History: Politics, War, and Revolution since 1945.* New Haven: Yale University Press, 1991.

Chomsky, Noam. *Rogue States: The Rule of Force in World Affairs.* Cambridge, Mass.: South End Press, 2000.

Chorbajian, Levon, and George Shirinian. *Studies in Comparative Genocide.* New York: St. Martin's Press, 1999.

Churchill, Ward. *A Little Matter of Genocide: Holocaust and Denial in the Americas, 1492 to the Present.* San Francisco: City Lights Books, 1997.

Dadrian, Vahakn. *The History of the Armenian Genocide: Ethnic Conflict from the Balkans to Anatolia to the Caucasus.* Providence, R.I.: Berghahn Books, 1995.

De Nike, Howard J., John Quigley, and Kenneth J. Robinson. *Genocide in Cambodia: Documents from the Trial of Pol Pot and Leng Sary.* Philadelphia: University of Pennsylvania Press, 2000.

Fein, Helen. *Genocide: A Sociological Perspective.* London: Sage Publications, 1990.

Giorgis, Dawit Wolde. *Red Tears: War, Famine, and Revolution in Ethiopia.* Trenton, N.J.: Red Sea Press, 1989.

Hovannisian, Richard G., ed. *The Armenian Genocide: History, Politics, Ethics.* New York: St. Martin's Press, 1992.

Kiernan, Ben. *The Pol Pot Regime: Race, Power, and Genocide in Cambodia under the Khmer Rouge, 1975–79.* New Haven: Yale University Press, 1996.

Kuper, Leo. *Genocide: Its Political Use in the Twentieth Century.* New Haven: Yale University Press, 1981.

Lemkin, Raphael. *Axis Rule in Occupied Europe: Laws of Occupation, Analysis of Government, Proposals for Redress.* Washington, D.C.: Carnegie Endowment for International Peace, 1944.

Melson, Robert. *Revolution and Genocide: On the Origins of the Armenian Genocide and the Holocaust.* Chicago: University of Chicago Press, 1992.

Riemer, Neal, ed. *Protection against Genocide: Mission Impossible?* Westport, Conn.: Praeger, 2000.

Rummell, R. J. *Death by Government.* New Brunswick, N.J.: Transaction Publishers, 1994.

———. *Statistics of Democide: Genocide and Mass Murder since 1900.* New Brunswick, N.J.: Transaction Press, 1999.

Vickery, Michael. *Cambodia, 1975–1982.* Boston: South End Press, 1984.

Articles and Reports

Australian Government. *Bringing Them Home: Report of the National Inquiry into the Separation of Aboriginal and Torres Strait Islander Children from Their Families.* Sydney: Human Rights and Equal Opportunity Commission, 1997.

Burkhalter, Holly J. "The Question of Genocide: The Clinton Administration and Rwanda." *World Policy Journal* 11 (winter 1995): 44–54.

Charny, Israel W. "Towards a Generic Definition of Genocide." In *Genocide: Conceptual and Historical Dimensions,* edited by George Andreopoulos, 64–94. Philadelphia: University of Pennsylvania Press, 1997.

———. "Innocent Denials of Known Genocides: A Further Contribution to a Psychology of Denial of Genocide." *Human Rights Review* 1, no. 3 (2000): 15–39.

Cushman, Thomas. "Critical Theory and the War in Croatia and Bosnia." *The Donald W. Treadgold Papers in Russian, East European and Central Asian Studies,* no. 13, July 1997, 7.

Fink, Clinton F. "Denials of the Genocide of Native Americans." In *Encyclopedia of Genocide,* ed. Israel W. Charny, 2:166. Santa Barbara, Calif.: ABC-CLIO, 1999.

Gurr, Ted Robert, Monty G. Marshall, and Deepa Khosla. *Peace and Conflict, 2001: A Global Survey of Armed Conflicts, Self-Determination Movements, and Democracy.* College Park, Md.: Center for International Development and Conflict Management, 2001.

Harff, Barbara, and Ted Robert Gurr. "Towards Empirical Theory of Genocides and Politicides: Identification and Measurement of Cases since 1945." *International Studies Quarterly* 32 (1988): 359–371.

———. "Systematic Early Warning of Humanitarian Emergencies." *Journal of Peace Research* 35, no. 5 (1998): 551–579.

———. "Genocide and Politicide in Global Perspective: The Historical Record and Future Risks." In *Just War and Genocide: A Symposium,* edited by Stan Windass. London: Macmillan, for the Foundation for International Security, forthcoming.

Heuveline, Patrick. "Between One and Three Million: Toward the Demographic Reconstruction of a Decade of Cambodian History, 1970–1979." *Population Studies* 52 (1998).

Hinton, Alexander. "A Head for an Eye: Revenge, Culture, and the Cambodian Genocide." Paper presented at the 1997 meeting of the Association of Genocide Scholars, Montreal, Canada.

Hovannisian, Richard G. "The Historical Dimensions of the Armenian Question, 1878–1930." In *History and Sociology of Genocide: Analyses and Case Studies,* edited by Frank Chalk and Kurt Jonassohn, 250–262. New Haven: Yale University Press, 1990.

Krieger, David. "International Criminal Court for Genocide and Major Human Rights Violations." In *Encyclopedia of Genocide,* edited by Israel W. Charny, 2:364. Santa Barbara, Calif.: ABC-CLIO, 1999.

Lilach, Beth. "From Southwest Africa to Auschwitz: German Imperialism and the Herero Genocide as an Antecedent to the Holocaust." Paper presented at the Interdisciplinary Workshop Symposium on Genocide in the Twentieth Century: Antecedent Causes, Victim Groups, and Possibilities for Intervention and Prevention, Center for Holocaust and Genocide Studies, Clark University, 19–21 October 2001.

Mirkov, Damir. "The Historical Link between the Ustasha Genocide and the Croato-Serb Civil War." *Journal of Genocide Research* 2, no. 3 (November 2000): 363–373.

Rummel, R. J. "The New Concept of Democide." In *Encyclopedia of Genocide,* edited by Israel W. Charny, 1:18–19. Santa Barbara, Calif.: ABC-CLIO, 1999.

———. "Power Kills, Absolute Power Kills Absolutely." In *Encyclopedia of Genocide,* edited by Israel W. Charny, 1:28–29. Santa Barbara, Calif.: ABC-CLIO, 1999.

Smith, David N. "The Psychocultural Roots of Genocide: Legitimacy and Crisis in Rwanda." *American Psychologist* 53, no. 7 (July 1998): 743–753.

Smith, Roger W. "Genocide and Denial: The Armenian Case and Its Implications." *Armenian Review* 42, no. 1 (spring 1989): 1–38.

Stanton, Gregory H. *The Seven Stages of Genocide.* Genocide Studies Program Working Paper Series, Working Paper GS 01. New Haven: Yale Center for International and Area Studies, 1998.

United Nations, International Criminal Tribunal for the Former Yugoslavia. "Indictment: Karadzic and Mladic." The Hague, Press and Information Office, 16 November 1995.

Van Schaak, Beth. "The Crime of Political Genocide: Repairing the Genocide Convention's Blind Spot." *Yale Law Journal* (May 1997): 202–230.

Web Sites

The Armenian Genocide
http://www.armenian-genocide.org

The Cambodian Genocide
http://www. DithPran.org; http://www.yale.edu/gsp

Genocide Against Native Americans
http://www.iwchildren.org/murderer1.htm

Genocide in Guatemala
http://www.amnestyusa.org/group/guate/what.html

The Rwandan Genocide
http://www.pbs.org/wgbh/pages/frontline/shows/evil

Documents

1. Convention on the Prevention and Punishment of the Crime of Genocide

Approved and proposed for signature and ratification or accession by General Assembly Resolution 260 A (III) of 9 December 1948, entered into force 12 January 1951

The full text is available at http://www.unhchr.ch/html/menu3/b/p_genoci.htm.

Extract

The Contracting Parties,

Having considered the declaration made by the General Assembly of the United Nations in its resolution 96 (1) dated 11 December 1946 that genocide is a crime under international law, contrary to the spirit and aims of the United Nations and condemned by the civilized world,

Recognizing that at all periods of history genocide has inflicted great losses on humanity, and

Being convinced that, in order to liberate mankind from such an odious scourge, international cooperation is required,

Hereby agree as hereinafter provided:

Article 1

The Contracting Parties confirm that genocide, whether committed in time of peace or in time of war, is a crime under international law which they undertake to prevent and punish.

Article 2

In the present Convention, genocide means any of the following acts committed with intent to destroy, in whole or in part, a national, ethnical, racial or religious group, as such:

(a) Killing members of the group;

(b) Causing serious bodily or mental harm to members of the group;

(c) Deliberately inflicting on the group conditions of life calculated to bring about its physical destruction in whole or in part;

(d) Imposing measures intended to prevent births within the group;

(e) Forcibly transferring children of the group to another group.

Article 3

The following acts shall be punishable

(a) Genocide;

(b) Conspiracy to commit genocide;

(c) Direct and public incitement to commit genocide;

(d) Attempt to commit genocide;

(e) Complicity in genocide.

2. Penal Code of the Empire of Ethiopia, Proclamation no. 158 of 1957

The full text is available at http://www.preventgenocide.org/law/domestic/ethiopia.htm.

Extract

TITLE II: OFFENCES AGAINST THE LAW OF NATIONS

Chapter 1 Fundamental Offences

Article 281 Genocide; Crimes against Humanity

Whosoever, with intent to destroy, in whole or in part, a national, ethnic, racial, religious or political group, organizes, orders or engages in, be it in time of war or in time of peace:

(a) killing, bodily harm or serious injury to the physical or mental health of members of the group, in any way whatsoever; or

(b) measures to prevent the propagation or continued survival of its members or their progeny; or

(c) the compulsory movement or dispersion of peoples or children, or their placing under living conditions calculated to result in their death or disappearance, is punishable with rigorous imprisonment from five years to life, or, in cases of exceptional gravity, with death.

GLOBAL WARMING

Chris Woodford

Global warming is perhaps the ultimate global problem. It is caused by everyone, affects everyone, and requires the cooperation of everyone for its solution. Mounting evidence suggests that a warming world could trigger a range of catastrophes, from refugee crises prompted by rising sea levels to famines caused by desertification. Yet national leaders have found it remarkably difficult to reach agreement on how to tackle this global challenge.

Historical Background and Development

Global warming is a deceptively simple problem. So-called greenhouse gases—notably carbon dioxide (CO_2), methane, water vapor, nitrous oxide, ozone, and chlorofluorocarbons—trap heat in Earth's atmosphere in much the same way that glass traps heat in a greenhouse. This natural effect keeps the planet around 30 degrees Celsius (86 degrees Fahrenheit), which is warmer than it would be otherwise. The amount of greenhouse gases in the atmosphere has, however, been on the rise since the Industrial Revolution and is causing a rise in average temperatures.

Although concern about climate change is widely considered a contemporary preoccupation, the science of global warming dates back to the nineteenth century. In 1827 French mathematician Jean-Baptiste Fourier noted the similarity between the warming of Earth's atmosphere and the workings of a greenhouse. Some thirty years later, Irish physicist John Tyndall showed how carbon dioxide and water vapor trap heat in Earth's atmosphere and proposed that ice ages—the flip side of global warming—might be caused by a reduction in atmospheric carbon dioxide.

The modern science of global warming was born in 1896, when Swedish chemist Svante Arrhenius calculated that a doubling of atmospheric carbon dioxide could increase Earth's temperature by around five to six degrees Celsius, which is roughly the estimate produced by the United Nations' Intergovernmental Panel on Climate Change in the late twentieth century. Arrhenius's prediction might have remained a purely theoretical concern without the later work of Charles Keeling. Since 1958 Keeling has made regular measurements of atmospheric carbon dioxide at the Mauna Loa observatory on Hawaii, demonstrating the trend of increasing amounts of carbon dioxide, a pattern that is confirmed by measurements of carbon dioxide in Antarctic ice cores. Since 1998 Keeling's measurements have been supplemented by a network of seventy carbon dioxide monitoring towers around the world.

International concern about rising levels of carbon dioxide was a major theme of the first World Climate Conference, held in 1979, and delegates at the conference, sponsored by the United Nations' World Meteorology Organization (WMO), called on nations to anticipate and avert changes in climate caused by humans. A wake-up call came in 1988, when one of the world's leading climate modelers, NASA's James Hansen, told Congress that there was strong evidence for global warming and argued that they and other leaders could no longer afford to procrastinate. That same year, with considerable uncertainty about the science of climate change prevailing, the United Nations Environment Programme (UNEP) and the WMO established the Intergovernmental Panel on Climate Change in 1988 to formulate an international scientific consensus on the subject.

Three IPCC assessments, released in 1990, 1995, and 2001, note with increasing conviction that global warming is a real phenomenon, that it is caused by human activities, and that drastic action is required to prevent damaging climate change. The IPCC's work was not the only indication of a mounting scientific consensus. In 1990 seven hundred members of the National Academy of Sciences, including forty-nine Nobel Prize winners, signed a declaration stating that greenhouse gases will cause climate change and urging that action soon be taken to avoid risk to future generations. In 1997 a similar declaration calling for urgent action was signed by fifteen hundred scientists, including one hundred four Nobel winners.

Popular concern about global warming has been fueled less by the science of climate change than by an apparent increase in the severity and frequency of extreme weather events. For example, almost every year in the 1990s was described as the hottest year since 1861, the first year such weather data was recorded. The 1990s were the hottest decade of the twentieth century; 1998 was the hottest year on record. Scientists have also discovered other phenomena that may point to a warming world, notably the disintegration of massive ice shelves in Antarctica. Catastrophic floods, droughts, and other disasters have been a regular feature of Earth's history, which leads some polar scientists to believe that the ice shelves may be collapsing for reasons other than global warming. Although Earth's climate is highly variable, and events of this kind could simply be coincidental, increasingly severe weather and melting polar ice caps are key predictors of climate models, and there is concern that they may be warning signs of irreversible climate change.

Uncertainties in climate science are mirrored by disagreements about how the international community should respond to a threat of unknown magnitude that may or may not present itself for decades or even centuries. Nevertheless, most nations have supported what environmentalists term the *precautionary principle,* which states that attention should be paid to potential threats and preventive measures planned even when scientific evidence is not entirely conclusive. In June 1993, one year after the acceptance of the UN Framework Convention on Climate Change (UNFCCC) in Rio de Janeiro at the "Earth Summit," 166 nations had signed the convention, the central objective of which was the "stabilization of greenhouse gas concentrations in the atmosphere at a level that would prevent dangerous anthropogenic [human-caused] interference with the climate system" (see Document 1). The convention officially went into effect 21 March 1994. Efforts to turn the convention into practical action, however, have proved more problematic.

The Kyoto Protocol to the United Nations Framework Convention on Climate Change extended the UNFCCC with, in part, a commitment by developed nations to cut greenhouse emissions, but it has led a troubled existence since it was agreed to in December 1997. In March 2001, amid fierce international criticism, U.S. president George W. Bush put the future of the protocol in doubt by withdrawing U.S. participation. Because the United States is the largest producer of greenhouse gases, its participation in significantly reducing emissions would be essential. Skeptics argue that international agreement on a collective response to global warming is premature, but environmentalists counter that continued delay could make the effects of climate change more severe and irreversible.

Current Status

Most climatologists believe that since the Industrial Revolution, the large-scale burning of fossil fuels—particularly coal, gas, and oil—has produced a heightened artificial greenhouse effect that has increased the concentration of atmospheric carbon dioxide from a preindustrial level of 280 parts per million per volume (ppmv) to a current level of 360 ppmv, the highest in the last four hundred thousand years (see Tables 1 and 2). Computer models suggest that the level of carbon dioxide will at least double during the twenty-first century, producing an estimated rise in the average global surface temperature of between 1.4 and 5.8 degrees Celsius (3.15 and 13.05 degrees Fahrenheit), an estimated average rise in sea level between 9 centimeters and 88 centimeters (3.5 inches to 34 inches), and drastic changes in the global climate.

Research

Although systemic measurements of carbon dioxide have been made only since 1958, climate scientists can measure the composition of the atmosphere in much earlier periods using Antarctic ice cores, ice samples that may be more than 2.5 kilometers (1 mile) long. These samples, extracted in thin borehole pipes and carefully stored in refrigerated warehouses, contain air bubbles that effectively preserve "memories" of earlier climates, thus allowing the air's chemical composition to be analyzed. Ice cores contain data for the last two hundred years or so. By examining ocean sediment, scientist can study the climate of the past million years.

The Intergovernmental Panel on Climate Change has the job of formulating the increasing volume of climate change research data into a form accessible to policymakers and the public so that it can be used to devise policies and programs. This collective of several hundred scientists and policy advisers has delivered increasingly pessimistic assessments summarizing the science and the likely effects of climate change.

The IPCC's third assessment *Climate Change, 2001* notes, "Emissions of greenhouse gases and aerosols due to human activities continue to alter the atmosphere in ways that are expected to affect the climate." It goes on to state, "Anthropogenic climate change will persist for many centuries" (see Document 2). Part of the report, published in February 2001, notes, "Projected changes in climate extremes could have major consequences" and "those [nations] with the least resources have the least capacity to adapt and are the most vulnerable."

In quantitative terms, the IPCC's findings seem more dramatic. As noted, the 1990s were the warmest decade, and 1998 the warmest year, since 1861. Snow, ice, and glacier cover has declined by 10 to 15 percent since the 1950s. Sea level rose an average of 10 to 20 centimeters (3.9 to 7.8 inches) during the twentieth century. Episodes of El Niño—the reversal of climate conditions in the Pacific that can disrupt much of the world's weather—have become more intense and longer lasting and occur three times more often than they did a century ago. In Asia and Africa, droughts now occur more regularly and are more severe.

According to the IPCC, the above changes strongly correlate with human activities, notably a 31 percent increase in atmospheric carbon dioxide since 1750, the beginning of industrialization, due to fossil fuel burning and deforestation. The IPCC underlines how extraordinary this change is in Earth's history. According to the UNEP press release for *Climate Change, 2001,* "The present CO_2 concentration has not been exceeded during the past 420,000 years and likely not during the past 20 million years. The current rate of increase is unprecedented during at least the past 20,000 years."

The scientific consensus regarding climate change has sometimes appeared fragile and strained, with a relatively small number of skeptical scientists attracting what IPCC scientists perceive to be disproportionate media coverage with their dissenting view that global warming is simply an artifact of incomplete computer modeling. By definition, computer models must be incomplete; models of global warming are imperfect because the computational complexity of modeling the world's climate exceeds the power of even the fastest supercomputers unless a number of simplifying assumptions are made. There are concerns among skeptics that these assumptions may not be justified or that the equations on which climate models are based do not accurately predict what happens in nature. Moreover, as leading U.S. climate scientists Thomas Karl and Kevin Trenberth have argued, there is a dearth of data to feed into the computer models, because the world's climate is not currently monitored in sufficient detail.

Climate models give skeptics particular cause for concern because the projections they make—accurate or otherwise—are used by environmental groups to argue for such changes in policy as major reductions in energy and automobile use, which, the skeptics argue, would drastically affect economic competitiveness. The environmentalists counter that the skeptics are simply mouthpieces for industrial vested interests, notably fossil fuel and automobile manufacturers. In the popular media, and perhaps in society as a whole, there is still a perception that global warming is an unresolved issue with environmentalists on one side, skeptics who may or may not be linked to industrial interests on the other, and climate scientists with imperfect computer models struggling to resolve the issue somewhere in between. Yet the scientific consensus that global warming is a real phenomenon has become increasingly robust during the first decade of the IPCC's existence. Supporters of the IPCC note that its reports are a peer-reviewed, international collaboration. The third IPCC assessment, for example, was written by some 640 contributing scientists from around the world. Yet even the IPCC is not without its critics. Political scientist Sonja Boehmer-Christiansen has argued that the IPCC is a self-perpetuating scientific elite that has exaggerated scientific uncertainty to ensure continued funding for research.

Disagreements over the science aside, attention is increasingly focused on global warming's likely effect on humans. Two-thirds of the world's 6 billion people live within 60 kilometers (37 miles) of a coast. A projected rise in sea level of up to 88 centimeters (34 inches) within a century is expected to prove disastrous for low-lying nations such as Bangladesh and islands and atolls around the world (see Table 3). According to the UNEP, a rise of this degree would subject around 100 million people a year to flooding (mostly in developing countries). Access to freshwater is expected to become one of the most pressing environmental problems of the twenty-first century, as encroaching seas threaten groundwater supplies in coastal areas and as global warming increases the severity of droughts and floods. A November 1999 report by the World Commission on Water for the 21st Century notes that more than half of the world's river systems are already overexploited and polluted and concludes, "Unless there are drastic changes, water shortages and environmental degradation will become the norm" (see FRESHWATER).

With 40 percent of the world's food produced on irrigated land, changes in water availability will necessarily affect agriculture and food production (see map, p. 263). A 1993 report by the Environmental Change Unit at Oxford University estimates a 5 percent increase in productivity in developed countries (due to longer growing seasons) offset by a 10 percent loss in productivity in developing countries (due to heat stress, desertification, and more intense monsoons). A 1999 report by the industry-sponsored Pew Center on Global Climate Change suggests that there will be regional shifts in food production with little overall loss or gain. Human health could suffer through increased heat stress and greater transmission of diseases through the spread of such pests as mosquitoes (see EPIDEMICS and HEALTH). The geographical reach of malaria, for example, is predicted to increase from 45 percent of the world's population to 65 percent toward the end of the twenty-first century. IPCC co-chair James McCarthy summed up the view of many when he delivered the group's third report in 2001: "Most of the earth's people will be on the losing side."

With the effects of climate change uncertain, attaching a financial cost to them might seem impossible. Yet, according to IPCC science co-chair Sir John

Houghton's *Global Warming,* the annual cost of climate change to the United States will be around $38 billion to $46 billion dollars per year and for most other countries is predicted to be around 5 percent of gross domestic product. A report compiled for UNEP by Munich Re, a leading insurance company, concludes that if atmospheric carbon dioxide doubles by 2050, the resulting climate change will prompt an increase in natural disasters costing $304 billion dollars a year.

Policies and Programs

Given the uncertainties in long-range computer climate models and the guarded wording of the IPCC's 1990 report, it is perhaps surprising that world leaders have reached any agreement at all on international policies to combat global warming. Yet, within a year of the acceptance of the UN Framework Convention on Climate Change at the Earth Summit in 1992, 166 countries had agreed to sign the convention.

Detailed agreements about how to accomplish the goals of the convention were left to subsequent meetings of the signatory states, or Conference of the Parties (COP). In the most important of these, COP3, held in Kyoto, Japan, in November 1997, 150 nations agreed to the Kyoto Protocol, which set legally binding targets for limits on the emission of greenhouse gases. These ranged from cuts of around 7 percent (for the United States) and 8 percent (for Europe) to allowable increases of 8 percent (for Australia) and 10 percent (for Iceland). Developing countries refused to accept and were exempted from specific cuts. The United States, despite being a signatory, refused to ratify the treaty until it included "meaningful participation" by developing countries.

Later COP sessions ran into difficulties over the "meaningful participation" of developing countries and over differing interpretations of how emissions cuts could be achieved using "flexibility mechanisms." These include emissions trading (in which countries with high greenhouse emissions can buy permits to emit from countries with lower emissions), joint implementation (in which developed countries might offset their emissions by, for example, investing in solar power in Africa), and net accounting (in which well-managed forests and soil "sinks" that help to remove carbon dioxide from the atmosphere count as "carbon credits" toward lower emissions).

Following the election of George W. Bush as president in 2001, the United States unilaterally withdrew support from Kyoto. According to a 11 June 2001 White House press release, Bush described the protocol as "fatally flawed," "unrealistic" and "not based on science." When Australia, Canada, and Japan sought a weakening of the protocol, the whole initiative seemed on the brink of collapse. Yet as climate negotiations progressed during 2001, it became apparent that the overwhelming majority of countries were determined to achieve a global agreement on greenhouse emissions. In June ministers from the European Union expressed their resolve to press ahead without the United States. Finally, at an international summit in Bonn on 23 July forty-five hundred delegates from 180 nations agreed to a compromise that would involve lower emissions cuts than those originally proposed at Kyoto in 1997. While diplomats expressed jubilation that they had reached an agreement at all, environmental groups, such as Greenpeace, blamed the fossil fuel industry, the Organization of Petroleum Exporting Countries, and the United States for "watering down" the original agreement. Crucially, the United States refused to sign even the revised agreement.

Programs for addressing climate change fall into two main categories—mitigation (reducing the effects) and adaptation (adjusting to the effects). Mitigation involves either cutting emissions directly, with improvements in energy use, or soaking up emissions with more carbon sinks (see DEFORESTATION). Energy improvement policies include energy efficiency and conservation measures, switching from fossil fuels that produce large amounts of carbon dioxide per unit of energy (such as coal) to more efficient fuels (such as natural gas), eliminating subsidies and tax concessions that favor the use of fossil fuels, and promoting the use of renewable energy technologies (such as solar power) that produce no carbon dioxide (see ENERGY). Carbon sink enhancements include planting large areas of forest and using low-till methods of soil management. The strongest form of mitigation, proposed by Greenpeace, is simply to abandon large amounts of fossil fuels underground.

By assuming that humans can and must adapt to climate change, adaptation is pragmatic but also controversial. Some climate scientists have already shifted the emphasis of their work toward helping developing countries plan ahead so that their people might survive and perhaps, in some cases, even benefit from a warmed world. Adaptation may be a meaningless and offensive concept, however, for the people of small island states and low-lying coastal areas who could lose their homelands entirely if forecasts of rises in sea level prove to be accurate.

Meanwhile, scientists continue to highlight the need for more powerful supercomputers that can run more detailed climate models using data from more extensive climate monitoring systems. In December 1999 in "The Human Impact on Climate," Thomas Karl and Kevin Trenberth comment that "the present outlook is grim: no US or international institution has the mandate or the resources to monitor long-term climate." Without the necessary financial investment in climate science, researchers' understanding of global warming will continue to be incomplete.

Regional Summaries

Although global warming is very much a long-term problem for Earth and its people, significant climate changes already appear to be occurring in every region of the planet.

North America

Canada and the United States are two of the world's largest emitters of greenhouse gases. At climate negotiations, they are part of an informal grouping called JUSCANZ—which stands for Japan, the United States, Canada, Australia, and New Zealand—that is notably hostile to the deep emissions cuts proposed by Europe. Some scientists believe that record heat waves in Florida, New York, and Texas during 1998 and 1999 and habitat and beach loss due to

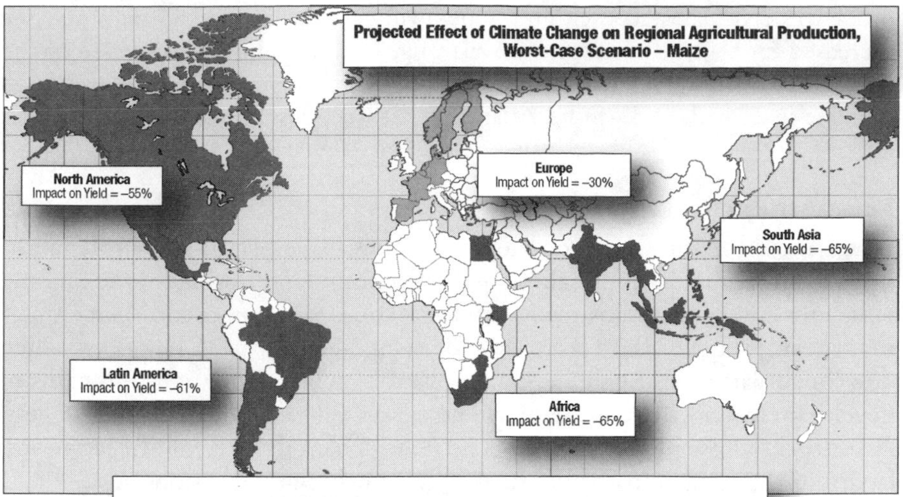

Projected Effect of Climate Change on Regional Agricultural Production, Range of Scenarios – Maize and Wheat

	Impact on Yields (%)			
	Maize	*Countries Analyzed*	*Wheat*	*Countries Analyzed*
North America	–55% to +62%	Canada and the United States	–100% to +234%	Canada and the United States
Latin America	–61% to an increase	Argentina, Brazil, Chile, Mexico	–50% to –5%	Argentina, Brazil, Uruguay
Former Soviet Union	NA	NA	–19% to +41%	All
Europe	–30% to an increase	France, Spain, Northern Europe	increase or decrease	France, United Kingdom, Northern Europe
Africa	–65% to +6%	Egypt, Kenya, South Africa, Zimbabwe	NA	NA
South Asia	–65% to –10%	Bangladesh, India, Philippines, Thailand, Indonesia, Malaysia, Myanmar	–61% to +67%	Bangladesh, India, Indonesia, Philippines, Thailand, Malaysia, Myanmar
Other Asia and the Pacific Rim		NA	NA –41% to +65%	Australia, Japan

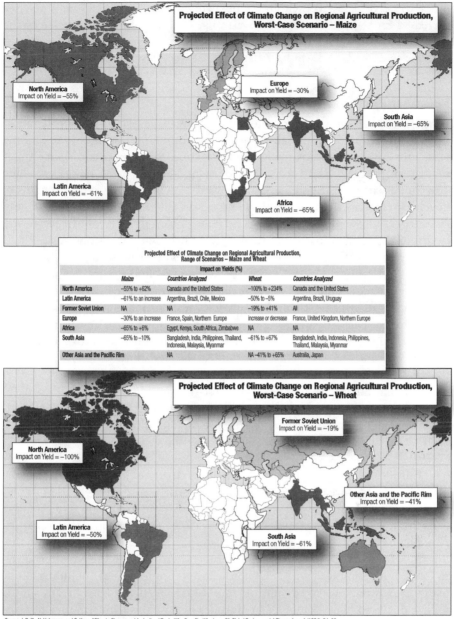

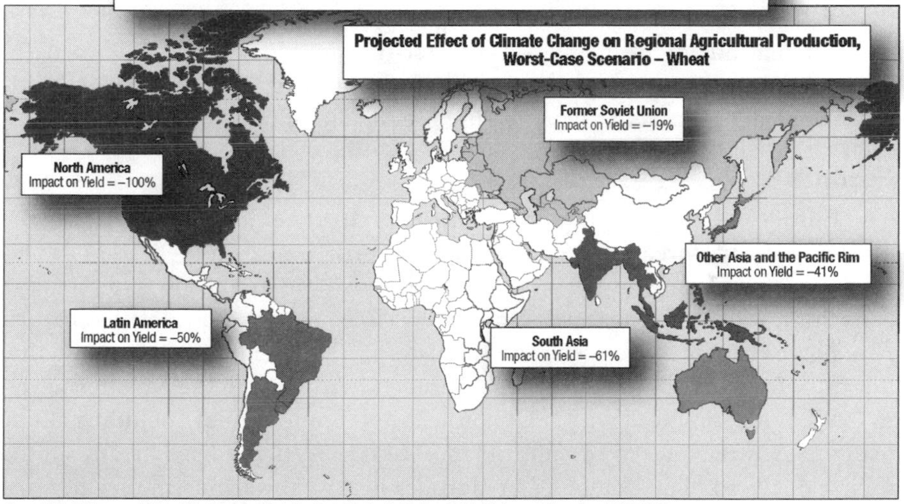

Source: J. Reilly, N. Hohmann, and S. Kane, "Climate Change and Agricultural Trade: Who Benefits, Who Loses?" *Global Environmental Change* 4, no. 1 (1994): 24–36.
Note: Models used assume environments in which carbon dioxide has doubled.

sea level rises in the Chesapeake Bay, Hawaii, and New Jersey may be early warnings of more drastic climate change effects in the future. Weather has intensified in North America, with record precipitation in California, Texas, and Washington state in 1998 and record droughts and forest fires in Florida, Louisiana, Mexico, and Texas that same year. In February 2001 researchers at Lawrence Berkeley National Laboratory in Berkeley, California, used a climate change model to predict serious water and power shortages for California and other western U.S. states within the next fifty years. Some U.S. states may see increased crop yields from global warming, but droughts will increase in the Great Plains and the Canadian Prairies. Coastal erosion and storm surges will increase in Florida and on the Atlantic coast (see Case Study—The Vanishing Arctic).

Latin America

Brazil and Argentina, large developing nations, have played a key role in climate negotiations, although they are exempt from (and hostile to) the binding emissions cuts proposed by the Kyoto Protocol. Brazil proposed a joint-implementation program, the Clean Development Mechanism (CDM), by which developed nations can help developing nations achieve low-emission paths to development and thereby claim credits against their own emissions targets. Argentina, whose representative Raul Estrada chaired the Kyoto negotiations, later said that Argentina would work toward voluntary emissions cuts.

The possible effects of global warming are evident in Peru, which already experiences extreme climate variations during El Niño events. Coral bleaching, in which corals die and turn white in high temperature ocean water as they expel the algae that keep them alive, is widespread in areas of the Caribbean and off Bermuda, Mexico, and Panama (and also in the Florida Keys). In Mexico and Central America, outbreaks of dengue fever—an infectious and painful tropical disease carried by mosquitoes—at higher altitudes than previously reported are consistent with global warming projections. Intensified weather phenomena include heat waves and forest fires in Mexico and Nicaragua in 1998. Future effects are expected to include declining crop yields, loss of deciduous tropical forests, and the increasing prevalence of new diseases.

Europe

The European Union, described by climate campaigner Jeremy Leggett as "the most progressive force at the climate negotiations," has taken the lead in implementing cuts in greenhouse gases. Europe, however, is already experiencing early indications of global warming. Media speculation that global warming could give Britain a "Mediterranean climate" has been tempered by devastating floods in England in 2000 and intense fires and droughts in the Mediterranean in 1998, both consistent with IPCC projections. Some species, including alpine plants in Austria, birds in Britain, and mollusks in Germany, have already shifted their habitats to higher latitudes or altitudes that have warmed in recent years. Future possible effects include increased river flooding, loss of permafrost (a permanently frozen layer of soil), glaciers (in the north), and the appearance of diseases never before seen in the region, such as malaria.

North Africa and the Middle East

The Organization of Petroleum Exporting Countries (OPEC) has frequently been accused of trying to frustrate climate negotiations that could spell a decline in the use of fossil fuels, yet North Africa and the Middle East, home to most OPEC nations, are no less subject to climate change than any other region. Record temperatures were recorded in Cairo in 1998, and coral bleaching has been reported in the Persian Gulf. Water shortages, are expected to be a key source of tension in the region. Former UN secretary-general Boutros Boutros-Ghali memorably noted in the 1980s, "The next war in the Middle East will not be over politics but over water."

Sub-Saharan Africa

Sub-Saharan Africa, the world's poorest region, produces the lowest greenhouse emissions, which are the result of the basic survival activities of cooking and keeping warm, yet they are among the most likely to be affected by climate change and the least well equipped to respond. The nations of sub-Saharan Africa have generally opposed emissions cuts for developing countries, and although they remain skeptical of flexibility mechanisms—seeing them as a means by which developed nations can escape cuts in greenhouse emissions—they have tended to embrace the proposed Clean Development Mechanism and the export of clean technologies from developed nations. Early indications of global warming include the disappearance of 92 percent of Kenya's Mount Lewis Glacier and 82 percent of ice on Tanzania's Mount Kilimanjaro during the twentieth century. The hottest decade ever recorded in the region was from 1985 to 1995. Malaria, already one of the region's biggest killers, has spread geographically in Kenya and Tanzania, as predicted by climate models. Rising sea level is already causing the loss of coastal areas in Senegal. Bleak predictions for the region include more desertification and drought, increasing stress on water resources, and a significant decrease in crop production.

Asia

Asia—with the world's densest population and most rapidly industrializing nations—might be regarded as the front line in the war against climate change. China and India, as developing nations, are exempted from the Kyoto Protocol, yet China is predicted to overtake the United States as the world's leading greenhouse gas polluter by 2010, as economic development prompts it to burn increasing amounts of its vast coal reserves. If China is excluded from statistics, Asia has relatively little greenhouse emissions, around 4 percent of those of North America. Asia, however, may be among the areas worst affected by climate change.

In 1991 and 1998 China experienced catastrophic flooding, ruining millions of acres of cropland and making more than 10 million people homeless on each occasion. A rise in sea level of half a meter could displace an estimated 30 million Chinese. Elsewhere in the region, a rise of one meter would displace approximately 7 million people from low-lying areas of Bangladesh. Early signs of global warming in the region include coral bleaching in the Indian Ocean and glacial retreat in the Himalayas and the Tien Shan Mountains of China. Extensive melting of glaciers in the Himalayas would cause devastating floods and water shortages for more than 500 million people.

The Pacific

The Pacific region includes the large developed nation of Australia plus many micro-states on low-lying islands and atolls that are particularly vulnerable to rising sea levels. Australia and New Zealand are part of the JUSCANZ grouping that is hostile to emissions cuts. Many Pacific islands support a different grouping, the Alliance of Small Island States (AOSIS), a collective of low-lying nations that argues powerfully that climate change threatens their very existence. Evidence of climate change includes widespread coral bleaching throughout the region (see Case Study—Coral Reefs in the Maldives), record temperatures in New Zealand in 1998, a rise in sea level and coastal erosion in Fiji and Western Samoa, and an extended geographical reach of malaria in Indonesia. The Great Barrier Reef, which is economically important to Australia, is particularly vulnerable to climate change.

Data

Table 1 Total and per Capita Carbon Dioxide Emissions in Selected Countries, 1980 and 1996

	Total (million metric tons)		Per Capita (metric tons)	
Country	1980	1996	1980	1996
Algeria	66.2	94.3	3.5	3.3
Argentina	107.5	129.9	3.8	3.7
Australia	202.8	306.6	13.8	16.7
Brazil	183.4	273.4	1.5	1.7
Canada	420.9	409.4	17.1	13.8
China	1,476.8	3,363.5	1.5	2.8
Colombia	39.8	65.3	1.4	1.7
Congo, Republic of	3.5	2.3	0.1	0.1
Egypt	45.2	97.9	1.1	1.7
France	482.7	361.8	9.0	6.2
Georgia	—	3.0	—	0.5
Germany	—	861.2	—	10.5
Guatemala	4.5	6.8	0.7	0.7
India	347.3	997.4	0.5	1.1
Indonesia	94.6	245.1	0.6	1.2
Israel	21.1	52.3	5.4	9.2
Japan	920.4	1,167.7	7.9	9.3
Russian Federation	—	1,579.5	—	10.7
Saudi Arabia	130.7	267.8	14.0	13.8
Spain	200.0	232.5	5.3	5.9
Sweden	71.4	54.1	8.6	6.1
Switzerland	40.9	44.2	6.5	6.3
Tajikistan	—	5.8	—	1.0
Thailand	40.0	205.4	0.9	3.4
Turkey	76.3	178.3	1.7	2.9
Uganda	0.6	1.0	0.1	0.1
United Kingdom	583.8	557.0	10.4	9.5
United States	4,575.4	5,301.0	20.1	20.0

Source: World Bank, *World Development Indicators, 2000* (Washington, D.C.: World Bank, 2000), table 3.8.

Table 2 Recent Trends in Greenhouse Gas Production in the United States

	1991	1992	1993	1994	1995	1996	1997	1998	Growth Rate[f] (%)
Atmospheric carbon dioxide[a]	100	101	101	101	102	102	103	104	0.4
Population[b]	101	102	103	104	105	106	107	108	1.0
Greenhouse gas emissions[c]	99	101	103	105	106	109	111	111	1.3
Energy consumption[d]	100	101	104	106	108	112	112	112	1.4
Fossil fuel consumption[d]	99	101	103	105	106	110	111	111	1.4
Electricity consumption[d]	102	102	105	108	111	114	116	119	2.2
GDP[e]	99	102	104	108	110	114	118	123	2.6

Source: U.S. Environmental Protection Agency, *Inventory of U.S. Greenhouse Gas Emissions and Sinks, 1990–1998* EPA 236-R-00-001, April 2000.

Note: Index: 1990 = 100. The index of 1990 represents the base year against which all other years are compared.

[a]Mauna Loa Observatory, Hawaii.

[b]U.S. Census Bureau, 1999.

[c]Weighted to take account of the different global warming potentials of different greenhouse gases.

[d]Energy content weighted values.

[e]Gross domestic product in chained 1992 dollars.

[f]Average annual growth rate.

Table 3 Projected Effects of Rising Sea Levels

Global/ Relative Rise (cm)	Effect	Approximate Year in Which Effect Occurs: High Growth Scenario[a]	Approximate Year in Which Effect Occurs: Medium Growth Scenario[b]
20	Annual storm surges affect 18 million extra people worldwide 2,700 km^2 of coastal Nigeria lost	2020	2050
30	20–40% of existing U.S. wetlands eroded or inundated	2040	2070
40	Erosion of most beaches in Alexandria, Egypt	2050	2085
50	10% of Bangladesh lost 3% of the Netherlands lost	2060	2100
60	In Japan, more than 1,400 km^2 of land sits below mean high tide level, 3 million people are vulnerable	2070	>2100
70	6% of Belize inundated 2% of Senegal lost	2080	>2100

Table 3 Projected Effects of Rising Sea Levels (*continued*)

Global/ Relative Rise (cm)	Effect	Approximate Year in Which Effect Occurs: High Growth Scenario[a]	Approximate Year in Which Effect Occurs: Medium Growth Scenario[b]
80	65% of the Marshall Islands and Kiribati inundated	2090	>2100
90	In China, more than a third of Shanghai is inundated 70 countries below the 100-year-storm-surge level 85% of Malé inundated	2095	>2100

Source: Stuart R. Gaffin, *High Water Blues: Impacts of Sea Level Rise on Selected Coasts and Islands* (New York: Environmental Defense Fund, 1997), fig. 1.

[a]Based on Intergovernmental Panel for Climate Change's IS92e emissions scenario.

[b]Based on Intergovernmental Panel for Climate Change's IS92a emissions scenario.

Case Study—Coral Reefs in the Maldives

The Maldives is an idyllic archipelago of some twelve hundred small, widely dispersed islands and atolls in the Indian Ocean. Its rich marine life includes a thousand species of fish, and along with coral reefs and attractive beaches they make tourism the backbone of the economy; tourism is estimated to provide around 18 percent of the Maldives' gross domestic product (GDP). With most islands low lying and approximately 80 percent of its land estimated to lie less than one meter above sea level, the Maldives is particularly at risk from global warming. The IPCC's predicted global rise in sea level of 9 to 88 centimeters (3.5 to 34 inches) could submerge much of the region before the end of the twenty-first century. Some of the lower-lying atolls are already submerged, even at low tide.

The coral reefs that attract 200,000 visitors to seventy-four resorts in the Maldives each year also, theoretically, offer one of its best defenses against climate change, for they grow upward at a rate of 3 to 5 millimeters (one-fifth of an inch to 1 inch) per year. If the corals can grow fast enough, they could mitigate the effects of a rising sea level. Yet here too, global warming may prove catastrophic, for corals tend to die off if ocean temperatures increase much above 29°C (84°F). Widespread coral bleaching in 1983, 1987, and 1998 killed off an estimated 90 to 95 percent of corals in North Malé and the Ari Atoll in the archipelago. Corals in shallow waters were the most severely affected, with the damage lessening in cooler, deeper water, and some reefs recovering rapidly.

The long-term prognosis for the Maldives' coral reefs is uncertain, as sea temperatures continue to rise. Experts from fifty-two countries gathered for the Ninth International Coral Reef Symposium in November 2000 and heard that global warming and pollution had killed an estimated one-fourth of the world's reefs. Predictions that all of the world's coral reefs could disappear within twenty years signal an economic as well as ecological disaster, for coral reefs annually generate an estimated $400 billion in fishing and tourism revenue worldwide. For the Maldives, the loss of coral reefs could drastically reduce tourist income, bringing economic hardship at a time when a rising sea level puts the region under great financial strain. The future cost of coastal protection in the Maldives is estimated to rise to more than 5 percent of GDP per year, with the cost of losses due to climate change estimated by Munich Re (in a report for UNEP in 2001) to be around 10 percent of GDP per year. A single sea wall built around Malé in the mid-1990s cost $30 million, but with the Maldives stretching more than 764 kilometers (474 miles), relatively little of the archipelago can be protected in this way.

Case Study—The Vanishing Arctic

The Arctic is a world away from the tropical paradise of the Maldives, and the effects of climate change there could be even more dramatic, for while the Maldives might *warm* significantly, large parts of the Arctic could *melt* completely. The process of melting may already have begun.

The third IPCC report, part of which was issued in January 2001, notes that spring and summer Arctic Sea ice cover had decreased by 10 to 15 percent since the 1950s, with a 40 percent reduction in autumnal sea ice thickness. The following month, Svein Tveitdal, a UNEP Arctic scientist, reported that rising temperatures were causing the Arctic permafrost to melt. Because permafrost is an important carbon sink—some 14 percent of the planet's carbon is stored in the Arctic—this melting could provide a powerful "positive feedback" to global warming, accelerating it and itself being accelerated by the process.

Melting polar ice caps have long been part of the doomsday scenario of climate change, but not without reason. In April 2000 scientists from the University of California at Berkeley calculated that if the glaciers of Greenland were to melt, as they did substantially during the interglacial period before the last ice age, around 120,000 years ago, sea levels would rise on average of about 4 to 6.1 meters (13 to 20 feet). With two-thirds of Earth's people living less than 60 kilometers (37 miles) from a coast, such a change could prove apocalyptic. Polar scientists do not know if all the changes to the Arctic are the result of natural variation (whose effects may reverse themselves in time without human intervention) or human-caused global warming (whose effects may already be irreversible).

Far from an inhospitable wilderness, the Arctic is actually home to many different indigenous peoples and to abundant wildlife, including polar bears, walruses, caribou, reindeer, seals, gulls, guillemots, and bowhead and beluga whales, at latitudes as high as 88°N. Climate change is already being felt throughout the region. On Banks Island, in the Canadian Arctic, the Inuit report fewer polar bears and seals and thinning ice and melting permafrost. Warmer and shorter winters have brought new species never before seen into the region, including robins and barn owls. Paradoxically, climate change models predict an overall increase in precipitation for high latitudes, like the Arctic, because increased moisture evaporating from lower latitudes is transported toward the poles. This has already been observed in Alaska and Northern Canada in recent decades.

In 1998 the Arctic Network and Greenpeace Alaska carried out a joint study of how climate change is affecting life in eight remote communities bordering the Bering and Chukchi Seas of the Arctic Ocean. Native peoples reported warmer winters and earlier springs, more open waters and thinner sea ice, less snow and snow disappearing earlier, more violent storms in winter and less summer rainfall, and a variety of other changes consistent with the projections of the IPCC. As noted in "Answers from the Ice Edge: The Consequences of Climate Change on Life in the Bering and Chukchi Seas," "The observations of Arctic people today not only match scientists' predictions, but are firsthand evidence that impacts of climate change are being felt now."

Biographical Sketches

Bert Bolin is a distinguished Swedish meteorologist who conducted pioneering research into the carbon cycle and later became the first chairman of the Intergovernmental Panel on Climate Change in 1988. Bolin is credited with steering the IPCC on a prudent middle course of scientific consensus, between exaggerated environmental claims on the one hand and the vested interests of the fossil-fuel lobby on the other.

James Hansen is the director of the NASA Goddard Institute for Space Studies in New York City and an influential researcher into the mechanisms of climate change. Hansen's testimony to Congress in 1988 is widely considered a defining moment in waking the world to global warming. In August 2000 Hansen and his colleagues argued controversially that controlling carbon dioxide emissions is less important than reducing emissions of other greenhouse gases, which, they said, have produced most of Earth's recent warming.

Sir John Houghton is an eminent British meteorologist and government adviser on environmental issues. As chair and later co-chair of the Scientific Assessment Working Group of the Intergovernmental Panel on Climate Change, he has steered the world's scientists toward a consensus on global warming. Houghton has contributed greatly to public understanding of the issue as the author of many scientific publications, including *Global Warming: The Complete Briefing.*

Jeremy Leggett is a British academic, environmental campaigner, and solar energy entrepreneur. His career reflects, in miniature, the revolution he has been trying to bring about in world energy consumption. Originally a lecturer in geology and a consultant to the oil industry, he became Greenpeace's director of climate science in 1990. A prominent figure at climate negotiations, Leggett has also popularized the issue of climate change through the best-selling *Global Warming: The Greenpeace Report* (1990) and *The Carbon War* (2000). Now a fellow of Oxford University, Leggett also runs a solar energy company called Solar Century.

Richard Lindzen is Alfred P. Sloan Professor of Meteorology at the Massachusetts Institute of Technology (MIT). As a distinguished meteorologist and climate scientist,

Lindzen is the most articulate and highly respected of the so-called climate skeptics. His views are summarized in an article he contributed to the Cato Institutes's *Regulation,* in which he states that "as a scientist, I can find no substantive basis for the warming scenarios being popularly described . . . [and] there would be little difficulty adapting to such warming if it were to occur."

Mohan Munasinghe is vice-chairman of the Intergovernmental Panel on Climate Change and professor of environmental management at the University of Colombo, Sri Lanka. An environmental adviser to the World Bank and the President's Council on Environmental Quality in the United States, Munasinghe has extensively explored the economics of climate change in numerous books and papers. His concept of sustainomics attempts to unite and trade off social, economic, and environmental concerns as a means of addressing climate change.

Directory

Environmental Defense, 257 Park Avenue South, New York, NY 10010. Telephone: (212) 505-2100, Email: contact@environmentaldefense.org, Web: http://www.edf.org/programs/GRAP
Environmental organization

Environmental Protection Agency, Ariel Rios Building, 1200 Pennsylvania Avenue NW, Washington, DC 20460. Telephone: (202) 260-2090, Email: public-access@epa.gov, Web: http://www.epa.gov/students/global_warming_us.htm
U.S. government agency responsible for environmental issues

European Commission Environment Directorate, 200 rue de la Loi / Wetstraat 200, 1049 Brussels, Belgium. Telephone: (32) 22991111, Email: envinfo@cec.eu.int, Web: http://europa.eu.int/comm/environment/climat/home_en.htm
EU body responsible for promoting environmental issues on behalf of member states

Global Climate Coalition, 1275 K Street NW, Washington, DC 20005. Telephone: (202) 682-9161, Email: gcc@globalclimate.org, Web: http://www.globalclimate.org
Alliance of business interests skeptical of global warming science and cuts in emissions

Greenpeace USA, 702 H Street NW, Suite 300, Washington, DC 20001. Telephone: (202) 462-1177, Email: greenpeace.usa@wdc.greenpeace.org, Web: http://www.greenpeace.org/~climate
Environmental organization

Hadley Centre for Climate Prediction and Research, Met Office London Road, Bracknell, Berkshire RG12 2SY, United Kingdom. Telephone: (44) 845 300 300, Email: hadleycentre@meto.gov.uk, Web: http://www.metoffice.gov.uk/research/hadleycentre
Part of the U.K. Meteorological Office responsible for developing climate models

Harvard Environmental School Center for Health and the Global Environment, Harvard Medical School, 260 Longwood Avenue, Room 262A, Boston, MA 02115. Telephone: (617) 432-0493, Email: chge@hms.harvard.edu, Web: http://www.med.harvard.edu/chge
Provides education and conducts research into health aspects of climate change

Intergovernmental Panel on Climate Change (IPCC), IPCC Secretariat, c/o World Meteorological Organization, 7bis Avenue de la Paix, P.O. Box 2300, 1211 Geneva 2, Switzerland. Telephone: (41) 22 730 8208, Email: ipcc_sec@gateway.wmo.ch, Web: http://www.ipcc.ch
UN agency responsible for climate change issues

NASA Goddard Institute for Space Studies, 2880 Broadway, New York, NY 10025. Telephone: (212) 678-5500, Email: info@giss.nasa.gov, Web: http://www.giss.nasa.gov
Division of NASA responsible in part for climate modeling and research

Pew Center on Global Climate Change, 2101 Wilson Boulevard, Suite 550, Arlington, VA 22201. Telephone: (703) 516-4146, Email: info@pewclimate.org, Web: http://www.pewclimate.org
Organization providing information about climate change policy

Sierra Club, 85 Second Street, 2d Floor, San Francisco, CA 94105-3441. Telephone: (415) 977-5500, Email: information@sierraclub.org, Web: http://www.sierraclub.org/globalwarming
Environmental organization

Union of Concerned Scientists, 2 Brattle Square, Cambridge, MA 02238-9105. Telephone: (617) 547-5552, Email: ucs@ucsusa.org, Web: http://www.ucsusa.org/environment/0warming.html
Organization presenting public and ethical concerns about scientific issues

United Nations Environment Programme (UNEP), United Nations Avenue, Gigiri, P.O. Box 30552, Nairobi, Kenya. Telephone: (254) 262 1234, Email: eisinfo@unep.org, Web: http://www.unep.org
Agency responsible for environmental issues of international importance

University of East Anglia Climatic Research Unit, University of East Anglia, Norwich NR4 7TJ, United Kingdom. Telephone: (44) 16 03 592722, Email: cru@uea.ac.uk, Web: http://www.cru.uea.ac.uk
Scientific institution specializing in global climate research

Further Research

Books

Drake, Frances. *Global Warming: The Science of Climate Change.* London: Arnold; New York: Oxford University Press, 2000.

Gelbspan, Ross. *The Heat Is On: The Climate Crisis, the Cover-up, the Prescription.* New York: Perseus Books, 1998.

Gore, Al. *Earth in the Balance.* New York: Houghton Mifflin, 1992.

Harvey, Danny. *Global Warming: The Hard Science.* Harlow and New York: Prentice Hall, 2000.

Hayes, Peter, and Kirk Smith, eds. *The Global Greenhouse Regime: Who Pays?* London: Earthscan and United Nations University Press, 1993.

Houghton, John. *Global Warming: The Complete Briefing.* New York and Cambridge: Cambridge University Press, 1997.

Jepma, Catrinus, and Mohan Munasinghe. *Climate Change Policy: Facts, Issues, and Analysis.* New York and Cambridge: Cambridge University Press, 1998.

Leggett, Jeremy. *The Carbon War.* New York and London: Penguin, 2000.

———, ed. *Global Warming: The Greenpeace Report.* New York and Oxford: Oxford University Press, 1990.

Mendlesohn, Robert. *The Impact of Climate Change on the United States.* New York: Cambridge University Press, 1999.

O'Riordan, T., and J. Jäger. *Politics of Climate Change: A European Perspective.* London: Routledge, 1996.

Articles and Reports

Asian Development Bank. *Environmental Management of the Republic of Maldives: An Overview.* Manila, Philippines: Asian Development Bank, 1999.

Boehmer-Christiansen, Sonja. "Global Climate Protection Policy: The Limits of Scientific Advice." *Global Environmental Change* 4, no. 2 (1994): 140.

Brown, Kathryn. "Taking Global Warming to the People." *Science,* 5 March 1999, 1440.

Calvin, William H. "The Great Climate Flip-Flop." *Atlantic Monthly,* January 1998, 47. Also available at http://www.theatlantic.com/issues/98jan/climate.htm.

Gelbspan, Ross, et al. *E Magazine.* September/October 2000. Special issue on global warming. Also available at http://www.emagazine.com/september-october_2000/0900feat1.html.

Gibson, Margie, and Sallie B Schullinger. "Answers from the Ice Edge: The Consequences of Climate Change on Life in the Bering and Chukchi Seas." 1998, http://www.greenpeace.org/~climate/arctic/reports/testimonies.pdf.

Hodges, Glenn. "The New Cold War: Stalking Climate Change by Sub." *National Geographic,* March 2000, 30.

Hoegh-Guldberg, Ove. "Climate Change, Coral Bleaching, and the Future of the World's Coral Reefs." Greenpeace USA, 6 July 1999, http://www.greenpeaceusa.org/media/publications/coral_bleaching.pdf.

Jones, Philip, and Tom Wigley. "Global Warming Trends." *Scientific American,* August 1990, 66.

Karl, Thomas, and Kevin Trenberth. "The Human Impact on Climate." *Scientific American,* December 1999, 62.

Kerr, Richard. "Will the Arctic Ocean Lose All Its Ice?" *Science,* 3 December 1999, 1828.

Lazaroff, Cat. "Global Warming Portends Water, Power Shortages in American West." Environment News Service, 2 February 2001, http://www.ens.lycos.com/ens/feb2001/2001L-02-02-06.html.

———. "Melting Arctic Permafrost May Accelerate Global Warming." Environmental News Service, 7 February 2001, http://ens-news.com/ens/feb2001/2001L-02-07-06.html.

Ledley, Tamara, et al. "Climate Change and Greenhouse Gases." *EOS,* 28 September 1999, 453. Also available at http://www.agu.org/eos_elec/99148e.html.

Lindzen, Richard S. "Global Warming: The Origin and Nature of the Alleged Scientific Consensus." *Regulation,* December 2001. Also available at http://www.cato.org/pubs/regulation/reg15n2g.html.

"Many Coral Reefs Nearly Dead." *Popular Science,* 24 October 2000.

McCarthy, James J., et al., eds. *Climate Change 2001: Impacts, Adaptation, and Vulnerability.* Cambridge and New York: Cambridge University Press, 2001.

National Resources Defense Council, "Polar Thaw: Global Warming in the Arctic and Antarctic." Photographs by Gary Braasch, http://www.nrdc.org/globalWarming/polar/polarinx.asp.

Niel, Laurenz. "Ocean Warming, Pollution Causing Death of Coral Reefs." *UniSci: Daily University Science News,* 29 November 2000, http://unisci.com/stories/20004/1129002.htm.

Pomerance, Rafe. "Coral Bleaching, Coral Mortality, and Global Climate Change." 5 March 1999. Report for U.S. Coral Reef Task Force, http://www.state.gov/www/global/global_issues/coral_reefs/990305_coralreef_rpt.html

Schneider, Stephen H. "Climate Modeling." *Scientific American,* May 1987, 72.

———. "The Coming Climate." *Scientific American,* September 1989, 38.

Socolovsky, Jerome. "Island Nations Desperate for Action." *Popular Science,* 17 November 2000.

United Nations Environment Programme. "Impact of Climate Change to Cost the World $US 300 Billion a Year," press release, 3 February 2001, http://www.unep.org/Documents/Default.asp?DocumentID=192&ArticleID=2758.

Watson, R. T., M. C. Zinyowera, and R. H. Moss, eds. *The Regional Impacts of Climate Change: An Assessment of Vulnerability.* New York: Cambridge University Press, 1998.

White, Robert M. "The Great Climate Debate." *Scientific American,* July 1990, 18.

World Water Vision Commission Report, "The Water Crisis: Where we are today and how we got there, November 1999," http://watervision.cdinet.com/pdfs/commission/cchpt2.pdf.

Web Sites

Climate Change Gazette
http://www.e5.org/pages/ccgar698.htm

Global Warning, Early Warning Signs
http://www.climatehotmap.org

IPCC Data Distribution Center
http://ipcc-ddc.cru.uea.ac.uk

NASA Goddard Institute for Space Studies, Spotlight: Global Warming in the 21st Century
http://www.giss.nasa.gov/about/spotlight

New Scientist, Frequently Asked Questions (FAQ) on Global Warming
http://www.newscientist.com/global/globalfaq.jsp

Pew Center on Global Climate Change, Reports and Environmental Policy Analysis
http://www.pewclimate.org/projects

UK Meteorological Office, Hadley Centre
http://www.metoffice.gov.uk/research/hadleycentre/pubs/brochures/B2000

UK Rivers Network, Finding Out about Climate Change and Global Warming: Student Research Resources
http://www.ukrivers.net/climate.html

United Nations Environment Programme, Climate Change Information Kit
http://www.unfccc.de/resource/iuckit/index.html

U.S. National Climate Data Center
http://www.ncda.noaa.gov

U.S. National Oceanic and Atmospheric Administration (NOAA), Climate Monitoring and Diagnostics Laboratory
http://www.cmdl.noaa.gov

World Meteorological Organization
http://www.wmo.ch/web/wcp/wcdmp/html/wcdmp.html

Documents

1. United Nations Framework Convention on Climate Change

Entered into force 21 March 1994

The full text is available at http://www.unfccc.de/resource/convkp.html.

Extracts

Article 2: Objective
The ultimate objective of this Convention and any related legal instruments that the Conference of the Parties may adopt is to achieve, in accordance with the relevant provisions of the Convention, stabilization of greenhouse gas concentrations in the atmosphere at a level that would prevent dangerous anthropogenic interference with the climate system. Such a level should be achieved within a time frame sufficient to allow ecosystems to adapt naturally to climate change, to ensure that food production is not threatened and to enable economic development to proceed in a sustainable manner.

Article 3: Principles
1. The Parties should protect the climate system for the benefit of present and future generations of humankind, on the basis of equity and in accordance with their common but differentiated responsibilities and respective capabilities. Accordingly, the developed country Parties should take the lead in combating climate change and the adverse effects thereof. . . .

3. The Parties should take precautionary measures to anticipate, prevent or minimize the causes of climate change and mitigate its adverse effects. Where there are threats of serious or irreversible damage, lack of full scientific certainty should not be used as a reason for postponing such measures, taking into account that policies and measures to deal with climate change should be cost-effective so as to ensure global benefits at the lowest possible cost. To achieve this, such policies and measures should take into account different socioeconomic contexts, be comprehensive, cover all relevant sources, sinks and reservoirs of greenhouse gases and adaptation, and comprise all economic sectors. Efforts to address climate change may be carried out cooperatively by interested Parties.

Article 4: Commitments
1. All Parties, taking into account their common but differentiated responsibilities and their specific national and regional development priorities, objectives and circumstances, shall:

(a) Develop, periodically update, publish and make available to the Conference of the Parties, in accordance with Article 12, national inventories of anthropogenic emissions. . . .

(b) Formulate, implement, publish and regularly update national and, where appropriate, regional programmes containing measures to mitigate climate change by addressing anthropogenic emissions . . . and measures to facilitate adequate adaptation to climate change;

(c) Promote and cooperate in the development, application and diffusion, including transfer, of technologies, practices and processes that control, reduce or prevent anthropogenic emissions of greenhouse gases . . . in all relevant sectors, including the energy, transport, industry, agriculture, forestry and waste management sectors;

(d) Promote sustainable management, and promote and cooperate in the conservation and enhancement, as appropriate, of sinks and reservoirs of all greenhouse gases . . . including biomass, forests and oceans as well as other terrestrial, coastal and marine ecosystems;

(e) Cooperate in preparing for adaptation to the impacts of climate change; develop and elaborate appropriate and integrated plans for coastal zone management, water resources and agriculture, and for the protection and rehabilitation of areas, particularly in Africa, affected by drought and desertification, as well as floods;

(f) Take climate change considerations into account, to the extent feasible, in their relevant social, economic and environmental policies and actions. . . .

(g) Promote and cooperate in scientific, technological, technical, socioeconomic and other research, systematic observation and development of data archives related to the climate system and intended to further the understanding and to reduce or eliminate the remaining uncertainties regarding the causes, effects, magnitude and timing of climate change and the economic and social consequences of various response strategies;

(h) Promote and cooperate in the full, open and prompt exchange of relevant scientific, technological, technical, socioeconomic and legal information related to the climate system and climate change, and to the economic and social consequences of various response strategies;

(i) Promote and cooperate in education, training and public awareness related to climate change and encourage the widest participation in this process, including that of non-governmental organizations.

2. Climate Change: The IPCC Working Group I, Third Scientific Assessment Report, Summary for Policymakers

Intergovernmental Panel on Climate Change, January 2001
Edited by R. T. Watson et al.

The full text is available at http://www.ipcc.ch/pub/spm22-01.pdf.

Extract

Summary Points

- An increasing body of observations gives a collective picture of a warming world and other changes in the climate system.

- The global-average surface temperature has increased over the 20th century by about 0.6°C.
- Temperatures have risen during the past four decades in the lowest 8 kilometres of the atmosphere.
- Snow cover and ice extent have decreased.
- Global average sea level has risen and ocean heat content has increased.
- Changes have also occurred in other important aspects of climate.
- Some important aspects of climate appear not to have changed.
- Emissions of greenhouse gases and aerosols due to human activities continue to alter the atmosphere in ways that are expected to affect the climate.
- Concentrations of atmospheric greenhouse gases and their radiative forcing have continued to increase as a result of human activities.
- Anthropogenic aerosols are short lived and mostly produce negative radiative forcing.
- Natural factors have made small contributions to radiative forcing over the past century.
- Confidence in the ability of models to project future climate has increased.
- There is new and stronger evidence that most of the warming observed over the last 50 years is attributable to human activities.
- Human influences will continue to change atmospheric composition throughout the 21st century.
- Global average temperature and sea level are projected to rise under all IPCC SRES [Special Report on Emission Scenarios].
- Anthropogenic climate change will persist for many centuries.
- Further action is required to address remaining gaps in information and understanding.

HEALTH

David E. Bloom and David Canning

The 1978 Alma-Ata Declaration, signed by representatives of the International Conference on Primary Health Care, defined health as "a state of complete physical, mental and social well-being, and not merely the absence of disease or infirmity." The signatories aimed to achieve world health for all by the year 2000. Despite significant improvements since the declaration, massive disparities are apparent in the health status of people who live in rich countries and those who live in poor countries. In the latter, public health care systems may be inadequate and underfunded, and private health care may be absent or unaffordable. In addition, some members of society tend to be more vulnerable to disease than others: the poor, those living in isolated rural areas; the elderly; infants and children; and women. Poor health, in turn, affects a country's economic development by, for instance, reducing the productivity of workers. Yet, in terms of health care costs, prevention is cheaper than cure. The increased attention given by many countries to solving health problems is a response to the recognition of the wide-ranging effects of poor health.

Historical Background and Development

Babylonian king Hammurabi's code of laws, written nearly four thousand years ago, provides one of the earliest known cases of state intervention in health. Echoes of its sliding scale of physicians' fees, where payment is determined by how much the patient can afford, can be found in many modern national health systems. Its code of conduct for physicians presages today's strict regulation of the medical profession. Recognition of the importance of health to society since Hammurabi's time has been erratic, however. Although the Romans built hospitals for their soldiers and slaves and introduced public sanitation measures, it was not until much later that states made consistent efforts to improve the health of their people.

In the middle ages, people's lives were dominated by the fear of illness and death. The practice of medicine, such as it was, relied heavily on the ancient studies of Galen, Avicenna, and Hippocrates, whose *Airs, Waters and Places,* published in 400 B.C., was the first known work to discuss the impact of environmental factors on disease. More than a thousand years later, physicians still had made no progress in combating the myriad of epidemics that killed vast swaths of population at increasingly frequent intervals. Such treatments as bloodletting had no positive impact on a patient's well-being beyond the psychological effect of having been treated. Trust in the medical profession was low, and people often turned instead to other forms of healing. Traveling vendors toured fourteenth-century England selling "wonder cures" to unsuspecting patients. Religious sects looked after the sick with faith healing, while many patients took matters into their own hands, ordering their physicians to bleed them despite the latter's advice to the contrary. Sickness was widely regarded as a message from God. Preachers persuaded their congregations that illness and early death were punishments from above or warnings to people to mend their evil ways. A wayward lifestyle, it was thought, would inevitably lead to some degree of physical discomfort, if not as a divine punishment then as a result of evil spirits or witches' spells.

Although the low standing of doctors forced most people to take individual responsibility for their own health, efforts were emerging in some parts of the world to provide for those who could not look after themselves. By the eleventh century, all major Muslim towns had hospitals, which were set up to care for the poor and travelers. Christian hospitals and almshouses also began to have an impact on health care. Asian children had been inoculated against smallpox for many centuries before the practice became common in Europe in the eighteenth century.

The advent of the Black Death—the plague that wiped out perhaps one-fourth of the population of Europe from the fourteenth to the sixteenth centuries—provided the first major impetus for states to become involved in protecting health. In the fifteenth century Italian doctors implemented a system to quarantine the plague; York, England, and other cities were closed off to prevent the plague from entering. Hospitals were built not only to look after the poor, but also to cordon off those with the plague from the rest of society. They also enabled physicians to better observe the symptoms of the disease and to track its progress. This greater knowledge eventually enabled more systematic responses to disease to evolve, which had the collateral effect of raising physicians' standing with their patients.

The Industrial Revolution provided the next great impetus to widespread health improvements. Mass labor was essential to the efficient functioning of industry, and as workers fell ill or became the victims of industrial accidents, their employers came to a greater realization of the benefits of a healthy populace. Many employers took steps to improve health via workplace medical insurance schemes or donations to hospital charities. Simultaneously, as increased wealth and productivity gave people more leisure time, their attentions turned to "luxuries," such as health. Demand for health care therefore grew.

The 1848 Public Health Act in England, which created a General Board of Health to deal with public health problems, was the natural result of the increasing importance given to health. The expansion of medical knowledge that was propelled by these major societal changes made possible Louis Pasteur's late-nineteenth-century discovery that germs were responsible for infectious disease. This was followed by other major breakthroughs, such as the discovery of the tubercle bacillus, the bacterium responsible for tuberculosis, and, in 1928, the discovery of penicillin. These developments meant that medicine could make a break from the methods of the ancients and focus on destroying the microorganisms that caused people to die. Physicians, who now possessed great stores of knowledge, were looked upon with a new respect. Public health administration, whose initial rumblings had facilitated the dramatic advances of science, now had a solid base from which to attack infectious disease.

In 1920 C. E. A. Winslow, one of the founders of modern public health in the United States, defined public health as "the science and art of preventing disease" and promoting health through community efforts and organization. The development of social machinery, he added, should "enable every citizen to realize his birthright of health and longevity." Public health, which is grounded not just in medicine but also in a variety of sciences ranging from epidemiology (the study of disease) to economics, encompasses a wide range of efforts directed toward protecting the health of entire populations. It also aims to link health to government and public policy, viewing health not in isolation, but as part of a broad effort to improve quality of life.

Systems such as Britain's National Health Service, established in 1948 to provide free health care to all who need it, and the World Health Organization (WHO), set up in 1946 by the United Nations, were the culmination of the progress achieved in health provision. The latter's successful global effort to eradicate smallpox in 1979 is the clearest signal yet of the potential of public health systems.

Current Status

Although the world as a whole has seen significant health improvements, the situation varies dramatically from country to country and region to region. Some areas have even seen a decline in overall health status.

Research

Researchers look at changes in populations' health status using a number of indicators. One common indicator of overall health is life expectancy—how long a child born in a particular year is likely to live. For example, based on UN population data, between 1975 and 1995 life expectancy rose in 163 of 184 countries for which data are available. According to the World Health Organization's healthy life expectancy data, a child born in Japan in 1999 can look forward to 74.5 years of healthy life. This contrasts dramatically with the 51 countries where children can expect less than 50 years of healthy life and with the 3 countries—Malawi, Niger, and Sierra Leone—where they can expect less than 30 years (see map, p. 286). Other indicators of a population's health status are mortality rates (what proportion of a population dies in a given period of time), morbidity rates (what proportion of a population is ill during a given period of time), proportions of children vaccinated, and expenditures on health (see Tables 1 and 2). According to *World Health Report, 2001,* global spending on health has risen, accounting for approximately 8 percent of the world's gross domestic product (GDP), but again, this figure hides large disparities between countries and regions (see INCOME INEQUALITY).

Some countries that had seen previous improvements in their health status are now seeing declines. For example, according to research conducted in 1998 by Charles Becker and David Bloom, life expectancies in some of the republics of the former Soviet Union have been declining since the 1950s. In another example, HIV/AIDS is having a devastating social and economic effect in many sub-Saharan African countries (see AIDS). Instances like these are drawing increased attention to global health. After a period of neglect, governments are refocusing attention on other infectious diseases, such as tuberculosis, which is staging a comeback in many parts of the industrial world.

According to research on the global burden of disease, two types of disease represent a majority of all deaths globally: chronic diseases, that is, conditions that can render people disabled or in pain for years, and "lifestyle" diseases, or conditions that arise as countries become wealthier, for example, when people switch from their previous more healthy diets to a diet higher in fat (see Table 3). Accidents and violence are also claiming more lives. By 2020 traffic accidents, suicide, violence, and war could rival infectious disease as a source of premature mortality worldwide.

The Alma-Ata Declaration provides three justifications for devoting resources to health: health is a basic human right, a vital social goal, and an essential ingredient for developing strong economies (see Document 1). Improved health leads to social and economic development, improves people's quality of life, and creates conditions that are more conducive to world peace. By declaring that health is a fundamental human right, the declaration asserts that people are entitled to a certain quality of life; that is, they are entitled to be well, not just to have access to remedies when they are sick. Governments, working as appropriate with the world community, are primarily responsible for fulfilling this entitlement. By signing on to a declaration that declares health to be a fundamental human right, governments implicitly recognize that health, like security, freedom of speech and freedom of thought, is something that the state owes its citizens.

This rights-based approach to health has several practical implications. First, it emphasizes the need for ongoing global action on health, because human rights can only be enforced in the presence of a global framework. As Gro Brundtland, director-general of the World Health Organization, suggests in *World Health Report, 1999,* the main reason for the failure of the Alma-Ata Declaration to meet its goal of health for all by 2000 was the lack of global leadership and advocacy. Second, a rights-based approach underscores the need for democracies that can be held responsible for safeguarding their people's rights. According to Amartya Sen's *Development as Freedom,* political freedoms are essential for ensuring that people can protect their quality of life, while large-scale, systematic abuse of human rights invariably results in social breakdowns and "new wars." Evidence supports the view that poor health can help lead to social breakdown. A study by Daniel Esty and his colleagues in 1998 found that high levels of infant mortality, along with other factors, including low openness to trade with other countries and low levels of democracy, are good predictors of state failure. Third, the rights-based approach underscores the importance of empowerment at the grass roots. For instance, the rapid spread of HIV/AIDS in many societies has been caused, in part, by young women's lack of control over sexual relations. Attempts to curb the spread of HIV/AIDS must therefore include a focus on extending women's rights and enforcing those rights.

In line with the Alma-Ata Declaration viewing improved health as a vital, worldwide, social goal, recent research has looked at the social determinants of health. Consider, for example, social inequality. G. B. Rodgers argued in 1999 that average life expectancy in an egalitarian society may be as much as ten years longer than in a nonegalitarian society. In other words, levels of health are related to people's social environment, as well as to how rich or poor the society in which they live is. Although inequality can affect health through such factors as lack of access to opportunities, lack of control, feelings of hopelessness, and chronic stress, the reverse is also true. Poor health contributes to these social factors, creating a situation in which people become trapped in a cycle of social exclusion.

Sen, in *Development as Freedom,* stresses, however, that a country does not have to be rich for its population to be healthy, and economic development alone is not sufficient for people's health status to improve. Although richer countries do tend to have healthier populations, the correlation is not automatic, but instead depends on such factors as how the society deploys its resources and what measure of control citizens have over their lives. In addition, sectors unrelated to health care contribute to improvements in health, including agriculture, education, and communications.

The social implications of health may also affect international relations. As noted, researchers have observed a link between health and political stability and also between health and war. Wars not only kill soldiers and civilians, but they also destroy infrastructure and social structures, which can lead to outbreaks of disease. Again, the reverse may also be true: prevalence of disease and poor health can, in turn, lead to conflict and war. Combatants in many modern conflicts are drawn from the socially excluded. Poor health, according to a 1983 article by Michael Doyle, shortens people's perceptions of their time horizons and makes them more likely to engage in conflict.

Research increasingly supports the Alma-Ata Declaration's assertion that a healthy population is a cornerstone of a strong and growing economy. The traditional view that wealth leads to health is complementary to, and does not contradict, this new research, since health and wealth can be mutually reinforcing. Although there is a broad correlation between per capita gross domestic product and life expectancy, researchers have been unable to fully demonstrate a causal link (in either direction) between wealth and health. For example, research conducted by David Bloom and David Canning in 2000 shows that there is little evidence that periods of rapid health improvement follow periods of high income growth. According to the 1999 *World Health Report,* other factors, such as access to health care technology, are more important than income growth for improving health outcomes. In the same vein, Richard Easterlin argues in a 1999 article that even though richer societies are in a better position to improve their population's health, they may not necessarily choose to do so. Regarding a potential causal link from health to wealth, Bloom and Canning argue that countries with educated, healthy populations are in a better position to prosper, but convincing causal inferences are difficult to make.

In the end, of course, research alone is insufficient for improving global health. The results of research must be applied. The development of new antibiotics against infectious diseases cannot be considered a major success if people in poor countries cannot afford to buy them, and investigation into how new or emerging diseases spread is not helpful if people are unaware of actions they can take to protect themselves. Investing in research is one thing, but deploying that knowledge to create change is what counts.

Policies and Programs

The complacency toward disease in the late twentieth century, when many assumed that diseases such as tuberculosis would continue retreating as health standards steadily increased, has been shaken (see EPIDEMICS). The fact that health standards are declining for many people is evolving as a political issue, and policymakers have become alarmed. In 2000 the United Nations Security Council debated the impact of AIDS on peace and security in Africa; it was the first time in fifty years that a health issue had been considered a security issue. Later that year the G-8, made up of eight of the major industrialized nations, pledged to cut deaths from tuberculosis by 50 percent by 2010 and the number of young people with HIV by 25 percent. The final declaration of the UN Millennium Summit committed heads of state and governments to reducing maternal mortality by 75 percent, lowering mortality among children under five by 67 percent, and reversing the spread of AIDS, malaria, and other major diseases by 2015.

Programs to control malaria, a disease that, according to *World Health Report, 2002,* kills at least 1 million people per year, are not new, but the most recent programmatic efforts for its containment combine an innovative approach employing the force of powerful collaborators: the United Nations Children's Fund (UNICEF), the United Nations Development Programme (UNDP), WHO, the World Bank, and a multitude of local and international partners. WHO's Roll Back Malaria program is two-pronged in that it attempts to control malaria and improve health services. According to a 1998 WHO press release, the goals of the program are to "strengthen health systems to ensure better delivery of health care, especially at the district and community levels; ensure the proper and expanded use of insecticide-treated mosquito nets; ensure adequate access to basic healthcare and training of healthcare workers; encourage the development of simpler and more effective means of administering medicines, such as training of village health workers, mothers and drug peddlers on early and appropriate treatment of malaria, especially for children; encourage the development of more effective and new anti-malaria drugs and vaccines."

Another major programmatic effort—primary health care—began with Alma-Ata. The primary health care approach includes a core set of services as spelled out in paragraph three of the declaration: "education concerning prevailing health problems and the methods of preventing and controlling them; promotion of food supply and proper nutrition; an adequate supply of safe water and basic sanitation; maternal and child health care, including family planning; immunization against the major infectious diseases; prevention and control of locally endemic diseases; appropriate treatment of common disease and injuries; and provision of essential drugs." This basic package changed health programming from one focused solely on medical treatment to one focused on the provision of largely prevention-based basic medical and public health measures. These services target those interventions that have proved to have the greatest impact on the long-term health of a population as a whole, such as maternal health care and immunizations for pregnant women and children.

The World Bank's *World Development Report, 1993: Investing in Health* was another pioneering step, as the first publication to present a complete, coherent case for applying rational decision making in the allocation of resources in the health sector. It concludes that world spending on health had been misallocated, inefficient, and substantially directed toward the affluent rather than the poor. It identifies five policy areas as particularly important for low-income countries: improving primary education, especially for girls; investing in highly cost-effective public health activities, such as immunization programs; investing in health care infrastructure at the district level to deliver a range of basic clinical services; reducing waste, especially through more effective use of pharmaceuticals; and decentralizing health systems to permit communities to have greater control over health expenditures.

When making decisions on the rational utilization of funds for the organization and provision of health services, policymakers and service providers can choose from various types of interventions. The primary health care approach initially promoted by the Alma-Ata Declaration demonstrates what is considered the basic package of primary health care services. *World Development Report, 1993* expanded this core package to include education, and not necessarily only health education. The introduction of non-health interventions and their potential effect on a population's health status are important to consider when planning for health. Essentially, policymakers have access to three different approaches to produce or protect good health. The first delivers medical interventions, such as vaccines, drugs, and primary health care centers. The second delivers non-medical health interventions, such as training medical personnel and devising more effective systems for procuring, storing, and developing pharmaceuticals and equipment. The third uses non-health interventions, such as providing clean water and improved sanitation facilities or better basic education. Each country needs to make its own decisions about relative investments in each of these areas.

Regional Summaries

Healthy conditions vary greatly across the world, and income is closely entwined with health. The poorest countries tend to suffer most from infectious diseases while economic development tends to bring chronic and lifestyle-related diseases to the fore.

Americas

As a region, the Americas have relatively high life expectancy rates (71.2 years) and low infant mortality rates (24.7 deaths per 1,000 live births), according to the U.S. Census Bureau. Due to differences in poverty rates, however, North America and South and Central America and the Caribbean face different health concerns and challenges.

WHO's and the Harvard School of Public Health's *Global Burden of Disease* estimates that the leading causes of death in the Americas are cardiovascular disease, accounting for 34 percent of all deaths, with cancer the second leading cause at 18 percent. According to studies by the Pan American Health Organization (PAHO), in North America aging, obesity, and heart disease are the leading causes of poor health. Diabetes and other diseases of the circulatory system are on the rise, due, in large part, to obesity and sedentary lifestyles.

PAHO also reports that this is in contrast to the significantly higher rates of communicable and infectious disease prevalent in South America. Mortality rates from diarrhea and respiratory disease, while dropping in most countries, remain high in Central America and the Andean region, particularly among children under five. Several departments of WHO are using the Integrated Management of Childhood Illness approach to target this vulnerable age group.

Europe

According to the International Data Base of the U.S. Census Bureau, Europe has the world's highest life expectancy (74.2 years) and lowest infant mortality rate (10.9 deaths per 1,000 live births). Although these may be indicators of relatively good health, there is a significant health divide in Europe, generally between the eastern and western parts of the region. This divide steadily increased in the 1990s. Eastern Europe now faces a variety of local health crises, including an AIDS epidemic.

According to WHO's "Global Burden of Disease, 2000," health risks facing Western Europeans are usually noncommunicable diseases, with cardiovascular diseases accounting for more than half of all deaths. WHO Europe notes that external causes of death, such as accidents, suicide, and homicide, account for approximately 30 percent of deaths, and cancer is responsible for about 25 percent.

Many countries in the east and southeast have seen civil unrest, political conflict, wars, and economic collapse in the last decade. As a result, the quality of health care and health services has dropped significantly, resulting in the reemergence of many diseases previously thought to have been eradicated,

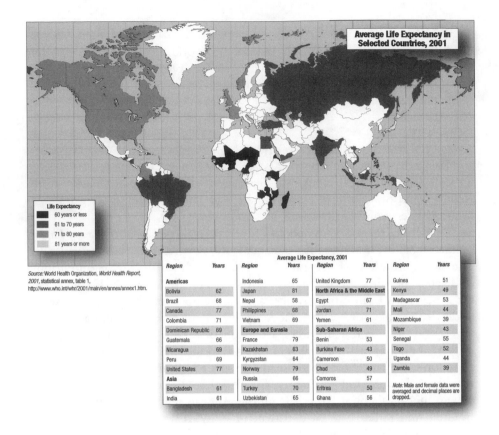

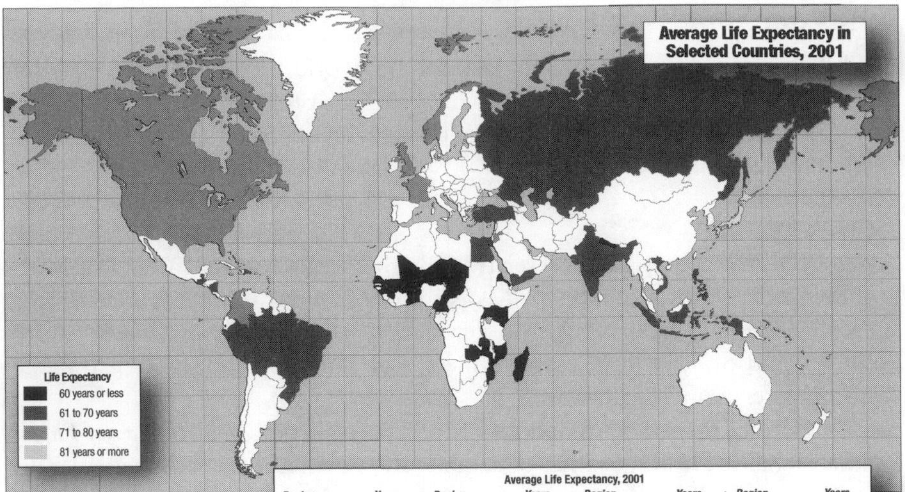

Source: World Health Organization, *World Health Report, 2001,* statistical annex, table 1, http://www.who.int/whr/2001/main/en/annex/annex1.htm.

Average Life Expectancy, 2001

Region	Years	Region	Years	Region	Years	Region	Years
Americas		Indonesia	65	United Kingdom	77	Guinea	51
Bolivia	62	Japan	81	**North Africa & the Middle East**		Kenya	49
Brazil	68	Nepal	58	Egypt	67	Madagascar	53
Canada	77	Philippines	68	Jordan	71	Mali	44
Colombia	71	Vietnam	69	Yemen	61	Mozambique	39
Dominican Republic	69	**Europe and Eurasia**		**Sub-Saharan Africa**		Niger	43
Guatemala	66	France	79	Benin	53	Senegal	55
Nicaragua	69	Kazakhstan	63	Burkina Faso	43	Togo	52
Peru	69	Kyrgyzstan	64	Cameroon	50	Uganda	44
United States	77	Norway	79	Chad	49	Zambia	39
Asia		Russia	66	Comoros	57		
Bangladesh	61	Turkey	70	Eritrea	50		
India	61	Uzbekistan	65	Ghana	56		

Note: Male and female data were averaged and decimal places are dropped.

including tuberculosis, as well as a rise in many other communicable diseases associated with poverty. HIV/AIDS has caused a major health crisis, particularly in Russia, and the region is currently experiencing the fastest-growing rate of HIV prevalence in the world. The *AIDS Epidemic Update,* produced by the Joint United Nations Programme on HIV/AIDS (UNAIDS), reports that there were 250,000 new infections in this region in 2001, bringing the number of those infected to 1 million.

North Africa and the Middle East

Although the region of North Africa and the Middle East has a relatively high life expectancy rate (67.9 years) according to the U.S. Census Bureau, the infant mortality rate is also high (49.4 deaths per 1,000 live births). Problems with infant and child health reflect underlying health problems that the relatively high life expectancy somewhat masks. For example, the percentage of children under age five who are underweight, according to the *Human Development Report, 2001,* is 11 percent in Iran, 13 percent in Algeria, and 26 percent in Pakistan; the percentage of infants with low birth weight is 10 percent, 9 percent, and 25 percent, respectively.

Plagued by war and civil unrest, North Africa and the Middle East have become a top priority for international health organizations. Iran and Iraq have both suffered through war and armed conflict in recent decades, resulting in populations with limited access to well-functioning health care systems. The situation is worst perhaps in Afghanistan, where the health care system is practically nonexistent and the shortage of health workers is severe. According to WHO, these dire conditions have boosted the maternal mortality rate in Afghanistan to the second highest in the world, at least 1,700 per 100,000 live births.

Sub-Saharan Africa

According to the U.S. Census Bureau, sub-Saharan Africa has the lowest life expectancy as well as the highest infant mortality rate on the planet. This troubling situation is associated with the severe poverty endemic to the region: according to the World Bank's *World Development Indicators, 2001,* nine of the ten poorest countries, as measured by national income per capita, are in sub-Saharan Africa.

WHO's "Global Burden of Disease, 2000" estimates that the leading cause of death in the region is HIV/AIDS—22.6 percent of all deaths, making sub-Saharan Africa the worst affected region in the world. According to a UNAIDS fact sheet, "An Overview of the HIV/AIDS Epidemic, 2001," there were 3.4 million new cases of HIV in 2001 in this region, 28.1 million Africans living with the virus, and 2.3 million deaths from AIDS. In several countries of southern Africa, one in five adults tests positive for HIV. Prevention efforts in some areas have slowed the transmission of HIV and therefore the spread of AIDS. In Uganda, for example, the number of pregnant women with HIV in urban areas has fallen for eight consecutive years, from 30 percent in 1992 to 11 percent in 2000. Unfortunately, overall increasing prevalence rates indicate that prevention efforts and improvements in educational efforts will only take effect gradually (see AIDS).

Another major health problem in sub-Saharan Africa is malaria. This tropical parasitic virus is responsible for more than 1 million deaths each year, 90 percent of which, according to the World Health Organization, occur in sub-Saharan Africa. The spread of the virus occurs under natural as well as man-made conditions, and it is especially prevalent in poor, rural areas with little access to health care and health services. Malaria makes its greatest impact among children. Sub-Saharan African children, according to a 1998 WHO fact sheet, suffer higher mortality from the disease than any other group. Children in rural areas of the region where health care is particularly limited are especially at risk.

Asia and the Pacific

Asia and the Pacific are divided by WHO into two areas: the Southeast Asian countries of Bangladesh, Bhutan, India, Indonesia, Maldives, Myanmar, Nepal, North Korea, Sri Lanka, and Thailand, and the western Pacific countries of China, Japan, and the rest of the countries of East Asia and the Pacific.

Southeast Asia has experienced a decrease in infant mortality rates in recent years and an increase in life expectancy. Nevertheless, some countries, such as India and Bangladesh, still have life expectancy rates that are relatively low compared to the countries of Europe and the Americas. The health conditions of Southeast Asia represent contradictions resulting from a gradual increase in economic status: the region is experiencing an increase in diseases typical of more developed countries, such as cardiovascular disease and cancer, but it still faces challenges typical of less developed countries, such as a variety of infectious diseases. Nevertheless, much progress has been made; polio, for instance, has been nearly eradicated. AIDS is also a major concern for Southeast Asia, with India, Myanmar, and Thailand experiencing 95 percent of the AIDS problem in the area.

The western Pacific displays some similarities to Southeast Asia in that it experiences health conditions typical of more developed countries as well as of less developed countries. Cancer is the leading cause of death in twenty-six countries, and circulatory disease is the leading cause of death in thirty-two nations. Although the area still struggles with infectious disease, success has been achieved in reducing malaria in the ten countries to which it is endemic, including Cambodia and China. Since the dengue fever epidemic of 1998, rates of this disease, while it is still prevalent, have declined. Life expectancy and infant mortality rates span a broad range and are mostly representative of the variations in socioeconomic conditions across the area. Australia and Singapore, for instance, have life expectancy rates of 79 and 78 years, respectively, while Laos and the Philippines have rates of 54 and 68 years, respectively.

Data

Table 1 Infant Mortality Rate and Childhood Vaccination Coverage in Selected Countries

Country and Date of Survey	Infant Mortality Rate (number of infant deaths per 1,000 live births)	Percentage of Children Fully Vaccinated
Asia		
Bangladesh, 1996/97	89.6	54.2
India, 1999	73.0	39.4
Indonesia, 1997	52.2	54.8
Nepal, 1996	93.0	43.3
Philippines, 1998	36.0	72.8
Vietnam, 1997	34.8	50.2
Europe and Eurasia		
Kazakhstan, 1995	40.7	23.4
Kyrgyzstan, 1997	66.2	69.7
Turkey, 1998	48.4	45.7
Uzbekistan, 1996	43.5	78.7
Latin America		
Bolivia, 1998	73.5	25.5
Brazil, 1996	48.1	72.5

Table 1 Infant Mortality Rate and Childhood Vaccination Coverage in Selected Countries (*continued*)

Country and Date of Survey	Infant Mortality Rate (number of infant deaths per 1,000 live births)	Percentage of Children Fully Vaccinated
Colombia, 1995	30.8	65.5
Dominican Republic, 1996	48.6	38.7
Guatemala, 1998/99	49.1	59.5
Nicaragua, 1997/98	45.2	72.6
Peru, 1996	49.9	63.0
North Africa and the Middle East		
Egypt, 1995	72.9	79.1
Jordan, 1997	29.0	20.5
Yemen, 1997	89.5	28.3
Sub-Saharan Africa		
Benin, 1996	103.5	55.6
Burkina Faso, 1998/99	108.6	29.3
Cameroon, 1998	79.8	35.8
Chad, 1996/97	109.8	11.3
Comoros, 1996	83.7	54.5
Eritrea, 1995	75.6	41.4
Ghana, 1998	61.2	62.0
Guinea, 1999	106.6	32.2
Kenya, 1998	70.7	59.5
Madagascar, 1997	99.3	36.2
Mali, 1996	133.5	31.5
Mozambique, 1997	147.4	47.3
Niger, 1998	135.8	18.4
Senegal, 1997	69.4	—
Tanzania, 1996	94.1	70.5
Togo, 1998	80.3	30.8
Uganda, 1995	86.1	47.4
Zambia, 1996	107.7	78.3

Source: Demographic and Health Surveys, STATcompiler, http://www.measuredhs.com.

Note: Infant and child mortality rates are for the ten-year period preceding the survey. Fully vaccinated children are those who have received bacille Calmette-Guérin, measles shots, and three doses of diptheria/pertussis/tetanus and polio (excluding polio 0).

Table 2 Health Expenditures per Capita in Selected Countries, 1998

Country	Per Capita (PPP $US)
Europe and Eurasia	
Kazakhstan	273
Kyrgyzstan	109
Uzbekistan	87
Latin America	
Bolivia	150
Brazil	453
Colombia	553
Dominican Republic	246
Guatemala	155
Nicaragua	266
Peru	278
South and Southeast Asia	
Bangladesh	51
Indonesia	44
Nepal	66
Philippines	136
Vietnam	81
Sub-Saharan Africa	
Benin	29
Burkina Faso	36
Chad	25
Ghana	85
Guinea	68
Kenya	79
Madagascar	16
Mali	30
Mozambique	28
Niger	20
Senegal	61
Tanzania	15
Togo	36
Uganda	65
Zambia	52

Source: United Nations Development Programme, *Human Development Report, 2001* (New York: Oxford University Press, 2001).

Note: Per capita expenditure is calculated according to the purchasing price parity (PPP) model.

Table 3 Leading Causes of Death, 2000

Rank	Cause of Death	Percentage of Total Deaths
1	Cardiovascular diseases	30.0
2	Malignant neoplasms	12.4
3	Respiratory infections	7.1
4	Respiratory diseases	6.4
5	Unintentional injuries	6.1
6	HIV/AIDS	5.3
7	Perinatal conditions	4.4
8	Diarrheal diseases	3.8
9	Digestive diseases	3.5
10	Tuberculosis	3.0
11	Intentional injuries	3.0
12	Childhood-cluster diseases	2.5
13	Malaria	1.9
14	Neuropsychiatric conditions	1.7
15	Genitourinary diseases	1.5

Source: Calculated from World Health Organization, *Global Burden of Disease, 2000,* version 1 estimates by subregion, http://www3.who.int/whosis/menu.cfm?path=evidence,burden,burden_gbd2000&language=english.

Case Study—Cambodia: Health, Wealth, AIDS, and Poverty

Health standards in Cambodia are poor, and its economic indicators are even worse. Like many of Cambodia's other problems, its population's poor health reflects the country's history of conflict, which stretches back fifty years. Although health standards improved following the ouster of the totalitarian Khmer Rouge in 1979, evidence suggests that these improvements have not been sustained, largely because of economic pressures.

Because of the lack of ready access to government health facilities, Cambodians seek treatment from legal and illegal pharmacies, where without a diagnosis and prescription they are likely to receive the wrong medication, the wrong dosage, or the wrong usage instructions. Traditional healers are not often qualified to handle serious illnesses. Private medical practitioners, whose services tend to be expensive, exploitative, and of poor quality, are another alternative for some. Corruption can also be a problem; even people who do have access to free public health care must pay bribes to corrupt, underpaid health workers.

As noted above, while poverty increases poor health, poor health increases poverty in a vicious cycle. For example, the poor health of a single family member can result in that family losing its land, and therefore its livelihood. As concerns HIV, women from poorer households are more likely to be sexually experienced at a young age, are less likely to practice safe sex, and are less likely to speak to their husbands about exposure to AIDS than women from wealthier households.

HIV was first detected in Cambodia in 1991, and it now has the highest prevalence rate in Asia, with 2.8 percent of residents HIV-positive. The economy experienced a boom in 1991–1993 with the presence of twenty-two thousand UN military and civilian observers in the country. This led to an explosive growth of the sex industry, fueled partly by the foreign peacekeepers, newly prosperous Cambodians, and uneducated, poor rural women who did not benefit from the economic development and provided a ready source of sex workers to meet the growing demand. Heterosexual sex is thus the dominant means of HIV transmission in Cambodia.

The government responded relatively rapidly to the AIDS epidemic, without the official denial witnessed in some African countries, and prevalence rates are dropping as more people die than are becoming infected. This trend is probably due to the growing use of condoms and information campaigns. The 100% Condom Use campaign, which aims to ensure universal condom use in brothels, exemplifies the positive information programs that the government has undertaken. A number of key problems exist, however: corruption, poor coordination among international donors, a poorly structured health care sector, and a lack of focus on rural areas, which leaves remote areas vulnerable to health, economic, and natural resource shocks.

Biographical Sketches

William Foege and **D. A. Henderson** played leading roles in the effort to eradicate smallpox, which was accomplished in 1979. They adopted the surveillance and containment approach to the disease and managed to eradicate it in much of the world through vaccination campaigns. Foege is a former director of the U.S. Centers for Disease Control, and Henderson is a former director of the World Health Organization's Smallpox Campaign.

James Grant is a former director of the United Nations Children's Fund (UNICEF) who mobilized the child survival and development revolution that promoted childhood immunization, oral rehydration therapy, and breast-feeding. During Grant's tenure, the UN General Assembly adopted the Convention on the Rights of the Child, a document he worked hard to get passed.

Richard Holbrooke was U.S. ambassador to the United Nations for the Clinton administration. He put HIV/AIDS on the Security Council agenda, focusing on the threat HIV/AIDS poses to international security. Holbrooke's efforts represented the first time that the Security Council had examined a health issue.

Nafis Sadik is a former executive director of the United Nations Population Fund (UNFPA) and the first woman to head one of the major voluntary-funded UN programs. Sadik is well known for successful family planning campaigns and for promoting affirmative action within the United Nations. Her contributions were affirmed by her appointment as the secretary-general of the International Conference on Population and Development, held in Cairo, Egypt, in 1994.

Mechai Viravaidya is a former member of the World Health Organization's Global Commission on AIDS who spearheaded the 1980s condom campaign in Thailand.

His social marketing campaigns promoted family planning and preventive measures against HIV/AIDS. As a result, the HIV infection rate in Thailand dropped more than any other country's. Mechai—which is now the colloquial term for "condom" in Thailand—currently serves as a Thai senator.

Directory

Bill and Melinda Gates Foundation, P.O. Box 23350, Seattle, WA 98102. Telephone: (206) 709-3140, Email: info@gatesfoundation.org, Web: http://www.gatesfoundation.org
Foundation that promotes global health equity

Pan American Health Organization, 525 23rd Street NW, Washington, DC 20037. Telephone: (202) 974-3000, Web: http://www.paho.org
World Health Organization regional office for the Americas

Rockefeller Foundation, 420 Fifth Avenue, New York, NY 10018-2702. Telephone: (212) 869-8500, Web: http://www.rockfound.org
Foundation dedicated to environmentally sustainable development with recent work focusing on combating the spread of HIV/AIDS

UNAIDS, Joint United Nations Programme on HIV/AIDS, 20 Avenue Appia, 1211 Geneva 27, Switzerland. Telephone: (41) 22 791 3666, Email: unaids@unaids.org, Web: http://www.unaids.org
Agency advocating worldwide action against HIV/AIDS

United Nations Children's Fund (UNICEF), 3 United Nations Plaza, New York, NY 10017. Telephone: (212) 326-7000, Email: unicef@unicef.org, Web: http://www.unicef.org
Agency working to resolve the problems related to the poverty and rights of children around the world

United Nations Population Fund (UNFPA), 220 East 42nd Street, 18th Floor, New York, NY 10017. Telephone: (212) 297-5020, Web: http://www.unfpa.org
Multilateral funding agency for population and development

U.S. Agency for International Development (USAID), Family Planning Programs, 1300 Pennsylvania Avenue NW, Washington, DC 20523-1000. Telephone: (202) 712-4810, Email: pinquiries@usaid.gov, Web: http://www.usaid.gov/pop_health
U.S. government agency for international assistance, including administering family planning programs

World Bank, 1818 H Street NW, Washington, DC 20433. Telephone: (202) 477-1234, Web: http://www.worldbank.org
International organization dedicated to the eradication of poverty worldwide

World Health Organization (WHO), 20 Avenue Appia, 1211 Geneva 27, Switzerland. Telephone: (41) 22 791 2111, Email: info@who.int, Web: http://www.who.int.
UN organization dedicated to improving health worldwide

Further Research

Books

Bloom, David E., Patricia H. Craig, and Pia N. Malaney. *Quality of Life in Rural Asia.* New York: Oxford University Press, 2001.

Jamison, Dean T., W. Henry Mosley, Anthony R. Meacham, and Jose Luis Bobadilla, eds. *Disease Control Priorities in Developing Countries.* New York: Oxford University Press, 1993.

McNeill, William H. *Plagues and Peoples.* New York. Monticello Editions, 1976.

Merson, Michael H., Robert E. Black, and Anne J. Mills, eds. *International Public Health.* Gaithersburg, Md.: Aspen, 2001.

Murray, Christopher J. L., and Alan D. Lopez, eds. *The Global Burden of Disease: A Comprehensive Assessment of Mortality and Disability from Diseases, Injuries, and Risk Factors in 1990 and Projected to 2020.* Cambridge, Mass.: Harvard School of Public Health on behalf of the World Health Organization, 1996.

Porter, Roy. *Disease, Medicine and Society in England, 1550–1860.* Cambridge: Cambridge University Press, 1993.

Savedoff, William D., and T. Paul Schultz. *Wealth from Health: Linking Social Investments to Earnings in Latin America.* Washington, D.C.: Inter-American Development Bank, 2000.

Sen, Amartya. *Development as Freedom.* Oxford: Oxford University Press, 1999.

Articles and Reports

Becker, Charles M., and David E. Bloom, eds. *World Development,* November 1998. Special issue.

Bloom, David E., and David Canning. "The Health and Wealth of Nations." *Science,* 18 February 2000.

Doyle, Michael. "Kant, Liberal Legacies, and Foreign Affairs: Part 1." *Philosophy and Public Affairs* 12 (1983): 213–215.

Easterlin, Richard A. "How Beneficent Is the Market? A Look at the Modern History of Mortality." *European Review of Economic History* 3 (1999): 257–294.

Esty, Daniel C., Jack Goldstone, Ted R. Gurr, Barbara Harff, Pamela T. Surko, Anan N. Unger, and Robert Chen. "The State Failure Project: Early Warning Research for U.S. Foreign Policy Planning." In *Preventive Measures: Building Risk Assessment and Crisis Early Warning Systems,* edited by John L. Davies and Ted R. Gurr. Boulder and Totowa, N.J.: Rowman and Littlefield, 1998.

Mann, Jonathan M., Lawrence Gostin, Sofia Gruskin, Troyen Brennan, Zita Lazzarini, and Harvey V. Fineberg. "Health and Human Rights." *Health and Human Rights* 1, no. 1 (1994).

Rodgers, G. B. "Income and Inequality as Determinants of Mortality." In *The Society and Population Health Reader.* Vol. 1, *Income, Inequality, and Health,* edited by Ichiro Kawachi, Bruce P. Kennedy, and Richard Wilkinson. New York: New Press, 1999.

Thomason, Jane A. "Health Sector Reform in Developing Countries: A Reality Check," http://www.acithn.uq.edu.au/conf97/papers97/Thomason.htm.

Winslow, C. E. A. "The Untilled Field of Public Health." *Modern Medicine* 2 (1920).

World Bank. *Assessing Aid: What Works, What Doesn't, and Why.* Washington, D.C.: World Bank, 1998.

———. *World Development Report, 1993: Investing in Health.* New York: Oxford University Press, 1993.
World Health Organization. *World Health Report, 1999.* Geneva: WHO, 1999.
———. *World Health Report, 2000.* Geneva: WHO, 2000.
———. *World Health Report, 2001.* Geneva: WHO, 2001.
———. *World Health Report, 2002.* Geneva: WHO, 2002.

Web Sites

Global Burden of Disease, 2000
http://www3.who.int/whosis/menu.cfm?path=evidence,burden,burden_gbd2000&language=english

United Nations, Electronic Library, Population Division of the Department of Economic and Social Affairs
http://www.un.org/popin/infoserv.htm

World Health Report
http://www.who.int/whr

Document

1. Alma-Ata Declaration

International Conference on Primary Health Care, Alma-Ata, Soviet Union, 6–12 September 1978

The full text is available at http://www.who.dk/policy/AlmaAta.htm.

Extract

The Conference strongly reaffirms that health, which is a state of complete physical, mental and social well-being, and not merely the absence of disease or infirmity, is a fundamental human right and that the attainment of the highest possible level of health is a most important world-wide social goal whose realization requires the action of many other social and economic sectors in addition to the health sector.

II
The existing gross inequality in the health status of the people particularly between developed and developing countries as well as within countries is politically, socially and economically unacceptable and is, therefore, of common concern to all countries.

III
Economic and social development, based on a New International Economic Order, is of basic importance to the fullest attainment of health for all and to the reduction of the gap between the health status of the developing and developed countries. The promotion and protection of the health of the people is essential to sustained economic and social development and contributes to a better quality of life and to world peace. . . .

VI
Primary health care is essential health care based on practical, scientifically sound and socially acceptable methods and technology made universally accessible to individuals

and families in the community through their full participation and at a cost that the community and country can afford to maintain at every stage of their development in the spirit of self-reliance and self-determination. . . .

VII

Primary health care:

1. reflects and evolves from the economic conditions and sociocultural and political characteristics of the country and its communities and is based on the application of the relevant results of social, biomedical and health services research and public health experience;
2. addresses the main health problems in the community, providing promotive, preventive, curative and rehabilitative services accordingly;
3. includes at least: education concerning prevailing health problems and the methods of preventing and controlling them; promotion of food supply and proper nutrition; an adequate supply of safe water and basic sanitation; maternal and child health care, including family planning; immunization against the major infectious diseases; prevention and control of locally endemic diseases; appropriate treatment of common diseases and injuries; and provision of essential drugs;
4. involves, in addition to the health sector, all related sectors and aspects of national and community development, in particular agriculture, animal husbandry, food, industry, education, housing, public works, communications and other sectors; and demands the coordinated efforts of all those sectors;
5. requires and promotes maximum community and individual self-reliance and participation in the planning, organization, operation and control of primary health care, making fullest use of local, national and other available resources; and to this end develops through appropriate education the ability of communities to participate;
6. should be sustained by integrated, functional and mutually supportive referral systems, leading to the progressive improvement of comprehensive health care for all, and giving priority to those most in need;
7. relies, at local and referral levels, on health workers, including physicians, nurses, midwives, auxiliaries and community workers as applicable, as well as traditional practitioners as needed, suitably trained socially and technically to work as a health team and to respond to the expressed health needs of the community.

VIII

All governments should formulate national policies, strategies and plans of action to launch and sustain primary health care as part of a comprehensive national health system and in coordination with other sectors. To this end, it will be necessary to exercise political will, to mobilize the country's resources and to use available external resources rationally.

IX

All countries should cooperate in a spirit of partnership and service to ensure primary health care for all people since the attainment of health by people in any one country directly concerns and benefits every other country. In this context the joint WHO/UNICEF report on primary health care constitutes a solid basis for the further development and operation of primary health care throughout the world.

X

An acceptable level of health for all the people of the world by the year 2000 can be attained through a fuller and better use of the world's resources, a considerable part of which is now spent on armaments and military conflicts. A genuine policy of independence, peace, détente and disarmament could and should release additional resources that could well be devoted to peaceful aims and in particular to the acceleration of social and economic development of which primary health care, as an essential part, should be allotted its proper share.

HUMAN RIGHTS

Daan Bronkhorst

The concept of human rights is arguably the most widely supported element of international law and the most widely shared ideal of the international community. The liberties and freedoms encompassed by this concept extend beyond simple civil rights—for instance, the right to free speech and to assemble—to cover such guarantees as the right to education and employment. The broadest conception of human rights, however, is not shared by all observers and analysts. Nevertheless, the high profile afforded blatant human rights abuses has been an invaluable tool in helping to stop, curtail, or at the very least, acknowledge some of the worst instances of man's inhumanity to man.

Historical Background and Development

The history of human rights entails Western and non-Western philosophies and traditions. Most of the concepts that have gradually been incorporated into modern international law, starting with the United Nations' 1948 Universal Declaration of Human Rights (UDHR) (see Document 1), are phrased in a terminology stemming from the European Enlightenment, the broad philosophical movement dealing with, among other things, the rationality of government. Among the movements propositions was the idea that the "general will" of the people should form the basis of the "social contract" between citizens and government.

Many basic principles of human social behavior can be found in all the world's religions and traditions. An elaborate comparative study of these was made during the preparation of the UDHR. According to that study and to further research, in Buddhist, Confucian, Christian, Hindu, Islamic, and Jewish texts one can find strikingly similar concepts of human dignity, fair treatment, protection against arbitrary violence by authorities, redress of injustices, protection of women and children, rights accorded to foreigners, and more.

No definitive history of human rights has been published, but stages of its development have been traced. First came the principle of the innate dignity of the human being, an idea that may date back five thousand years. The Sumerian Gilgamesh Epic contains the notion of the human being as one who has rights to security, freedom of opinion, and free will, even vis-á-vis the gods. Around 1771 B.C. the Babylonian king Hammurabi had his code of laws engraved in stone. Although Hammurabi's laws were harsh, they carried the promise of protecting the weak and prohibiting arbitrary decisions by authorities. Classical Athens of the sixth to fourth century B.C. is often regarded as the zenith of the concepts of traditional human dignity. Circa 590 B.C. Athens reformer Solon established new laws to alleviate poverty and give large groups of male and free citizens a vote in government and court decisions. It should be noted, however, that some of the most prominent Greek philosophers were highly discriminatory, authoritarian, and anti-democratic in their thinking. Plato sketched a utopian society in which only those of "merit"—apparently a very small proportion of the population—were allowed to rule and live as free citizens. Slaves were generally excluded from the attribution of human dignity, even by such "humane" philosophers as Aristotle.

Second, around 300 B.C. the idea of natural law evolved from Stoic philosophy. The presumption of natural, eternal principles of law gave rise to varying degrees of awareness that people should be considered equals, whatever their origin, station, or class. One of the most interesting figures of this school is the classical philosopher Panaetius, who in the second century B.C. developed the idea that "barbarians" were equal to Romans and that even slaves should be treated on an equal basis with free citizens.

Third, beginning in the late eighteenth century intellectual and popular movements prompted governments to abolish slavery, protect minimum rights to livelihood for workers, and set women on equal footing with men. This was partly the result of the Enlightenment, but also of the French and American Revolutions, upon which the British writer Thomas Paine put his mark with *The Rights of Man*. Paine justified these movements by citing human rights as the guiding principle of the American colonists' claim to independence and the French desire for parliamentary democracy.

Fourth, a body of international human rights law evolved during the twentieth century, particularly in the aftermath of World War II, of which UN conventions form the core. Major regional conventions followed, including the European Convention for the Protection of Human Rights and Fundamental Freedoms (1950), the American Convention on Human Rights (1969), and the African Charter on Human and People's Rights (1981). Their significance is being strengthened and their implementation advanced by a wide range of commissions, rapporteurs, and others. The primary institution concerning the issue is the UN Commission on Human Rights, which meets for six weeks each year in Geneva and discusses violations in particular countries and "themes," such as torture, extrajudicial executions, disappearances, and the rights of women.

Current Status

The concept of human rights is simultaneously clear-cut and vague. Its concrete nature takes the shape of the many forms of violations: discrimination, torture, genocide, political imprisonment, extrajudicial killings, and so on (see map, p. 305) (see GENOCIDE and INTERNATIONAL CRIMINAL JUSTICE). Its vagueness rests in the ongoing debate about what the sphere of human rights should include. For example, are claims of nations and peoples—such as the desire for political autonomy among ethnic Albanians in Macedonia, the Native Americans in Canada, or the Kurds in Turkey—covered under the umbrella of human rights? This debate does not necessarily point to a weakness in the concept of human rights, rather human rights ideals have gained such an international standing that a natural tendency to incorporate ever more rights has developed.

Research

Part of the complexity of the concept of *human rights* derives from the use of the term in three different manners. First, the concept of human rights is a tenet in international law that encapsulates more than a hundred different principles (see Table 1). These include various subcategories: integrity rights, such as those that protect life, body, and mind; political rights, such as those that allow participation in government; social and economic rights, including the rights to work, housing, and food; and cultural rights, such as copyright and the right to academic freedom. There is also a less-established category of collective rights, which include the rights of peoples and nations to self-determination, to the use of their own natural resources, and to their development as a group. Some experts feel that this last category is too distant from the older, individual-oriented human rights concept to be included under the human rights umbrella.

Second, human rights are used in monitoring and corrective campaigns as a tool of denunciation and in the political sphere by governments and, in particular, by nongovernmental organizations (NGOs) to put pressure on governments or to legitimate various forms of humanitarian or armed intervention. Denunciation campaigns can be honest and appropriate, but they can also be biased. For example, NGOs have legitimately documented political imprisonment, torture, use of the death penalty, and other violations in the People's Republic of China. The U.S. government voiced support for human rights improvements in China, but the government may well have ulterior motives. For instance, it can use the oppression of Chinese workers to ban imports from China and thus protect the interests of U.S. businesses.

Third, human rights are an ideological appeal to empathy, solidarity, and human dignity. From the perspective of many activists and thinkers, human rights have taken over the role previously played by religions and traditions. Buddhism, Christianity, Islam, Judaism, and other religions each lay claim to particular concepts of human dignity and to their own moral precepts. These various belief systems, however, do not satisfy a large portion of the world's population that wants a universal moral system. Human rights ideals fulfill such a desire for some people. They, indeed, have a worldwide appeal that is strongly rooted in universal feelings about justice and law. Human rights, however, lack much of what religions have to offer. They do not offer pronouncements on love or hate, on compassion or vengeance, or on hope or remorse, or values after or above human life. Clearly, the human rights ideal has limitations as the ultimate moral standard.

The literature on human rights is vast. Academic institutions worldwide produce thousands of reports on countries and issues annually, as well as a multitude of policy papers and official statements. In 1998 Human Rights Watch and Amnesty International issued extensive reports on human rights violations in the United States. The former organization focused on instances of police violence, including cases that may constitute torture. The latter presented an overview of police brutality, violations in prisons and jails, the death penalty, and the arms trade. Both organizations refer systematically to international law, under which torture and other human rights abuses are forbidden. Human rights organizations also point out that capital punishment is a violation of the right to life and the right to be protected from torture, arguing that even the most "humane" execution brings great suffering to the victim. (The United States has not ratified international conventions that outlaw the death penalty).

Journalists also publish field reports, often based on interviews. For instance, in 1998 Philip Gourevitch published an account of the aftermath of the 1994 genocide in Rwanda. He spoke with survivors on their perception of the healing and reconciliation process and interviewed local officials and the staff of international organizations about the failure to stop the "extrajudicial executions," which resulted in at least half a million deaths (see WAR CRIMES).

A growing number of academics now study the context of human rights violations, including options for prevention and remedies. In 2001 Priscilla Hayner published a book on the operations of truth commissions. Over a period of six years she interviewed hundreds of commission members, survivors, politicians, and academics and in her book she points to the shortcomings of various commissions, offering recommendations on how truth commissions can be improved (see INTERNATIONAL CRIMINAL JUSTICE).

At the United Nations, the Commission on Human Rights has commissioned special rapporteurs on a variety of issues. In 2000 Pakistani lawyer Hina Jilani was chosen to be the special rapporteur on human rights defenders. In 2001 in her first report, Jilani described dozens of cases of individuals who had been persecuted for their work in local human rights organizations. Many became prisoners of conscience, individuals detained solely for expressing their opinion. Others were held in administrative detention, that is, detained without trial. She appealed to governments to urge the protection of these individuals.

Policies and Programs

The roles of international law and monitoring and corrective campaigns in the development of human rights policy are fundamental (see INTERNATIONAL LAW). Intergovernmental organizations, in particular the United Nations, have adopted an array of conventions and declarations aimed at developing a body of international law on human rights issues. Their basis is in the Universal Declaration of Human Rights, which is simply a statement of principles and, therefore, cannot be legally enforced. The declaration has, however, led to a formulation of special legal instruments, covenants, which become legally binding when a country ratifies them. Five such instruments constitute the core of present-day *binding* human rights law.

The International Covenant on Civil and Political Rights (1966) and the International Covenant on Economic, Social and Cultural Rights (1966) derive nearly all their articles from the UDHR. The principles of the UDHR are, however, elaborated in much more detail in the covenants. For example, Article 3 of the UDHR states that "Everyone has the right to life, liberty and the security of the person." Article 6 of the Covenant on Civil and Political Rights has six paragraphs on the right to life, dealing with genocide, the death penalty, and pardons.

The First Optional Protocol (1966) is an annex convention to the International Covenant on Civil and Political Rights; an optional protocol is one that states party to a convention can opt to include in their ratification. The First Optional Protocol recognizes the right of an individual within the jurisdiction of a state party to the protocol to file a complaint with the Human Rights Committee, the UN body that supervises the observance of the convention. By ratifying the Second Optional Protocol (1989) states agree to abolish the death penalty.

The Convention against Torture and Other Cruel, Inhuman or Degrading Treatment or Punishment (1984) defines the crime of torture and the related abuses of "cruel, inhuman and degrading treatment" as acts that cause serious physical and mental suffering and that are committed or condoned by state functionaries or a state. It further describes the purposes of torture, which include obtaining information or a confession or punishing or intimidating a person. Most conspicuous among its many provisions is the article stating that torturers should be brought before a court or extradited when they are found within a nation's jurisdiction.

In these five instruments, as well as others of lesser importance, human rights are clearly and strictly defined, fostering their inclusion in the domestic law and jurisprudence of ratifying nations. In some countries national law is automatically overridden by international conventions that the government ratifies. Increasingly, judges of domestic courts are referring to international conventions and "common" international law in rulings on discrimination, women's rights, freedom of opinion, asylum policies, and other issues (see INTERNATIONAL LAW). For example, in deciding on asylum cases, judges in European Union countries have not only referred to international conventions, but also to nonbinding principles of the UDHR, such as those that guarantee the "right to enjoy asylum."

Yet the ratification of conventions is not an adequate reflection of the actual observance of human rights (see Table 2). For example, Colombia has ratified all major UN human rights conventions but in the 1990s was by far the worst violator of human rights in Latin America. Conversely, Singapore and Bhutan, which have not ratified any of the conventions, were relatively free of serious violations. In many cases, however, international instruments have proven highly effective. For example, on the basis of the Convention against Torture General Augusto Pinochet was arrested in London in 2000 for his responsibility in the torture of civilians while he was Chilean head of state.

The monitoring and corrective role of human rights has proved significant in the prevention of violations, in particular in the work of international and national NGOs. Arguably, the most important of these is Amnesty International, the only organization that systematically monitors human rights violations in all countries. Its work focuses on prisoners of conscience, fair trials for political prisoners (even if they may have used violence), and the abolition of torture, capital punishment, extrajudicial executions, and disappearances. Its campaign methods include writing letters to authorities, lobbying at national and international levels, publicity, awareness campaigns, human rights education, and more.

Human Rights Watch monitors a selection of countries, often with a focus on relations with the United States. Its reports deal with a scope of violations wider than those monitored by Amnesty International, including some social and economic rights, such as the right to nondiscrimination in employment, social benefits, and health care. Other organizations publish on a case-by-case basis. These organizations do not deal with all or most countries of the world systematically, but publish reports and advise governments according to their specific research capacities and country expertise. For example, the U.S.-based Lawyers Committee for Human Rights has initiated programs on human rights education, fact-finding by local human rights groups, and the human rights responsibilities of the U.S. business community.

The research and appeals of such organizations have often been followed up by governments and intergovernmental organizations. For example, the work of most monitors, or rapporteurs, assembled by the UN Commission on Human Rights is based almost entirely on nongovernmental input, and the U.S. State Department issues reports on human rights that are heavily dependent on the same nongovernmental sources.

A significant recent development is the application of monitoring and corrective human rights practice in formal governmental and judicial initiatives of redress. One example is the globalization of adjudication through the use of international tribunals and the establishment of a permanent International Criminal Court. Another example is the prosecution of foreign perpetrators on the basis of universal jurisdiction, of which the arrest of Pinochet in London was a groundbreaking case (see INTERNATIONAL CRIMINAL JUSTICE).

So far, the results of such international administrations of justice have been minimal, but the international judicial system is expected to grow rapidly. Another example of the system's use is that of the plethora of "truth commissions" and official inquiries concerning gross human rights violations. These commissions have been lauded as an effective tool for dealing with human rights in a transition to the rule of law, that is, for states emerging from civil war or recovering from a period of dictatorship. The process was used somewhat successfully in Argentina, Chile, and South Africa. In many cases, however, their results have been disappointing or even nonexistent. Many truth commissions have also exacerbated demands for "real justice" to be meted out in court rulings. For example, the UN-sponsored truth commission in El Salvador in 1992 provided little more than a summary of cases and the names of some of those responsible for violations. The publication of the report was followed almost immediately by a general amnesty releasing all individuals from any sort of punishment. Human rights organizations have since urged governments to investigate all mass killings and other atrocities and bring those responsible to justice.

For many people, the ideological appeal of human rights is such that these rights should be regarded as the ultimate standard of ethics and justice, a substitute for the wide variation in religious and political values. This trend toward universalism has been attacked by some governments, including China, Indonesia, and Iran, but NGOs and independent minds in those countries, including dissidents, political reformists, lawyers, journalists, and human rights activists, generally subscribe to it. Despite such advocacy, it is evident that human rights are for now far from capable of addressing the many aspects of morality, as they do not sufficiently touch on human emotions and everyday values.

Two trends in the conceptualization of human rights are distinguishable. One trend proposes the inclusion of certain rights and values into the human rights concept that currently are excluded, such as the aspirations and needs of groups and "peoples." This entails the risk of eroding the practical application of human rights. If human rights are considered too extensive with the addition of collective rights, governments may be less willing to seriously listen to the complaints of NGOs. The other trend is to restrict human rights mainly to the "classical" rights of individual integrity and personal liberty. Other claims would be relegated to debates about social, economic, and cultural development, where progress is being achieved by negotiation, increasing opportunities, and technical and intellectual advancements, rather than by reference to well-defined rights. The right to work is an instructive example. Employment involves the participation of employers, employees, and government. Businesses must be profitable in order for employment to be sustainable. In turn, sustainable employment depends on investment, economic conditions, the labor pool, worker skills, the market, and much more. The "employment contract" implied in the concept of the right to work establishes that employers offer opportunities and that employees offer good work. Stating that there exists a right to work may not mean very much if the implementation of that right depends on so many factors and so many parties.

Regional Summaries

The following information has been gathered from reports by Amnesty International and Human Rights Watch.

Americas

In most countries of the American continents the human rights situation has improved considerably since the 1980s. Argentina, Brazil, Chile, El Salvador,

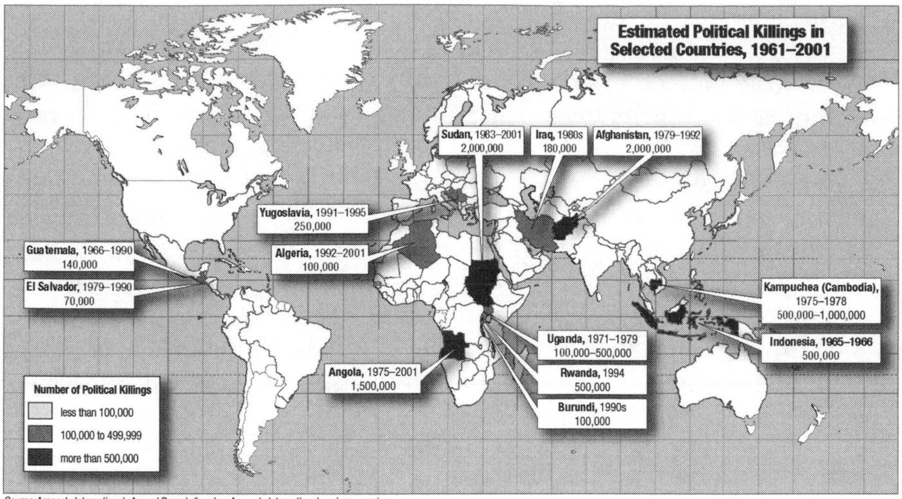

Source: Amnesty International, *Annual Reports* (London: Amnesty International, various years).

Guatemala, Honduras, Paraguay, and Suriname have made efforts to expose past abuses through truth commissions and other official bodies. Very few individuals, however, have been prosecuted for gross human rights violations. Serious violations have continued to occur in a number of countries. In Colombia, military, paramilitary, and armed opposition groups killed thousands of people annually in the 1990s. Violations continue on a wide scale today. In Peru there are reports of widespread torture and the detention of hundreds of people for acts of "treason," which are actually no more than denunciations of human rights violations. In Cuba, hundreds of people, including prisoners of conscience, are detained for political reasons. Human rights defenders are systematically harassed on occasion in most Latin American countries. In the United States, the application of the death penalty—a violation of the right to life enshrined in the Universal Declaration of Human Rights—is ever increasing. Eighty-five executions were carried out in 2000. Despite protection from torture—based on a variety of international conventions, including the UN Convention against Torture (see Document 2)—violence during arrest and detention, usually of ethnic minorities, is increasingly being exposed. Overall, the observation of human rights has improved since the mid-1980s throughout the Americas, yet some countries continue to have a record of wholesale violations.

Europe

In Western Europe the human rights situation is, generally speaking, in compliance with international norms. There are incidental reports from France, Germany, and Italy concerning mistreatment by police, mostly of foreigners and ethnic minorities. There are more systematic concerns regarding the treatment of asylum seekers—people seeking protection as refugees on the basis of a well-founded fear of political persecution—who are being "discouraged" from seeking refuge in this part of the world and are hampered in many ways, including by the degrading conditions found in reception centers (see REFUGEES). In most formerly communist countries of Eastern Europe the situation has significantly improved since the 1980s. In the Russian Federation, however, federal security forces killed thousands of people in Chechnya during the 1990s in the name of counterterrorism. In Belarus, hundreds of people were detained for peaceful opposition activities, and the death penalty is applied secretly. Belarus is the only European country, aside from Turkey, that has retained capital punishment; Turkey has kept the death penalty on its books, but it has not applied it in about a decade and is therefore considered by Amnesty International to have abolished it in practice. The gradual unification of Europe, in particular through the European Union, has clearly had a positive effect on the observance of human rights, as integration has made for closer mutual scrutiny of the law and the practice thereof in EU countries.

North Africa and the Middle East

The human rights situation in North Africa and the Middle East leaves much to be desired. An improvement, seen in the release of political prisoners and the suppression of torture, has been reported in Morocco and Syria. Israel, on the other hand, has continued to kill Palestinians during security operations in the areas under Israeli occupation in ostensible efforts to bring terrorism to a halt. Israel annually arrests thousands of Palestinians for political reasons. The Palestine Authority has also arrested hundreds of people and suppressed dissidents. Iraq has one of the world's worst human rights records, with the systematic torture and secret execution of hundreds of people each year. Egypt has detained thousands of people without charge or trial for alleged membership in Islamist groups. Iran executes people for a wide range of crimes, including prostitution and "acts of treason," and severely restricts freedom of expression, though a gradual loosening of such restrictions was witnessed during the 1990s.

The major obstacle for human rights in North Africa and the Middle East is the absence of democratic and civil society institutions (including free elections, independent political parties, autonomous judicial systems), independent NGOs, and human rights education. Only Israel can be labeled as a functioning democracy. Democratization in other countries has been a slow process or has been thwarted by civil strife, war, and most of all by strong traditions of autocratic rule and entrenched elite interests.

Sub-Saharan Africa

States of sub-Saharan Africa exhibit wide variations in their observance of human rights. Benin, Botswana, and Mali generally succeed in maintaining the principles and practices of the rule of law. South Africa, even given its history of systematic discrimination against its nonwhite population, has made progress since apartheid's abolition in the early 1990s. On the other hand, the continent was the scene of some of the worst atrocities of the 1980s and 1990s: the 1994 genocide in Rwanda claimed an estimated half a million to a million lives; since 1983 the civil war in Sudan has claimed 2 million lives; and innumerable and often anonymous people were killed in armed conflicts in Angola, Congo (Zaire), Liberia, Sierra Leone, and Somalia.

Regional organizations, including the Organization of African Unity and the Economic Community of West African States (ECOWAS), have hardly been able to make a difference. Wherever they have tried to intervene, as in the wars in Liberia and Sierra Leone, the situation has generally turned out only marginally better and sometimes worse. Although various African scholars and politicians assert that violations of the right to life are directly connected to violations of economic and social rights, there is, in reality, no direct correlation between the level of development and the application of the rule of law in African countries. For example, a very poor country like Mali has progressed in the protection of civil and political rights. Kenya, on the other hand, with a per capita income nearly three times that of Mali, still shows persistent patterns of extrajudicial killings, torture, political imprisonment, and press censorship. True civil society has not yet developed in most African states, due to the lack of education, a shortage of democratic safeguards, economic vulnerability, poverty, international intervention or neglect, and other factors.

Central and South Asia

Central and South Asia contain some small countries with a fair or reasonable human rights situation, such as Bhutan and Singapore, but in most countries violations are widespread. In Uzbekistan, there have been widespread arbitrary arrests and cases of torture. In Afghanistan, 2 million people have been killed and millions of others forced to flee the country during the political violence that has dominated the country since the 1980s. The country under the Taliban also had an extraordinarily bad record on women's rights. India, though the world's largest functioning democracy, is the scene of continuous political violence in the states of Assam, Punjab, Jammu, and Kashmir. Myanmar (Burma) is practically unique in its widespread use of slavery, whereby members of ethnic minorities are forced to work for the military government. The human rights and refugee situations in Cambodia, Laos, Thailand, and Vietnam are still affected by the aftermath of the wars of the 1970s and the devastation wrecked by ultra right and communist regimes.

East Asia and the Pacific

China has world record figures in judicial executions—more than a thousand in 2000—plus in its detention of some two thousand prisoners of conscience (according to Amnesty International's "Facts and Figures on the Death Penalty") and in the arbitrary administrative detention of an estimated 200,000 people. Freedom of expression has improved gradually, but the formation of independent political parties and NGOs is still fiercely repressed. Indonesia shows patterns of free press and politics alongside wholesale arbitrary violence by security forces that has claimed the lives of thousands in Aceh, Papua New Guinea, and East Timor. The main human rights concern in Australia is the arbitrary detention of asylum seekers and "boat people." Regional economic cooperation in the Pacific is increasing, but opinions about human rights principles and politics may be more diverse here than in any region of the world. Asia is the only continent that has not yet produced a regional human rights convention or a strong intergovernmental body for political deliberation.

Data

Table 1 International Human Rights Norms

The following rights and norms are recognized in key human rights documents and conventions, including the Universal Declaration of Human Rights (1948), the Convention on the Prevention and Punishment of the Crime of Genocide (1948), the Convention Relating to the Status of Refugees (1951), and the five conventions detailed in Table 2 below. Everyone has the right to the following:

General and Integrity Rights
- Enjoyment of all rights
- Equal protection by the law
- Equality before the law
- Recognition as a person before the law[a]
- Life[a]
- Integrity of the person
- Protection of privacy, home, and correspondence
- Protection of honor and reputation
- Freedom from torture and cruel treatment[a]
- Commutation of the death penalty
- Freedom from discrimination
- Freedom from national, racial, and religious hatred
- Freedom from war propaganda

Freedom Rights
- Liberty and security of the person
- Freedom of thought, conscience, and religion[a]
- Freedom to manifest religion
- Freedom to adopt religion
- Freedom to seek and impart information
- Peaceful assembly and association
- Freedom from coercion in membership associations
- Freedom from slavery and servitude[a]
- Free consent in marriage
- Liberty to ensure religious education
- Liberty to choose schools
- Consent in medical and scientific experiments
- Freedom of expression
- Freedom of the press
- Liberty of movement within one's own country

Participation Rights
- Vote and be elected in secret ballot
- Equal suffrage
- Take part in the conduct of public affairs
- Access public service
- Enjoy one's own culture
- Individual petition and complaints
- Nationality

Rights of Those Charged or Detained
- Effective remedies
- Freedom from arbitrary arrest
- Prompt informing of charges

Table 1 International Human Rights Norms (*continued*)

Fair and public hearing by an independent and impartial tribunal
Presumption of innocence until proven guilty
Adequate time and facilities for preparation of one's defense
Trial without undue delay
Legal assistance of one's own choosing
Legal assistance, if necessary without payment
Examination of witnesses
Free assistance of an interpreter
Not be compelled to confess guilt
Review of one's sentence by a higher tribunal
Not be tried again for the same offense
Not be held guilty for an offense that was not criminal at the time[a]
Compensation after a miscarriage of law
Not be imprisoned for failing to fulfill a contractual obligation[a]

Rights of Categories of Persons
Equal rights for men and women
Not be sentenced to death if under eighteen years of age
Not be sentenced to death if over seventy years of age[b]
Not be sentenced to death if pregnant
Special care for mothers and children
Protection of children from harmful work
Protection of the family
Equal rights within marriage

Rights of Aliens and Refugees
Leave and enter one's own country
Seek and enjoy asylum
Protection from *refoulement*[c]
Protection against collective expulsion of aliens[b]
Protection and support of migrants
Family reunion of migrants

Social and Economic Rights
Fair standard of living
Free choice of employment
Full employment
Protection against unemployment
Social security
Freedom of trade unions
Collective bargaining
Strike
Safe labor conditions
Rest and holidays
Equal payment for man and woman
Fair payment
Property
Food
Housing
Education
Public health services

Table 1 International Human Rights Norms (*continued*)

Cultural Rights
- Copyright
- Rectification
- Speak one's own language
- Carry one's own name
- Develop one's personality
- Freedom of scientific research
- Share in scientific progress

Collective Rights
- International peace and security
- Economic, social, and cultural development
- Self-determination of peoples
- Use of natural resources by peoples
- Liberation from colonization and oppression
- An environment beneficial to development[d]
- Cultures, languages, and religions of minorities[d]

Source: Daan Bronkhorst, *Prisma van de mensenrecht. Begrippen, documenten en activisten van A to Z* (Utrecht, Netherlands: Het Spectrum, 1992).

[a] A "non-derogatory right" (in the International Convention on Civil and Political Rights) that cannot be suspended, even in emergency situations.

[b] Only in the Inter-American Convention on Human Rights.

[c] To be sent back to a country where one has to fear persecution.

[d] Only in the African Charter of Human Rights.

Table 2 Ratification of UN Human Rights Conventions as of 1 January 2001

1 International Covenant on Economic, Social and Cultural Rights (1966)
2 International Covenant on Civil and Political Rights (1966)
3 First Optional Protocol to the International Covenant on Civil and Political Rights (right to individual petition by citizens)
4 Second Optional Protocol to the International Covenant on Civil and Political Rights (abolition of the death penalty)
5 Convention against Torture and Other Cruel, Inhuman or Degrading Treatment or Punishment (1984)

Afghanistan	1, 2, 5	Bahrain	5
Albania	1, 2, 5	Bangladesh	1, 2, 5
Algeria	1, 2, 3, 5	Barbados	1, 2, 3
Andorra	—	Belarus	1, 2, 3, 5
Angola	1, 2, 3	Belgium	1, 2, 3, 4, 5
Antigua and Barbuda	5	Belize	2, 5
Argentina	1, 2, 3, 5	Benin	1, 2, 3, 5
Armenia	1, 2, 3, 5	Bhutan	—
Australia	1, 2, 3, 4, 5	Bolivia	1, 2, 3, 5
Austria	1, 2, 3, 4, 5	Bosnia-Herzegovina	1, 2, 3, 5
Azerbaijan	1, 2, 4, 5	Botswana	2, 5
Bahamas	—	Brazil	1, 2, 5

Table 2 Ratification of UN Human Rights Conventions as of 1 January 2001 (*continued*)

Brunei	—	Iceland	1, 2, 3, 4, 5
Bulgaria	1, 2, 3, 4, 5	Ireland	1, 2, 3, 4
Burkina Faso	1, 2, 3, 5	India	1, 2
Burundi	1, 2, 5	Indonesia	5
Cambodia	1, 2, 5	Iran	1, 2
Cameroon	1, 2, 3, 5	Iraq	1, 2
Canada	1, 2, 3, 5	Israel	1, 2, 5
Cape Verde	1, 2, 3, 4, 5	Italy	1, 2, 3, 4, 5
Central African Republic	1, 2, 3	Ivory Coast	1, 2, 3, 5
Chad	1, 2, 3, 5	Jamaica	1, 2, 3
Chile	1, 2, 3, 5	Jordan	1, 2, 5
China	5	Kazakhstan	5
Colombia	1, 2, 3, 4, 5	Kenya	1, 2, 5
Comoros	—	Kiribati	—
Congo, Democratic Republic of	1, 2, 3, 5	Korea, Democratic People's Republic of	1, 2
Congo, Republic of the	1, 2, 3		
Costa Rica	1, 2, 3, 4, 5	Korea, Republic of	1, 2, 3, 5
Croatia	1, 2, 3, 4, 5	Kuwait	1, 2, 5
Cuba	5	Kyrgyzstan	1, 2, 3, 5
Cyprus	1, 2, 3, 4, 5	Latvia	1, 2, 3, 5
Czech Republic	1, 2, 3, 5	Laos	—
Denmark	1, 2, 3, 4, 5	Lebanon	1, 2, 5
Djibouti	—	Lesotho	1, 2, 3
Dominica	1, 2	Liberia	—
Dominican Republic	1, 2, 3	Libya	1, 2, 3, 5
Ecuador	1, 2, 3, 4, 5	Liechtenstein	1, 2, 3, 4, 5
Egypt	1, 2, 5	Lithuania	1, 2, 3, 5
El Salvador	1, 2, 3, 5	Luxembourg	1, 2, 3, 4, 5
Equatorial Guinea	1, 2, 3	Macedonia	1, 2, 3, 4, 5
Eritrea	—	Madagascar	1, 2, 3
Estonia	1, 2, 3, 5	Malawi	1, 2, 3, 5
Ethiopia	1, 2, 5	Maldives	—
Fiji	—	Malaysia	—
Finland	1, 2, 3, 4, 5	Mali	1, 2, 5
France	1, 2, 3, 5	Malta	1, 2, 3, 4, 5
Gabon	1, 2, 5	Marshall Islands	—
Gambia	1, 2, 3	Mauritania	—
Georgia	1, 2, 3, 4, 5	Mauritius	1, 2, 3, 5
Germany	1, 2, 3, 4, 5	Mexico	1, 2, 5
Ghana	1, 2, 3, 5	Micronesia	—
Greece	1, 2, 3, 4, 5	Moldova	1, 2, 5
Grenada	1, 2	Monaco	1, 2, 4, 5
Guatemala	1, 2, 3, 5	Mongolia	1, 2, 3
Guinea	1, 2, 3, 5	Morocco	1, 2, 5
Guinea-Bissau	1	Mozambique	2, 4, 5
Guyana	1, 2, 3, 5	Myanmar	—
Haiti	2	Namibia	1, 2, 3, 4, 5
Honduras	1, 2, 5	Mauru	—
Hungary	1, 2, 3, 4, 5	Nepal	1, 2, 3, 4, 5

Table 2 Ratification of UN Human Rights Conventions as of 1 January 2001 (*continued*)

Netherlands	1, 2, 3, 4, 5	St. Christopher and Nevis	—
New Zealand	1, 2, 3, 4, 5	St. Lucia	—
Nicaragua	1, 2, 3	St. Vincent and the Grenadines	1, 2, 3
Niger	1, 2, 3, 5		
Nigeria	1, 2	Sudan	1, 2
Norway	1, 2, 3, 4, 5	Suriname	1, 2, 3
Oman	—	Swaziland	—
Pakistan	—	Sweden	1, 2, 3, 4, 5
Panama	1, 2, 3, 4, 5	Switzerland	1, 2, 4, 5
Papua New Guinea	—	Syria	1, 2
Paraguay	1, 2, 3, 5	Tajikistan	1, 2, 3, 5
Peru	1, 2, 3, 5	Tanzania	1, 2
Philippines	1, 2, 3, 5	Thailand	1, 2
Poland	1, 2, 3, 5	Togo	1, 2, 3, 5
Portugal	1, 2, 3, 4, 5	Trinidad and Tobago	1, 2, 3
Qatar	5	Tunisia	1, 2
Romania	1, 2, 3, 4, 5	Turkey	5
Russian Federation	1, 2, 3, 5	Turkmenistan	1, 2, 3, 4, 5
Rwanda	1, 2	Tuvalu	—
Samoa	—	Uganda	1, 2, 3, 5
San Marino	1, 2, 3	Ukraine	1, 2, 3, 5
Sao Tomé and Principe	—	United Arab Emirates	—
Saudi Arabia	5	United Kingdom	1, 2, 4, 5
Senegal	1, 2, 3, 5	United States	2, 5
Seychelles	1, 2, 3, 4, 5	Uruguay	1, 2, 3, 4, 5
Sierra Leone	1, 2, 3	Uzbekistan	1, 2, 3, 5
Singapore	—	Vanuatu	—
Slovak Republic	1, 2, 3, 4, 5	Vatican	—
Slovenia	1, 2, 3, 4, 5	Venezuela	1, 2, 3, 4, 5
Solomon Islands	1	Vietnam	1, 2
Somalia	1, 2, 3, 5	Yemen	1, 2, 5
South Africa	2, 5	Yugoslavia	1, 2, 5
Spain	1, 2, 3, 4, 5	Zambia	1, 2, 3, 5
Sri Lanka	1, 2, 3, 5	Zimbabwe	1, 2

Source: Amnesty International, *Annual Report, 2001* (London: Amnesty International, 2001), 295–298. Annual reports are regularly updated and information posted on the Web site at http://www.unhchr.ch/html/intlinst.htm.

Case Study—China: Human Rights and the Business Community

The norms for the protection of workers and their rights have been elaborated in some two hundred conventions of the International Labour Organization (ILO). They deal with child labor, forced labor, fair wages, safe labor conditions, discrimination against women, holidays and rest periods, and other issues. In the mid-1970s various international statements of principles were drafted especially for the business community. Among these is the ILO's Tripartite

Declaration of Principles Concerning Multinational Enterprises and Social Policy (1977, and repeatedly amended and revised), concerning employment, working conditions, and training.

In 1989, six years after the People's Republic of China's first delegation attended an ILO annual conference, the Chinese spokesperson dismissed the possibility of being able to apply all ILO conventions and recommendations in China because of his country's size and lack of official mandate. In fact, two laws passed by the Chinese government, the Trade Union Law (1992) and the Labor Law (1995), both violate core ILO principles. The right to strike is not recognized.

China still has not ratified ILO Conventions 87 (Freedom of Association) and 98 (Collective Bargaining). After a series of complaints against China were lodged by international trade union representatives, the All-China Confederation of Trade Unions was voted out of a workers seat on the ILO Governing Body in 1990. The confederation was the only legal (and official) trade union in China. In the 1990s complaints backed by the International Transport Workers Federation and the International Confederation of Free Trade Unions referred to the Chinese government's denial of the right to freedom of association, ill-treatment of Chinese crewmen at sea, the detention of labor activists, and impediments to collective bargaining.

The Chinese government insists that international labor standards and ILO requirements are unfair. At a 1997 ILO conference, Labor Minister Li Boyong argued, "For developing countries which constitute the overwhelming majority in the membership, the existing labour standards, taken as a whole, do have the defect of being excessive in number and in criteria." As reported in "China and the ILO, Part 1," published by Hong Kong's independent *China Labour Bulletin,* he went on to say that developing countries' inability to live up to these standards "is not because of the lack of political will, but rather as a result of their limited capabilities." This prompted the *China Labour Bulletin* to comment in the report, "China has indeed learnt quickly how to use the ILO and this in turn raises serious doubts about the ILO's capacity to insist on its own principles. It also appears that the irony of a representative of a 'workers' state' arguing for diminishing labor standards while attending an international labor conference was lost on Mr. Li."

Since the late 1990s, NGOs for human rights and labor rights have pressed the international business community to help promote basic human rights in China. One approach is the application of an international standard called SA8000, an "auditable standard for third-party verification" of labor practices that was first published in 1997 by the U.S.-based Social Accountability International. The standard is based on core ILO conventions that guarantee protection from discrimination; protection from forced and bonded labor; freedom of association; the right to collective bargaining; minimum age requirements; occupational safety and health; fair wages; and decent working hours. Since China will host the Olympic Games in 2008, it is expected that trade and investment in China by the international business community will greatly increase.

Along with the promotion of objectively monitored standards, such contacts could have a significant impact on China's human rights performance.

Biographical Sketches

Baltasar Garzón is one of Spain's six investigating judges, assigned to gather evidence and evaluate whether cases should be brought to trial. Garzón's most prominent case thus far was the international warrant he issued against General Augusto Pinochet, the former head of state of Chile, for genocide, hostage taking, and conspiracy to commit murder. As a result of the warrant, Pinochet was detained for seventeen months in London, before being released on medical grounds.

Nelson Mandela was imprisoned from 1962 to 1990 by the South African government for his activities on behalf of black rights and in opposition to apartheid. After his release, he worked with President F. W. de Klerk, who had freed him, to bring about a peaceful transition to democracy and black majority rule. In 1994 Mandela was elected the first black president of South Africa. He organized the Truth and Reconciliation Commission, which over the course of more than five years worked to resolve the apartheid legacy of human rights violations.

Mary Robinson was Ireland's first woman president, from 1990 to 1997, and was appointed UN high commissioner for human rights in 1997. As commissioner she set an agenda that included not only civil and political rights, but also social and economic rights. Robinson is particularly noted for her efforts to include refugee issues within the conceptual parameters of human rights.

Aung San Suu Kyi is the leader of the opposition Burmese party that won an overwhelming victory in national elections held in 1990. The military junta annulled the results and placed Suu Kyi under house arrest. The daughter of Aung San, who led Burma (now Myanmar) to independence, Suu Kyi became an outspoken critic of the ruling junta. Her popularity among the Burmese has grown to enormous proportions. In 1991 she won the Nobel Peace Prize for her efforts to bring democracy to Burma.

Laurie Wiseberg established the Human Rights Internet in the 1970s as a resource for documenting the activities of a growing number of nongovernmental human rights organizations. For many years, particularly before the spread of the Internet, the organization's database was virtually the only source where activists, academics, and officials could find detailed information about the human rights movement in the West and in dozens of developing countries. Wiseberg was also instrumental in establishing professional standards for human rights workers.

Directory

Amnesty International, International Secretariat, 1 Easton Street, London WC1X 8DJ, United Kingdom. Telephone: (44) 207 413 5500, Email: aiusane@aiusa.org, Web: http://www.amnesty.org
Organization that systematically monitors human rights violations worldwide

Defence for Children International, P.O. Box 88, 1211 Geneva 20, Switzerland. Telephone: (41) 22 734 0558, Email: cdi-hq@pingnet.ch, Web: http://www.defence-for-children.org
Organization that promotes and protects the rights of children worldwide

Freedom House, 120 Wall Street, 26th Floor, New York, NY 10005. Telephone: (212) 514-8040, Email: goldfarb@freedomhouse.org, Web: http://www.freedom house.org
Organization that publishes reports on press freedom and civil liberties worldwide

Human Rights Internet, 8 York Street, Suite 302, Ottawa, ONT KIN 5S6, Canada. Telephone: (613) 789-7407, Email: hri@hri.ca, Web: http://www.hri.ca
Organization that documents the activities of human rights groups

Human Rights Watch, 350 Fifth Avenue, 34th Floor, New York, NY 10118-3299. Telephone: (212) 736-1300, Email: hrwnyc@hrw.org, Web: http://www.hrw.org
Organization that reports on human rights violations in selected countries

Index on Censorship, Lancaster House, 33 Islington High Street, London N1 9LH, United Kingdom. Telephone: (44) 207 278 1878, Web: http://www.indexonline.org
Resource center on freedom of the press and persecution of writers

International Commission of Jurists, P.O. Box 216, 81 A Avenue de Châtelaine, 1219 Geneva, Switzerland. Telephone: (41) 22 979 3800, Email: infor@icj.org, Web: http://www.icj.org
An independent group particularly strong on the inclusion of human rights law in domestic law, has national sections and affiliated legal organizations around the world

International Gay and Lesbian Human Rights Commission, 1360 Mission Street, Suite 200, San Francisco, CA 94103. Telephone: (415) 255-8662, Email: iglhrc@iglhrc.org, Web: http://www.iglhrc.org
Group that works to protect and advance human rights of all individuals and communities subject to discrimination on the basis of sexual orientation, gender identity, or HIV status

International League for Human Rights, 432 Park Avenue South, Room 1103, New York, NY 10016. Telephone: (212) 684-1221, Email: info@ilhr.org, Web: http://www.ilhr.org
The oldest general human rights organization, established in 1942, particularly defends human rights advocates

International Women's Rights Action Watch, University of Minnesota, 301 19th Avenue South, Minneapolis, MN 55455. Telephone: (612) 625-5093, Email: iwraw@hhh.umn.edu, Web: http://www.igc.org/iwraw
Monitoring group for worldwide adherence to women's human rights

Minority Rights Group International, 379 Brixton Road, London SW9 7DE, United Kingdom. Telephone: (44) 202 7978 9498, Email: minority.rights@mrgmail.org, Web: http://www.minorityrights.org
Organization that documents human rights violations that affect ethnic and other minorities worldwide

Office of the United Nations High Commissioner for Human Rights, 8-14 Avenue de la Paix, 1211 Geneva 10, Switzerland. Telephone: (41) 22 917 9000, Email: webadmin.hchr@unog.ch, Web: http://www.uhchr.ch
Office in charge of UN policymaking efforts relating to human rights protection around the world

U.S. State Department, Public Communication Division, Bureau of Public Affairs, Room 5827, 2201 C Street NW, Washington, DC 20520-6810. Telephone: (202) 647-6575, Email: AskPublicAffairs@state.gov, Web: http://www.state.gov
U.S. government agency responsible for foreign policy, tracks human rights worldwide, Web site has extensive annual reports on an array of human rights issues in most countries

Further Research

Books

Amnesty International. *"Disappearances" and Political Killings: Human Rights Crises of the 1990s. A Manual for Action.* Amsterdam: Amnesty International, 1994.

Gourevitch, Philip. *We Wish to Inform You That Tomorrow We Will Be Killed with Our Families: Stories from Rwanda.* New York: Farrar, Straus, Giroux, 1998.

Guest, Iain. *Behind the Disappearances: Argentina's Dirty War against Human Rights and the United Nations.* Philadelphia: University of Pennsylvania Press, 1990.

Hayner, Priscilla. *Unspeakable Truths: Confronting State Terror and Atrocity. How Truth Commissions around the World Are Challenging the Past and Shaping the Future.* New York: Routledge, 2001.

Kuper, Leo. *Genocide.* Harmondsworth: Penguin, 1981.

Laqueur, Walter, and Barry Rubin, eds. *The Human Rights Reader.* Rev. ed. New York: Meridian Books, 1989.

Lauren Gordon, Paul. *The Evolution of International Human Rights: Visions Seen.* Philadelphia: University of Pennsylvania Press, 1998.

Lewis, James R., and Carl Skutsch, eds. *The Human Rights Encyclopedia.* New York: Sharpe, 2001.

McGregor Burns, James, and Steward Burns. *A People's Charter. The Pursuit of Rights in America.* New York: Knopf, 1991.

Meltzer, Milton. *Slavery: A World History.* Rev. ed. New York: Da Capo Press, 1993.

Neyer, Aryeh. *War Crimes: Brutality, Genocide, Terror, and the Struggle for Justice.* New York: Random House, 1998.

Peters, Edward. *Torture.* Rev. ed. Philadelphia: University of Pennsylvania Press, 1996.

Poole, Hilary, ed. *Human Rights: The Essential Reference.* Phoenix: Oryx Press, 1999.

Rosenberg, Tina. *The Haunted Land: Facing Europe's Ghosts after Communism.* New York: Random House, 1995.

Weschler, Lawrence. *A Miracle, a Universe: Settling Accounts with Torturers.* Chicago: University of Chicago Press, 1998.

Witte, John, and Johan van de Vyver. *Religious Human Rights in Global Perspectives.* Dordrecht, Netherlands: Martinus Nijhoff, 1996.

Articles and Reports

Amnesty International. *Annual Reports.* A recording of human rights violations in all countries.

———. "Facts and Figures on the Death Penalty," http://www.web.amnesty.org/rmp/dplibrary.nsf/ff6dd728f6268d0480256aab003d14a8/46e4de9db9087e35802568810050f05f!OpenDocument.

"China and the ILO, Part 1." *China Labour Bulletin,* no. 58, January/February 2001, http://iso.china-labour.org.hk/iso/article.adp?article_id=1166#note9.

Human Rights Watch. *World Report.* Annual recording of human rights violations in select countries with additional information on international reactions to rights abuses.

Jilani, Hina. "Promotion and Protection of Human Rights: Human Rights Defenders," http://www.unhchr.ch/Huridocda/Huridoca.nsf/TestFrame/d6c1b351bf405ad3c1256a25005109bc?Opendocument.

Web Sites

Amnesty International Web Site Against the Death Penalty
http://www.web.amnesty.org/rmp/dplibrary.nsf/index?openview

Derechos
http://www.derechos.org

International Covenant on Civil and Political Rights
http://www.unhchr.ch/html/menu3/b/a_ccpr.htm

International Covenant on Economic, Social and Cultural Rights
http://www.unhchr.ch/html/menu3/b/a_cescr.htm

Social Accountability International
http://www.cepaa.org

Documents

1. Universal Declaration of Human Rights

United Nations General Assembly, 10 December 1948

The full text available is available at http://www.un.org/rights/50/decla.htm.

Extracts

Preamble

Whereas recognition of the inherent dignity and of the equal and inalienable rights of all members of the human family is the foundation of freedom, justice and peace in the world,

Whereas disregard and contempt for human rights have resulted in barbarous acts which have outraged the conscience of mankind, and the advent of a world in which human beings shall enjoy freedom of speech and belief and freedom from fear and want has been proclaimed as the highest aspiration of the common people,

Whereas it is essential, if man is not to be compelled to have recourse, as a last resort, to rebellion against tyranny and oppression, that human rights should be protected by the rule of law,

Whereas it is essential to promote the development of friendly relations between nations,

Whereas the peoples of the United Nations have in the Charter reaffirmed their faith in fundamental human rights, in the dignity and worth of the human person and in the equal rights of men and women and have determined to promote social progress and better standards of life in larger freedom,

Whereas Member States have pledged themselves to achieve, in co-operation with the United Nations, the promotion of universal respect for and observance of human rights and fundamental freedoms,

Whereas a common understanding of these rights and freedoms is of the greatest importance for the full realization of this pledge,

Now, Therefore,

THE GENERAL ASSEMBLY

proclaims

THIS UNIVERSAL DECLARATION OF HUMAN RIGHTS as a common standard of achievement for all peoples and all nations, to the end that every individual and every organ of society, keeping this Declaration constantly in mind, shall strive by teaching and education to promote respect for these rights and freedoms and by progressive measures, national and international, to secure their universal and effective recognition and observance, both among the peoples of Member States themselves and among the peoples of territories under their jurisdiction. . . .

Article 2
Everyone is entitled to all the rights and freedoms set forth in this Declaration, without distinction of any kind, such as race, colour, sex, language, religion, political or other opinion, national or social origin, property, birth or other status. . . .

Article 15
Everyone has the right to a nationality. No one shall arbitrarily be deprived of his nationality nor denied the right to change his nationality. . . .

Article 17
Everyone has the right to own property alone as well as in association with others. No one shall be arbitrarily deprived of his property.

Article 18
Everyone has the right to freedom of thought, conscience and religion; this right includes freedom to change his religion or belief, and freedom, either alone or in community with others and in public or private, to manifest his religion or belief in teaching, practice, worship and observance. . . .

Article 27
Everyone has the right to freely to participate in the cultural life of the community, to enjoy the arts and to share in scientific advancement and its benefits. Everyone has the right to the protection of the moral and material interests resulting from any scientific, literary, or artistic production of which he is the author.

2. Convention against Torture and Other Cruel, Inhuman or Degrading Treatment or Punishment

United Nations General Assembly, 10 December 1984

The full text is available at http://www.unhchr.ch/html/menu3/b/h_cat39.htm.

Extract

PART I

Article 1

1. For the purposes of this Convention, the term "torture" means any act by which severe pain or suffering, whether physical or mental, is intentionally inflicted on a person for such purposes as obtaining from him or a third person information or a confession, punishing him for an act he or a third person has committed or is suspected of having committed, or intimidating or coercing him or a third person, or for any reason based on discrimination of any kind, when such pain or suffering is inflicted by or at the instigation of or with the consent or acquiescence of a public official or other person acting in an official capacity. It does not include pain or suffering arising only from, inherent in or incidental to lawful sanctions.

2. This article is without prejudice to any international instrument or national legislation which does or may contain provisions of wider application.

Article 2

1. Each State Party shall take effective legislative, administrative, judicial or other measures to prevent acts of torture in any territory under its jurisdiction.

2. No exceptional circumstances whatsoever, whether a state of war or a threat of war, internal political instability or any other public emergency, may be invoked as a justification of torture.

3. An order from a superior officer or a public authority may not be invoked as a justification of torture.

Article 3

1. No State Party shall expel, return ("refouler") or extradite a person to another State where there are substantial grounds for believing that he would be in danger of being subjected to torture.

2. For the purpose of determining whether there are such grounds, the competent authorities shall take into account all relevant considerations including, where applicable, the existence in the State concerned of a consistent pattern of gross, flagrant or mass violations of human rights.

Article 4

1. Each State Party shall ensure that all acts of torture are offences under its criminal law. The same shall apply to an attempt to commit torture and to an act by any person which constitutes complicity or participation in torture.

HUNGER AND FOOD SECURITY

Suresh C. Babu

The world's farmers produce enough food to feed everyone on Earth, yet more than 800 million people suffer from chronic hunger and food insecurity because they do not have adequate food to eat on a daily basis. If the world produces enough food for everyone, why does widespread hunger continue to exist in many places? What can be done to move food from a region of abundance to a region of scarcity? How can surplus food be distributed to eliminate hunger or starvation? What technologies are needed to produce adequate food where the bulk of the world's poor live and produce it more efficiently without degrading natural resources? What policies and programs are needed to ensure that everyone is adequately fed to attain physiological and emotional well-being? What institutions are needed to protect the food insecure and the hungry and help them to increase their productive assets? These questions cover the scope and complexity of the problems surrounding hunger and food security and illustrate that there is not a single answer to the issues arising from world hunger.

Historical Background and Development

Famines have been a regular part of human history. The last major famine in the West was the Irish potato famine of the 1840s, resulting from a failure of the potato crop due to blight disease. The great Bengal famine of the 1940s, the Chinese famine of the 1950s, the Bangladesh famine of the 1970s, and the Horn of Africa famine in the 1970s and 1980s killed millions of people. Between 1983 and 1985 some 8 million people in Ethiopia were affected by drought that led to famine. An estimated 1 million of them died along with a large number of livestock. Famine and famine-like conditions continue to threaten several developing countries and regions.

Although famine prevention, food insecurity, and hunger are seemingly at the top of the current global development agenda, the first warning of the impact of population growth on food security was issued more than two hundred years ago. In 1798 Thomas Robert Malthus, a population scientist, predicted that population growth would outstrip food production. It was not until the 1960s, when the world population started to grow at an unprecedented rate of 2 percent per year, that Malthus's predictions generated renewed concern among policymakers.

The Food and Agriculture Organization (FAO) was founded in October 1945 under the auspices of the United Nations and charged with the mission to improve the food and agricultural situation at the global level. In 1960 FAO launched the Freedom from Hunger Campaign. During the 1960 U.S. presidential campaign, candidates Vice President Richard Nixon and Senator John Kennedy announced support for a multilateral food distribution system. In January 1961 President Kennedy established the Food for Peace office in the White House and appointed George McGovern as its first director. Also in 1961, an FAO conference passed a resolution establishing the World Food Programme (WFP) to oversee the use of surplus food in developed countries for emergency and development activities.

South Asian countries, particularly India, faced a major food crisis in the early 1960s and led a "ship to mouth" existence. India imported 10 million tons of food under Public Law 480 during 1965 and 1966. By 1970, through expanded use of high-yielding seeds, India and Pakistan increased their food production multifold, resulting in what is now called the Green Revolution. Between 1971 and 1975 Ethiopia experienced a major famine due to rain failures. An estimated 250,000 people died. Bangladesh faced a major famine in 1974. That year the first World Food Conference was held in Rome. The concept of food security originated at this conference, and delegates recognized the need for improved food policies. As result, the International Food Policy Research Institute (IFPRI) was established in 1975 to identify sustainable policy options for reducing hunger and food insecurity. FAO established the Global Information and Early Warning System to forewarn the global community of impending food shortages.

Three major events in the early 1990s—the UNICEF Children's Summit (1990), the Conference on Environment and Development (1992), and the International Conference on Nutrition (ICN) (1992)—addressed hunger and endorsed recommendations and targets for its reduction and elimination. In 1993 the World Bank organized the Conference on Overcoming Global Hunger, held in Washington, D.C. This conference highlighted the strong link between hunger and poverty alleviation. In 1994 the International Conference on Population and Development, organized by the United Nations Population Fund (UNFPA) and held in Cairo, identified high fertility rates and growing population as the major causes of increasing poverty and natural resource degradation in developing countries. Global Vision, a program to reduce food insecurity through the sustainable use of natural resources, was launched in 1995 by IFPRI. The 2020 Vision Conference, organized by IFPRI and held in October 1995, identified several key challenges, including overcoming complacency, lack of commitment, and political apathy to eradicate poverty and hunger and to protect the natural resource base.

In 1994 the conclusion of the Uruguay Round of the General Agreement on Tariffs and Trade (GATT) and the creation of the World Trade Organization

(WTO) provided opportunities to review food trade and food aid in a liberalized global economy. The 1995 UN World Summit on Social Development, held in Copenhagen, Denmark, and the Fourth World Conference on Women, held in Beijing, China, also in 1995, focused on food security and hunger issues as key development concerns. FAO organized the World Food Summit in 1996 in Rome. The Rome Declaration (see Document 1), agreed to by 186 countries, pledged to achieve food security for all and to eradicate hunger in all countries, with an immediate view to reducing the number of undernourished people by half by 2015.

By 2000 it was clear that the World Food Summit's goal of halving food insecurity would not be achieved. In 2001 IFPRI organized a major campaign to revitalize the efforts of the international community to place food security and hunger problems at the top of the development agenda. A 2020 Vision Conference held in Bonn, Germany, in 2001 helped to reestablish the commitment of donors to world food security. FAO has plans to organize a World Food Summit in 2002 to revisit the goal set in 1996 and to identify new opportunities for the future.

Current Status

As multifaceted as the problem of hunger is, fundamental and seemingly simple questions—for instance, "What is hunger"—must be addressed in order to explore the issue fully. Research geared toward understanding the nature and causes of food insecurity and hunger is the starting point from which broad-based and effective policies and programs can be developed.

Research

The current research on food security and hunger issues revolves around two major areas: quantifying and predicting food insecure and hungry populations, and identifying the causes of food insecurity in order to design and assess policy and program solutions to reduce food insecurity and hunger.

Quantifying and Predicting the Food Insecure and the Hungry. It is currently estimated that about 800 million people are food insecure. This figure is based on the Food and Agriculture Organization's measure of chronic food insecurity, which represents the number of people in each country who consume too few calories to meet their minimum dietary energy requirements. This measurement is based on three factors: per capita energy supply available in a country; distribution of energy consumption among the country's population; and the minimum per capita daily energy requirement. This measure of the food insecure is used as a benchmark for comparing changes in levels of hunger over time as well as across nations and regions. Although this approach has been under criticism, FAO's figures are widely used and extensively relied on by national planners and policymakers.

There are several other estimates of food security. In 2001 in "Ending Global Hunger in the Twenty-first Century: Projections of the Number of Food Insecure People," B. Senauer and M. Sur estimated that in 1996, about

1.11 billion persons, representing 19.1 percent of the world's population, were chronically food insecure. In sub-Saharan Africa and South Asia there were 285 million and 379 million food insecure people, respectively. S. Shapouri and S. Rosen, in their 1999 "Food Security Assessment: Why Countries Are at Risk," estimate that there were 1.1 billion food insecure people in 1998 and 865 million in 1999. A 2000 estimate of food insecurity by a research team led by M. Shane puts the number at approximately 1 billion people, as reported in "Economic Growth and World Food Insecurity: A Parametric Approach." Thus, the number of food insecure people ranges from 800 million to 1.1 billion, depending on the method of calculation, underlying assumptions about parameters, and the countries and regions included in the measurement.

Estimates and projections of the number of food insecure people provide insights into the number of the undernourished and the actions needed for reducing hunger in the long run (see Table 1). According to Senauer and Sur, there will be a decline in food insecurity from 1.1 billion to about 830 million people, representing 10.6 percent of the world's people, projected to be 7.8 billion in 2025. The Shane team estimates that by 2015, the number of the food insecure will have declined from the current level of 1.1 billion to 820 million. The International Food Policy Research Institute predicts that in developing countries the number of malnourished children under five years of age (who weigh less than the WHO standards for their age) will gradually decrease, from 166 million in 1997 to 132 million in 2020. In sub-Saharan Africa, the number of malnourished children is forecasted to increase by 18 percent from 1997 to 2020. This region is likely to remain vulnerable to hunger and malnutrition for years to come.

Although not precise, the above projections of global food insecurity provide an understanding of the direction and approximate magnitude of the problem at hand. A fundamental question that confronts food security planners and policymakers is whether the World Food Summit's goal of reducing the number of food insecure by half by 2015 can be achieved. According to analysis by Senauer and Sur, information on the factors underlying food security measurements indicate that this goal will not be met in 2015 or even by 2025 as long as the current trend in economic and population growth continues.

What is needed to achieve food for all by at least 2050? First, the world's poor, who are most vulnerable to food insecurity and hunger, must share in the broad benefits of economic growth. Second, the policies and programs of developing countries should address the basic needs of the poorest segments of society (see DEVELOPMENT AID and INCOME INEQUALITY). Third, investments in human capital—including universal primary education, health care, and productive activities for the poor—must be made to attain sustainable food security and the eradication of hunger. Fourth, programs and policies that increase the access of the poor to food by reducing prices are essential. Investment in agricultural research and development will play a crucial role in the quantity, quality, and affordability of food for the poor. Designing appropriate programs and policies will require a better understanding of the causes of food insecurity and hunger and of the options and strategies needed to improve the food security of the poor.

A Conceptual Framework for Understanding the Causes of Food Insecurity and Hunger. A complex set of factors determines food security and hunger outcomes. The conceptual framework in Figure 1 identifies the causes of food and nutrition security and the food policy and program linkages to them. It also identifies the points of entry for direct and indirect food security and nutrition programs and policy interventions as well as the human capacity gaps for analysis and evaluation of food and nutrition policies and programs.

This framework attempts to encompass the life-cycle approach to food security and nutrition, given the role of nutrition in the human life cycle. In addition, it includes the cause of food and nutrition security at the macro and micro levels. Achieving food security at the macro level requires economic growth that provides for poverty alleviation and increased equity in the distribution of income. For example, in a predominantly agrarian economy, economic growth is driven by increases in agricultural productivity and therefore depends on the availability of natural resources, agricultural technology, and human resources. These are depicted as potential resources at the bottom of Figure 1.

Technology and natural resources are necessary to generate dynamic agricultural growth, but they are not sufficient by themselves. Also needed are policies that appropriately price resources and allocate them efficiently and that stabilize investment in human and natural resources through political and legal institutions. These factors affect the underlying causes of nutrition security, i.e., food security, care, and health. Attaining food security is shown to be one of the key determinants of the nutritional status of individuals. According to the World Bank, food security is attained when all people have physical and economic access to sufficient food, at all times, to meet their dietary needs for a productive and healthy life. Although this definition is applied at national, subnational, and household levels, it is more meaningful at the household level. Resources for achieving food security are influenced by policies and programs that increase food production, provide income for food purchases, and establish the in-kind transfer of food through formal or informal support mechanisms.

In the "World Declaration on Nutrition" adopted at the 1992 International Conference on Nutrition, "care" was defined as the provision by households and communities of "time, attention, and support to meet the physical, mental, and social needs of children and other vulnerable groups" (see Document 2). Resources for the provision of care depend on policies and programs that increase caregivers' access to income, strengthen their control of income use, and improve their knowledge, adoption, and practice of care. Child feeding, health-seeking behavior, caring and supporting of mothers during pregnancy and breast-feeding are examples of caring practices. Resources for health can be improved through policies and programs that increase the availability of safe water, sanitation, health care, and environmental safety.

Food security that ensures a nutritionally adequate diet at all times plus a care and health environment that ensures the biological utilization of food determine the nutrition security of individuals. Thus, the components of nutrition security are dietary intake of macronutrients (energy, protein, and fat) and micronutrients (iodine, vitamin A, iron, zinc and folate) and health status. Adequate

Figure 1 A Policy-Focused Conceptual Framework for Analyzing Food and Nutrition Security

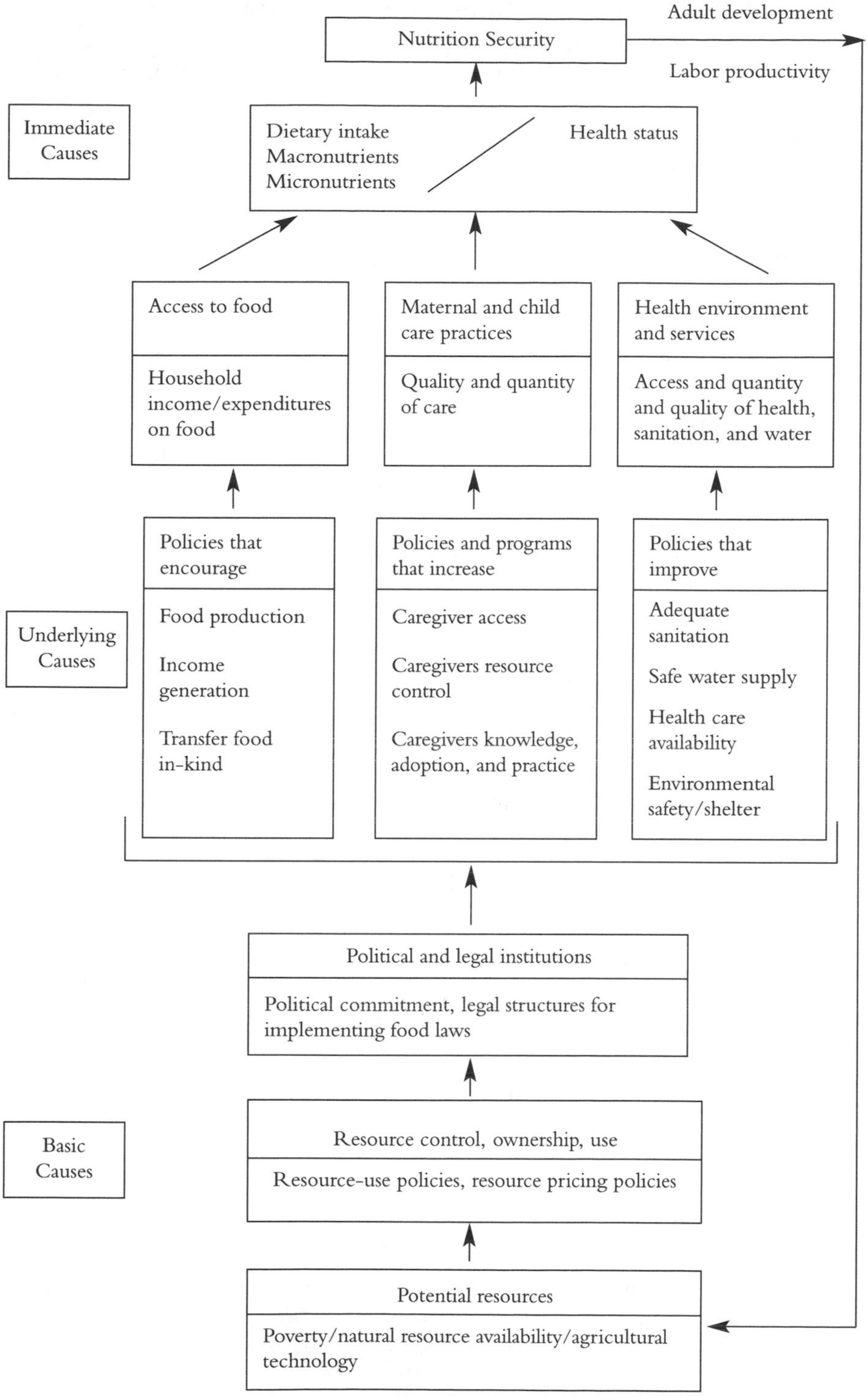

Source: Adapted from L. Smith and L. Haddad, *Explaining Child Malnutrition in Developing Countries: A Cross-Country Analysis* (Washington, D.C.: International Food Policy Research Institute, 1999).

nutrition security for children results in the development of healthy adolescents and adults and contributes to the quality of human capital. Healthy female adults with continuous nutrition security during pregnancy contribute to fewer incidences of low birth weight babies, thereby minimizing the probability of the infants becoming malnourished. In the case of adults, improved nutrition security in terms of timely nutrient intakes increases labor productivity (given opportunities for productive employment) thus resulting in reduced poverty. Lower poverty, in turn, increases the potential resources available for attaining nutrition security.

Policies and Programs

Many developing countries, particularly in sub-Saharan Africa, continue to experience slow and stagnant economic growth. This trend, combined with frequent natural disasters, has resulted in chronic food shortages. Food security remains a development problem even in regions and among groups of households that have shown considerable progress in combating poverty. A number of programs and policies designed to improve food and nutrition security have been implemented in these countries.

Trade and Macroeconomic Policies. Macroeconomic stability is undeniably a necessary condition for sustained economic growth. Conversely, macroeconomic imbalances invariably lead to rapid inflation, real exchange rate appreciation, and chronic balance of payment difficulties. According to research published in 1999 by food security economist Romeo Bautista, macroeconomic imbalances, sustained over time, may seriously undermine reforms undertaken in other sectors of the economy. Bautista's research team showed that trade policy reform alone would increase aggregate household income in Zimbabwe. Policies that encourage the generation of foreign exchange by focusing on a country's comparative advantage can help in achieving food security. The choice between increasing food supply through domestic food production and food import, however, should depend on the food supply on the world or regional markets, the cost of foreign exchange, and the comparative advantage of the country in international trade (see WORLD TRADE).

Targeted Food and Nutrition Interventions. Food and income transfers are nutrition interventions that directly affect malnutrition. Supplementary feeding programs that address the nutritional status of such vulnerable groups as pregnant women and preschool children have shown mixed results in sub-Saharan Africa. According to research conducted by Eileen Kennedy and Odin Knudsen, the impact of direct food transfers on nutritional status depends on several factors, including the quantity of food transferred, frequency of feeding, nutritional quality of the food supplied, timing of the intervention, and the availability of health and other services to complement the food.

Food-for-work programs that provide drought-affected households' access to food during periods of distress have not been effective in improving the nutritional status of the vulnerable groups. Poor targeting and high levels of leakage—pilfering of food from distribution centers that is then made available to consumers—have plagued food transfer programs. For example, in the case of Ethiopia and Sudan, which have frequently faced food shortages due to drought and famine, food-for-work programs have not reached the intended beneficiaries, as reported by Patrick Webb and J. von Braun in 1994.

Targeted interventions are more effective in transferring income to the poor compared to universal subsidies provided through public food distribution programs. Studies that have evaluated targeted intervention programs indicate that poor households change the quantity and quality of their food intake when they face changes in income and the price of rice; therefore, targeting the poor by the use of poor-quality rice, also known as self-targeting of commodities—since only the desperate will participate in the intervention program—is one way to reduce the cost involved in universal subsidies. Foods that are less preferred to staple foods are also useful as a self-targeting tool. Cash-based programs are more effective as income transfer mechanisms than food transfers, according to J. Low and associates in research published in 1999, because the cost of transportation and handling of food grains is at least 25 percent more expensive than cash transfer programs.

Geographical targeting of nutritionally vulnerable households in urban areas is the most widely used approach for increasing the cost-effectiveness of nutrition interventions. In a study of Accra and Abidjan, Margaret Armar-Klemesu and other researchers found, however, that geographical targeting would lead to wide-scale undercoverage of nutritionally vulnerable groups unless additional screening methods were used. Thus self-targeting food and nutrition intervention that are based on characteristics other than location of the residents may be more effective than geographical targeting alone

Food Price Stabilization. Stabilization of food prices continues to be an important element of food policy in many developing countries. Domestic food price stabilization has found a central place in the management of the food economy because of uncertainties in food production resulting from dependency on rainfall and international trade. Food economist Peter Timmer has determined that food price stabilization policies are designed to meet one or more of the following objectives:

- maintain food prices low enough to be affordable to most consumers
- maintain food prices high enough to meet production objectives
- provide stability of price levels to protect the poor from price shocks
- keep domestic prices close enough to world market prices to reduce distortions and illegal trade
- allow enough seasonal fluctuations to permit the domestic private sector to profitably operate in the market.

The stabilization of food prices, if accompanied by the provision of necessary investment in rural infrastructure and agricultural research, could contribute to macroeconomic stability and accelerated economic growth. Price stabilization can be cost-effective if it goes hand in hand with building an active and competitive private sector. The role of price stabilization agencies must be constantly modified to meet the changing role of food grains in the economy and to adjust to evolving domestic private marketing systems.

Food Aid and Public Works. The provision of food commodities to developing countries from donor countries in the form of food aid has been a major method of international assistance in improving food security. Food aid is usually classified according to three categories: program food aid, project food aid, and emergency food aid. Program food aid is used to generate local currency by selling surplus food in the recipient country's market. The funds generated through the local market operations are used for implementing development interventions. Project food aid provides food for programs specifically designed to help vulnerable groups in a recipient country to improve their food security. Targeted supplementary feeding programs and food-for-work programs in developing countries typify project food aid. Emergency food aid is the provision of food directly to the victims of manmade or natural disasters, including refugees and internally displaced people.

The share of food aid in official development assistance has declined over the past thirty years from 22 percent of total development assistance in 1965 to 3 percent in 1995. According to food aid researcher Edward Clay, the total shipment of cereals from donor countries declined from 15.1 million tons in 1992–1993 to 4.9 million tons in 1996–1997. The transition of food aid emergency interventions into development-oriented programs and policies has proved difficult due to the poor design of intervention programs. According to Clay and his associates, the food aid programs that distribute food to vulnerable groups through feeding camps have not been successful in targeting the most vulnerable and hence have shown little impact on improving the nutritional status of the beneficiaries.

Microfinance for Food Security and Nutrition. Microfinance programs that improve the access of the poor to credit, savings, and insurance services have the potential to reduce poverty and to increase household food security. Manfred Zeller and associates identified three different pathways through which access to financial markets can increase food and nutrition security: by generating income, smoothing consumption over time, and meeting immediate consumption needs. Access to credit increases the adoption of new technologies, such as improved seeds and chemical fertilizers, which in turn increase crop output. Higher crop yields result in increased income. Scarce access to financial services tends to result in high costs for the poor's informal savings, which they use for smoothing their consumption over time. Thus, increasing access to savings services microfinance programs could reduce this cost. Imperfections in labor, food, and other commodity markets, however, may also reduce the incentive for formal saving mechanisms that can be used to meet the immediate as well as long-term consumption needs of the poor.

Access to financial markets also reduces the cost of borrowing and protects poor households from food security shocks. Unless microfinance policies and programs address all these pathways, their effectiveness in contributing to household food security is likely to be lower. Access to formal credit for production and consumption purposes are necessary to increase household income and, thereby, reduce poverty and malnutrition. The magnitude of the impact of formal credit on income and food security, however, may be context specific. For example, A. Diagne reported in 1998 that access to formal credit had enabled the rural households studied in Malawi to reduce their borrowing from informal sources with high interest rates, but it did not have a significant impact on the food security and nutritional status of the borrowing households. Land scarcity and unfavorable agricultural terms of trade continue to be major constraining factors in increasing rural income. Thus complementary policies and institutions are needed to take full advantage of the availability of microfinance.

Food-Based Approaches for Nutritional Enhancement. Food-based approaches to nutritional enhancement include increasing nutrition availability, access to nutrient-rich foods, intake of such foods, and the bioavailability of these foods through improved home processing techniques and the better selection of dietary combinations and breeding methods. In 2001 researchers Marie Ruel and Carol Levin reviewed several studies that evaluate food-based approaches to nutrition. In Ethiopia, W. Z. Ayalew and a research team found that home gardening combined with nutrition education increased the knowledge, attitude, and practices related to vitamin A intake, which helps prevent night blindness. According to research reported by Vital Hagenimana and M. Anyango Oyunga in a 1999 report, in Kenya the introduction of new varieties of beta carotene–rich sweet potatoes and appropriate nutrition education increased the frequency of consumption of vitamin A–rich foods. Thus well-designed food-based interventions that combine production and nutrition education can significantly improve the nutritional status of the beneficiaries.

Urban agriculture has been shown to have a positive impact on the food security and nutritional status of low-income households. A 1998 formal study by a team led by Daniel Maxwell showed the positive and significant influence of urban agriculture on the height-for-age of children under five years old in urban households in Kampala, Uganda. The use of urban agriculture as a nutrition intervention, however, depends on the availability and accessibility of land in African cities for farming. Given the increasing migration from rural areas to urban centers in search of employment, this approach may not be a sustainable solution for urban child nutrition.

Nutrition Education and Care. The study in Accra by Armar-Klemesu and others showed that maternal education was the most consistent factor in providing child care, a major determinant of child nutrition. According to the research team, to achieve positive child nutrition outcomes, effective nutrition education is needed in addition to maternal education and knowledge. Furthermore, effective targeting of specific education messages to improve child-feeding practices and the use of preventive health care could have a major impact on child nutritional status. School nutrition programs, however, do not improve the nutritional status of young children unless the program contains an appropriate nutrition education component. The situation is similar in the case of nutrition supplementation programs, where effective communication measures are required for the successful implementation of the programs.

Regional Summaries

Food insecurity and hunger affect populations in every country. These problems are chronic in many developing regions (see map, p. 331). The following section focuses on the regions where the intensity of food insecurity is severe and needs the immediate attention of the global community. While the developed regions of North America and Europe continue to have pockets of hunger, the magnitude of their food problems are miniscule compared to the looming nature of food insecurity in Latin America, North Africa and the Middle East, sub-Saharan Africa, and Asia.

Latin America

Latin American countries rapidly expanded food and agricultural production in the 1990s, primarily through policies that resulted in macroeconomic expansion in the 1960s and 1970s. In the 1980s, however, unsustainable macroeconomic policies resulted in an economic crisis that affected the food and agricultural sectors. This led to reductions in agricultural research investments and negative growth in food production in the 1980s. According to Senauer and Sur, the FAO, and IFPRI, per capita cereal production declined from 262 kilograms per year in 1982 to 222 kilograms per year in 1990; it rose to 253 kilograms per year in 1997. The region is home to 481 million people, 77 million of whom are food insecure. The level of food insecurity is likely to decrease marginally to 71 million by the year 2025.

Although the food and agricultural sectors performed strongly in the 1990s, several countries in the region continued to face slow growth in crop yields. A large number of farm enterprises in Central America and northeastern Brazil and central and southern Mexico depend on small landholdings and the cultivation of a variety of crops to reduce risks. The major challenge in attaining food security among the vast majority of small landholders is the adoption of technology that will enhance the productivity of food systems while sustaining the use of the natural resource base.

North Africa and the Middle East

The vast majority of the population of North Africa and the Middle East live in widespread poverty. The exceptions are the 5 percent of the population that live in the oil-exporting countries. Because of low rainfall, this area faces severe challenges in expanding food and agricultural production. Among the population of 360 million people, about 40 million of them are food insecure. The number of food insecure people is likely to be the same in twenty-five years because the region has a limited resource base of arable land and water, low and erratic rainfall and frequent droughts, and low productivity growth. Past policies have encouraged the misuse of land and natural resources. In addition, skewed land distribution and insecure property rights have been important constraints on food and agricultural production.

Sub-Saharan Africa

Sub-Saharan African countries are faced with high population growth and an increasing growth in the demand for food that exceeds its modest increase in

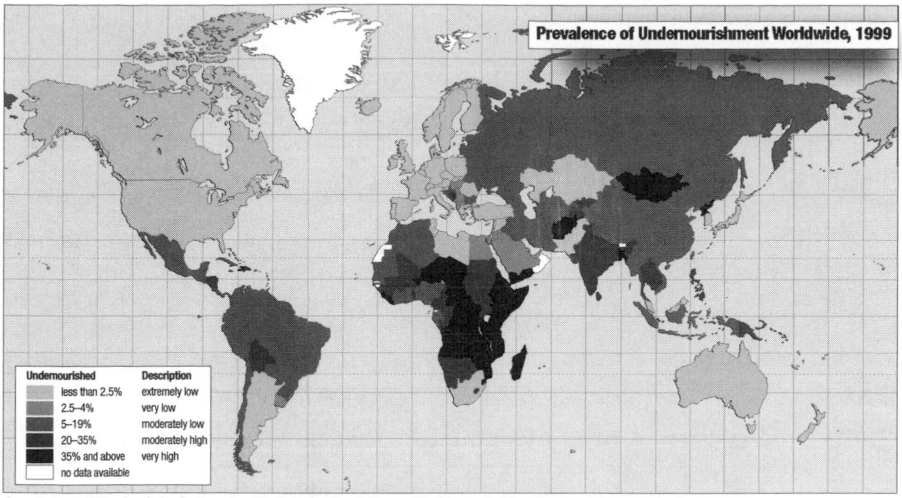

Source: Food and Agriculture Organization, *Food Insecurity—When People Must Live with Hunger and Fear Starvation: The State of Food Insecurity in the World, 1999* (Rome: FAO, 1999).

food production. Several factors condition the poor performance of the region in meeting its food needs. Poor resource endowment—such as poor land quality, large landlocked and inaccessible areas, endemic livestock diseases, and human diseases, including malaria and HIV/AIDS—reduces the food production potential of many countries. Years of colonial exploitation have negatively affected the development of agriculture. A poor policy environment and the lack of supporting institutions have consistently undermined agricultural development and food production. Recent studies show that in 1996, some 285 million of the 540 million people living in sub-Saharan Africa are food insecure. If the current population and economic trends continue, by the year 2025 this number will increase to 433 million. Sub-Saharan Africa is the only region in which the number of the food insecure and hungry is projected to increase.

Africa's food problem will not be solved by expanding the amount of land used for food production. Yields of food crops are indeed low and must grow at higher rates, but this is only one area that needs attention. Subsistence farmers must be encouraged to move toward market-oriented commercial food production, and the ongoing degradation and desertification that has devastated Africa's agricultural lands must be reversed with proper investment in soil and water management technologies. The policies of the 1980s and 1990s have not been helpful in reducing food insecurity and hunger. Renewed investment in agricultural research and extension along with institutional and market reforms will be necessary to meet the future food and nutritional needs of sub-Saharan Africa.

Asia and the Pacific

Asian food security can be understood better when disaggregated into three major regions. In 1996, 62 million people out of 483 million were food insecure in East Asia. About 195 million of the 1.24 billion people in China did not have adequate food. In South Asia, home to the largest number of food insecure people, 379 million out of 1.25 billion were food insecure. Rapid economic growth is likely to reduce dramatically the number of hungry people in Asia.

Although increased agricultural productivity through Green Revolution technologies has increased national food availability, high levels of food insecurity in South Asia still exist. This situation points to the challenge of increasing the entitlements of resource-poor households to meet their food needs. This challenge will require increasing the income of poor households through labor-intensive agricultural production activities. Appropriate research that improves the productivity of crops that poor households cultivate and consume provides a direct method of reducing poverty and food insecurity.

Data

Table 1 Prevalence of Undernourishment in Developing Regions

		Proportion of Undernourished Compared to Total Population (%)		
Region	Number of Undernourished 1996–97 (millions)	1979–81	1990–92	1995–97
Caribbean	9.3	19	25	31
Central America	5.6	20	17	17
North America[a]	5.1	5	5	6
South America	33.3	14	14	10
Near East	27.5	10	10	12
North Africa	5.4	8	4	4
Central Africa	35.6	36	37	48
East Africa	77.9	35	45	42
Southern Africa	35.0	32	45	44
West Africa	31.1	40	21	16
East Asia	176.8	29	17	14
Pacific	1.1	31	27	24
South Asia	283.9	38	26	23
Southeast Asia	63.7	27	17	13
Developing World	791.5	29	20	18

Source: Food and Agriculture Organization. *Food Security—When People Must Live with Hunger and Fear Starvation: The State of Food Insecurity in the World, 1999* (New York: FAO, 1999).

[a] Mexico only.

Case Study—Financial Crisis and Food Security in Asia

The 1997–1998 Asian financial crisis has had far-reaching effects on the food security of poor Asian households. Among Southeast Asian countries, Indonesia has been the most severely affected, as it continues to face downward trends in economic growth and likely increases in poverty and malnutrition levels. Developing program and policy responses to reduce the negative impact of these problems will require an understanding of recent trends in per capita food availability, calorie intake, income levels, and malnutrition. Designing policy responses to relieve acute food insecurity and malnutrition will also require ongoing up-to-date information on the impact of these policies. The institutional infrastructure that generates information in response to food-related emergencies is not functioning well in most developing Asian countries.

In Indonesia, the major impact of the financial crisis was on the per capita availability of food, which fell between 1997 and 1998. Dr. Soekirman of Bogor Agriculture University in Indonesia reported in 1999 that the production of rice, a major staple, decreased by 3.7 percent in 1997 and 8.8 percent in 1998. Retail prices of rice and wheat flour more than tripled between 1997 and 1998. These factors increased the instability of the food supply in the distribution system. Furthermore, expanding layoffs resulted in the reduction of workers' purchasing power, which exacerbated food insecurity.

The government of Indonesia intervened by deregulating the food trade and increasing local food production through agricultural input subsidies. These measures allowed for the free trade of food commodities and abolished the monopoly of Bulog, the food import agency. Food imports had increased significantly by 1998. For example, according to Soekirman, rice imports increased from 1.09 million tons in 1996 to 4.2 million tons in 1998. This explains, in part, the absence of widespread hunger and starvation in Indonesia following the crisis.

Case Study—Food Production and Food Security in South Asia

In the early 1960s, much of South Asia faced high levels of food insecurity and hunger. The countries of the region resolved to prevent famine and adopted measures to increase food production. For example, in the mid-1960s Indian minister for agriculture C. Subramanian designed a national strategy to produce adequate food, market it efficiently, and distribute it to reach the poor and hungry. In 1965 he established the Agricultural Price Commission for determining appropriate and remunerative prices for farmers. The Food Corporation of India was also established, to manage food stocks and stabilize the prices paid by consumers. On the food production front, Subramanian imported 250 tons of high-yielding wheat seeds from Norman Borlaug, a wheat breeder who would receive the Noble Peace Prize in 1970 for his work on the Green Revolution. The 250 tons of seed were multiplied into 5,000 tons of seed within a year. Additionally, 18,000 tons of high-yielding seeds were imported in 1966, and more than 1,000 demonstrations on how to grow these varieties of wheat were held throughout the country. As a result of intensive agricultural extension, India harvested 17 million tons of wheat, adding 5 million more tons than the previous best of 12 million tons. Indian scientists soon developed high-yielding varieties better adapted to local conditions, sowing the seed for the Green Revolution. Currently, India produces 75 million tons of wheat annually. It is self-sufficient in food grain production and has 40 million to 65 million tons in storage. Famine is history in India.

Although the increase in food production in the late 1960s and 1970s prevented mass starvation and famine conditions, food insecurity is still a development concern in India and much of South Asia. The level of poverty remains high, and the purchasing power of the poor does not allow them to meet their food requirements. Faster economic growth and well-targeted social safety net programs are needed to transfer national food self-sufficiency into household food and nutrition security.

Case Study—Famine Prevention and Early Warning Systems

Much of food insecurity and hunger can be prevented because planners and policymakers have access to information on impending food shortages. To generate information to predict reductions in food production in various parts of the world, a global food early warning system was initiated in 1975. Based on the pattern and quality of rainfall and the growth of standing crops, this approach has been able to predict food shortages with reasonable accuracy. Having information on food shortages, however, is no guarantee for timely action. The information on pending shortages must be assessed and analyzed for potential solutions, and action must be taken to reduce the severity of the reduction in food availability on the status of food security and hunger.

Early warning systems, also called food security and nutrition monitoring systems, have been successful in preventing mass starvation and hunger in several developing countries. In the early 1990s southern Africa experienced a major drought that lasted for several growing seasons. Food production in the region fell by more than 60 percent. Yet there was no mass famine, starvation, or death. Relief camps were not set up, there were no mass migrations from the affected areas, and no catastrophic outbreaks of disease.

Most developing countries have early warning systems with varying degrees of functional capacity and success. Addressing impending food shortages and preventing famine and mass starvation require a sustainable and user-friendly early warning system. The most likely system to be sustainable and successful is one that is simple, user-driven, based on existing institutional structures, and has the commitment of relevant decision makers for using the information in planning and policy design.

Biographical Sketches

Catherine Bertini is the executive director of the World Food Programme, which aims to reduce hunger through emergency and development food aid operations that benefit 80 million people in ninety developing countries. In April 2000 Bertini was appointed the UN special envoy on drought in the Horn of Africa. Under the leadership of Bertini, the WFP's share in world food aid rose from 22 percent in 1993 to 36 percent in 1998. Bertini is a recipient of the Leadership in Human Services Award from the American Public Welfare Association and of numerous other acknowledgments.

He Kang was China's minister of agriculture between 1979 and 1990. During his tenure, Kang was responsible for achieving food self-sufficiency for China, which is home to 22 percent of the world's population. Kang mapped out the agricultural reform strategies that enabled agricultural production to grow more than 8 percent annually in the early 1980s. As a result, rural income in China more than doubled, and poverty decreased dramatically. Kang was awarded the 1993 World Food Prize for his leadership in revitalizing China's food production system and for dramatically reducing the number of food insecure people in the world.

John Mellor is a former director of the International Food Policy Research Institute, which has developed a broad vision for achieving food security and the elimination of hunger through research-based policy advice in developing countries. In *The Economics of Agricultural Development* (1970) and *The New Economics of Growth: A Strategy for India and the Developing World* (1976) Mellor argues for an agricultural- and employment-led strategy of economic growth and poverty alleviation. As chief economist at the U.S. Agency for International Development, Mellor directly influenced U.S. foreign aid policy to focus on agriculture in developing countries.

Per Pinstrup-Andersen was director-general of the International Food Policy Research Institute in the mid-1990s, a time when international commitment and aid to agricultural development and reduction of food insecurity were at their lowest levels. In response, he organized IFPRI's researchers to alleviate apathy and complacency toward global poverty and hunger. Pinstrup-Andersen has been the driving force behind the 2020 Vision initiative to assist world leaders in focusing on food security and hunger in the twenty-first century. He is the recipient of the 2001 World Food Prize for his efforts to enable the governments of several developing countries to transform their food policies.

Nevin S. Scrimshaw is an authority on international nutrition and senior adviser to the World Hunger Programme of the United Nations University in Japan. As the founding director of the Institute of Nutrition for Central America and Panama in the 1950s, Scrimshaw studied kwashiorkar, a deadly protein deficiency disease, and developed cost-effective foods to alleviate it. Scrimshaw also addressed an iodine deficiency disorder that results in mental retardation, deafness, and dwarfism in newborns and developed a method of salt iodization. In 1975 Scrimshaw initiated and directed the World Hunger Programme and trained more than five hundred scientists from developing countries to address food and nutrition problems. He was awarded the Alan Shawn Feinstein Hunger Merit Award and the World Food Prize in 1991 for his lifelong dedication to alleviating hunger and malnutrition in developing countries.

Ismail Serageldin served as chairman of the Consultative Group on International Agricultural Research (CGIAR) between 1993 and 2000. The group is the world's largest ongoing cooperative effort to harness science for the promotion of sustainable agriculture for food security in developing countries. Serageldin launched a major renewal of the CGIAR by bringing in more members and redefining and sharpening the focus of its agenda.

Directory

Bread for the World, 50 F Street NW, Suite 500, Washington, DC 20001. Telephone: (202) 639-9400 or 1-800-82-BREAD, Email: bread@bread.org, Web: http://www.bread.org
Organization mobilizing resources and support for reducing food insecurity and malnutrition in developing countries primarily by sensitizing policymakers in the U.S. government

Consultative Group on International Agriculture Research, The World Bank, MSN G6-601, 1818 H Street NW, Washington, DC 20433. Telephone: (202) 473-8951, Email: cgiar@cgiar.org, Web: http://www.cgiar.org
Consortium of sixteen international agricultural research centers addressing global food security and hunger through scientific research and capacity strengthening

Food and Agriculture Organization (FAO), Viale delle Terme di Caracalla, 00100 Rome, Italy. Telephone: (39) 06 5705 1, Email: FAO-HQ@fao.org, Web: http://www.fao.org
UN agency devoted to alleviating poverty and hunger through food security

Food First, Institute for Food and Development Policy, 398 60th Street, Oakland, CA 94618. Telephone: (510) 654-4400, Email: foodfirst@foodfirst.org, Web: http://www.foodfirst.org
Development organization promoting alternative solutions for the food security problems of developing countries

Institute of Development Studies, University of Sussex, Brighton BN1 9RE, United Kingdom. Telephone: (44) 0 1273 606261, Email: ids@ids.ac.uk, Web: http://www.ids.ac.uk/ids
Center that conducts research on food security issues in developing countries

International Food Policy Research Institute, 2033 K Street NW, Washington, DC 20006-1002. Telephone: (202) 862-5600, Email: ifpri@cgiar.org, Web: http://www.ifpri.org.
Policy research and outreach institution identifying sustainable options of reducing food security, poverty, and natural resource degradation

Sasakawa Peace Foundation, The Nippon Foundation Building, 4th Floor, 1–2–2, Akasaka, Minato-ku, Tokyo, Japan. Telephone: (81) 3 6229 5400, Email: spfpr@spf.or.jp, Web: http://www.spf.org
Organization working to emulate the Asian success in food production in Africa through various field-based projects

World Food Programme, Via C. G. Viola 68, Parco dei Medici, 00148 Rome, Italy. Telephone: (39) 6 65131, Email: wfpinfo@wfp.org, Web: http://www.wfp.org
UN organization serving the food insecure in developing countries

Further Research

Books

Brown, L. R. *Who Will Feed China?: Wake-up Call for a Small Planet*. London: W. W. Norton, 1995.

Conway, G. *The Doubly Green Revolution*. Ithaca: Cornell University Press, 1997.

Dreze J., and A. Sen. *Hunger and Public Action*. Oxford: Clarendon Press, 1989.

Foster, P., and H. D. Leathers. *The World Food Problem*. Boulder: Lynne Rienner, 1999.

Hazell, P., and M. W. Rosegrant. *Rural Asia: Beyond Green Revolution*. Manila: Asian Development Bank, 1999.

Lappe, F. M., J. Collins, P. Rosset, and L. Esparaza. *World Hunger: Twelve Myths*. New York: Grove Press, 1998.

Low, J., et al. *Combating Vitamin A Deficiency through the Use of Sweet Potato*. Lima, Peru: International Potato Center and the Kenya Agricultural Research Institute, 1999.

McGovern, G. *The Third Freedom: Ending Hunger in Our Time*. New York: Simon and Schuster, 2001.

Measham, A. R., and M. Chatterjee. *Wasting Away: The Crisis in Malnutrition in India*. Washington, D.C.: World Bank, 1999.

Pinstrup-Andersen, P., and R. Pandya-Lorch. *The Unfinished Agenda: Perspectives on Overcoming Hunger, Poverty, and Environmental Degradation*. Washington, D.C.: International Food Policy Research Institute, 2001.

Rosegrant, M. W. *Global Food Projections to 2020: Emerging Trends and Alternative Futures*. Washington, D.C.: International Food Policy Research Institute, 2001.

Rosegrant, M. W., and P. B. R. Hazell. *Transforming the Rural Asian Economy: The Unfinished Revolution*. Oxford: Oxford University Press, 2001.

Sen, A. *Development as Freedom*. New York: Alfred A. Knopf, 1999.

Smil, V. *Feeding the World: A Challenge for the Twenty-first Century*. Cambridge, Mass.: MIT Press, 2000.

Timmer, C. P., W. P. Falcon, and S. R. Pearson. *Food Policy Analysis*. Baltimore: Johns Hopkins University Press, 1983.

Webb, P., and J. von Braun. *Famine and Food Security in Ethiopia: Lessons for Africa*. Chichester: John Wiley and Sons, 1994.

Wiebe, K., N. Ballenger, and P. Pinstrup-Andersen, eds. *Who Will Be Fed in the Twenty-first Century?: Challenges for Science and Policy*. Baltimore: Johns Hopkins University Press, 2001.

Articles and Reports

Armar-Klemesu, M. "Good Care Practices Can Mitigate the Negative Effects of Poverty and Low Maternal Schooling on Children's Nutritional Status: Evidence from Accra." *World Development* 27, no. 11 (1999): 1993–2010.

Ayalew, W. Z., G. Wolde, and H. Kassa. *Reducing Vitamin A Deficiency in Ethiopia: Linkages with a Women-Focused Dairy Goat Farming Project*. Washington, D.C.: International Center for Research on Women, 1999.

Babu, S. C., and P. Pinstrup-Andersen. "Food Security and Nutrition Monitoring: A Conceptual Framework, Issues and Challenges." *Food Policy* 19, no. 3 (1994): 218–233.

Babu, S. C., and A. Tashmatov. "Attaining Food Security and Nutrition in Central Asia." *Food Policy* 24, no. 4 (1999): 357–362.

Barrett, C. B. "Food Security and Food Assistance Programs." In *Handbook of Agricultural Economics*, edited by Bruce L. Gardner and Gordon C. Rausser. Amsterdam: Elsevier Science, 1999.

Bhalla, G. S., and P. Hazell. "Foodgrains Demand in India to 2020: A Preliminary Exercise." *Economic and Political Weekly* 32, no. 52 (1997): A150–A154.

Bread for the World Institute. *A Program to End Hunger: Hunger 2000—Tenth Annual Report on the State of World Hunger.* Silver Spring, Md.: BWI, 2000.

Clay, E., N. Pillai, and C. Benson. "Food Aid and Food Security in the 1990s: Performance and Effectiveness." Working Paper, Overseas Development Institute, London, 1999.

Delgado, C., M. W. Rosegrant, and H. Steinfeld. *Livestock to 2020: The Next Food Revolution.* 2020 Vision Discussion Paper 28. Washington, D.C.: International Food Policy Research Institute, 1999.

Diagne, A. *Impact of Access to Credit on Income and Food Security in Malawi.* Washington, D.C.: International Food Policy Research Institute, 1998.

Feng, Lu. "Grain Versus Food: A Hidden Issue in China's Food Policy Debate." *World Development* 26, no. 9 (1998): 1641–1652.

Food and Agriculture Organization. *Rome Declaration on World Food Security and World Food Summit Plan of Action.* Report of the World Food Summit, 13–17 November 1996. Rome: FAO, 1997.

———. *The State of Food Insecurity in the World, 1999.* Rome: FAO, 1999.

———. *Food Insecurity—When People Live with Hunger and Fear of Starvation: The State of Food Insecurity in the World, 2000.* Rome: FAO, 2000.

———. *Assessment of the World Food Security Situation.* Report by the Committee on World Food Security, Food and Agriculture Organization, Twenty-seventh Session, 28 May–1 June 2001 (CFS:2001/Inf.2), Rome, 2001.

———. *Fostering the Political Will to Fight Hunger.* Report by the Committee on World Food Security, Food and Agriculture Organization, Twenty-seventh Session, Rome, 28 May–1 June 2001 (CFS:2001/Inf.6), Rome, 2001.

———. *Mobilising Resources to Fight Hunger.* Report by the Committee on World Food Security, Food and Agriculture Organization, Twenty-seventh Session, Rome, 28 May–1 June 2001 (CFS:2001/Inf.7). Rome, 2001.

Haddad, L., E. Kennedy, and J. Sullivan. "Choice of Indicators for Food Security and Nutrition Monitoring." *Food Policy* 19, no. 3 (1994): 329–343.

Hagenimana, V., and M. Anyango Oyunga. *The Effects of Women Farmers' Adoption of Orange-Fleshed Sweet Potatoes: Raising Vitamin A Intake in Kenya.* Washington, D.C.: International Center for Research on Women, 1999.

International Food Policy Research Institute. *A 2020 Vision for Food, Agriculture, and the Environment: The Vision, Challenge, and Recommended Action.* Washington, D.C.: IFPRI, 1995.

International Fund for Agricultural Development. *Rural Poverty Report, 2001: The Challenge of Ending Rural Poverty.* New York: Oxford University Press, 2001.

Kennedy, E., and O. Knudsen. "A Review of Supplementary Feeding Programs and Recommendations on Their Design." In *Nutrition and Development,* edited by Margaret Biswas and Per Pintrup-Andersen. Oxford: Oxford University Press, 1985.

Levin, Carol, and Marie Ruel. *Assessing the Potential for Food-Based Strategies to Reduce Vitamin A and Iron Deficiencies: A Review of Recent Evidence.* Washington, D.C.: International Food Policy Research Institute and MOST, the USAID Micronutrient Project, 2001.

Maxwell, D., C. Levin, and J. Csete. "Does Urban Agriculture Help Prevent Malnutrition? Evidence from Kampala." *Food Policy* 23, no. 5 (1998).

Maxwell, S. "Saucy with the Gods: Nutrition and Food Security Speak to Poverty." *Food Policy* 23, nos. 3–4 (1998): 215–230.

Messer, E., M. Cohen, and J. D'Costa. *Food from Peace: Breaking the Links between Conflict and Hunger.* 2020 Vision Discussion Paper 24. Washington, D.C.: International Food Policy Research Institute, 1998.

Morris, S., et al. *Does Geographic Targeting of Nutrition Interventions Make Sense in Cities? Evidence from Abidjan and Accra.* Washington, D.C.: International Food Policy Research Institute, 1999.

Pinstrup-Andersen, P. *Food Policy Research for Developing Countries: Emerging Issues and Unfinished Business.* Washington, D.C.: International Food Policy Research Institute, 1999.

Pinstrup-Andersen, P., R. Pandya-Lorch, and M. Rosegrant. *World Food Prospects: Critical Issues for the Early Twenty-first Century.* Washington, D.C.: International Food Policy Research Institute, 1999.

Rosegrant, M. W., and P. Hazell. *Rural Asia Transformed: The Quiet Revolution.* Manila: Asian Development Bank, 1999.

Senauer, B., and M. Sur. "Ending Global Hunger in the Twenty-first Century: Projections of the Number of Food Insecure People." *Review of Agricultural Economics* 23, no. 1 (2001): 68–81.

Shane, M., L. Teigen, M. Gehlhar, and T. Roe. "Economic Growth and World Food Insecurity: A Parametric Approach." *Food Policy* 25, no. 3 (2000): 297–315.

Shapouri, S., and S. Rosen. "Food Security Assessment: Why Countries Are at Risk." *Agriculture Information Bulletin,* no. 754, U.S. Department of Agriculture, Economic Research Service, 1999.

Soekirman. "Protecting, Promoting and Fulfilling the Right to Food and Nutrition in the Economic Crisis: The Indonesian Perspective." Paper presented at the "The Substance and Politics of a Human Rights Approach to Food and Nutrition Policies and Programmes," a symposium by the Subcommittee on Nutrition, Geneva, 12–13 April 1999.

Svedberg, P. "841 Million Undernourished? On the Tyranny of Deriving a Number." Seminar Paper no. 656, Institute of International Economic Studies, Stockholm, 1998.

United Nations Administrative Committee on Coordination, Sub-Committee on Nutrition. *Fourth Report on the World Nutrition Situation.* Geneva: ACC/SCN in collaboration with the International Food Policy Research Institute, 2000.

U.S. Department of Agriculture, Economic Research Service. *Food Security Assessment,* GFA-11. Washington, D.C.: USDA, 1999.

U.S. Department of Agriculture, Foreign Agricultural Service. *U.S. Action Plan on Food Security: Solutions to Hunger.* Washington, D.C.: USDA, 1999.

World Bank. *Poverty and Hunger: Issues and Options for Food Security in Developing Countries.* Washington, D.C.: World Bank, 1986.

Zeller, M., et al. *Rural Finance for Food Security for the Poor: Implications for Research and Policy.* Washington, D.C.: International Food Policy Research Institute, 1997.

Web Sites

Demographic and Health Surveys
http://www.measuredhs.com

Economic Research Service, U.S. Department of Agriculture
http://www.ers.usda.gov/data

Living Standards Measurement, World Bank
http://www.worldbank.org/lsms

Use of Geographic Information Systems in Agricultural Research, United Nations Environment Program and the Consultative Group for International Agricultural Research
http://www.grida.no/cgiar

Documents

1. Rome Declaration on World Food Security

World Food Summit, Rome, 13 November 1996

The full text is available at http://www.fao.org/docrep/003/w3613e/w3613e00.htm.

Extract

We, the Heads of State and Government, or our representatives, gathered at the World Food Summit at the invitation of the Food and Agriculture Organization of the United Nations, reaffirm the right of everyone to have access to safe and nutritious food, consistent with the right to adequate food and the fundamental right of everyone to be free from hunger.

We pledge our political will and our common and national commitment to achieving food security for all and to an ongoing effort to eradicate hunger in all countries, with an immediate view to reducing the number of undernourished people to half their present level no later than 2015.

We consider it intolerable that more than 800 million people throughout the world, and particularly in developing countries, do not have enough food to meet their basic nutritional needs. . . . Food supplies have increased substantially, but constraints on access to food and continuing inadequacy of household and national incomes to purchase food, instability of supply and demand, as well as natural and man-made disasters, prevent basic food needs from being fulfilled. . . .

We reaffirm that a peaceful, stable and enabling political, social and economic environment is the essential foundation which will enable States to give adequate priority to food security and poverty eradication. Democracy, promotion and protection of all human rights and fundamental freedoms, including the right to development, and the full and equal participation of men and women are essential for achieving sustainable food security for all.

Poverty is a major cause of food insecurity and sustainable progress in poverty eradication is critical to improve access to food. Conflict, terrorism, corruption and environmental degradation also contribute significantly to food insecurity. . . .

We emphasize the urgency of taking action now to fulfill our responsibility to achieve food security for present and future generations. Attaining food security is a complex task for which the primary responsibility rests with individual governments. . . .

Food should not be used as an instrument for political and economic pressure. We reaffirm the importance of international cooperation and solidarity as well as the necessity of refraining from unilateral measures not in accordance with the international law and the Charter of the United Nations and that endanger food security. . . .

We are determined to make efforts to mobilize, and optimize the allocation and utilization of, technical and financial resources from all sources, including external debt relief for developing countries, to reinforce national actions to implement sustainable food security policies.

Convinced that the multifaceted character of food security necessitates concerted national action, and effective international efforts to supplement and reinforce national action, we make the following commitments:

- we will ensure an enabling political, social, and economic environment designed to create the best conditions for the eradication of poverty and for durable peace, based on full and equal participation of women and men, which is most conducive to achieving sustainable food security for all;
- we will implement policies aimed at eradicating poverty and inequality and improving physical and economic access by all, at all times, to sufficient, nutritionally adequate and safe food and its effective utilization;
- we will pursue participatory and sustainable food, agriculture, fisheries, forestry and rural development policies and practices in high and low potential areas, which are essential to adequate and reliable food supplies at the household, national, regional and global levels, and combat pests, drought and desertification, considering the multifunctional character of agriculture;
- we will strive to ensure that food, agricultural trade and overall trade policies are conducive to fostering food security for all through a fair and market-oriented world trade system;
- we will endeavour to prevent and be prepared for natural disasters and man-made emergencies and to meet transitory and emergency food requirements in ways that encourage recovery, rehabilitation, development and a capacity to satisfy future needs;
- we will promote optimal allocation and use of public and private investments to foster human resources, sustainable food, agriculture, fisheries and forestry systems, and rural development, in high and low potential areas;
- we will implement, monitor, and follow-up this Plan of Action at all levels in cooperation with the international community.

We pledge our actions and support to implement the World Food Summit Plan of Action.

2. World Declaration on Nutrition

International Conference on Nutrition, December 1992

The full text is available at http://www.fao.org/waicent/faoinfo/economic/esn/icn/icndec.htm.

Extract

1. We, the Ministers and the Plenipotentiaries representing 159 states and the European Economic Community at the International Conference on Nutrition (Rome, December 1992), declare our determination to eliminate hunger and to reduce all forms of malnutrition. Hunger and malnutrition are unacceptable in a world that has both the knowledge and the resources to end this human catastrophe. We recognize that access to nutritionally adequate and safe food is a right of each individual. We recognize that globally there is enough food for all and that inequitable access is the main

problem. Bearing in mind the right to an adequate standard of living, including food, contained in the Universal Declaration of Human Rights, we pledge to act in solidarity to ensure that freedom from hunger becomes a reality. We also declare our firm commitment to work together to ensure sustained nutritional well-being for all people in a peaceful, just and environmentally safe world.

2. Despite appreciable worldwide improvements in life expectancy, adult literacy and nutritional status, we all view with the deepest concern the unacceptable fact that about 780 million people in developing countries, 20 percent of their combined population, still do not have access to enough food to meet their basic daily needs for nutritional well-being.

3. We are especially distressed by the high prevalence and increasing numbers of malnourished children under five years of age in parts of Africa, Asia and Latin America and the Caribbean. Moreover, more than 2,000 million people, mostly women and children, are deficient in one or more micronutrients: babies continue to be born mentally retarded as a result of iodine deficiency; children go blind and die of vitamin A deficiency; and enormous numbers of women and children are adversely affected by iron deficiency. Hundreds of millions of people also suffer from communicable and non-communicable diseases caused by contaminated food and water. At the same time, chronic non-communicable diseases related to excessive or unbalanced dietary intakes often lead to premature deaths in both developed and developing countries. . . .

12. Policies and programmes must be directed towards those most in need. Our priority should be to implement people-focused policies and programmes that increase access to and control of resources by the rural and urban poor, raise their productive capacity and incomes and strengthen their capacity to care for themselves. We must support and promote initiatives by people and communities and ensure that the poor participate in decisions that affect their lives. We fully recognize the importance of the family unit in providing adequate food, nutrition and a proper caring environment to meet the physical, mental, emotional and social needs of children and other vulnerable groups, including the elderly. In circumstances where the family unit can no longer fulfil these responsibilities adequately, the community and/or government should offer a support network to the vulnerable. We, therefore, undertake to strengthen and promote the family unit as the basic unit of society.

INCOME INEQUALITY

James Heintz

While global integration has brought the economies of the world closer in significant ways, the economic distance between the well off and the poor has widened significantly. Global inequalities are not simply about fairness. Current research shows that income inequality affects many of today's crucial challenges: promoting economic development to eradicate poverty, maintaining a foundation of stable and secure well-being, and guaranteeing basic human rights and freedoms. Despite the importance of a politically viable strategy for addressing growing inequalities, one remains elusive.

Historical Background and Development

The history of income inequality is a long one. Archaeologists generally point to the rise of farming—which occurred approximately 10,000 years ago in the Fertile Crescent of the Eastern Mediterranean—as the key social development that supported an unequal distribution of economic production. When a community produces a storable surplus of agricultural goods, an accumulation of income and wealth becomes possible. The development of agriculture beyond subsistence, therefore, was accompanied by the emergence of sustained inequalities.

Modern thinking about inequality, however, is largely an outgrowth of the process of industrialization, which first occurred in Great Britain during the second half of the eighteenth century and expanded to other regions during the nineteenth and twentieth centuries. Although historical data on income distribution are patchy, some trends are evident. In Britain and the United States, inequality increased throughout much of the nineteenth century and decreased during the first half to three-fourths of the twentieth century. Inequality began to rise again during the 1970s. Much of continental Europe experienced a similar pattern of raising inequality in the nineteenth century and declining inequality during much of the twentieth century. The decline in inequality was particularly dramatic for the Nordic countries—Denmark, Finland, Norway, and Sweden—and, in some cases, occurred without a significant prior increase in inequality. As in Britain and the United States, in most of Europe inequalities have risen in recent years.

Government policies during the twentieth century offer a partial explanation of these trends. Some policies, most notably progressive income tax systems and transfer payments to low-income households, directly redistributed income. Other policies, such as the expansion of public education, the creation of a welfare state, and the pursuit of full-employment, increased the incomes of working people by improving their productivity and enhancing their ability to improve their living standards. Factors beyond government policies that had effects on inequality include the acquisition of skills across the workforce, due to changes in technology and the acquisition of skills on the job, and the strengthening of labor organizations, such as unions, which helped to protect the wages of workers and reduce the gap of wage inequality through the process of collective bargaining.

Historical patterns of colonization and domination directly affected the global distribution of income. During the age of imperialism, colonies were systematically underdeveloped and their economies structured to create dependence on the markets and capitals of the industrialized world long after independence. During the initial postcolonial period in the 1950s and 1960s, policies to increase domestic production and to promote development often failed. For example, import substitution industrialization aimed to reduce dependence on imported industrialized goods by encouraging domestic production in developing countries. These efforts, however, were often constrained by lack of finance, capital, and technology, and they frequently failed to produce high-quality industrial products. Other developing countries adopted socialist approaches to economic development, a good example of which is the vision of *ujamma,* a form of collective self-sufficiency, as developed by Julius Nyerere, the first president of independent Tanzania. Nyerere's policies of collectivized production failed to yield results in terms of sustainable improvements in productivity and incomes.

Beginning in the second half of the 1970s, many developing countries, particularly those in Latin America and Africa, experienced a rapid accumulation of foreign debt through loans extended by financiers and credit institutions in high-income countries. In the 1980s payments on the debts often exceeded new financial inflows, such as foreign investment or additional credit. Since new sources of finance were often not available, the indebted countries had to use their hard currency reserves or generate additional foreign exchange through exports in order to make their debt payments. Thus evolved a net transfer of financial resources from the heavily indebted countries to the industrialized world. The International Monetary Fund (IMF) frequently intervened, suggesting a policy mix—including export promotion, exchange rate devaluation, and reductions in government borrowing—that the fund claimed would stabilize the economies of these developing nations and promote growth. Despite these prescriptions, slow growth, economic instability, and income inequalities persist throughout the developing world and appear to have worsened in many regions in recent years.

Current Status

Measurements of income distribution generally compare the fractions of income that different segments of the population possess. For example, in 1999 in the United States, the richest 20 percent of households, ranked by income, received 46 percent of all income, while the bottom 20 percent received only 4.9 percent, according to a 2000 report by the U.S. Census Bureau.

The extent of inequality in a society can be summarized with a single number—a Gini coefficient (see Table 1). The Gini coefficient has values between 0 and 1, with 0 representing perfect equality. As the Gini coefficient increases, so does the extent of income inequality. Based on World Bank figures, in 1997 India had a Gini coefficient of 0.38, while Brazil's Gini was 0.59. Comparing money incomes across countries poses problems due to differences in prices. Although incomes can be expressed in a common currency using exchange rates—most often the U.S. dollar—such comparisons are misleading if prices differ substantially. Suppose that the average dollar price of food in Canada were twice that in Indonesia. Then half as much income would be needed in Indonesia to buy an identical quantity of food in Canada. Incomes are, therefore, often compared across countries using a purchasing power parity adjustment that takes into account price differentials (see Table 2).

Income comparisons across countries are often made using the gross domestic product (GDP), the total market value of all goods and services produced in a country during a year (see Table 3). GDP per capita—that is, total GDP divided by the population—gives an approximation of the average income per person in a particular country and can be used as a basis for comparing income levels among various economies. Per capita GDP, however, provides no information about how income is distributed within a given country. Average incomes can increase while the incomes of the poorest segment of the population fall. The result would be a larger per capita GDP but a higher level of inequality.

Income distribution should not be confused with the distribution of wealth, although the two concepts are closely related. In almost all circumstances, wealth—the ownership of physical assets, such as houses and cars, and financial assets, such as stocks and savings accounts—is more unequally distributed than income. Returns on investments can be a source of income. Likewise, earned income can be invested in order to build a stock of wealth. Therefore, income inequality is often directly connected to inequalities in wealth.

Research

International comparisons of income distribution frequently are made on two levels: differences in average incomes across countries and the degree of inequality within a particular country. Average income across countries reveal extreme global inequalities (see map, p. 352). For example, statistics compiled by the World Bank in *World Development Indicators, 2001* show that in 1999 the countries of sub-Saharan Africa had an average gross national income of $966 per person on a purchasing power parity basis compared to an average of

$25,690 in countries with highly developed economies. Today 2.8 billion people, nearly half the world's population, live on less than $2 a day, and 1.2 billion people live on less than $1 a day, according to the World Bank's *World Development Report, 2000–2001*. In contrast, the U.S. Census Bureau reports that average 1999 income per person in the United States exceeded $58 a day.

Although complete data is difficult to assemble, recent research suggests that global income inequality has grown. Robert Wade of the London School of Economics has estimated that worldwide Gini coefficients rose from 0.63 in 1988 to 0.67 in 1993. During the same period, the share of income going to the richest one-tenth of all countries grew from 48 percent to 52 percent. The share going to the poorest one-tenth dropped from 0.9 percent to 0.6 percent.

Growth rates of per capita consumption show that richer countries have been outpacing poorer ones. Between 1980 and 1998 the private consumption of goods and services per person increased by an average of 2.2 percent each year in the highest-income countries. Consumption increased by only 1.2 percent per year, however, in the lowest income countries. (In 1999, the World Bank defined high-income countries as those with per capita gross national product [GNP] in excess of $9,266. Low-income countries have GNP per capita of less than $756. The cutoffs are not adjusted for differences in price levels between countries.) During this time, consumption in Latin America increased by 0.6 percent a year, according to the *World Development Report, 2000–2001,* while in sub-Saharan Africa consumption declined at an annual rate of 1.2 percent.

Within-country inequalities appear to have worsened in recent years, but exceptions exist. Among industrialized countries, a review of the existing data shows that income inequality has generally risen since the early 1980s. According to evidence compiled by P. Gottschalk and T. M. Smeeding, the average growth rates of Gini coefficients were positive from 1980 to the mid-1990s for Australia, France, Germany, Japan, the Netherlands, Norway, Sweden, Taiwan, the United Kingdom, and the United States. A few industrialized countries, including Finland and Italy, showed little change in the degree of inequality during this period.

Many East Asian economies have been able to achieve high rates of economic growth while maintaining a relatively egalitarian income distribution. Duangkamon Chotikapanich and D. S. Prasada Rao report that in recent years, however, there has been evidence of growing inequalities in these economies. Developing countries in Africa and Latin America have also exhibited signs of worsening within-country inequality, but this trend is not universal. For example, *World Development Report, 2000–2001* shows that Brazil, a country with one of the most unequal income distributions, appears to have made slight improvements recently. Finally, many of the transitional economies of Eastern Europe and the former Soviet Union have encountered rapid growth in inequality due to a drop for a large number of households in their living standards—the level and quality of consumption that a particular level of income allows—and the emergence of a handful of extremely wealthy individuals.

In most of the industrialized world, the gap between the lowest-paying and the highest-paying jobs widened in the 1980s and 1990s. According to David

Rueda and Jonas Pontusson, this trend was particularly pronounced in Britain, Canada, and the United States, countries with fewer labor market regulations. High rates of unemployment plagued many highly regulated European countries during this same period. Adrian Wood reports similar patterns of greater wage inequality or rising joblessness in several developing economies, particularly in the countries of Latin American (see LABOR AND EMPLOYMENT).

The growth in global inequality has occurred during the era of globalization, in which the world's economies have become more closely integrated and often less regulated (see Document 1). Many observers argue that globalization has contributed to or at least has not stopped increases in inequality. Reactions to inequities in the global economy have triggered large-scale demonstrations and protests against the process of globalization.

What is the relationship between economic growth and income inequality? Many early economic thinkers, including Adam Smith in the eighteenth century, supported the idea that inequalities are necessary for economic growth, an argument that influences policy debates today. According to this theory, profits are the reward investors receive for the sacrifices they make and the risks they incur. Productive investments, however, require a prior accumulation of wealth and are only made by asset-owning classes. Efforts to redistribute income throughout a population weaken the incentive to invest and therefore reduce growth. This reasoning is consistent with the idea of an efficiency/equity trade-off, that is, the price of greater equality is a loss of efficiency. Less efficient economies, those that produce fewer goods and services with a given amount of labor and capital, enjoy fewer productivity gains and suffer slower growth, since low-productivity economies produce less with their resources.

Among the other approaches to economic development and inequality are Simon Kuznets' theory that as per capita income rises, inequality increases and then decreases. Growing income inequality occurs as people migrate out of agriculture and into industrial production, usually located in urban centers, giving rise to a growing income gap between agricultural workers, on the one hand, and industrial workers with higher earnings on the other. Industrial wages increase as development proceeds and as the demand for urban labor grows. Once industrial production is firmly established and the urban population stabilizes, inequalities diminish urbanization.

Research in the 1990s reversed the line of reasoning of Kuznets' theory. Instead of focusing on the impact of growth on income distribution, this research investigated the effects of inequality on growth. The results showed statistically significant relationships between inequality and growth. According to two reports, one by Alberto Alesina and Dani Rodrik and another by Torsten Persson and Guido Tabellini, countries with less inequality tend to grow faster. This finding contradicts the earlier idea of an efficiency/equity trade-off and could help explain differences in the growth experiences of developing countries. For example, in 1960 Argentina had a higher per capita income than Japan, but income inequality was much higher in Argentina. During the past forty years, however, the Japanese economy has consistently outperformed the Argentine economy. Such patterns of growth support the argument that less inequality contributes to relative success.

Theories of why inequality negatively affects growth have also been developed. One line of reasoning argues that in countries with highly unequal incomes and democratic political processes, there will be pressure to redistribute the income concentrated in relatively few households. Policies that tax the rich in order to transfer income through direct government grants—welfare programs—and provide services to the poor could discourage investment, according to Alesina and Rodrik. In contrast, Lorenzo Kristov, Peter Lindert, and Robert McClelland argue that in a situation of highly unequal income distribution, growth is negatively affected by the lack of social affinity for the poor and could lead to decreases in public investments in such services as health care and education that benefit low-income households. This lack of basic services or cutbacks in them for a large segment of the population could reduce growth since productivity would suffer in the face of pervasive health problems or a poorly educated workforce.

A second approach to explaining how inequality negatively affects growth focuses on access to credit. Low-income households generally have restricted access to credit because they are deemed to be high-risk borrowers. When income is unequally distributed, a large fraction of the population is unable to invest in educational or economic opportunities because of unequal access to credit markets. Such underinvestment can constrain growth, according to the research of Oded Galor and Joseph Zeira and of Ben Bernanke and Mark Gertler.

Another theory argues that unequal income distributions violate norms of fairness or justice to the extent that a high level of social and political conflict results. Studies by Alberto Alesina and Roberto Perotti and by Jakob Svensson contend that this type of conflict makes more difficult coordinating such productive activities as minimizing workplace disruptions and maintaining stable supplies of materials, increases uncertainty over the production process and profitability, and destabilizes important institutions, such as property rights, all of which could impede increased economic activity.

Taken together, these new growth theories provide important insights into the connections between income inequality and economic growth. Since closing the international income gap requires raising living standards in low-income countries relative to high-income countries, these new ideas have important implications for the global distribution of income. While recent trends point to an increasingly unequal distribution of income that could compromise economic development, more basic questions remain unanswered: Why should global inequality matter? As long as incomes are growing on average, why should anyone care about the distribution of income? What is a fair distribution of income?

Economist John Harsanyi and philosopher John Rawls have proposed similar ideas about fair income distribution. Suppose everyone, from the richest to the poorest, were faced with the prospect of swapping positions with another person in the world and the probability of selecting any particular person were the same across the population. Under these circumstances, what distribution of income would people freely choose? Rawls, in *A Theory of Justice,* argues that if people were unaware of the position they would occupy in society, and they could freely choose a set of rules governing income distribution, the principal of justice they would choose would be one that maximizes the welfare of the least advantaged. To see how Rawls' principal of justice works, consider a society in which everyone has an identical income. In this case, a person would only be allowed to occupy a privileged economic position if, by doing so, it improved the well-being of everyone else.

A narrow focus on income, however, can be misleading. Amartya Sen, a Nobel Prize–winning economist, suggests that an important goal is to improve individual opportunities and freedoms. A more equal distribution of income can be one means to this end. Sen, however, stresses that more income itself is not the ultimate goal, although it can improve such opportunities as access to education and life-prolonging health services (see Table 2). Similarly, many feminist economists, such as Nancy Folbre, argue that the emphasis on the market outcomes of wages and income misses important nonmarket sources of inequality, such as distribution of resources within a household.

Policies and Programs

At the UN Millennium Summit in September 2000, Secretary-General Kofi Annan pointed to the growing magnitude of global income inequality as a critical international concern (see Document 2). Annan called upon the countries of the world to halve the number of people living in the most extreme forms of poverty by the year 2015. Although such international declarations help call attention to the problem of increasing inequality, a well-developed, cooperative strategy to reduce poverty and inequality among the world's people has not yet materialized.

Traditionally, policies to reduce income inequalities exist mostly at the national level. Such policies have used a number of interrelated strategies: transferring income to disadvantaged citizens, creating social programs to help meet basic needs, and constructing a safety net to protect individuals who find themselves unemployed or in an economic emergency. *Welfare state* describes an integrated government strategy to protect the well-being of a nation's citizenry and employs these three types of policy mechanisms.

Welfare state policies are generally financed through a system of progressive taxation, in which high-income households pay a larger share of their earnings as taxes than do low-income households. A variety of social programs then transfers income or provides services to individuals and families. These programs include unemployment insurance, public pensions for the elderly, income subsidies and job programs for the disabled, child care services and grants to families raising children, health insurance, and the maintenance of a system of public education. In some countries, such programs are "means tested," that is, they are only available to individuals and families whose income fall below a certain level. An example of this would be Medicaid, the U.S. health insurance program for low-income families. In other countries, access to such programs is universal and does not depend on income. For example, Canada's policy of universal health care offers coverage to all.

During the final decades of the twentieth century, welfare state policies were progressively weakened. The process of globalization, the international character of production, and the rapid increase in financial mobility across borders placed constraints on government policies to redistribute income in developed and developing economies. Pressures to reduce taxes to avoid an outflow of investment or financial resources, for example, limited revenue available for welfare policies. Likewise, regulations that protected working people were seen as compromising competitiveness by raising labor costs. Many redistributive policies came to be viewed as wasteful, inefficient, or creating disincentives.

New forms of redistributive policies have emerged in response to the criticism of welfare state strategies. The redistribution of assets—such as land reform policies that break up large, concentrated holdings of land and promote a broader base of ownership or worker-ownership initiatives—has received attention for fostering egalitarian outcomes. For example, land reform in Taiwan has been credited with reducing within-country income inequality and improving economic growth. Likewise, programs that redistribute incomes in ways that enhance long-run productivity, such as investment in child care and education, are considered strategies. Better child care and improved educational opportunities can lead to a more productive labor force in the future, encouraging higher rates of growth and development. For example, according to Esther Duflo, in South Africa transfers of income have improved child health outcomes (see HEALTH and LITERACY EDUCATION).

Finally, policies that provide more equal access to economic resources, such as credit, can improve living standards (see DEVELOPMENT AID). Microcredit programs, which offer loans of small amounts of money to people who would otherwise be unable to borrow cash, have had a positive impact among rural women in several low-income communities. The most well known example of a successful microcredit program is the Grameen Bank in Bangladesh, which has improved economic opportunities in rural communities. Nevertheless, the ability of these often disjointed policies to counter overall trends toward greater inequality remains to be seen.

The World Bank and the International Monetary Fund have for decades shaped policies aimed at reducing global inequalities by improving economic performance in developing countries. Their market-oriented policies, which often include removing trade regulations, lowering government borrowing, privatizing government enterprises, and deregulating financial markets, have been dubbed the Washington consensus, because the headquarters of the World Bank and the IMF are located in Washington, D.C. Their strategies, however, have come under growing criticism in recent years. Critics argue that such policies have contributed to more global inequality rather than the stated goals of poverty reduction. They point out that Washington consensus policies focus almost exclusively on stabilization and economic growth without paying sufficient attention to the issues of poverty and inequality. For example, reducing government spending in order to achieve a more balanced budget might stabilize an economy from the point of view of investors, but it could also involve cutting important public programs. Likewise, liberalizing trade and investment could quickly integrate a country into the global economy, but it could also result in a loss of jobs and incomes for ordinary people. It is unclear what strategic shifts will be forthcoming in the future to tackle the growing gap between rich and poor.

Regional Summaries

North America

The United States and Canada enjoy some of the highest per capita incomes in the world. Furthermore, the growth rates of average income in the two countries have exceeded the world average over the past three decades. Between 1965 and 1999, per capita GDP grew at an annual rate of 2 percent in the United States and 1.9 percent in Canada.

Within-country income inequality is more pronounced in the United States than in Canada, although both countries have seen inequalities increase since the 1980s (see Case Study—The United States). According to *World Development Indicators, 2001,* the richest one-fifth of Canadians receive approximately 40 percent of all income, while the poorest one-fifth receive about 7.5 percent. In the United States the richest one-fifth receive about 49 percent, according to the U.S. Census Bureau, and the poorest one-fifth around 4 percent. More equality can lead to better social outcomes. Although the United States has a higher average income, the United Nations Development Programme (UNDP), in *Human Development Report, 2001,* ranks Canada above the United States in its human development index, which is a measure of well-being based on educational, health, and economic indicators.

Latin America

Over the past several decades, the development of Latin America and the Caribbean has been uneven. In most countries, periods of growth have been followed by years of crisis. On average, per capita GDP in Latin America increased at 1.4 percent per year from 1965 to 1999, a rate slightly below the world average according to *World Development Indicators, 2001.* Averages, however, hide the volatile nature of Latin American development.

Credit extended by industrialized countries in the second half of the 1970s led to a debt crisis throughout much of the region, which had serious consequences; average incomes stagnated or fell throughout much of the 1980s. In Brazil and Chile, authoritarian regimes that emerged in the 1970s and 1980s failed to manage economic policy in a way that would resolve economic crises and reduce inequalities. In the 1990s, serious financial crises in Argentina, Brazil, and Mexico threatened living standards throughout the region.

Latin America has, on average, the worst within-country income distributions in the world. Such widespread inequality has likely contributed to the region's political instability. In many countries, shifts toward market-oriented liberalization, such as reducing import restrictions, eliminating financial regulations, and limiting protections for workers without creating a social safety net

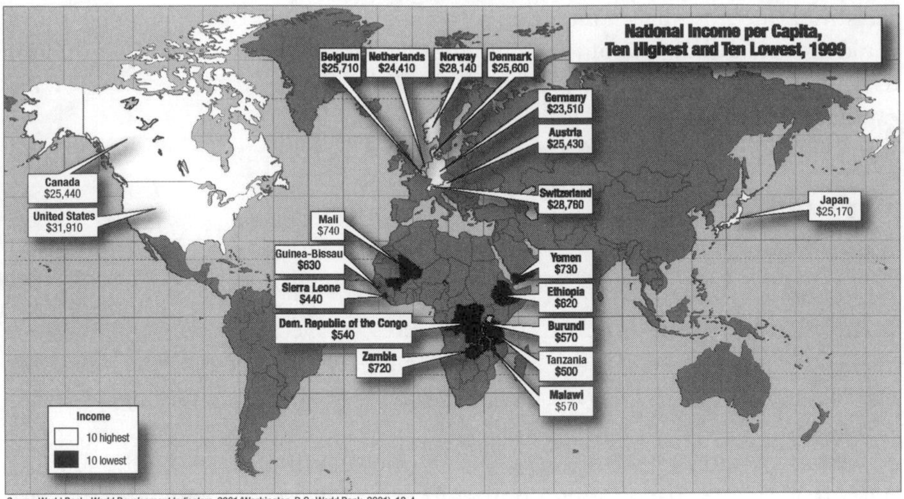

Source: World Bank, *World Development Indicators, 2001* (Washington, D.C.: World Bank, 2001), 12-4.
Note: Income figures are based on the purchasing power parity method of calculating comparable international income figures.

have been associated with worsening inequalities. The independent countries of the Caribbean generally have somewhat more equal income distributions but are often poorer than their Latin American counterparts.

Western Europe

The countries of Western Europe possess high average per capita incomes and a strong history of egalitarian policies. Because of their well-developed welfare states, the economies of Western Europe have some of the most equal income distributions in the industrialized world. In the years following World War II, the region enjoyed healthy rates of economic growth while maintaining low levels of inequality. Since the 1980s, however, slower economic growth and higher rates of long-term unemployment have emerged as significant problems.

The character of the welfare state differs across Western Europe. Not surprisingly, the Nordic countries, which have extensive welfare systems, have more equal income distributions than more liberalized, market-oriented economies, such as Great Britain's. Problems with poor economic performance and high levels of joblessness raise the question of whether traditional welfare-state policies are incompatible with the current pattern of globalization and the imperatives of international businesses for low-cost competitiveness.

Eastern Europe and Central Asia

Eastern Europe and Central Asia have experienced difficulties in the transition from centrally planned economies to more market-oriented systems. Average economic growth has been stagnant or negative since the late 1980s and early 1990s. The exceptions have been countries bordering Western Europe, including Hungary, Poland, and Slovenia. The countries of the Caucasus and Central Asia remain the poorest in the region. According to *World Development Indicators, 2001,* in 1999 the per capita GDP in Kazakhstan was $1,250; in Armenia $490; and in Tajikistan $280. In addition, the Balkan conflicts of the 1990s involving Serbia, Bosnia-Herzegovina, and other states of the former Yugoslavia were costly in terms of economic development and social stability in the region.

The countries of Eastern Europe and Central Asia possess a relatively equal distribution of income, despite poor economic performance. Less inequality likely contributes to the lower rates of infant mortality, the higher literacy rates, and the longer life expectancies in these countries compared to other countries in regions with similar levels of economic development. Recent data, however, suggest that within-country inequalities grew rapidly during the 1990s.

North Africa and the Middle East

Average growth rates of per capita income in the countries of North Africa and the Middle East have lagged behind world averages in recent decades, Egypt being a notable exception. *World Development Indicators, 2001* puts the average growth of per capita GDP in the region at just 0.1 percent a year between 1965 and 1999. Today most countries in the region possess middle-income economies—which, according to the World Bank, are those with an annual GNP per capita equivalent of more than $760 but less than $9,360 in 1998—roughly on par with countries in Latin America or Eastern Europe. Many of them remain dependent on extractive industries, such as mining and drilling for natural resources, most significantly, the petroleum industry.

The countries of North Africa and the Middle East generally have a more equal within-country distribution of income and a lower incidence of poverty compared to other countries at similar levels of development. Despite the prevalence of nondemocratic practices and political systems, several governments have maintained impressive levels of public assistance. For example, in Jordan transfer payments to women and elderly heads of households have helped reduce the degree of inequality.

Sub-Saharan Africa

The countries of sub-Saharan Africa are among the poorest in the world, and the average income of the region, relative to the rest of the world, has worsened in recent decades. Between 1965 and 1999 worldwide per capita GDP grew at an average annual rate of 1.6 percent, according to *World Development Indicators, 2001*; in sub-Saharan Africa per capita GDP dropped by 0.2 percent per year. Low incomes have taken their toll on human development; one-third of children under five are malnourished, and life expectancy in 1998 averaged forty-nine years for men and fifty-two for women.

Most African countries remained European colonies until the 1960s, and in some cases until the 1970s. In postcolonial Africa, many states experienced periods of political instability due to internal tensions and external conflicts, including cold war politics and in southern Africa efforts to sustain white minority rule. Decades of underdevelopment and social conflict have contributed to Africa's widespread poverty. The civil war in Mozambique that lasted from 1975 to 1992 left that country one of the poorest in Africa, with very low incomes, high rates of child mortality, and widespread poverty. With the end of the conflict and the establishment of democratic governance, however, Mozambique has enjoyed much more rapid rates of growth and development. While countries in Latin America and Asia have benefited from foreign investment in recent years, sub-Saharan Africa has been largely ignored. Currently the HIV/AIDS crisis in many places, including South Africa and Botswana, threatens to worsen the economic position of those hardest hit by the epidemic (see AIDS).

Within-country inequality can be extreme in sub-Saharan Africa. The legacy of apartheid in South Africa left that country with one of the most unequal income distributions in the world. Comparable statistics are incomplete, but current within-country inequality appears to be worse in southern Africa than in eastern or western Africa.

South Asia

Although the countries of South Asia have enjoyed good average rates of growth in recent decades, they remain some of the poorest in the world. Per capita GDP rose at an average annual rate of 2.4 percent from 1965 to 1999. In 1999, however, per capita GDP was just $370 in Bangladesh and $440 in India. On a purchasing power parity basis, average annual income for the entire region was equivalent to $2,110. Such poverty has real human costs. *World Development Indicators, 2001* reports that between 1993 and 1999, 47 percent of all children under age five in South Asia were malnourished.

Despite the fact that South Asia remains a poor region of the world, within-country income inequality is moderate. Among low-income regions of the world, the countries of South Asia have some of the most equal income distributions. The challenge facing the region is to raise average standards of living without adopting policies that will worsen existing inequalities by compromising social outcomes, such as improvements in health, education, and individual opportunities.

East Asia and the Pacific

Many of the countries of East Asia and the Pacific have enjoyed the fastest rates of economic growth in the world in recent decades. Moreover, rising within-country inequality generally did not accompany this rapid growth, although this has changed in the past few years. Between 1965 and 1999 the developing economies of East Asia grew at an average annual rate of 7.4 percent, with per capita GDP increasing by 5.6 percent each year, compared with the world average annual GDP growth rate of 3.3 percent and 1.6 percent growth in per capita GDP, according to *World Development Indicators, 2001.*

Several countries in East Asia—Indonesia, South Korea, and Taiwan, for example—achieved high rates of growth within the context of a relatively equal distribution of income. Many researchers have argued that prior redistributive policies, such as land reform, contributed to the region's success.

Globalization, however, has begun to pose significant challenges to the economic successes of East Asia. The financial crisis that began in 1997 drastically reduced economic growth. Furthermore, domestic currencies lost value, prices rose, and the standard of living of many households dropped. In addition to financial instability, longer-term trends of growing within-country income inequality, particularly wage inequality, have emerged, possibly as a result of the movement of production to poorer countries like Vietnam.

Data

Table 1 Within-Country Distribution of Income or Consumption in Selected Countries

Country and Year of Survey	Gini Coefficient	Share of the Poorest 10% of the Population (%)	Share of the Richest 10% of the Population (%)
North America			
Canada 1994	0.32	2.8	23.8
United States 1997	0.41	1.8	30.5
Latin America			
Brazil 1997	0.59	1.0	46.7
Chile 1996	0.58	1.4	46.9
Guatemala 1998	0.56	1.6	46.0
Western Europe			
France 1995	0.33	2.8	25.1
Germany 1994	0.30	3.3	23.7
Spain 1990	0.33	2.8	25.2
Sweden 1992	0.25	3.7	20.1
Switzerland 1992	0.33	2.6	25.2
United Kingdom 1991	0.36	2.6	27.3
Eastern Europe and Central Asia			
Georgia 1996	0.37	2.3	27.9
Russian Federation 1998	0.49	1.7	38.7
Uzbekistan 1993	0.33	3.1	25.2
Middle East and North Africa			
Algeria 1995	0.35	2.8	26.8
Egypt 1995	0.29	4.4	25.0
Israel 1992	0.36	2.8	26.9
Jordan 1997	0.36	3.3	29.8
Turkey 1994	0.42	2.3	32.3
Sub-Saharan Africa			
Nigeria 1996/1997	0.51	1.6	40.8
South Africa 1993/1994	0.59	1.1	45.9
Uganda 1996	0.37	3.0	29.8
South Asia			
India 1997	0.38	3.5	33.5
East Asia and the Pacific			
Australia 1994	0.35	2.0	25.4
China 1998	0.40	2.4	30.4
Indonesia 1999	0.32	4.0	26.7
Japan 1993	0.25	4.8	21.7
Thailand 1998	0.41	2.8	32.4

Source: World Bank, *World Development Indicators, 2001* (Washington, D.C.: World Bank, 2001), table 2.8.
Note: Gini coefficients range from 0, perfect equality, to 1, perfect inequality.

Table 2 Average Income, Income Distribution, Infant Mortality, and Life Expectancy, Selected Comparisons

Country	Average Gross Income per Person on a Purchasing Power Parity Basis (1999)	Income Share of the Poorest 20% of the Population[a]	Income Share of the Richest 20% of the Population[a]	Infant Mortality Rate per 1,000 Live Births (1999)	Life Expectancy For Men and Women (1998)
	Case A Countries with similar within-country income distributions but different average incomes: higher incomes associated with better human development outcomes				
Costa Rica	$7,880	4.5	51	14	M: 74 W: 79
Kenya	$1,010	5.0	50.2	118	M: 50 W: 52
	Case B Countries with similar average incomes but different within-country distributions: greater equality associated with better human development outcomes				
Brazil	$6,840	2.6	63.0	32	M: 63 W: 71
Lithuania	$6,490	7.8	40.3	12	M: 67 W: 77
	Case C Countries with similar human development outcomes: greater equality can compensate for lower average incomes				
United States	$31,910	5.2	46.4	8	M: 74 W: 80
Slovenia	$16,050	9.1	37.7	5	M: 71 W: 79

Source: World Development Indicators, 2001 (Washington, D.C.: World Bank, 2001), tables 1.1, 1.2, and 2.8; and World Bank, *World Development Report,* 2000–2001 (Washington D.C.: World Bank, 2001), Table 2.

[a] Most recent data available.

Table 3 Average Annual Growth Rates of per Capita Gross National Product by Region

Region	Rate % 1970–1990	Rate % 1990–1998
Latin America	0.1	1.9
Eastern Europe and Central Asia	N.A.	–4.3
North Africa and the Middle East	0.1	0.5
Sub-Saharan Africa	–0.9	–0.4
East Asia	7.1	7.1
South Asia	1.6	3.6
Southeast Asia and the Pacific	3.4	4.3
All developing countries	1.7	3.3
High-income countries	2.2	1.6

Source: United Nations Development Programme, *Human Development Report, 2000* (New York and Oxford: Oxford University Press, 2001), table 13.

Note: Gross domestic product (GDP) and gross national product (GNP) are measures of economic activity. GDP is a measure of the total market value of goods and services produced within a particular country, and GNP is a measure of the total value of goods and services produced by residents of a country regardless of where production occurs.

Case Study—The United States

Although average incomes in the United States, which has the largest economy in the world, rank among the highest anywhere, income distribution remains the most unequal of any industrialized country. The degree of income inequality has steadily worsened since the mid-1970s, and by the end of the 1990s it had reached its highest level in more than three decades.

While income distribution has became more unequal since the 1970s, the U.S. economy grew on average, suggesting that an unequal income distribution was the price to be paid for economic expansion. This argument cannot, however, explain the trends of the 1950s and 1960s. During these decades, the United States experienced some of the highest average growth rates of the post-World War II period while the distribution of income remained virtually unchanged.

One of the factors contributing to this growth in inequality is a widening gap between the wages of the lowest-paid and the highest-paid jobs. Researchers have suggested that technological changes and competition from low-wage imports caused the growth in the wage gap. Economist James Galbraith argues, however, that the erosion since the mid-1970s of public policies that supported a middle-class society is primarily responsible. These changes include a fall in the real value of the minimum wage (that is, the minimum wage adjusted for changes in the prices of goods and services), growing job insecurity, and a shift in macroeconomic policy. Beginning in the 1980s, macroeconomic policies emphasized controlling inflation instead of reducing unemployment.

Why is inequality more pronounced in the United States than in other industrialized countries? A less progressive tax system and a smaller social safety net are part of the explanation. The maximum tax rate is lower and the top tax bracket is higher in the United States than in other industrialized countries, including Germany, Italy, and Japan, and public support for families with children and unemployment benefits are less generous than in many European countries, including France and Sweden. Other factors include large inequalities in educational financing and few protections for low-wage workers. In addition, persistently lower incomes for African American, Latino, and Native American families reinforce existing social stratifications.

Unequal distribution of wealth in the United States also contributes to income inequality, since those who have access to wealth generally enjoy higher incomes. The U.S. Census Bureau reports that in 1997 the richest 10 percent of U.S. households owned 83 percent of the country's financial wealth. The rapid increases in U.S. stock prices during the 1990s greatly increased the value of this wealth, widening the economic distance between U.S. citizens still further.

Case Study—Kerala, India

The state of Kerala is located on the southwestern coast of India. Kerala's population numbers about 30 million people. Although this is relatively small by Indian standards, the state's population exceeds that of Canada and Sweden. Kerala's economy has traditionally depended on agriculture, spices, and fisheries, but numerous manufacturing industries also operate in the region.

Kerala is income poor by global standards, and the state's per capita income is not markedly different from the rest of India. What is remarkable about the region is its high level of social development. Its literacy rate, average life expectancy, and infant mortality rates are on par with most high-income, industrialized countries. Adult literacy exceeds 90 percent, and infant mortality is around 13 deaths per 1,000 live births, compared with all of India, which has an average literacy rate of between 50 and 70 percent, and an infant mortality rate of 71 deaths per 1,000 births. The life expectancy of men living in Kerala exceeds the life expectancy of African American men living in the United States.

How does Kerala do it? Most analysts point to a tradition of democratic redistribution that sustains relatively egalitarian social outcomes, although Kerala's egalitarian policies might have come at the expense of economic growth. The redistributive policies include land reform (reducing inequalities in land ownership and evictions), school and nursery lunch programs, emergency food stores, pensions for farm workers, and increased educational opportunities. Furthermore, Kerala has a tradition of encouraging community and worker engagement in the development of the state's economic policies. Taken together, the development strategies of Kerala have dramatically reduced inequality and improved human development.

While Kerala's policies of emphasizing redistribution have produced remarkable successes, there are potential problems. The economic growth rate, although positive on average, has lagged behind the average for India as a whole. Unemployment is about three times the average for India and remains a serious problem. Some people—for example, members of the fishing community—may have fallen through the cracks of Kerala's development strategy. Finally, recent policies, such as trade liberalization, threaten domestic economic activities, as cheap imports displace traditional, local producers. Nevertheless, Kerala remains a remarkable example of how redistributive strategies can dramatically improve social outcomes, even within the context of increasing globalization.

Biographical Sketches

Barbara Bergmann has made substantial contributions to research in the area of gender inequalities in income and earnings. Her research into the economic impact of gender roles on economic outcomes helped lay the foundation for subsequent work in the field.

François Bourguignon examines the macroeconomic foundations of the distribution of income. In particular, he examines the relationships between inequality, growth, and development. In addition, Bourguignon has written, with Anthony Atkinson, on the measurement of inequality.

Samuel Bowles and **Herbert Gintis** are economists and frequent collaborators on intellectual projects. Recently their work has included a reexamination of the supposed trade-off between efficiency and equity and a demonstration of how certain redistributive policies, such as asset redistribution, can be efficiency enhancing.

William Darity has examined inequalities in the distribution of income and earnings across different racial and ethnic groups. While he has written extensively on racial inequalities in the United States, he has also produced comparative studies of racial and ethnic inequalities in different countries.

James K. Galbraith has studied patterns of wage inequality as an important determinant of income inequality more generally. Not only has Galbraith analyzed the institutional factors behind shifts in wage inequality, he has also compiled a substantial database on U.S. wage differentials and global inequality.

John Rawls is a political philosopher who has written extensively on economic justice. He emphasizes the need to address individual liberty and material well-being. He has argued that a criterion for a just income distribution would be the distribution people would freely choose if they were ignorant of what their future socioeconomic position in society would be.

Directory

Drop the Debt, P.O. Box 5555, London SE1 0WG, United Kingdom. Telephone: (44) 20 7922 1111, Email: mail@dropthedebt.ord, Web: http://www.dropthedebt.org
Organization working for debt relief for heavily indebted developing countries

International Labour Organization, 4 Route des Morillons, 1211 Geneva 22, Switzerland. Telephone: (41) 22 799 6111, Email: ilo@ilo.org, Web: http://www.ilo.org
UN agency responsible for global human and labor rights

International Monetary Fund, 700 19th Street NW, Washington, DC 20431. Telephone: (202) 623-7000, Email: publicaffairs@imf.org, Web: http://www.imf.org
Global financial institution focusing on international financial stability

Jubilee Plus, New Economics Foundation, Cinnamon House, 6-8 Cole Street, London SE1 4YH, United Kingdom. Telephone: (44) 207 407 7447, Email: info.jubilee@neweconomics.org, Web: http://www.jubilee2000uk.org
Organization working in the area of debt relief for heavily indebted developing countries

Luxembourg Income Study, 44 Rue Emile Mark, P.O. Box 48, Differdange 4501, Luxembourg. Telephone: (352) 58 58 55 518, Email: caroline@lissy.ceps.lu, Web: http://lisweb.ceps.lu
Research organization that collects and analyzes income survey data

Oxfam International, Oxfam International Secretariat, 266 Banbury Road, Suite 20, Oxford OX2 7DL, United Kingdom. Telephone: (44) 1865 31 39 39, Email: information@oxfaminternational.org, Web: http://www.oxfam.org
Confederation of organization's specializing in global poverty

Political Economy Research Institute, Department of Economics, University of Massachusetts, Amherst, MA 01003. Telephone: (413) 545-6355, Web: http://www.umass.edu/peri
Research institute specializing in globalization, development, and labor markets

Society for International Development, 207 Via Panisperna, 00184 Rome, Italy. Telephone: (39) 064872172, Email: info@sidint.org, Web: http://www.sidint.org
Organization working on issues of sustainable development and poverty elimination

United Nations Development Program, 1 United Nations Plaza, New York, NY 10017. Telephone: (212) 906-5295, Email: aboutundp@undp.org, Web: http://www.undp.org
Agency responsible for human development and poverty programs

University of Texas Inequality Project, c/o James Galbraith, LBJ School of Public Affairs, University of Texas, Austin, TX 78713-8925. Telephone: (512) 471-1244, Email: galbraith@mail.utexas.edu, Web: http://utip.gov.utexas.edu
Research institute specializing in measuring and explaining changes in inequality

World Bank, 1818 H Street, NW, Washington, DC 20433. Telephone: (202) 477-1234, Email: askus@worldbank.org, Web: http://www.worldbank.org
Global financial institution specializing in development loans and research

World Institute for Development Economics Research, 6 B Katajanokanlaituri, 00160, Helsinki, Finland. Telephone: (358) 9 6159911, Email: wider@wider.unu.edu, Web: http://www.wider.unu.edu
Division of the United Nations University responsible for development and inequality research

Further Research

Books

Atkinson, Anthony B., and François Bourguignon, eds. *Handbook of Income Distribution*. Amsterdam: Elsevier Science, 2000.

Bowles, Samuel, and Herbert Gintis. *Recasting Egalitarianism*. Edited by Eric Olin Wright. New York and London: Verso, 1998.
Folbre, Nancy. *The Invisible Heart: Economics and Family Values*. New York: New Press, 2001.
Galbraith, James K. *Created Unequal: The Crisis in American Pay*. New York: Free Press, 1998.
Green, Philip. *Equality and Democracy*. New York: New Press, 1998.
Parayil, Govindan, ed. *Kerala: The Development Experience*. London: Zed Books, 2000.
Prakash, B. A., ed. *Kerala's Economic Development*. New Delhi and London: Sage Publications, 1999.
Rawls, John. *A Theory of Justice*. Cambridge, Mass.: Belknap, 1971.
Sen, Amartya. *Development as Freedom*. New York: Anchor Books, 1999.

Articles and Reports

Ahuja, V., B. Bidani, F. Ferreira, and M. Walton. *Everybody's Miracle? Revisiting Poverty and Inequality in East Asia*. Washington, D.C.: World Bank, 1997.
Alesina, Alberto, and Roberto Perotti. "Income Distribution, Political Instability, and Investment." *European Economic Review* 40 (1996): 1203–1228.
Alesina, Alberto, and Dani Rodrik. "Distributive Politics and Economic Growth." *Quarterly Journal of Economics* 109 (1994): 465–490.
Bernanke, Ben, and Mark Gertler. "Financial Fragility and Economic Performance." *Quarterly Journal of Economics* 105 (1990): 88–114.
Chotikapanich, Duangkamon, and D. S. Prasada Rao. "Inequality in Asia, 1975–1990: A Decomposition Analysis." *Asia Pacific Journal of Economics and Business* 2 (1998): 63–78.
Council of Economic Advisers. *Changing America: Indicators of Social and Economic Well-Being by Race and Hispanic Origin*. Washington, D.C.: Council of Economic Advisers for the President's Initiative on Race, 1998.
Duflo, Esther. "Child Health and Household Resources in South Africa: Evidence from the Old Age Pension Program." *American Economic Review* 90 (2000): 15–62.
Galor, Oded, and Joseph Zeira. "Income Distribution and Macroeconomics." *Review of Economic Studies* 60 (1993): 35–52.
Gottschalk, P., and T. M. Smeeding. "Empirical Evidence on Income Inequality in Industrial Countries." In *Handbook of Income Distribution,* edited by Anthony B. Atkinson and François Bourguignon, 261–307. Amsterdam: Elsevier Science, 2000.
Harsanyi, John C. "Cardinal Utility in Welfare Economics and in the Theory of Risk-Taking." *Journal of Political Economy* 61 (1953): 434–435.
Kanbur, Ravi. "Income Distribution and Development." In *Handbook of Income Distribution,* edited by Anthony B. Atkinson and François Bourguignon, 791–841. Amsterdam: Elsevier Science, 2000.
Kristov, Lorenzo, Peter Lindert, and Robert McClelland. "Pressure Groups and Redistribution." *Journal of Public Economics* 48 (1992): 135–163.
Kuznets, Simon. "Economic Growth and Income Inequality." *American Economic Review* 45 (1955): 1–28.
Lindert, P. H. "Three Centuries of Inequality in Britain and America." In *Handbook of Income Distribution,* edited by Anthony B. Atkinson and François Bourguignon, 167–216. Amsterdam: Elsevier Science, 2000.
Morrison, Christian. "Historical Perspectives on Income Distribution: The Case of

Europe." In *Handbook of Income Distribution,* edited by Anthony B. Atkinson and François Bourguignon, 217–260. Amsterdam: Elsevier Science, 2000.

Persson, Torsten, and Guido Tabellini. "Is Inequality Harmful for Growth?" *American Economic Review* 84 (1994): 600–621.

Pollin, Robert. "Can Domestic Expansionary Policy Succeed in a Globally Integrated Environment? An Examination of Alternatives." In *Globalization and Progressive Economic Policy,* edited by D. Baker, G. Esptein, and R. Pollin, 433–460. Cambridge: Cambridge University Press, 1998.

Rueda, David, and Jonas Pontusson. "Wage Inequality and Varieties of Capitalism." *World Politics* 52 (2000): 350–383.

Svensson, Jakob. "Investment, Property Rights, and Political Instability: Theory and Evidence." *European Economic Review* 42 (1998): 1317–1341.

United Nations Development Programme. *Human Development Report, 2001.* New York and Oxford: Oxford University Press, 2001.

U.S. Census Bureau. *The Changing Shape of the Nation's Income Distribution, 1947–1998.* Current Population Reports P60-204. Washington, D.C., June 2000.

———. *Money Income in the United States.* Current Population Report P60-209. Washington, D.C., September 2000.

Veron, René. "The 'New' Kerala Model: Lessons for Sustainable Development." *World Development* 29 (April 2001).

Wade, Robert. "Winners and Losers." *Economist,* 28 April 2001, 72–74.

Wolff, Edward. "Recent Trends in the Size Distribution of Household Wealth." *Journal of Economic Perspectives* 12 (1998): 131–150.

Wood, Adrian. "Wage Inequality in Developing Countries: The Latin American Challenge to East Asian Conventional Wisdom." *World Bank Economic Review* 11 (January 1997): 33–57.

World Bank. *World Development Indicators, 2001.* Washington, D.C.: World Bank, 2001.

———. *World Development Report, 2000–2001.* New York and Oxford: Oxford University Press, 2000.

Web Sites

Luxembourg Income Study
http://www.lisweb.ceps.lu

University of Texas Inequality Project
http://www.utip.gov.utexas.edu

U.S. Bureau of Labor Statistics Links
http://www.stat.bls.gov/oreother.htm?Lnav

U.S. Census Bureau
http://www.census.gov

WIDER World Income Inequality Database
http://www.wider.unu.edu/wiid/wiid.htm

Documents

1. Globalization and Its Impact on the Full Enjoyment of All Human Rights

United Nations General Assembly, Resolution 55/102, 2 March 2001

The full text is available at http://www.un.org/documents/ga/res/55/a55r102.pdf.

Extract

The U.N. General Assembly,

Guided by the purposes and principles of the Charter of the United Nations . . .

1. *Recognizes* that, while globalization, by its impact on, inter alia, the role of the Sate, may affect human rights, the promotion and protection of all human rights is first and foremost the responsibility of the State;

2. *Reaffirms* that narrowing the gap between rich and poor, both within and between countries, is an explicit goal at the national and international levels, as part of the effort to create an enabling environment for the full enjoyment of all human rights;

3. *Reaffirms also* the commitment to create an environment at both the national and global levels that is conducive to development and to the elimination of poverty through, inter alia, good governance within each country and at the international level, transparency in the financial, monetary and trading systems and commitment to an open, equitable, rule-based, predictable and non-discriminatory multilateral trading and financial system;

4. *Recognizes* that, while globalization offers great opportunities, its benefits are very unevenly shared and its costs are unevenly distributed, an aspect of the process that affects the full enjoyment of all human rights, in particular in developing countries;

5. *Recognizes also* that, only through broad and sustained efforts, including policies and measures at the global level to create a shared future based upon our common humanity in all its diversity, can globalization be made fully inclusive and equitable and have a human face, thus contributing to the full enjoyment of all human rights;

6. *Affirms* that globalization is a complex process of structural transformation, with numerous interdisciplinary aspects, which has an impact on the enjoyment of civil, political, economic, social and cultural rights, including the right to development;

7. *Affirms also* that the international community should strive to respond to the challenges and opportunities posed by globalization in a manner that ensures respect for the cultural diversity of all;

8. *Underlines* therefore the need to continue to analy[z]e the consequences of globalization for the full enjoyment of all human rights.

2. We the Peoples: The Role of the United Nations in the 21st Century

Kofi A. Annan, report of the UN secretary-general to the Millennium Assembly, September 2000

The full text is available at www.un.org/millennium/sg/report.

Extract

While more of us enjoy better standards of living than ever before, many others remain desperately poor. Nearly half the world's population still has to make do on less than $2 per day. Approximately 1.2 billion people—500 million in South Asia and 300 million in Africa—struggle on less than $1. . . . People living in Africa south of the Sahara are almost as poor today as they were 20 years ago. With that kind of deprivation comes pain, powerlessness, despair and lack of fundamental freedom—all of which, in turn, perpetuate poverty. Of a total world [labor] force of some 3 billion, 140 million workers are out of work altogether, and a quarter to a third are underemployed.

The persistence of income inequality over the past decade is also troubling. Globally, the 1 billion people living in developed countries earn 60 percent of the world's income, while the 3.5 billion people in low-income countries earn less than 20 percent. Many countries have experienced growing internal inequality, including some of those in transition from communism. In the developing world, income gaps are most pronounced in Latin America, followed closely by sub-Saharan Africa.

Extreme poverty is an affront to our common humanity. It also makes many other problems worse. For example, poor countries—especially those with significant inequality between ethnic and religious communities—are far more likely to be embroiled in conflicts than rich ones. Most of these conflicts are internal, but they almost invariably create problems for neighbours or generate a need for humanitarian assistance.

Moreover, poor countries often lack the capacity and resources to implement environmentally sound policies. This undermines the sustainability of their people's meager existence, and compounds the effects of their poverty.

Unless we redouble and concert our efforts, poverty and inequality may get worse still. World population recently reached 6 billion. It took only 12 years to add the last billion, the shortest such span in history. By 2025, we can expect a further 2 billion—almost all in developing countries, and most of them in the poorest. . . . We must act now.

I call on the international community at the highest level—the Heads of State and Government convened at the Millennium Summit—to adopt the target of halving the proportion of people living in extreme poverty, and so lifting more than 1 billion people out of it, by 2015. I further urge that no effort be spared to reach this target by that date in every region, and in every country.

History will judge political leaders in the developing countries by what they did to eradicate the extreme poverty of their people—by whether they enabled their people to board the train of a transforming global economy, and made sure that everyone had at least standing room, if not a comfortable seat. By the same token, history will judge the rest of us by what we did to help the world's poor board that train in good order.

INTERNATIONAL CRIMINAL JUSTICE

Eric Stover

At the dawn of the new millennium, the international community has demonstrated a renewed commitment to the pursuit of international criminal justice. More than one hundred thirty countries have signed the Rome Statute of the International Criminal Court (ICC), and as of 1 October 2001 thirty-seven countries had ratified it (see map, p. 373 and Document 1). At the end of 2001 two ad hoc international criminal tribunals sat in judgment for war crimes and genocides committed in Rwanda and the former Yugoslavia (see GENOCIDE and WAR CRIMES). Efforts to pursue justice for international crimes in domestic courts also gained momentum. In June 2001 a Belgian court convicted and sentenced two Rwandan women, both Roman Catholic nuns, to up to fifteen years in prison for their complicity in the 1994 Rwandan genocide. In 1998 a Spanish court had tried unsuccessfully to extradite General Augusto Pinochet from Great Britain to stand trial for human rights violations allegedly committed in Chile in the 1970s while he was head of state. An Argentine court in 2001 made a similar effort. At issue concerning the growing emphasis on international justice is whether such attempts at universal legal accountability will help make the twenty-first century less bloody than the twentieth.

Historical Background and Development

The first international trial for war crimes took place in Breisach, Germany, in 1474, when twenty-seven judges of the Holy Roman Empire ruled that Peter van Hagenback had violated the "laws of God and man" by allowing his troops to rape, murder, and pillage. The court sentenced him to death. Hagenback's conviction underscored one of the defining ideas of civilized society since antiquity: even in war unnecessary suffering inflicted on civilians is strictly forbidden. It was not until the nineteenth century, however, that formal international agreements embodying this principle were accepted and ratified by governments.

The codification of the "laws of war" date back to the mid-1800s, when several countries established internal codes of conduct. U.S. president Abraham

Lincoln, for example, authorized the War Department to promulgate guidelines—the Lieber Code—consisting of 159 articles, to govern the conduct of the army during the Civil War. The first international agreement on the laws of war, the Convention for the Amelioration of the Condition of the Wounded in Armies in the Field, was signed by twelve European governments in Geneva in 1864. Thirty-five years later, in 1899, the Convention with Respect to the Laws and the Customs of War on Land was adopted at The Hague, codifying generally accepted principles of customary international law, promulgating, among other things, the protection of civilians and civilian institutions, such as hospitals and churches.

The world's second attempt at prosecuting war crimes followed World War I, but the effort was abandoned as the Allies feared that the search for justice would look like victor's revenge and shatter Germany's chances of making an orderly postwar transition to democracy. On 20 November 1945, a little more than six months after the end of World War II, the trial of the Major War Criminals of the European Axis before the International Military Tribunal, now known as the Nuremberg trials, took place (see Document 2 and WAR CRIMES). Among the twenty-two high-ranking Nazis who stood trial were Hitler's successor, Hermann Goering, and deputy Rudolf Hess and foreign policy adviser Joachim von Ribbentrop. Allied armies were instrumental in capturing suspects and retrieving evidence from buildings previously under the control of the Nazi regime. Three defendants were acquitted; seven were sentenced to ten years to life; and twelve were sentenced to hang.

In Tokyo between May and November 1946, the International Military Tribunal for the Far East prosecuted twenty-eight Japanese military and civilian leaders for war crimes. The tribunal's charter was influenced by the Nuremberg trials, but significant differences affected the outcomes in Tokyo. For instance, while the judges of the Nuremberg Tribunal were from the four major Allied powers, judges from thirteen nations sat on the Far East tribunal, resulting in less than unanimous decisions concerning sentencing and other matters.

In the wake of World War II, one might think that nations would have had an interest in suppressing massive violations of human rights because of their possible threat to world peace. In a world largely divided into communist and noncommunist camps, however, the Chinese, Soviet, and U.S. governments, claiming national and regional security interests, promoted and maintained authoritarian governments no matter how abusive they were of their citizens. It was only in 1991 that the idea of punishing war criminals resurfaced.

After Iraq's invasion of Kuwait, U.S. president George Bush and British prime minister Margaret Thatcher called for a UN tribunal to try Iraqi leader Saddam Hussein and Iraqi military officers for crimes committed during the invasion. The political will of European and U.S. leaders soon faded. During the 1980s the West had provided massive aid to Hussein, whose government had served as a counterweight to the anti-Western Islamic Republic of Iran. While supplying Iraq with financial assistance and weaponry, the West turned a blind eye to the generally repressive nature of Hussein's government in addition to such extraordinary acts as the use of chemical weapons against Kurdish citizens. For some Western leaders, the idea that this hypocrisy would surface in an international trial was reason enough to dampen their pursuit of the Iraqi leader.

A half century after the Nuremberg and Tokyo trials, the United Nations breathed new life into the pursuit of international criminal justice when it created the International Criminal Tribunal for the Former Yugoslavia at The Hague in May 1993 to investigate alleged war crimes committed during the wars there following the disintegration of the Yugoslav state. After a Hutu-led slaughter claimed the lives of hundreds of thousands of people between April and July 1994 in Rwanda, the UN Security Council established the International Criminal Tribunal for Rwanda in Arusha, Tanzania, in November 1994 to prosecute war crimes and acts of genocide.

These ad hoc UN tribunals emerged in far less propitious circumstances than their predecessors following World War II. The Yugoslav and Rwandan tribunals, in contrast to those following World War II, do not have political or military authority over the territory in which the alleged war crimes were committed, and they do not have police powers to arrest suspects. Instead, they have had to rely on the goodwill of national governments, UN member states, and regional organizations, such as the North Atlantic Treaty Organization (NATO), to locate and arrest suspected war criminals. Governments, with a few exceptions, initially hindered the tribunal's investigative work by failing to provide adequate funding and intelligence information. They were also unwilling to risk the safety of their troops by removing land mines and guarding suspected mass gravesites, let alone arrest indicted war criminals. Some of these problems—inherent in the ad hoc status of these tribunals—were addressed on 25 November 1992, when the UN General Assembly adopted a resolution calling on the International Law Commission to draft a statute for a permanent international criminal court.

Current Status

International criminal tribunals derive their authority from the notion that certain crimes—genocide, crimes against humanity, and war crimes—concern the entire international community and consequently should be subject to universal jurisdiction. Inherent in the notion of relinquishing sovereignty to an international criminal court is the conviction that certain crimes are so abominable that they violate not only the individual victims but also all of humanity. These crimes are defined under international law as deportation, extermination, enslavement, mass murder, and other inhumane acts committed against any civilian population, before or during a war, or persecutions on political, racial, or religious grounds. Those who commit such crimes are to be considered *hostis humani generis,* enemies of all humankind, over which all governments shall have jurisdiction.

International criminal justice has at least three distinct levels or applications. On the international level, ad hoc tribunals—and eventually the permanent International Criminal Court—convened under the authority of the UN

Security Council, will pursue war criminals across borders. In bilateral situations, extradition procedures can be invoked when alleged perpetrators travel or live abroad; extradition provisions in international criminal law treaties and the growing authority of the principle of universal jurisdiction allow states to apprehend and try individuals of serious international crimes. Finally, foreign courts may also obtain civil jurisdiction over defendants charged with international crimes when lawyers for the victims file for damages. In the United States, for instance, the Alien Tort Claims Act and Torture Victim Protection Act allow civil damage suits against foreign defendants for torture, summary execution, and other "torts in violation of the law of nations."

Research

The Yugoslav and Rwanda tribunals and movement toward the International Criminal Court has spawned a growing body of research and debate among legal scholars, political theorists, and social scientists about the efficacy of international criminal tribunals and their objectives. So-called realists, such as former U.S. secretary of state Henry Kissinger, oppose such courts because they believe that governments, and by extension diplomats, might be shackled by the overextension of international law. They have long regarded the pursuit of international justice as a potentially dangerous extravagance that could threaten peace and international stability and jeopardize U.S. national security interests. The realists fear that, as the international community turns increasingly to international criminal courts to solve what are inherently issues of state politics and diplomacy, it runs the "risk of substituting the tyranny of judges for that of governments," to quote Kissinger from "The Pitfalls of Universal Jurisdiction: Risking Judicial Tyranny." From the realists' perspective, war crimes tribunals are nothing more than the crude application of state power, something the victors who decisively win a war inflict on the defeated.

Proponents of international criminal courts argue that without justice there can be no enduring peace following conflict. They consider the tribunals for Rwanda and the former Yugoslavia, in the words of human rights activist Aryeh Neier in *War Crimes: Brutality, Genocide, Terror, and the Struggle for Justice,* "the most dramatic innovations in international law to protect human rights in half a century." Justice and international order, Neier argues in the same work, are best served through "the disclosure and acknowledgment of abuses, the purging of those responsible from public office, and the prosecution and punishment of those who commit crimes against humanity." The Yugoslav tribunal, in its 1994 annual report, states that its work is essential to peace and security in the former Yugoslavia: "[I]t would be wrong to assume that the Tribunal is based on the old maxim *fiat justitia et pereat mundus* (let justice be done, even if the world were to perish). The Tribunal is, rather, based on the maxim propounded by German philosopher Georg Hegel in 1821: *fiat justitia ne pereat mundus* 'let justice be done lest the world should perish.'"

Liberal law theorists and human rights activists argue that justice, like the pursuit of rights, is a universal, historic practice that exists above politics (see HUMAN RIGHTS). Thus, justice can moderate desires for revenge and foster respect for democratic institutions by demonstrating that no individual—whether a foot soldier or high government official—is above the law. Insofar as legal proceedings confer legitimacy on otherwise contestable facts, trials make it more difficult for individuals and societies to take refuge in denial and avoid the truth. Criminal trials, even of a few arch criminals, followed by convictions and appropriate punishment, constitute an acknowledgment of the suffering inflicted on the victims. Some liberal legal theorists, including Mark Osiel, view trials as a moral pedagogy. They contend that international tribunals, through their ability to distinguish between proper and improper conduct, can help postwar societies foster tolerance and reconciliation, forge a "shared truth" of past events, and reshape national identities.

The Nuremberg trials introduced the concept that individuals—and not society as a whole—should be held accountable for crimes committed in war. Thus, one function of an international postwar trial of government leaders is to differentiate between the criminal leaders of a nation and their deceived populations. "Crimes against international law," the Nuremberg Tribunal states in its judgment, "are committed by men, not by abstract entities, and only by punishing individuals who commit such crimes can the provision of international law be enforced." For public attitudes to shift in postwar societies, writes political scientist Gary Jonathan Bass in *Stay the Hand of Vengeance: The Politics of War Crimes Tribunals,* "criminal leaders must be tried—their aura of mystery shattered by showing their weaknesses and stupidities, and their prestige deflated by the humiliation of standing in the dock." Bass warns, however, that tribunal justice "is inevitably symbolic: a few war criminals stand for a much larger group of guilty individuals. Thus, what is billed as individual justice actually becomes a de facto way of exonerating many of the guilty."

Some social scientists take issue with the sweeping claims—or what historian Michael Ignatief calls articles of faith—made by international lawyers and human rights activists about the virtues of international criminal justice. They contend that such high-flown rhetoric fails to recognize that courts, like all institutions, exist because of, and not in spite of, politics. People and entire communities can interpret a tribunal's decisions, procedures (modes and manner of investigation, selection of cases, timing of trials, types and severity of punishments), and even its very existence in a variety of ways. Even the idea that war crimes tribunals will individualize guilt is fraught with ambiguity, especially in the wake of a genocide like in Rwanda, where so many people planned and carried out the killing and where so much of the violence was localized, pitting community against community, neighbor against neighbor.

The reality is that ad hoc international tribunals have limited mandates and resources, restricted powers of subpoena, and no authority to make arrests. With such limitations, they can never come close to meting out justice to all war criminals. The logic of law, as the social critic Hannah Arendt warns, can never make sense of the logic of atrocity or how it is interpreted by survivors and perpetrators. The picture that emerges from strictly legal interpretations of wartime atrocities, especially when they are committed by all sides to a conflict, often can be skewed. While victims and their communities may feel some measure of vindication from international trials, the communities from which the perpetrators came may feel as if they have been made the scapegoats.

"[A]lthough most people have a sense that prosecuting war criminals is a morally good thing to do," writes Bass in *Stay the Hand of Vengeance,* "there is no reliable proof that so doing will always have good results." In fact, there is a paucity of research on the role, whether good or bad, that international justice plays in communities torn asunder by genocide and ethnic violence. Without systematic empirical studies of the effects that international criminal courts have had on postwar communities, says Bass, "we are left with only our scruples and our hunches." In 2000 researchers from the University of California, Berkeley, in collaboration with universities and research institutes in Rwanda and the former Yugoslavia, launched a study to examine how communities in these countries perceive and interpret the work of the international war crimes tribunals. Their findings will be published in 2003.

Policies and Programs

The move to create an International Criminal Court is, in the words delivered by UN secretary-general Kofi Annan at the ceremony celebrating the adoption of the court, "a giant step forward in the march towards universal human rights and the rule of law." The treaty establishing the court was agreed to in Rome on 17 July 1998, with 120 nations voting in favor, 7 voting against, and 21 abstaining (see Document 1). Despite such support, the court is yet to become a reality, because sixty nations must first ratify the treaty, which can, in many countries, require passing a bill in parliament. In July 2001 the Netherlands became the thirty-seventh country to ratify the treaty. Another twenty-three ratifications are needed before the court can begin operations.

The ICC—to be headquartered at The Hague—will prosecute individuals for war crimes, crimes against humanity, and genocide, including crimes committed in international and local armed conflicts. As a permanent entity, the court's supporters argue, the body's very existence will be a deterrent, sending a strong warning to would-be perpetrators. It will also encourage states to investigate and prosecute egregious crimes committed in their territories or by their nationals, for if they do not, the ICC will exercise its jurisdiction. Consistent with international human rights standards, the ICC has no competence to impose a death penalty. It can impose lengthy terms of imprisonment, including life, if so justified by the gravity of the case. The court may, in addition, order a fine, forfeiture of proceeds, property, or assets derived from the crimes committed. Some aspects of the court are groundbreaking in terms of international law, including the recognition of sexual violence as a crime against humanity (which was first recognized by the tribunal for the former Yugoslavia), special services to victims and witnesses, and the court's independence from the UN Security Council. Some of the key legal principles governing the ICC include the following:

- all persons have the right to a fair trial, and all persons are innocent until proven guilty; the burden of proof lies with the prosecution, and guilt must be proven beyond a reasonable doubt;
- intent to commit a crime must be proven;

- persons cannot be tried twice for the same alleged offense;
- alleged crimes that occurred before the court takes effect cannot be tried;
- the court cannot try anyone who committed the alleged offense while under age 18;
- there is no statute of limitations on the crimes covered by the court;
- an accused person has certain rights upon arrest, such as the right to legal advice, the right to remain silent, and freedom from coercion or degrading punishment;
- accused persons cannot use "following orders" as a defense except in the rarest of circumstances;
- convicted persons have the right to a review of their sentence after serving two-thirds of it; and
- the court can try any person regardless of their official status or any immunity from prosecution they may ordinarily enjoy because of that status.

The ICC's creation is fraught with controversy. The United States is opposed to the court, arguing that it challenges national judicial sovereignty, and U.S. armed forces personnel may face politically motivated trials. Proponents of the ICC counter that checks and balances are built into the process. Still, some U.S. legislators introduced a bill that would withdraw military assistance from states that ratify the ICC treaty. Other countries are opposed to the treaty because some of its provisions conflict with their constitutions. Most notably, heads of state are not immune from prosecution by the ICC. Other issues with the ICC treaty that may have constitutional implications for countries include the absence of a statute of limitations and the right to a trial by jury, as well as extradition requirements.

For the ICC to operate effectively and provide for fair trials, it must be able to secure the cooperation of its state parties in surrendering suspects and in procuring the witnesses and evidence necessary for a successful investigation and prosecution. Thus, it is likely that many states willing to cooperate with the ICC will need to alter or modify their national laws and regulations. First, states will need to ensure that they have effective provisions for the extradition of persons indicted by the ICC. Second, the ICC will require access to prosecution and defense witnesses. Securing unwilling witnesses could prove extremely difficult for the court and for the country where the potential witness resides if neither the witness nor the state wants the witness to testify. Third, like domestic courts, the ICC will need to have access to documentary evidence if it is to be fair to victims and defendants alike. Article 93 of the Rome Statute states that the court can request certain documentary evidence from governments; it, however, has no effective enforcement options if states refuse to cooperate.

States and their citizens can turn to other forms of international and domestic mechanisms to hold human rights violators and war criminals accountable for their crimes. Depending on the prevailing political conditions, they can pursue human rights abusers residing in their own countries through the establishment of truth commissions or through domestic or regional courts. Victims whose human rights have been violated in another country can use extradition agreements to have offenders transferred to a national court. If an alleged offender travels to certain countries, such as the United States, victims residing there can file for civil damages for their suffering.

Regional Summaries

The International Criminal Court will not be instated for several years. In the meantime, numerous countries are struggling to come to terms with the past in the wake of communal violence, genocide, or prolonged civil war. Some of these countries have brought human rights offenders to trial, while others have formed local or UN-led truth and reconciliation commissions to investigate and expose patterns of atrocity, lines of responsibility, and complicity.

North America

The United States has in its history incidents of crimes against humanity, of which the most significant—slavery and massacres of Native Americans—ended in the nineteenth century. Many have argued, and continue to argue, that the U.S. bombing of Hiroshima and Nagasaki on 6 and 9 August 1945, respectively, was a war crime and a crime against humanity. While military targets were no doubt destroyed, nonmilitary targets suffered the overwhelming brunt of the bombs, which killed more than two hundred thousand civilians.

More recently, in the 1990s, the United States and Canada played key roles in the creation of the ad hoc International Criminal Tribunals for the Former Yugoslavia and Rwanda, but they took divergent paths when it came to the creation of the International Criminal Court. The Canadian government has signed and ratified the Rome Statute establishing the court, and a Canadian, Philippe Kirsch, chairs the Preparatory Committee for the International Criminal Court, which has overall responsibility for thrashing out issues involving the jurisdiction and operations of the institution.

Although the Clinton administration initially supported the establishment of a permanent war crimes tribunal, in an about face the United States became one of only seven countries to vote against the Rome Statute in 1998. The strongest pressure on the Clinton administration against the ICC (which would continue under President George W. Bush) came from military officials, who couched their public objections in terms of sovereignty, claiming that the court would infringe on U.S. jurisdiction. Many observers interpret this argument, however, as the military's desire for a guarantee that no American will ever be prosecuted by the court. The government's official stance is that the statute puts U.S. military personnel at risk of frivolous prosecution and hinders the president's ability to deploy armed forces. On 31 December 2000, the deadline for signing the Rome Statute, outgoing president Bill Clinton put his signature on the document, but his action was not seen as an endorsement of the ICC. Rather, his signing was perceived as a maneuver for the U.S. government to retain influence over the future shape of the court. If the United States had not signed on by the end of 2000, it would have lost its seat on the preparatory committee responsible for laying the groundwork for the court. The Bush administration has indicated that it firmly opposes the ICC, and its ratification in the Senate seems unlikely.

Latin America

By the mid-1980s, as the cold war began to thaw, entrenched authoritarian regimes in Latin America began to relinquish power to elected civilian

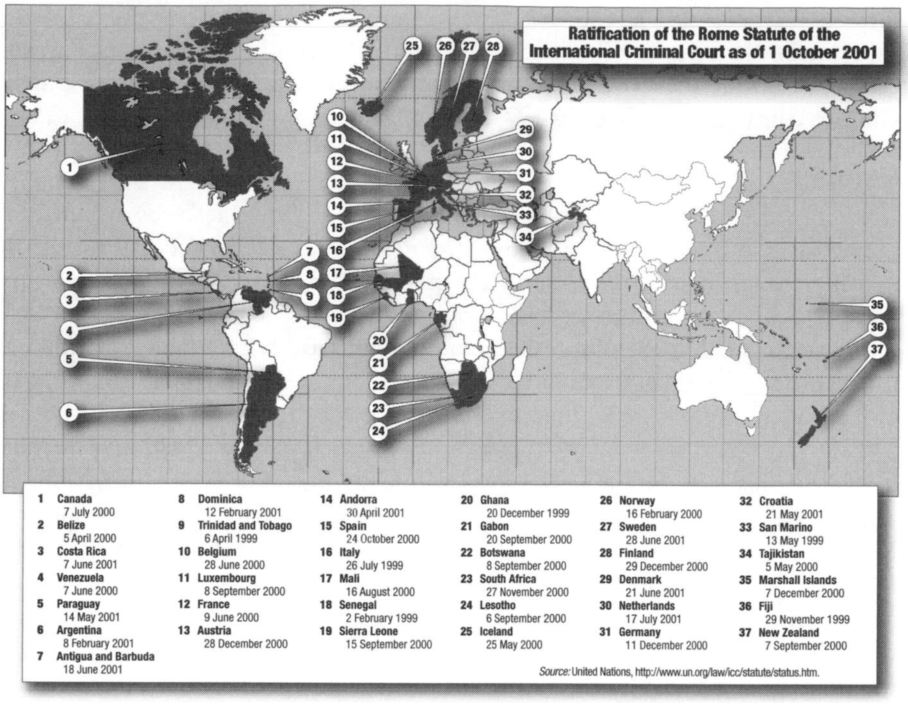

Source: United Nations, http://www.un.org/law/icc/statute/status.htm.

governments. Most of these new governments emerged after years of repressive military and sometimes civilian rule under which systematic violations of human rights took place. In Brazil the military thwarted any possibility of trials for such violations by passing de facto amnesties absolving themselves of past crimes. The fledgling civilian governments of Bolivia, Chile, Ecuador, El Salvador, Guatemala, and Uruguay, where the military retains substantial power, set up truth commissions to expose state abuses by gathering victims' testimonies, holding public hearings, and issuing reports of their findings. Argentina is the only country that has pursued trials of past military leaders in addition to a truth commission process. Chile, Guatemala, and Honduras also have held trials—though few and with limited success—of past human rights offenders.

Perhaps the most well publicized case in the region involves former Chilean dictator General Augusto Pinochet. Human rights activists praised Pinochet's arrest in London on 16 October 1998 in response to an extradition request by Spanish magistrate Baltasar Garzón, who had indicted the former military ruler for human rights abuses committed in Chile in the 1970s. A year later, a British magistrate ordered Pinochet's extradition to Spain, but in early 2000 the British government released the general, because of his declining health, and allowed him to return to Chile.

Earlier attempts had been made to bring Pinochet to justice. Since 1989 a Chilean judge had been trying to prosecute Pinochet on charges that he covered up the killings of political opponents by a death squad shortly after he seized power in 1973. In July 2001, however, an appeals court ruled that

Pinochet was not well enough to stand trial. A month later, the Chilean supreme court rejected a request by Argentina to extradite Pinochet to answer questions about his possible involvement in the assassination of an exiled Chilean army general there in 1974.

Europe

Ironically, the most significant event in Europe that would lead toward greater universal accountability for wartime atrocities took place largely because UN member states feared taking definitive military action to stop a bloody war. Thus, on 22 February 1993, as "ethnic cleansing" raged in Bosnia, the UN Security Council in Resolution 808 voted unanimously to establish an ad hoc international criminal tribunal to prosecute "persons responsible for serious violations of international humanitarian law committed in the territory of the former Yugoslavia since 1991." To date, forty-three people, including former Yugoslav president Slobodan Milosevic, are in the custody of the tribunal awaiting trial or serving sentences (see Case Study—The Trial of Slobodan Milosevic). Two of the court's major indictees, former Bosnian Serb president Radovan Karadzic and his top military commander, General Ratko Mladic, remain in hiding. The two men are charged for their role in the bombardment of civilians in Sarajevo, where approximately ten thousand people died during the three-and-a-half year siege, and for the massacre of seven thousand Muslim men and boys during the fall of Srebrenica in July 1995. Among the offenses listed in the indictment is the most heinous of all state-sponsored crimes: genocide. By characterizing the wide-scale killing of Bosnian Muslims as an act of genocide, the tribunal asserted that the two Bosnian Serb leaders were not engaged merely in a quest for territory but also to destroy—or at least eliminate—a large proportion of the Muslim population of Bosnia.

The tribunal's work has introduced a new dimension to global affairs. The tribunal, once an institution openly scorned or ignored by world leaders, now commands not only the attention of many political and national security thinkers, but also their respect. As former chief prosecutor Louise Arbour said in a press conference, as reported by UN Wire, "[W]e have moved international criminal justice . . . to a point of no return."

North Africa and the Middle East

The most significant application of international criminal justice to violations of human rights in this region has been a lawsuit filed in a Belgian court in June 2001 by twenty-three plaintiffs charging Israeli prime minister Ariel Sharon and other Israeli officials for "command responsibility" in the killing and disappearance of hundreds—and possibly thousands—of Palestinian civilians in the Sabra and Shatila refugee camps in Beirut, Lebanon, in 1982. A 1983 Israeli inquiry found that Sharon, who was at the time defense minister, bore indirect responsibility for the massacre, during which Israeli troops ringed the camps while about 150 heavily armed, pro-Israeli Christian militiamen slaughtered refugees inside. The plaintiffs—all survivors of the massacre—claim in the suit that the Israeli army, commanded by Sharon, was in constant contact with the Christian militia leaders, was aware of the events taking place in the camps, and had the power to stop the killings. The Geneva Conventions of 1949 and the 1998 statute of the International Criminal Court maintain that military commanders are liable for crimes that they know to be occurring or should have known about if they were committed by forces under their command and control.

Since the late 1980s, the United Nations and international human rights organizations have amassed significant evidence revealing that the Iraqi army was responsible for the disappearance and deaths of thousands of civilians during its military campaigns in the mid-1980s to quash Kurdish resistance groups in northern Iraq. Despite requests to the United Nations by human rights organizations, including Human Rights Watch, to establish a commission of inquiry to examine the evidence and, if appropriate, an ad hoc international criminal tribunal to try Iraqi leaders, neither has materialized.

Sub-Saharan Africa

The central African nation of Rwanda has become the focus of the second experiment in international criminal justice since the Nuremberg and Tokyo trials. On 8 November 1994, the UN Security Council established the International Criminal Tribunal for Rwanda in Arusha, Tanzania, to investigate and prosecute persons responsible for the 1994 genocide that largely destroyed Rwanda. The potential defendants can be divided into three groups. The first consists of the leaders who ordered the genocide—close associates of the late president Juvenal Habyarimana, military and militia leaders, mayors, and officials of Radio de Milles Colines. The second group, numbering in the tens of thousands, consists of lower-level municipal and administrative officials who were not part of the core group of instigators but who used their authority to order mass killings.

Many of these potential defendants are now held in jails throughout Rwanda and are being tried by national courts. The third group is comprised of people who were caught up in the fighting or were forced to kill or be killed. Many of them will be tried under a traditional form of justice, *gacaca,* predating the arrival of Europeans in Africa. Under gacaca, judges chosen from the community will accompany the accused to crime scenes in the hope that the guilty will confess and ask forgiveness. Those who insist on their innocence will be allowed to return to the community; those who profess innocence but are found guilty face life imprisonment or the death penalty. So far, the Arusha tribunal has secured the arrest of fifty persons, of which eight have been tried and sentenced to prison terms ranging from twelve years to life. Of these, Jean-Paul Akayesu, the former district mayor of Taba in central Rwanda, has received the severest sentence—three life sentences for genocide and crimes against humanity, plus eighty years for other violations that included torture and rape (see Case Study—The Trial of Jean-Paul Akayesu).

In July 2001 the creation of a second ad hoc international war crimes tribunal on the African continent gained momentum when the UN Security Council dispatched a planning delegation to Sierra Leone to form a tribunal to prosecute some twenty leaders accused of atrocities during that country's ten-year civil war. Ethiopia continues to use its own courts to pursue people who committed crimes under the Mengistu regime that controlled the state from 1974 to 1991. Mozambique declined to pursue trials or a truth commission process following the conclusion of its sixteen-year civil war, which ended in a peace agreement in 1992. Ten days after the signing of the accord, the parliament declared a general amnesty for "crimes against the state." At various times in their troubled pasts, Uganda (1974 and 1986), Zimbabwe (1985), Chad (1990), South Africa (1994), Sierra Leone (1999), and Nigeria (1999) have formed national truth commissions (with decidedly mixed results) in an effort to come to terms with the past and promote reconciliation.

In February 2000 a Senegalese court indicted Hissene Habre, Chad's exiled former dictator, on torture charges and placed him under house arrest. It was the first time that an African had been charged with atrocities against his own people by the court of another African country. Five months later, the court dismissed the case, ruling that Senegal had not enacted legislation to implement the Convention against Torture and therefore had no jurisdiction to pursue the charges because the crimes were not committed in Senegal. Habre reportedly spent lavishly to influence the outcome of the case.

Asia and the Pacific

Cambodia's Constitutional Council approved legislation in August 2001 to establish a "special court" to try former Khmer Rouge leaders for crimes against humanity, clearing a hurdle in the effort to prosecute for some of the worst human rights atrocities in Asia since World II. The legislation establishes a unique framework for foreign and local judges to try surviving Khmer Rouge leaders, who are blamed for the deaths of an estimated 1.7 million to 2 million people—roughly 20 percent of Cambodia's population—in the late 1970s (see GENOCIDE). Such progress notwithstanding, the United Nations must still approve the tribunal's statute before the court can begin functioning.

In October 2001 the Indonesian government announced that it would set up a special court to prosecute soldiers and officials behind the bloodshed surrounding East Timor's 1999 vote for independence. Human Rights Watch and other international human rights organizations are highly skeptical that the Indonesian court will ever prosecute high-ranking military commanders who were responsible for abuses or who took no action to stop them. They have urged the UN Security Council to establish an international tribunal before crucial evidence is lost by the passage of time. Meanwhile, courts created by the United Nations Transitional Administration in East Timor are investigating war crimes and crimes against humanity committed in 1999. In September 2001 Mohamed Chande Othman, the UN chief prosecutor for East Timor, indicted two Indonesian soldiers and nine East Timorese militia members for the crime of extermination in the killings of sixty-five people in Oecussi, an isolated enclave, in 1999.

Case Study—The Trial of Jean-Paul Akayesu

On 2 September 1998 the International Criminal Tribunal for Rwanda found Jean-Paul Akayesu, the former district mayor of the Taba commune in central

Rwanda, guilty on nine of fifteen counts of genocide, direct and public incitement to commit genocide, and crimes against humanity. A month later, Judge Laity Dama of Senegal sentenced the former mayor to three life sentences. The 294-page judgment made Akayesu the first person to be found guilty of genocide by an international tribunal. His case also represented the first conviction in which rape—one of the most ancient of war crimes—would be held by a court of law to be an act of genocide and a crime against humanity.

Akayesu was arrested in Zambia on 10 October 1995 and handed over to the Arusha tribunal. His detention came not at the behest of the tribunal but because his name appeared on a list of suspected war criminals wanted by the Rwandan government. Under the tribunal's rules, prosecutors had ninety days to decide whether to file charges. From the start, they sought to frame their case around the charge of mass murder, linking the defendant to the more than two thousand deaths in Taba. Tribunal investigators, mostly male, often unconsciously failed to ask about rape or did not consider it important enough to ask about it. Women from Taba did not volunteer that they had been raped. It was not therefore surprising that the first indictment lodged against Akayesu on 26 February 1996 made no mention of rape.

The Akayesu indictment caused a furor in feminist and human rights circles, as Elizabeth Neuffer notes in *The Key to My Neighbor's House: Searching for Justice in Bosnia and Rwanda*. Human Rights Watch, in a 1996 report based on its own investigations in Rwanda, concluded that rape had been widespread in the Taba commune. The first mention of rape in the Akayesu trial surfaced unexpectedly in January 1997, when a protected witness on the stand described Akayesu's role in various murders. During her testimony she mentioned that her six-year-old daughter had been raped by three members of the Interahamwe, the Hutu militia group responsible for much of the death and destruction in Rwanda. Two months later, another protected witness testified that Hutu military and militia had raped women at Taba's Bureau Communale. Astounded that the prosecution had not pursued these allegations, Judge Navanethem Pillay, a respected women's advocate who had served on South Africa's Truth and Reconciliation Commission, and Swedish judge Lennert Aspegren peppered the witness with questions aimed at determining the mayor's responsibility for the rapes.

When the court reconvened months later, the prosecutor announced that he wanted to amend the indictment against Akayesu to include three additional charges of rape and sexual violence. The judges agreed. In ensuing months, more than a dozen women from Taba came forward to describe the rapes and other crimes that they had witnessed or suffered at the hands of the Interahamwe. Their testimony proved that Akayesu had not only ordered that the Tutsi residents of Taba give themselves up and go to the Bureau Communale, but that he had also been present on the second day of the rapes there.

In February 2001 judges at the International Criminal Tribunal for the Former Yugoslavia referred to the precedent set in the Akayesu judgment when issuing their verdict against three Bosnian Serb commanders found guilty of raping Bosnian Muslim women and girls, some as young as twelve and fifteen years old, in the town of Foca in eastern Bosnia. Two of the accused were also found guilty of sexual enslavement, a crime against humanity, by holding women and girls captive in de facto detention centers near Foca. Forced prostitution, though common in the Far East during World War II, was never prosecuted in the international tribunals following the war. The Akayesu and Foca judgments are historic developments in international criminal law, and should encourage individual nations to treat sexual violence more seriously.

Case Study—The Trial of Slobodan Milosevic

Slobodan Milosevic will figure high on any list of the dozen or so men who symbolize the barbarity of the last decades of the twentieth century. The International Criminal Tribunal for the Former Yugoslavia indicted Milosevic and four other high-ranking government officials on 24 May 1999, at the height of the Kosovo crisis, when Milosevic was still president of Yugoslavia. The tribunal charged Milosevic with crimes against humanity and war crimes, including the destruction of ten cities in Kosovo and the killing of 314 ethnic Albanians in the province between January and May 1999. Chief prosecutor Carla del Ponte's most difficult task in building her case against Milosevic's actions in Kosovo will be establishing command responsibility—namely, that Milosevic had either ordered or, having known that systematic and widespread crimes were taking place, had failed to take all reasonable measures to prevent or repress subordinates from committing such acts. Prosecutors have evidence that Milosevic, at a meeting with senior officials in late March 1999, ordered his security forces to cover up any evidence of crimes that might be of interest to the tribunal. By September 2001 the Serbian police had unearthed several mass graves throughout Yugoslavia containing the bodies of some one thousand ethnic Albanians believed killed by Yugoslav forces during the war in Kosovo.

Milosevic first appeared before the tribunal on 3 July 2001. Refusing legal counsel, he sought to turn the arraignment into an attack on the court's legitimacy and on the North Atlantic Treaty Organization for its bombing of Serbia. The tribunal indicted Milosevic a second time, on 29 October 2001, for crimes he allegedly committed in Croatia. The indictment charges him with multiple counts of murder, torture, detention, deportation, and other atrocities committed during a Serb attempt to ethnically cleanse Croatia from 1991 to 1992. On 11 December 2001 the tribunal issued a third indictment against Milosevic for crimes in Bosnia. The indictment includes one count of genocide, one count of complicity with genocide, and an additional twenty-seven counts of war crimes and crimes against humanity arising from the conflict in Bosnia between 1992 and 1995.

In Serbia and other parts of the former Yugoslavia, the question that now arises is What impact will the trial of Milosevic have on the public sense of responsibility for the crimes of the past decade? In July 2001 a survey by the weekly Serbian-language news magazine *NIN* found that 48 percent of Serbs approved of Milosevic's defiance at The Hague, while only 21 percent were critical. Seventy-two percent said the tribunal was "illegitimate," even though most respondents, 57 percent, said that Milosevic was responsible for war crimes. Whether the trial of Milosevic will awaken a sense of responsibility that has thus far seemed dormant in Serbia or, alternatively, whether it will produce a sense of absolution, is difficult to foretell. It depends in part on the way the trial at The Hague is conducted and whether more indictees, including Milosevic's four co-defendants, can be brought before the court. Putting these men on trial would demonstrate that Milosevic was aided and abetted by many others. In turn, their trials could expand public awareness in Serbia that other political and military leaders, though not directly responsible for ordering or carrying out war crimes, bear political responsibility because they actively supported the commission of these crimes or because they knew of them and failed to attempt to stop them.

Biographical Sketches

Louise Arbour is a judge on the Ontario Court of Appeals and a former criminal law professor who replaced Richard Goldstone as chief prosecutor of the International Criminal Tribunals for the Former Yugoslavia and Rwanda in 1996. She introduced the practice of secret indictments, which resulted in more suspected war criminals turning themselves in to the Yugoslav tribunal.

Richard J. Goldstone has been a justice of the Constitutional Court of South Africa since 1994 and has served as chairperson of the Commission of Inquiry Regarding the Prevention of Public Violence and Intimidation in South Africa. He was appointed chief prosecutor of the International Criminal Tribunals for the Former Yugoslavia and Rwanda in 1994. In *For Humanity: Reflections of a War Crimes Investigator,* Goldstone provides an intimate account of his progression from a young activist opposing South Africa's racial policies to the world's first independent war crimes prosecutor.

Gabrielle Kirk McDonald began her career as a civil rights lawyer in 1966 with the National Association for the Advancement of Colored People (NAACP). In 1979 she became the first African American to be appointed a federal court judge in Houston, Texas. In 1993 the UN General Assembly appointed her as a judge on the International Criminal Tribunal for the Former Yugoslavia. From 1997 to 2000 she served as the tribunal president.

Aryeh Neier is a human rights activist and writer who fled Nazi Germany as a child. He is an ardent supporter of international justice and, as director of Human Rights Watch in the early 1990s, played a key role in garnering support among American and European diplomats for the creation of the International Criminal Tribunals for the Former Yugoslavia and Rwanda. He is currently president of the Soros Foundation and its Open Society Institute.

Navanethem Pillay was a defense attorney for members of the African National Congress until 1995, when she was elected judge of the International Criminal Tribunal for Rwanda. In 1999 she was elected tribunal president. Pillay was instrumental in prompting tribunal prosecutors to investigate widespread reports of rape during the 1994 genocide in Rwanda.

Directory

Amnesty International, 99-119 Rosebery Avenue, London EC1R 4RE, United Kingdom. Telephone: (44) 207 814 6200, Email: info@amnesty.org.uk, Web: http://www.amnesty.org
Organization working to promote the human rights enshrined in the Universal Declaration of Human Rights and other international standards

Coalition for International Justice, 740 Fifteenth Street NW, 8th Floor, Washington, DC 20005-1009. Telephone: (202) 505-2100, Email: coalition@cij.org, Web: http://www.cij.org
Organization working to support the war crimes tribunals for Rwanda and the former Yugoslavia

Crimes of War, American University, 4400 Massachusetts Avenue NW, Washington, DC 20016-8017. Email: infor@crimesofwar.org, Web: http://www.crimesofwar.org
Collaboration of journalists, lawyers, and scholars raising awareness of the laws of war and the human consequences when armed conflict becomes entrenched

Human Rights Watch, 350 Fifth Avenue, 34th Floor, New York, NY 10118-3299. Telephone: (212) 290-4700, Email: hrwnyc@hrw.org, Web: http://www.hrw.org
Organization dedicated to protecting the human rights of people around the world

Institute for War and Peace Reporting, Lancaster House, 33 Islington High Street, London N1 9LH United Kingdom. Telephone: (44) 2 07 713 7130, E-mail: info@iwpr.net, Web: http://www.iwpr.net
Educational charity that supports democratization and development in crisis zones throughout the world

International Criminal Tribunal for the Former Yugoslavia, 1 Churchillplein, 2501 EW, The Hague, Netherlands. Telephone: (31) 0 70 512 8656, Web: http://www.un.org/icty
UN-sanctioned tribunal to prosecute persons responsible for serious violations of international humanitarian law committed in the former Yugoslavia

International Criminal Tribunal for Rwanda, Arusha International Conference Centre, P.O. Box 6016, Arusha, Tanzania. Telephone: Arusha (255) 27 250 4369 or 4372, New York (212) 963-2850, Web: http://www.ictr.org
UN-sanctioned tribunal to prosecute persons responsible for genocide and other serious violations of international humanitarian law committed in the territory of Rwanda between 1 January 1994 and 31 December 1994

International Crisis Group, 400 Madison Avenue, Suite 11C, New York, NY 10017. Telephone: (212) 813-0820, Email: icgny@crisisweb.org, Web: http://intl-crisis-group.org
Organization committed to strengthening the capacity of the international community to anticipate, understand, and act to prevent and contain conflict

Office of the United Nations High Commissioner for Human Rights, 8-14 Avenue de la Paix, 1211 Geneva 10, Switzerland. Telephone: (41) 22 917 9000, Email: webadmin.hchr@unoq.ch, Web: http://www.unhchr.org
Office that oversees the work of several agencies promoting and protecting human rights and fundamental freedoms

South Asian Human Rights Documentation Centre, B-6/6 Safdariang Enclave Extension, New Delhi 110029, India. Telephone: (91) 11 619 1120, Email: hrdc online@hotmail.com, Web: http://www.hri.ca/partners/sahrdc
Network of individuals across South Asia working to investigate, document, and disseminate information about a wide range of human rights issues

United States Institute of Peace, 1200 17th Street NW, Suite 200, Washington, DC 20036-3011. Telephone: (202) 429-3828, Email: usip_requests@usip.org, Web: http://www.usip.org
Independent, nonpartisan federal institution created and funded by Congress to strengthen the nation's capacity to promote the peaceful resolution of international conflict

Further Research

Books

Arendt, Hannah. *Eichman in Jerusalem: A Report on the Banality of Evil.* Middlesex, England: Penguin Books, 1964.

Ball, Howard. *Prosecuting War Crimes and Genocide: The Twentieth-Century Experience.* Lawrence: University Press of Kansas, 1999.

Bass, Gary Jonathan. *Stay the Hand of Vengeance: The Politics of War Crimes Tribunals.* Princeton, N.J.: Princeton University Press, 2000.

Bassiouni, M. Cherif, and Peter Manikas. *The Law of the International Criminal Tribunal for the Former Yugoslavia.* Irvington-on-Hudson, N.Y.: Transnational Publishers, 1966.

Chang, Iris. *The Rape of Nanking: The Forgotten Holocaust of World War II.* New York: Basic Books, 1997.

Goldstone, Richard J. *For Humanity: Reflections of a War Crimes Investigator.* New Haven: Yale University Press, 2000.

Gourevitch, Phillip. *We Wish To Inform You That Tomorrow We Will Be Killed With Our Families: Stories from Rwanda.* New York: Farrar, Straus and Giroux, 1998.

Gutman, Roy, and David Rieff, eds. *Crimes of War: What the Public Must Know.* New York: W. W. Norton, 1999.

Hayner, Priscilla B. *Unspeakable Truths: Confronting State Terror and Atrocity.* New York: Routledge, 2001.

Jaspars, Karl. *The Question of German Guilt.* New York: Dial Press, 1948.

Kritz, Neil J. *Transitional Justice: How Emerging Democracies Reckon with Former Regimes.* Washington, D.C.: United States Institute of Peace Press, 1995.

Minnow, Martha. *Between Vengeance and Forgiveness: Facing History and Genocide and Mass Violence.* Boston: Beacon Press, 1998.

Muller, Ingo. *Hitler's Justice: The Courts of the Third Reich.* Cambridge, Mass.: Harvard University Press, 1991.

Neier, Aryeh. *War Crimes: Brutality, Genocide, Terror, and the Struggle for Justice.* New York: Times Books, 1998.

Neuffer, Elizabeth. *The Key to My Neighbor's House: Searching for Justice in Bosnia and Rwanda.* New York: Picador, 2001.

Osiel, Mark. *Mass Atrocity, Collective Memory, and the Law.* New Brunswick, N.J.: Transaction Publishers, 1997.

Rosenberg, Tina. *The Haunted Land: Facing Europe's Ghosts after Communism*. New York: Random House, 1995.

Stover, Eric, and Gilles Peress. *The Graves: Srebrenica and Vukovar.* Zurich: Scalo, 1998.

Tanaka, Yuki. *Japanese War Crimes in World War II.* Boulder: Westview Press, 1996.

Taylor, Telford. *Nuremberg and Vietnam: An American Tragedy.* New York: A New York Times Book, 1970.

———. *The Anatomy of the Nuremberg Trials.* New York: Alfred A. Knopf, 1992.

Articles and Reports

Akhavan, Payam. "Justice in The Hague, Peace in the Former Yugoslavia? A Commentary on the United Nations War Crimes Tribunal." *Human Rights Quarterly* 20, no. 4 (1998): 737–816.

Alvarez, Jose E. "Lessons from the Akayesu Judgment." *ILSA Journal of International and Comparative Law* 5, no. 2 (1999): 359–370.

"Balkans: Arbour Wants Local Courts to Try Some War Criminals." UNWire, http://www.unfoundation.org/unwire/archives/UNWIRE990719.asp.

Cohen, David. "Beyond Nuremberg: Individual Responsibility for War Crimes." In *Human Rights in Political Transitions: Gettysburg to Bosnia,* edited by Carla Hesse and Robert Post. New York: Zone Books, 1999.

Crawford, James. "First Report on State Responsibility." A report of the International Law Commission, Fifth Session, http://www.un.org/law/ilc/sessions/50/english/n9812606.pdf.

Farer, Tom J. "Restraining the Barbarians: Can International Criminal Law Help?" *Human Rights Quarterly* 22, no. 1 (2000): 90–117.

Human Rights Watch. "Justice in the Balance: Recommendations for an Independent and Effective International Criminal Court." June 1998, http://www.hrw.org/reports98/icc.

———. "Milosevic in The Hague," August 2001, http://www.hrw.org/campaigns/Serbia.

Human Rights Watch and the Fédération Internationale des Ligues des Droits de l'Homme. "Shattered Lives: Sexual Violence during the Rwandan Genocide and Its Aftermath," 1 September 1996, http://www.hrw.org/reports/1996/Rwanda.htm.

International Criminal Tribunal for the Former Yugoslavia. *Annual Report, 1994.* New York, General Assembly of the United Nations, 1994, http://www.un.org/icty/rappannu-e/1994/index.htm.

Katz Cogan, Jacob. "The Problem of Obtaining Evidence for International Criminal Courts." *Human Rights Quarterly* 22, no. 2 (2000): 404–427.

Kissinger, Henry A. "The Pitfalls of Universal Jurisdiction: Risking Judicial Tyranny." *Foreign Affairs* 80, no. 4 (2001): 86–96.

Neier, Aryeh. "What Should Be Done about the Guilty?" *New York Review of Books,* 1 February 1990.

Orentlicher, Diane F. "Settling Accounts: The Duty to Prosecute Human Rights Violations of a Prior Regime." *Yale Law Journal* 100 (1991): 2538–2618.

Osiel, Mark J. "Why Prosecute? Critics of Punishment for Mass Atrocity." *Human Rights Quarterly* 22, no. 1 (2000): 118–147.

Roht-Arriaza, Naomi. "Institutions of International Justice." *Journal of International Affairs* 52, no. 2 (1999): 474–491.

Stover, Eric. "Dreamtime of Vengeance in Kosovo." Crimes of War Project, August 2001, http://www.crimesofwar.org/mag_stover.html

Trueheart, Charles. "A New Kind of Justice." *Atlantic Monthly,* April 2000, 80–90.

Web Sites

Akayesu Judgment and Sentence, International Criminal Tribunal for Rwanda
http://www.ictr.org/english/cases/akayesu/judgement.htm

Milosevic Hearing and Trial Transcripts, British Broadcasting Corporation
http://news.bbc.co.uk/hi/english/world/europe/newsid_1419000/141007.stm

Milosevic Indictment, International Criminal Tribunal for the Former Yugoslavia
http://www.un.org/icty/indictment/english/mil-ii990524e.htm

Rome Statute of the International Criminal Court
http://www.un.org/law/icc/statute.htm

War Criminal Watch (Rwanda and Yugoslavia), Coalition for International Justice
http://www.wcw.org

Documents

1. Rome Statute of the International Criminal Court

United Nations Diplomatic Conference of Plenipotentiary on the Establishment of an International Criminal Court, Rome, 17 July 1998

The full text is available at http://www.un.org/law/icc/statute/romefra.htm.

Extract

Preamble

The States Parties to this Statute,

Conscious that all peoples are united by common bonds, their cultures pieced together in a shared heritage, and concerned that this delicate mosaic may be shattered at any time,

Mindful that during this century millions of children, women and men have been victims of unimaginable atrocities that deeply shock the conscience of humanity,

Recognizing that such grave crimes threaten the peace, security and well-being of the world,

Affirming that the most serious crimes of concern to the international community as a whole must not go unpunished and that their effective prosecution must be ensured by taking measures at the national level and by enhancing international cooperation,

Determined to put an end to impunity for the perpetrators of these crimes and thus to contribute to the prevention of such crimes,

Recalling that it is the duty of every State to exercise its criminal jurisdiction over those responsible for international crimes,

Reaffirming the Purposes and Principles of the Charter of the United Nations, and in particular that all States shall refrain from the threat or use of force against the territorial integrity or political independence of any State, or in any other manner inconsistent with the Purposes of the United Nations,

Emphasizing in this connection that nothing in this Statute shall be taken as authorizing any State Party to intervene in an armed conflict or in the internal affairs of any State,

Determined to these ends and for the sake of present and future generations, to establish an independent permanent International Criminal Court in relationship with the United Nations system, with jurisdiction over the most serious crimes of concern to the international community as a whole,

Emphasizing that the International Criminal Court established under this Statute shall be complementary to national criminal jurisdictions,

Resolved to guarantee lasting respect for and the enforcement of international justice.

2. Principles of International Law Recognized in the Charter of the Nuremberg Tribunal and in the Judgment of the Tribunal

International Law Commission of the United Nations, 1950

The full text is available at http://www.un.org/law/ilc/texts/nurnberg.htm.

Extract

Principle I
Any person who commits an act which constitutes a crime under international law is responsible therefore and liable to punishment.

Principle II
The fact that internal law does not impose a penalty for an act which constitutes a crime under international law does not relieve the person who committed the act from responsibility under international law.

Principle III
The fact that a person who committed an act which constitutes a crime under international law acted as Head of State or responsible Government official does not relieve him from responsibility under international law.

Principle IV
The fact that a person acted pursuant to order of his Government or of a superior does not relieve him from responsibility under international law, provided a moral choice was in fact possible to him.

Principle V
Any person charged with a crime under international law has the right to a fair trial on the facts and law.

Principle VI
The crimes hereinafter set out are punishable as crimes under international law:

a. Crimes against peace

i. Planning, preparation, initiation or waging of a war of aggression or a war in violation of international treaties, agreements or assurances;
ii. Participation in a common plan or conspiracy for the accomplishment of any of the acts mentioned under (i).

b. War crimes
Violations of the laws or customs of war which include, but are not limited to, murder, ill-treatment or deportation to slave-labor or for any other purpose of civilian population of or in occupied territory; murder or ill treatment of prisoners of war, of persons on the [s]eas, killing of hostages, plunder of public or private property, wanton destruction of cities, towns, or villages, or devastation not justified by military necessity.

c. Crimes against humanity
Murder, extermination, enslavement, deportation and other inhuman acts done against any civilian population, or persecutions on political, racial or religious grounds, when such acts are done or such persecutions are carried on in execution of or in connection with any crime against peace or any war crime.

Principle VII
Complicity in the commission of a crime against peace, a war crime, or a crime against humanity as set forth in Principle VI is a crime under international law.

INTERNATIONAL LAW

Bruce Cronin

International law is the body of legal rules, customs, and norms that regulate activities carried on beyond the borders of individual states, primarily those between governments. International law developed gradually over several centuries and is derived from a highly diverse collection of lawmaking treaties, customary practices, and judicial opinions that states accept as binding obligations. Although the scope of international law's jurisdiction is limited, it covers a wide range of practices, including the use of force, the behavior of military combatants, the distribution and use of territory, and waterways, and diplomatic interaction. All countries are legally bound to adhere to its principles as a condition of their participation in the international community.

Historical Background and Development

International law evolved with the development of the nation-state system during the sixteenth and seventeenth centuries. The nation-state system consists of sovereign countries throughout the world that carry on formal political and diplomatic relations with one another. Drawing from Roman and medieval legal traditions, international law was originally based on a view that all sovereigns were subject to a natural law that consisted of universal principles of right and wrong. Over time, philosophers, political leaders, and legal scholars began to move away from natural law doctrines and toward a positivist approach that saw international law as the product of human will grounded in voluntary consent. Legalists began to examine the behavior of states and tried to determine from it which practices had become accepted as obligations in the international community. From this they developed a set of legal principles that came to be known as customary law, which was considered to be binding on all states specifically because it reflected a set of consistent practices that states had viewed as obligatory over a long period of time. For example, the tenet that all ships have a right to free navigation on the high seas derives from the fact that countries had long espoused and accepted this principle as a legal obligation in international relations.

As the nation-state system expanded, political leaders gradually realized that they needed a more formal set of rules to regulate their relations and a stable environment for trading, resolving disputes, and minimizing suffering. Yet they had to confront a tension between increasing international obligations and their desire to assert their independence and autonomy. This created problems in the development of a coherent "law of nations," another term for international law used in this period. States are legally sovereign entities and are therefore not subject to legal sanction by a higher authority. They jealously guard their sovereignty and are reluctant to submit to external, or international, judgment.

On this basis, political realists long argued that international law is not in fact law, but rather positive morality that states only follow when it is in their interest to do so. Given what political scientist and diplomat George Kennan describes as "chaotic and dangerous aspirations of governments" coupled with the lack of a central authority to protect individual states, governments can ultimately only rely on their own resources to promote their interests. States do not "obey" international law because there is no law to obey. Rather, strong states follow the rules when it is convenient, and weak ones follow them when they are forced to. For these reasons, studies by realist legal scholars and political scientists have tended to focus on the role of the great powers in making and enforcing the rules of order.

This bleak view remained dominant until the twentieth century. After World War I many political leaders and transnational nongovernmental organizations began to explore the possibility of creating a stronger system of international law through the establishment of international organizations, such as the League of Nations. Article 12 of the league covenant, which is legally considered a treaty, prohibited states from using force until a determination was made by a court of arbitration. This was strengthened in 1929, when Belgium, Czechoslovakia, France, Germany, Great Britain, Italy, Japan, Poland, and the United States signed the Treaty for the Renunciation of War, also known as the Kellogg-Briand Pact, in an ambitious attempt to make warfare illegal (see Table 1). Nongovernmental organizations, such as the International Law Society, and international institutions, such as the Permanent Court of International Justice, supported these efforts and tried to reorganize international relations as a society of states based on the rule of law.

Ultimately, a variety of factors, including trade conflicts and economic depression, undermined these efforts. In addition, since the main point of the League of Nations was to prevent aggression, the fact that it was unable to stop German and Italian aggression in the 1930s essentially meant its functional end. Also, the United States, beset by isolationist concerns, never joined the league. The Treaty for the Renunciation of War technically remained in effect, but had no effective force. Following World War II and the onset of the cold war, efforts to expand international law became subordinate to power politics and, outside of Western Europe, was no longer considered to be a major factor in international relations.

At the same time, the success of Western European integration and the rise of economic interdependence among the industrialized states convinced many government officials and leaders within nongovernmental organizations to initiate new efforts toward greater international cooperation and legalization. Moreover, the creation and expansion of the United Nations spurred a proliferation of new lawmaking treaties. Thus, during the cold war there was significant growth in the number and strength of international organizations and multilateral agreements, at least in the West. The most comprehensive agreement on the treatment of prisoners of war was concluded in Geneva in 1949 (see Document 1). Accompanying this expansion of intergovernmental organizations was an increase in the influence of transnational nongovernmental organizations, such as Greenpeace and Amnesty International. Such groups sought to expand the scope of international law by promoting greater legal commitments to human rights and environmental protection.

All of this activity led to the ascendancy of the institutionalist and internationalist approaches to the study and practice of international law during the 1980s. Specifically, an increasing number of scholars and political leaders began to explore the various conditions that lead states to cooperate with each other toward the attainment of common goals. In developing this approach, internationalists argued that states formed a type of international community in which they were bound by a common set of rules in their relations with one another.

The end of the cold war brought a new optimism among academics and policymakers that international law and organizations could play an increasingly important role in regulating the relations of states. The ensuing consensus on the basic principles of international order raised expectations unseen since the end of World War I. Although the rapid spread of nationalist conflict and civil war in Africa, Eastern Europe, and the Middle East has since dampened this optimism, international law has assumed an important place in international relations.

Current Status

According to legal scholar John Austin, law consists of a command issued by a sovereign power and backed by a sanction. Unlike most national legal systems, international law operates within a global environment that lacks a central government with the authority to enact legislation, adjudicate disputes, and punish transgressors. As a result, international law is highly decentralized. Its main functions are not primarily provided by global legal institutions, but by individual states that often must interpret and enforce the rules themselves. When conflicts over interpretation arise, they are usually addressed through political and diplomatic means rather than legal ones.

This situation is complicated by the fact that political leaders are wary of making commitments to follow general principles that would apply in unforeseen future circumstances—the very essence of a legal obligation. States jealously guard their sovereignty and will not easily cede their authority to a higher power, be it a legal norm or global institution. For these reasons, there has been a long-standing debate among legal scholars and political leaders over the degree to which international law can be considered "law" in the traditional sense. Indeed, many researchers ask why nations obey international law at all.

Research

Despite the above roadblocks, international law has expanded in the range of issues that fall within its jurisdiction and the number of institutions that administer it. Increased economic integration, or globalization, and the dramatic spread of democratization have led to a rising demand for more precise and binding commitments by states. The degree to which international law may be assuming a greater role in regulating relations among states is thus of great concern to legal scholars, political scientists, and officials from international institutions and nongovernmental organizations. Current research and policy analysis is primarily concerned with three questions: How well do states comply with existing international law? What are the barriers to greater "legalization" of international relations? How are changing international norms increasing the range of issues that fall within the scope of international law?

According to a number of recent studies, despite the absence of strong enforcement mechanisms, states have demonstrated a remarkably high rate of compliance with the provisions of international law. Research conducted by Thomas Franck and Abram and Antonia Chayes suggests that most states consistently meet their obligations under international law. Although disputes over interpretation often arise, there are few documented cases of blatant violations. These findings have been confirmed by a number of empirical studies in the areas of trade and the environment. While there is now little disagreement over whether states comply with international law, there is, however, a spirited debate over the reasons for this.

A statistical study by George Downs, for example, suggests that much of the documented compliance would have occurred *without* international agreements. He argues that since governments tend to establish and agree to international rules that they intend to follow anyway, international law *reflects* state preferences and behavior rather than shapes them. Anne Marie-Slaughter takes a slightly different approach, linking compliance not to the power of international legal institutions but to the proliferation of liberal democratic states and domestic politics. Such states, she argues, are far more likely to conduct their international relations according to the rule of law than are authoritarian ones. At the same time, an empirical study by Martin Friedland and his associates suggests that there is no single overriding factor determining compliance; states comply for a wide variety of reasons, including habit, belief in the legitimacy of the rules, self-interest, fear of sanction, socialization, and domestic politics.

Many recent studies have moved beyond the seemingly endless debate about compliance to the issue of whether international relations are in fact becoming "more legalized." A 2000 issue of *International Organization* brought together a dozen law scholars and political scientists to consider whether the post–cold war era is witnessing a "legalization of world politics." In particular, the authors explore the conditions under which states have attempted to do so by (1) translating nonlegal norms into binding rules; (2) increasing their ability to develop a more coherent system for creating new rules; and (3) formalizing adjudication and compliance mechanisms through the creation of international courts; and (4) formalizing the rules by integrating international law into domestic legal systems. Their conclusions, and those of other researchers, offer a mixed evaluation.

There is little doubt that there has been a dramatic increase in the use of legal mechanisms to solve the problems of collective action. Between 1899 and 1950, for example, states signed approximately forty legally binding multilateral treaties and conventions. From 1951 to 2001, this figure was closer to two hundred. Moreover, these agreements expanded from the traditional focus on diplomatic relations and conduct during war to include trade, arms control, limitations on the use of force, human rights, and the environment (see Table 2). In addition, since the creation of the European Union, the United Nations, the World Trade Organization, and other transnational and international entities, there has also been a dramatic increase in the types of mechanisms for creating new obligations and implementing existing ones. This increase in new mechanisms for implementing international law has not prevented the use of coercion and violence to achieve state goals, but it has modified it.

Policies and Programs

Traditionally, international law has focused primarily on issues related to diplomatic relations, behavior in wartime, the use of such common pool resources as the high seas, and the rights and duties of states. Efforts to expand the scope of international law and strengthen the world's legal institutions have been initiated by a variety of international institutions and nongovernmental organizations. The most active is the International Law Commission, which was established by the United Nations General Assembly in 1947 to promote the development and codification of international law. Although the founding members of the United Nations were overwhelmingly opposed to granting the organization legislative power to enact binding rules of international law, there was strong support for giving the General Assembly the more limited powers of study and recommendation. As a result, the commission has been the central player in conducting research and drafting recommendations on strengthening international law in select issue areas, such as state responsibility, unilateral acts of states, diplomatic protection, jurisdiction with regard to crimes committed outside national territory, and defining aggression.

The International Law Commission examines existing law to determine its adequacy in addressing specific issues in international relations and then submits detailed reports to the General Assembly. Sometimes the commission will propose a specific treaty or convention for consideration by the UN membership. These reports often lead to General Assembly resolutions, and sometimes they become the basis for organizing international conferences where proposed treaties are negotiated. For example, the commission was the driving force in developing such landmark treaties as the Vienna Convention on Diplomatic Relations (completed in 1961 and ratified by 174 countries). In doing so, the convention took a hodgepodge of customary law that had developed over hundreds of years and organized it into a coherent treaty defining the various types of diplomats, stipulating their rights and duties, providing for their immunities, and articulating a precise set of rules for the conduct of diplomatic relations.

Although the General Assembly lacks the legal authority to create new international law, it often acts as a vehicle for drafting legally binding treaties and conventions. Some of the most ambitious attempts to expand international law into the areas of the environment, intellectual property, organized crime, terrorism, arms control, and human rights have emanated from UN agencies. For example, the 1996 United Nations Diplomatic Conference on an International Total Ban on Anti-Personnel Land Mines produced a legally binding convention outlawing the use of land mines. Each signatory state must adhere to the convention after ratifying it (usually through some form of domestic legislation) and officially informs the UN secretary-general of its ratification. The convention is only binding on those states that have ratified it. Participating governments can be held accountable for complying with its provisions by their own national courts and (if they voluntarily agree) by the International Court of Justice. The land mine convention was signed by 135 states; China, Russia, and the United States have refused to sign. Similarly, the 1992 United Nations Framework Convention on Climate Change led to the approval of the Kyoto Protocol, a legally binding agreement on reducing ozone depletion to which eighty-four countries have signed on (see GLOBAL WARMING).

Not all General Assembly efforts have been successful. For example, the Conference on the Illicit Trade in Small Arms and Lights Weapons failed to produce an anticipated treaty banning international trade in small weapons. The limits of international law undoubtedly will be seriously tested by its effectiveness in helping states cope with international terrorism (see Table 3). In particular, states and international organizations will likely assess the effectiveness of existing international legal instruments relating to terrorism, such as the International Convention for the Suppression of Terrorist Bombings.

Perhaps the most ambitious attempt to expand the scope of international law is in the area of human rights (see HUMAN RIGHTS). Traditionally, international law has been restricted to regulating the relations *between* states, not *within* them, such as through the Vienna Convention on Diplomatic Relations and the Declaration on Rights and Duties of States, also known as the Montevideo Convention (see Document 2). With support from such nongovernmental organizations as Amnesty International and the Lawyers Committee for Human Rights, regional and international organizations have begun to work toward making human rights treaties a key part of international law. Although this has been a slow and uneven process, the United Nations and regional organizations have developed several legally binding conventions, including the Covenants on Civil and Political Rights and on Social and Economic Rights, which put into a legal framework many of the nonbinding principles enshrined in the Universal Declaration of Human Rights passed by the General Assembly in 1948. At the regional level, such organizations as the European Union, the Organization of American States, and the Organization of African Unity each have legally binding charters and conventions that provide for the protection of human rights. Although the mechanisms for implementing these guarantees vary widely, from simple standard setting to coercive enforcement, in all cases the signatories accept them as legal obligations.

In addition to expanding law into new areas, international and regional organizations have worked to strengthen transnational adjudication mechanisms through the creation of international courts and tribunals. The UN-sponsored International Court of Justice, created in 1945, has had a limited mandate and thus cannot act as a "world court." During the 1990s, however, the United Nations created new mechanisms for holding individuals and political leaders responsible for violations of international law, including through the proposed International Criminal Court (ICC) and several ad hoc tribunals to try war criminals in the Balkans and Rwanda (see INTERNATIONAL CRIMINAL JUSTICE and WAR CRIMES). The ICC was created through a multilateral treaty that has yet to take effect, and the war crimes tribunals were initiated by the UN Security Council under its authority to act against breaches of the peace.

In addition to the international courts and tribunals that have been established by the United Nations, a number of treaties provide for adjudication in specific areas of international law. For example, as part of the 1994 World Trade Organization (WTO) agreement, all member states are required to submit to the authority of the organization's Dispute Settlement Body in all matters within the jurisdiction of the WTO. Similarly, under the various treaties of the European Union, all members are subject to decisions issued by the European Court of Justice and, under the European Convention for the Protection of Human Rights and Fundamental Freedoms, the European Court of Human Rights. Unlike the jurisdiction of most international courts, in EU courts individuals and private organizations have legal standing along with states. Signatories to the American Convention on Human Rights, drafted by the Organization of American States and signed by twenty-six of its member countries, are under the limited jurisdiction of the Inter-American Court of Human Rights. Despite these advancements, however, in international adjudication, most issues of international law are addressed not by transnational courts but by national ones.

Regional Summaries

The expansion of international law and the growth of international organizations has been uneven around the world. While virtually all states are members of the United Nations and signatories to the most important diplomatic agreements, there is a wide disparity in the level of legalization from region to region. International law tends to be strongest where there are regional arrangements as defined by the UN Charter. According to Chapter VIII, "regional arrangements or agencies" that address matters relating to the

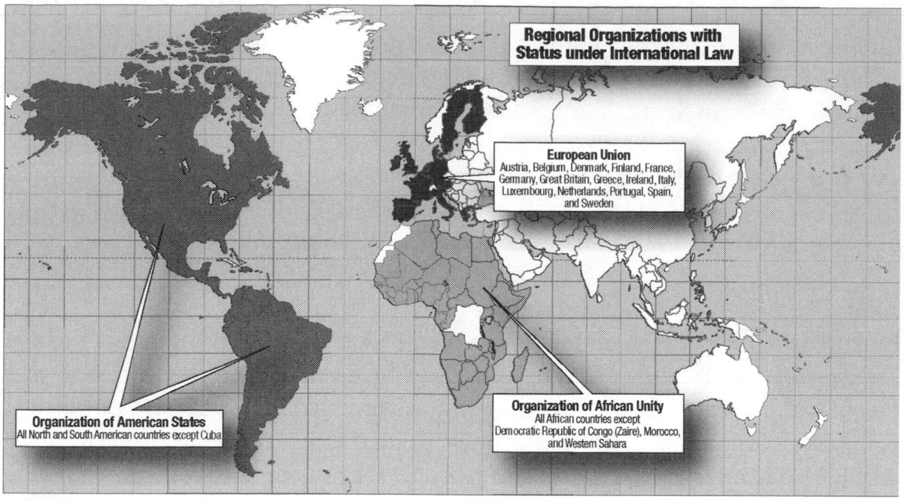

Source: Bruce Cronin.

maintenance of international peace and security are permitted, but all regional organizations must gain approval from the Security Council before undertaking any enforcement action. These regional arrangements are strengthened by the fact that their charters tend to be legal documents imposing domestic obligations on its members (see map).

Americas

International law has long played a role in relations among the American states, but it has also been hampered by the great disparity in power and wealth between North America and South America. In addition, the role of law was restrained by the rise of authoritarian governments in South America during the 1960s and 1970s. By the late 1980s, however, several factors increased the role of international law in the Americas. First, virtually all of the authoritarian regimes in Latin America either resigned or were overthrown and replaced by democratic governments. This turn of events coupled with the end of the cold war made states more likely to implement human rights agreements. Second, the conclusion of the North American Free Trade Agreement (NAFTA) in 1994 created a new transnational legal system in the areas of trade and investment. While at present NAFTA is restricted to Canada, Mexico, and the United States, the number of members is likely to expand over the next decade.

All American states except Cuba are members of the Organization of American States. Although dominated by the United States, the organization's charter nevertheless guarantees sovereign equality among its members and parallels many of the provisions of the UN Charter in addressing nearly all facets of economic and political life in the region. While this has not led to the development of a regional legal system, it has facilitated the conclusion of the legally binding American Convention on Human Rights and the creation of the Inter-American Court of Human Rights. Both institutions impose a weak set of obligations on their members, although the treaty and the court have grown stronger in recent years. Two additional regional bodies are the Organization of Central American States, which resolves disputes between member states, and the Andean Court of Justice, which was created by the 1969 Treaty of Bogotá (commonly known as the Andean Pact) and whose judgments are directly enforceable in the national courts of member states.

Europe

Europe has the most developed international legal system in the history of the nation-state system. The twelve-member European Union is the closest that the world has come to a transnational government. Although the union was originally formed as a common economic market, it gradually evolved into a complex organization with the authority to set policies and create laws binding on member states. European law is superior to state law in the areas of its jurisdiction, which have moved far beyond economic activity to include immigration, social policy, labor relations, human rights, and local governance. The laws and regulations passed by the various EU legal bodies have direct effect, meaning that they are not only binding on the member states but are binding also for individuals and organizations within these states. The European Court of Justice and the European Court of Human Rights have compulsory jurisdiction over EU states and can order them to change their laws to conform to EU policy.

In addition to the EU network, several other structures impart quasi-legal obligations. The Council of Europe, established in 1949, is an intergovernmental organization comprised of states committed to democratic governance, human rights, and the rule of law. Toward this end the council developed two human rights treaties, the European Convention for the Protection of Human Rights and Fundamental Freedoms and the European Social Charter, both of which are legally binding on their signatories. The former is enforced by the European Court of Human Rights. The North Atlantic Treaty Organization (NATO)—the world's largest military alliance, which includes members outside of Europe, including the United States—was formed through treaty, thereby imposing legal obligations on its members. By definition, however, military treaties are exclusive—that is, only certain countries can sign—and they are only binding in regard to military matters. Thus, military alliances are not considered in discussions of international law. Nevertheless, NATO has worked with the United Nations and the Organization for Security and Cooperation in Europe (OSCE) to undertake military enforcement missions, such as those conducted in Bosnia and Kosovo in the 1990s. The legality of the missions in the Balkans is questionable, since technically NATO has no legal status in international law, and only the United Nations or a regional arrangement is permitted to engage in military action (aside from immediate self-defense). The fifty-five-member OSCE includes, despite its name, all states "from Vancouver to Vladivostok," covering Canada, the United States, the states of Europe, and most of the former Soviet republics. The OSCE lacks international legal standing and in fact was not created through a treaty. It is, nonetheless, recognized by the United Nations as a Chapter VIII regional arrangement and thus has the authority to carry out various peacekeeping and peacemaking missions.

Africa

African states, which tend to be politically, economically, and militarily weak, benefit from international law inasmuch as it places legal constraints on stronger powers from intervening in their internal affairs. Among the most basic principles in international law are the legal equality of states and the right of all states to territorial integrity and nonintervention. Thus, weak states benefit from international law because in its absence strong states have no legal limits. In 1963 the Organization of African Unity (OAU) was formed, and all independent states on the continent became members. Its primary purpose is to promote self-government and social progress throughout Africa. The OAU charter commits members to pursue the "peaceful settlement of disputes" and the renunciation of all "subversive activities." To this end, the organization has established a commission to mediate disputes among its members. As a legal organization, the OAU is weak. It imposes few legal obligations on its members, and it lacks the resources and cohesion to stabilize the continent.

In 1991 OAU members concluded a new treaty that sought to expand the mission of the organization to create an economic community. The 1986 Ganjul Charter on Human Rights offers minimal protection for individuals, although it tends to focus more on responsibilities of individual citizens to their governments than it does on "rights" as we have come to understand them. The African Commission on Human Rights, which was created by the charter, has the power to investigate, report, and make recommendations, but it has no enforcement authority.

Asia and the Pacific

As in Africa, regional international law in Asia is weak. The two regional organizations—the Association of Southeast Asian Nations (ASEAN) and the Asia-Pacific Economic Cooperation forum (APEC)—help to facilitate economic cooperation, but impose few legal obligations on their members. Although most Asian states have signed various international human rights treaties, unlike Africa, the Americas, and Europe, they have no human rights charter of their own. Moreover, the states of the region lack a security organization other than memberships in the United Nations.

Data

Table 1 Treaties and Conventions Regulating Warfare

The execution of a treaty involves three processes. First, it is signed by the heads of state from the countries that negotiated the treaty. These are the original signers, or parties, to the agreement, but other countries can later join by "acceding." Second, the treaty needs to be ratified by each country. The ratification process differs significantly from country to country. (The United States requires a two-thirds vote of the Senate.) Third, once a specified number of countries has ratified the treaty—the number is contained within the treaty—it is considered "in force" and becomes legally binding on those who have ratified it. The last step, which has only been in place since 1945, is registering the treaty with the secretary-general of the United Nations. This last step is required by the UN Charter, which is itself a legally binding treaty.

Treaty or Convention	Year Signed
Convention (I) for the Pacific Settlement of International Disputes	1899
Convention (II) with Respect to the Laws and Customs of War on Land	1899
Convention (II) for the Pacific Settlement of International Disputes	1907
Convention (III) Relative to the Opening of Hostilities	1907
Convention (IV) Respecting the Laws and Customs of War on Land	1907
Convention (V) Respecting the Rights and Duties of Neutral Powers and Persons in Case of War on Land	1907
Convention (VI) Relating to the Status of Enemy Merchant Ships at the Outbreak of Hostilities	1907
Convention (VII) Relating to the Conversion of Merchant Ships into War-Ships	1907
Convention (VIII) Relative to the Laying of Automatic Submarine Contact Mines	1907
Convention (IX) Concerning Bombardment by Naval Forces in Time of War	1907
Convention (X) for the Adaptation to Maritime War of the Principles of the Geneva Convention	1907
Convention (XI) Relative to Certain Restrictions with Regard to the Exercise of the Right of Capture in Naval War	1907
Convention (XIII) Concerning the Rights and Duties of Neutral Powers in Naval War	1907
Protocol for the Prohibition of the Use in War of Asphyxiating, Poisonous or Other Gases, and of Bacteriological Methods of Warfare	1925
Convention on the Prevention and Punishment of Genocide	1948
Geneva Convention (I) for the Amelioration of the Condition of the Wounded and Sick in Armed Forces in the Field	1949
Geneva Convention (II) for the Amelioration of the Condition of Wounded, Sick and Shipwrecked Members of Armed Forces at Sea	1949
Geneva Convention (III) Relative to the Treatment of Prisoners of War	1949
Geneva Convention (IV) Relative to the Protection of Civilian Persons in Time of War	1949
Convention for the Protection of Cultural Property in the Event of Armed Conflict	1954
Treaty Banning Nuclear Weapon Tests in the Atmosphere, in Outer Space and Under Water	1963
Treaty on the Non-Proliferation of Nuclear Weapons	1968
Treaty on the Prohibition of the Emplacement of Nuclear Weapons and Other Weapons of Mass Destruction on the Seabed and the Ocean Floor and in the Subsoil Thereof	1971
Convention on the Prohibition of the Development, Production and Stockpiling of Bacteriological (Biological) and Toxin Weapons and on Their Destruction	1972
Convention on the Prohibition of Military or Any Other Hostile Use of Environmental Modification	1976

Table 1 Treaties and Conventions Regulating Warfare (*continued*)

Treaty or Convention	Year Signed
Protocol Additional to the Geneva Conventions of 12 August 1949, and Relating to the Protection of Victims of International Armed Conflict (Protocol I)	1977
Protocol Additional to the Geneva Conventions of 12 August 1949, and Relating to the Protection of Victims of Non-International Armed Conflict (Protocol II)	1977
Convention on Prohibitions or Restrictions on the Use of Certain Conventional Weapons Which May Be Deemed to Be Excessively Injurious or to Have Indiscriminate Effects	1980
South Pacific Nuclear Free Zone Treaty	1985
Treaty on Conventional Armed Forces in Europe	1990
Treaty on Open Skies	1992
Convention on the Prohibition of the Development, Production, Stockpiling and Use of Chemical Weapons and on Their Destruction	1993
Comprehensive Test Ban Treaty	1996
United Nations International Convention for the Suppression of Terrorist Bombings	1998

Source: United Nations Treaty Series, available at http://untreaty.un.org/English/treaty.asp (by subscription) or at United Nations depository libraries.

Table 2 Multilateral Treaties and Conventions by Issue Area

Treaty or Convention	Number
Maritime and coastal	52
Human rights	40
Environment*	36
Trade and commercial relations	32
Rules of warfare	22
Atmosphere and space	17
Cultural protection	12
Control on weapons	9
Diplomatic relations	4

Source: Multilaterals Project, Edwin Ginn Library, Fletcher School of Diplomacy, Tufts University.

*Excluding those that specifically address the atmosphere and space.

Table 3 Multilateral Treaties and Conventions on Terrorism

Treaty or Convention	Year Signed
Tokyo Convention on Offenses and Certain Other Acts Committed On Board Aircraft	1963
Hague Convention on the Suppression of Unlawful Seizure of Aircraft	1970
Montreal Convention for the Suppression of Unlawful Acts Against the Safety of Civil Aviation	1971
Convention on the Prevention and Punishment of Crimes Against Internationally Protected Persons [diplomats]	1973
Convention against the Taking of Hostages	1979
Convention for the Suppression of Unlawful Acts Against the Safety of Maritime Navigation Located on the Continental Shelf	1988
Convention on the Marking of Plastic Explosives for the Purposes of Detection	1991
Ottawa Ministerial Declaration on Countering Terrorism	1995
International Convention for the Suppression of Terrorist Bombings	1998

Source: United Nations Treaty Series, available at http://untreaty.un.org/English/treaty.asp (by subscription) or at United Nations depository libraries.

Case Study—Limitations on the Use of Force

Perhaps the greatest advancement in international law since World War II has been the prohibition on the use of force and the mandate that states pursue the peaceful resolution of disputes. Although these obligations have obviously not prevented military conflict and aggression—just as domestic laws against murder have not prevented people from killing—for the first time since the beginning of the nation-state system, states have collectively established these principles as a legal obligation. In a sense, efforts to curb aggression and violence demonstrate the limits and the promises of international law. Preventing the use of force in cases where states deem such use to be in their self-interest is the greatest challenge for international institutions. The basic problem, of course, is that states may accept many obligations, but the mechanisms for ensuring that they meet these obligations are weak.

The primary legal document limiting the use of force in international relations is the UN Charter, Article 2(4) of which mandates that all members refrain "from the threat or use of force" against other states. This article is one of the most fundamental principles in international law, yet political leaders and legal scholars often disagree on the conditions under which it applies. The problem is complicated further by disagreement over the meaning of Article 51, which provides for the "inherent right of individual or collective self-defense." This article has been used by states to justify almost every military action, thereby allowing them to claim compliance even as they engage in warfare. For example, when the United States invaded Panama and arrested its leader, Manuel Noriega, in 1989, Washington claimed that it was acting in self-defense, arguing that Noriega was involved in smuggling drugs into the United States. Many countries have challenged the validity of this claim. Although the self-defense exemption is technically limited to cases in which an "armed attack" has occurred, many political leaders and legal scholars have argued that this includes the right to take preemptive action, commonly known as anticipatory self-defense. Moreover, since military reprisals for hostile actions have been a common practice of states for centuries, many argue that they have achieved some legitimacy (consensus by action) and are thus legal under customary international law (even if they are not under the UN Charter or other international legal instruments).

Although debates over interpretation and problems of compliance are a major impediment to fulfilling the spirit of the charter, the greatest challenge lies in enforcement. The UN Charter gives the Security Council tremendous authority to determine when a violation has occurred and almost free rein in taking steps to respond. Chapter VI grants to the council the authority to investigate and recommend actions to resolve any conflict that is brought before it. Chapter VII allows it to "determine the existence of any threat . . . or breach of the peace or act of aggression." It further provides the council with the authority to take action, including the use of military force to restore the peace or stop an aggressor. In practice, the council has only used this power twice: during the Korean War in 1950 and as a prelude to the Persian Gulf War in 1991. During the cold war the Security Council was paralyzed by the veto power of the Soviet Union and the United States. Neither state would permit UN action against countries with which they were allied or supporting. After 1990 the council became more active, but it still hesitates using its authority.

As a result of states' reluctance to take action when their parochial interests are not at stake, the Security Council, with the help of various secretaries-general, has developed alternative methods of enforcement: economic sanctions, peacekeeping, peacemaking, and peacebuilding (see PEACEMAKING AND PEACEBUILDING). The use of sanctions is one of the tools made available to the council in Chapter VII of the UN Charter. In 1965 the council levied a mandatory arms embargo and ban on trade with Rhodesia, the first time such sanctions were imposed. It later banned arms sales to South Africa (1977); all economic activity with Iraq (1990); airline traffic and arms sales to Libya (1992); and the sale of oil, coal, and steel to Serbia (1992). It also initiated similar though less-comprehensive sanctions against the states of the former Yugoslavia (1991), Somalia, Haiti, and Angola (1993), Rwanda (1994), Liberia (1995), Sudan and Burundi (1996), and Sierra Leone (1997).

The Security Council has rarely used collective force to oppose aggression. Instead it has chosen conflict resolution and the maintenance of cease-fires after a truce has already been declared. Using the authority granted it in Chapter VII, the council has steadily increased its involvement in regional conflicts through peacekeeping missions. Although peacekeeping was originally designed as a mechanism to keep warring parties separated after a truce is declared, the council has expanded the role of the peacekeepers to include state building, establishing civil administrations, facilitating democratization, promoting human rights, disarming militias, protecting populations from attack, and caring for displaced persons. Between 1991 and 1999 the United Nations initiated peacekeeping missions in Bosnia-Herzegovina, the Congo, Croatia, East Timor, Georgia, Kosovo, Prevlaka, Macedonia, Mozambique, Sierra Leone, and the Western Sahara.

In many cases, however, the Security Council has not acted directly. Rather it has contracted out its authority to various regional organizations, such as the Organization for Security and Cooperation in Europe and the Organization of American States; in some cases it has approved a single country or coalition of countries to carry out missions. For example, the council authorized the OAS (primarily the United States) to intervene in Haiti in 1994 to restore a democratically elected leader who had been overthrown in a military coup. Similarly, in 1998 it ceded its authority to Australia to stop military aggression by Indonesia in East Timor. In other cases, the council remained uninvolved, leaving it to regional groups to take action on their own. This was the case in 1990, when the Economic Community of West African States sent troops into Liberia to stop the civil war there.

Case Study—The Recognition of States

The creation, breakup, amalgamation, and reorganization of states has been a persistent feature in world history. It has also been a major source of conflict. In a world in which virtually all territory has been allocated to some sovereign entity, the creation of a new state can in most instances only come at the expense of an existing one. Although some new state formations have been voluntary—for example, the breakup of Czechoslovakia into the Czech Republic and the Slovak Republic in 1993—most are the result of forced secession, international war, or revolution. The breakup of the Soviet Union and Yugoslavia in the early 1990s led to the creation of more than a dozen new states. This process sparked a series of civil wars and nationalist conflicts, as opposing claims threatened the cohesion of the new entities. At the same time, a number of long-standing claims for statehood remain, including those of the Palestinians and Kurds in the Middle East, the Basques in Spain, the Québécois in Canada, and the Catholics in Northern Ireland.

The idea of legal recognition is a relatively new concept in international law. In past centuries, states were usually formed out of violent conflict or, as in the case of Italy and Germany, voluntary amalgamation. Recognition was extended as a de facto acknowledgment, not as a matter of law. The twentieth century saw efforts to formalize this process. Yet the creation of new states has been challenged by two contradictory principles in international law: the right to continued existence for all states and the right of self-determination for all peoples. In general, international law has long been biased toward maintaining the cohesion and unity of existing states. Beginning in the aftermath of World War I, however, countries began to accept the principle of national self-determination even if it meant breaking up an existing state. Yet after World War II, neither the major national powers nor the United Nations recognized secession as a legitimate method for securing this right.

International law does offer some guide for state policy. Under the 1933 Montevideo Convention on Rights and Duties of States, signed by nearly all countries, any group claiming statehood must first meet the following criteria: (1) a permanent population; (2) a defined territory; (3) independence from other states; and (4) the capacity to enter into relations with other states (in short, a functioning government that is in control of a territory). A U.S. federal court affirmed this position by arguing in part that "any government, however violent and wrongful in its origin, must be considered a *de facto* government if it was in the full and actual exercise of sovereignty over a territory."

Still, there is much controversy over whether official recognition is required for a state to be accepted into the international community. According to the constitutive theory of recognition, without de jure (legal) recognition, a political community cannot expect the rights that go with sovereign statehood. The declaratory approach, however, holds that recognition is not a legal act but an acknowledgment of an existing fact. From this perspective, states and international institutions do not have the right to withhold recognition from a state that meets the criteria cited in the Montevideo Convention. In practice, since the end of World War II, legal recognition has been granted through the United Nations, which acts as the principal body for conferring legitimacy on new states by admitting them to the organization.

These are not abstract or academic issues. States assume a wide range of rights and duties under international law that can have serious consequences. For example, a group that attempts to secede from an existing state cannot claim to be a victim of international aggression when attacked if it is not recognized as a sovereign state. In fact it was the recognition of Croatia by the European Union in 1992 that turned the civil war in Yugoslavia into an international conflict. Prior to this act, any military actions taken by the central government of Yugoslavia was an internal matter, technically a police action. Once recognition was extended, however, the boundary separating the Croatian region of Yugoslavia from the rest of the country became a national border. After that, Yugoslavia's military forces were prohibited by international law from violating Croatia's territorial integrity.

Biographical Sketches

Abram and Antonia Chayes have produced a vast body of scholarship on the architecture of international organizations and patterns of treaty compliance in the areas of arms control and the environment. Abram was a legal adviser to the U.S. State Department, and Antonia was an undersecretary of the U.S. Air Force. The Chayes, paving the way for the development of the international process school of international law, argue that states comply with international law as part of a general diplomatic process through which they conduct their international relations. To understand compliance, then, is to understand how and why states interact with one another.

Thomas Franck is a professor of international law at New York University. He is one of the foremost proponents of new thinking in international law. Franck's theories focus on how international law has been transformed since World War II and more recently since the end of the cold war. His influential *Power of Legitimacy among Nations* established a new school of thought in international law, arguing that compliance is not based on state self-interest but on a widespread acceptance of the law's legitimacy in international affairs.

Louis Henkin is professor emeritus at the Columbia University School of Law, former president of the American Society of International Law, and one of the foremost scholars on international law. His co-authored *International Law: Cases and Materials* is standard in most law schools. A passionate advocate for the rule of law in international relations, he helped to keep the field alive when many had abandoned it during the cold war. His most influential work, *How Nations Behave,* was the first authoritative book to argue that "almost all nations observe almost all principles of international law and almost all of their obligations almost all of the time."

Anne-Marie Slaughter is a professor at Harvard University and one of the few international law scholars bridging the disciplinary divide between political science and international law. Slaughter combines Kantian philosophy, which bases legal principles on moral imperative, with practical politics. Her chief contribution to the development of international law theory is the provocative thesis that liberal states act according to the rule of law in their relations with each other, but operate according to the rule of power politics when dealing with nonliberal states. Such behavior has obvious implications for the future of international law in a rapidly democratizing world.

Directory

American Society of International Law, 2223 Massachusetts Avenue NW, Washington, DC 20008. Telephone: (202) 939-6000, Email: mclincy@asil.org, Web: http://www.asil.org
Private organization that educates and engages the public in international law

Amnesty International, 322 8th Avenue, New York, NY 10001. Telephone: (212) 807-8400, Email: admin-us@aiusa.org, Web: http://www.aiusa.org
Advocacy and research nongovernmental organization that deals with human rights and the application of international standards of behavior regarding nations' relationship with their citizens

Center for Human Rights and Humanitarian Law, American University, Washington College of Law, 4801 Massachusetts Avenue NW, Washington, DC 20016. Telephone: (202) 274-4000, Email: humlaw@wcl.american.edu, Web: http://www.wcl.american.edu/pub/humright/home.htm
Research organization dealing with human rights and humanitarian law

Center for International Environmental Law, 1367 Connecticut Avenue NW, Suite 300, Washington, DC 20036. Telephone: (202) 785-8700, Email: info@ciel.org, Web: http://www.ciel.org
Nongovernmental organization that works to increase compliance with international environmental law

Court of Justice of the European Communities, Palais de la Cour de Justice, Boulevard Konrad Adenauer, 2925 Kirchberg, Luxembourg. Telephone: (352) 4303 3367, Email: info@curia.eu.int, Web: http://curia.eu.int/en
Court for members of the European Union

European Court of Human Rights, Council of Europe, 67075 Strasbourg, France. Telephone: (33) 03 88 41 20 18, Email: Webmaster@echr.coe.int, Web: http://www.echr.coe.int
Court adjudicating issues related to the European Convention on Human Rights

Inter-American Court of Human Rights, P.O. Box 6906-1000, San Jose, Costa Rica. Telephone: (506) 234 0581, Email: corteidh@sol.racsa.co.cr, Web: http://www.corteidh.or.cr
Agency of the Organization of American States that deals with human rights issues and cases of its member states

International Court of Justice, Peace Palace, 2517 KJ The Hague, Netherlands. Telephone: (31) 0 70 302 2323, Email: information@icj-cij.org, Web: http://www.icj-cij.org
UN agency that settles legal disputes between states according to international law and advises recognized international agencies on legal questions

International Law Association, Charles Clore House, 17 Russell Square, London WC1B 5DR, United Kingdom. Telephone: (44) 20 7323 2978, Email: info@ila-hq.org, Web: http://www.ila-hq.org
Private organization promoting the study of international law

International Law Institute, 1615 New Hampshire Avenue NW, Washington, DC 20009. Telephone: (202) 483-3036, Email: training@ili.org, Web: http://www.ili.org
Educational organization that sponsors training sessions and conferences on international law

International Law Students Association, 1615 New Hampshire Avenue NW, Washington, DC 20009. Telephone: (202) 299-9101, Email: ilsa@iamdigex.net, Web: http://www.ilsa.org
Private organization for students studying international law

Permanent Court of Arbitration, International Bureau, Peace Palace, 2 Carnegieplein, 2517 KJ The Hague, Netherlands. Telephone: (31) 0 70 302 4165, Email: bureau@pca-cpa.org, Web: http://www.pca-cpa.org
International organization that settles disputes between states on a voluntary basis

Project on International Courts and Tribunals, Center on International Cooperation, New York University, 418 Lafayette Street, Suite 543, New York, NY 10003. Telephone: (212) 998-3680, Email: cr28@acf2.nyu.edu, Web: http://www.pict-pcti.org/home.html.
Private advocacy organization that addresses legal, institutional, and financial issues arising from the proliferation of international courts and tribunals

United Nations Commission on International Trade Law, Vienna International Centre, P.O. Box 500, 1400 Vienna, Austria. Telephone: (43) 1 26060 4061, Email: uncitral@uncitral.org, Web: http://www.uncitral.org
Agency dealing with international law relating to trade

World Trade Organization, Centre William Rappard, 154 Rue de Lausanne, 1211 Geneva 21, Switzerland. Telephone: (41) 22 739 51 11, Email: enquiries@wto.org
Organization that imposes binding obligations on members in all areas of international trade

Further Research

Books

Arend, A., and R. Beck, eds. *International Law and the Use of Force.* London: Routledge, 1993.

Brierly, J. L. *The Law of Nations: An Introduction to the International Law of Peace.* New York: Oxford University Press, 1963.

Cassese, Antonio. *International Law in a Divided World.* Oxford: Clarendon Press, 1986.

———. *Self-Determination of Peoples: A Legal Reprisal.* Cambridge: Cambridge University Press, 1995.

Charlesworth, Hilary, Richard Falk, and Burns Weston. *International Law and World Order.* St. Paul, Minn.: West Group, 1997.

Chayes, Abram, and Antonia Handler Chayes. *The New Sovereignty: Compliance with International Regulatory Agreements.* Cambridge, Mass.: Harvard University Press, 1995.

Damrosch, L., ed. *Enforcing Restraint: Collective Intervention in International Conflicts.* New York: Council on Foreign Relations, 1993.

Damrosch, L., and David Scheffer. *Law and Force in the New International Order.* Boulder: Westview Press, 1991.

Ehrilich, T., and M. O'Connell. *International Law and the Use of Force.* Boston: Little, Brown and Company, 1993.

Franck, Thomas. *The Power of Legitimacy among Nations.* New York: Oxford University Press, 1990.

———. *Fairness in International Law and Institutions.* Oxford: Clarendon Press, 1995.

Ginsburgs, George. *From Soviet to Russian International Law: Studies in Continuity and Change.* The Hague: Martinus Nijhoff Publishers, 1998.

Henkin, Louis. *How Nations Behave: Law and Foreign Policy.* New York: Columbia University Press, 1979.

Henkin, Louis, et al. *International Law: Cases and Materials.* St. Paul, Minn.: West Publishing Company, 1993.

Janis, Mark, and John Noyes. *Cases and Commentary on International Law.* St. Paul, Minn.: West Group, 1997.

Joyner, Christopher, ed. *The United Nations and International Law.* Cambridge: Cambridge University Press, 1997.

Ku, Charlotte, and Paul Diehl, eds. *International Law: Classic and Contemporary Readings.* Boulder: Lynne Rienner, 1998.

Malanczuk, Peter. *Akehurst's Modern Introduction to International Law.* New York: Routledge, 1997.

McCormack, T. *Self-Defense in International Law: The Israeli Raid on the Iraqi Reactor.* Jerusalem: Magnes Press, 1996.

Rosenne, Shabtai. *The World Court: What It Is and How It Works.* Dordrecht: M. Nijhoff, 1995.

Wallace-Bruce, and Nii Lante. *Claims to Statehood in International Law.* New York: Carlton Press, 1994.

White, N. D. *Keeping the Peace: The United Nations and the Maintenance of International Peace and Security.* Manchester: Manchester University Press, 1997.

Zartman, I. William. *Collapsed States: The Disintegration and Restoration of Legitimate Authority.* Boulder: Lynne Rienner, 1995.

Articles and Reports

Arend, Anthony Clark. "Do Legal Rules Matter? International Law and International Politics." *Virginia Journal of International Law* 38 (1998).

International Law Commission. *Report on the Work of the Fifty-fifth Session,* United Nations General Assembly, Official Records, Fifty-fifth Session, Supplement 10 (A/55/10).

Keohane, Robert. "International Relations and International Law: Two Optics." *Harvard International Law Journal* 38 (1997).

Lobel, J., and M. Ratner. "Bypassing the Security Council: Ambiguous Authorizations to Use Force, Ceasefires, and the Iraqi Inspection Regime." *American Journal of International Law* 93 (1999).

Web Sites

International Convention for the Suppression of Terrorist Bombings
http://fletcher.tufts.edu/multi/texts/terror.txt

International Law Commission
http://www.un.org/law/ilc

International Law Dictionary and Directory
http://www.august1.com/pubs/dict/index.shtml

International Law Links, E. B. Williams Law Library, Georgetown University
http://www.ll.georgetown.edu/intl/intl.html

International Law Page
http://users.bart.nl/~bethlehem/law.html

International Law Research on the Web
http://lic.law.ufl.edu/~willipam/intlweb.htm

International Law Resources, Westminster Law Library, University of Denver
http://www.law.du.edu/library/research_links/intl/intl_res.htm

Legal Research on International Law Issues Using the Internet
http://www.lib.uchicago.edu/~llou/forintlaw.html

Multilaterals Project, The Fletcher School, Tufts University
http://fletcher.tufts.edu/multilaterals.html

Statute of the International Court of Justice
http://www.icj-cij.org/icjwww/ibasicdocuments/ibasictext/ibasicstatute.htm

Treaties, U.S. State Department
http://www.state.gov/s/1/trtyact

United Nations Charter
http://www.un.org/Overview/Charter/contents.html

United Nations International Law
http://www.un.org/law

Documents

1. Geneva Convention Relative to the Treatment of Prisoners of War

Conference for the Establishment of International Conventions for the Protection of Victims of War, Geneva, 12 August 1949

The full text is available at http://fletcher.tufts.edu/multi/texts/BH240.txt.

Extract

Article 3

In the case of armed conflict not of an international character occurring in the territory of one of the High Contracting Parties, each Party to the conflict shall be bound to apply, as a minimum, the following provisions:

(1) Persons taking no active part in the hostilities, including members of armed forces who have laid down their arms and those placed hors de combat by sickness, wounds, detention, or any other cause, shall in all circumstances be treated humanely, without any adverse distinction founded on race, colour, religion or faith, sex, birth or wealth, or any other similar criteria. To this end the following acts are and shall remain prohibited at any time and in any place whatsoever with respect to the above-mentioned persons:

(a) violence to life and person, in particular murder of all kinds, mutilation, cruel treatment and torture;
(b) taking of hostages;
(c) outrages upon personal dignity, in particular, humiliating and degrading treatment;
(d) the passing of sentences and the carrying out of executions without previous judgment pronounced by a regularly constituted court affording all the judicial guarantees which are recognized as indispensable by civilized peoples.

(2) The wounded and sick shall be collected and cared for. . . .

Article 13

Prisoners of war must at all times be humanely treated. Any unlawful act or omission by the Detaining Power causing death or seriously endangering the health of a prisoner of war in its custody is prohibited, and will be regarded as a serious breach of the present Convention. In particular, no prisoner of war may be subjected to physical mutilation or to medical or scientific experiments of any kind which are not justified by the medical, dental or hospital treatment of the prisoner concerned and carried out in his interest.

Likewise, prisoners of war must at all times be protected, particularly against acts of violence or intimidation and against insults and public curiosity.

Measures of reprisal against prisoners of war are prohibited.

2. Convention on Rights and Duties of States (Montevideo Convention)

Montevideo, 26 December 1933

The full text is available at http://www.yale.edu/lawweb/avalon/intdip/interam/intam03.htm.

Extract

Article 3

The political existence of the state is independent of recognition by the other states. Even before recognition the state has the right to defend its integrity and independence, to provide for its conservation and prosperity, and consequently to organize itself as it sees fit, to legislate upon its interests, administer its services, and to define the jurisdiction and competence of its courts.

The exercise of these rights has no other limitation than the exercise of the rights of other states according to international law.

Article 4

States are juridically equal, enjoy the same rights, and have equal capacity in their exercise. The rights of each one do not depend upon the power which it possesses to assure its exercise, but upon the simple fact of its existence as a person under international law. . . .

Article 8

No state has the right to intervene in the internal or external affairs of another. . . .

Article 9

The jurisdiction of states within the limits of national territory applies to all the inhabitants.

Nationals and foreigners are under the same protection of the law and the national authorities and the foreigners may not claim rights other or more extensive than those of the nationals. . . .

Article 11

The contracting states definitely establish as the rule of their conduct the precise obligation not to recognize territorial acquisitions or special advantages which have been obtained by force whether this consists in the employment of arms, in threatening diplomatic representations, or in any other effective coercive measure. The territory of a state is inviolable and may not be the object of military occupation nor of other measures of force imposed by another state directly or indirectly or for any motive whatever even temporarily.

LABOR AND EMPLOYMENT

Scott B. Martin

Most people work locally, but today employment is increasingly affected by global economic processes. Greatly increased cross-border flows of trade and investment—economic globalization—have had a considerable impact on the quantity and quality of work, the nature of working conditions, and the collective rights of workers. Yet scholars, policymakers, and advocates concerned with labor and employment issues disagree on whether these developments are more positive or negative and on appropriate programs and policies to respond to them. Particular areas of contention are employment generation, job security, and international labor rights in the context of multinational corporations and international economic agreements.

Historical Background and Development

Policies and norms governing conditions of work and employment have emerged and evolved over time in response to changing technological circumstances and shifting international economic and political conditions. International and national initiatives and debates have continually shaped each other. The Industrial Revolution brought masses of impoverished laborers together in often highly unsafe and exploitative conditions in the first workshops and factories. While transforming Europe and the United States in the mid- to late-nineteenth century, the revolution also generated national and international reform movements and the first workers' organizations. The International Workingmen's Association (First International), which lasted from 1864 to 1870, and the subsequent Second International, founded in the late 1880s and lasting through World War I, voiced revolutionary socialist demands and promoted international working-class solidarity.

The first national labor federations, or centrals, were formed in Europe in the latter decades of the nineteenth century. Also, the first national laws regulating conditions of work emerged during this period in the industrializing countries of Europe and in the United States, focusing on limiting child labor, women's labor, and hours of work; creating a weekly day of rest and limiting night work; and regulating dangerous occupations. The right to form trade unions and engage in strikes, however, was not formally established and was mostly restricted in practice. Based on the earlier work of European industrialists interested in promoting intergovernmental cooperation on labor laws, and responding to growing pressure from an emerging working class, the first international labor treaties—regulating working hours for women and children and night work by children—were drafted on the eve of World War I. They were not adopted or ratified, however, because of the war.

The momentum for the adoption of international labor norms survived the war, as the International Labour Organization (ILO) was founded in 1919, in large part through the efforts of trade unions from the Allied powers to include an international labor charter in the Treaty of Versailles, which officially concluded World War I. A tripartite commission of government, union, and employer representatives established nine principles to guide the new organization, including the right of association, equal pay for equal work, an eight-hour workday (or forty-eight-hour workweek), the abolition of child labor, and equitable economic treatment of immigrant labor. Between the two World Wars, the ILO functioned as an autonomous part of the League of Nations, the short-lived predecessor to the United Nations. With the end of World War II and the creation of the United Nations, the ILO became in 1946 the first of the specialized UN agencies, with specific responsibilities in the areas of labor and social policy, such as employment conditions, labor relations, social security, and vocational training. The ILO has continued to be organized under the principle of tripartism, with equal representation for member governments and national trade union and employer organizations.

On the national front, the interwar and immediate post-World War II periods were marked by considerable trade union activism and political and social conflict over the role of workers in society, particularly in the industrialized countries of the West but also in some of the industrializing countries of the Southern Hemisphere. The central place of labor in modernizing economies was recognized in an expanding network of labor laws improving working conditions and guaranteeing trade union and bargaining rights, as well as in newly created or expanded social benefits in the areas of retirement pensions, health care, education, and housing. U.S. examples are the Wagner Act of the mid-1930s, which guaranteed the right to organize and strike, and New Deal social legislation, both of the Roosevelt era. Meanwhile in socialist countries, such as the Soviet Union and China, social rights were formally guaranteed and benefits were expanded, but labor rights to freedom of association and political rights to free speech and assembly were sharply curtailed.

Although the workings of the ILO were at times stymied by a relatively small budget and staff and by cold war rivalries, the organization nevertheless remained at the center of international efforts to regulate conditions of work and employment in the post-World War II decades. In recent years, the end of the cold war, the burgeoning debate about the social impact of globalization, and the high profile of the ILO's leadership have focused renewed attention on the organization's role. Its official functions not only include setting international norms but also engaging in international technical cooperation with governments, unions, and employers, as well as promoting public education and conducting research. Nearly all nation-states are ILO members. Core international labor standards have been negotiated in a series of international conventions subject to ratification by member states and binding upon ratifying countries (see Table 1 and Documents 1 and 2). These agreements cover basic principles, such as the abolition of forced labor, freedom of association of workers through trade unions, rights to collective bargaining, anti-discrimination, and limits on child labor. The United Nations, in addition to sponsoring ILO conventions, adopted the Universal Declaration of Human Rights in 1948, Article 20 of which protects "the right to freedom of peaceful assembly and association" and establishes that "no one may be compelled to belong to any association."

Current Status

Research and policy efforts relating to global and comparative employment and labor trends are complicated by the complex, difficult-to-measure connections between global processes and national and local employment patterns, as well as the unusual joining of new and old forms of work that globalization has wrought. For instance, in developing countries, grinding historic problems of poverty and wealth and income inequality persist, reflected in phenomena such as gender, ethnic, and racial discrimination in pay and employment and children being sent to work to support impoverished families. Yet, these problems take on a new cast under globalization, for studies show that an increasing share of the large segment of the workforce who have long eked out a living in the "informal sector," the unregulated, underground economy, now work directly or indirectly in globalized economic activities. Women are disproportionately represented in the informal sector, particularly as declining family incomes as well as (in some cases) shifting cultural values lead them to enter the workforce as part of household survival strategies (see Table 2 and map, p. 418). Thus, for instance, street vendors may well sell imported consumer goods, and industrial home workers and laborers in clandestine workshops and factories, usually female, may stitch together pieces of garments or make ceramics that are then sold internationally, often under name brand labels. Such low-skilled laborers are just as engaged in the globalizing economy as are the workers in the high-tech sectors of the information economy that are often more commonly associated in the media with globalization.

Research

The most direct and immediate impact of global integration on labor and employment has been the enormous growth in the 1980s and 1990s of transnational corporations (TNCs), foreign direct investment (FDI), and complex international networks of production and trade centering on transnational firms. In 2000 there were approximately 63,000 parent firms operating some 690,000 foreign affiliates in almost every country and economic sector.

Through direct investment, these companies route flows of money across national boundaries to establish offices and factories and managerial control of overseas employees. Examples of such companies are McDonald's, Shell Oil, and Volkswagen.

Direct investment by TNCs has become more diverse in terms of the location and nature of jobs it supports, but remains concentrated within the United States, Western Europe, and Japan—almost three-fourths by 1999—meaning that, for instance, an increasing number of U.S. jobs depend directly or indirectly on investment in the United States by non-American firms. Yet FDI-related employment grew fastest in the 1980s and 1990s in developing and transitional economies. Twenty of these economies accounted for 83 percent of the bulk of the capital inflows into the so-called emerging markets by 1998, with those of Brazil, China, Mexico, and Singapore leading the way.

The effect of international trade on employment has also grown dramatically (see WORLD TRADE). From 1965 through 1989, the global growth rate of total world trade volume ranged between 3 and 5 percent per year. In the 1990s the rate increased to between 5 and 10 percent per year. Even in the United States—which because of the sheer size of its domestic market has tended to be internally oriented economically—more than 12 million jobs now depend on exports. In smaller national economies, such as those of Western Europe and East and Southeast Asia, a much higher percentage of jobs are trade related. One downside of this trend is that slumps in export markets are quickly felt at home. For instance, export-oriented economies, such as those of Hong Kong, Korea, and Taiwan, experienced rising unemployment as their key export markets in Europe, Japan, and the United States experienced an economic slowdown in 2001.

International portfolio investment—purchases of stocks and other private financial instruments that do not usually imply direct managerial control over workers by the purchaser—has grown a great deal in scale but has also been subject to dramatic fluctuations in recent decades. By nature these investments are more liquid than are direct investment monies tied up in physical assets. From 1989 to 1996, during the boom in emerging markets, such short-term, sometimes speculative flows from wealthy to developing countries grew tenfold (1,000 percent). New jobs were thus indirectly generated in the process, as firms had greater financing to initiate new activities or expand older ones. Portfolio investment flows then declined 70 percent during 1997 to 1999, when a financial crisis struck Asia and moved on to Russia and parts of Latin America. This downturn had a major negative effect on employment, working conditions, and job security in the countries affected.

Research evaluating the impact of globalization on the quantity and quality of work is somewhat less polarized than the current contentious public debate between views of globalization as a panacea and globalization as a race to the bottom. Complex trade-offs among competing goals and different social groups are a frequent theme. The United Nations Conference on Trade and Development (UNCTAD)—a traditional critic of TNCs—has documented that they generally provide better pay and benefits, more training, greater job security, and more stimulus for innovation by local business partners than do domestically owned firms. This is because they are generally larger and more competitive firms that place a premium on the stability provided by more institutionalized human resources practices. This does not, however, always extend to cultivating working relations with unions, since transnational subsidiaries adapt closely to national regulatory frameworks. In many countries, particularly in the developing world, there are formal and informal restrictions on independent union organization and labor–management collective bargaining over terms of employment. Moreover, transnational firms are capital intensive, so they tend to generate fewer jobs per unit of investment or output. Furthermore, human resource advantages do not always hold true for export-oriented affiliates in such lower-end industries as apparel, toys, some consumer electronics, and industries in tax-favorable export processing zones (EPZs) in regions of developing nations, such as those in southern China and northern Mexico. In EPZs, pay, working conditions, and job security are notoriously poor, freedom of association is seldom respected, and the primary workers are typically young women and other recent arrivals from the countryside, where material conditions are even more dire than in the new manufacturing centers.

Mainstream economists recognize international trade's aggregate benefits of promoting growth in world output and living standards, as well as providing benefits to consumers through lower trade barriers. Even these economists, however, agree that there are definite distributional effects for employment: workers in export-oriented industries and regions gain while those in import-sensitive areas lose, at least in the short term. Certain industries—such as the textile, shoe, and garment sectors in the United States and other developed countries—are particularly sensitive to import competition due, in part, to their labor intensity, smaller firm size, and slimmer profit margins. Displaced workers may or may not recover secure employment at similar wages in another firm or industry in the medium to long term; their fate depends on their age, skills, and the availability of government assistance. In the meantime their families and communities may endure great hardship.

Mainstream economists also argue that in the long term it is technology, not trade, that determines the demand for and price of labor. Critics, however, point to evidence that technological change interacts in complex ways with openness to trade, producing a growing skills gap in which less-educated and less-skilled workers increasingly fall behind the rest as their employability and wages decline. During the two decades beginning in the late 1970s, for instance, the real (inflation-adjusted) hourly wages of young U.S. males with a high school education or less—for many decades the backbone of the country's working class turned middle class—dropped by 20 percent, recovering only somewhat in the late 1990s at the end of the country's longest peacetime expansion in history. Competition with lower-wage competitors overseas, critics suggest, helps spur firms to invest in labor-saving technology (such as automation and robotics); even well-trained industrial workers from many developing and transitional economies, however, can suffer greatly in the face of lower wages and more efficient production from overseas.

By this same line of reasoning, one of the effects of the globalization of production and of trade has been to shift bargaining power dramatically from labor to capital, as firms can increasingly make credible threats to move production overseas, away from union pressure. In the 1997 report "Trade Unions: Battered but Rising to the Challenges of Globalization," the ILO suggests that globalization is a major reason why it found significant drops in the percentage of the workforce organized into unions from the 1980s through 1995. In forty-eight of ninety-two countries surveyed in 1997, union members had fallen to less than 20 percent of the workforce over the previous decade, and in all but twenty countries membership levels had fallen (see Table 3).

Another alleged impact of increased global integration and related portfolio capital flows is growing pressure on the ability of national governments to finance welfare states. Pension programs, health care, education, housing, and other social benefits have been part of an implicit social contract with citizens since the Great Depression and World War II in wealthy and, on a smaller scale, many transitional and some developing countries. Capital assets, the argument goes, will move to those geographic locations where they earn the highest return (and suffer the least taxation), whereas labor is by nature limited in its mobility; hence, contemporary tax burdens will increasingly fall on wage earners whom states can more easily reach, say, through income or sales taxes. With more of the tax burden shifted to workers, political support for welfare state programs, particularly those seen as benefiting only certain groups in society, erodes. Skeptics find this argument faulty, arguing that even under such constraints different nation-states make different political choices about maintaining strong welfare states (as in France, Germany, and Scandinavia) or reducing them substantially (as in Great Britain and the United States).

Policies and Programs

One can identify, roughly speaking, three general approaches to policies regarding labor and employment issues in a globalizing economy. The mainstream perspective is strongly pro-market, pushing for labor market flexibility and less intrusive government policies. It rejects any linkage between labor rights and international trade and investment agreements and advocates for a deepening of globalization. The reformist perspective calls for more active domestic and international measures to regulate global integration to cushion its social impact and give voice to organizations that speak for workers and other groups disadvantaged by globalization. The anti-globalization perspective advocates a radical rollback or halt to continuing global integration and the domestic and international policies that foster it. Critiques of unfettered globalization from the latter two perspectives, as well as signs of a mounting social gap between winners and losers of globalization within and across countries, have motivated subtle but important shifts in mainstream positions in recent years.

Flexible labor markets has been the watchword used by mainstream policymakers and analysts for the type of reforms they advocate. They call for private transactions and decisions to dictate the terms of wages, skill formation, and the hiring and dismissal of workers. Such reforms, adopted on a significant international scale in the 1980s and 1990s, sought to make it easier for employers to fire workers for economic motives, decentralize labor–management negotiations to the firm level, make it more difficult for unions to strike, foster part-time and temporary work contracts, and reduce minimum wages and their role in wage setting in the broader economy.

Labor market flexibility has also been seen as a key ingredient of a larger package of broad economic reforms, sometimes referred to as the Washington consensus, embodying greater economic openness, less government spending and intervention, and increasing privatization. Many developing and transitional economies have adopted some or all of these reforms because of pressures from the World Bank and the International Monetary Fund (IMF), both of which are heavily influenced by the United States, and changing economic doctrines among governing elites (see DEVELOPMENT AID and INCOME INEQUALITY). Many Western European nations (with their strong welfare states and significant labor movements) as well as Japan (with its corporate-centered system of lifetime employment in large companies) have pursued labor market reforms only selectively or timidly, even while generally moving toward more market- and outward-oriented macroeconomic policies.

The 1990s brought alarming and growing signs that Washington consensus reforms, even while restoring some growth and healthy government finances in many countries, were leaving many citizens behind in transitional and developing economies. The series of financial crises affecting East and Southeast Asia, Latin America, and Russia added considerable weight to these concerns. Creditor countries and international financial institutions, while not abandoning market-oriented macroeconomic and labor market policies, responded in part by pushing for more active "pro-poor" policies. They advocated targeted spending on at-risk groups (such as women and the rural poor), generating income through micro-entrepreneurship, and strengthening the property rights of poor people over productive assets (like their residences, often lacking title), among other measures. Somewhat at odds with these new policies was a heightened focus on the need to restructure social security systems in response to growing pressures on government budgets from aging workforces. Among proposed changes were such measures as limiting benefits, increasing retirement ages, and privatizing pensions. These new policy orientations are still decidedly pro-market.

On the employment front, lending policies began to focus on measures that would foster human capital, the stock of abilities and skills of the population, through reform and expansion of basic education, vocational training, and school-to-work transitions. On the financial front, there have been limited initiatives to forgive the debt of a few highly indebted developing countries instituting rigorous market reforms, as well as some initial efforts to rethink the policies and roles of the World Bank and IMF in light of growing criticism from many quarters.

Reformists and anti-globalists raise strong practical and philosophical objections to the mainstream policy agenda for employment and labor reform.

Reformists, however, sometimes agree with specific new pro-poor initiatives. They generally believe that countries can and should balance high levels of social protection and strong labor rights with efficiency, innovation, and quality, while anti-globalists fundamentally question the social efficacy of the market system. Whereas mainstream analysts insist that income testing or work requirements for particular social benefits are necessary to promote personal responsibility, their reformist and anti-globalists critics view such measures as punitive procedures that blame individuals for systemic socioeconomic problems, such as the growing scarcity of well-paying work for less-educated people in wealthy countries. Reformists and anti-globalists regard radical efforts to overhaul social security systems through privatization as undermining the principle of intergenerational solidarity—today's workers pay taxes to support yesterday's workers who are now retired—and creating a danger of widening inequalities. They also express skepticism over whether the best-conceived pro-poor policies can deal with the structural inequalities generated by market-oriented developed and unregulated global integration.

Critics of mainstream reforms also argue that measures to strengthen collective bargaining between management and labor, tripartite government-business-labor consultation on economic and social polices, and collective representation of workers through unions can contribute to economic growth with enhanced social equity, as such policies have done in much of Western Europe. For instance, a Socialist government in France and a Social Democratic administration in Germany implemented reforms that strengthened worker representation and in the former reduced working hours while pursuing a generally market-friendly economic posture.

Internationally, two broad areas of activism and proposed reforms have emerged loosely from the reformist and anti-globalist perspectives. One is the effort to promote responsible labor (and other social) practices by globally active corporations through consumer-focused campaigns. Examples are the "clean clothes" movement in Europe and the burgeoning anti-sweatshop movement in the United States; fair trade initiatives to promote sales by small-scale, developing country producers (for instance in the coffee sector) that do not pass through powerful TNC intermediaries; and campaigns for socially responsible investing that take into account corporations' labor and other practices in choosing stocks. These efforts, in turn, have spurred initiatives by individual companies to improve their images through voluntary codes of conduct—corporate social responsibility—as well as initiatives by governments, international organizations, and unionists and other advocates to create industry-wide or pan-industry codes, such as the Fair Labor Association in the U.S. apparel industry.

Corporations have also responded to or contributed to intergovernmental and governmental initiatives that seek to elaborate acceptable labor practices, such as the ILO's 1996 Tripartite Declaration on Multinational Enterprises and Social Policy, which calls for respect for worker rights of association and bargaining, and the Organization for Economic Cooperation and Development's (OECD) 2000 revised Guidelines for Multinational Enterprises, which call for consultation with worker representatives and governments in cases of mass layoffs and facility closures. Moreover, activist campaigns around the issue of child labor in export manufacturing, particularly in South Asia, helped give impetus to the 1999 adoption by the ILO of the Convention concerning the Prohibition and Immediate Action for the Elimination of Worst Forms of Child Labour.

Many trade unionists and anti-sweatshop activists criticize such efforts as well intentioned but limited only to the most egregious abuses, such as unsafe work environments, forced overtime, and gender discrimination. These efforts fall short on two counts. First, the independence and rigor of outside monitoring of corporate labor practices can be limited. Second, some voluntary codes and admonitions omit the core labor right of freedom of association and avoid such economic issues as payment of "living wages." Loftier labor standards are set by initiatives such as the Worker Rights Consortium in the United States, and in a different way, by company framework agreements between international trade unions and a dozen or so European-based TNCs.

Another related area of activism and debate concerns efforts to rewrite the rules of major institutions of global and regional economic integration. Calls for the explicit linkage of labor (and other social) standards to international trade and investment agreements have grown in the past decade and have had some effect in shaping the debate. Under a European Union directive, large European transnational companies have recently implemented work councils, which represent all the firms' workers regardless of national boundaries. Meanwhile, in 1993, Canada, Mexico, and the United States negotiated side agreements to the North American Free Trade Agreement to promote enforcement of domestic environmental and labor laws (see Case Study—North American Integration and Labor Rights). Later in the decade, U.S. proposals for a World Trade Organization working group to study labor standards and trade—in large part a response to pressure from unionists and other labor advocates—were rejected in 1998 and 1999 by other WTO member states, particularly developing countries, fearing that they were a protectionist attempt to keep their cheaper goods out of rich markets. Labor standards are one of the several issues causing problems in the advancement of new international and regional trade agreements.

In the United States, advocates' efforts to pressure for trade and labor issues in the formulation of trade policy have had mixed results. Connecting labor rights to access by developing countries to the U.S. market for specific products is typically invoked only selectively and on the basis of broader diplomatic and political considerations. Only countries with poor relations with the United States tend to be singled out. Although a bilateral free trade agreement reached with Jordan in 2000 and ratified in 2001 was seen as a pioneering achievement—because it explicitly incorporated core labor standards as the basis for greater bilateral market access—the agreement seems unlikely to serve as a model for future trade agreements during the George W. Bush administration.

Other efforts are in the works to improve labor and employment conditions. Initiatives for trade union revitalization include merging competing unions into larger entities, involving national confederations of unions in national negotiations, and reaching out to previously underrepresented segments of the workforce. It is premature, however, to gauge the success of such efforts. Another strand of activity combines development research and policy as exemplified by the ILO's International Institute for Labour Studies. This effort focuses on policies and strategies that play on the tendency of particular economic activities to cluster in specific geographic locations but are in turn linked to global production, trading, and sales networks. Local policymakers, unions, industry associations, and activists from nongovernmental organizations are urged to foster development alliances that can "upgrade" the position of localities and regions within global industries, moving them into higher-value-added activities with more stable long-term growth paths. Such an upgrade would generate more and better employment, improved working conditions, and an expanded tax base.

Regional Summaries

Employment and labor trends exhibit some common tendencies in relation to globalization, but with significant differences across regions.

North America

Growing integration into the global economy is increasingly shaping the conditions of employment creation and labor relations in Canada and the United States. According to the *Economist* and the *Economist Intelligence Unit,* in the 1990s the United States fared much better on the employment front, with unemployment rates in the 5 to 6 percent range during the first half of the decade and in the 4 percent range by the decade's end; in Canada unemployment rates remained stubbornly high at 8 to 9 percent. The United States was considered by many observers to be a great "job-creating machine" during its protracted boom of the mid- to late 1990s, when it outperformed industrialized countries in Europe as well as Japan. The United States' flexible labor markets are built upon the ease with which employers can hire and fire workers; comparatively weak unemployment and other benefits and an employer-based health care system that together strongly discourage long periods of unemployment; and restrictions on labor organizing. The U.S. Department of Labor's Bureau of Labor Statistics reported that in 2000 only 9 percent of the private sector labor force was organized, a rate among the lowest in the industrialized world.

Amid the U.S. economic expansion, critics of its allegedly benign distributional impact point to stubbornly high poverty rates even among the employed—the working poor—particularly among blacks and Latinos, people in inner cities, and female-headed households; the hollowing out of the manufacturing-based middle class; the highest rates of inequality of wealth and income among industrialized countries; and eroding inflation-adjusted minimum wages and income for workers. The labor movement, which entered a period of revitalization in 1995, has barely held its own on the organizing front.

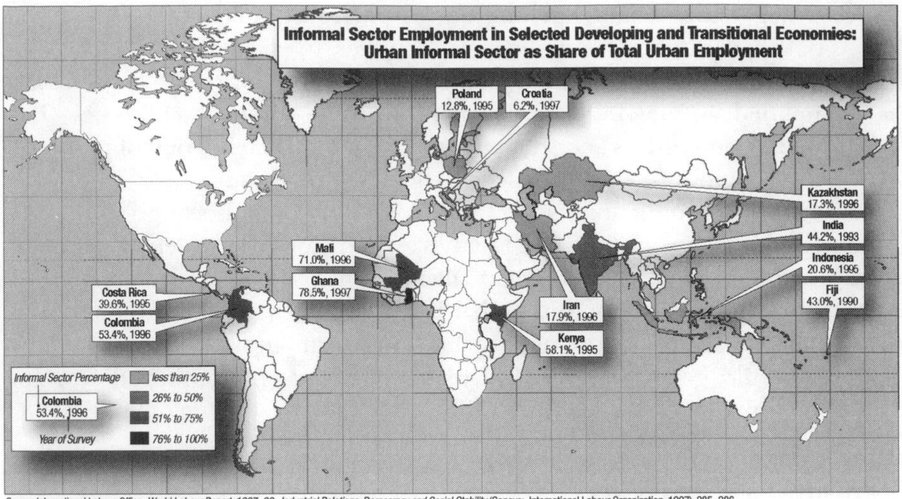

Source: International Labour Office, *World Labour Report, 1997–98: Industrial Relations, Democracy and Social Stability* (Geneva: International Labour Organization, 1997), 285–286.
Note: The criteria for selection of the countries involved depicting the "modal" range of rates within regions and including at least one country from the major relevant subregions.

It lost members in the heavily unionized (and increasingly globalized) manufacturing sectors as fast as it could recruit new members among janitors, home health care workers, public servants, and the like.

Canada, by contrast, has much lower poverty rates, somewhat higher rates of union density (though lower than much of Europe), and a much more extensive welfare state, including universal health care. Efforts to pare back state social spending have gained ground in recent years. As in the United States, Canada has increasing trade and investment links with Mexico under the North American Free Trade Agreement.

Latin America

The phenomenon of jobless growth is a problem for Latin America. Despite 3.7 percent average annual growth in economic output from 1990 to 1997, employment grew at only 2.2 percent, 0.7 points less than it had during the previous decade, according to Barbara Stallings and Wilson Peres in *Growth, Employment and Equity*. In a study covering 1990 to 1998, only two countries—Chile and Bolivia—experienced a decline in overall unemployment rates, while six countries—Argentina, Brazil, Colombia, Jamaica, Mexico, and Peru—documented increases. Only Costa Rica maintained the same level of unemployment. These figures do not take into account the region's very high levels of informal sector employment—in the range of 30 to 55 percent in the mid-1990s—activities that constitute "disguised" unemployment or "underemployment" and have kept official unemployment rates relatively low. Growth brought moderate improvements in average real wages in the formal sector in the 1990s, though 1998 levels remained 9.5 percent lower than 1980 levels.

Meanwhile during the 1980s and 1990s, there was a general trend toward more flexible labor markets in practice (even if few laws changed). Combined with increased competition for domestic firms from imports and increased pressure to cut costs to be competitive on export markets, this trend encouraged employment shedding through restructuring in privatized and tradable goods sectors and in the state bureaucracy, longtime bastions of union strength. The layoffs resulted, in turn, in a general decline in union density rates. Two other factors also probably help explain the region's disappointing employment picture: weaknesses in human capital formation in terms of basic education and vocational training and competition policies to promote adjustment by domestic firms plus greater labor market flexibility in terms of ease of hiring and firing. Finally, as a result of weak job growth, the growing commercialization of agriculture, the increasing concentration of landownership, and inadequate social policies, the region's levels of inequality—rivaled only by those of Africa according to Gini coefficients—actually increased slightly during the 1990s (see INCOME INEQUALITY).

Europe

Europe has a diverse set of employment and labor trajectories as a result of national differences in levels of development and economic integration. Albeit with considerable national variations, European Union member states from northern, western, and to some extent southern Europe have the world's most developed welfare states, the most institutionalized systems of union rights and collective bargaining, and the most tightly regulated labor markets. Persistently high unemployment levels have been a major issue since the early 1990s. Slow economic growth, high wages and high payroll taxes to fund social programs, and increased competition from lower-cost manufacturers in Asia are among the causes widely cited for European unemployment. The role of the labor market "flexibilization" urged by conservative observers is controversial, particularly since the two countries that have pursued it most forcefully since the 1980s—Spain and the United Kingdom—have suffered on the unemployment front as well.

Most countries on the continent have resisted reforms in protective labor laws. In lieu of flexible labor reforms, these countries have variously tinkered with strengthening active labor market policies, such as retraining, job search assistance, and the like, and existing bargaining mechanisms, such as Germany's proposed extension of the works council system of employee representation to smaller firms. The poorer southern European countries that entered the European Community, now the European Union, in the 1980s, plus the United Kingdom and Italy, all had poverty rates of 20 percent or more, a level of magnitude approaching the United States,' which had a poverty rate of 27.3 by the mid-1990s. Among the EU members whose more generous social assistance cushioned the social hardship of high unemployment, rates were 10 to 20 points lower.

The countries of Eastern and Central Europe, the Baltics, and the Russian Federation have suffered the social dislocations of "marketization" and integration into the global capitalist economy. The Balkan states have also suffered economically from interethnic strife. Some countries clearly fared better than the rest in attracting foreign investment, creating market institutions, and stabilizing democratic structures, which are necessary (if not essential) conditions for retaining and creating jobs. These countries, which include the Czech Republic, Hungary, Poland, and Slovenia, have become key outposts for production and key markets for transnational corporations. Yet, according to the *Economist,* even in these countries joblessness either steadily increased in the 1990s (as in the Czech Republic and Slovenia) or reached or stayed at double-digit levels (as in Poland and Hungary). Poverty rates crept upward due to unemployment and cuts in social safety nets. For instance, in the mid-1990s, 20 percent of Poles were living on the equivalent of less than $4 a day, and 55 percent of Czechs were living on less than $2.

Other non-EU countries, particularly the Russian Federation, fared much more poorly in terms of economic growth, employment generation, and social equity. The *Economist* reports that from the fall of communism in 1989 through 1999, annual income in dollar equivalents fell about 44 percent, from $1,059 to $591 per person. These figures subsequently improved slightly in 2001, rising to an estimated $706 per person based on the first two quarters. Real wages in the formal sector have been erratic but with a downward tendency. The levels in 2000 were 59.3 percent lower than those in 1990.

North Africa and the Middle East

According to UNCTAD's *World Investment Report,* in 1980 North Africa's foreign direct investment (inward and outward) as a share of gross domestic product was 9.6 percent. In 1998 it totaled 15.9 percent compared to 20 percent in developing countries as a whole. Comparable UNCTAD figures for the Middle East in 2000 were a quite low 7.6 percent, a slight drop from 1985. Economies in North Africa and the Middle East grew poorly during the 1990s because of stagnant or deteriorating prices for export commodities and a lack of demand for higher-value-added products, investment capital, and technological and managerial know-how. The *Economist* reports that per capita income in the Middle East increased by 0.9 percent annually in the aggregate during the 1990s, improving somewhat from a slight contraction in the 1980s. This masked great cross-national disparities, with—to focus on three of the largest countries—a decline in Saudi Arabia (at 1.3 percent annualized) contrasted with gains in Iran (2.2 percent) and Egypt (2.3 percent).

Unemployment statistics are unevenly available, but figures for Arab countries in *World Labour Report, 2000* are alarming—26.4 percent in Algeria (1997), 17.8 percent in Morocco (1997), and 11.1 percent in Egypt (1995). Recent data on the size of the informal sector are also lacking. Most available poverty statistics are from the early 1990s and for only six countries. They reveal rates that range from a low of 13.1 percent in Morocco to a high of 57 percent in Mauritania, with Algeria, Jordan, Tunisia, and Yemen in the 14 to 23 percent range. Repression of independent trade union organization and worker collective action is widespread.

A wealthier Israel fared much better on the employment front. According to the *Economist* and *World Labour Report, 2000,* real per capita output grew unevenly, but averaged a healthy 2.3 percent from 1990 to 2000, while real personal disposable income grew by a robust average of 4 percent from 1991 to 2000. This reflected a combination of expansion and a dramatic reduction in inflation, which reached single-digit levels in the late 1990s, after a hyperinflationary period in the 1980s of three- and four-digit annual levels. A big part of this story was a substantial increase in Israel's international integration, as foreign trade and inward and outward investment grew rapidly.

Sub-Saharan Africa

Global integration is problematic for the generation of more and better jobs in Africa. The region's mostly agricultural and extractive economies are dependent on foreign trade and investment, and its countries' foreign debt burdens are among the highest of the world's poor and indebted nations. Drops in real commodity prices for many staple agricultural and mineral exports have devastated the region, and severely limited the capacity of these sectors to maintain jobs, let alone create new ones. According to the *Economist,* total goods exported in 1998 grew 3.1 percent, more slowly than in any other poor region of the world. Famine, political instability, and civil and international strife in a number of countries, as well as the scourge of HIV/AIDS, have also played their part in ravaging employment prospects (see AIDS).

Outside of a few notable exceptions, such as South Africa and Mauritius, foreign direct investment in manufacturing, which has boomed in many developing and transitional economies, and new private inflows of portfolio capital have been notably absent on the African continent. Thus, the *Economist* reports, growth remains weak—inflation-adjusted output grew by 2 percent in the 1990s and 1.8 in the 1980s—and continues to fall behind increases in the size of the labor force because of high population growth and a youthful age structure. The total regional unemployment rate was 14.2 percent in 1995, the most recent year for which data are available. The most recent national surveys, from the early to mid-1990s, show that anywhere from 24 percent of residents (in Mauritius) to 83.7 percent of the people (in Uganda) earn a living in the informal sector, outside of Botswana and South Africa, which have even lower levels. As a result of these trends, poverty rates in Africa are the world's highest. In one sample of eighteen countries (based on data mostly from the early 1990s), 50.2 percent of the people of Guinea-Bissau and South Africa lived on the equivalent of $2 per day, according to *World Labour Report, 2000,* as did 98.1 percent of the population in Zambia.

Asia

Economic trends across Asia and the Pacific have been uneven on a country by country basis despite the economic dynamism seen in much of the region as a result of global and intraregional integration. Several countries experienced the downside of global integration in the form of the financial crises in the late 1990s, which were followed by a global economic slowdown that eroded demand for the region's exports and left employment security and creation at risk. The *Economist* reports that average annual growth in exports from

1989 to 1998 was 12.7 percent in East Asia and the Pacific and 10.2 percent in South Asia, compared to 8.4 percent for all developing countries and 6.4 percent for the world. Japanese growth was sluggish in the 1990s, down to 1.3 percent annually. Unemployment rates had risen to the 5 percent range by 2001, up from 2.1 in 1990, as the vaunted lifetime employment system of Japan's large corporations began to fray.

China continues its rapid process of capitalist reform and industrialization, which is built to a significant degree on direct investment from Japan and other Asian economies. Employment and incomes are rising for many Chinese, but this trend is accompanied by large social dislocations and creeping social inequalities. India, just behind China in terms of total population, has gradually opened up to large-scale foreign investment and moved to become more active as an exporter. Its growth rates have been more modest at 3.8 percent in the 1990s, according to the *Economist.* Economic crisis since the onset of the Asian financial decline in 1997 has interrupted or slowed the trend of high growth and improving earnings and per capita incomes in countries such as Thailand, Indonesia, Malaysia, and South Korea.

Other countries in the region are variously reconnecting with the capitalist global economy under communist rule and cautious market reform (Cambodia, Laos, and Vietnam), dealing with civil strife (Sri Lanka), political instability (Pakistan), or famine (Bangladesh), or emerging from Soviet domination as independent but very poor republics (Azerbaijan, Georgia, Kyrgyzstan, Tajikistan, Turkmenistan, and Uzbekistan and Mongolia, a Soviet satellite). Poverty rates among the region's developing countries are the world's highest in large part because of such countries—ranging from 68.1 percent in Azerbaijan (in 1995) to 13.1 in Thailand (in 1992). Moreover, working poverty under informal conditions in a developing capitalist economy like that of the Philippines is in some ways different from the working poverty that exists under a transitional or a still nominally socialist economy like that of Vietnam in terms of what survival strategies and state resources households have at their disposal. A general, region-wide problem for workers is the weakness of trade union density, with, according to *World Labour Report, 2000,* rates outside agriculture varying from 4.3 percent in Bangladesh to 27.9 percent in Taiwan, and hence of the extent of workers covered by collective bargaining, 2.6 percent in Malaysia, 3.4 percent in Taiwan, 3.7 percent in the Philippines, 18.8 percent in Singapore, and 26.7 percent in Thailand. This weakness has led to the exclusion of organized workers as partners in national development strategies in some cases and repression of union activity in socialist and transitional economies in others.

The Pacific

Australia and New Zealand have increased their global economic ties since the 1980s. Australia did so particularly through increased trade and investment links with Asia. Australia's economic growth rate of 2.9 percent annually over the course of the 1980s and 1990s outpaced population growth, even with substantial influxes of immigrants from Asia and increases in the labor force. This translated into solid gains in gross domestic product per capita. According to the *Economist,* by the late 1990s, however, unemployment still crept up to the 8 percent range in Australia and 6 to 7 percent in New Zealand, mirroring trends characteristic of most of the industrialized world outside the United States during that time period.

In the mid-1980s, the density of union membership was in the 40 percent range, moderately high by the standards of industrialized countries, but it had fallen by roughly half in New Zealand and by 30 percent in Australia by the mid-1990s, according to *World Labour Report, 1997–98.* This reflected a heavy loss of manufacturing jobs because of trade liberalization, declining competitiveness, and weak government support for retention of such industries. The *Economist* records poverty rates in Australia—17.5 percent in 1994 on the order of Canada or the wealthier countries of Europe. Fewer hard data are available on the less developed microstates of Oceania. Their per capita incomes, in 1997 dollar purchasing power equivalents, ranged from $2,230 in the Solomon Islands to $2,500 in Papua New Guinea to $6,159 in Fiji.

Data

Table 1 Ratification of the Core Labor Rights Conventions as of August 2001

Convention Title and Number	Year Adopted	Number of Countries
Forced or Compulsory Labor (29)	1930	158[a]
Freedom of Association and Protection of the Right to Organise (87)	1948	137
Right to Organise and Collective Bargaining (98)	1949	149
Equal Remuneration for Work of Equal Value (100)	1951	153
Discrimination in Employment and Occupation (111)	1958	151
Minimum Age for Employment (138)	1973	111
Elimination of the Worst Forms of Child Labour (182)	1999	93[a]

Source: International Labour Organization, August 2001, http://webfusion.ilo.org/public/db/standards/normes/appl/index.cfm?lang=EN.

[a]Conventions ratified by the United States.

Table 2 Female Labor Force Participation Rates, 2000

Region	Rate %
Africa	57.4
East Africa	72.5
Central Africa	63.1
North Africa	36.7
South Africa	50.5
West Africa	58.1
Asia	62.0
East Asia	77.3
South Central Asia	46.5
Southeast Asia	64.0
West Asia	41.6
Europe	64.0
Eastern Europe	70.0
Northern Europe	69.2
Southern Europe	51.6
Western Europe	60.9
Latin America	45.2
Caribbean	53.5
Central America	42.0
South America	45.5
North America	70.2
Canada	72.1
United States	70.0
Pacific	66.2
Australia and New Zealand	67.0
Melanesia	60.0
Micronesia	60.0
Polynesia	46.7

Source: International Labour Office, *World Labour Report, 2000: Income Security and Social Protection in a Changing World* (Geneva: International Labour Organization, 2000), 267–271.

Table 3 Trade Union Density in Selected Countries as a Share of the Nonagricultural Labor Force

Country	Year	Density (%)	Change since 1980s (Points)
Argentina	1995	25.4	–23.3 (1986–95)
Australia	1995	28.6	–12.0 (1985–95)
Belarus	1995	96.1	–3.9 (1985–95)
Brazil	1991	32.1	—
Canada	1993	31.0	–0.2 (1985–93)
Chile	1993	15.9	4.3 (1985–93)
China	1995	54.7	–4.6 (1985–95)
Colombia	1995	7.0	–4.2 (1985–95)
Egypt	1995	29.6	–9.3 (1985–95)
France	1995	6.1	–5.5 (1985–95)
Germany	1995	29.6	–1.1 (1991–93)
Guatemala	1994	4.4	–3.7 (1985–94)
India	1991	5.4	–1.2 (1980–91)
Indonesia	1995	2.6	—
Israel	1995	23.1	–76.9 (1985–95)
Italy	1994	30.6	–2.3 (1985–94)
Japan	1995	18.6	–4.0 (1985–95)
Korea, Republic of	1995	9.0	0.4 (1985–95)
Mexico	1991	31.0	–23.1 (1989–91)
Peru	1991	7.5	—
Russian Federation	1996	74.8	—
South Africa	1995	21.8	6.3 (1985–95)
Spain	1994	11.4	4.1 (1985–94)
Sweden	1994	77.2	–2.1 (1985–94)
Thailand	1995	3.1	–0.2 (1985–95)
Uganda	1995	3.9	–3.9 (1985–95)
United Kingdom	1995	26.2	–9.8 (1985–95)
United States	1995	12.7	–2.3 (1985–95)

Source: International Labour Office, *World Labour Report, 1997–98: Industrial Relations, Democracy and Social Stability* (Geneva: International Labour Organization, 1997), 237–240.

Case Study—North American Integration and Labor Rights

In 1992 the governments of Canada, Mexico, and the United States entered into the North American Free Trade Agreement (NAFTA), eliminating most trade barriers among them and creating the world's largest free trade area. Proponents argued that it would expand prosperity and employment in all three countries. Labor, consumer, and environmental advocates criticized the agreement on the grounds that it covered only trade and investment, ignoring such issues as labor rights, environmental protection, and democracy and human rights in Mexico. In order to ensure congressional approval of the agreement, the incoming administration of Bill Clinton negotiated labor and environmental side agreements to the basic text in 1993. The North American Agreement on Labor Cooperation (NAALC), the labor side agreement, was criticized at the time as lacking enforcement capacity in the form of trade sanctions, but it was nonetheless novel in establishing a formal link between a wide variety of labor rights, including for migrant laborers, and trade and in committing the three member nations to respect existing domestic labor rights.

NAFTA's impact is undisputed in terms of its multiplying trade and investment flows among the three neighbors, but it has been the object of strongly conflicting evaluations in regard to its effect on employment and labor. Employment losses and gains due to imports and exports are notoriously difficult to estimate, much less document, with any precision. The trilateral, government-to-government NAFTA Free Trade Commission reported that in 2000 2.9 million U.S. jobs were "supported by" merchandise exports to Mexico, up from 914,000 in 1993, before NAFTA. Yet it remained silent on the exact number of jobs lost to imports from Mexico beyond the roughly 356,000 U.S. workers who, it reported, were officially certified for job training and income support by July 2001 under NAFTA's Transitional Adjustment Assistance (TAA), according to "NAFTA at Seven." Instead, it simply pointed to the record-setting employment creation in the U.S. economy during the NAFTA years, even though it is difficult to separate the effects of NAFTA from the general economic expansion. In principle, high levels of turnover, or churning, in the U.S. labor market meant that job creation coexisted with widespread job destruction. Trade unions and other critics argued that officially certified NAFTA-related unemployment represented only a small fraction of true job losses. In doing so, they pointed out that indirect job losses to supplier firms and other companies dependent on lost jobs were not counted; only 57 percent of the people petitioned about TAA actually were found to qualify for the program's narrow criteria, according to Public Citizen Global Trade Watch's *NAFTA Trade Adjustment Assistance*; and many workers did not know about TAA or apply under other generic trade assistance packages.

"NAFTA at Seven" reports that more than half of the new jobs generated in Mexico were export related, mostly due to NAFTA. An assessment of employment impacts in Mexico, however, must also balance gains in jobs tied to exports to losses in import-sensitive industries, such as small and medium-sized manufacturers, which were clearly evident but not well quantified. Moreover, the prosaic reality is that many of the jobs that left the United States were probably, in effect, redirected by NAFTA to Mexico and away from other low-wage offshore sites with less favorable access to the U.S. market. This is what one might infer from the fervent zeal with which African, Caribbean, and Central American nations have complained about favoritism toward Mexico under NAFTA and demanded "NAFTA parity" for their own exports.

A detailed study of the NAALC by Human Rights Watch finds it to be "underutilized" due to a lack of "political will" on the part of the member countries and the lack of an independent oversight body. Nonetheless, this and other studies have found surprisingly frequent use of the complaint mechanism against countries, with twenty-three cases so far of nongovernmental organizations alleging violations of domestic labor laws in one of the other two member states. On a number of occasions, such complaints have helped mobilize public pressure against corporations to desist from particular actions, such as harassing independent union organizers. This has happened through unprecedented and often quite innovative cross-national alliances among unionists and human rights and women's rights activists, which are virtually necessary if, say, U.S.-based organizations are to bring a meaningful complaint in the U.S. regarding alleged Mexican violations. Although most complaints have been directed against Mexico, focusing in particular on organizing rights, health and safety, and forced pregnancy testing in the export-processing industry, or *maquiladora,* a handful of complaints have been filed against Canada (freedom of association for provincial public employees) and the United States (migrant labor health and safety and organizing rights in telecommunications).

As documented by Human Rights Watch's *Unfair Advantage: Workers' Freedom of Association in the United States under International Labor Standards* and other literature, respect for organizing rights in the United States is quite relative, given the legal delays, permanent replacement workers, intimidation of activists, state right-to-work laws, and other tools that anti-union employers have at their disposal. Thus, another unexpected result of the NAALC has been to highlight the fact that the United States—in recent years a leading voice for attaching labor standards to global trading agreements—does not always speak with a consistent voice on labor rights issues domestically and internationally. Meanwhile, in Mexico the creation of a national independent labor central, the Unión Nacional de Trabajadores, and the breakthrough in national politics with the unseating of the long-standing PRI (Partido Revolucionario Institucional) in 2000 have created some hope that there can be progress made on labor rights.

Biographical Sketches

Jagdish Bhagwati is a professor of economics at Columbia University who has written widely in defense of multilateral free trade unencumbered by formal labor rights and other social linkages, stressing in particular trade's benefits for developing countries but also defending their right to regulate capital flows for national development. He is a leader of the Academic Consortium on International Trade, an organization of pro–free trade legal and economic scholars.

Mike Moore is director-general of the World Trade Organization and a former prime minister of New Zealand. He has sought to consolidate the organization since the controversy surrounding it that erupted during the 1999 Seattle summit. He has criticized "globaphobes [who] think that they could put a halt to globalization and rewrite the rules of the world economy on their terms," while at the same time calling for "civilized discourse" with critics and establishing new contacts with nongovernmental organizations. Moore has pushed vigorously for a new round of global trade liberalization talks, arguing that poor countries need greater access to Western markets for agricultural and manufactured goods.

Juan Somavia is secretary-general of the International Labour Organization. He has raised the ILO's profile, criticizing those who "see workers' rights as an obstacle to growth" and insisting that such rights are "essential to making the global economy work for everyone." Particular initiatives have been approval and ratification of the child labor convention, a determined effort to push ratification and enforcement of the various established ILO conventions on labor rights, and a focus on women as an at-risk group and on the plight of poor countries in general.

John Sweeney is president of the American Federation of Labor–Congress of Industrial Organizations (AFL-CIO). Since coming to power in 1995 on the groundswell of an internal reform movement, Sweeney has devoted greater resources to the organizing of new workers, particularly women, people of color, and immigrants. Under his leadership, the organization has reversed its long-standing opposition to amnesty for undocumented immigrant workers, joined in anti-sweatshop coalitions, and advocated strong labor rights provisions for international trade agreements involving the United States.

Lori Wallach is the director of Global Trade Watch, a division of the Washington-based group Public Citizen. She has been a leading articulator of domestic and international opposition to trade agreements lacking social protection for workers and the environment, including a proposed new round of WTO negotiations, China's accession to the WTO, and the proposed Free Trade Agreement of the Americas. Wallach has also lobbied intensely to prevent U.S. presidents from gaining fast-track authority that would enable them to negotiate international trade agreements not subject to congressional amendment and considered only on an up-or-down basis.

Directory

American Federation of Labor–Congress of Industrial Organizations (AFL-CIO), 815 16th Street NW, Washington, DC 20006. Telephone: (202) 637-5000, Email: feedback@aflcio.org, Web: http://www.aflcio.org
Umbrella organization of U.S. unions

Center for Responsibility in Business, 30 Irving Place, New York, NY 10003. Telephone: (212) 420-1133, Email: pradford@cfrib.org, Web: http://www.cfrib.org
Organization concerned with corporate social responsibility and social monitoring, formerly the Council on Economic Priorities

Fair Labor Association, 1420 K Street NW, Suite 400, Washington, DC 20005. Telephone: (202) 898-1000, Email: sambrown@fairlabor.org, Web: http://www.fairlabor.org
Organization that administers an industry-wide conduct and monitoring system for the apparel industry

Institute of Development Studies, University of Sussex, Brighton BN1 9RE, United Kingdom. Telephone: (44) 127 360 6261, Email: ids@ids.ac.uk, Web: http://www.ids.ac.uk/ids
Leading international center for academic research on third world economic and social development

International Confederation of Free Trade Unions, 5 Boulevard Roi Albert II, 1210 Brussels, Belgium. Telephone: (32) 2 224 0211, Email: internetpo@icftu.org, Web: http://www.icftu.org
International grouping of 221 national trade union confederations and other union organizations from 148 countries representing 155 million workers

International Organisation of Employers, 26 Chemin de Joinville, 1216 Geneva, Switzerland. Telephone: (41) 22 798 1616, Email: ioe@ioe-emp.org, Web: http://www.ioe-emp.org
Confederation of 132 national employer organizations in 129 countries

Office of the United States Trade Representative, 600 17th Street NW, Washington, DC 20508. Telephone: (202) 395-3230, Email: contactustr@ustr.gov, Web: http://www.ustr.gov
Executive branch agency charged with negotiating international trade agreements

Organization of Economic Cooperation and Development (OECD), Directorate for Education, Employment, Labour and Social Affairs, 2 Rue André Pascal, 75775 Paris, France. Email: els.contact@oecd.org, Web: http://www.oecd.org/els/employment
International organization of the leading industrialized nations

School of Industrial and Labor Relations, Cornell University, Ives Hall, Ithaca, NY 14853. Web: http://www.ilr.cornell.edu
Center for research, education, and outreach on issues of employment relations and human resources

Worker Rights Consortium, 5 Thomas Circle NW, 5th Floor, Washington, DC 20005. Telephone: (202) 387-4884, Email: wrc@workersrights.org, Web: http://www.workersrights.org
Organization formed by university anti-sweatshop activists and administrators to promote worker rights

World Trade Organization, 154 Rue de Lausanne, 1211 Geneva 21, Switzerland. Telephone (41) 22 739 51 11, Email: enquiries@wto.org, Web: http://www.wto.org
Organization dealing with the rules of trade among nations

Further Research

Books

Bhagwati, Jagdish N. *A Stream of Windows: Unsettling Reflections on Trade, Immigration, and Democracy.* Cambridge, Mass.: MIT Press, 1998.

Candland, Christopher, and Rudra Sil, eds. *The Politics of Labor in a Global Age: Continuity and Change in Late-Industrializing and Post-Socialist Economies.* Oxford and New York: Oxford University Press, 2001.

Held, David, Anthony McGrew, David Goldblatt, and Jonathan Perraton. *Global Transformations: Politics, Economics, and Culture.* Stanford: Stanford University Press, 1999.

International Labour Office. *International Labour Standards: A Workers' Education Manual.* 4th ed. Geneva: International Labour Organization, 1998.

Rodrik, Dani. *Has Globalization Gone Too Far?* Washington, D.C.: Institute for International Economics, 1997.

Ross, Andrew, ed. *No Sweat: Fashion, Free Trade and the Rights of Garment Workers.* New York: Verso, 1997.

Sassen, Saskia. *Globalization and Its Discontents.* New York: New Press, 1998.

Stallings, Barbara, and Wilson Peres. *Growth, Employment, and Equity: The Impact of the Economic Reforms in Latin America and the Caribbean.* Washington, D.C.: United Nations Economic Commission for Latin America and the Caribbean and Brookings Institution Press, 2000.

Articles and Reports

Compa, Lance. "The Multilateral Agreement on Investment and International Labor Rights: A Failed Connection." *Cornell International Law Journal,* no. 10 (1998).

Evans, Peter. "Fighting Marginalization with Transnational Networks: Counter-Hegemonic Globalization." *Contemporary Sociology: A Journal of Reviews* 29, no. 1 (January 2000): 230–241.

"The Face of Globalism: A Special Report on Globalization and Its Critics," supplement of *American Prospect,* summer 2001.

Featherstone, Liza, and Doug Henwood. "Clothes Encounters: Activists and Economists Clash over Sweatshops." *Lingua Franca,* March 2001, 27–33.

Gereffi, Gary, Ronie Garcia-Johnson, and Erika Sasser. "The NGO-Industrial Complex." *Foreign Policy,* July–August 2001.

"Global Capitalism: Can It Be Made to Work Better?" *Business Week,* 6 November 2000, 72–99.

Human Rights Watch. *Trading Away Rights: The Unfulfilled Promise of NAFTA's Labor Side Agreement,* April 2001, http://www.hrw.org/reports/2001/nafta.

———. *Unfair Advantage: Workers' Freedom of Association in the United States under International Human Rights Standards,* August 2000, http://www.hrw.org/reports/2000/uslabor.

International Labour Office. *World Employment Report.* Geneva: International Labour Organization, various years. Annual reports with a thematic focus and statistics.

———. *World Labour Report.* Geneva: International Labour Organization, various years. Annual reports with a thematic focus and statistics.

"NAFTA at Seven: Building on a North American Partnership." Joint Statement of the NAFTA Free Trade Commission, January 2001, http://www.ustr.gov/naftareport/nafta7_brochure-eng.pdf.

Portes, Alejandro. "The Informal Economy and Its Paradoxes." In *The Handbook of Economic Sociology,* edited by Neil Smelser and Richard Swedberg, 426–449. Princeton, N.J.: Princeton University Press, 1994.

Public Citizen Global Trade Watch. "Down on the Farm: NAFTA's Seven-Years War on Farmers and Ranchers in the U.S., Canada and Mexico," June 2001, http://www.tradewatch.org/nafta/reports/naftaAG/NAFTAAGREPORT.htm.

———. *NAFTA Trade Adjustment Assistance,* July 2001, http://www.citizen.org/trade/nafta/index.cfm.

Tilly, Charles, et al. "Scholarly Debate: Globalization Threatens Labor's Rights." *International Journal of Working Class History* 47 (spring 1995): 1–55. Special issue on global flows of capital and labor.

Trubeck, David M., and Jeffrey S. Rothstein. *Transnational Regimes and Advocacy in Industrial Relations: A "Cure" for Globalization?* Working Paper Series on Political Economy of Legal Change no. 4. Madison: University of Wisconsin, Global Studies Program, 1998.

United Nations Conference on Trade and Development (UNCTAD). *World Investment Report.* New York and Geneva: various years. Annual reports with a thematic focus and statistics.

United Nations Development Programme (UNDP). *Human Development Report.* New York and Geneva: various years. Annual reports with a thematic focus and statistics.

World Bank. *World Development Report.* New York and Washington, D.C.: Oxford University Press: various years. Annual reports with a thematic focus and statistics.

Web Sites

Academic Consortium on International Trade
http://www.spp.umich.edu/rsie/acit

Brookings Institution
http://www.brook.edu/globalization

Economic Policy Institute
http://epinet.org

The Economist
http://www.economist.com

The Economist Intelligence Unit
http://www.eiu.com

Electronic Policy Network
http://epn.org/jobs/index.html

European Trade Union Confederation
http://www.etuc.org

International Forum on Globalization
http://www.ifg.org

U.S. Department of Labor, Bureau of Labor Statistics
http://www.bls.gov/home.htm

Documents

1. Convention concerning Freedom of Association and Protection of the Right to Organise

International Labour Organization, Convention 87, General Conference of the ILO, San Francisco, 1948

The full text is available at http://ilolex.ilo.ch:1567/scripts/convde.pl?C87.

Extract

Article 1
Each Member of the International Labour Organi[z]ation for which this Convention is in force undertakes to give effect to the following provisions.

Article 2
Workers and employers, without distinction whatsoever, shall have the right to establish and, subject only to the rules of the organisation concerned, to join organisations of their own choosing without previous authorisation.

Article 3
1. Workers' and employers' organisations shall have the right to draw up their constitutions and rules, to elect their representatives in full freedom, to organise their administration and activities and to formulate their programmes.

2. The public authorities shall refrain from any interference which would restrict this right or impede the lawful exercise thereof.

Article 4
Workers' and employers' organisations shall not be liable to be dissolved or suspended by administrative authority.

Article 5
Workers' and employers' organisations shall have the right to establish and join federations and confederations and any such organisation, federation or confederation shall have the right to affiliate with international organisations of workers and employers.

2. Convention concerning the Prohibition and Immediate Action for the Elimination of the Worst Forms of Child Labour

International Labour Organization, Convention 182, ILO General Conference, Geneva, 17 June 17 1999

The full text is available at http://www.ilo.org/public/english/standards/ipec/ratification/convention/text.htm.

Extract

Considering that the effective elimination of the worst forms of child labour requires immediate and comprehensive action, taking into account the importance of free basic education and the need to remove the children concerned from all such work and to provide for their rehabilitation and social integration while addressing the needs of their families, and . . .

Recognizing that child labour is to a great extent caused by poverty and that the long-term solution lies in sustained economic growth leading to social progress, in particular poverty alleviation and universal education . . .

Article 1
Each Member which ratifies this Convention shall take immediate and effective measures to secure the prohibition and elimination of the worst forms of child labour as a matter of urgency.

Article 2
For the purposes of this Convention, the term *child* shall apply to all persons under the age of 18.

Article 3
For the purposes of this Convention, the term *the worst forms of child labour* comprises:

(a) all forms of slavery or practices similar to slavery, such as the sale and trafficking of children, debt bondage and serfdom and forced or compulsory labour, including forced or compulsory recruitment of children for use in armed conflict;

(b) the use, procuring or offering of a child for prostitution, for the production of pornography or for pornographic performances;

(c) the use, procuring or offering of a child for illicit activities, in particular for the production and trafficking of drugs as defined in the relevant international treaties;

(d) work which, by its nature or the circumstances in which it is carried out, is likely to harm the health, safety or morals of children.

Article 4

1. The types of work referred to under Article 3(d) shall be determined by national laws or regulations or by the competent authority, after consultation with the organizations of employers and workers concerned, taking into consideration relevant international standards, in particular Paragraphs 3 and 4 of the Worst Forms of Child Labour Recommendation, 1999. . . .

Article 5

Each Member shall, after consultation with employers' and workers' organizations, establish or designate appropriate mechanisms to monitor the implementation of the provisions giving effect to this Convention.

Article 6

1. Each Member shall design and implement programmes of action to eliminate as a priority the worst forms of child labour.

2. Each Member shall, taking into account the importance of education in eliminating child labour, take effective and time-bound measures to:

(a) prevent the engagement of children in the worst forms of child labour;

(b) provide the necessary and appropriate direct assistance for the removal of children from the worst forms of child labour and for their rehabilitation and social integration;

(c) ensure access to free basic education, and, wherever possible and appropriate, vocational training, for all children removed from the worst forms of child labour;

(d) identify and reach out to children at special risk; and

(e) take account of the special situation of girls. . . .

LITERACY AND EDUCATIONAL ACCESS

Anya Hogoboom

According to the United Nations Educational, Scientific and Cultural Organization (UNESCO), an estimated 872 million of the world's people are illiterate. Nearly two-thirds of them are women. A main source of illiteracy is the lack of primary education, and although the United Nations declared education to be a fundamental human right in 1948, UNESCO reports that an estimated 113 million school-age children do not attend school. Literacy empowers people personally, and having a literate population is important to a country economically, making UNESCO's commitment to worldwide literacy a powerful tool for individual and national development.

Historical Background and Development

The Greek and Roman civilizations are examples of ancient societies that developed systems of writing, but it has been found that the general populations of these societies were probably not literate. Although there were village schools, they seem to have been limited in number, and no true network of schools for the masses existed in either society. The Protestant Reformation played a large role in promoting mass literacy. Priests in the Catholic Church at the time read and wrote Latin rather than local languages, or vernaculars. The Church, in fact, was against mass literacy, because it was linked to heresy; if a people read scriptures for themselves, they might form an opinion in opposition to the teachings of the Church. Martin Luther, leader of the Reformation, published the Small Catechism, which became basic reading for his followers. The first mass literacy campaign took place in Sweden in the seventeenth century as an effort to increase Bible reading and study.

It is interesting to note that functional literacy has not always been part of the goal of primary education. In France, reading skills were taught three hundred years before writing was of instructional concern, because a population that is able to read is relatively nonthreatening, but the ability to write gives a person a tool with which to challenge established norms and the parties in power. Although many European countries passed legislation that addressed universal primary education in the eighteenth century, in most cases it took around one hundred years for this goal to be seriously pursued. Prior to 1800 countries in the north and west of Europe had generally literate societies with respect to the ability to read. The countries in the south and east of the continent had significantly fewer literates and literate communities.

General education came of age in Europe during the nineteenth century. Although all European countries made gains in the 1800s, at the century's end the literacy rate in Hungary, Italy, Russia, and Spain lagged far behind the rest of the continent. In the early twentieth century wide differences remained in the literacy rates between different areas of many nations. According to *The Rise of Mass Literacy,* in 1911 Piedmont, an urbanized region in the industrialized north of Italy, had an illiteracy rate of 11 percent compared to 70 percent in Calabria, a rural area in the far south of the country.

Sub-Saharan Africans colonized by the British began to see the benefits associated with literacy in the nineteenth century. The demand for printed material in many British-occupied African countries rose during this period. Actual literacy campaigns in these countries, however, did not begin until some years after independence. Japan stands out as a non-Western country that addressed education and literacy in the nineteenth century. By 1910 Japan had achieved 90 percent enrollment of children in its six-year schooling system. The achievement of mass literacy in Japan is thought to be due to the primary education system. The Japanese language is logographic, that is, based on symbols rather than an alphabet. Alphabetic writing systems are thought to be superior to those based on logographs, especially in regard to the efficiency of teaching them and learning them. The Japanese education system's success at improving literacy casts some doubt on this long-standing belief.

Access to basic education became a fundamental human right in 1948 through its inclusion in the Universal Declaration of Human Rights as Article 26, which guarantees the right to free primary education (see HUMAN RIGHTS). Since then, literacy and educational access have been of prime concern to the United Nations. UNESCO was established in 1945 to foster world peace through educational and cultural exchanges and programs. From 1969 to 1974 UNESCO oversaw the Experimental World Literacy Program (EWLP) with funding from the United Nations Development Programme (UNDP). This was the first major mass literacy campaign on an international scale, and although the EWLP had no stated aim of world literacy, it was harshly criticized in the press for failing to end illiteracy. More recently, 1990 was declared the International Year of Literacy. As a consequence of UNESCO's efforts over the latter part of the twentieth century, developing countries have benefited from numerous literacy and educational programs.

Current Status

The question of what constitutes literacy poses a major difficulty for researchers and workers in the field as well as for government and international policymakers. Should being able to read and write in one's native language or dialect be considered sufficient or should one also be able to read and write in the official language designated by government? Further, different governments use different criteria for determining literacy, from being able to write one's name to being able to read and write in any situation needed in society. UNESCO and others often use the term *functional literacy* for the latter definition. This definition allows for differences between communities—as, for example, the functional level of literacy in industrialized nations is higher than in developing countries—making an international literacy standard difficult. Comparisons and statistics should be viewed with these words of caution in mind. Increasingly, literacy and illiteracy are not seen as static states, but as being on a continuum, and researchers are beginning to speak in terms of degrees of literacy rather than literacy versus illiteracy.

Research

Literacy and basic education are often blurred, so in the literature and research on literacy it can be unclear what is a benefit or effect of literacy specifically and what is a benefit or effect of basic education generally. Basic education can mean primary schooling or it can mean nonformal education, such as adult literacy programs. Schooling is considered formal education. Often, people (and organizations) speak of literacy as though it were the sole end and measure of basic education. Of course, there are other important aspects of basic education. For example, numeracy, the basic awareness and use of mathematics, has begun to gain attention in the research on literacy and in nonformal basic education programs.

According to the *UNESCO Annual Statistical Yearbook, 1999,* in 1995 there were 174 million illiterate people in the less developed countries and 13 million in the more developed countries. This illustrates that literacy is strongly tied to financial constraints (see Table 1). Developing countries have less money to spend on primary education (see map, p. 440), and many families in developing countries cannot afford school supplies and such basic items as shoes. They therefore do not send their children to school (see INCOME INEQUALITY).

UNESCO measures a country's primary school enrollment rate in two ways. The gross enrollment rate is measured by dividing the total number of students enrolled in primary school, which includes late enrollments and retentions (that is, students who have been held back to repeat a grade), by the number of children of primary school age; gross enrollment rates can therefore be more than 100 percent. The net enrollment is calculated by dividing the number of students enrolled in primary school who are of the official age for first grade by the number of children in the age group that officially corresponds to primary school. Collectively, the more developed countries have a gross enrollment rate of 106 percent and a net enrollment rate of 98 percent, according to UNESCO figures for 1998. The less developed countries, by contrast, have a gross enrollment rate of 96 percent and a net enrollment rate of 82 percent (see Table 2). In the less developed countries, not only do a smaller percentage of children attend school than do those in developed countries, but there is also a wider gap between gross and net enrollments, reflecting a larger number of students who are not age-appropriate for the first grade.

Globally, there is a gender gap in education and in literacy. Proportionally, more boys than girls attend primary school, and more men than women are literate. This has been overwhelmingly true historically and is due to traditions that keep girls and women at home with little or no access to education. The gender gap has all but disappeared in the more developed countries and has narrowed in Central and East Asia, Central and Eastern Europe, and Latin America. Other literacy gaps include the social gap—reflecting that people in higher social classes tend to have better access to education and higher literacy rates than people in lower classes—and the rural-urban gap—which indicates that the literacy rate is often significantly higher in urban areas than it is in rural areas. It is easier to set up schools and programs that are accessible to higher concentrations of people.

As can be seen above, literacy and education are not isolated issues. They are linked to poverty, employment, health, fertility rates, and infant mortality, among other factors. For instance, a strong link has been found between parental education and child health. Although both parents' level of education corresponds to better health in their children, the mother's has the greater impact. The reason for this is unclear, but Shireen Jejeebhoy's explanation of the correlation between woman's education and child health is that education makes women more autonomous, thereby giving them greater control over the health decisions regarding their children. In keeping with Jejeebhoy's analysis, it has been suggested that the reason this correlation does not hold as strongly in sub-Saharan Africa is because women there have a higher degree of autonomy, regardless of their level of education. Even a small amount of education can make a positive difference in the health of offspring and the lowering of fertility rates and infant mortality rates (see HEALTH).

There are macro and micro rationales for fostering literacy. On the macro level the expectation is that increased literacy will help the economic development of a nation because of the increased potential for meaningful employment and for productivity gains (see LABOR AND EMPLOYMENT). In fact, one school of thought claims that the economic situation of a country cannot improve unless higher literacy rates are attained. Educated and literate workers are able to perform more work that requires advanced skills, enabling a country to produce more. Doubts exists, however, regarding this correlation between literacy and economic growth, because, for example, if a newly literate person takes the job of a less literate person, nothing has been altered except for the people directly involved. In short, having more literate people does not automatically create more work requiring advanced skills. The micro effects of literacy are clearer. Literacy often leads to increased social status and respect from peers. Also, the ability to perform such functions as reading medicine bottles and writing checks increases a person's ability to function successfully in daily life.

Primary education is one of the main routes to literacy. Much of the literacy rate increase in some countries, such as Mexico in recent years, is due to the increase in primary school attendance rather than to nonformal programs. Because a person has attended school does not, however, mean that he or she is literate. Many countries have problems with high dropout rates, which means that many children are leaving school before literacy has been attained or at least before a high level of literacy has been reached. UNESCO reports that Cambodia, Colombia, India, Laos, Madagascar, Pakistan, and Togo all have a dropout rate of more than 40 percent before the fifth grade. Literacy is not a static state and needs to be used and reinforced to be retained or improved. Therefore, children who drop out of school with only a basic level of literacy are less likely to become functionally literate adults.

Literacy statistics are often based on the number of years of schooling received. For example, in gathering literacy statistics many countries assume that a person who has attended school for at least four or five years is literate; four or five years is generally considered the minimum number of years necessary for literacy to be achieved. This is not an absolute correlation, however, as some people are able to attain literacy in less time while others need more time. Many countries struggle with high retention rates. If children only go to school for a few years, a high retention rate means that children are potentially not completing enough schooling to acquire literacy. For example, in South American countries, children go to school for a regional average of five years, but because of the high retention rate, less than five grades are completed by the average child. Schooling that does not result in literacy is called wastage. This means that literacy statistics based on the number of years of schooling are not necessarily accurate.

Although the acquisition of literacy is generally thought to be an empowerment, it can also be a tool of oppression. Many countries with low literacy rates have multiple languages within their borders. This is particularly true of sub-Saharan African nations and of the Pacific islands. National literacy campaigns tend to focus on one language. Thus a person's native language is devalued, and the individual is forced to adopt the national language chosen by the ruling party. National literacy campaigns highlighting a particular language can, however, serve to bring about a sense of national unity.

Policies and Programs

UNESCO is the premier international organization concerned with promoting basic education and achieving literacy worldwide. It advocates a two-pronged approach to raising literacy rates. The first is to provide quality education to all children, and the second is to provide literacy classes for adults. UNESCO has pursued these goals largely through its Education for All (EFA) initiative. This project, through which a large number of countries are now committed to providing primary education to all school-age children and resources for adult education, was launched at the World Conference on Education for All in Jomtien, Thailand, March 1990, in conjunction with the UN-declared International Year of Literacy. The conference was attended by representatives from 155 governments. The result of the conference was a World Declaration on Education for All calling for a rise in global literacy rates and a broadening of education parameters to encompass all basic learning functions, such as oral expression and problem solving (see Document 1).

Following-up on the world declaration, a major evaluation of basic education in more than 180 countries was undertaken. The general opinion is that governments have not lived up to the promises they committed themselves to in Jomtien. A renewed effort is now taking place to fulfill EFA goals. A framework for action was adopted at the World Education Forum in Dakar, Senegal, in April 2000 (see Document 2). The agreement was approved by 181 nations, thus committing their governments to achieving the goals set forth by 2015. The targets include expanding primary education to all children (with special emphasis on bridging the education gap for girls, ethnic minorities, and the disadvantaged) and bringing about a 50 percent improvement in the literacy rate of adults (see Table 3). The main responsibility for meeting these goals rests with national governments. Each country is to have a comprehensive Education for All plan by the end of 2002 that includes a sustainable financial framework for addressing the goals of the Dakar agreement. The Dakar framework states that "no countries seriously committed to education for all will be thwarted in their achievement of this goal by a lack of resources." Therefore, once countries adopt an approach, partners in the international community are to help them successfully carry out their plan if they lack the resources to do it alone. Priority for international assistance is to be given to the least developed countries. Annual meetings are planned to assess progress made since the Dakar forum.

A variety of literacy campaigns are being initiated by governments and nongovernmental organizations. These programs take many different approaches. The government of India oversees a national literacy program of community-based projects. Literacy programs targeting the family have been developed in many countries. Some such programs emphasize strengthening childhood education by helping parents learn how to facilitate their children's learning, whereas others focus on illiterate or barely literate parents. Programs in some countries tie literacy to other issues. For example, in the Philippines and in Nepal family literacy and health-promoting programs are combined.

Many adult literacy programs are administered by nongovernmental organizations (while national governments tend to invest in primary schooling). Programs for illiterate adults are changing in important ways. In contrast to the traditional thinking that illiterate adults also lack such skills as critical thinking and problem solving and that they are "blank pages," many programs now take into consideration what skills illiterate adults already possess as well as the topics they find valuable. Many argue that adults' interest will only be held by literacy programs that address topics that are immediately relevant to their everyday lives.

Regional Summaries

North America

According to 1995 data from the World Bank, Canada and the United States have literacy rates of 99 percent, and according to UNESCO figures for 1997, North America as a whole has a gross enrollment rate of 101.1 percent. Broken down by gender, males have a gross enrollment rate of 101.4 percent and females have a rate of 100.8 percent. The United States and Canada have very high attendance in their systems of free, compulsory education, yet problems of functional illiteracy persist. Functional illiteracy is now recognized as a

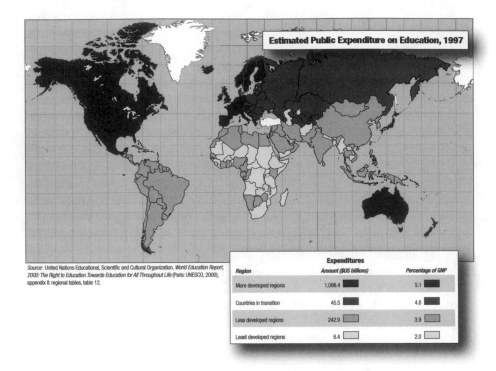

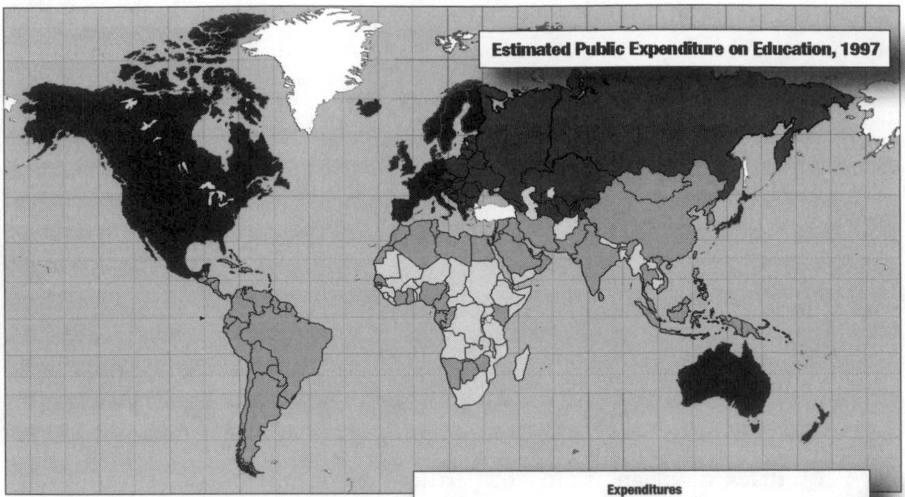

	Expenditures	
Region	*Amount ($US billions)*	*Percentage of GNP*
More developed regions	1,098.4	5.1
Countries in transition	45.5	4.8
Less developed regions	242.9	3.9
Least developed regions	6.4	2.0

Source: United Nations Educational, Scientific and Cultural Organization, *World Education Report, 2000: The Right to Education. Towards Education for All Throughout Life* (Paris: UNESCO, 2000), appendix II: regional tables, table 12.

problem because there is not as much demand for unskilled labor due to continuing automation, which leaves many functional illiterates without means of employment. According to the U.S. National Adult Literacy Survey from 1993, African Americans, American Indians and Alaskan Natives, Asian and Pacific islanders, and Hispanics demonstrated lower levels of literacy than whites. Using figures based on the 1980 census, the Rural Clearinghouse for Lifelong Education and Development reports that 28 percent of the U.S. population lived in rural areas and accounted for 48 percent of the functionally illiterate adults in the nation. A pressing issue regarding the education of ethnic minorities is whether their native language or dialects should be incorporated in the curricula. Canadian literacy surveys have found that the lowest levels of literacy correspond with low educational attainment. Canada also has a rural-urban gap, as access to education beyond the primary level is limited in very rural areas of the country.

Latin America

According to UNESCO figures from 1997, Latin America has a regional gross enrollment rate of 113.6 percent; by gender, the rate is 116.9 percent for males and 110.2 percent for females. The male net enrollment rate is 94 percent, and for females the rate is 93 percent. Most Central and South American countries have succeeded in expanding their primary education systems, and according to UNESCO's 2000 assessment, all of Latin America is making steady progress toward universal primary education. As a result, illiteracy rates are dropping. Brazil, for instance, has seen impressive increases in its literacy rate, largely due to improvements in its education system. According to Brazil's Education for All report, the illiteracy rate dropped from 20.1 percent in 1991 to 14.7 percent in 1996.

Adult illiteracy in the region remains highly problematic. Literacy rates are lowest among native populations. Bolivia, Ecuador, and Peru have particularly high populations of Indians and the highest illiteracy rates in South America. A large percentage of South American children enter primary school, but many drop out before basic literacy is achieved. UNESCO reports an 87.5 percent literacy rate for the region based on 1997 data. The illiteracy rate for Mexico is 9.6 percent, for Argentina 3.4 percent, and for Jamaica 14.4 percent.

Europe

Because mass literacy has been part of Western European society for more than a century, there is a feeling that residual illiteracy is shameful. Based on international standards of literacy, the illiteracy rate is about 1 percent. In industrial countries, however, functional literacy involves more skills than in developing countries, because the level of literacy needed for day-to-day living, transportation, employment, and commercial transactions is much higher. Although most European countries do not have a literacy gender gap, they do have a social gap. Some countries have instigated positive discrimination policies to try to compensate for social inequalities. France and Portugal, for example, have similar programs in which poorer areas receive extra financial and human resources and are encouraged to take the needs of the children in their area into account when planning their educational programs. According to UNESCO figures for 1997, Western, Central, and Eastern Europe as a whole have a gross enrollment rate of 107.2 percent, 107.2 percent for males and 107.3 percent for females.

With the end of the cold war, the education systems of Central and Eastern Europe required some overhauling, such as updating teaching methods and materials. The governments, however, have lacked the resources to make many needed changes because recovery from the economic downturn in the early and mid-1990s has been slow. On a positive note, the illiteracy rate is generally low in these areas. For example, the Russian Federation has an illiteracy rate of 0.5 percent, according to UNESCO figures for 1997.

Central and Eastern European countries are able to provide (near) universal primary education, but the United Nations Children's Fund (UNICEF) reports that available statistics indicate decreases in national spending on education between 1990 and 1996 that ranged from 25 percent in Bulgaria to 78 percent in Hungary. Teachers' salaries suffered more than the average wage decline. In addition to limited government resources, households had less to spend on education, particularly in the former Yugoslavia, as many people were displaced by war. The Romany (Gypsy) population remains one of the most disadvantaged groups educationally, having suffered high dropout and retention rates in primary and secondary school, as well as decreased attendance rates in the 1990s.

North Africa and the Middle East

According to UNESCO figures for 1997, the gross enrollment rate for North Africa and the Middle East is 84.7 percent, 92.1 percent for males and 76.9 percent for females. The net enrollment rate is 80 percent for males and 71 percent for females. The countries in this region show a great difference between their gross and net primary enrollments. According to UNESCO, net enrollment remains problematic in most of these countries, with only five (out of twenty)—Iraq, Jordan, Libya, Palestine, and the United Arab Emirates—having a net enrollment of more than 90 percent, and three countries—Djibouti (26.2 percent), Sudan (43 percent), and Morocco (48.8 percent)—falling below 50 percent.

The illiteracy rate in North Africa and the Middle East—recorded by UNESCO in 1995 at 43.8 percent—is the third worst in the world, following Southern Asia and sub-Saharan Africa. One serious impediment to higher literacy is that the official language of all of these countries, Modern Standard Arabic, or *fusha,* is no one's native language and is difficult to learn. This, however, is the language that is used in all official documents, as well as in literature and in the media. Additionally, the gender gap remains a serious problem. Egypt and Tunisia, for example, share a high female illiteracy rate (43.5 percent and 59.3 percent, respectively, according to 1997 data from UNESCO), in part due to cultural values and traditions that discriminate against women. The regional literacy rate is 58.5 percent, 70.6 percent for males and 50.1 percent for females. Enrollment rates for girls have improved. The female gross enrollment rate in Egypt rose from 86 percent to 94 percent between 1990 and 1996, according to UNESCO.

Sub-Saharan Africa

According to UNESCO data for 1997 as reported in the *World Education Report, 2000,* 45 million school-age children do not attend school in sub-Saharan Africa, a large percentage of the global estimate of 113 million. The gross enrollment rate for the region is 74.8 percent. Males have a gross enrollment rate of 84.1 percent, and females have a rate of 69.4 percent, illustrating the gender gap that exists not only in education but in literacy as well. Regionally, males have a literacy rate of 66.7 percent, whereas the female literacy rate is 50.1 percent. UNESCO's 2000 assessment found that although primary school attendance is up globally, it has fallen in some African counties, including Botswana, Lesotho, and Mozambique, largely due to civil wars. Many sub-Saharan countries have a high retention rate—more than one-third of primary school students are retained in Chad, the Comoros islands, the Republic of Congo, and Gabon—a symptom of, among other things, overcrowded classrooms and insufficiently trained teachers. Several countries have large discrepancies between rural and urban enrollment figures. According to UNESCO, the gap ranges from 26 percentage points in the Central African Republic to 49 percentage points in Burkina Faso.

Central and South Asia

According to UNESCO data for 1997, the gross enrollment rate for Central and South Asia is 95.4 percent. A large gender gap is evident: the gross enrollment rate of males is 106.8 percent, compared to 83.3 percent of females. The fast-growing populations of many countries in this region have strained educational funding. UNESCO reports that this region has one of the lowest levels of literacy in the world—53.2 percent in 1997—and the highest literacy gender gap—64.8 percent of males are literate compared to 41 percent of females—but that these issues are beginning to be addressed. Adult illiteracy in India is a continuing struggle despite multiple national campaigns in the latter half of the twentieth century. The literacy rate in India is 54.9 percent, 66.5 percent for males and 42.5 percent for females. There is a large rural-urban literacy gap in the region. Literacy rates in urban areas of Bangladesh are approximately twice as high as those in rural areas. Adults who become literate often slip back into illiteracy because of the absence of support systems for neo-literates. For this reason, and because many children complete primary school without having reached sustainable levels of literacy, wastage is high in this region.

East Asia and the Pacific

Primary school attendance has made general gains in Asia over the last decade, and universal primary education in East Asia is beginning to look plausible. The gross enrollment rate of more developed Asia and the Pacific, which includes Australia, Japan, and New Zealand (as well as Israel), is 98.8 percent, 98.9 percent for males and 98.7 percent for females, according to UNESCO data for 1997. Gross enrollment in less developed East Asia and Oceania, which includes all other countries of East Asia and the Pacific, is 118 percent, 118.3 percent for males and 117.6 percent for females. The literacy rate for less developed eastern Asia and Oceania is 84.3 percent, 91.1 percent for males and 77.3 percent for females. China has a gross enrollment rate of 122.8 percent, 122.5 percent for males and 123 percent for females, and a literacy rate 82.2 percent, 90.3 percent for males and 73.7 percent for females. Japan has a gross enrollment of 101 percent, with no gender gap, and, according to the World Bank data for 1995, a literacy rate of 99 percent.

Many countries in East Asia and the Pacific have rapidly increasing populations and therefore need continuing expansion of their primary education systems. The populations in many Pacific nations, for example, Indonesia, are spread unevenly across small islands, presenting further challenges. The countries in this region tend to be internally culturally diverse, so there are large numbers of people who use a language other than the official language or languages. For many people in the South Pacific, literacy remains unincorporated into their daily lives, and personal reading is regarded as antisocial. Australia and New Zealand have very high literacy rates—99 percent in 1995 for both, according to the World Bank—but have only recently begun to consider the needs of the indigenous populations of Aborigines and Maori, respectively.

Data

Table 1 Estimated Literate and Illiterate Populations Aged 15 and Over in Less Developed Regions, 2000 (millions)

	Literate		Illiterate	
Region	Males	Females	Males	Females
Arab states	65	43	24	43
East Asia and the Pacific	645	544	54	138
Latin America	155	159	19	23
South Asia	322	199	160	255
Sub-Saharan Africa	122	98	54	84

Source: United Nations Educational, Scientific and Cultural Organization, *World Education Report, 2000: The Right to Education. Towards Education for All Throughout Life* (Paris: UNESCO, 2000), 37, Fig. 2.2.

Table 2 Duration, Population, and Enrollment Ratios for Primary Education in Selected Countries, 1996

	Duration (years)		School-age Population (1,000)	Gross Enrollment Ratio (%)			Net Enrollment Ratio (%)		
Country	Compulsory Education	Primary Education		Total	Male	Female	Total	Male	Female
Algeria	9	6	4,349	107	113	102	94	97	91
Argentina	10	7	4,633	113	114	113	—	—	—
Australia	10	7	1,828	101	101	101	95	95	95
Brazil	8	8	27,472	125	—	—	90	—	—
Canada	10	6	2,402	102	103	101	95	96	94
China	9	5	114,017	123	122	123	100	100	100
Colombia	5	5	4,370	113	113	112	85	—	—
Congo, Democratic Republic of	—	6	7,500	72	86	59	—	—	—
Egypt	8	5	8,153	101	108	94	93	98	88
France	10	5	3,813	105	106	104	100	100	100
Georgia	9	4	332	88	89	88	90	88	91
Germany	12	4	3,715	104	104	104	86	86	87
Guatemala	6	6	1,754	88	93	82	72	76	69
India	8	5	110,650	100	109	90	—	—	—
Indonesia	9	6	25,946	113	115	110	95	96	93
Israel	11	6	644	98	—	—	—	—	—
Japan	9	6	7,748	101	101	101	100	100	100
Russian Federation	9	3	7,325	107	108	107	93	93	93
Saudi Arabia	—	6	2,970	76	77	75	61	63	60
Spain	10	6	2,491	109	109	108	100	100	100
Sweden	9	6	648	107	106	107	100	100	100
Switzerland	9	6	—	—	—	—	—	—	—

Table 2 Duration, Population, and Enrollment Ratios for Primary Education in Selected Countries, 1996 (*continued*)

Country	Duration (years)		School-age Population (1,000)	Gross Enrollment Ratio (%)			Net Enrollment Ratio (%)		
	Compulsory Education	Primary Education		Total	Male	Female	Total	Male	Female
Tajikistan	9	4	621	95	96	94	—	—	—
Thailand	6	6	6,797	87	—	—	—	—	—
Turkey	8	5	5,949	109	111	104	99	100	96
Uganda	—	7	3,917	74	81	68	—	—	—
United Kingdom	11	6	4,605	116	115	116	99	98	99
United States	10	6	23,619	102	102	101	95	94	95

Source: United Nations Educational, Scientific and Cultural Organization, *World Education Report, 2000: The Right to Education. Towards Education for All Throughout Life* (Paris: UNESCO, 2000), appendix III: world education indicators, table 4.

Note: Duration of compulsory education: Number of years of compulsory education, according to the regulations of each country. *Duration of primary education:* Number of grades (years) in primary education, according to the education system of each country in 1996. *School-age population:* Population of the age group that officially corresponds to primary schooling. *Gross enrollment ratio/Net enrollment ratio:* The gross enrollment ratio is the total enrollment in primary education, regardless of age, divided by the population of the age group that officially corresponds to primary schooling. The net enrollment ratio only includes the enrollment of the age group corresponding to the official age range for primary education, divided by the population of school-age children.

Table 3 Estimated Adult Illiteracy in Countries With More Than 10 Million Illiterate Adults in 1970

Country	1970				2000				Proportion of Total Illiterate Adults	
	Number of Illiterate Adults (millions)	Adult Illiteracy Rate (%)			Number of Illiterate Adults (millions)	Adult Illiteracy Rate (%)			1970 (%)	2000 (%)
China	244	49	34	64	152	16	8	24	28	17
India	221	67	53	81	289	43	32	55	26	33
Indonesia	30	44	32	56	19	13	8	18	3	2
Pakistan	28	79	68	91	49	54	40	69	3	6
Bangladesh	28	76	65	88	49	59	48	70	3	6
Nigeria	22	80	69	90	23	36	28	44	3	3
Brazil	18	32	28	36	18	15	15	15	2	2
Egypt	14	69	54	83	20	45	33	56	2	2
Ethiopia	14	87	81	94	21	62	56	67	2	2
Subtotal	618	57	43	71	640	29	20	38	72	73
World Total	858	37	29	45	875	21	15	26	100	100

Source: United Nations Educational, Scientific and Cultural Organization, *World Education Report, 2000: The Right to Education. Towards Education for All Throughout Life* (Paris: UNESCO, 2000), 38, figure 2.4.

Case Study—A Successful Literacy Effort in Rural Nepal

South Asia has one of the highest illiteracy rates in the world. From 1981 to 1992 the rural areas along the Seti River in western Nepal were the focus of a successful literacy campaign. Among South Asian nations, Nepal has the highest adult illiteracy rate, 61.9 percent of the population aged 15 and above in 1997, according to UNESCO. Nepal also has a high gender gap, with an illiteracy rate of 44.2 percent for men compared to 79.4 percent for women, again based on UNESCO figures for 1997. This gap is due in part to families relying on the work girls perform at home, which leaves little time for school attendance, and also because women are the subject of social and legal discrimination.

The UNESCO-supervised Seti Project, officially called Education for Rural Development in the Seti Zone, grew out of the national Equal Access of Girls to Education program, which began in Nepal in 1970. Girls who participated in the Seti Project had the highest rates of academic success and achievement. Based on the results of the effort, another national program, the Basic and Primary Education Project (BPEP), was developed. The BPEP is a larger-scale attempt to repeat the success of the Seti Project.

One of the aspects that made the Seti Project so successful was its practical instruction, which related directly to the participants' daily lives. The program itself focused on issues of health and hygiene and taught literacy as it conveyed information on these issues to young girls and women. The program is also thought to have been effective because of its multifaceted approach, as it included improving school conditions, supplying materials for literacy training and postliteracy support, and short- and long-term teacher training. The program was also different in that administrators at the local level were only paid when they showed positive results.

The young girls, who had classes for two hours every morning, would share the practical information they learned with their families and thus improve the general heath of their households. The women were likewise taught skills, as well as community health practices and literacy-promoting activities. Village reading centers were established to support postliteracy skills. Because of such programs and their positive effects, the Seti Project is often held up as a particularly successful effort to educate people in a very impoverished area.

Case Study—Literacy Options in Norway

Norway has a largely heterogeneous population of around 4.5 million people. Numerous dialects of Norwegian are spoken nationwide. The Sami (Laplanders) are a significant minority in the northern part of the country as well as in the north of Sweden, Finland, and the northwest section of the Russian Federation. There are three Sami languages, which are not mutually understandable. Norway also has other ethnic minorities, largely due to refugee immigration. The country thus faces difficult education issues and is noteworthy for its response to them.

Most governments only provide literacy instruction in the official language of the country, so Norway is distinguished in its efforts in this area. In the 1850s a Norwegian language based on the dialects of the country was formed. This stood in contrast to the official written language of the time, Danish; Norway was under Danish rule for some four hundred years. Written Danish in Norway has been influenced by spoken Norwegian and is called *bokmål* (book language). The language made to reflect Norwegian dialects was given the name *nynorsk* (New Norwegian). In the late 1800s nynorsk was given equal legal status with bokmål, so children could then be taught in either language. This is the situation today, but whether a child is taught primarily in one language rather than the other often depends on the preferences of local government. Additionally, in the 1960s Sami began to be used in Sami district schools, and now all Sami children in Norway can receive their first ten years of education in Sami. More recently, all children were given the right to receive literacy instruction in their native language. In practice, around 38 percent of linguistic minorities receive initial literacy instruction either solely in their native language or in their native language and in either nynorsk or bokmål. Norway's success with this approach is evident in its 99 percent literacy rate, which is according to 1995 World Bank 1995 figures. Additionally, the 2000 Education for All report cites a nearly 100 percent completion rate for Norway's ten-year compulsory schooling.

There is a substantial body of research that shows that literacy acquisition in a second language is more difficult than attaining it in a native language because the learner is learning literacy and the language at the same time. Therefore, programs that base literacy instruction in a child's native language, such as those used in Norway, are instrumental in helping children acquire literacy and also help preserve cultural roots.

Biographical Sketches

Paulo Freire is an adult educator who established national adult literacy programs first in Brazil and later in Chile, where he was forced into exile in 1964. In the 1970s Freire worked to establish adult literacy programs in newly independent nations, including Guinea-Bissau and Tanzania. He felt that illiteracy was closely related to oppression and worked to liberate people through literacy. He has published more than twenty-five works on literacy, his most famous being *Pedagogy of the Oppressed* (1970).

Nancy Hornberger is a professor at the University of Pennsylvania who is concerned with minority education and literacy programs as they pertain to indigenous populations and immigrants. Her research focuses on South America and the United States. In the 1990s Hornberger served as a consultant to the United Nations on education programs in El Salvador and Bolivia.

Shoichi Noma is a publisher who has worked to make books available in developing countries and to promote reading there. He established the Noma Prize, which is awarded each year to the writer of an outstanding (children's or academic) book published in Africa.

Nelly Stromquist is a professor of international development education at the University of Southern California and a former president of the Comparative and International Education Society. Her research focus is gender inequality in education as applied through programs and policies, especially in Latin America and West Africa. Her research also includes the social and practical obstacles women face in becoming literate.

Daniel Wagner is a professor at the University of Pennsylvania School of Education who also serves as the director of the National Center on Adult Literacy and of the International Literacy Institute. He has published many articles on children and adult literacy acquisition. He is the co-editor of *Literacy: An International Handbook* (1999) and *Literacy among African-American Youth: Issues in Learning, Teaching, and Schooling* (1995).

Directory

Dhaka Ahsania Mission, P.O. Box 3674, New York, NY 10017. Telephone: (718) 658-3870, Email: Ahsania@banglanet.com, Web: http://www.ahsania.org
Organization headquartered in Bangladesh dedicated to economic development through education

Global Campaign for Education, c/o Education International, 5 Boulevard Roi Albert II, 8th Floor, 1210 Brussels, Belgium. Telephone: (32) 2 224 06 11, Email: global.edu.campaign@ei-ie.org, Web: http://www.campaignforeducation.org
Organization that urges governments to follow through on promises of education for all

International Association for the Evaluation of Educational Achievement, Herengracht 487, 1017 Amsterdam, Netherlands. Telephone: (31) 20 625 3625, Email: department@iea.nl, Web: http://www.iea.nl
Independent international cooperative of research centers concerned with the educational policies and practices of its members

International Bureau of Education, P.O. Box 199, 1211 Geneva 20, Switzerland. Telephone: (41) 22 917 78 00, Email: c.braslavsky@ibe.unesco.org, Web: http://www.ibe.unesco.org
UNESCO affiliate that observes and assists education efforts worldwide

International Literacy Institute, Literacy Research Centers, University of Pennsylvania, Graduate School of Education, 3910 Chestnut Street, Philadelphia, PA 19104-3111. Telephone: (215) 898-2100, Email: editor@literacy.upenn.edu, Web: http://www.literacy.org
A collaboration of UNESCO and the University of Pennsylvania Graduate School of Education involved in education research and development around the world

International Reading Association, 800 Barksdale Road, P.O. Box 8139, Newark, DE 19714-8139. Telephone: (302) 731-1600, Email: pubinfo@reading.org, Web: http://www.reading.org
Organization promoting high levels of literacy and quality literacy instruction

National Center for Family Literacy, 325 West Main Street, Suite 200, Louisville, KY 40202-4251. Telephone: (877) 326-5481, Email: ncfl@famlit.org, Web: http://www.famlit.org
Organization supporting family literacy in the United States

United Nations Children's Fund (UNICEF), UNICEF House, 3 United Nations Plaza, New York, NY 10017. Telephone: (212) 326.7000, Email: unicef@unicef.org, Web: http://www.unicef.org
Agency concerned with the welfare of the world's children

United Nations Educational, Scientific and Cultural Organization (UNESCO), 7 Place de Fontenoy, 75352 Paris, France. Telephone: (33) 1 45 68 10 00, Email: unesco@unesco.org, Web: http://www.unesco.org
Agency promoting justice and peace in the world through international collaboration in the scientific, educational, and cultural arenas

World Education, 44 Farnsworth Street, Boston, MA 02210. Telephone: (617) 482 9485, Fax: (617) 482 0617, Email: wei@worlded.org, Web: http://www.worlded.org
Organization committed to helping the poor through education development

Further Research

Books

Arnove, Robert, and Harvey Graff. *National Literacy Campaigns: Historical and Comparative Perspectives.* New York: Plenum Press, 1987.

Gallego, Margaret, and Sandra Hollingsworth, eds. *What Counts as Literacy: Challenging the School Standard.* New York: Teacher's College Press, 2000.

Graff, Harvey. *The Labyrinths of Literacy: Reflections on Literacy Past and Present.* Rev. and expanded ed. Pittsburgh: University of Pittsburgh Press, 1995.

Harris, William V. *Ancient Literacy.* Cambridge, Mass.: Harvard University Press, 1989.

Heward, Christine, and Sheila Bunwaree, eds. *Gender, Education and Development: Beyond Access to Empowerment.* London: Zed Books, 1999.

Jejeebhoy, Shireen. *Women's Education, Autonomy, and Reproductive Behaviour: Experience from Developing Countries.* Oxford: Clarendon Press, 1995.

King, Elizabeth, and M. Anne Hill, eds, *Women's Education in Developing Countries: Barriers, Benefits, and Polices.* Baltimore: Johns Hopkins University Press for the World Bank, 1993.

Olson, David R. *The World on Paper: The Conceptual and Cognitive Implications of Writing and Reading.* Cambridge: Cambridge University Press, 1994.

Verhoeven, Ludo, and Aydin Durgunoglu, eds. *Literacy Development in a Multilingual Context: Cross-Cultural Perspectives.* Mahwah, N.J.: Lawrence Erlbaum Associates, 1998.

Vincent, David. *The Rise of Mass Literacy: Reading and Writing in Modern Europe.* Cambridge: Polity Press, 2000.

Wagner, Daniel, Richard Venezky, and Brian Street, eds. *Literacy: An International Handbook.* Boulder: Westview Press, 1999.

Articles and Reports

Ainscow, Mel, and Memmenasha Haile-Giorgis. *The Education of Children with Special Needs: Barriers and Opportunities in Central and Eastern Europe.* Innocenti Occasional Papers, Economic and Social Policy Series, no. 67. Florence: UNICEF International Child Development Centre, 1998. Also available at http://www.unicef-icdc.org/publications/pdf/eps67.pdf.

"Basic Education: Gaps on the Map." *UNESCO Courier,* March 2000, http://www.unesco.org/courier/2000_03/uk/dossier/intro03.htm.

Education for All: Schools Reach Out. UNESCO Courier, March 2000, http://www.unesco.org/courier/2000_03/uk/somm/intro.htm.

Helander, Elina. "The Sami of Norway," 1992, http://odin.dep.no/odinarkiv/norsk/dep/ud/1997/annet/032005-990462/index-dok000-b-f-a.html.

Hvenekilde, Anne. "Literacy Training for Linguistic Minorities in Norway." In *Literacy Development in a Multilingual Context: Cross-Cultural Perspectives,* edited by Ludo Verhoeven and Aydin Durgunoglu. Mahwah, N.J.: Lawrence Erlbaum Associates, 1998.

Karki, Arjun. "Rural Poverty in Nepal," *International Communication Project Newsletter,* July 1996, http://www.comlink.apc.org/fic/newslett/eng/nl27/nepal.htm.

Maslak, Mary Ann. "The 'SWAP': One Financial Strategy for Educational Development in Nepal." *Current Issues in Comparative Education,* 1 May 2002. Also available at http://www.tc.columbia.edu/cice/vol03nr2/mamart1.htm.

"One Billion Illiterates: A Challenge for Our Time." *UNESCO Courier,* July 1990.

United Nations. A United Nations Literacy Decade: Education for All. Fifty-fourth Session, Resolution 54/122 of 20 January 2000, http://www.un.org/documents/ga/res/54/a54r122.pdf.

United Nations Educational, Scientific and Cultural Organization. "The Dakar Framework for Action: Education for All. Meeting Our Collective Commitments." The World Education Forum, Dakar, Senegal, 26–28 April 2000, http://unesdoc.unesco.org/images/0012/001202/120240e.pdf.

———. "Education for All: Central and Eastern Europe, Synthesis Report," http://www.unesco.org/education/efa/efa_2000_assess/cee.doc.

———. "Education for All: The Year 2000 Assessment, Regional Report on Education for All in Asia and the Pacific," http://www.unesco.org/education/efa/efa_2000_assess/asia.doc.

———. "Education for All: The Year 2000 Assessment, Regional Report on Education for All in Spanish, Portuguese and French Speaking African Countries," http://www2.unesco.org/wef/en-docs/findings/westafricaeng.doc.

———. "Education for All: The Year 2000 Assessment, Regional Report on Education for All in the Arab States," http://www.unesco.org/education/efa/efa_2000_assess/arab_states.doc.

———. *Education for All: 2000 Assessment. Statistical Document.* Nîmes: Société Provence, 2000. Also available at http://unesdoc.unesco.org/images/0012/001204/120472e.pdf.

———. "Education for All: Warsaw Regional Conference," 6–8 February 2000, working document, http://www.unesco.org/education/efa/efa_2000_assess/europe_eng.doc.

———. "EFA 2000 Assessment, Country Reports: Norway," http://www2.unesco.org/wef/countryreports/norway/rapport_1.htm.

———. *UNESCO Annual Statistical Yearbook, 1999.* Lanham, Md.: Bernan Press, 1999.

———. "World Declaration on Education for All and Framework for Action to Meet Basic Learning Needs." World Conference on Education for All: Meeting Basic Learning Needs, Jomtien, Thailand, 5–9 March 1990. Paris: UNESCO, 1990. Also available at http://www.unesco.org/education/information/nfsunesco/pdf/JOMTIE_E.PDF.

———. *World Education Report, 2000: The Right to Education Towards Education for all Throughout Life.* Paris: UNESCO, 2000.

Verhoeven, Ludo. "Second Language Reading." In *Literacy: An International Handbook,* edited by Daniel Wagner, Richard Venezky, and Brian Street. Boulder: Westview Press, 1999.

Wagner, Daniel, and Laurel Puchner. "World Literacy in the Year 2000." *Annals of the American Academy of Political and Social Science,* 520 (March 1992).

Web Sites

Building the Basics for Lifelong Learning, Public Broadcasting System
http://www.pbs.org/literacy

International Literacy Explorer
http://litserver.literacy.upenn.edu/explorer/overview.html

Seti Project, Nepal, Young Girls' and Women's Literacy through Basic Skills Education
http://litserver.literacy.upenn.edu/explorer/seti_back.html

SIL International
http://www.sil.org

UNESCO, Education for All
http://www.unesco.org/education/efa/index.shtml

UNESCO in Nepal
http://www.unesco.org.np

United Nations Literacy Decade
http://www.unesco.org/education/litdecade

Documents

1. World Declaration on Education for All: Meeting Basic Learning Needs

World Conference on Education for All: Meeting Basic Learning Needs, Jomtien, Thailand, 5–9 March 1990

The full text is available at http://www2.unesco.org/wef/en-conf/Jomtien%20Declaration%20eng.shtm.

Extract

EDUCATION FOR ALL: THE PURPOSE

Article I Meeting Basic Learning Needs

1. Every person—child, youth and adult—shall be able to benefit from educational opportunities designed to meet their basic learning needs. These needs comprise both essential learning tools (such as literacy, oral expression, numeracy, and problem solving) and the basic learning content (such as knowledge, skills, values, and attitudes) required by human beings to be able to survive, to develop their full capacities, to live and work in dignity, to participate fully in development, to improve the quality of their lives, to make informed decisions, and to continue learning. The scope of basic learning needs and how they should be met varies with individual countries and cultures, and inevitably, changes with the passage of time.

2. The satisfaction of these needs empowers individuals in any society and confers upon them a responsibility to respect and build upon their collective cultural, linguistic and spiritual heritage, to promote the education of others, to further the cause of social justice, to achieve environmental protection, to be tolerant towards social, political and religious systems which differ from their own, ensuring that commonly accepted humanistic values and human rights are upheld, and to work for international peace and solidarity in an interdependent world.

3. Another and no less fundamental aim of educational development is the transmission and enrichment of common cultural and moral values. It is in these values that the individual and society find their identity and worth.

4. Basic education is more than an end in itself. It is the foundation for lifelong learning and human development on which countries may build, systematically, further levels and types of education and training.

EDUCATION FOR ALL: AN EXPANDED VISION AND A RENEWED COMMITMENT

Article II Shaping the Vision

To serve the basic learning needs of all requires more than a recommitment to basic education as it now exists. What is needed is an "expanded vision" that surpasses present resource levels, institutional structures, curricula, and conventional delivery systems while building on the best in current practices. New possibilities exist today which result from the convergence of the increase in information and the unprecedented capacity to communicate. We must seize them with creativity and a determination for increased effectiveness. As elaborated in Articles III–VII, the expanded vision encompasses:

Universalizing access and promoting equity;

Focusing on learning;

Broadening the means and scope of basic education;

Enhancing the environment for learning;

Strengthening partnerships.

The realization of an enormous potential for human progress and empowerment is contingent upon whether people can be enabled to acquire the education and the start needed to tap into the ever-expanding pool of relevant knowledge and the new means for sharing this knowledge. . . .

Article IX Mobilizing Resources

1. If the basic learning needs of all are to be met through a much broader scope of action than in the past, it will be essential to mobilize existing and new financial and human resources, public, private and voluntary. All of society has a contribution to make, recognizing that time, energy and funding directed to basic education are perhaps the most profound investment in people and in the future of a country which can be made.

2. Enlarged public-sector support means drawing on the resources of all the government agencies responsible for human development, through increased absolute and proportional allocations to basic education services with the clear recognition of competing claims on national resources of which education is an important one, but not

the only one. Serious attention to improving the efficiency of existing educational resources and programmes will not only produce more, it can also be expected to attract new resources. The urgent task of meeting basic learning needs may require a reallocation between sectors, as, for example, a transfer from military to educational expenditure. Above all, special protection for basic education will be required in countries undergoing structural adjustment and facing severe external debt burdens. Today, more than ever, education must be seen as a fundamental dimension of any social, cultural, and economic design.

2. Dakar Framework for Action: Education for All. Meeting Our Collective Commitments

World Education Forum, Dakar, Senegal, 26–28 April 2000

The full text is available at http://www2.unesco.org/wef/en-conf/dakframeng.shtm.

Extract

2. The Dakar Framework is a collective commitment to action. Governments have an obligation to ensure that EFA goals and targets are reached and sustained. This is a responsibility that will be met most effectively through broad-based partnerships within countries, supported by cooperation with regional and international agencies and institutions. . . .

7. We hereby collectively commit ourselves to the attainment of the following goals:

(i) expanding and improving comprehensive early childhood care and education, especially for the most vulnerable and disadvantaged children;

(ii) ensuring that by 2015 all children, particularly girls, children in difficult circumstances and those belonging to ethnic minorities, have access to and complete free and compulsory primary education of good quality;

(iii) ensuring that the learning needs of all young people and adults are met through equitable access to appropriate learning and life skills programmes;

(iv) achieving a 50 per cent improvement in levels of adult literacy by 2015, especially for women, and equitable access to basic and continuing education for all adults;

(v) eliminating gender disparities in primary and secondary education by 2005, and achieving gender equality in education by 2015, with a focus on ensuring girls' full and equal access to and achievement in basic education of good quality;

(vi) improving all aspects of the quality of education and ensuring excellence of all so that recognized and measurable learning outcomes are achieved by all, especially in literacy, numeracy and essential life skills.

8. To achieve these goals, we the governments, organizations, agencies, groups and associations represented at the World Education Forum pledge ourselves to:

(i) mobilize strong national and international political commitment for education for all, develop national action plans and enhance significantly investment in basic education;

(ii) promote EFA policies within a sustainable and well-integrated sector framework clearly linked to poverty elimination and development strategies;

(iii) ensure the engagement and participation of civil society in the formulation, implementation and monitoring of strategies for educational development;

(iv) develop responsive, participatory and accountable systems of educational governance and management;

(v) meet the needs of education systems affected by conflict, national calamities and instability and conduct educational programmes in ways that promote mutual understanding, peace and tolerance, and help to prevent violence and conflict;

(vi) implement integrated strategies for gender equality in education which recognize the need for changes in attitudes, values and practices;

(vii) implement as a matter of urgency education programmes and actions to combat the HIV/AIDS pandemic;

(viii) create safe, healthy, inclusive and equitably resourced educational environments conducive to excellence in learning with clearly defined levels of achievement for all;

(ix) enhance the status, morale and professionalism of teachers;

(x) harness new information and communication technologies to help achieve EFA goals;

(xi) systematically monitor progress towards EFA goals and strategies at the national, regional and international levels; and

(xii) build on existing mechanisms to accelerate progress towards education for all.

PEACEMAKING AND PEACEBUILDING

Erin McCandless and Mary Hope Schwoebel

Peacekeeping, peacemaking, peacebuilding, and preventive diplomacy are four strategic approaches to catalyzing peace in countries and regions in conflict. These terms, popularized by UN secretary-general Boutros Boutros-Ghali in the 1992 Agenda for Peace, provide the conceptual and practical basis for international, national, and local peace and conflict resolution efforts. While all are useful in different contexts and in many cases complementary, the trend toward a greater emphasis on peacebuilding reflects the nature of contemporary wars. Compared to conflicts in previous eras, today's wars are more violent and protracted, more destructive of social, political, and economic infrastructure, result generally in more civilian than combatant deaths, and employ child soldiers. Peacebuilding addresses these aspects of war, targeting the context of the conflict and supporting the structures that will solidify the peace.

Historical Background and Development

Attempts to end war have traditionally been the terrain of statesmen. Diplomacy has its roots in *realpolitik,* or political realism of the mid-1990s, which prioritizes the pursuit of national interests and the exercise of economic and military power. Deterrence—security through the threat of force and the balancing of power—and the formation of alliances became pillars of political realism (see INTERNATIONAL CRIMINAL JUSTICE). Civil war was considered nonthreatening to the world order and of little concern to anyone outside of the state affected, given the overriding international principles of sovereignty and nonintervention across state borders.

The field of international relations, however, brought forth ideas in the 1970s about the interdependence of states in the global system and the need for the international community to become more involved in civil wars, particularly in cases involving large-scale abuses of human rights and humanitarian disasters. The concept of peacemaking—the use of diplomatic means to persuade parties in conflict to cease hostilities and to negotiate a peaceful settlement of disputes—brought new thinking, challenging strategies rooted in zero-sum competition in favor of cooperation, collaboration, and the potential for "win-win" outcomes. Proponents of peacemaking reasoned that beneath bargaining positions were interests which were far more negotiable. They emphasized improving relations and achieving cease-fires and peace agreements. Multilateral diplomatic missions applied the concept, often employing problem-solving approaches through negotiation and mediation. At the same time, other challenges within mainstream international relations theory addressed notions of peacebuilding. The World Order Models Project (WOMP) identified the need for an intercultural dialogue to agree on basic values: peace, environmental and economic well-being, social justice, and democratic governance.

The field of conflict resolution emerged in the 1960s and challenged traditional notions even more. As a critique of power politics in international relations, conceptual foundations for conflict resolution were emerging within industrial organizational theory and practice, and then in the 1970s and 1980s in the human relations field within social psychology. Conflict was perceived as a natural, even productive, positive force for social change, and skills were needed to create win-win solutions. Debates focused on causes of conflict and methods for resolution. A consensus was emerging, however, around the idea that resolving conflict, if indeed possible, required addressing its roots, a pillar of the peacebuilding approach. Advocates of realpolitik preferred the idea of conflict management, assuming that conflicts could ultimately not be resolved.

Peace theory became a strong force in the 1970s. Its emphasis on values, aims, and methods laid the foundation for present-day notions of peacebuilding. In the 1970s, Johan Galtung and Adam Curle spoke passionately about the need for peace to embrace equitable development, distributive justice, conscientization, and just social, economic, and political relations and institutions. Most recently, John Paul Lederach outlined the building blocks of peacebuilding, theorizing from his own practice and experience as a peacebuilding trainer in the 1990s. Contemporary conflicts necessitate changing destructive relationship patterns into constructive systemic change rooted in cooperative and mutually beneficial relationships. Peacebuilding, Lederach argues, is a holistic strategy that encompasses, generates, and sustains the full array of processes, approaches, and stages needed for this task.

Current Status

Peacemaking and peacebuilding are concepts gaining widespread understanding and usage by the international community. Research in these areas is driven by practice and the changing nature of war. The idea that violent conflicts can be "terminated" or "resolved" through Track I processes—those involving only political leaders—has been discredited during the last decade by cease-fires and peace agreements that have not held, in part because they failed to address the roots of conflict and the needs of the societies involved. Left unaddressed, such conflicts resurface around old and new issues, leading to greater distrust, cynicism, and hopelessness.

Research

The traditional mandates and methods of international intervention came under increasing question after the international community's failure to achieve peace and reestablish a legitimate central government in Somalia and after the failure to intervene to prevent genocide in Rwanda (because of the Somalia experience). Wars are now very different than they were in the past, usually involving civilian targets and casualties, attacks on humanitarian personnel, child soldiers and victims, vast numbers of internally displaced people and refugees, more violence and less adherence to rules of engagement, and the rampant use of land mines.

The new face of war demanded new conceptual tools and practices, so the idea of peacebuilding found a home among diplomats, policymakers, and relief and development workers. Peacebuilding focuses on the context of the conflict—the attitudes and socioeconomic circumstances of the people who are affected by war and will build the peace—rather than the military and the issues that divide the parties (see DEVELOPMENT AID and INCOME INEQUALITY). This is a logical refocusing if one considers that the majority of war casualties are now civilians rather than combatants, who were the majority of war casualties at the beginning of the twentieth century. This holistic approach focuses on the multitude of processes and actors that are required to build, make, and sustain a peace agreement. Other key principles include the following:

- causes of violent conflict are relational, that is, identity based, and structural, meaning economic and politically based, so approaches to peace must address both sources;
- cease-fires and peace agreements alone are insufficient to sustain peace, so it is crucial to rebuild infrastructures and institutions;
- conflict and peace develop and are sustained within particular cultures and societies, so it is necessary to draw upon cultural and social resources;
- local ownership of the processes and outcomes of peace offers the best chance for success, so the participation of communities in the design, implementation, and evaluation of efforts is critical;
- interplay between theory, research, and practice keep the field of peaceamaking relevant and appropriate, so the development of policy must be informed by all of them.

Peacebuilding activities have come to include generating contact and dialogue between communities, initiating reconciliation, identifying overarching goals between communities, undertaking confidence-building measures, institutionalizing respect for human rights, promoting political pluralism and the rule of law, accommodating ethnic minorities and ethnic diversity, strengthening the capacity of state structures and promoting good governance, and supporting participation, community, and human development (see ETHNIC AND REGIONAL CONFLICT).

While the emphasis on peacebuilding for such intergovernmental institutions as the United Nations and the World Bank is postconflict, many theorists, practitioners, and policymakers view peacebuilding as an ongoing process to be undertaken during all phases of a conflict. Although preventive diplomacy has always been a component of peacemaking, new thinking increasingly views peacemaking as the key to conflict prevention—before violent conflict breaks out and in the postconflict phase—to ensure that conflict does not resurface. In *Breaking Cycles of Violence,* Janie Leatherman and her colleagues identify the need for structural, institutional, economic, and cultural solutions aimed at addressing roots of conflict based in these spheres.

Peacekeeping and peacemaking play important, complementary roles to peacebuilding. Researchers point to the necessity of peacekeeping in monitoring a cease-fire, stopping violence, and generally providing a buffer between contending parties. Peacekeepers also can prevent the looting of humanitarian assistance and help implement peace agreements, such as overseeing or observing demobilization and disarmament. Debates have focused on the various roles peacekeepers might assume, including as activists in constructing the peace or maintainers of the status quo. The UN Agenda for Peace affirms active interpretation, whereby peacekeeping "expands the possibilities for both the prevention of conflict and the making of peace" (see Document 1). Peacemaking is the tool designed to settle disputes, end hostilities, and rejuvenate positive interaction. It excludes the use of force against one of the parties to enforce an end to hostilities, an activity that in UN parlance is referred to as "peace enforcment." Secretary-General Boutros-Ghali pointed out that peacebuilding is crucial to the success of peacemaking, since it includes activities that aim to address the underlying causes of conflict and to support structures that will strengthen and solidify peace.

New directions in research into peacebuilding and peacemaking include their intersections with religion, culture, and non-Western thinking and practice, aid and development, the roles of reconciliation and justice, and the role of civil society, including nongovernmental organizations (NGOs) and the media. Peacemaking research has focused on the impact of culture on the effectiveness of negotiation and mediation, while peacebuilding literature has given priority to the importance of creating space for indigenous approaches. Kevin Avruch, in *Culture and Conflict Resolution,* and John Paul Lederach, in *Preparing for Peace,* emphasize the role of culture in influencing how people understand conflict and practice conflict resolution. In "From Conflict Resolution to Sustainable Democracy," Tim Murithi points to the growing school of thought which maintains that indigenous approaches to conflict resolution and traditional structures of leadership have a vital role to play in the building of sustainable frameworks for governance, which are central to the making and building of peace.

In the area of religion and peacebuilding, scholars are identifying resources for peace within their faiths. Mohammed Abu-Nimer highlights the textual and practical ways in which Islamic values parallel and enrich those of peacebuilding. Marc Gopin is doing the same within Judaism. Such research is often done alongside practical efforts to contribute to the dialogue within countries where religion is a factor in violence and therefore must be a factor in peacebuilding.

Innovations in peacebuilding and development literature are responding to contextual trends: wars are primarily occurring in developing countries; development aid is too often exacerbating and even catalyzing conflict; the growth and spread of poverty is causing and resulting from conflict; and the unequal distribution of the benefits and burdens of globalization and of high export value resources, such as oil and diamonds, is a source of conflict (see Document 2).

The impact and effectiveness of peacebuilding and peacemaking are also topics of research. A number of efforts are under way to evaluate these areas and to develop guidelines for best practices, accountability to all stakeholders, and codes of ethics for intervention. Much of this research is being developed within and between nongovernmental organizations. These include Lessons Learned in Peacebuilding, a program of the European Platform for Conflict Prevention, and Reflecting on Peace Practice, a project of the Collaborative for Development Action and the Life and Peace Institute. Although trends are emerging through case study research, practitioners and researchers are generally in agreement that peacemaking and peacebuilding are not scientific experiments. Rather, they are dynamic processes rooted in particular contexts. This notion raises a challenge for the professionalization of the field to "walk the talk" of these principles.

Policies and Programs

Peacemaking and peacebuilding policies and programs are moving onto numerous governmental and intergovernmental agendas. While areas of consensus are clearly emerging, such as the need for prevention, there are also challenges that accompany the proliferation of policies and practices at different levels. Civil society organizations, including NGOs and community-based organizations and religious groups, research and academic institutions, and networks and coalitions are actively spearheading this movement. The discussion here is limited to intergovernmental policies.

The United Nations. Collective global security is the organizing precept of the UN Charter. The end of the cold war has presented new challenges for the United Nations, perhaps the greatest of which has been choices about when and where to intervene in violent conflicts in the face of limited resources. The UN secretary-general implements the peace and security mandates issued by the Security Council and the General Assembly and works with special representatives and envoys and other emissaries to fulfill them. At the same time, however, the United Nations can play a role only if the parties to a dispute agree that it should do so.

Preventive diplomacy and action are increasingly favored as means of preventing human suffering and as alternatives to costly politico-military operations to resolve conflicts after they have erupted. Although diplomacy is a well-tried means of preventing conflict, recent experience points to the utility of other forms of preventive action, including deployment, disarmament, humanitarian action, and peacebuilding. This more comprehensive approach to prevention has generated a shift in terminology from "preventive diplomacy" to "preventive action." Among UN member states, there are increasing linkages between preventive action and peacebuilding.

Department of Political Affairs (DPA). The UN Department of Political Affairs provides advice and support on all political matters to the UN secretary-general in the exercise of that office's global responsibilities under the UN Charter relating to the maintenance and restoration of peace and security. This involves monitoring and analyzing political developments and latent and manifest conflicts globally, recommending appropriate actions, and executing approved activities and policies to be carried out in the areas of preventive diplomacy, peacemaking, peacekeeping, and peacebuilding. Specific DPA activities include fact finding, mediation and negotiation, undertaking goodwill and other missions, establishing partnerships with funds and programs as well as other agencies in the UN system, supporting Track II processes (involving civil society organizations or citizens' initiatives) where the United Nations is not able to play a direct role, assisting in elections (including providing technical help and support for national electoral institutions and processes), cooperating with regional organizations, and reaching out to civil society organizations and the media.

Office for the Coordination of Humanitarian Affairs (OCHA). The mission of the Office for the Coordination of Humanitarian Affairs is to mobilize and coordinate effective and principled humanitarian action in partnership with national and international actors to alleviate human suffering in disasters and emergencies, advocate for the rights of people in need, promote preparedness and prevention, and facilitate sustainable solutions. OCHA often has a presence in conflict settings before UN or regional peacekeeping or peacemaking efforts have been launched. As the coordinator of humanitarian aid for all UN agencies, and in theory, of all government and nongovernmental aid organizations, OCHA often becomes the primary link between political and military leaders of different parties to a conflict concerning the needs and interests of vulnerable civilian populations, including refugees and internally displaced persons.

Department of Peacekeeping Operations (DPKO). Peacekeeping operations are based on the principle that an impartial UN presence on the ground can ease tensions and facilitate the implementation of a peace agreement. In the past, such operations normally fell into two categories: military observer missions composed of relatively small numbers of unarmed officers charged with such tasks as monitoring cease-fires, verifying troop withdrawals, or patrolling borders or demilitarized zones; and peacekeeping forces composed of national contingents of troops deployed to carry out tasks similar to those of military observers and, often, to act as a buffer between hostile parties. In response to new contexts and situations, peacekeeping operations now increasingly fit into a third category: complex deployments composed of military personnel, civilian police, and other civilian personnel, such as human rights monitors, electoral experts and observers, deminers trained to identify and eliminate land mines, and specialists in civil affairs and communications. Together, these peacekeepers work alongside governments and civil society organizations to provide emergency relief, demobilize and reintegrate former fighters into society, clear mines, organize and conduct elections, create new political institutions and broaden their bases, and promote sustainable development practices.

Peacekeeping missions are perhaps the most visible UN operations in conflict zones, but many other UN agencies and offices are usually present. These include the Children's Fund (UNICEF), the Office of the United Nations High Commissioner for Human Rights, United Nations High Commissioner for Refugees, and the World Food Programme, all of which work closely with peacekeepers. Together, they help alleviate suffering, deal with the problems of refugees and displaced persons, and contribute to reconciliation and reconstruction. Often a special representative of the secretary-general is appointed to direct and coordinate the work of the peacekeeping operation and other UN bodies present, maintaining political momentum toward peace.

World Bank. The World Bank's Conflict Prevention and Reconstruction Team, formerly the Post-Conflict Unit, seeks to ease the transition to sustainable peace and support socioeconomic development in conflict-affected countries. The bank assesses the degree to which poverty reduction activities may have a negative effect on economic and social stability and human security where these elements are preconditions for sustainable development. It also looks at whether poverty reduction activities are being negatively affected by war-related destruction and destabilization of normal socioeconomic activity and by the diversion of public resources from development purposes to military and other expenditures incurred in waging war.

Recognizing that the dominant model of development—one based on a linear progression through stages—does not reflect reality in conflict-affected countries, the bank may utilize different approaches besides or in addition to a Country Assistance Strategy (CAS), the instrument the bank usually employs in development settings. One of these alternative instruments is a Watching Brief, which provides support for activities beyond the monitoring activities prescribed in a CAS. Another is a Transitional Support Strategy (TSS), a short- to medium-term plan for which there is no CAS or the CAS no longer represents a responsive strategy because of ongoing conflict. Here the bank may become involved incrementally by, for instance, supporting the objectives and sequencing of priorities of peace accords and rehabilitation plans in peaceful areas of a country. The TSS may incorporate activities in neighboring countries that are not directly engaged in hostilities to support regional peace. Finally, the bank may provide Emergency Recovery Assistance, which is a tool for financing countries in transition from conflict.

Governmental and Civil Society Organizations. Governments have their own policies and programs related to peacemaking and peacebuilding globally, regionally, or nationally. The United Kingdom's Department for International Development (DFID) addresses conflict through its Conflict and Humanitarian Affairs Department. DFID attempts to address the underlying causes of conflict stemming from social inequality and poverty. It conducts conflict appraisals when preparing country assistance programs, into which it integrates conflict reduction objectives that build the political and social means to enable the equitable representation of different interest groups, promotion of human rights, and resolution of disputes and grievances without recourse to violence.

In 1994 the United States Agency for International Development (USAID) established the Office for Transition Initiatives (OTI) to provide assistance in conflict-prone and postconflict settings for the types of activities outside the mandate of the Office for Foreign Disaster Assistance (OFDA), which provides short-term emergency assistance, and USAID's regular long-term development activities. OTI works with local partners to promote peaceful, democratic change and to address the causes of conflict with fast, flexible, short-term assistance. OTI has programs for reintegrating former combatants, demining, resettling refugees and internally displaced persons, and establishing transparency and good governance. It also assists with civil society development, civilian-military relations, human rights, policy reform, conflict management, community relations, and reconciliation.

Civil society organizations (CSOs), in addition to facilitating the design and adoption of peacebuilding and prevention strategies, implement their own peacebuilding, peacemaking, and conflict prevention programs in such areas as training and education, dialogue, citizen diplomacy, action research, nonviolent action, and collaborative community development. These groups, which include nongovernmental and community-based organizations, are also successfully forging alliances with intergovernmental organizations, particularly in the areas of peacebuilding and conflict prevention, as their critical role in envisioning and actualizing new strategies that meet local needs is increasingly recognized.

Regional Summaries

There are many actors involved in peacemaking and peacebuilding activities globally. The focus here is primarily on subregional actors and the United Nations. These institutions, however, are historically not the first to respond to conflict or the last to remain involved in postconflict stages.

Americas

The primary peacebuilding activities of the Organization of American States (OAS) are its postconflict demining program in Central America and the joint OAS-UN International Civil Mission in Haiti (MICIVIH). A commitment to human rights is realized through the Inter-American Court of Human Rights and the Inter-American Commission on Human Rights. During the 1980s and 1990s, when Latin American governments became more democratic, the OAS successfully defended democracies from military overthrow in Guatemala, Haiti, and Peru. Its approach involved deploying electoral observation missions to numerous countries.

There are presently no UN peace operations in the Americas, although the Colombian conflict—which involves the government, right-wing paramilitary troops, left-wing revolutionary forces, and drug cartels—is one of the most violent in the world. Over the years, the United Nations has had eight peace operations in five countries in the Americas; four of these were carried out in Haiti between September 1993 and March 2000. Other missions were deployed to the Dominican Republic, from May 1965 to October 1966; Central America, from November 1989 to January 1992; El Salvador, from July 1991 to April 1995; and Guatemala, from January 1997 to May 1997.

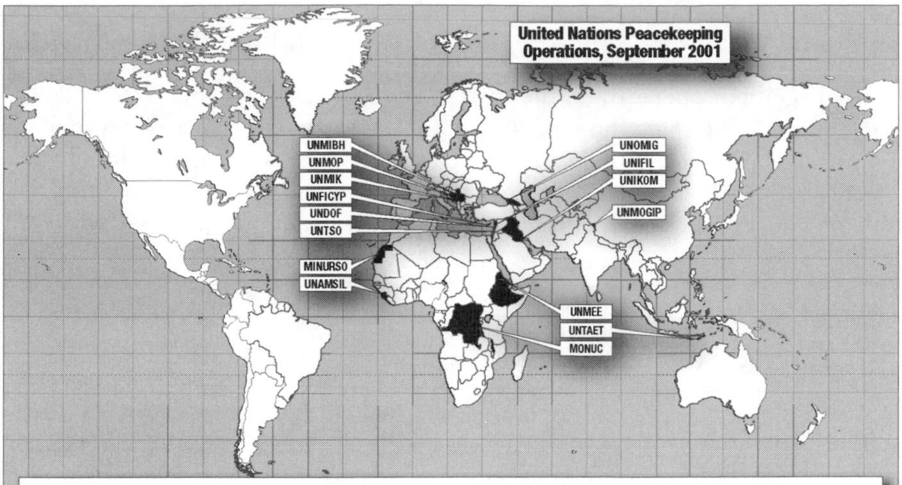

UNMIBH
United Nations Mission in Bosnia and Herzegovina
Began December 1995
Strength: 1,680 civilian police plus military and civilian personnel
Fatalities: 8
Appropriation 07/01–06/02: $144.7 million (gross)
Budget figures include UNMIBH, UNMOP, and UN liaison offices at Belgrade and Zagreb

UNMOP
United Nations Mission of Observers in Prevlaka
Began January 1996
Military strength: 27
Appropriation included in UNMIBH

UNMIK
United Nations Interim Administration Mission in Kosovo
Began June 1999
Strength: 4,332 civilian police plus military and civilian personnel
Fatalities: 13
Appropriation 07/01–06/02: $413.4 million (gross)

UNFICYP
United Nations Peacekeeping Force in Cyprus
Began March 1964
Military strength: 1,251
Fatalities: 170
Appropriation 07/01–06/02: $42.4 million (gross) including voluntary contributions from Cyprus and Greece

UNDOF
United Nations Disengagement Observer Force [Syrian Golan Heights]
Began June 1974
Military strength: 1,039
Fatalities: 40
Appropriation 07/01–06/02: $35.7 million (gross)

UNTSO
United Nations Truce Supervision Organization [Middle East]
Began June 1948
Military strength: 153
Fatalities: 38
Appropriation for year 2001: $22.8 million

MINURSO
United Nations Mission for the Referendum in Western Sahara
Began April 1991
Military strength: 229
Fatalities: 10
Appropriation 07/01–06/02: $50.5 million (gross)

UNAMSIL
United Nations Mission in Sierra Leone
Began October 1999
Military strength: 16,654
Fatalities: 46
Commitment authority 07/01–12/01 (six months): $293.4 million (gross), but revision in budget expected

UNOMIG
United Nations Observer Mission in Georgia
Began August 1993
Military strength: 106
Fatalities: 3
Appropriation 07/01–06/02: $27.9 million (gross)

UNIFIL
United Nations Interim Force in Lebanon
Began March 1978
Military strength: 4,486
Fatalities: 244
Commitment authority 07/01–12/01 (six months): $106.2 million (gross)*

UNIKOM
United Nations Iraq-Kuwait Observation Mission
Began April 1991
Military strength: 1,099
Fatalities: 14
Appropriation 07/01–06/02: $52.8 million (gross) including voluntary contributions of $33.7 million from Kuwait

UNMOGIP
United Nations Military Observer Group in India and Pakistan
Began January 1949
Military strength: 45
Fatalities: 9
Appropriation for year 2001: $7.3 million

UNMEE
United Nations Mission in Ethiopia and Eritrea
Began July 2000
Military strength: 3,866
Fatalities: 2
Commitment authority 07/01–12/01 (six months): $96.0 million (gross), but revision in budget expected

UNTAET
United Nations Transitional Administration in East Timor
Began October 1999
Military strength: 8,125
Fatalities: 16
Commitment authority 07/01–12/01 (six months): $300.8 million (gross), but revision in budget expected

MONUC
United Nations Organization Mission in the Democratic Republic of the Congo
Began December 1999
Military Strength: 2,398
Fatalities: 2
Appropriation 07/01–12/01 (six months): $209.1 million (gross), but revision in budget expected

Source: United Nations, Department of Public Information, Peace and Security Section, *United Nations Peacekeeping Operations, Background Note 15 September 2001*, http://www.un.org/Depts/dpko/dpko/cu_mission/body.htm.

Europe

The fifty-three-nation Organization for Security and Cooperation in Europe (OSCE) is often held up as an infrastructural model for regional peace and security. During the cold war, the OSCE secured agreements for arms control, security, and human rights and assisted civil societies in Eastern and Central Europe and the republics of the former Soviet Union in challenging their governments. Today the OSCE's Conflict Prevention Center serves as the focal point for the organization's prevention and peacebuilding activities. The OSCE currently has missions and field activities in the central, eastern, and southeastern areas of the continent and in the Caucasus and Central Asia. The focus of these operations are institution and democracy building and human rights. Special envoys and observer missions are regularly sent to member states to work directly with governments and opposition groups dealing with minority problems and other internal conflicts.

A new impetus to strengthen the European Union's conflict prevention and crisis management infrastructure resulted from Europe's failure to lead the crisis management operation in the former Yugoslavia. A number of peacekeeping, civil disaster, and humanitarian assistance exercises and operations are coordinated regionally under the direction of NATO's Partnership for Peace, established in 1994, and its Euro-Atlantic Partnerships Council, established in 1997. The Partnership for Peace has established multinational peacekeeping battalions for deployment in UN and NATO peace missions.

Africa

Africa has more institutions devoted to preventing and resolving conflicts than any other region, but a severe lack of financial capacity has hampered the effectiveness of these outfits to date. The Organization of African Unity's (OAU) peace infrastructure includes the Mechanism for Conflict Prevention, Management and Resolution, the Mechanism for Negotiation, Mediation and Conciliation, and the Peace Fund. OAU heads of state are committed to implementation of the OAU Early Warning System.

In recent years, the OAU has served as lead mediator in a joint effort with the United Nations and the United States to end the war between Ethiopia and Eritrea that, according to the *Stockholm International Peace Research Institute Yearbook, 2000,* has killed 70,000 people and displaced another 500,000. The OAU supported the regional peace process led by the Southern African Development Community (SADC) that led to the signing of the Lusaka ceasefire agreement in the Democratic Republic of Congo. The United Nations has completed fifteen peace operations in eleven African countries. Perhaps the most well-known of these were the United Nations Operations in Somalia I and II (UNOSOM I and II), the missions to Somalia from April 1992 to March 1995. The United Nations currently has four peace operations in Africa (see map, p. 463).

Uneven development is a root cause of problems in southern Africa and has become the increasing focus of peacebuilding efforts. In Mozambique, a post–civil war peacebuilding effort by the international community has been relatively successful in assisting with disarmament efforts, demobilization and reintegration procedures, and infrastructure reconstruction. Repeated interventions in Angola, however, including four UN missions, have failed to end the ongoing conflict there. More hopeful is the strengthening civil society movement that is spearheading, in consultation with international civic actors, a Referendum on War or Peace to authoritatively establish the desires of the Angolan people.

SADC has an Organ on Politics, Defense, and Security committed to the peaceful settlement of disputes by negotiation, mediation, and arbitration. According to Article 4 of the SADC Treaty, military intervention "shall be decided upon only after all possible remedies have been exhausted in accordance with the OAU and UN Charters." The war involving the Democratic Republic of Congo and its neighbors has been a real test for SADC and has split SADC members.

The Common Market for Eastern and Southern Africa (COMESA) is gathering views from the private sector and civil society for a peace and security policy and striving to develop mechanisms for collaborations. Southern African peace and conflict nongovernmental organizations are collaborating through the Southern African Conflict Prevention Network (SACPN), a new regional nongovernmental organization. The network is establishing an agenda for a coordinated approach by NGOs to conflict prevention in the region.

Eastern and central Africa have been the sites of numerous peace efforts since the first peacekeeping mission to the Congo from 1960 to 1964. The failed UNOSOM missions to Somalia focused on the provision of security for the delivery of humanitarian assistance and developed into a major effort to assist Somalis in rebuilding political and economic institutions and achieve national reconciliation. The Intergovernmental Authority on Development was established in 1996 to unite East African states in a regional economic initiative. Although its conflict prevention and management capacity has yet to be developed, the authority's efforts in Sudan have resulted in an agreement by the Islamist government and the Sudan People's Liberation Army to use the authority's Declaration of Principles as the foundation for initiating peace talks. The declaration acknowledges the right of southerners to self-determination and proposes a four-year transition period to be followed by a southern referendum on unity. A conflicting parallel effort has been initiated by Egypt and Libya with the support of the government and its northern allies. In Somalia, the authority is focusing on the development of civil society as the foundation for peace. This strategy has support from the UN Security Council, but conflicts between member states have caused major setbacks.

In the 1990s West Africa suffered from numerous conflicts, many of which remain problems for the region today. The Economic Community of West Africa States (ECOWAS) was formed in 1975 by sixteen West African states to coordinate the gradual economic and political integration of the region. ECOWAS adopted a nonaggression protocol in 1978 and a Mutual Assistance Protocol in 1981 and established the ECOWAS Monitoring Group (ECOMOG) to respond to the Liberian civil war in 1990 and later to the war in Sierra Leone. Other responses included the United Nations Observer Mission in Liberia (UNOMIL) from 1993 to 1997 as well as to Sierra Leone from 1993 to 1999. The United Nations Observer Mission in Sierra Leone (UNOMSIL) replaced UNOMIL in 1999. ECOMOG has since also intervened in Guinea-Bissau.

In 1999 ECOWAS's conflict prevention and resolution mechanism divided West Africa into four zones for the purpose of gathering conflict-related data for the secretariat's analysis and transmission to governments. The mechanism includes a stand-by force and mediation and judicial instruments and has a moratorium on the import, export, and manufacture of light weapons. Efforts are under way by NGOs and donors to enhance collaboration with ECOWAS in peacebuilding and prevention activities, which could include mechanisms for information gathering and sharing and rapid response. The West African Network for Peacebuilding coordinates many national peacebuilding and peacemaking civic efforts in the region.

Central Asia and the Caucasus

The former Soviet Central Asian republics have been plagued by violence, political instability, and economic hardship since gaining independence in 1991. The 1992–1997 civil war in Tajikistan was particularly destructive, but the peace process has managed to accommodate divergent interests and to create some space for the development of political cooperation; violent skirmishes, however, persist. Cease-fires in the Caucasus have, for the most part, held for several years, although military engagement remains a method of conflict resolution. Peacemaking efforts have been undertaken by the Organization for Security and Cooperation in Europe and the United Nations, through the bilateral and multilateral involvement of a number of states, and through civic initiatives by international and local nongovernmental organizations. Regardless, little progress has been made in the Georgia and Nagorno-Karabakh conflicts. These situations are complex and have been exacerbated by difficulties in coordination, negotiating mandates, and cautious diplomacy in the face of a multiplicity of actors and precarious balances of power.

Southeast Asia

The violence surrounding East Timorese independence from Indonesia highlights the ineffectiveness of institutional peace and security frameworks in Southeast Asia. In June 1999 the UN Security Council passed Resolution 1272 establishing the United Nations Transitional Administration in East Timor (UNTAET) as an integrated, multidimensional peacekeeping operation fully responsible for the administration of East Timor during its transition to independence, pending a favorable referendum on ending Indonesian control of the territory. In elections held in August 1999, 98 percent of registered voters went to the polls and cast ballots in favor of independence. As a result of ongoing violence by Indonesian anti-independence militias, in September 1999 the Security Council authorized the International Force in East Timor (INTERFET), under a unified command structure headed by Australia, to restore peace and security and to protect and support UNTAET in carrying out its mission. In February 2000 INTERFET transferred command for military operations to UNTAET.

Case Study—Postconflict Peacebuilding in Somaliland: The War-Torn Societies Program

In May 1991, four months after the collapse of the government of the Somali Democratic Republic and the flight of its president, Mohamed Siyad Barre, the Republic of Somaliland declared independence from the rest of Somalia. A decade of oppression and conflict had left the country and its people devastated by war. Within months, however, fighting broke out in Somaliland between and within various clans. Power struggles erupted within the Somali National Movement (SNM) between the military and political wings for control of the government. Conflicts ensued over control of the country's main revenue-generating resources, and organized and random criminal violence was perpetrated by unemployed and armed youth, many of them demobilized SNM fighters.

Somaliland is well known to peace and conflict researchers and practitioners for its success in employing traditional conflict resolution practices for peacebuilding and state building. Between 1991 and 1997 Somaliland's traditional clan leaders sponsored a series of reconciliation conferences that brought an end to all but random criminal violence and established a two-year transitional rule, an interim constitution, and a two-house legislature (one comprised of elected officials and the other of traditional clan leaders).

At the close of 2001, however, monumental tasks remained, including preparing a constitution and holding a national referendum on it, continued sovereignty for Somaliland or reunification with Somalia, establishing political parties, holding a national election, constructing infrastructure, establishing financial institutions, and developing a social services sector. The two houses of the legislature continued to struggle over the constitutional handling of decentralization and power sharing between the executive and the legislature and between elected officials and traditional clan leaders.

It is to these tasks that the War-Torn Societies Program (WSP) addresses itself. WSP was initiated by the United Nations Research Institute for Social Development and operates in five postconflict countries—Eritrea, Guatemala, Mozambique, Somalia, and Somaliland—to facilitate policy-oriented dialogue between representatives of societal sectors: national and local government, civil society organizations, traditional leaders, and others associated with specific dialogue topics. This postconflict peacebuilding process is designed to engage members of society vertically (levels of society) and horizontally (sectors, clans, and regions).

WSP began with the goal of finding solutions to the difficulties faced by the international community in responding to the challenges of postconflict rebuilding in general. Other goals included the following:

- facilitating a national rebuilding process in which dialogue and research are used together to set priorities and identify policy options;
- ensuring that international assistance contributes to peacebuilding, rather than to more conflict;
- promoting participatory action research as a vehicle for democratizing development and empowering communities;
- strengthening the capacity of national and local government and civil society organizations to contribute to state building and reconstruction;
- learning about the relationships between research and policy formulation and the application of action research at the micro and macro levels; and
- providing lessons about tools that positively affect the way external organizations plan, implement, and coordinate their activities in countries emerging from conflict.

The first phase of WSP in Somaliland involved research into the political, economic, and social situation of the country. This drew on existing documentation and the findings of focus groups from urban and rural communities throughout Somaliland. Four broad themes, or entry points, emerged as priorities for policy-directed research: the media (objectivity and responsibility), governance (decentralization and taxation), livestock regulation (internal and external marketing), and the family (the impact of the war and the impact of *khat,* a stimulant widely used in Somaliland, especially by men). Workshops were held in communities throughout Somaliland with participation from representatives of the relevant stakeholder groups.

In Somaliland WSP contributed to the important first steps in the state-building and reconstruction processes. WSP participatory action research created the space for Somalilanders to articulate the issues and challenges confronting them; acquire a better understanding of the paradoxes and tradeoffs involved in these processes; explore alternatives that may lead to win-win solutions to problems; and begin to build consensus around priorities and approaches, facilitate local ownership of and responsibility for these processes, raise consciousness about the roles, rights, and responsibilities of citizens and government, and demonstrate that there are peaceful ways of resolving differences of opinion and conflicting needs and interests. These issues are at the core of peacebuilding, as bottom-up processes are the foundation of sustainable peace.

Case Study—Interfaith Peacebuilding in Niger State: The Women Opinion Leaders' Forum

Based on research carried out by Chom Bagu

Niger state is located in north central Nigeria. It is home to a large number of Muslims and a larger population of Christians and other non-Muslims. In January 2000 the newly elected civilian government passed legislation establishing *sharia,* Islamic law, in Niger state. In response, the Women Opinion Leaders' Forum (WOLF)—seeking to prevent violent conflict along religious and communal lines, as had recently occurred between Christians and Muslims in Kaduna state—designed and implemented a peacebuilding intervention.

WOLF is a membership civil society organization that aims to increase women's roles in public affairs. It has twenty-three offices and conducts workshops on civic education, interfaith mediation, and conflict resolution. In Niger state, WOLF's peacebuilding and conflict prevention strategy centered around an interfaith mediation program to encourage religious tolerance, dialogue, and consultation. In preparation, WOLF conducted visits to government representatives and traditional and religious leaders to sensitize them to the issues involved and to solicit support for their initiative. Working with the Kaduna-based Interfaith Mediation Center, WOLF held workshops in three Senate districts during three weeks in May 2001. Participants included Christian and Muslim groups, youth and women leaders, traditional and religious leaders, journalists, security personnel, and representatives of labor unions. The organization simultaneously carried out a radio and television campaign, which through jingles and discussion programs explored contentious issues and presented moderate views from Christian and Muslim perspectives. The intervention concluded with a policy dialogue on sharia on 1 June 2001 that was attended by representatives from government, traditional chiefs' councils, the police, and many other stakeholder groups. During the dialogue, Christians and other non-Muslims expressed their concerns about the implementation of sharia and made recommendations for amendments. The police explained their difficulties in enforcing the law, and the forum jointly debated possible changes. They agreed on creating a forum for regular consultation on sharia and related issues as a means of preventing violent conflict in Niger state.

WOLF's efforts highlight many of the important facets of peacebuilding, including the constructive leadership role that women can play. Group members focused on the contribution of dialogue among various stakeholder groups, and they created an ongoing process, rather than a one-time workshop that people would forget about after it had ended. Their media campaign and workshops generated consciousness about the need for tolerance and for future dialogue to address group differences. Moreover, members of the general public were able to speak with policymakers and to contribute to establishing mechanisms to prevent conflict.

Biographical Sketches

Edward Azar is a political scientist who has facilitated understanding of third world protracted social conflicts rooted in identity, inequality, and the international development system. He has sought to shift international relations away from its superpower bias and toward a focus on the other two-thirds of the world and the need for humanistic study in which security and stability are based on human dignity, quality of life, and genuine peace. Azar was active in efforts to resolve conflicts in the Middle East during the 1960s, 1970s, and 1980s.

Elise Bjorn-Hansen Boulding is a sociologist, professor, peace activist, researcher, writer, and speaker. She has served as the secretary-general of the International Peace Research Association and board member for several leading peace institutions. Boulding is the author of nineteen books and hundreds of articles addressing critical peace and conflict issues, including democracy, development, and women in society. She was nominated for the 1990 Nobel Peace Prize.

John Burton is a leading pioneer in the field of conflict resolution. He catalyzed the shift in thinking about conflict's causes from positions and interests (international relations thinking) to frustrated needs. Burton's revolutionary theory posited that conflict results from frustration by social institutions of the universal, basic (nonnegotiable) human needs of individuals. If these needs are denied, people will rebel against the responsible institutions, even "irrationally," or against all odds. Burton also introduced the pluralist paradigm—the world society perspective—emphasizing the values and relationships of multiple actors in the global system.

Johan Galtung is considered by many observers to be the "father of peace studies." In *Essays in Peace Research* (1975), Galtung put forth the tripartite classification of conflict resolution strategies: peacekeeping, peacemaking, and peacebuilding. He has written more than fifty books and more than a thousand articles advancing the field of peace and conflict resolution. In 1959 he established the International Peace Research Institute in Oslo, Norway, the first peace research institute in the world, and served as its director for ten years. Galtung also founded the *Journal of Peace Research* and TRANSCEND: A Peace and Development Network, which he directs. In 1987 he was awarded the Alternative Nobel Peace Prize.

Herbert Kelman is a professor best known for his groundbreaking efforts to develop a social psychology of international relations and to apply social-psychological concepts to conflict analysis and social-psychological methods to conflict resolution. As a practitioner, Kelman developed problem-solving workshops with John Burton involving a social-psychological approach to intervention. He practiced these new approaches in the Middle East during the 1970s, 1980s, and 1990s.

Directory

Conflict, Development and Peace Network, Dean Bradley House, 6th Floor, 52 Horseferry Road, London SW1P 2AF, United Kingdom. Telephone: (44) 020 7799 2477, Email: kathleena@codep.org.uk, Web: http://www.codep.org.uk
Group of nongovernmental organizations, consultants, academics, and donors who work in development, human rights, and peacebuilding exploring the causes of conflict and its impact on people and improving practice

Copenhagen Peace Research Institute, 18 Fredericiagade, 1310 Copenhagen, Denmark. Telephone: (45) 3 345 5050, Email: bmoeller@copri.dk, Web: http://www.copri.dk/ipra/ipra.html
Organization that promotes debate on issues related to peace and security studies through research, seminars, and publications

European Platform for Conflict Prevention and Transformation, P.O. Box 14069, 3508 Utrecht, Netherlands. Telephone: (31) 30 253 7528, Email: euconflict@euconflict.org, Web: http://www.euconflict.org
Network of European nongovernmental organizations involved in the prevention and resolution of violent conflicts

Initiative on Conflict Resolution and Ethnicity, Aberfoyle House, Northland Road, Londonderry BT48 7JA, Northern Ireland, United Kingdom. Telephone: (44) 1504 375 500, Email: INCORE@incore.ulst.ac.uk, Web: http://www.incore.ulst.ac.uk
Center for the study and resolution of conflict that combines research, training, and other activities to inform and influence national and international organizations working in the field of conflict resolution

International Peace Research Institute, 11 Fuglehauggata, 0260 Oslo, Norway. Telephone: (47) 22 54 77 00, Email: info@prio.no, Web: http://www.prio.org
Organization that focuses on conditions of war and peace, conflict resolution, peacebuilding and ethics, and norms and identities, publishes the Journal of Peace Research *and* Security Dialogue

Life and Peace Institute, P.O. Box 1520, 751 45 Uppsala, Sweden. Telephone: (46) 18 169 500, Email: info@life-peace.org, Web: http://www.life-peace.org
Ecumenical research institution that aims to further the causes of justice, peace, and reconciliation through a combination of research and action

Responding to Conflict, 1046 Bristol Road, Selly Oak, Birmingham B29 6LJ, United Kingdom. Telephone: (44) 121 415 5641, Email: enquiries@respond.org, Web: http://www.respond.org
Organization that provides advice, cross-cultural training, and long-term support to people working for peace, development, human rights, and humanitarian assistance in societies affected or threatened by violent conflict

Stockholm International Peace Research Institute, 9 Signalisgatan, 169 70 Solna, Sweden. Telephone: (46) 8 655 97 00, Email: sipri@sipri.se, Web: http://www.sipri.se
Organization for research on questions of conflict and cooperation of importance for international peace and security

Transnational Foundation for Peace and Future Research, 25 Vegagatan, 224 57 Lund, Sweden. Telephone: (46) 46 145 909, Email: tff@transnational.org, Web: http://www.transnational.org
Organization for applied peace research and global networking

Further Research

Books

Abu-Nimer, Mohammed, ed. *Reconciliation, Justice and Co-Existence.* Lanham, Md.: Rowman and Littlefield Publishing Group, 2001.

Ausburger, David. W. *Conflict Mediation across Cultures.* Louisville, Ky.: John Knox Press, 1992.

Avruch, Kevin. *Culture and Conflict Resolution.* Washington, D.C.: United States Institute for Peace, 1998.

Azar, Edward E. *The Management of Protracted Social Conflict: Theory and Cases.* Dartmouth, Mass.: Aldershot Publishing, 1990.

Curle, Adam. *Tools for Transformation.* London: Hawthorne Press, 1990.

Durch, William, ed. *The Evolution of UN Peacekeeping: Case Studies and Comparative Analysis.* New York: St. Martin's Press, 1993.

Galtung, Johan. *Essays in Peace Research.* Vol. 1. Oslo: International Peace Research Institute, 1975.

———. *Peace by Peaceful Means.* Oslo: Sage Publications, 1996.

Gopin, Marc. *Between Eden and Armageddon: The Future of World Religions, Violence and Peacemaking.* Oxford: Oxford University Press, 2000.

Jeong, Howon. *Peace and Conflict Studies: An Introduction.* Burlington, Vt.: Ashgate, 2000.

Leatherman, Janie, William DeMars, Patrick D. Gaffney, and Raimo Vayrynen. *Breaking Cycles of Violence: Conflict Prevention in Intrastate Crises.* West Hartford, Conn.: Kumarian Press, 1999.

Lederach, John Paul. *Preparing for Peace: Conflict Transformation across Cultures.* Syracuse: Syracuse University Press, 1995.

Reychler, Luc, and Thania Paffenholz, eds. *Peacebuilding: A Field Guide.* Boulder: Lynne Rienner, 2001.

Smith, Dan, et al. *The State of War and Peace Atlas.* Oslo: International Peace Research Institute, 1997.

Articles and Reports

Abu-Nimer, Mohammed. "Framework for Nonviolence and Peacebuilding in Islam." *Journal of Law and Religion* 15, no. 1–2 (2000–2001): 217–266.

Adisa, Jinmi. "Problems of Peacemaking and Peacebuilding for Africa's Post-Conflict States: A Research Note." *Africa Peace Review* 1, no. 2 (1997): 16–25.

Goodhand, Jonathan, and David Hulme. "From Wars to Complex Political Emergencies: Understanding Conflict and Peacebuilding in the New World Disorder." *Third World Quarterly* 20, no. 1 (1999): 13–26.

Murithi, Tim. "From Conflict Resolution to Sustainable Democracy: State Collapse and

Post-Conflict Peace Building in Africa." In *Africa towards the Millennium: An Agenda for Mature Development,* edited by S. Bakut and S. Dutt. London: Macmillan, 1999.

Nathan, Laurie. "The Four Horsemen of the Apocalypse: The Structural Causes of Crisis and Violence in Africa." *Peace and Change* 25, no. 2 (2000): 188–207.

Web Sites

African Journal on Conflict Resolution
http://www.accord.org.za/publications/journal.htm

Coexistence Chronicle
http://www.co-net.org/Chronicle.htm

Conflict, Development and Peace Network
http://www.codep.org.uk

Conflict Prevention Newsletter
http://www.euconflict.org/euconflict/publicat/newslett.htm

Cooperation and Conflict
http://www.sagepub.co.uk

ECMI Journal on Ethnopolitics and Minority Issues in Europe
http://www.ecmi.de/doc/public.html

International Journal of Peace Studies
http://www.ecmi.de/doc/public.html

International Journal on World Peace
http://www.pwpa.org/IJWP/index.html

Journal for Peace and Change
http://webs.cmich.edu/peaceandchange

Journal of Conflict Resolution
http://www.library.yale.edu/un/un2f1a1.htm

Journal of Peace Research
http://www.sagepub.co.uk or http://www.prio.no/publications

Online Journal of Peace and Conflict Resolution
http://www.trinstitute.org/ojpcr

Peace and Conflict Studies
http://www.gmu.edu/academic/pcs

Peace Research Abstracts Journal
http://www.sagepub.co.uk/journals/details/j0029.html

Peace Review
http://www.usfca.edu/peacereview

Security Dialogue
http://www.sagepub.co.uk or http://www.prio.no/publications

Self-Determination in Focus
http://www.fpif.org/selfdetermination/index.html

Transcend: A Peace and Development Network
http://www.transcend.org

Documents

1. An Agenda for Peace: Preventive Diplomacy, and Peace-keeping

United Nations, report of the secretary-general, 17 June 1992

The full text is available at http://www.un.org/Docs/SG/agpeace.html.

Extract

15. . . . Our aims must be:

- To seek to identify at the earliest possible stage situations that could produce conflict, and to try through diplomacy to remove the sources of danger before violence results;
- Where conflict erupts, to engage in peacemaking aimed at resolving the issues that have led to conflict;
- Through peace-keeping, to work to preserve peace, however fragile, where fighting has been halted and to assist in implementing agreements achieved by the peacemakers;
- To stand ready to assist in peace-building in its differing contexts: rebuilding the institutions and infrastructures of nations torn by civil war and strife; and building bonds of peaceful mutual benefit among nations formerly at war;
- And in the largest sense, to address the deepest causes of conflict: economic despair, social injustice and political oppression. It is possible to discern an increasingly common moral perception that spans the world's nations and peoples, and which is finding expression in international laws, many owing their genesis to the work of this Organization.

16. This wider mission for the world Organization will demand the concerted attention and effort of individual States, of regional and non-governmental organizations and of all of the United Nations system, with each of the principal organs functioning in the balance and harmony that the Charter requires. The Security Council has been assigned by all Member States the primary responsibility for the maintenance of international peace and security under the Charter. In its broadest sense this responsibility must be shared by the General Assembly and by all the functional elements of the world Organization. Each has a special and indispensable role to play in an integrated approach to human security. The Secretary-General's contribution rests on the pattern of trust and cooperation established between him and the deliberative organs of the United Nations.

17. The foundation-stone of this work is and must remain the State. Respect for its fundamental sovereignty and integrity are crucial to any common international progress. The time of absolute and exclusive sovereignty, however, has passed; its theory was never matched by reality. It is the task of leaders of States today to understand this and to find a balance between the needs of good internal governance and the requirements of an ever more interdependent world. Commerce, communications and environmental matters transcend administrative borders; but inside those borders is where individuals carry out the first order of their economic, political and social lives. The United Nations has not closed its door. Yet if every ethnic, religious or linguistic group claimed statehood, there would be no limit to fragmentation, and peace, security and economic well-being for all would become ever more difficult to achieve.

18. One requirement for solutions to these problems lies in commitment to human rights with a special sensitivity to those of minorities, whether ethnic, religious, social

or linguistic. The League of Nations provided a machinery for the international protection of minorities. The General Assembly soon will have before it a declaration on the rights of minorities. That instrument, together with the increasingly effective machinery of the United Nations dealing with human rights, should enhance the situation of minorities as well as the stability of States.

19. Globalism and nationalism need not be viewed as opposing trends, doomed to spur each other on to extremes of reaction. The healthy globalization of contemporary life requires in the first instance solid identities and fundamental freedoms. The sovereignty, territorial integrity and independence of States within the established international system, and the principle of self-determination for peoples, both of great value and importance, must not be permitted to work against each other in the period ahead. Respect for democratic principles at all levels of social existence is crucial: in communities, within States and within the community of States. Our constant duty should be to maintain the integrity of each while finding a balanced design for all.

2. An Agenda for Development

United Nations, report of the secretary-general, 6 May 1994

The full text is available at http://www.un.org/Docs/SG/agdev.html.

Extract

22. Peace-building means action to identify and support structures which will tend to strengthen and solidify peace in order to avoid a relapse into conflict. As preventive diplomacy aims to prevent the outbreak of a conflict, peace-building starts during the course of a conflict to prevent its recurrence. Only sustained, cooperative work on the underlying economic, social, cultural and humanitarian problems can place an achieved peace on a durable foundation. Unless there is reconstruction and development in the aftermath of conflict, there can be little expectation that peace will endure.

23. Peace-building is a matter for countries at all stages of development. For countries emerging from conflict, peace-building offers the chance to establish new institutions, social, political and judicial, that can give impetus to development. Land reform and other measures of social justice can be undertaken. Countries in transition can use peace-building measures as a chance to put their national systems on the path of sustainable development. Countries high on the scale of wealth and power must hasten the process of partial demobilization and defense conversion. Decisions made at this stage can have an immense impact on the course of their societies and the international community for future generations.

24. The most immediate task for peace-building is to alleviate the effects of war on the population. Food aid, support for health and hygiene systems, the clearance of mines and logistical support to essential organizations in the field represent the first peace-building task.

25. At this stage too, it is essential that efforts to address immediate needs are undertaken in ways that promote, rather than compromise, long-term development objectives. As food is provided there must be concentration on restoring food production capacities. In conjunction with the delivery of relief supplies, attention should be given to road construction, restoration and improvement of port facilities and establishment of regional stocks and distribution centers. . . .

29. As conflict typically takes a heavy toll on the mechanisms of governance, post-conflict efforts must pay special attention to their repair. Key institutions of civil society, judicial systems, for example, may need to be reinforced or even created anew. This means assistance for a variety of governmental activities, such as a fair system for generating public sector revenue, a legislative basis for the protection of human rights, and rules for the operation of private enterprise.

30. Pulling up the roots of conflict goes beyond immediate post-conflict requirements and the repair of war-torn societies. The underlying conditions that led to conflict must be addressed. As the causes of conflict are varied, so must be the means of addressing them. Peace-building means fostering a culture of peace. Land reform, water-sharing schemes, common economic enterprise zones, joint tourism projects and cultural exchanges can make a major difference. Restoring employment growth will be a strong inducement to the young to abandon the vocation of war.

POLLUTION

Chris Woodford

Pollution respects no geographical boundaries. When the Chernobyl nuclear power plant exploded in the Ukraine in 1986, a cloud of radioactive fallout was deposited over much of northern Europe, contaminating an area of more than 160,000 square kilometers (64,000 square miles). Sometimes pollution travels even farther. Toxic chemicals thought to have originated in Europe and North America have been found in the tissue of polar bears in remote parts of the Arctic. Incidents such as these highlight the transboundary nature of pollution, an often global problem that requires local and global solutions.

Historical Background and Development

Although pollution is considered to be a particularly modern phenomenon, the problem actually dates back several thousand years, to when people first began to live in cities. The world's first landfill is believed to have been constructed in Knossos, Crete, circa 3000 B.C., and in Athens circa 500 B.C. it was decreed that municipal waste should be transported to a landfill one mile beyond the city gates. Yet it was the Industrial Revolution, which began in Britain in the eighteenth century and later spread to continental Europe and North America, that marked the true beginning of the modern age of pollution. As coal-fired industry marched on, cities and towns were choked with smoke, and poor sanitation and polluted water supplies led to severe health problems. England had passed a law as early as 1297 requiring households to keep the front of their homes free of refuse, and its Public Health Acts of 1848 and 1875 were among the world's first major pieces of anti-pollution legislation, introducing, among other things, methodical sewage treatment and the concept of "smokeless zones" to reduce pollution in urban areas.

Increasing awareness of the causes and effects of pollution prompted a progressive cleanup by many industrial nations during the twentieth century, not least because of a number of serious (and often fatal) incidents. For example, people became acutely aware of the need to tackle air pollution after severe cases of smog in Donora, Pennsylvania, in 1948 (when 20 people died and nearly 6,000 others became ill), in London in 1952 (when an estimated 4,000 people died), and in New York in 1963 and 1966 (when 405 and 168 people died, respectively). Indeed, the 1952 episode in London led directly to England's 1956 Clean Air Act. Pollution proved much harder to tackle, however, where the effects were more widely distanced from the cause. Such was the problem with Minamata disease, a degenerative and often fatal type of mercury poisoning that became epidemic in Minamata Bay, Japan, in the 1950s, after a chemical factory discharged mercury into the bay. Although the factory opened in 1938, ecological changes were noted only in 1950, and the effects on humans only in 1953. Yet it was not until 1968 that Minamata disease was linked to the chemical factory, by which time two thousand people had been poisoned from eating contaminated fish. Forty-three people subsequently died, and more than seven hundred people were left disabled.

Rachel Carson's crusade against toxic pesticides and insecticides in *Silent Spring* is another example of how long it can take for society to address the effects of pollution even after the source has been identified. Although declining bird populations had been noted since the late 1950s, and Carson's book was published in 1962, it was not until 1971 that production of DDT, one of the chemicals whose misuse she highlights, ceased in the United States. It may take even longer before recent attempts by Sandra Steingraber and others to link environmental chemicals to such health problems as cancer lead to successful curbs of other toxic pollutants. Even establishing a causal link between a particular type of pollution and its effects may not be enough to prompt a cleanup. The method by which coal-fired power plants produce acid rain—rain that turns into acid after passing through oxides of nitrogen and sulfur contained in air pollution—was established in the 1960s, yet acidification remains a major problem in New York's Adirondack Mountains, downwind of power plants in the Midwest. The number of acidified lakes in the Adirondacks is expected to double by 2040.

There has been no shortage of environmental legislation in recent years. Notable attempts to tackle marine pollution have included the 1972 Convention on the Prevention of Marine Pollution by Dumping of Wastes and Other Matter (also called the London Dumping Convention) and the 1978 International Convention for the Prevention of Pollution from Ships (MARPOL). Other international initiatives have shaped recent policy, including the 1979 Geneva Convention on Long-Range Transboundary Air Pollution (see Table 1), the 1987 Montreal Protocol on Substances That Deplete the Ozone Layer, the 1989 Basel Convention on Hazardous Waste, and the 1982 Convention on the Law of the Sea, which was signed by more than 120 nations.

There is a clear expectation that many global problems will one day be solved. For example, doctors may find a vaccine for HIV/AIDS, and world leaders may be forced to agree to measures for tackling climate change. Pollution, however, is a more diffuse problem that will likely always affect humankind, not least because human ingenuity is constantly introducing new forms of pollution. Weapons that use depleted uranium, a very dense by-product of nuclear power that can penetrate armor plating, are just one example.

These weapons, first deployed in the 1991 Persian Gulf War, attracted much more attention following their use in the 1999 Kosovo bombing campaign, when NATO was estimated to have fired more than 30,000 depleted uranium shells. Concerns were later expressed by the World Health Organization (WHO) and the United Nations that civilian populations might be exposed to the effects of the uranium for years to come. Decades of progress in fighting pollution through technological improvements, international legislation, and growing environmental consciousness can be undermined in a matter of days or weeks by actions such as these.

Current Status

It is now four decades since the world's attention was focused on the problems of the polluted environment described in Carson's groundbreaking *Silent Spring.* Since then more has been discovered about the causes and effects of pollution, and considerable effort has been devoted to preventing pollution through regulation, economic instruments, and technological solutions.

Research

Views have sometimes differed sharply on exactly what constitutes "pollution," but the generally accepted definition is the introduction into the natural and human environment of harmful substances and organisms that do not belong there. In Carson's mind, there was no doubt about the effects of chemical pesticides and insecticides: "As crude a weapon as the cave man's club, the chemical barrage has been hurled against the fabric of life." In response, chemical companies vigorously defended the value of their products in fighting pests and diseases, increasing crop yields, and helping to combat such problems as world hunger.

Yet since *Silent Spring,* and partly thanks to Carson's wake-up call, some of yesterday's champion chemicals have become today's toxics (see Table 2). Numerous pesticides and insecticides widely used in Carson's time are now banned in many countries and generally referred to as persistent organic pollutants (POPs). Among them are aldrin, chlordane, DDT, dieldrin, endrin, heptachlor, hexachlorobenzene, polychlorinated biphenyls (PCB), and toxaphene. Not only do these chemicals not readily biodegrade, they systematically bioaccumulate—that is, they become more and more concentrated in organisms higher up the food chain—presenting a greater danger to humans than their ordinary concentration in the environment might suggest. Such heavy metals as lead, cadmium, and mercury have similarly fallen into disfavor. Lead, until recently a major gasoline additive, has been banned as an additive in many countries after several studies confirmed a correlation between high lead levels in the environment and reductions in childhood IQ. According to the World Resources Institute, lead poisoning is the most preventable condition related to environmental toxicity. PCBs, once widely used to make electronic equipment, have also been added to the blacklist. A number of studies found significant traces of PCBs in fish, birds, and mammals in remote parts of the Arctic, thousands of miles from their presumed places of origin. Once described as "miracle compounds" because of their numerous industrial uses, chlorofluorocarbons (CFCs) are now known to destroy Earth's ozone layer, though they are not actually toxics per se.

Potentially harmful substances are still routinely discharged into the environment in large quantities. According to the United Nations Environmental Programme's (UNEP) *Global Environment Outlook, 2000* (GEO-2000), worldwide production of hazardous wastes—harmful by-products of industrial processes that often form the source of environmental pollution—had reached around 440 million tonnes (400 million tons) per year by the early 1990s, 75 percent of it produced by developed countries through industrial processes ranging from mining to papermaking. Everyday human exposure to toxics can be high for other reasons as well. In 1980 Wayne Ott and Lance Wallace of the U.S. Environmental Protection Agency (EPA) began a major study of the exposure to environmental toxics of three thousand carefully chosen human subjects. Their surprising discovery was that many citizens suffer greatest chemical exposure not through industrial pollution, which accounts for only around 3 percent of total exposure, but from a variety of sources *inside* their homes, such as household cleaning products, paints, tobacco smoke, and dust. A 1999 study by environmental engineers at the University of Texas confirmed the dangers of volatile organic compounds—or VOCs, carbon-based chemicals that evaporate at low temperatures—originally contained in tap water, and turned into potentially harmful indoor air pollution when boiled off by dishwashers and showers.

Not all forms of pollution are easily recognizable as such. Fertilizers have played a major role in increasing world food production, but as GEO-2000 notes, worldwide fertilizer use rose more than tenfold between 1950 and 1988. The report further states that human activities have doubled the amount of nitrogen on the planet: "We are fertilizing the Earth on a global scale and in a largely uncontrolled experiment" (see map, p. 485). The consequences include nitrogen-contaminated water supplies, acid rain, photochemical smog, and harmful algal blooms, of which "red tides" in coastal areas are the most familiar example. One of the most spectacular worldwide demonstrations of algal blooms is the so-called dead zone in the Gulf of Mexico. Each summer, where the nutrient-rich Mississippi and Atchafalaya Rivers empty into the gulf, a massive algal growth is induced that causes oxygen levels to drop to just two parts per million, a level so low that the water can no longer support marine life. The dead zone covers an area of 15,500 to 18,500 square kilometers (6,200 to 7,400 square miles), an area roughly the size of New Jersey.

Chemicals, "natural" and otherwise, are only one form of pollution. A less obvious form involves the introduction of living organisms into ecosystems where they do not naturally occur. The coastal waters of numerous countries have been affected by so-called alien species (see Table 3). The Mediterranean, for example, has been swamped by a "killer algae," *Caulerpa taxifolia*. On the French Côte d'Azur it spread from an area of just 1 square meter (1.2 square yards) in 1984 to around 6,000 hectares (15,000 acres) in 1999. In the Black

Sea, the jellyfish-like *Mnemiopsis leidyi* decimated fish stocks by 90 percent after being introduced by a ship's ballast water in 1989. A 1999 study by Cornell University's David Pimentel estimates that alien species cost the U.S. economy $123 billion a year. Recent concern over the introduction of genetically modified organisms (GMOs) into the environment is the flip side of the same coin. While proponents argue that genetic engineering overcomes the inherent drawbacks of a system of natural selection that can no longer keep pace with human needs, opponents counter that GMOs are effectively a form of alien species pollution with the potential to decimate natural ecosystems.

If introducing "unnatural" substances and organisms into the environment is the cause of pollution, the effects are water and air pollution on a global and local scale. Pollution of freshwater sources compounds the wider problem of meeting the world's growing demand for water (see FRESHWATER). In November 1999, the World Commission on Water for the 21st Century reported that more than half of the world's five hundred major rivers were polluted or overexploited or both, citing the leaching of fertilizers, pesticides, sewage, and industrial chemicals as the main cause. Many rivers flow through more than one nation, so transboundary water pollution is an international issue. For example, the New River flows from Mexico into California's Imperial Valley, bringing with it 76 million to 95 million liters (20 million to 25 million gallons) of raw sewage every day in violation of EPA pollution standards by several hundred times. Even pristine rivers are not always safe from pollution. On 30 January 2000, the entire ecosystem of Hungary's Tisza River was wiped out by a 40-kilometer (25-mile) cyanide spill from a Romanian mine that subsequently flowed into the drinking water supplies of Hungary and Yugoslavia. Not all water pollution occurs by accident. Arsenic contamination of drinking water, primarily caused by geological factors, is a major hazard in Bangladesh (where 19 percent of wells tested have unacceptably high arsenic levels), as well as in Argentina, Chile, China, India, Mexico, Thailand, and the United States.

Inland waterways are often used as high-speed drains or sewers and ultimately pollute the oceans. According to the Joint Group of Experts on the Scientific Aspects of Marine Environmental Protection (GESAMP), around 80 percent of marine pollution comes from land-based sources, while the remainder comes from air pollution. In winter 1998–1999 the *Earth Island Journal* reported that during the last three decades of the twentieth century, two large chemical plants at Usolye and Sayansk in Russia released a total of more than 500 tonnes (550 tons) of mercury into the Angara River and thence into the Arctic's Kara Sea, posing a major threat to the entire Arctic ecosystem. Sewage, persistent organic pollutants, PCBs, fertilizers, and alien species also find their way into the oceans eventually. Stricken oil tankers may provide the most spectacular incidents of marine pollution, yet the publicity they receive contrasts markedly with the scale of the global problem they pose compared to, for example, sewage discharges, which are the priority issue for most coastal regions.

Once pollution is in the ocean, it becomes a transboundary issue. The Sellafield nuclear plant on Britain's northwest coast reprocesses waste nuclear fuel from around the world, arguably therefore making the world a cleaner place. The plant, however, discharges radioactive effluent into the Irish Sea that is then carried by ocean currents to Ireland, Scandinavia, and farther afield. In March 2001 the Norwegian government called for the plant to be closed after a report showed that radiation levels along the Norwegian coast had risen sixfold in the previous five years. Much ocean pollution causes concern because of its long-lasting nature. Nuclear waste, POPs, and PCBs all fall into this category. So too does plastic waste, which, being light, buoyant, and generally nonbiodegradable, can be considered a perfectly designed form of transboundary ocean pollution. Plastic waste has now been carried by the seas to all corners of the globe. It is estimated to kill at least a million seabirds a year, and around 100,000 seals and cetaceans; one-fourth of the world's seabirds are thought to have traces of ingested plastic in their systems. Some of the ocean's pollution—a majority of its mercury and cadmium, for example—derives from air pollution via atmospheric deposition. GESAMP reports that most nitrogen entering the oceans on the east coast of the United States originates from cities and power plants in the Midwest, some 1,000 kilometers (600 miles) away (see Document 1).

Smokestacks belching into the sky and car exhaust polluting the streets also make air pollution a local problem. Notoriously air-polluted cities, such as Athens, Beijing, Delhi, Los Angeles, Mexico City, Paris, and Rome, make their own air pollution. According to GEO-2000, "Urban air pollution problems are reaching crisis dimensions in many cities in the developing world." Yet even in developed countries, such as the United States, air pollution remains a major problem. In 2000 the American Lung Association reported that half of the nation's urban areas exceeded smog requirements, potentially putting 132 million people at risk from asthma, bronchitis, and other lung diseases. Air pollution is also a transboundary issue. One of the most spectacular recent examples occurred following substantial forest fires that burned in East Kalimantan and Sumatra in 1997 and 1998, spreading dense smoke over six neighboring countries and ultimately reaching as far south as Darwin, Australia. According to UNEP, 70 million people were affected by the fires, which cost Southeast Asia an estimated $1.4 billion. All told, air pollution is one of the world's biggest killers. According to World Health Organization estimates, 3 million people die from air pollution every year, with more than 90 percent of these deaths occurring in developing countries and 80 percent of them among children under five years of age. Ninety-three percent of deaths are caused by indoor air pollution, most of them from a heavy reliance on biomass and coal fuels in badly ventilated homes in developing nations.

Policies and Programs

Pollution can be viewed from a variety of perspectives and solved in as many different ways. From an environmentalist point of view, pollution is an inherently bad thing: toxic chemicals and wastes do not occur naturally in the environment, so they should not be introduced by humans or industrial processes in the first place. Pollution can also be seen as a technical problem requiring such engineering solutions as catalytic converters or electrostatic "scrubbers" to prevent it from entering the environment. (Wayne Ott and John Roberts report that simply wiping your feet on a doormat reduces lead pollution on household carpets by a factor of six, a very effective, low-tech solution.) From an economic perspective, pollution is arguably a necessary by-product of industrial development; no one pollutes the environment intentionally but there is a greater economic incentive to pollute than not to; it is generally cheaper to pump chemical waste untreated into rivers or seas than to clean it up. In *Through Green-Colored Glasses,* Oxford University economist Wilfred Beckerman has argued that economic growth is an absolute prerequisite for tackling environmental and social problems and that the "small-is-beautiful" approach of environmentalists, which seeks to limit problems such as pollution by limiting growth, is really a case of "small is stupid." Finally, because pollution is often a transboundary, global issue, it can be viewed as a diplomatic problem whose solution lies in international anti-pollution laws and agreements motivated as much by the need to maintain good international relations as by the desire to preserve the environment. Inevitably, these perspectives are oversimplifications, and solutions advocated by various groups often combine approaches from different perspectives.

Many environmentalists, for example, believe in the "polluter pays" principle, an economic solution that seeks to reduce pollution by levying its costs on the people who cause it. Other solutions advocated by environmentalists may include imposing a public relations cost on polluters through the publication of a register of who pollutes, where, and by how much. Generally, solutions to pollution combine environmental, economic, technological, and legislative or regulatory factors.

From a global perspective, it has traditionally been assumed that pollution is a necessary consequence of industrialization. Developing nations are not only condemned to repeat the grossly polluted past of such nations as the United Kingdom and the United States, but they will be unable to address the problem until they reach a comparable level of affluence. Yet *Greening Industry,* a major report published by the World Bank in 1999, questions this assumption, citing studies from a variety of developing nations, including China, India, and Brazil: "These experiences have persuaded us that the conventional wisdom is wrong: Economic development and industrial pollution are not immutably linked. We are convinced that developing countries can build on the new model to reduce industrial pollution significantly, even if they grow rapidly during the coming decade."

Greening Industry confirms that communities, markets, and governments can act together to help poorer nations take a cleaner path toward development. For example, the Indonesian government's PROPER program involves publishing information about how factories pollute the environment so that communities and markets can put pressure on companies to clean up (see Case

Study—PROPER Pollution Control in Indonesia). There has long been a concern that developing nations could become "pollution havens" for waste exported by developed countries because of developing nations' lower labor costs, less stringent environmental legislation, lower environmental awareness, and need to earn foreign currency. Prior Informed Consent (PIC), a system operated by the FAO and UNEP, aims to reduce this dangerous trade by providing developing nations with more information about the potentially damaging effects of waste that might be exported to them.

Local *and* national initiatives are essential for tackling pollution problems. Global initiatives have proved essential in addressing transboundary pollution. A number of international agreements have targeted specific forms of pollution, including the London Dumping Convention, MARPOL, and the Geneva Convention on Long-Range Transboundary Air Pollution as well as the 1990 International Convention on Oil Pollution Preparedness, Response and Cooperation. One of the most successful recent global initiatives for tackling pollution has been the Montreal Protocol to cut worldwide production of chlorofluorocarbons that deplete the ozone layer. Now generally heralded as a model of how international environmental legislation can be swiftly and effectively implemented, the protocol cut global CFC consumption from 1.1 million tonnes (1.2 million tons) in 1986 to 110,000 tonnes (121,000 tons) in 1996, according to UNEP. Yet the protocol has not been completely successful. CFCs are still produced in developing countries, tough restrictions on their use have produced a significant black market in the United States, and alternative, more damaging ozone-depleting chemicals, such as halons, are now being produced in greater quantities by China.

There are several key components to policies and programs that aim to control pollution. Information and education feature in most of them. It is essential to disseminate the established risks of using and disposing of chemicals in the environment. One problem, however, is that the long-term risk of using some chemicals is unknown, especially if they cause genetic mutations, which may not appear in the current generation. Another problem is the difficulty of proving without long-term, large-scale epidemiological studies that chemicals in the environment cause particular health problems, especially when transboundary pollution is involved. This last problem has proved a major stumbling block for environmental lawyers keen to seek compensation for communities affected by pollution.

Apart from information about pollution, most programs aim to put information about specific polluters into the hands of the communities that are most affected by them. Typically this means establishing registers of who is discharging what, where, when, and in how great a quantity and instituting freedom of information laws that allow ordinary people to inspect these registers. As the World Bank's *Greening Industry* argues in the context of cutting pollution in developing nations, "Armed with good information, poor citizens can work with environmental agencies and elect political leaders willing to pressure factories to curb emissions, as regions and countries make the transition to greener industry."

In successful pollution programs, economic instruments also feature strongly. The idea of a global "commons" that can be freely polluted at no charge is replaced by the polluter pays principle, in which factories are charged for polluting (either fined directly or indirectly through bad publicity and community or shareholder action) or given incentives not to pollute. Equally, purist environmentalists are sometimes obliged to accept that when it comes to pollution control, industry can only justify investments in what is sometimes called the best-practicable environmental option—that is, the most cost-effective solution. Finally, programs to address local pollution problems also need to bear in mind such broader problems as the risk of forcing polluting factories to move to less-regulated nations and the illegal trafficking in chemicals banned in certain nations (see Document 2).

Regional Summaries

Because of the transboundary nature of pollution, few places on Earth have escaped its effects. Developed nations generally pollute less than they used to, and developing nations are trying to follow cleaner paths to development although not always successfully.

North America

The United States and Canada enjoy relatively high quality water supplies, yet water pollution problems persist in both countries. GEO-2000 reports that, according to the Council on Environmental Quality, the water supplies for 20 percent of the American population (or some 40 million people) suffered health violations during 1994. In March 1999 the American Waterworks Association called for a fivefold reduction in permitted arsenic levels for 2000 to improve the standards of the nation's 56,000 water supply systems and reduce cancer risks for millions of people. Proposals by the Clinton administration to achieve this 80 percent reduction, however, were scrapped by the Bush administration in 2001. According to the U.S. Geological Survey, groundwater pollution by volatile organic compounds is estimated to affect 42 million Americans, mostly in eastern states. Most Canadians also enjoy good water quality, though pollution of groundwater by nitrates and bacteria is commonplace. Canadian government estimates from 1997 suggest that 20 to 40 percent of all rural wells may be contaminated.

According to UNEP and WHO, two U.S. cities, Los Angeles and New York, suffer "world class" air pollution problems. Long-range air pollution has been a major problem in the northeastern United States and southeastern Canada, with thousands of lakes and inland waters contaminated by acid rain from power plants and industries in the Midwest. Despite substantial reductions in emissions during the 1980s and 1990s, many lakes remain too acidic to support fish. In Toronto, smog-related illnesses are estimated to kill three hundred people a year, according to the city's environment task force. In the

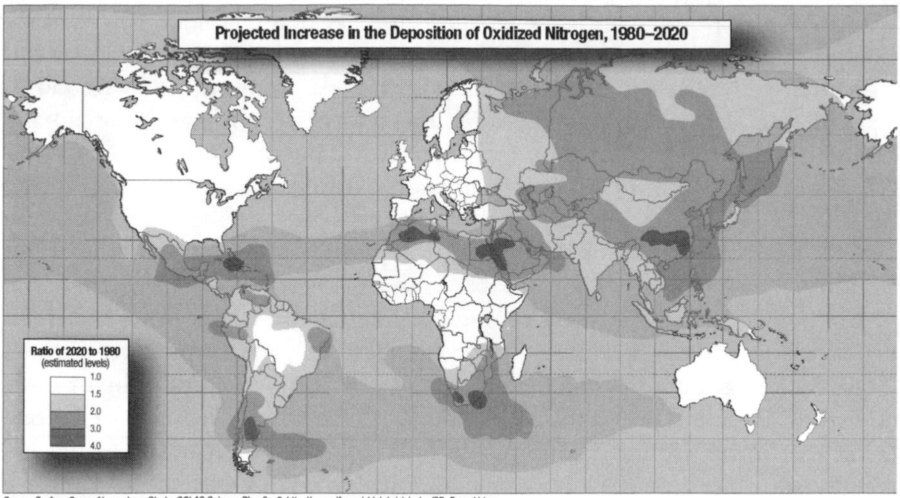

Source: Surface Ocean Atmosphere Study, *SOLAS Science Plan*, fig. 9, http://www.ifm.uni-kiel.de/ch/solas/SP_Focusl.htm.

United States, the Clean Air Act of 1990 is expected to produce benefits that exceed costs by four to one, based on the assessment of the EPA, which used a computer model to calculate that the legislation will prevent 23,000 premature deaths and more than 1,700,000 attacks of asthma each year.

Latin America

Latin America's abundant water resources are compromised by pollution in industrializing areas. The activities of an estimated 1 million informal miners contribute substantially to heavy metal pollution, notably mercury. Inadequate disposal of wastewater and industrial chemicals has led to widespread surface and groundwater pollution. Coastal areas suffer from inadequate sewage disposal that imperils the abundant coral reefs of the Caribbean, which constitute 12 percent of the world's reefs.

The smoke produced by slash-and-burn deforestation has contributed greatly to air pollution problems in the region. Unlike such rapidly industrializing nations as China and India, Brazil produces more than two-thirds of its electricity from hydroelectricity, avoiding substantial sulfur dioxide and greenhouse gas emissions. Deregulation of the electricity industry in Brazil and elsewhere in the region, however, is driving an increase in energy production from fossil fuels.

Europe and Central Asia

Eutrophication is the biggest water pollution problem in Europe and Central Asia. This process of overnutrification simulates the production of algae, sometimes killing off all other types of marine life, and is caused by inadequate sewage disposal and increasing fertilizer use. Nitrates contaminate surface water and groundwater in many European nations, despite European Union legislation introduced in 1991 that sets strict levels on nitrate concentrations. Scandinavian lakes continue to suffer the effects of acid rain substantially caused by fossil fuel power plants in Britain and mainland European countries. Groundwater pollution by industry and agriculture is a major problem in the Russian Federation, particularly in the industrial areas of the Ukraine where heavy metal contamination has forced the closure of many drinking water facilities.

Air pollution has improved through a gradual shift away from coal-fired power plants and the decline of heavy industry in parts of Western Europe. Considerable growth in vehicle use, mainly cars, is now responsible for most emissions. Pollution hot spots have gradually shifted from the north of Europe to the east and the south. Economic decline in the east and central regions has recently produced marked improvements in air quality, yet these gains are likely to prove short-lived as economic recovery takes priority over environmental protection.

North Africa and the Middle East

Water quality problems in North Africa and the Middle East relate substantially to the region's relatively low water availability (see FRESHWATER). Large parts of the region are supplied by shallow fossil aquifers. Excessive extraction of water has caused a drop in water tables and has led to such pollution problems as the inundation of some coastal agricultural areas with saltwater from the sea. In Bahrain, for example, UNEP estimates that saltwater inundation is encroaching inland at a rate of 75 to 130 meters (246 to 426 feet) per year. Nitrate pollution of water supplies is also common due to agricultural discharges, inadequate wastewater treatment, and industrial pollution; some domestic wells in the West Bank and Gaza have nitrate levels five times greater than WHO recommends. Coastal pollution is an ever-increasing problem in the region, with the Mediterranean basin now one of the most polluted bodies of water in the world, according to UNEP assessments. Transportation of oil through the Indian Ocean and the Red Sea poses another threat to coastal areas.

The abundance of oil reserves in the region has produced substantial growth in vehicle ownership (and fuel emissions) since World War II. This development, along with the growth of heavy industries and fossil-fueled power stations, has led to grave air pollution problems in Baghdad, Beirut, and Damascus. Smog is a particular problem near the Persian Gulf. Leaded fuel is still widely used throughout the region, often in old and inefficient cars, which according to the World Bank contribute 90 percent of atmospheric lead emissions.

Sub-Saharan Africa

Air pollution is currently less of a problem in most African states than in such rapidly developing nations as India, but the World Bank estimates that emissions from thermal power stations will increase elevenfold and emissions from vehicles fivefold by 2003. Heavy dependence on coal-fired power plants accounts for most air pollution, with mining making a major contribution. South Africa produces around two-thirds of all sulfur emissions in the region. Biomass provides 80 percent of energy in sub-Saharan Africa. Reliance on biomass for cooking is a major factor in the high incidence of respiratory diseases in the region.

Water pollution problems in Africa stem from eutrophication, industrial and wastewater discharges into inland waterways and the sea, and the spread of invasive, alien plants. The water hyacinth (*Eichhornia crassipes*) has contaminated some of the continent's major waterways, including Lake Victoria and the Nile, where it disrupts power generation, fishing, and water supplies. Lake Victoria has also been contaminated by the Nile perch (*Lates niloticus*), which has killed off more than five hundred native fish species.

Asia and the Pacific

Asia and the Pacific islands are home to many of the world's rapidly industrializing nations. The region suffers considerably from pollution. Between 1980 and 1996, sulfur dioxide emissions in Asia almost doubled between 1980 and 1996—rising four times faster than in any other region—and are predicted by the World Resources Institute to triple by 2010. The region's two great industrializing nations, China and India, both rely heavily on cheap and abundant coal for electricity generation, contributing to substantial sulfur dioxide and greenhouse gas emissions. According to statistics from the Chinese Environmental Bureau, quoted in a 1999 story from the Environment News Service, Beijing experiences winter air pollution levels that are 20 to 30 percent worse than those in Mexico City, widely considered to be the world's most polluted city. Ten of the region's eleven megacities exceed WHO guidelines on levels of particulates—organic and inorganic matter found in the atmosphere in liquid or solid form—by a factor of at least three. According to the World Bank, around ten thousand people die prematurely each year from exposure to particulates in the four Chinese cities of Beijing, Chongqing, Shanghai, and Shenyang.

The biggest potential for marine pollution in the region comes from the high concentration of large cities along coastlines, which were predicted to house nearly half the world's total population by early in the twenty-first century. Coastal development has led to a variety of problems, notably the discharge of industrial waste and untreated sewage directly into the sea (damaging fisheries and causing red tides) and such related problems as the destruction of mangrove swamps and other important habitats (see FRAGILE ECOSYSTEMS).

Data

Table 1 Pollutants Emitted by Countries That Have Signed the 1979 Convention on Long-Range Transboundary Air Pollution

	Sulfur Dioxide (1,000 metric tons)			Nitrogen Oxides (1,000 metric tons)			Carbon Monoxide (1,000 metric tons)		
Country	1980	1990	1996	1980	1990	1996	1980	1990	1996
Armenia	X	72	2	X	46	11	X	304	125
Austria	400	91	52	231	194	163	1,690	1,287	1,021
Belarus	740	637	246	234	285	173	X	1,722	1,242
Belgium	828	322	240	442	343	334	X	1,631	1,434
Bosnia-Herzegovina	X	480	X	X	X	X	X	X	X
Bulgaria	2,050	2,020	1,420	X	376	259	X	891	613
Canada	4,643	3,236	2,722	1,959	2,104	2,011	10,273	10,596	X
Croatia	150	180	58	X	87	67	X	651	375
Czech Republic	2,257	1,876	946	937	742	432	894	1,055	886
Denmark	450	182	186	282	282	288	681	794	597
Finland	584	260	105	295	300	267	660	556	430
France	3,338	1,298	1,031	1,823	1,585	1,641	9,216	10,736	8,850
Germany	7,514	5,313	1,543	3,334	2,693	1,887	14,046	11,165	6,717
Greece	400	509	543	X	343	374	X	1,338	1,334
Hungary	1,633	1,010	673	273	238	196	1,019	767	727
Iceland	18	24	X	X	20	X	X	26	X
Ireland	222	178	147	73	115	121	X	429	307
Italy	3,757	1,651	X	1,638	1,938	X	7,588	8,003	X
Latvia	X	119	59	X	93	35	X	388	176
Lithuania	311	222	93	152	158	65	541	521	312
Macedonia	X	X	X	X	X	X	X	X	X
Moldova	308	231	X	58	39	X	136	193	X
Netherlands	490	202	135	583	580	501	X	1,143	903
Norway	140	53	34	189	222	223	896	858	720
Poland	4,100	3,210	2,368	1,229	1,280	1,154	X	7,406	4,837
Portugal	266	362	X	X	348	X	X	1,020	X
Romania	1,055	1,311	X	523	546	X	3,245	3,186	X
Russian Federation	7,161	4,460	2,685	1,734	3,600	2,467	13,520	13,174	9,312
Slovak Republic	780	543	227	X	225	130	X	487	346
Slovenia	234	194	110	51	62	70	68	79	95
Spain	3,319	2,266	X	950	1,177	X	X	4,752	X
Sweden	491	119	83	404	338	302	X	1,210	1,082
Switzerland	116	43	30	170	166	130	1,280	707	485
Turkey	860	X	X	275	497	X	X	X	X
Ukraine	3,849	2,782	1,293	1,145	1,097	467	X	8,141	2,567
United Kingdom	4,862	3,731	2,017	2,511	2,686	2,029	7,642	7,111	5,000
United States	23,501	20,989	17,339	22,501	21,584	21,222	105,872	87,576	80,579
Yugoslavia	406	508	434	47	66	57	X	X	X

Source: Compiled by the World Resources Institute from data supplied by the Co-operative Programme for Monitoring and Evaluation of the Long-Range Transmission of Air Pollutants in Europe, 1998, http://www.emep.int.

Note: X indicates that statistics are not available. The 1980 figures for Germany are the combined figures from the German Democratic Republic and the Federal Republic of Germany.

Table 2 Chemicals Widely Distributed in the Environment and Reported to Have Reproductive and Endocrine-Disrupting Effects

Fungicides	Herbicides	Industrial Chemicals	Insecticides	Metals	Nematocides
Benomyl	2, 4-D	Dioxin (2,3,7,8-TCDD)	a-HCH	Mercury	Aldicarb
HCB	2, 4, 5-T		b-HCH	Cadmium	DBCP
Mancozeb	Alachlor	PBBs	Carbaryl	Lead	
Maneb	Amitrole	PCBs	Chlordanes		
Metiram-complex	Atrazine	PCP	Dicofol		
	Metribuzin	Alkylphenols	Dieldrin		
TBT	Nitrofen	Phthalates	DDT+metabolites		
Zineb	Trifluralin	Styrenes	Endosulfan		
Ziram			Heptachlor		
			Methomyl		
			Methoxychlor		
			Mirex		
			Parathion		
			Synthetic pyrethroids		
			Toxaphene		

Source: Joint Group of Experts on the Scientific Aspects of Marine Environment Protection (GESAMP) and the Advisory Committee on Protection of the Sea, *Protecting the Oceans from Land-Based Activities* (Nairobi: United Nations Environment Programme, 2001).

Table 3 Examples of Introduced (Alien) Species Water Pollution since the 1980s

Species	Origin	Area
Comb jellyfish (Ctenophora) *Mnemiopsis leidyi* American comb jellyfish	North America	Black and Azov Seas
Crabs (Decapoda) *Charybdis helleri* Indo-Pacific swimming crab	Mediterranean	Colombia, Cuba, United States, and Venezuela
Dinoflagellates *Gymnodinium catenatum*	Japan	Australia
Mussels and clams (Bivalvia) *Ensis americanus* American razor clam	North America Japan	Western and northern Europe New Zealand
Musculista senhousia Japanese mussel	Black Sea	Eastern North America and the Great Lakes
Dreissena polymorpha Zebra mussel		

Table 3 Examples of Introduced (Alien) Species Water Pollution since the 1980s (*continued*)

Species	Origin	Area
Polychaete worms (Annelida) *Marenzilleria viridis* Spionid tubeworm	North America	Western and northern Europe
Seastars (Asteroidea) *Asterias amurensis* North Pacific seastar	Japan	Australia

Source: Joint Group of Experts on the Scientific Aspects of Marine Environment Protection (GESAMP) and the Advisory Committee on Protection of the Sea, *Protecting the Oceans from Land-Based Activities* (Nairobi: United Nations Environment Programme, 2001).

Case Study—The Crumbling Taj Mahal

"A teardrop on the face of eternity" was how Indian poet Rabindranath Tagore described the seventeenth-century Taj Mahal. Built from white marble and inlaid with precious stones, the mosque was constructed by twenty thousand workers over twenty-two years for the Mogul emperor Shah Jahan in memory of his wife Mumtaz Mahal, who died during childbirth. After the building was complete, Shah Jahan reputedly ordered the thumbs of his craftsmen to be cut off so that they could never again create such beauty. In 1983 the United Nations Educational, Scientific and Cultural Organization designated the monument a World Heritage Site, calling it "the most perfect jewel of Moslem art in India and . . . one of the universally admired masterpieces of the world's heritage."

Today, the Taj Mahal's beauty prompts a different kind of teardrop. Agra, where the building stands, is classified by the World Health Organization as a "pollution intensive zone," thanks to numerous iron foundries, coal-burning power plants, and severe traffic congestion. Several decades of chronic air pollution have now brought the Taj Mahal to the brink of collapse. So-called marble cancer has turned Shah Jahan's pristine white marble to a dirty yellow and riddled it with cracks. The nearby Jumna River, which once cooled and helped to preserve the building, has become sluggish and polluted and now exacerbates the building's problems. Visiting Agra in March 2000, President Bill Clinton commented, "Pollution has managed to do what 350 years of wars, invasions and natural disasters have failed to do. It has begun to mar the magnificent walls of the Taj Mahal. I can't help wondering that if a stone can get cancer, what kind of damage can this pollution do to children?"

Steps have now been taken by Indian authorities in a desperate attempt to save the building. In 1994 the Supreme Court prohibited motorized vehicles within 4 square kilometers (1.6 square miles) of the monument. In 1997 the court ordered 292 small and medium-sized foundries in the city either to switch their fuel from coal to less-polluting natural gas or to relocate away from the monument. When 53 foundries refused to comply, the court ordered their closure in 1999. It also required that more trees be planted within 456 meters (500 yards) of the site to absorb the worst of the pollution. Other initiatives include a cooperative venture between Indian and U.S. transport engineers to produce an improved, pedal-powered rickshaw. The hope is that the easier-to-pedal, more comfortable vehicles will stem the growth of gas-powered auto-rickshaws and help cities such as Agra cut pollution. Meanwhile, craftsmen from India's archaeological service are systematically working to replace the Taj Mahal's damaged marble blocks.

Some of these measures have proved highly controversial. Foundry owners, for example, complained that the Supreme Court's orders threatened the jobs of some seven thousand workers. Indian environmental lawyer M. C. Mehta, who prompted the action by the court, countered, "The cultural heritage of the country is much more important than the economic interests. . . . [T]he Taj Mahal is not only a monument but it has much more economic value because even if we consider the Taj Mahal as an industry, this single industry is giving employment to more than a hundred thousand people, it is bringing enormous foreign exchange to the country and we have to keep this monument, protect it and preserve [it]."

Case Study—PROPER Pollution Control in Indonesia

When it comes to controlling pollution, conventional wisdom suggests that developed countries are the most effectively regulated. Indeed, there is a strong correlation between a country's gross domestic product and its degree of air and water regulation. Developing countries have nevertheless pioneered some highly effective programs for tackling pollution. Indonesia's PROPER initiative—PROgram for Pollution Control Evaluation and Rating—has been held up as a model of how industrial pollution can be swiftly and effectively reduced.

Developed in the early 1990s by BAPEDAL, the Indonesian environmental regulation agency, with help from World Bank consultants, PROPER measures emissions from factories and makes public the results. The pilot phase of the project began in early 1995, and by the summer of that year water pollution from 187 plants had been assessed and ranked using a color system: black represented no pollution control and severe environmental damage; red meant some pollution control efforts, but below the necessary standard; blue represented a company that had met the minimum standard; green meant that the standards had been exceeded, and there was good control; and the top award, gold, indicated exceptional performance. Early results were disappointing, with two-thirds of factories assessed falling into the blue, red, and black categories.

Gross polluters were not immediately "named and shamed," however. Instead, the five best performers were invited to an awards ceremony with Vice President Tri Sutrisno; the remainder of the factories were mailed their results and informed that unless they cleaned up, they would be named as the country's worst polluters six months later. This news prompted panic and a flurry of activity among the noncompliant companies. Six months later, major changes had occurred. One of the award-winning green companies had lost its status, after being discovered secretly dumping waste at night. Other results were more encouraging. There was a 50 percent drop in black (grossly polluting) companies, a 6 percent drop in red (noncompliant) companies, and an 18 percent increase in blue (compliant) companies. Improvements continued over the following eighteen months: where there had been 113 plants in the red and black groupings in December 1995, by July 1997 there were just seventy-five, and, overall, pollution in the pilot group of factories was down by 40 percent.

Spurred on by the success of the pilot project, BAPEDAL planned to assess around two thousand factories in a major extension of the program, "2000 by 2000." The project has been held up by the World Bank as a model for emissions reduction, and other countries, including Colombia, Mexico, and the Philippines, have developed similar programs. The key to PROPER's success is not its ratings system per se, but the way in which publicly available information can be used to bring pressure on polluting companies by communities and markets or, as BAPEDAL officials describe the approach, "no shame, no gain."

Biographical Sketches

Shakeb Afsah is senior policy adviser for the U.S.-Asia Environmental Program. He is one of the architects of the Indonesian PROPER pollution control program and previously worked as an environmental economist at the World Bank, where he collaborated with national governments on environmental monitoring programs. Afsah has also worked in rain forest conservation and on research projects in a number of developing countries.

Wilfred Beckerman is emeritus fellow of economics, Balliol College, Oxford University, and formerly a member of the Royal Commission on Environmental Pollution. He is a leading skeptic of environmentalism, arguing that economic growth and wealth creation are the only credible methods of solving social and environmental problems, especially those facing developing nations.

F. Sherwood Rowland and **Mario Molina** published a groundbreaking scientific paper in *Nature* on 28 June 1974 explaining how chlorofluorocarbons (CFCs) were rapaciously destroying the ozone layer. Rowland is a professor of chemistry at the University of California, Irvine, and Molina, once Rowland's student, is now a professor of chemistry at the Massachusetts Institute of Technology. Their findings were initially greeted with skepticism but later accepted when a hole in the ozone layer was discovered in 1985. Ten years later, they were awarded the 1995 Nobel Prize in Chemistry for their work.

Sandra Steingraber came to prominence in 1997 with the publication of *Living Downstream: An Ecologist Looks at Cancer and the Environment*. Combining a scientific argument that toxins in the environment cause cancer with a poignant and poetic account of her own battles against the disease, Steingraber's book made her the natural successor to Rachel Carson and earned her numerous plaudits. She also served on the Clinton administration's National Action Plan for breast cancer.

David Wheeler is lead economist in the Environment Unit of the World Bank's Development Research Group. He has spent much of his life researching and formulating policy on pollution control in developing countries and has worked with pollution control agencies in Brazil, China, Colombia, India, Indonesia, Mexico, and the Philippines. He has published widely on environmental and development issues.

Directory

American Lung Association, 1740 Broadway, New York, NY 10019. Telephone: (212) 315-8700, Email: info@lungusa.org, Web: http://www.lungusa.org
Organization concerned with issues related to lung disease, including environmental pollution

Environmental Defense, Environmental Health Program, 257 Park Avenue South, New York, NY 10010. Telephone: (212) 505-2100, Email: contact@environmentaldefense.org, Web: http://www.environmentaldefense.org/programs/Health
Environmental organization dedicated to research and policy solutions on a wide range of environmental concerns

Friends of the Earth USA, Community, Health, and Environment Program, 1025 Vermont Avenue NW, Washington, DC 20005. Telephone: (877) 843-8687, Email: foe@foe.org, Web: http://www.foe.org/ptp/PtP.html
Network devoted to promoting the health and diversity of Earth by championing environmental issues

Joint Group of Experts on the Scientific Aspects of Marine Environmental Protection (GESAMP), 4 Albert Embankment, London SE1 7SR, United Kingdom. Telephone: (44) 207 587 3119, Email: ksekimizu@imo.org, Web: http://gesamp.imo.org
International body established by various UN organizations in 1967 to advise on marine pollution

National Pollution Prevention Roundtable, 11 Dupont Circle NW, Suite 201, Washington, DC 20036. Telephone: (202) 466-7272, Email: info@p2.org, Web: http://www.p2.org
Forum for discussing pollution prevention by bringing together leading pollution experts

United Nations Economic Commission for Europe (UNECE), Environment and Human Settlements Division, Palais des Nations, 1211 Geneva 27, Switzerland. Telephone: (41) 229 172 370, Email: air.env@unece.org, Web: http://www.unece.org/env/lrtap
Agency responsible for administering the 1979 Convention on Long-Range Transboundary Air Pollution

United Nations Environment Programme (UNEP), Secretariat of the Basel Convention, Geneva Executive Center, 15 Chemin des Anemones, Building D, 1219 Chatelaine, Switzerland. Telephone: (41) 229 799 111, Web: http://www.basel.int
Agency responsible for administering the Basel Convention, which calls for monitoring the transboundary movement and disposal of hazardous wastes

U.S. Environmental Protection Agency, 1200 Pennsylvania Avenue NW, Washington, DC 20460. Telephone: (202) 260-2090, Email: public-access@epa.gov, Web: http://www.epa.gov
U.S. government agency responsible for assessing environmental issues

World Bank, Environment Program, 1818 H Street NW, Washington, DC 20433. Telephone: (202) 477-1234, Email: feedback@worldbank.org, Web: http://www.worldbank.org/environment
International organization aiming to relieve poverty by financing development projects

World Health Organization, 20 Avenue Appia, 1211 Geneva 27, Switzerland. Telephone: (41) 22 791 2111, Email: info@who.int, Web: http://www.who.int
UN agency responsible for drawing attention to health problems and promoting health programs around the world

Further Research

Books

Alloway, B. J., and D. C. Ayres. *Chemical Principles of Environmental Pollution*. London and New York: Blackie/Chapman and Hall, 1997.

Beckerman, Wilfred. *Through Green-Colored Glasses: Environmentalism Reconsidered*. Washington, D.C.: Cato Institute, 1996.

Carson, Rachel. *Silent Spring*. New York: Houghton-Mifflin, 1962.

Farmer, Andrew. *Managing Environmental Pollution*. London and New York: Routledge, 1997.

Gourlay, K. A. *Poisoners of the Seas*. London: Zed Books, 1980.

———. *World of Waste*. London: Zed Books, 1992.

Steingraber, Sandra. *Living Downstream: An Ecologist Looks at Cancer and the Environment*. London: Virago, 1999.

Articles and Reports

"Alien Species Cost US $123 Billion a Year," Environment News Service, http://ens.lycos.com/ens/jan99/1999L-01-25-05.html.

Borgese, Elisabeth. "The Law of the Sea." *Scientific American*, March 1983, 28.

"Clean-Air Allies: Rickshaws Get a Lift." *Science News*, 20 November 1999, 333.

"Clinton Awed by Taj Mahal, Dismayed by Pollution." Reuters, 23 March 2000, http://www.climateark.org/articles/2000/1st/dismatpo.htm.

Cohen, Margot. "Indonesia—Day of Shame for Polluters." *TimesNet ASIA*, 1 November 1995, http://web3.asia1.com.sg/timesnet/data/ab/docs/ab0511.html.

Deere-Jones, Tim. "Back to the Land: The Sea-to-Land Transfer of Radioactive Pollution." *Ecologist*, January/February 1991, 18.

Greening Industry: New Roles for Communities, Markets, and Governments. A World Bank Policy Research Report. New York: Oxford University Press, 1999. Also available at http://www.worldbank.org/nipr/greening.

Gumbel, Andrew. "Closing Surf City." *E Magazine*, January–February 2000, http://www.emagazine.com/january-february_2000/0100ib_surfcity.html.

Joint Group of Experts on the Scientific Aspects of Marine Environmental Protection (GESAMP). *The State of the Marine Environment*. Oxford and New York: Blackwell, 1990.

Joint Group of Experts on the Scientific Aspects of Marine Environmental Protection (GESAMP) and the Advisory Committee on Protection of the Sea. *Protecting the Oceans from Land-Based Activities*. Nairobi: United Nations Environment Programme, 2001.

Malakoff, David. "Death by Suffocation in the Gulf of Mexico." *Science,* 10 July 1998, 190–192.

"Mercury Pollution Threatens Siberia and the Arctic Ocean," *Earth Island Journal* 14, no. 1 (1998–1999), http://www.earthisland.org/eijournal/winter99/wn_winter99 merc.html.

Ott, Wayne, and John Roberts. "Everyday Exposure to Toxic Pollutants." *Scientific American,* February 1998. Also available at http://www.sciam.com/1998/0298issue/0298ott.html.

Pan, Hu. "Air Pollution Blocks Beijing's Sky," Environment News Service, http://www.ens.lycos.com/ens/sep99/1999L-09-01-02.html.

Ryan, Heather E. "Sandra Steingraber: Living Downstream and Fighting Back." *E Magazine,* November–December 1999, http://www.emagazine.com/november-december_1999/1199conversations.html.

Scheierling, Susanne M. "Overcoming Agricultural Water Pollution in the European Union." *World Bank,* September 1996, http://www.worldbank.org/fandd/english/0996/articles/0100996.htm.

"Smog Threatens to Destroy Taj Mahal." *Daily Telegraph* (London), 3 October 1999.

Tenenbaum, David J. "Focus: Northern Overexposure." *Environmental Health Perspectives,* February 1998, http://ehpnet1.niehs.nih.gov/qa/106-2focus/focus.html

Wheeler, David, and Shakeb Afsah. "Going Public on Polluters in Indonesia: BAPEDAL's PROPER PROKASIH Program." *East Asian Executive Reports,* May 1996. Also available at http://www.worldbank.org/nipr/work_paper/proper.

Web Sites

UK Rivers Network
http://www.ukrivers.net/pollution.html

United Nations Environment Programme, *Global Environment Outlook, 2000* (GEO-2000)
http://www.unep.org/Geo2000

U.S. Fish and Wildlife Service, Environmental Contaminants Program
http://contaminants.fws.gov/Issues/EndocrineDisruptors.cfm

World Bank, *Pollution Prevention and Abatement Handbook, 1998: Toward Cleaner Production*
http://wbln0018.worldbank.org/essd/essd.nsf/Docs/PPAH

World Resources Institute, Heavy Metals and Health
http://www.wri.org/wri/wr-98-99/metals.htm

World Wildlife Fund, Global Campaign to Reduce the Use of Toxic Chemicals
http://www.worldwildlife.org/toxics

Documents

1. Protecting the Oceans from Land-Based Activities

Joint Group of Experts on the Scientific Aspects of Marine Environmental Protection (GESAMP) and the Advisory Committee on Protection of the Sea, 2001

The full text is available at http://gesamp.imo.org.

Extract

Executive Summary

Environmental processes are complex in nature. Interactions occur both within the biosphere and the abiotic environment and between them. Consequently, environmental problems are inextricably linked to, or influenced by, one another and do not recognize political boundaries. This is particularly the case for the problems of the marine environment. They cannot be remedied without taking into account the ecological interdependence of the oceans, the coastal areas and the freshwater systems associated with them.

Environmental processes and ecological systems are strongly influenced by social and economic systems and, in turn, influence them. A high proportion of the world's population lives in coastal areas, and many more of its people derive benefit from the use of marine and coastal resources, from employment linked with coastal and maritime activities, and from coastal recreational opportunities. However, population pressure, consumption patterns, and increasing demands for space and resources—combined with poor economic performance and the impoverishment of a large part of the global population—undermine the sustainable use of oceans and coastal areas, and of their resources.

Globally, both the environmental problems of the oceans and coastal areas, and their causes, have remained largely unchanged for several decades. Although there have been some notable successes in addressing problems caused by some forms of marine pollution, and in improving the quality of certain coastal areas, on a global scale marine environmental degradation has continued and in many places even intensified.

Persistent Problems

Marine pollution stemming from land-based sources and activities has previously been of predominant concern. However, improved appreciation of the scale of other forms of damage and threats to the marine and coastal environment has resulted in a more balanced perspective. Today, aside from the impacts expected in the long-term from global climate change, the following are considered to be the most serious problems affecting the quality and uses of the marine and coastal environment:

- alteration and destruction of habitats and ecosystems;
- effects of sewage on human health;
- widespread and increased eutrophication;
- decline of fish stocks and other renewable resources; and
- changes in sediment flows due to hydrological changes.

2. Agenda 21

Declaration on Environment and Development, Rio de Janeiro, 3–14 June 1992

The full text is available at http://www.unep.org.

Extract

Chapter 19 Environmentally Sound Management of Toxic Chemicals including Prevention of Illegal International Traffic in Toxic and Dangerous Products

Introduction

19.1. A substantial use of chemicals is essential to meet the social and economic goals of the world community and today's best practice demonstrates that they can be used widely in a cost-effective manner and with a high degree of safety. However, a great deal remains to be done to ensure the environmentally sound management of toxic chemicals, within the principles of sustainable development and improved quality of life for humankind. Two of the major problems, particularly in developing countries, are (a) lack of sufficient scientific information for the assessment of risks entailed by the use of a great number of chemicals, and (b) lack of resources for assessment of chemicals for which data are at hand.

19.2. Gross chemical contamination, with grave damage to human health, genetic structures and reproductive outcomes, and the environment, has in recent times been continuing within some of the world's most important industrial areas. Restoration will require major investment and development of new techniques. The long-range effects of pollution, extending even to the fundamental chemical and physical processes of the Earth's atmosphere and climate, are becoming understood only recently and the importance of those effects is becoming recognized only recently as well.

19.3. A considerable number of international bodies are involved in work on chemical safety. In many countries work programmes for the promotion of chemical safety are in place. Such work has international implications, as chemical risks do not respect national boundaries. However, a significant strengthening of both national and international efforts is needed to achieve an environmentally sound management of chemicals.

19.4. Six programme areas are proposed:

(a) Expanding and accelerating international assessment of chemical risks;

(b) Harmonization of classification and labeling of chemicals;

(c) Information exchange on toxic chemicals and chemical risks;

(d) Establishment of risk reduction programmes;

(e) Strengthening of national capabilities and capacities for management of chemicals;

(f) Prevention of illegal international traffic in toxic and dangerous products.

POPULATION

Ulla Larsen

The population of the world is at an all time high of 6.1 billion humans. Nonetheless, in recent years the rate of global population growth has declined. The populations of several European countries are declining because of fewer annual births than deaths and little net migration, whereas in some African countries the AIDS epidemic has caused severe population and development concerns. In fact, for the most part, the dire predictions of the *Population Bomb,* written in 1966 by Paul Ehrlich, have not occurred. Despite more than thirty years of research since Ehrlich's publication, the precise relationship between population growth, economic development, and consequent effects on the environment has proven to be complex and situation dependent. In some circumstances, increases in population appear coupled with economic growth, as the generation of new knowledge is able to overcome environmental deterioration; in other instances, however, rapid population growth has led to economic and environmental decline. Thus, although population growth has not caused insurmountable problems to date, there is a consensus among population researchers that a finite limit to population growth exists, and a better understanding of the balance between population, development, and the environment is essential.

Historical Background and Development

Population growth did not achieve its current types of rates until around 1800, when the world's population reached 1 billion people for the first time. According to the Population Division of the United Nations Department of Economic and Social Affairs, the subsequent two hundred years witnessed such unprecedented growth that the next 5 billion people were born in increments of 1 billion in 1927, 1960, 1974, 1987, and 1999. The source of this accelerated growth was a decline in death rates later followed by a reduction in birth rates. The mortality decline was due to medical innovations (such as vaccination against smallpox), improved hygiene (such as new provisions for clean water and sewage systems and better personal hygiene), and better social and economic conditions (such as more dependable food supplies). After World

War II improved medical technologies played the biggest role in further reducing mortality rates.

The highest reliably recorded level of fertility in a population is about ten births per woman among seventeenth- and eighteenth-century French Canadians and mid-twentieth-century North American Hutterites, a religious sect that prohibits all forms of fertility control. Below maximum fertility in historical populations has been rendered by such customs as late entry into marriage and permanent abstinence from sexual intercourse. For instance, in Western Europe before its fertility decline in the modern era, the mean age of marriage was twenty-five years or more; only 10 to 15 percent of women remained unmarried at age 50.

At the end of the eighteenth and the beginning of the nineteenth century, economist and population scientist Thomas Robert Malthus expressed concern that the world's population would eventually exceed Earth's capacity for subsistence, so he recommended fertility control through "moral constraint." That is, people should delay marriage so that the number of children born would keep population growth within the limits of the planet's natural resources. (Malthus was a Protestant clergyman who explicitly rejected contraception.) In Europe and North America, fertility began to decline in the mid- to late nineteenth century. Reduced fertility was achieved largely by male withdrawal before ejaculation, or *coitus interruptus.* Modern contraceptives, including the pill and other hormonal methods, became available in the 1960s. Subsequently, the development of new birth control methods and the spread of knowledge and use of contraception have been foci for government and nongovernment agencies concerned with population control.

In the 1950s demographers noted that many low-income countries were experiencing a drop in mortality, while fertility remained the same or only declined slightly. This demographic pattern led to concerns that increased population growth in these less developed countries would impede their economic development. The relationship between population and economic development soon became a popular subject for scientific inquiry. An example of this research is the 1958 case study of India and Mexico by U.S demographer Ansley Coale and U.S economist Edgar Hoover at Princeton University. In the case of Mexico, they made projections of future population size using the following assumptions: mortality would decline gradually, and by 1985 life expectancy at birth would be seventy years; fertility would remain unchanged or it would be reduced by 50 percent from 1955 to 1980 or it would decline by 50 percent from 1965 to 1980. They then analyzed the differential effects on economic growth. The study concluded that the projected income per adult consumer would be about 40 percent higher if fertility were reduced by half. (Coale reevaluated the situation in Mexico in the late 1970s and in the 1980s and largely drew the same conclusions as the original study.) Mexico ultimately experienced a multistage response to population growth: First, the economy expanded to meet the needs of the increasing population; second, there was an increase in internal migration from rural to urban areas (especially to Mexico City); and third, out-migration became prevalent (especially to the United

States). Coale and Hoover's study was an important influence on scientific research and public policy on population and development in the 1960s and 1970s.

Popular and scientific concerns about a population crisis were heightened by the publication of Ehrlich's *Population Bomb,* in which he used such phrases as "too many people," "too little food," and "environmental degradation." In 1990 Ehrlich, with his wife Anne Ehrlich, published a follow-up, *The Population Explosion,* in which they argue that the destruction of the environment, including depletion of nonrenewable resources, climate change, and increasing international tensions had become much worse since 1968. The negative consequences of population growth were also the primary focus of international debates, including at the United Nations World Population Conferences in 1974 (in Bucharest) and 1984 (in Mexico City), but less so for the International Conference on Population and Development (ICPD) in 1994 (in Cairo).

The debate at the 1974 conference was polarized between the perspective of developing countries and that of the United States and other developed countries. The latter argued that developing countries should establish growth rate targets and that these targets should be met through family planning programs. The developing countries, however, wanted to discuss and implement new ways of integrating population programs with economic development programs. This disagreement aside, all the delegates agreed to a World Population Plan of Action, which was largely an international program for promoting family planning (see Document 1). The phrase "development is the best contraceptive"—meaning that increased schooling and labor force participation of women and men, industrialization, and urbanization would automatically result in fewer births per woman—originated at this conference. At the 1984 conference, the United States proposed that population growth is a neutral factor. That is, population growth does not have an effect on economic development. (This position was inspired by the late professor Julian Simon's influence in the Reagan administration and its support by groups opposed to abortion. Simon's main thesis was that population growth does not hinder economic progress and eventually raises standards of living.) The Recommendations for the Further Implementation of the World Population Plan of Action passed at Mexico City raised concerns about the environment, the role and status of women, and meeting the need for family planning, but the overall consensus was that the 1974 World Population Plan of Action was still valid.

The 1994 ICPD resulted in the Programme of Action, which covered a wide range of topics. The conference was preceded by several meetings sponsored by the United Nation, gatherings called by nongovernmental organizations, and numerous books, articles, newspaper columns, and radio and television segments assuring the world that a broad section of people had an input in the development and formulation of the Programme of Action. Of importance, at these preliminary meetings women's organizations had a chance to participate and to make women's voices and concerns part of the final program, which was not the case at the 1974 and 1984 meetings. Throughout the

Programme of Action there is a strong commitment to improving women's reproductive health and securing their reproductive rights (see Document 2). Women's concerns about fertility control were broadened to include all aspects of reproductive health (see WOMEN).

Current Status

The welfare of individuals is affected by and has an effect on population growth and the environment. Recent research on this topic has aimed to enhance the understanding of inter-relations between population, development (especially economic development), and the environment and to ascertain whether population trends are sustainable (see map, p. 507). The 1990s saw women's organizations and their supporters shift the values and priorities of the population and development debate away from demographic target setting by placing equity, gender, and human rights at the center of the discussion and by proposing a more holistic agenda for action. Thus, the 1990s population policy debate emphasized the role of women's health and women's empowerment and how these affect population growth, development, and the environment.

Research

The twentieth century experienced an unprecedented rate of population growth and economic improvement. The economic performance of individual countries bore a modest relation to the intensity of its population growth. According to the World Bank, world gross domestic product per capita—based on international U.S. dollars using purchasing power parity conversion rates, or GDP per capita in PPP—increased eightfold between 1950 and 2000. (The World Bank defines GDP per capita in PPP as "the number of units of a country's currency required to buy the same amount of goods and services in the domestic market as one dollar would buy in the United States.") Also between 1950 and 2000 world population grew from 2.5 billion to 6.1 billion resulting in a threefold increase in GDP per capita in PPP.

Economic growth was uneven, and disparities in income widened between countries (see INCOME INEQUALITY). During the 1980s and 1990s there was almost no change in economic growth in North Africa, the Middle East, or sub-Saharan Africa; by far the greatest increase in per capita income occurred in the industrialized countries of the Organization for Economic Cooperation and Development (OECD). The World Bank estimates that GDP per capita in PPP in 1998 ranged from almost $30,000 in the United States to $480 in Tanzania and $458 in Sierra Leone. Further evidence suggests that income inequalities widened within many countries, raising concerns about the effects of this growing disparity.

The relationship between population growth and economic development is complicated by the presence of other factors, such as the availability of natural resources, institutional conditions, and the timing of the start of the population growth process. Edward Crenshaw and his colleagues, in a 1997 study published in *American Sociological Review,* show that in developing countries an increase in the child population hinders economic progress, while an increase in the adult population fosters economic development. They suggest that a decline in the average number of children per woman results in an increase in economic development because rapid labor force growth occurs in the presence of a growing adult population and reduced youth dependency. This pattern is illustrated by the population and economic trends in Japan after World War II, where there were steep declines in mortality and fertility followed by an economic boom.

It is well known that a host of environmental problems are linked to population and economic growth, as described so vividly by Ehrlich in *Population Bomb.* These include global warming, resulting from increases in carbon dioxide emissions and greenhouse effects; deforestation, resulting from the expansion of cropland and the harvesting of wood for fuel; and water shortages, resulting from increased pressure on watersheds (see DEFORESTATION, FRESHWATER, and GLOBAL WARMING). The challenge remains to determine the complex and sometimes harmful effects that population and economic growth have on the environment. Esther Boserup documented that increased population pressure has traditionally led to new technologies aimed at intensifying agriculture production and increasing agricultural yields. Julian Simon advanced this school of thought, suggesting that in the long run societies adjust to additional people. The debate remains whether there are possible limits to how intense food production can become before resources are degraded.

In October 1993 at the Population Summit of the World's Scientific Academies in New Delhi, Samuel Preston presented the results of an in-depth study on population and the environment. Among his findings, published in 1994 as "Population and the Environment: The Scientific Evidence," he concluded, "Population growth is not the only factor capable of affecting the extent of resource degradation. Depending on time, place and criterion, it may not be the most important factor. Because they have multiple origins, it would be foolhardy to think that problems of food production and resource maintenance can or should be solved by population policy alone." At the Population Summit Jane Menken also presented her thoughts on the impact of population growth on development. In her study, published as "Demographic-Economic Relationships and Development," she concluded the following:

1. Population growth has important effects on economic development, but it is, in some cases, not as great as was thought in the past.
2. Feedback mechanisms are important, because societies adapt; if this is not taken into account, the impact of population growth can be vastly overestimated in forecasts.
3. Population growth has not prevented economic growth, although it may have reduced it.
4. The effects of population growth depend upon the situation of individual countries; for example, concerns about self-sufficiency in food production are quite different for Kuwait, which has oil to trade on international markets, than for Bangladesh, for which trade is far less likely to compensate for internal shortages.

5. No singly directed policy can address all the ills of society. Reducing population growth through declining fertility is not a panacea; it will not, in and of itself, make a poor country rich. Rather, rapid population growth exacerbates problems, but it is not a root cause of many of the deterrents to economic development.
6. Reducing population growth has direct effects, by, for example, affecting some aspects of economic development, and indirectly, by "buying time" so root causes of development deterrents can be addressed.
7. Economic change can affect population growth and change.

Preston's and Menken's statements about the relationships between population, environment, and development were substantiated later in the 1990s by additional empirical data and research generated and reported by, among others, the National Research Council's Board on Sustainable Development and Policy and the National Research Council's Forum on Biodiversity Committee, as well as in the United Nations Development Programme's annual *Human Development Report,* and the World Bank's annual *World Development Report.*

Although annual global population growth rates have declined steadily since the late 1960s, the total number of people continues to grow (see Tables 1, 2, and 3). For instance, the annual growth rate of 1.3 percent between 1995 and 2000 added about 80 million people to the population each year. At the core of the "population problem" lies the concern of how many people Earth can support, or its human "carrying capacity." In a 1995 study, Joel Cohen showed that estimates of Earth's carrying capacity varied widely, from less than 1 billion to more than 1,000 billion people; about two-thirds of the estimates fell in the range of 4 billion to 16 billion people; the median value was 12 billion. In 2000, the United Nations projected that the global population would reach 9.3 billion in 2050 based on the assumption that by 2050 each woman, on average, would have 2.1 children. Future population size, however, is sensitive to small deviations in annual population growth rates, and the global population projection in 2050 would be 7.9 billion or 10.9 billion if the fertility assumption were half a child lower or half a child higher than 2.1 children per woman. Cohen did not attempt to estimate the carrying capacity of Earth, but he did stress that it depends on natural constraints and human choices, including everything from food and the environment to lifestyles. The National Research Council's Board on Sustainable Development echoed Cohen's concerns about the validity of measures of carrying capacity and requested that more work be done on this concept, either in terms of a scientific foundation supporting the idea of "safe limits" for world population size or alternative concepts for efforts to attain sustainability. The general consensus at the end of the 1990s was that the prevailing level of population growth was not sustainable and that trends toward zero population growth were desirable and should be promoted.

Policies and Programs

There is a general consensus in the international population community that the 1994 ICPD represented a paradigm shift in the population and development discourse. Ruth Dixon-Mueller and Adrienne Germain described eloquently the strides made in population policies and programs following the conference by contrasting a more traditional, narrow demographic approach—as illustrated by John Bongaarts' recommendations for achieving the highest demographic impact—to the Programme of Action signed by the delegates. Shortly before the ICPD, Bongaarts proposed in *Science* that governments pursue three policy options for reducing population growth: reduce unwanted pregnancies by strengthening family planning programs and addressing unmet contraception needs; reduce the need or demand for large families by investing in human development, such as education, improvements in women's status, and infant and child survival; and slow the momentum of population growth by raising the average age of childbearing. In contrast, the Programme of Action emphasized, with respect to childbearing decisions, that the manipulation of the decision-making process, whether concerning a person's decision to use contraception or address broader socioeconomic issues, should be guided not by demographic objectives but by the primacy of health, empowerment, and human rights (see HEALTH and HUMAN RIGHTS). It is in this sense, argued Dixon-Mueller and Germain, that ICPD moved beyond family planning and even beyond demography to encompass a broader range of political, developmental, and ethical concerns. In general, the post-Cairo perspective shifted population policies away from slowing population growth to improving the lives of individuals, in particular, women, and that family planning should be provided in the broader context of reproductive health. Underlying this new perspective was a belief that enhancing individual health and rights would ultimately lower fertility and slow population growth.

The Cairo consensus was supported by the 1995 World Summit for Social Development in Copenhagen and the 1995 Fourth World Conference on Women in Beijing, where many women's organizations were active and helped to ensure that similar policies were adopted. In 1999, five years after Cairo, the United Nations held several meetings to discuss population and development policies and to review progress made since 1994. The review, ICPD^{+5}, resulted in *Key Actions for the Further Implementation of the Programme of Action of the International Conference on Population and Development,* which included new benchmarks for 2015 and sharpened the goals of the 1994 Programme of Action. Three of the pivotal benchmarks involved family planning, maternal mortality, and prevention of sexually transmitted diseases (STDs) (see EPIDEMICS).

ICPD^{+5} concluded that the use of contraception was up. For instance, in India the use of contraception increased from 41 to 48 percent from 1993 to 1998–1999, and in Cameroon from 20 to 24 percent from 1991 to 1998. Concerns were raised about whether there were adequate supplies of affordable contraceptives and whether prevailing levels of aid could keep pace with the growing demand for them. Price discounts and donations of contraceptives had been made possible by funding from the World Bank and developed countries, but it was deemed inadequate.

The 1994 ICPD called for maternal death ratios below 60 per 100,000 births, and ICPD^{+5} added that at least 60 percent of all deliveries should be assisted by trained health personnel. The level of maternal mortality in developing countries is not well documented, but UN data suggest that in the early 1990s maternal mortality ratios per 100,000 births were about 880 in Africa, 410 in Asia, 180 in Latin America and the Caribbean, and 10 in more developed countries. The World Bank has exhibited a long-term and ongoing commitment to safe motherhood, but progress has been slow, partly because of insufficient funding, lack of political support, and weak health care systems in many developing countries. It is helpful to keep in mind that ICPD^{+5} only covers a five-year period, and discernable improvements in maternal health may require a longer time frame.

Concerns about STDs, including HIV/AIDS, increased during the 1990s (see AIDS). The United Nations estimated that 36.1 million people were living with HIV/AIDS in 2001. The potentially destabilizing effects of the HIV/AIDS epidemic led the Security Council to declare in 2000 that AIDS was a global security concern. ICPD^{+5} urged governments to ratchet up all efforts to combat the epidemic, including expanding national and community-level programs and supporting interventions for those who are most vulnerable. Specifically, it recommended that governments, with assistance from UNAIDS and donors, ensure that by 2005 at least 90 percent of men and women aged 15 to 24 have access to the education, information, and services necessary to reduce their vulnerability to infection by HIV and that 95 percent of this age group have them by 2010. The services provided should include access to female and male condoms, voluntary HIV testing, and counseling and follow through.

According to the World Bank, more than one adult in ten worldwide acquires an STD each year, and some 333 million new infections occur annually. Gonorrhea and chlamydia are two common STDs that often do not show any symptoms. In women they can spread and cause scarring and blockage of the fallopian tubes, leading to infertility. Syphilis is another prevalent STD that can cause miscarriage in women and at an advanced stage mental illness in both sexes. HIV-prevention strategies and programs often include all STDs. It has been difficult to evaluate the effectiveness of such programs because the ICPD population-based data about STDs and HIV are rare and generally of poor quality.

At the time of ICPD^{+5} in 1999, many developing countries still had high rates of unwanted childbearing, maternal mortality, and STD and HIV infection, suggesting that the agenda of the 1994 Programme of Action had not yet been realized, despite recorded progress. ICPD^{+5} concluded that the shortcomings in the implementation of the program were partly due to insufficient funding. During the 1990s there had been an overall decline in funding from governments and multilateral organizations, such as the World Bank. Only Denmark, Norway, and the Netherlands met the financial commitments made in Cairo, while several countries, including the United States and Japan, lagged far behind in their contributions. The United States is the largest single contributor to population and reproductive health programs and is an important influence on assistance availability. After the Republican Party won a majority in Congress in 1994, the United States shifted away from supporting international family planning programs, so funds for family planning were cut. In the 2000 U.S. budget, the global "gag rule" was enacted, denying U.S. funding to private organizations overseas if they provided abortion services or counseling or lobbied for changes in abortion laws in their country. In January 2001, after taking office, President George W. Bush reinstated the so-called Mexico City policy imposed by the Reagan administration, forcing overseas organizations to steer clear of abortion issues or forego receiving U.S. funding.

ICPD^{+5} emphasized that despite funding shortages, progress had been made and nongovernmental organizations, religious and community leaders, and the private sector had been instrumental in implementing the ICPD agenda. It also noted that many countries had modified their laws in favor of women's empowerment and health and concluded that the international debate on population and development might had led to national debates. For instance, many European countries extended maternity leave and increased the monetary benefits provided to couples with children. Brazil made reproductive health care a part of primary health care, to which all citizens have free access.

Some environmental scientists, including Paul Ehrlich, expressed concern that the post-Cairo policy debate had lost sight of the links between population growth, pollution, and natural resource depletion. Bongaarts and his colleagues commented in *Environment* in 1997 that the 1995 assessment of the Intergovernmental Panel on Climate Change had paid almost no attention to the role of population growth in global warming and that by not addressing population growth the debate missed the opportunity to simultaneously promote developmental and environmental benefits. In this context, it is noteworthy that UN secretary-general Kofi Annan, in his address to the special session of the General Assembly on the Follow-up to the International Conference on Population and Development, expressed a clear affirmation of the importance of the quantitative dimension of the population issue: "[W]e have to stabilize the population of this planet. Quite simply, there is a limit to the pressures our global environment can stand." Annan's statement is notable because it was made to the delegates reviewing the 1994 Programme of Action, which in popular terms states that "population is not about numbers."

Regional Summaries

Although the problems of population growth, development, and possible depletion of Earth's natural resources are global, they have taken significantly different forms in different regions of the world. The data reported in these summaries are from John Week's *Population: An Introduction to Concepts and Issues,* and the United Nations Population Division's *Population, Environment, and Development, 2001* and *World Population Prospects: The 1998 Revision.*

North America

At the end of the twentieth century, the United States and Canada had a population of about 317 million people, or 5 percent of the world's total. Women had on average 2.0 children each in the United States and 1.6 in Canada; these

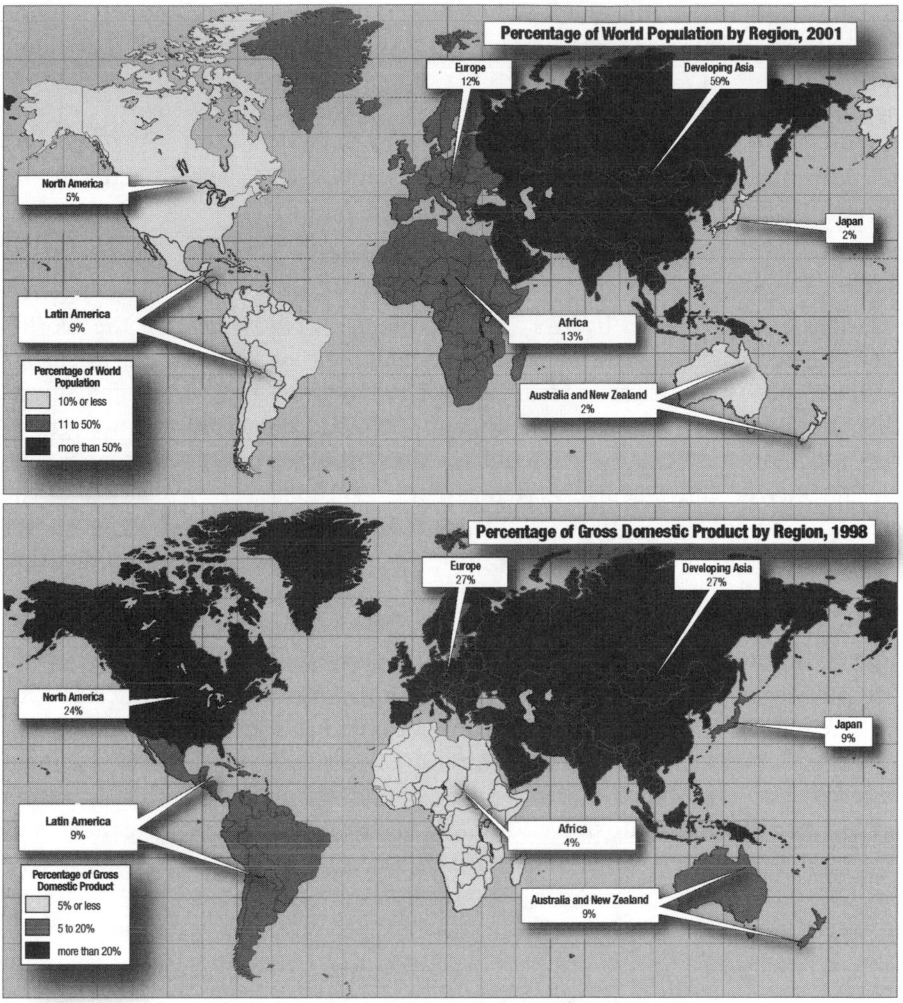

Source: United Nations, Department of Economic and Social Affairs, Population Division, *Population, Environment and Development, 2001* (New York: United Nations, 2001).

children could expect to live until the age of 77 and 79, respectively (see Tables 2 and 3). Thus, in both countries fertility and mortality were low, but even so the annual growth rate was about 0.9 percent because of immigration. In the United States the majority of immigrants came from Latin America. Many settled in urban areas, where in some situations they essentially remained segregated from native-born Americans. In 1998 the World Bank documented that residents of the United States had the world's highest purchasing power, that Canadians' purchasing power ratio to Americans' was 0.76, and that North America accounted for 24 percent of the world's GDP per capita in PPP.

The average U.S. annual population growth was 1.6 percent during the period 1965 to 1998. Increasing population and economic growth rates in North America, however, took their toll on the environment. For instance, in 1997 the United States had the world's highest ecological deficit—a measurement estimating the land and water area required to support indefinitely the material standard of living of a given human population, using prevailing technology—at 3.6 hectares per capita, while Canada had a surplus of 1.9 hectares. North America contributed 26 percent of the world's carbon dioxide emissions, one of the main causes of global warming. According to the World Resources Institute, the United States and Canada ranked first and third in carbon dioxide emissions per capita.

Latin America

In 2001 Latin America had 527 million people, or 9 percent of the world's population. At the end of the twentieth century mortality had declined significantly, life expectancy at birth had reached the age of 69, the average number of children per woman had declined to 2.7, and the population was growing at an annual rate of 1.4 percent. The decline in mortality was steeper than the fertility decline and had started earlier, so the relatively young age of the population contributed to the region's rapid population increase.

Mitigating the effects of rapid population growth, Mexico and several other countries experienced substantial rural to urban migration, as well as outmigration, which reduced under- and unemployment. The rapid and unplanned growth of the urban population is one of the gravest problems in this region because this growth has led to huge slums. In 1998 Latin America contributed 9 percent of the world's GDP per capita in PPP, and Brazil and Mexico ranked number nine and ten among the worlds largest economies as measured by GDP per capita in PPP. In terms of environmental impact, 6 percent of the world's carbon dioxide emissions came from this region. Mexico's ecological deficit was not negligible at 1.2 hectares per capita.

Europe

In 2001 Europe's population reached 726 million, or 12 percent of the world's population. Mortality was low, although some Eastern European countries, including Russia, experienced increasing mortality in the late 1980s and early 1990s at the time of the dissolution of communist rule in the east. For a couple of decades, many European countries have had below replacement fertility, with couples having fewer than the approximately two children needed to beget the next generation. From 1995 to 2000 Spain ranked the lowest, with a total fertility of 1.15, followed by Romania, the Czech Republic, and Italy, with rates of 1.17, 1.19, and 1.20, respectively. In populations with low mortality rates for pre-childbearing ages, each woman needs to have a total of about two children to reach replacement. Thus, fertility was below replacement from 1995 to 1999 in most European countries, and the population growth rate hovered around zero except in Eastern Europe, where it was negative.

In 1997 the United Nations held a meeting on below replacement fertility where it was suggested that efforts to increase fertility to replacement levels should possibly be linked to efforts to improve the empowerment of women. The evidence for this argument was found in Sweden, where fertility had increased in the late 1980s in response to favorable population policies and laws but then declined in the early 1990s, when public benefits were reduced and the economy entered a mild recession. Europe was confronted with an increasingly aging population and a declining proportion of people in the productive age range of 15 to 64.

In the 1980s and early 1990s West Germany became the home of a large number of immigrant guest workers from Greece, Italy, Turkey, and Yugoslavia, while England, France, and the Netherlands received migrant laborers mainly from their former colonies. It proved difficult to integrate these new arrivals, however, and in the late 1990s the European Union restricted legal immigration while encouraging internal migration within member countries. In 1998 Europe produced 27 percent of the world's GDP, documenting that it was possible to have high economic productivity in times of stagnant or negative population growth. Several European countries, however, exceeded their carrying capacity, as indicated by an ecological deficit of 2.3 for Russia and 3.5 for the United Kingdom. Also, pollution was not insubstantial, as seen by the fact that Europe was responsible for 25 percent of carbon dioxide emissions in the world.

North Africa and the Middle East

North Africa and the Middle East counted about 360 million people in 2001, representing 6 percent of the world's total. Egypt is the most populous country in the region, followed by Turkey. There are 69 million Egyptians, and Egypt's annual growth rate is 2 percent. Mortality has dropped significantly in Egypt since World War II, while fertility remained high until recently. Similar trends of mortality and fertility have prevailed throughout the region, causing it to have a youthful population. Economic development, however, has not followed rapid population growth. Today youth unemployment is high, and the political situation in many parts of the region is unstable. Large numbers of young people have left the area in search of work in Europe and North and South America.

Sub-Saharan Africa

In 2001, 10 percent of the world's population, or 635 million people, lived in sub-Saharan Africa. This region had the highest levels of mortality and fertility, as well as the highest annual population growth rate. In most African countries, mortality declined gradually from the 1960s to the 1980s, while fertility remained unchanged until around 1980, resulting in an unprecedented growth rate. The onset of fertility decline was earliest and most pronounced in southern Africa, where at the end of the 1990s women had on average 3 to 4 children, compared to about 5.5 in western Africa, 6.2 in central Africa, and 5.8 in eastern Africa. Today, most sub-Saharan African countries have experienced a fertility decline, albeit a modest one. The HIV/AIDS epidemic has halted or reversed mortality trends throughout the region. The Population Division of the United Nations Department of Economic and Social Affairs estimates that during the period 2000 to 2005, life expectancy at birth will be no more than 36 years in Botswana, in contrast to 70 without AIDS (that is, if all deaths from AIDS were eliminated in the event of a cure). In 2001 Botswana had the highest HIV/AIDS prevalence rate, more than 40 percent.

Internal labor migration was prevalent in sub-Saharan Africa in the 1990s, with rural to rural and male migration being dominant (except where marriage migration was common). In contrast, international migration appeared to be modest, but the evidence is poor. Africa accounted for 4 percent of the world's GDP per capita in PPP, and for many sub-Saharan African countries the GDP per capita in PPP ratio to that of the United States was 0.03 or lower. This region had poorly developed farming techniques, as suggested by the finding that in 1993 the percentage of irrigated land to cropland—hectares per person—was 7 in Africa relative to 17 in the world, and that fertilizer use—kilograms per hectare of cropland—was 21 relative to 83. Economic development was also low in sub-Saharan Africa, as was carbon dioxide emissions, which constituted 3 percent of the world's total. The region, however, suffered from other environmental problems, including deforestation and water shortages.

Asia

In 2001 Asia was the most populous region, with 3.5 billion people, or 58 percent of the world's population. The people of China constituted 36 percent and India 29 percent of that total. Asia is diverse in terms of population, development, and environmental impact. Japan had the world's lowest mortality, below replacement fertility, and 0.01 percent population growth. China had the world's largest population, almost 1.3 billion people, relatively low mortality, below replacement fertility (partly the result of a coercive government population policy in place since about 1970), and a growth rate of 0.7 percent. India, the second most populous country after China, with slightly more than 1 billion people, had higher mortality and fertility rates than China but a similarly high growth rate of 1.5 percent. The Asian countries with the most rapid decline in fertility are currently experiencing problems with how to care and provide for the elderly because state services and institutional supports are not yet available to replace the care previously provided by children and relatives.

In 1998 Japan had the second largest economy (after the United States), and the GDP per capita in PPP ratio to the United States was 0.84, while the ratio for China was 0.12 and for India 0.06. The ecological deficits were 0.4 in China and 0.03 in India, while carbon dioxide emissions per capita were 9.2 tons in Japan, 2.8 tons in China, and 1.1 tons in India, reflecting the gravity of pollution and environmental problems in this region.

The Pacific

The population of the Pacific was 31 million in 2001. Mortality and fertility were low in countries with peoples of mainly European origin. For example, women in Australia and New Zealand on average had 1.8 children, and at birth from 1995 through 2000 these children could expect to live until the age of 78. In contrast, countries with people primarily of largely indigenous origin had high mortality and fertility rates. For example, in Melanesia and Micronesia each woman had an average of 5.8 and 5.9 children, respectively, and the children could expect to live 50.5 years in Melanesia and 57.5 in Micronesia. Similarly, economic development was also higher in countries with mainly European populations. In these states, there was no shortage of land, and there were large surpluses of underutilized cropland. Pollution, including levels of carbon dioxide emissions, however, was high in Australia and New Zealand, but minor in most of Polynesia and Melanesia.

Data

Table 1 Total Population and Annual Growth Rate in Selected Countries

Country	Total (thousands) 2001	Projected Annual Growth Rate, 2000–2005 (%)		
		Total	Urban	Rural
Algeria	30,841	1.8	3.2	0.4
Argentina	37,488	1.2	1.5	–1.3
Australia	19,338	1.0	0.9	0.7
Brazil	172,559	1.2	1.8	–1.4
Canada	31,015	0.8	1.1	0.3
China	1,284,927	0.7	2.3	–0.1
Colombia	42,803	1.6	2.2	0.1
Congo, Democratic Republic of	52,552	3.3	4.5	2.3
Egypt	69,080	1.7	2.3	1.2
France	59,453	0.4	0.6	–0.7
Georgia	5,239	–0.5	0.8	–1.2
Germany	82,007	0.0	0.2	–1.5
Guatemala	11,687	2.6	3.4	2.0
India	1,025,096	1.5	2.8	0.8
Indonesia	214,840	1.2	3.6	–0.6
Israel	6,172	2.0	1.8	0.6
Japan	127,335	0.1	0.3	–0.7
Russian Federation	144,664	–0.6	0.2	–1.7
Saudi Arabia	21,028	3.1	3.4	–0.1
Spain	39,921	0.0	0.2	–1.2
Sweden	8,833	–0.1	0.3	–0.3
Switzerland	7,170	–0.1	0.6	0.1
Tajikistan	6,135	0.7	1.3	1.3
Thailand	63,584	1.1	2.7	0.3
Turkey	67,632	1.3	2.6	–2.5
Uganda	24,023	3.2	5.7	2.8
United Kingdom	59,542	0.2	0.2	–0.6
United States	285,926	0.9	1.0	–0.4
More developed regions	1,193,861	0.2	0.5	–0.8
Less developed regions	4,940,274	1.5	2.7	0.6
Least developed countries	674,954	2.5	4.5	1.6
World	6,134,135	1.2	2.0	0.4

Source: United Nations, Department of Economic and Social Affairs, Population Division, *Population, Environment and Development, 2001* (New York: United Nations, 2001).

Table 2 Life Expectancy at Birth in Selected Countries, 1970–2000

	1970–1975 (years)			1995–2000 (years)		
Country	Male	Female	Both Sexes	Male	Female	Both Sexes
Algeria	53.5	55.5	54.5	67.5	70.3	68.9
Argentina	64.1	70.8	67.1	69.7	76.8	72.9
Australia and New Zealand	68.5	75.1	71.7	75.2	80.9	78.0
Brazil	57.6	62.2	59.6	63.1	71.0	66.8
Canada	69.7	76.8	73.2	76.1	81.8	79.0
China[a]	62.5	63.9	63.2	67.9	72.0	69.8
Colombia	59.7	63.9	61.6	67.3	74.3	70.4
Congo, Democratic Republic of	44.4	47.6	46.1	49.2	52.3	50.8
Egypt	50.8	53.4	52.1	64.7	67.9	66.3
France	68.6	76.3	72.4	74.2	82.0	78.1
Georgia	65.0	72.9	69.2	68.5	76.8	72.7
Germany	67.9	73.8	71.0	73.9	80.2	77.2
Guatemala	52.4	55.4	53.7	61.4	67.2	64.0
India	51.2	49.3	50.3	62.3	62.9	62.6
Indonesia	48.0	50.5	49.3	63.3	67.0	65.1
Israel	70.1	73.3	71.6	75.7	79.7	77.8
Japan	70.6	76.2	73.3	76.8	82.9	80.0
Russian Federation	63.1	73.5	68.2	60.6	72.8	66.6
Saudi Arabia	52.4	55.5	53.9	69.9	73.4	71.4
Spain	70.2	75.7	72.9	74.5	81.5	78.0
Sweden	72.1	77.5	74.7	76.3	80.8	78.5
Switzerland	70.8	77.0	73.8	75.4	81.8	78.6
Tajikistan	60.8	65.9	63.4	64.2	70.2	67.2
Thailand	57.7	61.6	59.6	65.8	72.0	68.8
Turkey	55.9	60.0	57.9	66.5	71.7	69.0
Uganda	44.9	48.1	46.5	38.9	40.4	39.6
United Kingdom	69.0	75.2	72.0	74.5	79.8	77.2
United States	67.5	75.3	71.3	73.4	80.1	76.7
Uzbekistan	60.7	67.4	64.2	64.3	70.7	67.5
More developed regions[b]	67.6	74.7	71.2	71.1	78.7	74.9
Less developed regions[c]	53.9	55.5	54.7	61.8	65.0	63.3
Least developed countries	42.9	44.5	43.7	49.6	51.5	50.5
World	56.5	59.4	58.0	63.2	67.6	65.4

Source: United Nations, Department of Economic and Social Affairs, Population Division, *World Population Prospects: The 1998 Revision*, vol. 1, *Comprehensive Tables* (New York: United Nations, 1999).

[a]Data do not include Hong Kong.

[b]Comprising Australia, Europe, Japan, New Zealand, and North America.

[c]Comprising Africa, Asia (excluding Japan), Latin America and the Caribbean, and Melanesia, Micronesia, and Polynesia.

Table 3 Fertility Rate per Woman in Selected Countries, 1970–2000

Country	1970–1975	1995–2000
Algeria	7.38	3.81
Argentina	3.15	2.62
Australia and New Zealand	2.58	1.83
Brazil	4.72	2.27
Canada	1.97	1.55
China[a]	4.86	1.80
Colombia	5.00	2.80
Congo, Democratic Republic of	6.30	6.43
Egypt	5.54	3.40
France	2.31	1.71
Georgia	2.60	1.92
Germany	1.64	1.30
Guatemala	6.45	4.93
India	5.43	3.13
Indonesia	5.10	2.58
Israel	3.77	2.68
Japan	2.07	1.43
Russian Federation	1.98	1.35
Saudi Arabia	7.30	5.80
Spain	2.89	1.15
Sweden	1.89	1.57
Switzerland	1.82	1.47
Tajikistan	6.83	4.15
Thailand	4.99	1.74
Turkey	5.04	2.50
Uganda	6.90	7.10
United Kingdom	2.04	1.72
United States	2.02	1.99
Uzbekistan	6.01	3.45
More developed regions[b]	2.11	1.57
Less developed regions[c]	5.43	3.00
Least developed countries	6.71	5.05
World	4.48	2.71

Source: United Nations, Department of Economic and Social Affairs, Population Division, *World Population Prospects: The 1998 Revision*, vol. 1, *Comprehensive Tables* (New York: United Nations, 1999).

[a]Data do not include Hong Kong.

[b]Comprising Australia, Europe, Japan, New Zealand, and North America.

[c]Comprising Africa, Asia (excluding Japan), Latin America and the Caribbean, and Melanesia, Micronesia, and Polynesia.

Case Study—Below Replacement Fertility in Italy

Sustained below replacement fertility will lead to population decline and eventual extinction. To prevent this bleak prospect, European policymakers and researchers are attempting to understand the social and economic forces behind low fertility in order to implement policies aimed at encouraging people to have more children. In 1997 the United Nations convened a meeting devoted to low fertility in Europe. The delegates' findings are described here using the case of Italy.

By European standards, Italy had a relatively high fertility rate until around 1970–1975, when the rate was 2.3. From 1995 through 1999, it declined to 1.2. This trend resulted in a population at the end of the twentieth century with almost no large families (four or more children), with two-child families the norm, but one-child and childless families rapidly becoming more common. In 1996 for women born in 1963, 18 percent of their families were childless, and 27, 39, and 16 percent had one, two, or three or more children, respectively. Low fertility was even more prevalent in northern Italy, where, for example, 24 percent remained childless; in the Emilia-Romagna region, 40 percent had one child. Northern Italy has traditionally had lower fertility rates than the rest of Italy and has in the past been a harbinger of future trends for the whole of Italy. Demographer Antonio Golini has speculated within this context whether there is a fertility threshold below which a population does not go and whether the fertility recorded in some northern Italian regions can be considered to have reached the minimum.

Several factors have contributed to Italy's low fertility rate. More than 90 percent of women use contraception, and abortion is legal and available. Thus, there is little unwanted fertility. Almost all children are born within marriage (92 percent in 1995), the age at marriage is going up, and childbearing is being postponed, resulting in some cases in a reduction of children per couple. The postponement of marriage can be explained, in part, by the fact that people are waiting until they finish their education, youth unemployment is high, and housing is expensive. Finally, Italians' desired fertility—the number of children that people say they would like to have—is low, at about two children per couple.

It is difficult to fully explain the factors behind Italians' below replacement fertility. An opinion poll from 1991 suggests that Italians believed that they had very low fertility because women needed to work, the high cost of rearing children, and the increased appreciation for individual fulfillment and freedom. Italian gender roles had not kept pace with women's entry into the workforce. Women continued to be the primary caretakers of children and the home, and access to quality day care was limited. Furthermore, the business sector had not adjusted to women's increasing participation in the workforce, so opening hours of retail stores and public offices remained generally limited to standard business hours, making it difficult for working people (women) to find time to shop and do other errands, such as go to the post office and the doctor.

The main demographic consequences of below replacement fertility are an aging and declining population. In the case of Italy, if it is assumed that fertility stays at the 1997 level until 2047, the total Italian population will decline by 16.3 million, to 41.1 million in 2047 (a fall of 21.5 million for people under 60 and an increase of 5.2 million for people 60 and above); the working age population will fall to less than the number of people above age 60 (17.4 million people aged 20 to 59 and 18.3 million above age 60); 45 percent of the population will be over 60; there will be about five times more people over 80 compared to under age 5.

Given the above circumstances, one may question whether Italy will be able to maintain its current standard of living if the working age population is reduced by some 50 percent. Drastic changes in the social security system will be needed as the proportion of retired people grows. The system could collapse. Also, children will grow up surrounded mainly by adults and old people, providing for very different interpersonal relations.

Italy's demographic and socioeconomic problems resulting from below replacement fertility can probably not be solved by increased immigration in light of the fact that Italy has historically had difficulties integrating immigrants. Furthermore, a level of immigration much higher than that experienced in the past would be needed to prevent the total population from declining. In conclusion, the current situation is unsustainable, and the Italian population risks disappearing if fertility stays at the low level recorded in the 1990s. The Italian government and other institutions in Italian society have not taken measures to correct this critical problem, although recently there have been signs of increased awareness of the current and future problems the state is facing due to low fertility rates.

Biographical Sketches

John Bongaarts is vice president of the Population Council, Research Division. His research has focused on a variety of population issues, including the determinants of fertility, population-environment relationships, the demographic impact of the HIV/AIDS epidemic, and population policy options in the developing world. He is a member of the Royal Dutch Academy of Sciences and a fellow of the American Association for the Advancement of Science.

John Caldwell is professor emeritus at the Australian National University. His research has focused on understanding fertility decline, childbearing decisions, intergenerational relationships, sexual behavior, and other issues critical to population conditions in developing countries, particularly in Bangladesh, India, and Nigeria. From 1993 to 1997 he was president of the International Union for the Scientific Study of Population.

Ansley Coale is professor emeritus at Princeton University. His research has included methods of indirect estimation, demographic transitions in Europe and elsewhere, and the demography of China. He taught and was a mentor to an entire generation of demographers. He is a member of the U.S. National Academy of Sciences and the

American Academy of Arts and Sciences. From 1977 to 1981 he was president of the International Union for the Scientific Study of Population.

Paul Ehrlich is a population biologist and ecologist with a distinguished research record on population and the environment. He is a professor of biology at Stanford University, and his work on overpopulation has been widely debated in the scientific and popular press. Ehrlich is the author of the influential *Population Bomb* (1968) and co-author of *Population Explosion* (1990).

Jane Menken is a professor of sociology and demography at the University of Colorado, Boulder. Her research focuses on mathematical modeling, microsimulation and empirical analyses of child survival, and the determinants of fertility. She authored the influential "Demographic-Economic Relationships and Development" (1994). Menken was elected to the U.S. National Academy of Sciences in 1989, the American Academy of Arts and Sciences in 1990, and the Institute of Medicine in 1995.

Samuel H. Preston is Frederick J. Warren Professor of Demography and dean of the School of Arts and Sciences at the University of Pennsylvania. He has written on mortality patterns, world urbanization, and the history of child health, among other subjects. He advises the U.S. government on the reform of the social security system and is an authority on the methodologies applied in the U.S. census. He is a member of the U.S. National Academy of Sciences.

Directory

Alan Guttmacher Institute, 120 Wall Street, 21st Floor, New York, NY 10005. Telephone: (212) 248-1111, Email: info@guttmacher.org, Web: http://www.agi-usa.org
Organization that conducts research on contraceptive use, fertility, and other reproductive health issues

European Association for Population Studies, EAPS Secretariat, P.O. Box 11676, 2502 The Hague, Netherlands. Email: eaps@nidi.nl, Web: http://www.nidi.nl/eaps
Association of European population scientists, publishes the European Journal of Population

International Union for the Scientific Study of Population, 3-5 Rue Nicolas, 75890 Paris 20, France. Telephone: (33) 1 56 06 21 73, Email: iussp@iussp.org, Web: http://www.iussp.org
Association for population scientists that organizes meetings and working groups on topics of interest to the population field

MEASURE DHS+, ORC Macro Inc., 11785 Beltsville Drive, Suite 300, Calverton, MD 20705. Telephone: (301) 572-0958, Email: MEASURE@macroint.com, Web: http://www.measuredhs.com
A project funded by the U.S. Agency for International Development that assists developing countries in collecting and using data to monitor and evaluate population, health, and nutrition programs

Population Association of America, 8630 Fenton Street, Suite 722, Silver Spring, MD 20910. Telephone: (301) 565-6710, Email: info@popassoc.org, Web: http://www.popassoc.org
Association for population scientists, publishes Demography

Population Council, One Dag Hammarskjold Plaza, New York, NY 10017. Telephone: (212) 339-0500, Email: pubinfo@popcouncil.org, Web: http://www.popcouncil.org
Research organization that focuses on population and social policy, reproductive health, and family planning and other areas

Population Reference Bureau, 1875 Connecticut Avenue NW, Suite 520, Washington, DC 20009. Telephone: (800) 877-9881, (202) 483-1100, Email: popref@prb.org, Web: http://www.prb.org
Research organization that focuses on population trends, the environment, reproductive health, and HIV/AIDS

United Nations Department of Economic and Social Affairs, Population Division, 2 United Nations Plaza, Room DC2-1950, New York, NY 10017. Telephone: (212) 963-3183, Web: http://www.un.org/esa/population
Section that houses the Population Division and produces population-related data and research

U.S. Census Bureau, Washington, DC 20233. Telephone: (301) 457-4608, Email: webmaster@census.gov, Web: http://www.census.gov
U.S. government agency that conducts a census every ten years, distributes information about population trends, and provides data for administrative planning and policy

Further Research

Books

Bongaarts, John, and Rodolfo A. Bulatao, eds. *Beyond Six Billion: Forecasting the World's Population*. Washington, D.C.: National Academy Press, 2000.

Boserup, Esther. *Population and Technological Change.* Chicago: University of Chicago Press, 1981.

Bouvier, Leon F., and Jane T. Bertrand. *World Population: Challenges for the Twenty-first Century.* Santa Ana, Calif.: Seven Locks Press, 1999.

Coale, Ansley J., and Edgar Hoover M. *Population Growth and Economic Development in Low-Income Countries.* Princeton, N.J.: Princeton University Press, 1958.

Cohen, Joel. *How Many People Can the Earth Support?* New York: W. W. Norton, 1995.

Eberstadt, Nicholas. *Prosperous Paupers and Other Population Problems.* New Brunswick, N.J., and London: Transaction Publishers, 2000.

Ehrlich, Paul R. *The Population Bomb.* New York: Ballantine Books, 1968.

Ehrlich, Paul R., and Anne Ehrlich. *The Population Explosion*. New York: Simon and Schuster, 1990.

Ehrlich, Paul R., Anne Ehrlich, and Gretchen C. Daily. *The Stork and the Plow: The Equity Answer to the Human Dilemma.* New York: G. P. Putnam's Sons, 1995.

Graham-Smith, Francis, ed. *Population: The Complex Reality.* Cambridge: Cambridge University Press, 1994.

Jain, Anrudh, ed. *Do Population Policies Matter?* New York: Population Council, 1998.

Livi Bacci, Massimo. *A Concise History of World Population*. 3d ed. Oxford: Blackwell Publishers, 2001.

National Research Council, Board on Sustainable Development Policy Division. *Our Common Journey: A Transition toward Sustainability.* Washington, D.C.: National Academy Press, 1999.

National Research Council, Forum on Biodiversity Committee. *Nature and Human Society: The Quest for a Sustainable World.* Washington, D.C.: National Academy Press, 2000.

Presser, Harriet B., and Gita Sen, eds. *Women's Empowerment and Demographic Processes: Moving beyond Cairo.* Oxford: Oxford University Press, 2000.

Simon, Julian L. *Population and Development in Poor Countries: Selected Essays.* Princeton, N.J.: Princeton University Press, 1992.

———, ed. *The Economics of Population: Key Modern Writings.* Cheltenham: Edward Elgar Publisher, 1997.

———, ed. *The Economics of Population: Classic Writings.* New Brunswick, N.J.: Transaction Publishers, 1998.

Tsui, Amy, Judith Wasserheit, and John Haaga, eds. *Reproductive Health in Developing Countries.* Washington, D.C.: National Academy Press, 1997.

Weeks, John R. *Population: An Introduction to Concepts and Issues.* 7th ed. Belmont, Calif.: Wadsworth Publishing, 1999.

Articles and Reports

Ashford, Lori S. "New Population Policies: Advancing Women's Health and Rights." *Population Bulletin* 56, no. 1 (March 2001).

Bongaarts, John. "Population Growth and Global Warming." *Population and Development Review* 18, no. 2 (1992): 229–319.

———. "Population Policy Options in the Developing World." *Science,* 11 February 1994, 771–776.

Bongaarts, John, Brian C. O'Neill, and Stuart R. Gaffin. "Global Warming Policy: Population Left Out in the Cold." *Environment* 39, no. 9 (1997): 40–41.

"Conversations: Paul and Anne Ehrlich," November–December 1996, http://www.emagazine.com/november-december_1996/1196conv.html.

Council of Europe. *Recent Demographic Developments in Europe, 1999.* Strasbourg: Council of Europe Publishing, 1999.

Crenshaw, Edward M., Ansari Z. Ameen, and Matthew Christenson. "Population Dynamics and Economic Development: Age-Specific Population Growth Rates and Economic Growth in Developing Countries, 1965 to 1990." *American Sociological Review* 62 (December 1997): 974–984.

Dixon-Mueller, Ruth, and Adrienne Germain. "Reproductive Health and the Demographic Imagination." In *Women's Empowerment and Demographic Processes: Moving beyond Cairo,* edited Harriet B. Presser and Gita Sen, 69–94. Oxford: Oxford University Press, 2000.

Foster, Caroline. "The Limits to Low Fertility: A Biosocial Approach." *Population and Development Review* 26, no. 2 (2000).

Frejka, Thomas, and Gerard Calot. "Cohort Reproductive Patterns in Low-Fertility Countries." *Population and Development Review* 27, no. 1 (2001).

Kohler, Hans-Peter, ed. *European Journal of Population* 17, no. 1 (2001). Special issue on low fertility.

Malthus, Thomas Robert. *An Essay on Population,* http://www.ecn.bris.ac.uk/het/malthus/popu.txt.

Menken, Jane. "Demographic-Economic Relationships and Development." In *Population: The Complex Reality,* edited by Francis Graham-Smith, 59–70. Cambridge: Cambridge University Press, 1994.

Preston, Samuel. *Population and the Environment.* Distinguished Lecture Series on Population and Development. Liege, Belgium: International Union for the Scientific Study of Population, 1994.

———. "Population and the Environment: The Scientific Evidence." In *Population: The Complex Reality,* edited by Francis Graham-Smith, 85–92. Cambridge: Cambridge University Press, 1994.

"Think Tank with Ben Wattenberg: Is Population a Problem?" June 1994, http://www.pbs.org/thinktank/show_112.html. Interviews with John Bongaarts, Samuel Preston, and Julian Simon.

United Nations, Department of Economic and Social Affairs, Population Division. Recommendations for the Further Implementation of the World Population Plan of Action, Mexico City 6–14 August 1984, UN document E/CONF.76/19, 1984. Reprinted in *Population and Development Review* 10, no. 4 (1984): 758.

———. "Below Replacement Fertility." *Population Bulletin of the United Nations,* nos. 40/41 (1999).

———. *The Demographic Impact of HIV/AIDS.* Report on the Technical Meeting, New York, 10 November 1998. New York: United Nations, 1999.

———. *Demographic Yearbook, 1998.* New York: United Nations, 2000.

———. *Population, Environment and Development: The Concise Report.* New York: United Nations, 2001.

———. *World Population Prospects: The 2000 Revision, Highlights.* New York: United Nations, 2001.

———. *World Urbanization Prospects: The 1999 Revision. Data Tables and Highlights.* Working Paper, no. 161. New York: United Nations, 2001.

World Bank. *World Development Report, 2000–2001.* New York: Oxford University Press, 2001.

World Resources Institute. *World Resources, 1996–97.* New York: Oxford University Press, 1997.

World Resources Institute et al. *World Resources, 2000–2001.* New York: Oxford University Press, 2001.

Web Sites

Futures Group International
http://www.tfgi.com/software/spec.htm

Population and Development Review
http://www.popcouncil.org/publications/pdr/pdrabs.html

U.S. Census Bureau, International Programs Center
http://www.census.gov/ipc/www/world.html

Zero Population Growth
http://www.zpg.org

Documents

1. World Population Plan of Action

United Nations World Population Conference, Bucharest, Romania, 1974

The full text is reprinted in Population and Development Review *1, no. 1 (1975): 163.*

Extracts

17. Countries which consider that their present or expected rates of population growth hamper their goals of promoting human welfare are invited, if they have not yet done so, to consider adopting population policies, within the framework of socio-economic development, which are consistent with basic human rights and national goals and values. . . .

37. In light of the principles of this Plan of Action, countries which consider their birth rates detrimental to their national purposes are invited to consider setting quantitative goals and implementing policies that may lead to the attainment of such goals by 1985. Nothing herein should interfere with the sovereignty of any Government to adopt or not to adopt such quantitative goals. . . .

97. This Plan of Action recognizes the responsibility of each Government to decide on its own policies and devise its own programmes of action for dealing with the problems of population and economic and social progress.

2. Programme of Action

International Conference on Population and Development, Cairo, Egypt, 1994

The full text is reprinted in Population and Development Review *21, no. 1 (1995): 187; 21, no. 2 (1995): 437.*

Extracts

3.4 The objectives are to fully integrate population concerns into:

(a) Development strategies, planning, decision-making and resource allocation at all levels and in all regions, with the goal of meeting the needs, and improving the quality of life, of present and future generations;

(b) All aspects of development planning in order to promote social justice and to eradicate poverty through sustained economic growth in the context of sustainable development. . . .

4.3 The objectives are:

(a) To achieve equality and equity based on harmonious partnership between men and women and enable women to realize their full potential;

(b) To ensure the enhancement of women's contributions to sustainable development through their full involvement in policy- and decision-making processes at all stages and participation in all aspects of production, employment, income-generating activities, education, health, science and technology, sports, culture and population-related activities and other areas, as active decision makers, participants and beneficiaries;

(c) To ensure that all women, as well as men, are provided with the education necessary for them to meet their basic human needs and to exercise their human rights. . . .

6.3 Recognizing that the ultimate goal is the improvement of the quality of life of present and future generations, the objective is to facilitate the demographic transition as soon as possible in countries where there is an imbalance between demographic rates and social, economic and environmental goals, while fully respecting human rights.

This process will contribute to the stabilization of the world population, and, together with changes in unsustainable patterns of production and consumption, to sustainable development and economic growth. . . .

15.1 As the contribution, real and potential, of nongovernmental organizations gains clearer recognition in many countries and at regional and international levels, it is important to affirm its relevance in the context of the preparation and implementation of the present Programme of Action. To address the challenges of population and development effectively, broad and effective partnership is essential between Governments and non-governmental organizations (comprising not-for-profit groups and organizations at the local, national and international levels) to assist in the formulation, implementation, monitoring and evaluation of population and development objectives and activities.

REFUGEES

Stephen C. Lubkemann

At the start of 2000 approximately one out of every five hundred people were refugees, but many others who did not fit the standard definition of a refugee were displaced within their home countries or outside of them. Since World War II a growing body of international law and international humanitarian organizations have developed to assist and protect refugees and other displaced people. Forced migration and resolution of conflicts that cause displacement became central geopolitical concerns during the last decade. There has also been growing awareness of the traumatizing and dehumanizing conditions experienced by displaced people. Displacement thus represents not only a growing global policy concern but also one of the international community's most pressing moral and ethical challenges for the twenty-first century.

Historical Background and Development

Throughout history people have been forced to flee their homes to escape war, persecution, and natural disasters. During the twentieth century, however, for the first time on a global scale particularly massive forced migrations resulted from political and economic processes, including the growth of ethnonationalism, the demise of colonial rule, and the confrontation between capitalism and communism.

While attempts to assist uprooted people have been constant throughout history, it was only in the twentieth century that attempts were made to create international standards and institutions for protecting displaced people. The first international effort to assist refugees occurred after World War I, when the newly formed League of Nations appointed its first high commissioner for refugees in 1921. Although initially limited to assisting stateless refugees fleeing the Russian Revolution, the office of the commissioner eventually assisted millions of other displaced minorities expelled from countries in Eastern Europe that were attempting to create ethnically homogeneous nations. The political weakness of the League of Nations, however, limited its ability to prevail upon nations to receive asylum seekers. Most notably it failed to assist German Jews, millions of whom later perished in the Holocaust.

During and after World War II, the Allies, through the recently established United Nations, organized several efforts to assist the estimated 30 million to 45 million people displaced by the war. In 1950, as postwar reconstruction in Europe progressed, the United Nations High Commissioner for Refugees (UNHCR) was created to assist those who had not been resettled under previous UN programs. In 1951 the United Nations Convention Relating to the Status of Refugees established the basic definition of "refugees" recognized by international law today and specified the rights of this population and the obligations of states to uphold those rights (see Document 1) (see INTERNATIONAL LAW). These include freedom of thought, freedom of movement, freedom from torture or degrading treatment, freedom from *refoulement* (repatriation against one's will), and the right to safe asylum and to education and medical care. Also according to the convention, refugees must uphold the laws of their host countries and be civilians.

The UNHCR and the 1951 convention were initially limited in scope to Europe. Prior to the late 1950s displacement outside of Europe was only addressed on an ad-hoc basis through the creation of specialized UN agencies. For example, the United Nations Relief and Works Agency for Palestine Refugees in the Near East (UNRWA) was created in 1948 to assist the more than 700,000 Palestinians displaced in the creation of Israel and during the first Arab-Israeli war, and the United Nations Korean Reconstruction Agency (UNKRA) was created to assist civilians displaced by the Korean War. In contrast, the displacement of more than 14 million people during the violent partition of India and creation of Pakistan in 1947 was never addressed by a largely Eurocentric international community that felt few of its geostrategic interests were at stake.

By the late 1950s the emergence of new nations in the third world and the growing displacement of people during anticolonial struggles shifted the focus of international assistance to refugees outside of Europe. In Africa alone, the refugee population more than doubled, rising above one million during the 1960s. The UNHCR undertook its first activities outside Europe in 1958, when it assisted more than 150,000 Algerian refugees who had fled to Morocco and Tunisia during the war against French colonialism. It was only in 1967, however, that an international protocol made UNHCR's mandate and the terms of the 1951 convention applicable worldwide (see Document 2).

In 1969 the Organization of African Unity (OAU) drafted its own regional refugee convention that broadened the UN convention's definition of a refugee by including all people fleeing general conditions of war, violence, or danger resulting from public disorder. Most of these types of refugees were self-settled and received assistance from sympathetic populations, often of the same ethnic group, or by governments in neighboring countries that had recently fought anticolonial wars. Throughout the 1970s the UNHCR worked with host governments in Africa to create more than 100 planned settlement schemes for refugees that were integrated into national rural development projects.

The end of several major anticolonial struggles in Africa and the conclusion of the Pakistani civil war that led to the creation of Bangladesh allowed significant repatriations to take place. These positive developments, however, were offset in the 1970s and 1980s by the intensification of the cold war. Proxy wars fought with superpower backing produced massive new refugee flows in Afghanistan, Angola, Cambodia, El Salvador, Ethiopia, Mozambique, and Nicaragua. External interference also contributed to the displacements produced by ethnic conflicts in Burundi, Iran, Iraq, Lebanon, Rwanda, Sri Lanka, Sudan, and Uganda.

The massive scale of refugee flows significantly affected international policies toward the displaced. Policies of so-called humane deterrence, in which refugees were intercepted and turned back or simply refused entry into another country, became more commonplace. Large-scale refugee displacements were increasingly dealt with through the creation and management of huge refugee camps. Many refugees were forced into a semi-detained status and dependent on aid, sometimes for decades. Refugees in such conditions became particularly susceptible to the appeals of political factions organizing armed resistance movements, sometimes with superpower support, as in the cases of Afghans and Palestinians. Consequently camps increasingly became military targets during conflicts, endangering the lives of civilians.

The demise of the cold war raised hopes that many conflicts would end, and large-scale refugee repatriations might be possible. The end of apartheid in South Africa contributed to the resolution of conflicts in Mozambique and Namibia and, indeed, led in the early 1990s to successful large-scale repatriations. Lacking Soviet support, Vietnam withdrew its forces from Cambodia, paving the way for a peace settlement in 1991 and the largely successful repatriation of more than 360,000 refugees. In Central America the negotiated settlement of long-standing civil wars in El Salvador, Guatemala, and Nicaragua and the military defeat of an insurgency in Peru resulted in largely self-organized repatriations and resettlement of displaced populations.

Elsewhere, however, expectations that the end of the cold war would reduce the level of armed conflict and result in a dramatic decrease in displacement proved unfounded. Major displacement-producing conflicts in Afghanistan, Angola, Eritrea, Ethiopia, Palestine, Sri Lanka, Somalia, and Sudan persisted and even intensified, driven by agendas other than those of cold war rivalry. Meanwhile in the 1990s, a new wave of massive displacements resulted from the Persian Gulf War, the disintegration of the former Yugoslavia, the Rwandan genocide, and from civil wars in Burundi, Colombia, East Timor, Haiti, the Democratic Republic of Congo, Liberia, Sierra Leone, and in several of the former Soviet republics in Central Asia. By 2001 it was estimated that more than 35 million people were displaced worldwide (see ETHNIC AND REGIONAL CONFLICT).

Current Status

As defined by the 1951 UN convention, refugees are "individuals who are outside their own country and are unable to return as a result of a well-founded fear of persecution on grounds of race, religion, nationality, political opinion, or membership of a social group." The majority of people forcibly uprooted from their homes, however, do not fit the legal definition of a "convention refugee," either because they are forced to move for reasons other than those specified in the convention or they are displaced internally. The latter, people uprooted within their own countries, are referred to as internally displaced persons (IDPs). Displacement is thus a process that includes but is not limited to refugees. Moreover, individuals and groups adversely affected by displacement often include people other than those who are forced to move, such as the host populations in the impoverished third world nations where most uprooted people are resettled (see Table 1 and map, p. 533). The causes of displacement today are related to the global historical trends of the twentieth century, such as the changing structure of global geopolitics during and since the cold war, the rise of ethnonationalism, global environmental degradation, and such international development policies as structural adjustment.

Research

During the last three decades of the twentieth century, refugees attracted attention from various disciplines as the relationship between displacement and a wider variety of processes—for example, conflict resolution, development, demographic change, immigration, ethnonationalism, public health, and the environment—was increasingly recognized. The development of refugee and humanitarian studies as specialized interdisciplinary subfields in their own right is a response to the heightened international visibility of complex emergencies and growing concern about how to prevent and solve displacement. Current research examines the different types of displacement and their causes; the psychological, social, and public health effects of displacement on refugees; the broader political and economic effects of displacement; how to assist and protect the uprooted; and how these challenges are changing as a result of worldwide political and economic developments and trends.

Typically, people fleeing wars and political violence have been regarded as "involuntary migrants" and distinguished from "voluntary migrants" who move in order to improve their economic situation. Increasingly, however, researchers have questioned this distinction, pointing out that political conflict and economic well-being are often closely related. Many researchers argue that people are still displaced if they migrate because their economies have been devastated by warfare, even if they have not been targeted for violence. Cases such as Sudan and Ethiopia—where governments have forbidden the distribution of food aid within insurgent areas in an effort to starve populations thought to be harboring enemy troops—demonstrate how economic and political processes are often interrelated.

Wars can also produce forced migration by limiting options in the face of adverse environmental conditions. During the Mozambican civil war, the inability of internally displaced people to move from rural areas held by one warring faction to urban areas held by the other made it impossible to implement mechanisms for coping with drought that had worked in peacetime. The massive exodus across international borders that resulted was thus not caused solely by environmental hardship, but also by political conditions that constrained and hampered traditional coping mechanisms.

One area of recent but growing interest considers the relationship between the environment and displacement. Researchers conducting microlevel studies in Bangladesh and throughout Africa have coined the term *environmental refugees,* arguing that environmental insecurity can also be a cause of displacement. Work in this area is just beginning to consider the potential effects of worldwide environmental trends, such as global warming, on possible future displacement (see DEFORESTATION, FRAGILE ECOSYSTEMS, and GLOBAL WARMING). A related body of research focuses on how earthquakes, floods, and volcanic eruptions produce displacement. The effects of these natural disasters have been shown also to be related to broader social, political, and economic factors, since people who are economically and politically marginalized are more likely to have to live in areas that are more vulnerable to catastrophic events. Another dimension of this research examines displacement caused by development. It is estimated that the ongoing construction of the Three Gorges Dam on China's Yangtze River will displace up to 10 million people (see FRESHWATER).

While causes for displacement other than political violence and war have attracted increased attention, researchers and policymakers have also become increasingly concerned with categories of displaced people other than those who are officially categorized as refugees. Internally displaced persons are estimated to be almost twice as numerous as convention refugees, and the fact that wars are increasingly internal rather than between states has placed this population at the center of broader conflict resolution, peacebuilding, and human rights agendas (see PEACEMAKING AND PEACEBUILDING and HUMAN RIGHTS). Research on IDPs is harder to conduct because, unlike refugees, the internally displaced remain in war zones and are thus much less accessible. It is difficult to even reliably estimate their numbers.

As policymakers and aid practitioners have recognized that refugees are a part of a broader set of challenges that must be assessed and confronted jointly as "complex emergencies," researchers have also examined how displacement affects other populations, such as hosts. The rapid arrival of large numbers of destitute and desperate refugees can have far-reaching and often negative economic effects on host populations. This is especially true in developing countries, which bear the brunt of the world's refugee burden and where poverty may already be widespread. Social scientists working with refugees in Burundi, the Democratic Republic of Congo, Guinea, Kenya, Macedonia, Rwanda, Turkey, and Uganda have also examined how national political stability can be affected when population movements influence ethnic composition and balances of power.

The political effects of displacement on refugees themselves have also been studied, particularly situations in which refugee status has become particularly prolonged. Millions of Afghans, Palestinians, and Rwandans have been living in camps or other forms of exile for decades, with multiple generations born and reaching adulthood as refugees. In these cases, social identities can come to be tied to political objectives that paradoxically contribute to perpetuating the conflicts that produced displacement in the first place. Not surprisingly, refugee camps in Palestine and Lebanon have proved to be fertile grounds for recruitment by military groups fighting against Israeli occupation and in Afghanistan for groups engaged in that country's drawn-out civil war. In the case of the latter, the Taliban and its opponents originated in Afghan refugee communities in Pakistan.

Considerable research has been conducted on how displacement affects social organization, personal identities, and psychological well-being. In many refugee situations women and children comprise more than 80 percent of the population, and there is evidence that wartime violence and displacement often have more negative economic and social effects on women than on men. For example, refugee women are usually more vulnerable to predatory sexual violence than refugee men (see INTERNATIONAL CRIMINAL JUSTICE and WAR CRIMES). A great deal of policy research has attempted to identify the most vulnerable groups within displaced populations, such as women-headed households, children, the elderly, and people with disabilities, in order to devise ways to provide them with greater assistance and protection. Some nongovernmental and UN organizations focus exclusively on assisting vulnerable populations. UNICEF, for example, focuses on children and their mothers. The challenges of ensuring the safety of those assisted and those who assist them has also led to more research not only on how to protect refugees, but also on how to promote their human rights. The Social Science Research Council and several nongovernmental organizations have since 1999 been involved in a collaborative project on this topic.

The psychological effects of exposure to violence and displacement are attracting increased attention from mental health experts. The trauma of displacement can make adaptation to new and unfamiliar social and cultural environments particularly difficult. Differences between refugee cultural norms and those of host societies often create further tensions within refugee families, between spouses or between children and parents. The challenges of adaptation may be exacerbated by the uncertainty and insecurity of refugee status or by a sense of being highly constrained in a refugee camp environment. Prolonged reliance on aid while in refugee camps can also lead to diminished self-esteem and a sense of dependency and disempowerment.

One of the most fruitful recent areas of collaboration between researchers and organizations assisting refugees has been in understanding and improving humanitarian reactions to the health problems faced in complex emergencies. The catastrophic mortality rates in the Rwandan refugee camps in what was formerly Zaire (and subsequently renamed the Democratic Republic of Congo) sounded a wake-up call within the humanitarian community that has since sparked greater collaboration with the Centers for Disease Control and Prevention and research and training programs on refugee health at leading schools of public health, including Johns Hopkins and Columbia Universities. In 1999 the National Research Council Committee on Population created a Roundtable on Forced Migration to assess and encourage research on the demographic effects of displacement. Research on refugee mortality and morbidity represents only the first step in a much-needed examination of the broader demographic effects of forced migration. It is worth noting that Africa is the continent with the greatest number of IDPs and the world's highest fertility rates, fastest urban growth, and highest rates of HIV (see POPULATION and AIDS), yet the relationship of forced migration to these demographic processes has scarcely been examined.

With the growing reluctance of governments worldwide to take in immigrants, legal research has increasingly examined the relationship between refugees and immigration policies. In North America, considerable debate has revolved around the question of how "social groups" are defined and, in particular, whether women who face gender discrimination in their home countries qualify as refugees on the basis of their gender—that is, can "women" be considered a "social group." To date, court rulings have been inconsistent regarding this matter, even in cases where women face considerable physical danger, such as the threat of genital mutilation.

Another area of growing research is the field of humanitarian studies, which examines the activities of organizations that provide assistance. Humanitarian organizations have been confronted with research that is critical of how their activities are often more responsive to external pressures, such as funding, and to interorganizational rivalry and competition than to the needs of refugees themselves. Similarly, researchers have shown that humanitarian assistance that does not create sustainable solutions or use local capacities often cause considerable harm instead of helping refugee populations.

Policies and Programs

The United Nations High Commissioner for Refugees plays a leading role in international efforts to assist and protect refugees and displaced people worldwide. The number of "persons of concern" to the UNHCR in 2000 was 22.12 million, according to the UNCHR's *2000 Global Refugee Trends.* Increasingly the majority of forced migrants do not meet the 1951 convention's restrictive criteria for who is recognized as a refugee under international law. The members of this group tend to be denied refugee status because they are internally displaced within their own countries, and thus have not crossed an international border, or because they have fled general conditions of insecurity or oppression rather than targeted or individualized political persecution. Of the 22.12 million people considered to persons of concern to the UNCHR, approximately one-third were IDPs or others who did not qualify as convention refugees.

Although regional international bodies such as the Organization of African Unity and the Organization of American States have extended the definition of a refugee to include individuals and groups forced to flee their countries because of conditions of generalized violence and insecurity rather than because of individual, specific persecution, at best these criteria have only been applied within these regions. In practice, countries throughout the world increasingly follow the lead of Western European and North American governments in limiting the number of refugees allowed to settle within their borders.

Such policies are a reaction by industrialized nations to two decades of rapid growth in the immigration of people fleeing deteriorating political and economic conditions in the developing world, such as Haiti, Mexico, and Nigeria, and the former communist bloc, such as Romania and Nicaragua. These immigrants relocated in search of greater opportunity in the West. Such flows have been fed by the globalization of mass communication, which has increased awareness of and aspirations for the opportunities available in many industrialized nations, and by international transportation systems that facilitate transcontinental travel.

Since the UNCHR can only advise individual states on how to interpret the refugee convention's criteria to individuals seeking asylum within their borders, governments have been able to restrict whom they accept as refugees in ways that serve their political and economic interests. Fears of the negative economic effects of excessive immigration have led industrialized nations to interpret the convention's criteria in ever more restrictive terms. Thus, for example, some North America courts in the 1990s recognized that asylum seekers had fled their homes because of a legitimate fear of violence but still denied them refugee status because it was determined that they were being persecuted for "nonpolitical" reasons, such as sexual orientation or gender.

Governments have also developed ways to provide temporary relief for people fleeing insecurity without incurring the legal obligations implied in granting convention refugee status. Throughout Europe and North America, different forms of temporary protection status (TPS) have been created that provide haven for displaced people fleeing generalized violence until it is safe for them to return. During their stay, they are usually not afforded the social benefits to which refugees are entitled, such as education and employment or the possibility of seeking asylum or permanent resettlement. Although such policies were put forth initially as a short-term measure, prolonged insecurity and challenging conditions, as in, for example, Liberia and Guatemala, have led to annual renewals of TPS status for up to a decade for some displaced populations in the United States.

In the most extreme cases, industrialized nations have resorted to more severe measures to prevent immigrant flows from forced migration. European Union states have refused entry to some asylum seekers on the grounds that they had already passed through "safe countries" en route from their countries of origin. Heavy fines have been imposed on airlines that transport asylum seekers who do not already have visas. Even more draconian and legally dubious measures have involved intercepting refugees before they arrive on host country shores and turning them back without asylum hearings. This was the U.S. government's policy toward thousands of Haitian boat people who sought to land on U.S. shores during the 1990s. These increasingly restrictive measures represent a policy of "containment," often seen as an attempt to create "fortress" regions, that make access to forced and other migrants more difficult.

Such policies have not stemmed the rising tide of forced migrants, but instead has produced greater levels of clandestine immigration into industrialized nations while deferring the economic burden of displacement to less industrialized countries, which are even more adversely affected by massive refugee influxes. Meanwhile, the level of financial assistance that industrialized nations provide to international organizations and third world nations to assist refugees has also diminished. With the unwillingness of governments everywhere to host refugees, violence and hostility from host populations and governments toward them has grown. Even governments that have long proven to be generous hosts, such as Iran and Tanzania, carried out large-scale forced repatriations during the late 1990s and sealed their borders against further refugee flows.

Restrictions on asylum are also reducing the options for the displaced in ways that subject them to greater risk of violence. One example is the creation of so-called safe zones, or safe havens, within areas of conflict as an alternative to allowing refugees to cross international borders. EU countries already overwhelmed by massive population influxes that resulted from the fall of the Berlin Wall urged the creation of safe zones in Bosnia-Herzegovina because of their reluctance to receive refugees from the former Yugoslavia. Insufficient military means for ensuring refugees' safety, however, led to notorious calamities in 1995 as the safe zones in Srebrenica and Zepa were overrun, and thousands of Bosnian civilians were massacred.

The appointment in 1992 of the first UN special representative on internally displaced persons represented a critical step in institutionalizing international concern about this group of people. Although the UNHCR's mandate technically does not extend to IDPs, in practice the agency with more frequency has been authorized on a case-by-case basis to extend its "good offices" in order to assist IDPs. At the same time other international organizations, such as the International Organization for Migration (IOM), have come to play a major role in assisting IDPs, often in conjunction with or support from the UNCHR.

Assisting and protecting internally displaced persons pose particularly thorny challenges to the international community because, as noted above, these populations tend to be in areas where wars are still actively being fought. National governments, often parties in these conflicts, are sometimes reluctant to allow food or other aid to be provided to civilians whom they believe are harboring or supporting rebel factions. Conversely, insurgent groups may see assistance as tacitly supporting the regimes that they are trying to overthrow when it is only provided to government-controlled areas or through government-approved channels.

The increase in the number of IDPs and the fact that fortress policies do not successfully contain forced migration flows has led the international community to consider how to prevent displacement in the first place. In the 1990s the international community took unprecedented steps by intervening in the internal affairs of countries, for example, in Iraq and Serbia, in order to protect displaced people and to prevent forced migration flows across international borders. There remained, however, a reluctance on the part of most states and international organizations to challenge the principle of national sovereignty by interfering in countries' internal affairs. The issue of how to assist displaced populations thus presented new challenges to policymakers in addressing conflicts that produced large numbers of IDPs, such as in Bosnia-Herzegovina, Chechnya, Colombia, Iraq, Liberia, Rwanda, Sierra Leone, and Sri Lanka. The fact that the United Nations is an organization premised on the sovereignty of its members along with the requirement that the UNCHR act at the request and with the permission of sovereign governments have made it particularly difficult for the UNCHR to provide assistance in some of these cases. Although the international community of nongovernmental organizations remains divided on this issue, some groups have taken positions that clearly prioritize assistance at the expense of considerations of national sovereignty. This was the case in Liberia, Sierra Leone, and Somalia.

It is important to note that over the last three decades, nongovernmental organizations such as CARE, Catholic Relief Services, Doctors Without Borders, the International Rescue Committee, Oxfam International, and Save the Children have come to play a pivotal role in organizing and providing assistance to displaced and war-affected people worldwide. Many of these organizations work with the UNCHR, sometimes doing much of the operational work on the ground. Often they have also influenced policymakers and national governments by bringing the plight of displaced people to the attention of the media, as in the cases of Rwanda and Kosovo.

The nature of post–cold war conflicts presents considerable new challenges to organizations that want to assist the displaced. Many civil wars—such as those in the former Yugoslavia and Rwanda—have been driven by ethnonationalist sentiments in which military forces have directly targeted civilian populations in an effort to eliminate or uproot minorities, a process called ethnic cleansing. In these cases humanitarian efforts to assist the displaced do not serve the interest of warring parties and therefore are often hindered. Long-term solutions to the displacement produced by ethnically driven violence may be particularly difficult to find. Repatriation efforts that bring ethnic groups back into contact often spark renewed violence, "revenge killings," and new displacement, as was witnessed in Kosovo.

In other situations, warring parties have an interest in the persistence of conflict. The "blood diamond trade" in Sierra Leone and narcotrafficking in Colombia are cases in which the targeting of populations and ongoing displacement help perpetuate the conditions of violence, instability, and insecurity upon which illegal profitable activities thrive. Finally, in some places, as in Somalia, humanitarian aid itself is appropriated by combatants, transforming assistance intended for refugees into a means of supporting the conflict that is producing displacement.

As policymakers and humanitarian organizations have struggled with the challenges of assisting people who remain in harm's way and may even be purposely targeted, there has been a shift away from a primary focus on assistance to a greater consideration of how to ensure that those assisted and those assisting are also protected from violence. Some organizations in the international humanitarian community have started to place greater emphasis on promoting the human rights of the displaced. Thus, Doctors Without Borders—recipient of the 2000 Nobel Peace Prize—publicly denounces human rights violations, even if it insults governments or controlling entities and thereby prevents them from carrying out assistance activities. In some situations in which assistance has been diverted to serve the interests of combatants (such as in the Rwandan refugee camps in eastern Zaire) or where human rights violations have been particularly grave (such as the Taliban's mistreatment of women in Afghanistan), some organizations have ceased their assistance activity. Other groups, such as the International Committee of the Red Cross, have chosen not to comment on human rights violations and to remain politically neutral in order to continue to provide assistance, even if it is diverted or has unintended and undesired consequences.

There have been important recent collaborative attempts to improve humanitarian action and advocacy despite a considerable range of positions within the humanitarian community and problems of coordination among independent and often competing organizations. Important developments in this direction include the establishment in the mid-1990s of Interaction, a coalition of more than 165 associations involved in humanitarian work, and the SPHERE initiative, the project to draft a voluntary charter with standards and ethical principles for humanitarian action.

Humanitarian assistance is only one component necessary for the solution of the challenges arising from the creation of refugees and internally displaced persons and the set of interrelated political, economic, and military problems that together constitute complex emergencies. Although international humanitarian assistance efforts continue to gradually expand in scope to provide aid to all populations affected by displacement—including IDPs, hosts, and even those left behind by forced migrants in devastated war zones, or the "displaced in place"—it has become increasingly evident that humanitarian action can only be effective if the more fundamental political and economic roots of displacement and conflict are also addressed.

Regional Summaries

North America

In contrast to other regions of the world, North America consistently has been a receiver of refugees rather than a producer of displacement. Throughout the cold war, the United States pursued an immigration policy in line with its strategic political objectives by granting asylum almost exclusively to people fleeing communist bloc countries, including Cuba, Nicaragua, and Vietnam, while generally refusing to assist people fleeing violence in countries with U.S.-supported regimes, such as El Salvador. In the 1980s strong negative public reaction against the wave of Cubans arriving in the Mariel boatlift, Indochinese refugees, and rising illegal Mexican immigration sparked the U.S. government to introduce measures aimed at restricting refugee intake, a trend that has gained momentum since. New policies included intercepting Haitian refugees at sea before they reached U.S. territorial waters, detaining them or turning them back without asylum hearings. Narrowing interpretations of the

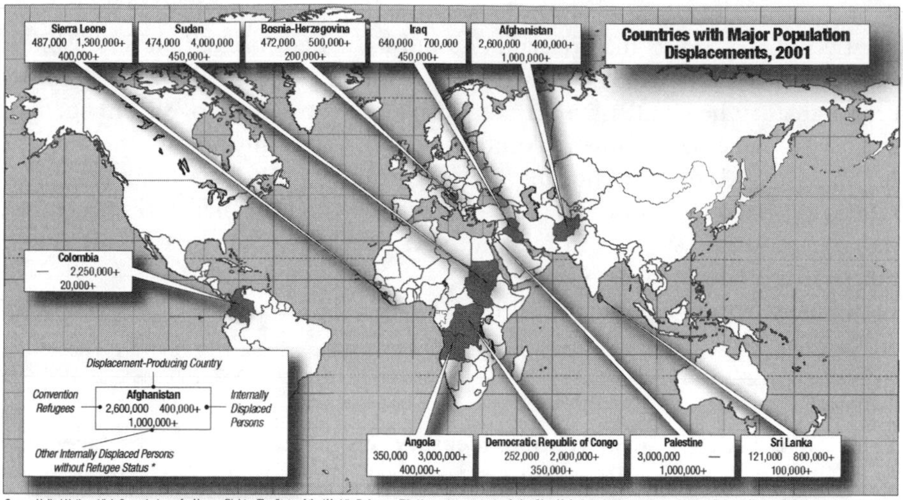

Source: United Nations High Commissioner for Human Rights, *The State of the World's Refugees: Fifty Years of Humanitarian Action* (New York: Oxford University Press, 2000); U.S. Committee on Refugees, *World Refugee Survey* (Washington, D.C.: USCR, 2001); and other resources.

refugee convention placed difficult burdens of proof on asylum seekers. Canada pursued policies aimed at restricting the influx of immigrants, but its government has proven more even-handed in granting refugee status to people fleeing coercive regimes.

In the aftermath of the attacks against the United States on 11 September 2001, further restrictive measures are likely as officials struggle to find constitutional methods to increase control over U.S. borders. In the 1990s Canada and the United States introduced temporary protection status to assist asylum seekers without granting them refugee status on the assumption that they would eventually return home. The unforeseen prolongation of insecurity in some refugees' countries of origin has created problems for them. Many have lived in the United States for almost a decade, during which time their social ties back home have eroded, and their attachment to their host society has grown.

Convention refugees hosted in region: 650,000
IDPs: not applicable

Latin America

During the 1990s, after three decades of widespread political violence that produced massive displacements, Latin America crafted political or military resolutions for a number of conflicts that allowed displaced populations to return home. The most alarming exception to this trend is the escalating civil war in Colombia, where in 2001 more than 2.1 million people are estimated to be internally displaced, according to the U.S. Committee for Refugees's "World Refugee Information, Country Report: Colombia," the third largest group of IDPs worldwide, thousands more have fled to neighboring countries. This decades-old civil war involving left-wing guerrillas, right-wing paramilitary groups, and narcotraffickers has significantly escalated as the result of the

U.S. government's controversial decision to provide more than $1 billion in mostly military aid to the government and its armed forces. The intensification of the civil war has increased displacement, in particular from rural to urban areas, where IDPs live in conditions of worsening poverty in shantytowns. Displacement across Colombia's border is also threatening the stability of neighboring countries hosting growing numbers of forced migrants. Elsewhere in Latin America, internal conflicts producing smaller displacement flows continue to simmer in the southern Mexican province of Chiapas, in neighboring Guatemala, and in Peru.

Convention refugees hosted in region: 61,000
IDPs: more than 2,300,000

Europe

The last decade of the twentieth century witnessed massive displacement within Europe, primarily resulting from the disintegration of the former Yugoslavia in successive waves of ethnonationalist strife. Beginning in 1991 ethnic conflict in Croatia, one of the former constituent states of Yugoslavia, produced more than 200,000 refugees and 350,000 IDPs, followed by civil war in Bosnia-Herzegovina, which produced almost 1.2 million refugees and 1.3 IDPs between 1992 and 1995. The conflict in Kosovo has produced more than 1 million refugees and 300,000 IDPs since 1998. Unrest in Kosovo also sparked further ethnonationalist tensions in neighboring Macedonia. These conflicts were motivated by nationalist ideologies, also witnessed earlier in the century, that espouse the creation of ethnically homogenous nations, if necessary by ethnic cleansing.

Western European governments responded to their diminishing need for immigrant labor, rising xenophobia among their citizens, and massive immigration from former Eastern bloc countries by instating policies making it harder to obtain asylum and to enter EU countries in the first place. One example of this latter policy is diverting refugees to safe third countries through which they passed en route from their countries of origin. Throughout the 1990s EU states sought to harmonize their asylum and border control policies through a series of agreements, including the Dublin and Schengen Conventions. The overall trend has been toward narrower interpretations of the 1951 refugee convention and a barrage of measures that hinder refugees from resettling in what is now often described as "Fortress Europe."

Convention refugees hosted in region: 2,600,000
IDPs: 1,600,000

Africa

In 2001 Africa was estimated to have approximately 30 percent of the world's refugees and 50 percent of the world's IDPs. With only 12 percent of the world's total population, Africa, the most impoverished region of the world, hosts 38 percent of all uprooted people. Displacement on the continent is concentrated in four subregions that have experienced political violence for more than a decade: West Africa, an area affected by protracted civil wars in Liberia and

Sierra Leone; the Great Lakes region in the central and eastern part of the continent, where civil and interstate conflicts in Burundi, the Democratic Republic of Congo, Rwanda, and Uganda have produced massive forced migration flows; in and around Angola, where a twenty-five-year civil war continues to rage; and in the northeastern Horn, where reignited and intensified civil conflict persists within Ethiopia, between Ethiopia and Eritrea, and in Sudan and Somalia. Smaller pockets of displacement in northwest Africa have resulted from civil wars in Algeria and in the Western Sahara. Southern Africa has proven to be the one "bright spot" for the continent during the last decade, with the resolution of conflicts in Mozambique, Namibia, and South Africa that led to largely successful repatriation efforts. With the end of anticolonial struggle and a deterioration in economic conditions throughout the continent, however, African governments are increasingly reluctant to host refugees, who are seen as a growing threat to national security and economic development.
Convention refugees hosted in region: 3,523,000
IDPs: approximately 12,000,000

Middle East and Central Asia

The Middle East and Central Asia have the world's largest number of convention refugees—more than 8 million—and two of the world's three largest producers of displacement: Afghanistan and Palestine, both the source of more than 4 million refugees each. This area hosts approximately half of the world's total convention refugees, with more than 2 million refugees from Afghanistan living in Pakistan and Iran, and 1.6 million Palestinian refugees—as well as another 800,000 displaced without official status—living in Jordan alone. The Palestinians are also the world's longest-standing refugee population, dating back in origin to the events surrounding the creation of Israel and the 1948 Arab-Israeli war. This ethnoreligious and political conflict has proven to be one of the most intractable problems of the last half century and has continually produced displacement throughout the region, most recently as a result of the al-Aqsa intifada in Palestine, the uprising that erupted in September 2000 against Israeli occupation of East Jerusalem, Gaza, and the West Bank.

Massive new waves of Afghan refugees were reported in the wake of U.S. military actions against the Taliban regime in Afghanistan after the 11 September 2001 attacks against the United States. These forced migrants joined an estimated 400,000 people who had fled Afghanistan's civil war earlier during the year and more than 3 million fellow citizens who were already living as displaced persons in Iran and Pakistan. Faced with such overwhelming numbers, neighboring regimes have proven unwilling to receive more Afghans and have even carried out forcible repatriations.

Another major refugee-producing country in the region is Iraq, with more than 450,000. Meanwhile, conflicts within and among several of the former Soviet Central Asian republics and the Chechen conflict within the Russian Federation account for more than 1 million displaced people, only a small fraction of whom are convention refugees. In another of the world's longest displacements, hundreds of thousands of Kurds remain displaced primarily within

Iran, Iraq, Syria, and Turkey. There are at least 200,000 stateless Kurds in Syria alone.
Convention refugees hosted in region: 3,700,000 (excluding 4,000,000 Palestinians administered by UNRWA)
IDPs: more than 4,000,000

South Asia, East Asia, and the Pacific

The resolution of several major conflicts in Indochina during the early 1990s led to major repatriations that significantly reduced the number of refugees in this region to fewer than 800,000. Slightly fewer than 300,000 refugees and more than 250,000 IDPs resulted from the violence that followed East Timor's successful referendum for independence from Indonesia in1999 , as anti-independence militia and the Indonesian military collaborated in a crackdown after the voting. Although the majority of IDPs and refugees had returned home by the end of 2000, more than 120,000 refugees—many of whom are related to former civil servants of the Indonesian regime—remained displaced in West Timor. Meanwhile, more than 250,000 refugees and an estimated equal number of illegally settled displaced persons from Burma's oppressive military junta remained in neighboring countries.

The number of the region's IDPs has risen dramatically because of the persistence of long-entrenched civil war in Sri Lanka, where more than 200,000 new forced migrants brought the total number of internally displaced people to more than 750,000 in 2000, and in Indonesia, where new strife between Christians and Muslims produced an estimated 800,000 IDPs in 1999–2000. The ongoing secessionist movements in Punjab and Kashmir in northern India are also estimated to have produced a significant if uncertain number of IDPs.
Convention refugees hosted in region: 830,000
IDPs: 3,900,000

Data

Table 1 Refugee Populations in Selected Host Countries, 2001

Host Country	Number of Refugees
Jordan	1,600,000 (plus approx. 1,000,000 without status)
Germany	975,000 (plus 264,000 asylum seekers)
Guinea	501,000
Indonesia	162,000
Iran	1,835,000
Pakistan	1,200,000
Sudan	391,000
Tanzania	622,000
United States	513,000 (plus 580,000 asylum seekers)
Yugoslavia	500,000

Source: United Nations High Commissioner for Human Rights, *The State of the World's Refugees: Fifty Years of Humanitarian Action* (New York: Oxford University Press, 2000); U.S. Committee on Refugees, *World Refugee Survey* (Washington, D.C.: USCR, 2001); and other resources.

Case Study—Rwandans in Zaire 1994–1996: The Political Effects of Displacement and the New Dilemmas of Humanitarian Assistance

Throughout late 1994 and into 1995, the world was captivated by the media spectacle of the deplorable living conditions and appalling death rates experienced by hundreds of thousands of Rwandan Hutu refugees who had fled into Zaire, now the Democratic Republic of Congo. The media and even the international organizations assisting this population failed, however, to sufficiently examine the root causes of this displacement, which eventually led to disastrous consequences for the political stability of central Africa as a whole.

In early 1994 the Hutu-led government of Rwanda had incited the Hutu majority to engage in the genocidal killing of more than 800,000 members of the Tutsi ethnic minority that led in turn to the intensification of a Tutsi-led insurgency against the government. The eventual success of this insurgency resulted in the flight of more than 2 million Hutus into neighboring countries, including a large number of the extremists who had incited and perpetrated the genocide. Throughout eastern Zaire, the extremists quickly gained power in the largest refugee camps, leading to their militarization and use as bases for continued aggression against Rwanda in direct violation of the 1951 refugee and 1969 OAU conventions as well as to numerous human rights violations within the camps. No government was willing to take the military action necessary to separate the combatants from the civilians being used as "human shields."

Humanitarian organizations were thus forced to choose between withdrawing assistance critical for civilians' survival or continuing to provide assistance, knowing that they were also supporting war criminals who continued to fight and were actually controlling the flow of aid to civilians in order to control these noncombatants. Eventually the use of these camps as bases led to the camps being attacked by Rwandan government troops in alliance with insurgents in Zaire, leading in turn to that country's degeneration into a civil war that has since spilled over into or involved in some way most neighboring countries.

This case clearly demonstrates how the resolution of refugee problems is implicated in broader political issues that require resolution in order to effectively allow for the protection and assistance of the displaced. The intentional targeting and strategic manipulation of civilian populations by combatants in contemporary warfare creates dilemmas for humanitarian efforts, often forcing zero-sum game choices among equally important goals, such as assistance, protection, ensuring justice, and upholding human rights. The Rwandan case also provides an example of how displacement increasingly factors as a key *cause* of conflict rather than simply being a by-product.

Biographical Sketches

Francis Deng is a diplomat and former minister of foreign affairs for Sudan. Since 1992 he has served as the first special representative of the UN secretary-general for internally displaced persons. In this position, as a former senior research fellow at the

Brookings Institution and as a faculty member of the Graduate School at the City University of New York, Deng has been the most important scholarly and policy voice focusing international attention on the growing phenomenon of internal displacement. He is co-author of the landmark volumes *Masses in Flight: The Global Crisis of Internal Displacement* (1998) and *The Forsaken People: Case Studies of the Internally Displaced* (1998).

Barbara Harrell-Bond founded the first and largest contemporary refugee studies program, at Oxford University in the early 1980s, and continues to play a key role in the institutionalization and intellectual direction of refugee studies as an interdisciplinary subfield. While director of the refugee program at Oxford, Harrell-Bond founded the *Journal of Refugee Studies* and conducted anthropological research with refugees throughout Africa. Her seminal *Imposing Aid* (1986) established the baseline for the critical study of humanitarian practices and international policy toward refugees. Harrell-Bond is the most recognizable advocate for including refugee voices and perspectives in policymaking and research and against forms of aid that disempower refugees.

Larry Minear is the director of the Humanitarianism and War Project, currently based at Tufts University. He organized and co-directed the project in 1990, after working more than two decades as a humanitarian aid practitioner. The project has produced arguably the most thorough critical assessment of humanitarian action through a series of more than forty case-based studies drawing on more than 100 of the top specialists and leading practitioners and policymakers in the field. The Humanitarianism and War Project has played a significant role in stimulating reflection among humanitarian aid organizations and in the way humanitarian assistance is provided to refugees and other populations affected by complex emergencies.

Sadako Ogata is a scholar and former chair of the UNICEF executive board. In 1990 she became the first academic and female UN high commissioner for refugees, an office she held until 2000. Her tenure was marked by an expansion of the UNCHR's activities to encompass the growing number of displaced and war-affected people who are not recognized as convention refugees, in particular internally displaced persons. In part through her efforts, the link between international security and refugees was increasingly recognized.

Directory

Amnesty International, 322 8th Avenue, New York, NY 10001. Telephone: (212) 807-8400, Email: www.aiusa.org, Web: http://www.amnesty.org
Organization dedicated to promoting the rights of refugees and prisoners of conscience worldwide

CARE, 151 Ellis Street NE, Atlanta, GA 30303. Telephone: (800) 521-CARE, ext. 999, Email: info@care.org, Web: http://www.care.org
Organization that provides assistance in complex emergencies worldwide

Catholic Relief Services, 209 West Fayette Street, Baltimore, MD 21201-3443. Telephone: (410) 625-2220, Email: webmaster@catholicrelief.org, Web: http://catholicrelief.org
Faith-based organization that assists displaced and disadvantaged people worldwide

Center for Gender and Refugee Studies, University of California, Hastings College of the Law, 200 McAllister Street, San Francisco, CA 94102. Telephone: (415) 565-4720, Web: http://www.uchastings.edu/cgrs
Academic research, advocacy, and education center providing legal resources for female asylum seekers

Center for Migration Studies, 209 Flagg Place, Staten Island, NY 10304-1199. Telephone: (718) 351-8800, Email: cms@cmsny.org, Web: http://www.cmsny.org/index.htm
Nonprofit independent education and research institute focusing on the interdisciplinary study of international migration and refugees

Centre for Refugee Studies, 4700 Keele Street, York University, York Lanes Building, Suite 322, Toronto, ONT M3J1P3, Canada. Telephone: (416) 736-5663, Email: crs@yorku.ca, Web: http://www.yorku.ca/crs
Academic-based policy and research institute for refugee issues

Doctors Without Borders, 2040 Avenue of the Stars, 4th Floor, Los Angeles, CA 90067. Telephone: (310) 277-2793, Web: http://www.doctorswithoutborders.org
International organization dedicated to providing medical assistance in complex emergencies

European Council on Refugees and Exiles, 110 Clifton Street, Clifton Center, Unit 22, 3d Floor, London EC2A 4HT, United Kingdom. Telephone: (44) 171 729 5252, Web: http://www.ecre.org
Umbrella organization of seventy refugee-assisting agencies in twenty-five European countries

Human Rights Watch, 350 Fifth Avenue, 34th Floor, New York, NY 10118. Telephone: (212) 216-1221, Web: http://hrw.org
Organization advocating for human rights worldwide, including those of refugees, asylum seekers, migrants, and internally displaced persons

Humanitarianism and War Project, Feinstein International Famine Center, Tufts University, 11 Curtis Avenue, Somerville, MA 02144. Telephone: (617) 627-5949, Web: http://hwproject.tufts.edu
Academic research program focused on interdisciplinary analysis of humanitarian action

Interaction—American Council for Voluntary International Action, 1717 Massachusetts Avenue NW, Suite 801, Washington, DC 20036. Telephone: (202) 667-8227, Web: http://www.interaction.org
Umbrella organization of 165 voluntary agencies involved in humanitarian action and relief

International Federation of the Red Cross and Red Crescent Societies, Public Information Centre, 19 Avenue de la Paix, 1202 Geneva, Switzerland. Telephone: (41) 22 734 6001, Web: http://www.ifrc.org
World's largest humanitarian organization dedicated to improving the lives of vulnerable people

International Organization for Migration, 17 Route des Morillons, P.O. Box 71, 1211 Geneva 19, Switzerland. Telephone: (41) 22 717 9111, Web: http://www.iom.int
Intergovernmental organization working to provide humane responses to migration and displacement worldwide

International Rescue Committee, 122 East 42nd Street, 12th Floor, New York, NY 10168-1289. Telephone: 877-REFUGEE, Web: http://www.interscom.org/index.cfm
International organization dedicated to assisting people fleeing persecution or uprooted by violence

Jesuit Refugee Services, 1616 P Street NW, Suite 400, Washington, DC 20036. Telephone: (202) 462-0400, Web: http://www.JesRef.org
Faith-based organization that assists, accompanies, and defends the rights of people forcibly displaced worldwide

Johns Hopkins University School of Public Health Refugee and Disaster Studies Program, Bloomberg School of Public Health, 615 North Wolfe Street, Baltimore, MD 21205. Telephone: (410) 955-6878, Web: http://www.jhsph.edu/research/emergencies
Academic research and training program focusing on public health issues in complex emergencies and among forced migrants

Mailman School of Public Health, Program on Forced Migration and Health, Columbia University, 722 West 168th Street, New York, NY 10032. Telephone: (212) 305-3927, Web: http://cpmcnet.columbia.edu/dept/sph/popfam/rp/forced_health.html#1
Academic research and training program focusing on public health issues in complex emergencies and among forced migrants

Oxfam International, 26 West Street, Boston, MA 02111-1206. Telephone: (800) 77-OXFAM, Web: http://www.oxfam.org
Confederation of twelve nongovernmental organizations that provides emergency relief in developing countries

Refugee Studies Centre, Oxford University, Queen Elizabeth House, University of Oxford, 21 St. Giles, Oxford OX1 3LA, United Kingdom. Telephone: (44) 1865 270 725, Web: http://www.qeh.ox.ac.uk/rsp
Academic research center focusing on the interdisciplinary study of forced migration and related issues

Refugees International, 1705 N Street NW, Washington, DC 20036. Telephone: (202) 828-0110, Email: ri@refintl.org, Web: http://www.refintl.org
A nongovernmental organization responding to the needs of refugees and displaced and dispossessed people

United Nations High Commissioner for Refugees, P.O. Box 2500, 1211 Geneva 2, Switzerland. Telephone: (41) 22 739 8111, Web: http://www.unhcr.ch
UN agency involved in refugee assistance and protection worldwide

U.S. Committee for Refugees, 1717 Massachusetts Avenue NW, Suite 701, Washington, DC 20036. Telephone: (202) 347-3507, Web: http://www.refugees.org
Organization dedicated to defending the rights of uprooted people

Women's Commission for Refugee Women and Children, 112 East 42nd Street, New York, NY 10168. Telephone: (212) 551-3089, Web: http://www.womenscommission.org
Organization that advocates for the protection and well-being of displaced women, children, and adolescents

Further Research

Books

Allen, Tim, and Hubert Morsink, eds. *When Refugees Go Home.* Trenton, N.J.: Africa World Press,1993.

Black, Richard. *Refugees, Environment, and Development.* New York: Longman, 1998.

Black, Richard, and Khalid Koser, eds. *The End of the Refugee Cycle? Refugee Repatriation and Reconstruction.* New York: Berghahn, 1999.

Chimni, B. S., ed. *International Refugee Law: A Reader.* New Delhi: Sage Publications, 2000.

Cohen, Roberta, and Francis Deng. *Masses in Flight: The Global Crisis of Internal Displacement.* Washington, D.C.: Brookings Institution, 1998.

Daniel, E. V., and J. Knudsen, eds. *Mistrusting Refugees.* Berkeley: University of California Press, 1995.

Hanes, David W., ed. *Refugees in America in the 1990s: A Reference Handbook.* Westport, Conn.: Greenwood Press, 1996.

Harrell-Bond, Barbara. *Imposing Aid: Emergency Assistance to Refugees.* Oxford: Oxford University Press, 1986.

Indra, Doreen, ed. *Engendering Forced Migration: Theory and Practice.* New York: Berghahn, 1999.

Krufeld, Ruth M., and L. MacDonald Jeffrey. *Power, Ethics, and Human Rights: Anthropological Studies of Refugee Research and Action.* New York: Rowman and Littlefield Publishers, 1998.

Loescher, Gil. *Beyond Charity.* Oxford: Oxford University Press, 1993.

MacCrae, Joanna, and Anthony Zwi, eds. *War and Hunger: Rethinking International Responses to Complex Emergencies.* London: Zed Books, 1995.

Malkki, Liisa H. *Purity and Exile: Violence, Memory, and National Cosmology among Hutu Refugees in Tanzania.* Chicago: University of Chicago Press, 1995.

McDowell, Christopher, ed. *Understanding Impoverishment: The Consequences of Development-Induced Displacement.* New York: Berghahn Press, 1996.

Minear, Larry, and Tom Weiss. *Mercy under Fire: War and the Global Humanitarian Community.* Boulder: Westview, 1997.

Richmond, Anthony. *Global Apartheid.* Oxford: Oxford University Press, 1994.

Van Hear, Nicholas. *New Diasporas: The Mass Exodus, Dispersal and Regrouping of Migrant Communities.* London: University College London Press, 1998.

Zolberg, Aristide, Astri Suhrke, and Sergio Aguayo. *Escape from Violence: Conflict and the Refugee Crisis in the Developing World.* Oxford: Oxford University Press, 1989.

Articles and Reports

Crisp, Jeff. "Africa's Refugees: Patterns, Problems, and Policy Challenges." *Journal of Contemporary African Studies* 18, no. 2 (2000).

Dowty, A., and Gil Loescher. "Refugee Flows as Grounds for International Action." *International Security* 2, no. 1 (1996).

Kibreab, Gaim. "Environmental Causes and Impacts of Refugee Movements: A Critique of the Current Debate." *Disasters* 2, no. 1 (1997).

Malkki, Liisa. "National Geographic: The Rooting of Peoples and the Territorialization of National Identity among Scholars and Refugees." *Cultural Anthropology* 7, no. 1 (1992): 24–43.

Martin, Susan F. "Forced Migration and the Evolving Humanitarian Regime." *UNHCR New Issues in Refugee Research Working Papers,* no. 20, July 2000.

United Nations High Commissioner for Refugees. *The State of the World's Refugees: A Humanitarian Agenda.* Oxford: Oxford University Press, 1997.

———. *2000 Global Refugee Trends.* Geneva: United Nations High Commissioner for Refugees, 2001.

U.S. Committee for Refugees. "World Refugee Information, Country Report: Colombia," http://www.refugees.org/world/countryrpt/amer_carib/colombia.htm.

Waldman, Ronald, and G. Martone. "Public Health and Complex Emergencies: New Issues, New Conditions." *American Journal of Public Health* 89, no. 10 (1999): 1483–1485.

Weiner, Myron. "The Clash of Norms: Dilemmas in Refugee Policies." *Journal of Refugee Studies* 11, no. 4 (1998): 433–453.

Web Sites

Global IDP Survey
http://www.idpproject.org

International Association for Study of Forced Migration
http://www.uni-bamberg.de/~ba6ef3/iasfm.htm

Documents

1. UN Convention Relating to the Status of Refugees, 1951

Entered into force 22 April 1954

The full text is available at http://www.ufsia.ac.be/~dvanheul/genconv.html.

Extracts

The High Contracting Parties

Considering that the United Nations has, on various occasions, manifested its profound concern for refugees and endeavoured to assure refugees the widest possible exercise of these fundamental rights and freedoms,

Noting that the United Nations High Commissioner for Refugees is charged with the task of supervising international conventions providing for the protection of refugees, and recognizing that the effective co-ordination of measures taken to deal with this problem will depend upon the co-operation of States with the High Commissioner,
Have agreed as follows:

Article 1

Definition of the term "Refugee"

For the purposes of the present Convention, the term "refugee" shall apply to any person who:

As a result of events occurring before 1 January 1951 and owing to a well-founded fear of being persecuted for reasons of race, religion, nationality, membership of a particular social group or political opinion, is outside the country of his nationality and is unable or, owing to such fear, is unwilling to avail himself of the protection of that country; or who, not having a nationality and being outside the country of his former habitual residence as a result of such events, is unable or, owing to such fear, is unwilling to return to it.

The provisions of this Convention shall not apply to any person with respect to whom there are serious reasons for considering that:

(a) he has committed a crime against peace, a war crime, or a crime against humanity, as defined in the international instruments drawn up to make provision in respect of such crimes;

(b) he has committed a serious non-political crime outside the country of refuge prior to his admission to that country as a refugee;

(c) he has been guilty of acts contrary to the purposes and principles of the United Nations.

Article 2

General obligations

Every refugee has duties to the country in which he finds himself, which require in particular that he conform to its laws and regulations as well as to measures taken for the maintenance of public order. . . .

Article 33

Prohibition of expulsion or return ("refoulement")

No Contracting State shall expel or return ("refouler") a refugee in any manner whatsoever to the frontiers of territories where his life or freedom would be threatened on account of his race, religion, nationality, membership of a particular social group or political opinion.

The benefit of the present provision may not, however, be claimed by a refugee whom there are reasonable grounds for regarding as a danger to the security of the country in which he is, or who, having been convicted by a final judgment of a particularly serious crime, constitutes a danger to the community of that country.

2. Protocol Relating to the Status of Refugees of 31 January 1967

United Nations General Assembly, 4 October 1967

The full text is available at http://www.mapleconsult.com/pages/en/ref2.html.

Extract

Considering that the Convention relating to the Status of Refugees done at Geneva on 28 July 1951(hereinafter referred to as the Convention) covers only those persons who have become refugees as a result of events occurring before 1 January, 1951,

Considering that new refugee situations have arisen since the Convention was adopted and that the refugees concerned may therefore not fall within the scope of the Convention,

Considering that it is desirable that equal status should be enjoyed by all refugees covered by the definition in the Convention irrespective of the dateline 1 January 1951,
Have agreed as follows:

Article 1

General provision

The present Protocol shall be applied by the States Parties hereto without any geographic limitation, save that existing declarations made by States already Parties to the Convention in accordance with Article 1 B (1)(a) of the Convention, shall, unless extended under Article 1 B (2) thereof, apply also under the present Protocol.

TERRORISM

David Leheny

In early 1995, when a Japanese religious cult released sarin, a poison gas, on subway cars in Tokyo, government officials and security experts believed that they had seen the new face of terrorism. In the years following, as governments planned for the possibility of terrorist attacks with chemical or biological weapons, no one prepared for suicide missions to hijack airplanes and crash them into buildings, as happened at the World Trade Center towers in New York and the Pentagon, outside Washington, D.C. Terrorism surprises because it is designed to do just that. Although much discussed, terrorism is still poorly understood and difficult to confront. If the United States does lead an international war on terrorism, it may turn out to be the most important global issue facing policymakers during the next decade.

Historical Background and Development

The history of terrorism is in many ways a history of the reconstruction of the term as an unmitigated negative one. In the late nineteenth century, Russian anarchists opposing the czar's autocratic government freely used the term *terrorist* to describe themselves. They sought to replace an authoritarian government that protected the rich with one of their own, which would terrorize the rich. By forming clandestine organizations dedicated to the use of revolutionary violence, they aspired to use terror as a means of creating what they considered to be a more just political order.

With the development of revolutionary and postcolonial nationalist movements in much of the world after World War II, the use of terrorism expanded, and political actors sought to adapt it it to their more complex struggles. Political groups from Latin America to Africa to Southeast Asia began to incorporate the use of terror attacks into their campaigns to reorder social and political structures and extend their military advantage. In Lebanon, Hizballah (the Party of God) used car bombings against American troops stationed there in the 1980s; at the conclusion of Lebanon's civil war, Hizballah developed a political wing that advocates social policies to help religious groups and the poor in the southern part of the country.

For most of the industrialized world, terrorism became a hotly debated topic in the 1960s and 1970s for two reasons. First, groups protesting U.S. involvement in the Vietnam War increasingly turned to violence to bring down what they viewed as inherently exploitative and corrupt capitalist governments. Groups such as the Weathermen in the United States, the Red Army Faction in West Germany, the Red Army in Japan, and other groups, often made up of radical university students or recent graduates, carried out bombings, assassinations, and kidnappings to get their message out.

Probably more important over the long term was the decision of several nationalist movements from the developing world to present their causes on a global stage. Black September took hostage eleven Israeli athletes at the 1972 Olympic Games in Munich to publicize the plight of the Palestinians. Over the course of several days, the world watched the drama unfold on television, including the firefight that took the lives of nine hostages, five Black September members, and a German police officer.

Reference to the "stage" and the "drama" underscores one of the central aspects of what terrorism has become: it is today designed to reach an audience, and governments and terrorists alike ultimately perform roles as the world watches, fascinated. This has been particularly true in the case when the United States is under attack. The global reach of the U.S. government, the country's ostentatious wealth and power, and the ubiquity of its news media have made Americans valuable targets for terrorist groups in recent years. When members of the Palestine Liberation Front captured the *Achille Lauro* cruise ship in 1985, they could be confident that with several Americans on board their actions would be broadcast globally and their cause would receive more attention than it would have through nonviolent protest or polite requests for support from governments and media outlets.

The 1970s and 1980s also witnessed the recognition of "state terror," or the use of terrorist-style tactics by governments against their opponents. Examples include violence by left-wing governments, such as the Soviet Union, and by right-wing governments, such as Chile under General Augusto Pinochet (see INTERNATIONAL CRIMINAL JUSTICE and WAR CRIMES). Discussion of "state terrorism" is highly controversial, however, because governments are reluctant to accuse their allies of being terrorists, and they certainly do not consider their own actions terrorist in nature. The double standard in which government opponents are terrorists and governments ostensibly are not has left many doubtful about the fundamental utility of the terms *state terror* or *state terrorism* in politics.

Since the end of the cold war, terrorism has taken on new dimensions. As noted above, some specialists argue that so-called new terrorists are committed to millennial violence through the use, if possible, of weapons of mass destruction. Less controversial is the contention that networks of organizations using terrorist violence are increasingly connected through training, financing, and cooperation and are aided by the rapid transmission of information. The primary example of this type of organization is Osama Bin Laden's al-Qaeda network, which operated out of Afghanistan among other places until the United States disrupted it during its military campaign following the 11 September

2001 attacks on the World Trade Center and the Pentagon. With an international black market in arms, rapid transfer of funds through legitimate institutions as well as money-laundering operations, and the growing ability of organizations to use the Internet to recruit and to spread their message, terrorism is a truly global phenomenon. The 2001 attacks on the United States bear this out. The hijackers came from different nations and were loosely linked to a terrorist network with cells operating across a range of regions including Central Asia, North America, the Middle East, and Western Europe. They moved money across borders and lived openly in places such as Florida, where a multiethnic community made it difficult to discern anything suspicious about them.

Current Status

Research on terrorism has never been far removed from policy concerns and crises involving terrorism. Anti-terrorism policies and research on terrorism are both complicated by the fact that no one agrees precisely on what terrorism is. People who commit what might be considered a terrorist act do not view themselves as terrorists. Numerous academic and policy debates on the issue have devolved into rows over terminology such as who can rightfully be considered a terrorist. For the purposes here, a value-neutral perspective is used that views terrorism as a tactic whereby actors use politically motivated violence against targets primarily of symbolic value. The goal of a terrorist attack exceeds the immediate loss of life and destruction of property by also aiming to intimidate opponents by creating a crisis that commands attention and alerts an audience to the potential harm that might come to them.

Research

A terrorist act, designed to command attention, is considered a failure if no one watches. Indeed, attacks such as the Japanese Red Army's massacre at Lod Airport in 1972, the seizure of the *Achille Lauro* by the Palestine Liberation Front in 1985, and the kidnapping and murder of former Italian prime minister Aldo Moro by the Red Brigades in 1983 were compelling news stories around the world.

Debate has raged over whether there is something fundamentally new about terrorism in its most recent manifestations. Two concerns underscore research on the "new terrorism": millennial attacks and the use of weapons of mass destruction (see ARMS CONTROL). First, the spate of attacks by so-called millennial terrorist organizations seem designed not to achieve a discrete political result but to cause catastrophic damage in the hope of bringing about fundamental transformations in world politics and the social order. One might view the 1999 attacks on the U.S. embassies in Kenya and Tanzania in this light or Timothy McVeigh's 1995 bombing of the Alfred P. Murrah Federal Building in Oklahoma City. Some experts argue that unlike previous terrorist campaigns, in which limited actions were undertaken in the pursuit of clearly defined goals, the new terrorism knows no limits and the new terrorists kill as many people as possible in the pursuit of broader religious or ideological quests.

Second, with the end of the cold war and the development of an international black market for chemical, nuclear, and biological weapons, many observers are concerned that terrorists will be able to unleash incurable plagues or detonate nuclear devices in their millennial struggles. Ironically, the only confirmed case of a terrorist group's use of a weapon of mass destruction in an effort to kill thousands was entirely homegrown. The sarin attack by the Aum Shinrikyo (Supreme Truth) cult on the Tokyo subway in 1995 was made possible not because of the international arms market, but because the cult's members included several chemists trained at Japan's best universities. The attack killed eleven people, but had the group's timing and luck been somewhat different, hundreds or thousands more could easily have died. Some argue that the growth in broad-based religious and ideologically driven terrorist groups increases the likelihood that weapons of mass destruction will be used in terrorist attacks.

Not all terrorism specialists agree about the changing nature of terrorism. Some think that "old-fashioned terrorism" is very much alive and well, and that the vast majority of attacks will remain limited, carried out with conventional weapons, and tied to political struggles (see map, p. 551). As an example, they would likely refer to Osama Bin Laden's explicit political goal—to force the United States to withdraw its armed forces from bases in the Persian Gulf.

In addition to such debates about the face of terrorism, officials and experts also are delving deeper into what motivates terrorists to act. Most terrorism specialists, including Martha Crenshaw and Bruce Hoffman, take an eclectic approach that examines the political, psychological, and organizational issues of terrorism. If terrorism is viewed as a tactic, the conclusion could be reached that terrorism is no more easily eradicable than are war and disease. Researchers and policymakers have thus focused their efforts on two approaches. First, they have tried to establish reliable law enforcement and military techniques to prevent or respond to individual terrorist attacks. Second, they take into consideration the political context within which terrorism occurs. Although terrorist activities have some common elements, a solution that works to reduce terrorist violence between Catholics and Protestants in Northern Ireland might be wholly ineffective in curbing the large-scale training and financing of terrorists in failed states like Afghanistan, where the plot of the 11 September attacks on the United States were facilitated.

Policies and Programs

As a public policy issue, terrorism resembles crime. When it decreases, everyone wants to take credit; when it increases, everyone points fingers. As a general rule, there is no reliable way of assessing which anti-terrorism policies are most effective. Instead, governments have begun adhering to a series of international agreements designed to make it more difficult for terrorist groups to operate (see INTERNATIONAL LAW). Well-established and widely accepted UN conventions, such as the Convention against the Taking of Hostages (adopted in 1979), have helped to define categories of outlawed violence, while states continue to debate appropriate adherence to the International Convention for the Suppression of the Financing of Terrorism (adopted in 1999, but only signed and ratified by a small number of nations).

Global condemnation of terrorism and adherence to international conventions does not, however, mean that terrorism can be eradicated. Even in "safe" countries, crime still exists (see Documents 1 and 2). The goals of counterterrorism policies are to reduce terrorist violence and to make it easier for states to identify and eliminate the threat. For democratic states, it can be difficult to balance such policies with the rights of their citizenry (see HUMAN RIGHTS). In 1995, over intense objections from left-leaning activists, the British government passed a counterterrorism act largely aimed at constraining the actions of the Irish Republican Army (IRA) and its various offshoots. In the aftermath of the 11 September attacks on the United States, the Justice Department pushed for new counterterrorism measures that would give the government broader powers to establish wiretaps and to detain immigrants and other noncitizens without filing charges against them. Members of Congress, Democrats *and* Republicans, questioned whether these limitations on privacy and individual freedoms could be justified and whether they would really improve security. Similarly, after the sarin attack, the Japanese government—constrained by constitutional protections on the freedom to organize, to worship, and to speak freely—passed a law that specifically targeted the cult that carried out the attack but had little utility beyond that. Japanese civil liberties advocates, who invoke the extent to which the country's military government in the 1930s suppressed political and religious groups, have pushed strongly to limit the state's ability to investigate terrorist groups broadly.

For most states confronted with potential terrorist attacks, policy choices can be grouped loosely into three related and often complementary categories. The first is the military option, whereby government forces attempt to eliminate terrorist threats as they would an invading army. Most governments have special forces trained to deal specifically with clandestine groups that might be harboring weapons, holding hostages, or planning assaults. Israel's General Security Services and military force are good examples of this kind of force. This option is often popular because it appears to the public that the government is taking a "hard line" against terrorism. For instance, terrorists who attack Israel face the serious threat that their organizations or families will be targeted for retribution. It is not clear, however, that Israel has experienced a reduction in terrorist violence as a result of its use of the military option. Such tactics might instead radicalize political opponents, because innocent civilians can be killed and political options eschewed.

Another option available to states is to treat terrorism as a criminal matter best handled by law enforcement authorities through the criminal justice system. This approach essentially delegitimizes the terrorists' political aims by treating them as being no different from any other violent criminal. Most democratic states approach domestic terrorist threats in this way, and dedicate special divisions in police agencies primarily to counterterrorism, as is the case with the Federal Bureau of Investigation (FBI). The United States successfully pushed for the arrest and trial in 2000 of two Libyans accused of the 1988 bombing of Pan Am Flight 800 over Scotland in which more than two hundred people died. Although this was a largely peaceful conclusion to the investigation, the time lag, the acquittal of one defendant, and the absence of attention on Libyan leader Mu'ammar al-Qadhafi, who many believed was the mastermind behind the attack, made it an unsatisfying outcome for many American critics of the law-and-order approach.

Finally, states will acknowledge under some circumstances the political demands of terrorist groups and will enter into negotiations with them. Usually this is possible only when the government determines that it cannot easily defeat the movement using military or police tactics. This approach can be risky. Negotiations, even in good faith, can produce splinter groups that will continue to use acts of terror against old and new targets alike. Talks between the British government and the IRA seemed designed to create a lasting peace, for example, but peace in Northern Ireland has been elusive, in part because groups such as the IRA often have radical members who oppose any sort of compromise.

In practice, states often use a combination of measures to combat terrorism. Israel entered into negotiations with the Palestine Liberation Organization (PLO) and created the Palestinian Authority under the leadership of PLO chairman Yasir Arafat. Even so, it continues to use military force against Palestinian groups. The U.S. government has sometimes relied on legal approaches, such as the Pan Am case, but has also resorted to military force, as in the 2001–2002 air strikes and military attacks on Afghanistan.

As noted above, what makes terrorism such a tricky issue is that it is a bad word. Neither the IRA nor the various Palestinian groups would use the word *terrorist* to describe themselves, but would instead use the word to characterize their opponents while claiming that their actions are legitimate forms of resistance. The U.S. government maintains a list of "foreign terrorist organizations" and another of "state sponsors of terrorism," which are those governments that allegedly lend support to terrorist groups. These lists are, however, terribly political and are contested and debated whenever the U.S. government releases a new list or engages in any dialogue on international counterterrorism.

Regional Summaries

Americas

Until 2001 terrorism from abroad was not regarded as a major security threat in North America. In Canada, an extremist wing of the Québécois separatist movement calling itself the Front for the Liberation of Quebec has occasionally carried out low-level acts of political violence. In 1995 Timothy McVeigh, a right-wing extremist and U.S. army veteran, detonated a truck bomb at the Alfred P. Murrah Federal Building in Oklahoma City, killing 168 people. McVeigh had become increasingly tied to a right-wing militia movement that considers the federal government illegitimate and part of a Zionist conspiracy to dominate the globe. He viewed his attack as the moment that would catalyze

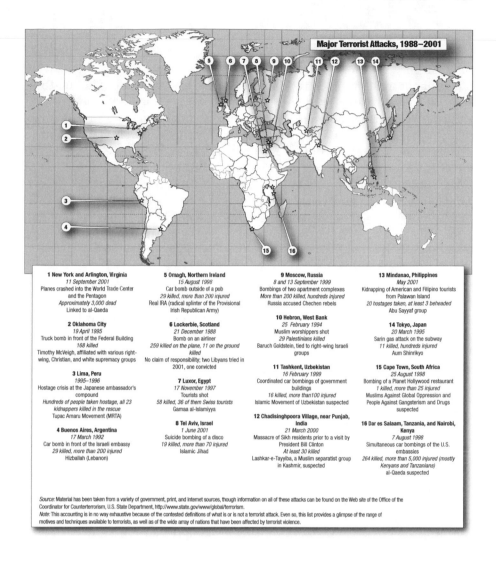

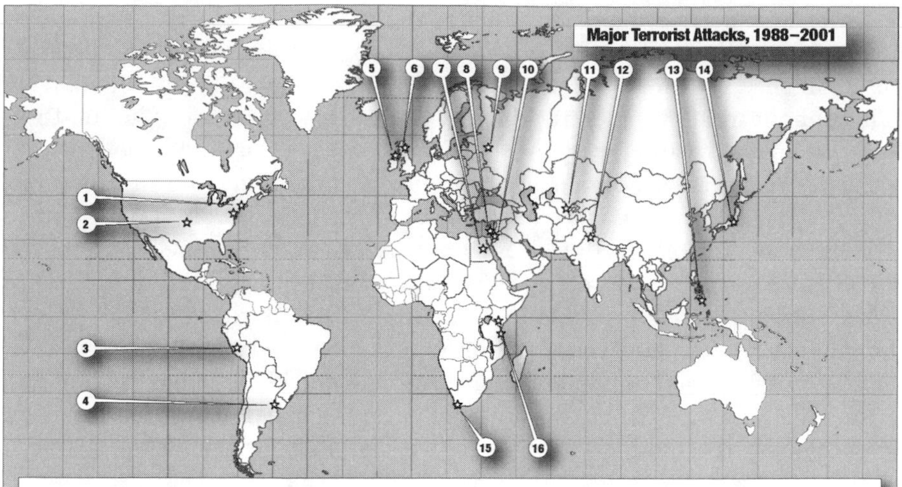

1 New York and Arlington, Virginia
11 September 2001
Planes crashed into the World Trade Center and the Pentagon
Approximately 3,000 dead
Linked to al-Qaeda

2 Oklahoma City
19 April 1995
Truck bomb in front of the Federal Building
168 killed
Timothy McVeigh, affiliated with various right-wing, Christian, and white supremacy groups

3 Lima, Peru
1995–1996
Hostage crisis at the Japanese ambassador's compound
Hundreds of people taken hostage, all 23 kidnappers killed in the rescue
Tupac Amaru Movement (MRTA)

4 Buenos Aires, Argentina
17 March 1992
Car bomb in front of the Israeli embassy
29 killed, more than 200 injured
Hizballah (Lebanon)

5 Omagh, Northern Ireland
15 August 1998
Car bomb outside of a pub
29 killed, more than 200 injured
Real IRA (radical splinter of the Provisional Irish Republican Army)

6 Lockerbie, Scotland
21 December 1988
Bomb on an airliner
259 killed on the plane, 11 on the ground killed
No claim of responsibility; two Libyans tried in 2001, one convicted

7 Luxor, Egypt
17 November 1997
Tourists shot
58 killed, 36 of them Swiss tourists
Gamaa al-Islamiyya

8 Tel Aviv, Israel
1 June 2001
Suicide bombing of a disco
19 killed, more than 70 injured
Islamic Jihad

9 Moscow, Russia
8 and 13 September 1999
Bombings of two apartment complexes
More than 200 killed, hundreds injured
Russia accused Chechen rebels

10 Hebron, West Bank
25 February 1994
Muslim worshippers shot
29 Palestinians killed
Baruch Goldstein, tied to right-wing Israeli groups

11 Tashkent, Uzbekistan
16 February 1999
Coordinated car bombings of government buildings
16 killed, more than100 injured
Islamic Movement of Uzbekistan suspected

12 Chadisinghpoora Village, near Punjab, India
21 March 2000
Massacre of Sikh residents prior to a visit by President Bill Clinton
At least 30 killed
Lashkar-e-Tayyiba, a Muslim separatist group in Kashmir, suspected

13 Mindanao, Philippines
May 2001
Kidnapping of American and Filipino tourists from Palawan Island
20 hostages taken, at least 3 beheaded
Abu Sayyaf group

14 Tokyo, Japan
20 March 1995
Sarin gas attack on the subway
11 killed, hundreds injured
Aum Shinrikyo

15 Cape Town, South Africa
25 August 1998
Bombing of a Planet Hollywood restaurant
1 killed, more than 25 injured
Muslims Against Global Oppression and People Against Gangsterism and Drugs suspected

16 Dar es Salaam, Tanzania, and Nairobi, Kenya
7 August 1998
Simultaneous car bombings of the U.S. embassies
264 killed, more than 5,000 injured (mostly Kenyans and Tanzanians)
al-Qaeda suspected

Source: Material has been taken from a variety of government, print, and Internet sources, though information on all of these attacks can be found on the Web site of the Office of the Coordinator for Counterterrorism, U.S. State Department, http://www.state.gov/www/global/terrorism.
Note: This accounting is in no way exhaustive because of the contested definitions of what is or is not a terrorist attack. Even so, this list provides a glimpse of the range of motives and techniques available to terrorists, as well as of the wide array of nations that have been affected by terrorist violence.

a Christian war to replace the government. Although the Oklahoma City bombing shocked Americans, it would pale in comparison to the 2001 attacks on the World Trade Center towers and the Pentagon, in which some three thousand people died.

Unlike North America, Central and South America have been vulnerable to terrorism for decades. Throughout the 1960s and 1970s, left-wing radical movements, often made up of university students, carried out terrorist attacks, including kidnapping the U.S. ambassador to Brazil in 1969. These groups were cited as justification for the consolidation of right-wing military governments in Brazil, Chile, and Argentina. Once established, these regimes institutionalized state terror and killed more people than the alleged terrorists they sought to eradicate. The precise numbers of victims will probably never be known.

Cold war strategies helped to support the civil wars of Central America in the 1970s and 1980s, including in Nicaragua and El Salvador, where terrorist-style violence was employed by the state and its opponents in both countries. Throughout the 1980s in Peru, the Maoist Sendero Luminoso (Shining Path) killed thousands before being crushed by a police and military crackdown in the early 1990s. More durable, however, has been the brutal war in Colombia, where the U.S.-backed government has confronted the Revolutionary Armed Forces of Colombia (FARC). Rightist militias with connections to the Colombian military have carried out brutal attacks, slaughtering villages of FARC supporters as warnings to other potential adversaries. FARC, which is funded largely through its cooperation with narcotraffickers, has scarcely been better, carrying out bombings, assassinations, and kidnappings in order to ensure that supporters of the government never feel safe. Colombia is currently experiencing the most devastating use of terrorism in the Western Hemisphere.

Europe

Although radical groups, often emanating from universities, posed a threat to democratic governments in Europe in the 1970s, the most durable conflicts have proven to be nationalist in nature. European separatist organizations that employ terrorism are usually surrounded by communities of potential supporters and recruits, people from a minority who believe themselves to be treated unfairly by their government. In Spain, for example, the revolutionary secessionist Basque Homeland and Freedom movement (ETA) has for decades employed bombings, assassinations, and killings. In recent years, the government's efforts to give more power to state and local governments has reduced some support for ETA, which was also weakened by the arrest of some of its top officers.

The conflict in Northern Ireland, in which Catholics seek secession from the United Kingdom and unification with the Republic of Ireland, has witnessed violence carried by Protestant and Catholic. "The Troubles" resulted in the deaths of more than three thousand people in the 1970s and 1980s, with the late 1990s bringing concerted efforts toward peace on the part of Catholic and Protestant activists alike. Even so, a splinter group from the Irish Republican Army, the Real IRA, bombed a bar in Omagh in August 1998, killing twenty-nine people, the single worst terrorist attack in the history of the Troubles. Protestant paramilitaries responded with terrorist violence of their own, including a series of bombings in 2001.

Middle East

The use of terrorist violence has been a mainstay of conflict in the Middle East for decades. Palestinians seeking self-determination have long used bombings, hijackings, kidnappings, and assassinations to end the Israeli occupation of their land, bring attention to their cause, and some say to destroy Israel. The Israeli government too has used assassinations as well as other tactics that can be described as terrorist. Additionally Israeli extremists have carried out terrorist attacks, as evidenced by Baruch Goldstein's 1994 massacre of Muslim worshippers in Hebron and Yigal Amir's 1995 assassination of Israeli prime minister Yitzhak Rabin, who was at the time negotiating a peace with Palestinian Authority leader Yasir Arafat.

Today Hamas, the Islamic Resistance Movement, uses bombings, suicide attacks, and killings against Israeli targets. The Israeli government, meanwhile, sees itself as besieged by terrorist groups and responds by assassinating Palestinian leaders and attacking Palestinian Authority infrastructure and Palestinian towns and villages, in actions that some observers label state terrorism. The use of political violence in the Israeli-Palestinian conflict by each side is inflammatory, with each side leveling the terrorist label against the other. This has created a mutual hostility that makes peace in this region elusive.

Former Soviet Union and Central Asia

Because of the authoritarian quality of the Soviet government and the tight control it wielded over its citizens, the Soviet Union suffered far less from terrorism than did the United States in the 1970s and 1980s; after all, it did not have to obey democratic rules when dealing with regime opponents who might have considered terrorism an option. Since the Soviet Union's collapse, however, the region has witnessed an upsurge in terrorist violence, largely linked to secessionist and religious conflicts. In particular, in the Russian Federation the efforts of secessionist rebels from the southwestern provinces of Chechnya and Dagestan, many of whom are Islamists, involve tactics some observers call terrorist. In the most notorious case, several Moscow apartment buildings were bombed in 1999, killing more than two hundred people. The Russian government immediately blamed Chechen guerillas, though some skeptics believe that the Russian government might have planted the bombs in order to justify wider military action in Chechnya.

Three of Russia's Central Asian neighbors and former Soviet republics—Kyrgyzstan, Tajikistan, and Uzbekistan—have suffered from the use of terrorist violence by Islamists attempting to overthrow their mostly secular governments. Partially supported in the past by the Taliban in Afghanistan, these groups (especially the Islamic Movement of Uzbekistan) killed regime supporters and engaged in bombing campaigns and hostage taking. The governments, especially Uzbekistan's, responded with violent, draconian measures that have only increased support among the Muslim population for an Islamist alternative. These conflicts have at times approached full-scale civil war. The 2001–2002 U.S.-led attacks on Afghanistan launched in part from Uzbekistan and Tajikistan may add to the danger in the short run.

Africa

Three factors have distanced Africa from terrorism in westerners' minds. First, much of the violence that one can specifically call terrorism has taken place in North Africa—for example, Egypt, where al-Jihad assassinated President Anwar Sadat in 1983—which is often considered part of the Middle East. Second, terrorist campaigns in sub-Saharan Africa have involved attacks by groups from abroad, rather than indigenous organizations. Third, a great deal of the political violence in sub-Saharan Africa has gone beyond anything that might be categorized as terrorism. Cold war–era civil wars in Angola and elsewhere occasionally featured terrorist violence, but it is usually thought of as insurgent actions. Similarly, the 1998 genocide of some 800,000 Tutsis by Hutus in Rwanda exceeded in brutality any terrorist attack. This Hutu campaign is conceptually separated from terrorism because the purpose of the violence appears to have been to annihilate a population rather than to intimidate it into political concessions (see INTERNATIONAL CRIMINAL JUSTICE and WAR CRIMES).

According to the U.S. State Department, only one major terrorist organization—PAGAD, People Against Gangsterism and Drugs—is based in sub-Saharan Africa. This group operates primarily in Cape Town, South Africa. The region's most notorious terrorist incidents in recent years were the bombings of the U.S. embassies in Nairobi, Kenya, and Dar es Salaam, Tanzania, in 1998 by members of the al-Qaeda network. Although U.S. diplomatic installations were the target, the vast majority of the hundreds killed were Kenyans and Tanzanians. American authorities believe that Islamist groups based elsewhere are able to operate easily in Africa but that terrorist violence there is only occasionally linked to local organizations. The relatively low profile of terrorism in Africa, however, should not be taken to mean that there is an absence of political violence. It merely takes different forms.

Central and South Asia

The political conflicts in Central Asia have been fueled by developments to their south, especially the training of Islamic militants in camps in Afghanistan and Pakistan presumably run by allies of Afghanistan's former ruling Taliban regime. Having defeated a Soviet-backed government in the 1980s, Taliban-allied and -supported militants throughout the region still view Russians and their supposed allies as enemies. The Taliban's enemies, however, were not limited to the Central Asian nations of the former Soviet Union. Indeed, the training camps in Afghanistan are alleged to have trained militants for struggles in Africa, Southeast Asia, and against the United States.

The international community tried to isolate the Taliban by imposing sanctions, especially in response to overwhelming evidence that Osama Bin Laden's network was behind the attacks on the U.S. embassies in Kenya and Tanzania in 1998. The U.S. military campaign to destroy the Taliban following the 2001 attacks in the United States was seemingly effective, at least in its initial phases, but the situation is far from resolved.

South Asia exemplifies the potential of terrorism to cause harm beyond individual attacks. Pakistan and India, long-time rivals and both of which are now nuclear powers, have fought two wars over Kashmir, the territory controlled by India but populated largely by Muslims with greater loyalty to Pakistan. Pakistan was one of the few nations that maintained diplomatic relations with the Taliban, and India has charged that terrorists trained in Afghanistan have engaged in bombings and assassinations in Kashmir. If a terrorist attack were to instigate armed conflict between these two powers, the consequences could be catastrophic, as could a takeover of the fragile Pakistani government by factions affiliated more closely with Bin Laden or the Taliban. South Asia has also been home to one of the longest-running and most brutal conflicts. Rebels of the Liberation Tigers of Tamil Eelam have used more suicide attacks than any other organization in their efforts to break away from Sri Lanka.

East Asia and the Pacific

China's Xinjiang province is home to millions of Uighurs, a Turkic-language-speaking Muslim minority that has been generally supportive of secession. The Chinese government has long alleged that Uighur activists have carried out terrorist bombings, although the figures are sketchy. At considerably greater risk for terrorism are poor Southeast Asian nations, especially the Philippines and Indonesia. For decades the authoritarian rule of Indonesian president Suharto made terrorist activities difficult to carry out, but secessionist conflicts since his removal from office in 1998 have included bombings and assassinations, especially in Aceh and East Timor. In East Timor, Indonesian-backed militias were responsible for the most brutal violence, using massacres to intimidate Timorese into staying away from the polls during their 1999 referendum for independence.

The Philippines has been a consistent site of terrorism by such Marxist groups as the New People's Army and the Islamist groups such as the Moro Islamic Liberation Front in the Mindanao region. In 2000 the Abu Sayyaf group, an offshoot of the Moro movement, kidnapped dozens of Filipino schoolchildren and Western tourists, releasing most of them only after ransoms had reportedly been paid. Although the Abu Sayyaf group maintains that its aims are political and religious, its odd elements—such as a leader named Commander Robot, because he evidently can imitate Michael Jackson's style of dancing—and its focus on ransom payments have suggested to some that it is more appropriately classified as an organized crime outfit.

Data

There are no commonly accepted statistics on terrorism for two reasons. First, terrorism is an inherently political phenomenon, so few statisticians agree on what ought to be counted or coded as terrorist. Second, numerous attacks that might be considered terrorism are kept state secrets, and some private decisions, such as settling a political kidnapping by paying ransom, are never made public. The illustrative figures here are from perhaps the most widely cited source on terrorism, the U.S. State Department (see Table 1). Significantly, the number of casualties in North America, which was zero from 1998 to 2000, rose to close to three thousand in 2001, because of the deaths from the attacks on the World Trade Center towers and the Pentagon. Few scholars or policymakers rely on counterterrorism statistics as anything other than rough guides.

Table 1 Casualties of Terrorist Violence by Region, 1998–2000

Region	1998	1999	2000
Africa	5,379	185	102
Asia	635	690	898
Eurasia	12	103	103
Latin America	195	9	20
Middle East	68	31	69
North America	0	0	0
Western Europe	405	16	4

Source: U.S. State Department, *Patterns of Global Terrorism, 2000* (Washington, D.C.: U.S. State Department, 2000).

Case Study—Negotiating to End Terrorism in Ethnic and Religious Conflicts

An early-twentieth-century independence struggle led to the partition of Ireland in 1920. The island was divided into the independent Republic of Ireland in the south and Ulster, comprised of six counties in the north controlled by the United Kingdom and known collectively as Northern Ireland. Militants on both sides of the dispute have used violence to intimidate their opponents. A particularly intense wave of violence broke out in the early 1970s, when Catholics in Belfast held demonstrations, inspired by the civil rights movement in the United States. The Protestant majority responded with violence, and the British army entered Northern Ireland, principally to protect Catholics. The Republicans (allied with the Catholics and promoting the reunification of the entire island under the Irish government) viewed the British as an occupying army. A group called the Provisional Irish Republican Army, sometimes referred to as the Provos, broke away from the somewhat impotent "official" IRA. Within years, the Provos had become adept at assassinating and bombing opponents. Protestant paramilitary groups responded with similar tactics, and credible evidence indicates that the British army and the Northern Irish police forces were complicit in some anti-Catholic attacks. More than three thousand people have died in the conflict.

The Northern Irish conflict shows how difficult it is to end terrorist violence. Since the mid-1990s, virtually all parties to the conflict have been involved in complicated negotiations to bring about a peaceful resolution. Protestant leader David Trimble and Catholic moderate leader John Hume shared the 1998 Nobel Peace Prize for their efforts. Even so, Sinn Fein, the political wing of the IRA that negotiated on its behalf, found it difficult to guarantee that militant elements would honor a compromise. When a small group calling itself the Real IRA split from the Provos and killed twenty-nine people in a 1998 pub bombing in Omagh, it led many observers to believe that terrorism was perhaps ineradicable; even if the largest groups laid down their weapons, smaller, more fanatical groups could still wreak havoc. Continuing peace negotiations might undermine some of the causes of terrorism and in the long term diminish support for such violence against Catholic and Protestant communities alike. Even small numbers of politically disgruntled activists, with limited arms, can still carry out attacks with terrible consequences.

Like the Northern Ireland conflict, the struggle between Israelis and Palestinians appears intractable in part because of the willingness of extremists on both sides to derail efforts at compromise. PLO chairman Yasir Arafat has been implicated in several acts of terrorism in the struggle for Palestinian self-rule, as had Menachem Begin while trying to establish Israel in the 1940s. In his role as head of the Palestinian Authority, Arafat is now in the position of having to distance himself and his administration from attacks by members of extremist Islamic groups determined to oppose Israeli occupation by violence. The most extreme reject any compromise that would leave Israel in control of any part of historic Palestine.

The largest of these Islamist organizations is Hamas. While it is portrayed in the West as little more than a terrorist group, Hamas also operates as a social services organization, providing basic needs to the poorest Palestinians, in part to woo them to their fundamentalist vision of a Palestinian state. To Hamas, the Palestinian Authority has erred by negotiating with Israel and by operating as a secular entity. Hamas wants a Palestinian state governed by Islamic law, or *sharia.* Motivated in part by Israel's ongoing building of settlements and confiscation of Palestinian land in the occupied territories of East Jerusalem, Gaza, and the West Bank, Hamas has engaged in killings, bombings, and suicide attacks designed to undermine the fragile peace process. By most accounts, Hamas has received financial and operational support from Iran.

Although Hamas militants have killed Israeli police, military, and civilians, the group possibly poses an even graver threat to the Palestinian Authority. If the PA is seen to compromise too much with Israel, Hamas's suicide attacks can provoke heavy-handed Israeli responses that will make the PA's position untenable. Even though moderates on both sides are interested in peace, Palestinian extremists, as well as Jewish hard-liners, can jeopardize the chances by polarizing their communities.

Case Study—Millennial Terrorism: Catastrophic Attacks to Provoke Transformation in the Social Order

For reasons that are hotly debated, Japan has been home to a staggeringly large number of new religious movements, often considered cults. With their economy in a free-fall and the collapse of social bonds and general security, many Japanese have turned to religious communities promising spiritual fulfillment. The most infamous of these is Aum Shinrikyo, the creation of a blind cleric named Shoko Asahara (originally Chizuo Matsumoto). Especially adept at recruiting members from Japan's top technical universities, the Aum (Supreme Truth) cult began to terrorize its own members and even murdered some who appeared ready to leave the group. Using a hodge-podge of religious prophecies about the end of the world, Asahara and his associates began a crash program, carried out in testing grounds Aum owned in Japan and overseas, in developing chemical weapons. The most potent of these was sarin, a deadly gas.

The group first used sarin in an attack in Matsumoto City that killed seven people. Authorities initially mistook the attack as an accidental gas leak from a chemical factory. The cult then decided to use the gas on a grander stage. In 1995 three Aum members released the gas on subway cars converging at Tokyo's Kasumigaseki Station, the stop closest to the main offices of the Japanese government. Only eleven people died, although the death toll could have been vastly higher if the gas had traveled farther through the subway system. Several Aum members were arrested, and the government passed a bill allowing it to crack down on this particular cult. The law refers to groups that "have committed acts of indiscriminate mass murder," which boils down to just Aum). Some Aum members have already been sentenced to death, and it seems likely that Asahara's lengthy trial will end with the same result.

Aum lends itself to pondering whether its members are "new terrorists" or whether they are terrorists at all. Aum had no clear political aspirations, and it did not carry out attacks in order to intimidate the government into making concessions. Rather, the group followed a millennial religious calling that told them to initiate the apocalypse. Even if Aum members were not terrorists in the political sense, most terrorism specialists argue that their attack on the Tokyo subway was one of the most important in terms of its influence on counterterrorism policy. Whether these new policies will be effective is hard to tell, but since the Tokyo attack, new "consequence management" programs have spread around the world, as governments have sought ways to cope with the effects of possible attacks with weapons of mass destruction.

Ideological zealots who try to use catastrophic violence to effect transformation in the political and social order can, however, pursue their goals with thoroughly conventional weapons. In April 1995, a massive truck bomb exploded in front of the Alfred P. Murrah Federal Building in Oklahoma City, Oklahoma. Although suspicion immediately fell on Islamist groups, the FBI quickly learned that the bomb had been planted by an extremist right-wing American with ties to Christian fundamentalists and hate groups. The bomber, Timothy McVeigh, a decorated veteran of the Persian Gulf War, said that the bombing was to avenge the federal government's 1993 siege of the Branch Davidian compound in Waco, Texas, an operation in which the FBI took part and more than eighty people died. McVeigh's bomb killed 168 people. Motivated by a belief that the attack would instigate a civil war to replace the federal government with Christian militias, McVeigh had targeted the Murrah building because FBI offices in the building represented the agency's presence in the U.S. heartland.

Although the Aum attack demonstrated that a small, highly trained group might be able to develop weapons of mass destruction, McVeigh's more conventional attack was in many ways more unsettling. Although McVeigh had received some help from at least one friend, here was an individual who carried out an attack almostly completely on his own using nothing more exotic than fertilizer and simple detonation techniques that can be easily and quickly learned. McVeigh killed far more people than Aum Shinrikyo managed to.

Could the U.S. government have prevented McVeigh's attack? The FBI has for decades surveilled extremist groups in the United States in order to preempt attacks. With constitutional guarantees of freedom of association, hate groups and other extremists are free to organize and to speak out. It is difficult to balance citizens' right to free speech, privacy, and association with the public need for safety. In the case of crazed loners, the surveillance necessary to head off a McVeigh-type attack would have to be almost overbearing.

Case Study—The Bombing of the U.S.S. *Cole* and the Difficulties of International Cooperation against Terrorism

Most terrorist groups used to claim responsibility for their acts; indeed, what was the purpose of carrying out an attack unless one could use it to publicize one's cause and the lengths to which one were willing to go? In the case of attacks linked to Saudi financier Osama Bin Laden, however, there have tended to be no such claims. The evidence gathered by the United States concerning Bin Laden's role in the 1998 embassy bombings in Dar es Salaam and Nairobi, in which more than two hundred people were killed, was so compelling that the United Nations Security Council adopted Resolution 1267 in 1999, imposing sanctions on the Taliban government of Afghanistan until it agreed to extradite Bin Laden to the United States. The Taliban, calling Bin Laden a "guest," refused to do so and responded that, anyway, Bin Laden was prohibited from carrying out terrorist attacks while residing in Afghanistan.

U.S. officials quickly concluded that Bin Laden was behind the October 2000 attack by three suicide bombers on the U.S.S. *Cole* while it was docked in Yemen. Seventeen sailors died in the operation. U.S. investigators immediately headed to the site. Although FBI officials were allowed to interrogate some suspects, the agents claimed that the Yemeni government shut down their investigation before they could do much more than ascertain the identities of the bombers. Their efforts to look into a broader conspiracy were largely unsuccessful. If the Yemeni government were to cooperate enthusiastically with the United States, it might become a prime target of Islamists; its behavior is, therefore, in many ways understandable if not justifiable. By the same token, the Yemenis' refusal to allow the FBI to probe more deeply demonstrates the political nature of terrorism and that its criminalization works only if governments are willing to pursue culprits.

Why would Bin Laden and his organization attack a naval vessel in Yemen? If the hypothesis that Bin Laden was behind the attack is correct, it would appear that he wanted to raise the costs of the U.S. presence in the Middle East. Bin Laden asserts that he wants U.S. forces to leave the Middle East, especially its bases in Saudi Arabia because of their proximity to the Islamic holy city of Mecca. Such tactics, it should be pointed out, are hardly unproven. In 1983, after President Reagan had deployed marines to participate in peacekeeping operations in Lebanon, a suicide bomber from Hizballah detonated a bomb that killed more than two hundred marines. Although Reagan spoke of never giving in to terrorists, the U.S. public was disheartened by the loss of American lives in a distant land in a conflict they barely understood. Within a few months of the attack, U.S. forces withdrew. If, as seems likely, Bin Laden was behind the attack on the *Cole* (and the 11 September attacks in New York and outside Washington), it is perhaps because he truly believes that the U.S. government can be intimidated into withdrawing its military presence from the Middle East.

Biographical Sketches

Richard Clarke was a member of the National Security Council under Presidents George Bush, Bill Clinton, and George W. Bush. He ultimately earned the title national coordinator for counterterrorism. Clarke has pushed for a hard line by the U.S. government against terrorism and has emphasized the importance of preparing for terrorist attacks with weapons of mass destruction. A controversial figure, Clarke has been accused by his critics of trying to turn the United States into something akin to a prison state, though his supporters argue that the threat is sufficient to merit a strong response.

Martha Crenshaw is a professor at Wesleyan University who helped to pioneer the field of terrorism studies after completing her doctoral research at the University of Virginia on the use of terrorism in the Algerian war of independence. Often sought after by policymakers and the media for her views, Crenshaw calls attention to the politics behind terrorist conflicts and actions.

Jerrold Post is one of the more well known scholars researching terrorism. As a psychologist for twenty years with the Central Intelligence Agency, he has been at the forefront of research on the psychology of terror. Post has interviewed dozens of accused terrorists. Some terrorism experts, however, believe that psychological research thus far has failed to yield much useful information and has drawn attention away from more important political and organizational factors.

Ehud Sprinzak is a professor at Hebrew University in Jerusalem and is a leading expert on the politics of terrorism. He has written on extremist violence among Jewish and Palestinian communities and has argued against oversimplifying terrorism, including drawing attention to the diverse motives and psychological profiles of suicide bombers.

Jessica Stern is a lecturer at Harvard University and a leading expert on terrorist groups and their possible use of weapons of mass destruction. Her research focuses on Islamist organizations, particularly in Pakistan.

Paul Wilkinson is an academic studying terrorism and has served as an adviser on terrorism to British political figures. He is the author of *Terrorism and the Liberal State* (1977), which argues that liberal democratic nations face special problems in fighting terrorism and that their solutions should be consistent with the basic freedoms guaranteed to citizens.

Directory

Canadian Security Intelligence Service, P.O. Box 9732, Postal Station T, Ottawa, ONT K1G 4G4, Canada. Web: http://www.csis-scrs.gc.ca/eng/operat/ct_e.html
Canadian government agency responsible for counterterrorism

Centre for the Study of Terrorism and Political Violence, Department of International Relations, University of St Andrews, St Andrews KY16 9AL, Scotland. Web: http://www.st-and.ac.uk/academic/intrel/research/cstpv
Independent academic research center focusing on terrorism, maintains databases on terrorist incidents and organizations

International Policy Institute for Counter-Terrorism, Interdisciplinary Center, P.O. Box 167, Herzlia 46150, Israel. Web: http://www.ict.org.il
Think tank focusing on counterterrorism

National Domestic Preparedness Office, Federal Bureau of Investigation, Room 5214, 935 Pennsylvania Avenue NW, Washington, DC 20535. Web: http://www.ndpo.gov
Main coordinating center for U.S. domestic counterterrorism programs

Office of the Coordinator for Counterterrorism, U.S. Department of State, 2201 C Street NW, Washington, DC 20520-6810. Web:http://www.state.gov/s/ct
U.S. agency that provides information on U.S. foreign policies against terrorism

Further Research

Books

Bell, J. Bowyer. *The IRA, 1968–2000: Analysis of a Secret Army.* London: Frank Cass, 2000.

Chalk, Peter. *West European Terrorism and Counterterrorism: The Evolving Dynamic.* London: Macmillan, 1996.

Crenshaw, Martha. *Terrorism, Legitimacy, and Power.* Middletown, Conn.: Wesleyan University Press, 1983.

Crenshaw, Martha, and John Pimlott, eds. *Encyclopedia of World Terrorism.* Armonk, N.Y.: Sharpe, 1997.

Esposito, John L. *Political Islam: Revolution, Radicalism, or Reform?* Boulder: Lynne Rienner, 1997.

Green, Michael. *Terrorism: Prevention and Preparedness—New Approaches to U.S.-Japan Security Cooperation.* New York: Japan Society, 2001.

Heymann, Philip B. *Terrorism and America: A Commonsense Strategy for a Democratic Society.* Cambridge, Mass.: MIT Press, 1998.

Hubbak, Andrew. *Apocalypse When? The Global Threat of Religious Cults.* London: Research Institute for the Study of Violence and Terrorism, 1997.

Juergensmeyer, Mark. *Terror in the Mind of God.* Berkeley: University of California Press, 2000.

Laqueur, Walter. *Terrorism.* Boston: Little, Brown, 1997.

Lesser, Ian O., et al. *Countering the New Terrorism.* Washington, D.C.: RAND, 1999.

Lifton, Robert J. *Destroying the World in Order to Save It: Aum Shinrikyo, Apocalyptic Violence, and the New Global Terrorism.* New York: Henry Holt, 1999.

Michel, Lou, and Dan Herbeck. *American Terrorist: Timothy McVeigh and the Oklahoma City Bombing.* New York: Regan Books, 1999.

Mishal, Shaul, and Avraham Sela. *The Palestinian Hamas: Vision, Violence, and Coexistence.* New York: Columbia University Press, 2000.

Nusse, Andrea. *Muslim Palestine: The Ideology of Hamas.* Amsterdam: Harwood Academic Publishers, 1998.

O'Doherty, Malachi. *The Trouble with Guns: Republican Strategy and the Provisional IRA.* Belfast: Blackstaff, 1998.

Post, Jerrold M. *Political Paranoia: The Psychopolitics of Hatred.* New Haven: Yale University Press, 1997.

Reader, Ian. *Religious Violence in Contemporary Japan: The Case of Aum Shinrikyo.* Honolulu: University of Hawaii Press, 2000.

Reinares, Fernando, ed. *European Democracies against Terrorism.* Brookfield, Vt.: Ashgate, 2000.

Rubin, Barry, ed. *The Politics of Terrorism.* Washington, D.C.: Johns Hopkins School of Advanced International Studies, 1989.

Turner, Stansfield. *Terrorism and Democracy.* Boston: Houghton Mifflin, 1991.

Wilkinson, Paul, and Brian Jenkins, eds. *Aviation Terrorism and Security.* Portland, Ore.: Frank Cass, 1999.

Articles and Reports

Ball, Terrence, and Richard Dagger. "Inside the Turner Diaries: Neo-Nazi Scripture." *PS: Political Science and Politics* 30, no. 4 (December 1997): 717–718.

Bell, J. Bowyer. "Ireland: the Long End Game." *Studies in Conflict and Terrorism* 21, no. 1 (January 1998): 5–28.

Burns, John F. "Cole Inquiry Stalled." *New York Times,* 26 August 2001, 2.

Calabresi, Massimo, et al. "Evidence, and Bin Laden News, Hard to Come By." *Time,* 6 November 2000, 40.

Kristianasen, Wendy. "Challenge and Counterchallenge: Hamas to Oslo." *Journal of Palestine Studies* 28, no. 3 (Spring 1999): 19–26.

Metraux, Daniel P. "Religious Terrorism in Japan: The Fatal Appeal of Aum Shinrikyo." *Asian Survey* 35, no. 12 (December 1995): 140–156.

National Commission on Terrorism. *Countering the Changing Threat of International Terrorism.* Report to the105th Congress, 2000, http://w3.access.gpo.gov/nct.

Web Sites

Emergency Response and Research Institute
http://www.emergency.com/cntrterr.htm

Studies in Conflict and Terrorism
http://www.tandf.co.uk/journals/tf/1057610X.html

Terrorism and Political Violence
http://www.frankcass.com/jnls/tpv.htm

Terrorism Research Center
http://www.terrorism.com

Documents

1. International Convention for the Suppression of the Financing of Terrorism

United Nations General Assembly, 9 December 1999

The full text is available at http://untreaty.un.org/English/Terrorism/Conv12.pdf.

Extract

[States must undertake]:

(b) Measures requiring financial institutions and other professions involved in financial transactions to utilize the most efficient measures available for the identification of their usual or occasional customers, as well as customers in whose interest accounts are opened, and to pay special attention to unusual or suspicious transactions and report transactions suspected of stemming from a criminal activity. For this purpose, States Parties shall consider:

(i) Adopting regulations prohibiting the opening of accounts the holders or beneficiaries of which are unidentified or unidentifiable, and measures to ensure that such institutions verify the identity of the real owners of such transactions;

(ii) With respect to the identification of legal entities, requiring financial institutions, when necessary, to take measures to verify the legal existence and the structure of the customer by obtaining, either from a public register or from the customer or both, proof of incorporation, including information concerning the customer's name, legal form, address, directors and provisions regulating the power to bind the entity;

(iii) Adopting regulations imposing on financial institutions the obligation to report promptly to the competent authorities all complex, unusual large transactions and unusual patterns of transactions, which have no apparent economic or obviously lawful purpose, without fear of assuming criminal or civil liability for breach of any restriction on disclosure of information if they report their suspicions in good faith;

(iv) Requiring financial institutions to maintain, for at least five years, all necessary records on transactions, both domestic or international.

2. States Parties shall further cooperate in the prevention of offences set forth in article 2 by considering:

(a) Measures for the supervision, including, for example, the licensing, of all money-transmission agencies;

(b) Feasible measures to detect or monitor the physical cross-border transportation of cash and bearer negotiable instruments, subject to strict safeguards to ensure proper use of information and without impeding in any way the freedom of capital movements.

2. Declaration on Measures to Eliminate International Terrorism

United Nations General Assembly, Resolution 49/60, 9 December 1994

The full text is available at http://www.un.org/law/terrorism/english/a_49_60e.pdf.

Extract

The General Assembly,

Recalling its resolution 46/51 of 9 December 1991 and its decision 48/411 of 9 December 1993,

Taking note of the report of the Secretary-General,

Having considered in depth the question of measures to eliminate international terrorism,

Convinced that the adoption of the declaration on measures to eliminate international terrorism should contribute to the enhancement of the struggle against international terrorism,

1. Approves the Declaration on Measures to Eliminate International Terrorism, the text of which is annexed to the present resolution. . . .

ANNEX

Declaration on Measures to Eliminate International Terrorism

The General Assembly, Guided by the purposes and principles of the Charter of the United Nations, . . .

Deeply disturbed by the world-wide persistence of acts of international terrorism in all its forms and manifestations, including those in which States are directly or indirectly involved, which endanger or take innocent lives, have a deleterious effect on international relations and may jeopardize the security of States, . . .

Convinced of the desirability of keeping under review the scope of existing international legal provisions to combat terrorism in all its forms and manifestations, with the aim of ensuring a comprehensive legal framework for the prevention and elimination of terrorism,

Solemnly declares the following:

I

1. The States Members of the United Nations solemnly reaffirm their unequivocal condemnation of all acts, methods and practices of terrorism, as criminal and unjustifiable, wherever and by whomever committed, including those which jeopardize the friendly relations among States and peoples and threaten the territorial integrity and security of States;

2. Acts, methods and practices of terrorism constitute a grave violation of the purposes and principles of the United Nations, which may pose a threat to international peace and security, jeopardize friendly relations among States, hinder international cooperation and aim at the destruction of human rights, fundamental freedoms and the democratic bases of society;

3. Criminal acts intended or calculated to provoke a state of terror in the general public, a group of persons or particular persons for political purposes are in any circumstance unjustifiable, whatever the considerations of a political, philosophical, ideological, racial, ethnic, religious or any other nature that may be invoked to justify them;

II

4. States, guided by the purposes and principles of the Charter of the United Nations and other relevant rules of international law, must refrain from organizing, instigating, assisting or participating in terrorist acts in territories of other States, or from acquiescing in or encouraging activities within their territories directed towards the commission of such acts;

5. States must also fulfil their obligations under the Charter of the United Nations and other provisions of international law with respect to combating international terrorism and are urged to take effective and resolute measures in accordance with the relevant provisions of international law and international standards of human rights for the speedy and final elimination of international terrorism, in particular:

(a) To refrain from organizing, instigating, facilitating, financing, encouraging or tolerating terrorist activities and to take appropriate practical measures to ensure that their respective territories are not used for terrorist installations or training camps, or for the preparation or organization of terrorist acts intended to be committed against other States or their citizens;

(b) To ensure the apprehension and prosecution or extradition of perpetrators of terrorist acts, in accordance with the relevant provisions of their national law;

(c) To endeavour to conclude special agreements to that effect on a bilateral, regional and multilateral basis, and to prepare, to that effect, model agreements on cooperation;

(d) To cooperate with one another in exchanging relevant information concerning the prevention and combating of terrorism;

(e) To take promptly all steps necessary to implement the existing international conventions on this subject to which they are parties, including the harmonization of their domestic legislation with those conventions. . . .

10. The Secretary-General should assist in the implementation of the present Declaration by taking, within existing resources, the following practical measures to enhance international cooperation:

(a) A collection of data on the status and implementation of existing multilateral, regional and bilateral agreements relating to international terrorism, including information on incidents caused by international terrorism and criminal prosecutions and sentencing, based on information received from the depositaries of those agreements and from Member States;

(b) A compendium of national laws and regulations regarding the prevention and suppression of international terrorism in all its forms and manifestations, based on information received from Member States;

(c) An analytical review of existing international legal instruments relating to international terrorism, in order to assist States in identifying aspects of this matter that have not been covered by such instruments and could be addressed to develop further a comprehensive legal framework of conventions dealing with international terrorism;

(d) A review of existing possibilities within the United Nations system for assisting States in organizing workshops and training courses on combating crimes connected with international terrorism.

URBANIZATION

Chris Woodford

In 1987 the World Commission on Environment and Development (WCED) announced in *Our Common Future* that "the future will be predominantly urban and the most immediate environmental concerns of most people will be urban ones." Almost twenty years later, around half the world's people live in urban areas: 76 percent of the population in developed countries are urbanized, as are 40 percent of the population in less developed countries. Forecasts predict that urbanization will increase significantly in both areas. Although urbanization is a potent force for economic, social, and cultural development, these benefits are sometimes won only at considerable environmental and social costs that frequently have international and sometimes global implications.

Historical Background and Development

The urban environment may seem a quintessential feature of the modern world, but even ancient civilizations had cities. Mohenjo-Daro in the Indus Valley (ca. 3000 B.C.), Kahun in Egypt (ca. 2000 B.C.), and Miletus in Greece (ca. 500 B.C.) were methodically laid out in what were probably the earliest examples of urban planning. By the time of the ancient Greeks, theories of urban planning had been formalized by Plato, Hippocrates, and Aristotle. Centuries later, the Roman writer Vitruvius wrote the first major treatise on architecture, *De architectura,* which greatly influenced urban planning in the centuries that followed.

Cities span history, yet urbanization is a much more recent phenomenon, closely tied to the spread of industrial development from the middle of the nineteenth century to the present. Urbanization brought such problems as pollution, high infant mortality, and a massive increase in slum dwellings. It also brought responses in the form of public health legislation, such as England's Health of the Towns Act (1868), which allowed local government authorities to set standards for sewage disposal and the general condition of housing. It also led to theories of how to build better settlements, where people could live and work at high population densities without suffering the usual problems created by urbanization.

Nineteenth- and twentieth-century architects proposed numerous solutions to these problems. The Chicago School of architects pioneered skyscrapers during the mid-nineteenth century. Sir Ebeneezer Howard (in Britain) and his disciples Clarence Stein and Henry Radburn (in the United States) offered a new vision of the "garden city," a small urban settlement permanently surrounded by countryside. Modernist architects, notably Le Corbusier (from Switzerland), sketched visions that replaced existing cities with massive tower blocks separated by roads and surrounded by parkland.

Nevertheless, architectural utopias have little to offer in solving the most fundamental urban problem of all: satisfying the basic human right to shelter as enshrined in the 1948 Universal Declaration of Human Rights. During the second half of the twentieth century, informal shantytowns became defining features of most cities in developing countries, housing an estimated 30 to 60 percent of the urban population. Since the 1987 World Commission on Environment and Development's Brundtland Report, or *Our Common Future,* popularized the term *sustainable development,* it has become fashionable to speak of "sustainable cities" as the solution to the urban crisis. A major advance toward urban sustainability was made when 171 governments adopted the Istanbul Declaration and the Habitat Agenda at the Second United Nations Conference on Human Settlements (Habitat II) in June 1996. Although the Habitat Agenda contained numerous broad goals, it provided no specific targets or timetables for achieving these goals. The extent to which progress has been made globally and locally will become clear only after analysis has been completed for the follow-up to Habitat II, scheduled by the United Nations General Assembly in June 2001.

Current Status

Urbanization is not itself a bad thing. As the World Bank's *Cities in Transition* argues, "The urban transition offers significant opportunities to improve the quality of life for all individuals, but whether this potential is realized depends critically on how cities are managed and on the national and local policies affecting their development." In other words, whether urbanization results in benefits or problems depends on whether it is managed through effective policies and programs or simply allowed to proceed in a laissez-faire manner, unplanned and unchecked.

Research

In February 2001 the American Association for the Advancement of Science published a series of satellite maps called the Atlas of Population and Environment that revealed the extent of humankind's influence on the natural environment. According to the association's data, around half of Earth's surface has been transformed for humankind's use. Although just 2 to 3 percent has been urbanized for industry, housing, services, and transportation, a much greater area has been transformed by the farming, commercial forestry, and pastures needed to support an increasingly urban population (see POPULATION).

Megacities—areas with 10 million inhabitants or more—cover vast amounts of territory; the world's largest metropolis, Tokyo, has more than 26 million residents. Yet megacities' "ecological footprint"—the area of land needed to feed the people of an area, provide energy, and dispose of their waste—may be vastly greater. For example, urbanization expert Herbert Girardet has estimated that London's ecological footprint is 125 times greater than the area occupied by the city itself.

Because different regions are in different stages of development, urbanization presents different problems around the world. In the developed countries of Western Europe and North America, for example, there is a net movement away from many urban areas. Here, one of the main problems of urbanization is to reconcile the progressive deterioration of urban areas with the gradual "suburbanization" of the rural areas that surround them. In rapidly industrializing nations such as China and India, urbanization may bring other problems, such as pollution or excessive stress on natural resources, including water supplies needed to support a growing urban population (see FRAGILE ECOSYSTEMS, FRESHWATER, and POLLUTION). The worst effects of urbanization, however, often fall on developing nations, the least equipped to cope with them, and, within these nations, disproportionately on the growing underclass of urban poor (see INCOME INEQUALITY). According to the World Bank's *Cities in Transition,* in the two most urbanized regions, Latin America and Europe/Central Asia, half the poor live in urban areas, and the proportion will increase to two-thirds by 2025. Urbanization therefore implies not only the extension of cities, but also the growth of the urban poor within them, people who are disproportionately affected by problems such as pollution, poor sanitation, and natural disasters. According to the United Nations Environmental Programme's (UNEP) *Global Environment Outlook, 2000* (GEO-2000), "While large cities in some developing countries have been growing at rates of up to 10 percent per annum, slums and squatter settlements in some of them are growing twice as fast."

Adverse social and environmental impacts have saddled the term *urbanization* with a negative connotation. Author and critic Christopher Morley wrote, "All cities are beautiful, but the beauty is grim." The frequent pairing of the word *urban* with terms such as *decay, renewal,* and *regeneration* insinuates that the urban dream has condemned millions of people to lives of poverty and degradation. According to a 1996 estimate by the United Nations Centre for Human Settlements (UNCHS, now the United Nations Human Settlements Programme, UN-HABITAT), around 100 million of the world's urban poor are homeless. A further 600 million people in Africa, Asia, and Latin America occupy shantytowns and squatter settlements on the fringes of megacities with little or no access to safe water and sanitation, let alone electricity (see Table 1). Often the first urban living environment for rural migrants, shanty settlements provide a significant proportion of the accommodations for poor people in many large cities of the developing world. According to a 1986 estimate by UNCHS, 59 percent of Bogotá's population dwelled in shantytowns, 32 percent of São Paulo's, 40 percent of Mexico City's, and 47 percent of Manila's.

Shantytowns, usually constructed illegally by the people who live there, are perhaps the most obvious example of unplanned urbanization, yet even in developed countries, cities continue to evolve in a largely inefficient and haphazard way. Pioneers of modernist architecture, such as Le Corbusier, may have sketched gleaming urban dream cities as "machines for living in," but they invariably started with blank sheets of paper. The reality of the modern metropolis is more likely to be unplanned sprawl, reinvented over many decades or even centuries, using land and environmental resources in an inefficient and therefore unsustainable manner, and often lacking overall cohesiveness. Writer Dorothy Parker once famously described Los Angeles as "72 suburbs in search of a city."

In developing countries, a lack of financial support for urban planning and development is substantially to blame (see DEVELOPMENT AID). According to the United Nations Agenda 21, presented at the 1992 Earth Summit in Rio de Janeiro, only 1 percent of the UN system's total grant-financed expenditures in 1988 had gone toward human settlements, and in 1991 the World Bank and the International Development Association had devoted just 5.4 percent of their total lending to urban development and 5.4 percent to water supply and sewerage. The cities in developed countries are older and more constrained and therefore evolve with more difficulty. It is often cheaper and easier to develop "greenfield" areas bordering suburbs than to recycle "brownfield" sites in city centers, so market incentives tend to favor urban sprawl over urban regeneration. Despite sound environmental reasons for coordinating housing, office developments, and transportation links in an approach known as integrated land-use planning, economic imperatives may favor large out-of-town developments accessible only by automobile. Multiple-use cities that mix housing, urban developments, and open space may gradually be replaced by concentric circles of "ghettoization," with the business district at the center surrounded by the downtown "no-go" ghettos and high-security residential suburbs on the periphery. Without effective policies and programs to control urbanization, the social and environmental problems associated with human settlements become self-perpetuating and mutually reinforcing.

What of the future? According to the UN Population Division's *World Urbanization Prospects: The 1999 Revision,* almost all population growth between 2000 and 2030 will occur in urban areas, and most of this will be in developing countries (see Tables 2 and 3). While the urban population of developed countries will increase only slightly during this period, from 0.9 billion people to 1.0 billion, the urban population of developing countries is predicted to double, from 1.9 billion to 3.8 billion (see map, p. 573). Rural-urban migration and the urbanization of rural settlements will be the main causes of this trend. Although megacities, with their 10 million or more inhabitants, such as New York and Beijing, attract more attention, they house just 4.3 percent of the world's people; smaller cities, such as Bogotá, Madras, and Lima, with 5 million to 10 million people, house 2.6 percent. By 2015, cities with 5 million or more inhabitants will still house only 8.7 percent of the total population. Currently, around

28.5 percent of people live in cities of 1 million inhabitants or fewer, such as Agra and Calgary, and this proportion is expected to rise to 30.6 percent by 2015. Such smaller cities are expected to show the most significant population growth between 2000 and 2015.

Policies and Programs

In 1987 the World Commission on Environment and Development's groundbreaking Brundtland Report formalized the concept of sustainable development, ensuring that humankind "meets the needs of the present without compromising the ability of future generations to meet their own needs." With urbanization being such a potent force for environmental and social transformation, the WCED focused on the challenge of addressing what it called "a crisis in Third World cities." Among the policies it recommended were the development of national urban strategies with "an explicit set of goals and priorities" to restrain the uncontrolled development of megacities and promote the development of small- and medium-sized urban centers instead. The WCED also recommended concentrating effort and resources where they can most effectively solve the problems of the urban poor, with strengthened authority to effectively tackle problems on a local scale and greater empowerment and involvement of ordinary citizens in the planning process.

Similar themes were explored in more detail at the 1992 Earth Summit, whose Agenda 21, a blueprint for sustainable development, identified eight major program areas, one of which was a program for the development of sustainable human settlement (see Document 1). With the right to shelter recognized as a basic human right in the 1948 Universal Declaration of Human Rights, the first objective of Agenda 21's human settlements program became "providing adequate shelter for all." In 1988 the UN General Assembly adopted a Global Strategy for Shelter to the Year 2000 as a key step toward realizing this objective.

Considering adequate shelter to be a human right is not alone sufficient to ensure the sustainability of human settlements. The second objective in Agenda 21's human settlements program, therefore, was "improving human settlement management" through national and local urban strategies. Greater local involvement may be the key to better management of settlements, but international initiatives also have a part to play. Important efforts include the Sustainable Cities Program managed by the United Nations Human Settlements Programme and the World Health Organization's Healthy Cities Program. Another important initiative is the Best Practices Database, launched in 1996 by UNCHS and other organizations. It focuses on the effectiveness of the local approach to urban sustainability, detailing more than a thousand examples of urban improvement from 120 countries.

One of the best ways to ensure that settlements are more manageable is to plan them that way. Hence, Agenda 21's third objective was "promoting sustainable land use planning and management." Key features of this objective include managing and reconciling the various activities that compete for land use and making it easier for communities to own and manage their land.

Better land use planning and management overlap considerably with Agenda 21's fourth and fifth objectives, "promoting the integrated provision of environmental infrastructure" (such as water supply, sanitation, and waste disposal) and "promoting sustainable energy and transport systems." Improved water supply systems, for example, may mean that agricultural land can be used more productively through better irrigation, whereas investment in public transportation systems typically reduces the need to build highways that exacerbate a number of urban problems, such as physically dividing communities, discouraging children from playing outside, and producing pollution-related health problems.

The fragility of urban life for many poor people leaves them particularly at risk when disasters such as earthquakes and floods strike. In the two decades prior to the 1992 Earth Summit, natural disasters caused some 3 million deaths and affected another 800 million people, with annual losses typically reaching $30 million to $50 billion. With this in mind, Agenda 21's sixth objective became "promoting human settlement planning and management in disaster-prone areas." The General Assembly declared the 1990s the International Decade for Natural Disaster Reduction.

Disasters are not the only large-scale forces shaping the urban environment. Humankind's activities have the power to effect equally drastic changes. From highways to factories and hydroelectric dams to shopping malls, large-scale construction projects are the engines of urbanization. Agenda 21's seventh objective was therefore "promoting sustainable construction industry activities." Recognizing the economic importance of many construction projects, planners, contractors, politicians, and other stakeholders should carefully assess the potential impact of major developments on surrounding communities and avoid construction in fragile ecosystems, use recycled materials to reduce the effects of mining and quarrying, and use local materials to reduce transportation impacts.

Agenda 21's eighth and final objective was "promoting human resource development and capacity-building for human settlement development" that is, making more effective use of the people and skills available to make settlements better places to live. This includes identifying the important role that women, youth, and community groups and nongovernmental organizations can play in developing sustainable settlements.

If the Brundtland Report laid the foundation for Agenda 21, the agenda in turn laid the foundation for the global plan of action on urbanization adopted at Habitat II in Istanbul in 1996 (see Document 2). At the conference, 171 nations signed on to the Istanbul Declaration calling on their governments to identify and resolve problems of urbanization, including resource consumption, excessive population concentration, homelessness, poverty, urban degradation and violence, and vulnerability to disasters. More significant, the conference proposed a detailed "roadmap" for sustainable urban development, the Habitat Agenda (see Document 3). Focused on the twin themes of achieving "adequate shelter for all" and "sustainable human settlements development in an urbanizing world," the Habitat Agenda includes proposals similar to

Agenda 21, but it also draws attention to the role of international cooperation and coordination. Much of the responsibility for this falls on UNCHS, which is charged with overseeing implementation of the Habitat Agenda. In line with the recommendations of Agenda 21 and the Habitat Agenda, UNCHS has encouraged considerable stakeholder participation, inviting local authorities, businesses and commercial industries, nongovernmental organizations, and private individuals to take an active part in urban reform. Another important element of the Habitat Agenda is the need to monitor the progress of policies and programs and to adjust them accordingly.

Regional Summaries

Patterns of urbanization vary dramatically around the world. In Europe and the Americas, roughly 80 percent of the population live in urban areas. Elsewhere in the world, notably in East Africa, levels of urbanization remain as low as 6 percent.

North America

In North America during the early part of the twentieth century, immigration, population growth, and the development of transportation systems such as railroads and highways spurred considerable urban and suburban development; by 1980 around three-fourths of the population in the United States and in Canada lived in urban areas. This rapid growth slowed substantially toward the end of the century, but UN Population Division estimates suggest that further significant urbanization will occur during the early part of the twenty-first century, leaving the United States with 85 percent of its population in urban areas by 2025 and Canada with 81 percent of its population similarly situated. Cities with major urban problems include Los Angeles and New York, which rank among the world's most heavily polluted cities. Los Angeles is also notable for the way its neighborhoods have become increasingly segregated in recent decades.

Latin America

Latin America experienced dramatic urbanization during the second half of the twentieth century, with the urban population growing from 43 percent in 1950 to 73.4 percent in 1995, according to UN population figures. This population is expected to reach 83 percent by 2030. Spectacular urban growth occurred in a number of megacities; some of the world's largest cities are in this region, including Bogotá, Buenos Aires, Mexico City, Rio de Janeiro, and São Paulo. In 1987 the WCED estimated that population growth between 1950 and 2000 would be nearly ninefold for Mexico City and São Paulo, and sixteenfold for Bogotá. Rural immigrants continue to swell the population of Mexico City by as many as eighty thousand per month. Substantial population growth is now occurring in small and medium-sized cities too. Bogotá, Mexico City, Rio de Janeiro, and São Paulo are among the cities suffering the

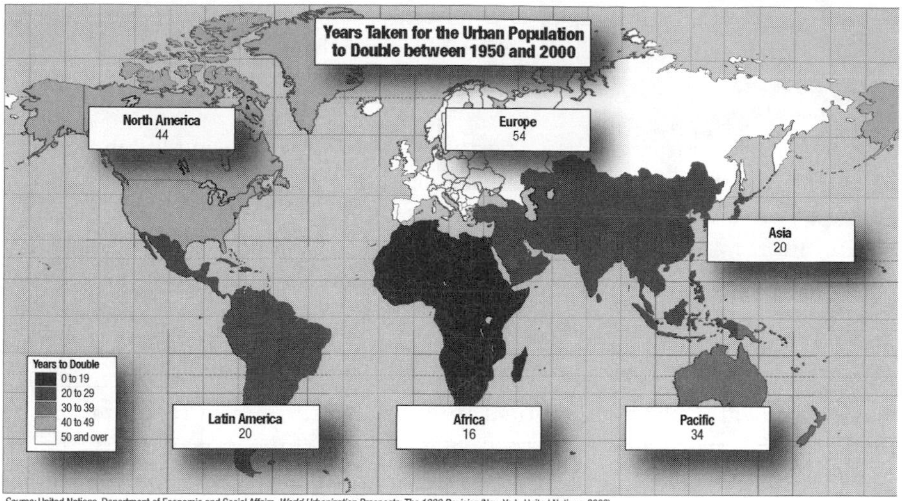

Source: United Nations, Department of Economic and Social Affairs, *World Urbanization Prospects: The 1999 Revision* (New York: United Nations, 2000).

strains of urbanization, including chronic air pollution. Caracas, La Paz, Lima, Rio de Janeiro, and São Paulo, among other cities, have severe urban sanitation problems.

Europe and Central Asia

Roughly three-fourths of the population in this region currently live in urban areas. Despite massive urban and suburban growth throughout the twentieth century, current rates of urbanization have slowed virtually to zero except in Central Asia, where urban growth continues, and Eastern Europe, where urban growth is now negative. In Europe, the rate of urbanization from 1995 to 2015 is predicted to be around a third of the rate between 1975 and 1995. Nevertheless, some 83 percent of Europeans will live in urban areas in 2030, compared to just 67 percent in 1975. In Western Europe, the decline of city centers has continued in tandem with increasing suburbanization since the 1960s. A similar phenomenon has now spread to Eastern Europe. London typifies cities trying to deal with gridlocked roads, expensive real estate, huge economic disparities, crime, and health problems associated with pollution.

North Africa and the Middle East

Urbanization is much greater in North Africa (where roughly half the people live in urban areas) than in the sub-Sahara (where urbanization stands at roughly 40 percent). In the Middle East, urbanization has occurred partly through a gradual drift of population from rural to urban regions and, in the Arabian Peninsula, partly because of the sudden industrialization prompted by the postwar oil boom. In 2000 the urban population of the Middle East was estimated to be around 70 percent, while in North Africa, half. Cities in the region continue to experience urbanization problems. In Amman, Sanaa, and many other cities, for example, only around 50 percent of the garbage generated is actually collected, which presents a major health hazard.

Sub-Saharan Africa

The twentieth century marked a period of substantial change for sub-Saharan Africa. At the start of the century, just 5 percent of Africans lived in towns and cities. Since 1970, however, Africa as a whole has had the highest rate of urbanization in the world—roughly 4 percent per annum. By 2000, roughly 40 percent of residents were classed as urban dwellers, with UN predictions forecasting urbanization of 43 percent by 2010. Yet this figure disguises dramatic variations in levels of urbanization from country to country. In some nations, such as Djibouti and South Africa, as much as half the population is now urbanized. Elsewhere, particularly in the east, levels of urbanization are closer to what they were for the region as a whole at the start of the twentieth century: for example, in Rwanda and Burundi, urbanization is only around 7 percent. Cities with major urbanization difficulties in the region include Lusaka, where two-thirds of the population lack adequate sanitation, and Kinshasha, which grew sevenfold between 1950 and 1980 and whose 4 million people have no garbage collection.

Asia and the Pacific

Asia and the Pacific continue to experience dramatic urbanization, with the urban population growing by about 260 percent (or 560 million people) over the last thirty years. It is projected to grow by another 250 percent (or 1.45 billion people) over the next thirty years. The region has a pattern of urbanization quite different from other regions. It has the highest rural population (and will continue to until around 2030), and the proportion of the population living in urban areas is less than half that of most other regions. Only slightly more than a third of the people in Asia and the Pacific live in urban areas, yet the region contains almost half of the world's major cities, including nine of the world's fourteen megacities. In other words, the region has more dramatic concentrations of population than the other regions. According to UNEP's GEO-2000, "Urbanization is one of the most significant issues facing Asia and the Pacific," with major concerns including the disposal of waste, water and air pollution, and unchecked traffic growth. Urbanization has brought difficulties to many cities. More than three hundred of China's cities, for example, have experienced water shortages, while only 20 percent of the country's sewage is adequately treated.

Data

Table 1 Percentage of Housing Units with Facilities in Selected Countries, 1985–1994

Country	Piped Water			Toilet			Electric Lighting			Kitchen		
	Total	Urban	Rural	Total	Urban	Rural	Total	Urban	Rural	Total	Urban	Rural
Algeria	X	X	X	X	X	X	73.4	X	X	X	X	X
Argentina	92.5	X	X	X	X	X	X	X	X	X	X	X
Brazil	X	82.6	X	X	X	X	X	X	X	X	X	X
Canada	99.9	100.0	99.4	99.6	99.7	99.1	X	X	X	100.0	X	X
Colombia	70.5	94.5	X	X	X	X	77.1	X	X	X	X	X
France	99.9	X	X	95.8	X	X	96.6	X	X	93.7	X	X
Germany, Federal Republic of	X	X	X	100.0	100.0	100.0	100.0	100.0	100.0	99.3	99.3	99.3
Guatemala	X	58.2	X	X	X	X	X	X	X	X	X	X
India	32.3	65.1	20.6	23.6	63.6	8.8	43.0	75.9	31.1	X	X	X
Indonesia	13.0	33.0	4.6	17.2	X	X	47.0	85.8	30.8	X	X	X
Japan	X	X	X	98.8	98.5	99.8	X	X	X	98.8	98.5	99.8
Mexico	76.4	X	X	74.8	X	X	87.5	X	X	91.0	X	X
Russian Federation	62.1	81.3	19.0	X	X	X	100.0	100.0	100.0	100.0	100.0	100.0
Spain	98.7	X	X	97.1	X	X	99.2	X	X	99.3	X	X
Switzerland	X	X	X	X	X	X	X	X	X	99.5	X	X
Thailand	29.7	84.5	16.8	87.6	99.1	85.0	89.3	98.6	87.1	X	X	X
Ukraine	44.8	68.2	4.3	43.3	66.4	3.4	100.0	100.0	100.0	X	X	X
United Kingdom	X	X	X	X	X	X	X	X	X	98.7	X	X
United States	99.7	X	X	97.7	X	X	100.0	X	X	99.0	X	X
Venezuela	81.4	87.4	48.7	X	X	X	93.0	91.8	100.0	X	X	X

Source: United Nations Center for Human Settlements, *Human Settlements Basic Statistics, 1997,* May 2001, http://www.unchs.org/unchs/english/stats/contents.htm.

Note: X indicates not available.

Table 2 Urban and Total Population Distribution, 1950–2030

Area	Population (millions)			Growth Rate (%)	
	1950	2000	2030	1950–2000	2000–2030
	Urban Population				
North America	110	239	314	1.6	0.9
Latin America	69	391	604	3.5	1.5
Europe	287	545	571	1.3	0.2
Africa	32	297	766	4.4	3.2
Asia	244	1,352	2,605	3.4	2.2
Pacific	8	21	31	2.0	1.2

Table 2 Urban and Total Population Distribution, 1950–2030 (*continued*)

Area	Population (millions)			Growth Rate (%)	
	1950	2000	2030	1950–2000	2000–2030
	Total Population				
North America	172	310	372	1.2	0.6
Latin America	167	519	726	2.3	1.1
Europe	547	729	691	0.6	–0.2
Africa	221	784	1,406	2.5	1.9
Asia	1,402	3,683	4,877	1.9	0.9
Pacific	13	30	41	1.8	1.0

Source: Department of Economic and Social Affairs, United Nations, Population Division, *World Urbanization Prospects: The 1999 Revision* (New York: United Nations, 2000).

Table 3 Urban and Rural Population Changes in Selected Countries

	Population Distribution, 2000 (%)		Average Annual Rate of Change in Population, 1995–2000 (%)	
Country	Urban	Rural	Urban	Rural
Algeria	60	40	3.57	0.51
Argentina	90	10	1.60	–1.55
Australia	85	15	1.02	1.02
Brazil	81	19	2.04	–1.58
Canada	77	23	1.11	0.65
China[a]	32	68	2.47	0.22
Colombia	74	26	2.46	0.30
Congo, Democratic Republic of	30	70	3.63	2.13
Egypt	45	55	2.28	1.59
France	76	24	0.60	–0.36
Georgia	61	39	–0.31	–2.27
Germany	88	12	0.38	–1.48
Guatemala	40	60	3.18	2.29
India	28	72	2.84	1.19
Indonesia	41	59	4.22	–0.30
Israel	91	9	2.31	1.20
Japan	79	21	0.37	–0.44
Russian Federation	78	22	0.30	–1.68
Saudi Arabia	86	14	4.08	–0.40
Spain	78	22	0.33	–0.99
Sweden	83	17	0.30	–0.02
Switzerland	68	32	0.68	0.65
Tajikistan	28	72	1.47	1.47
Thailand	22	78	2.50	0.52

Table 3 Urban and Rural Population Changes in Selected Countries (*continued*)

Country	Population Distribution, 2000 (%)		Average Annual Rate of Change in Population, 1995–2000 (%)	
	Urban	Rural	Urban	Rural
Turkey	75	25	3.35	–2.75
Uganda	14	86	5.23	2.42
United Kingdom	90	10	0.23	–0.30
United States	77	23	1.11	–0.08

Source: Department of Economic and Social Affairs, United Nations, Population Division, *World Urbanization Prospects: The 1999 Revision* (New York: United Nations, 2000).

[a]The data for China do not include Hong Kong, Macao, or Taiwan.

Case Study—Urban Dreams: Brasília versus Curitiba

The Brazilian cities of Brasília and Curitiba offer contrasting approaches to realizing urban dreams, through a grand overarching design, on one hand, and through active citizen participation on the other. In 1956 in an attempt to relieve pressure on the burgeoning capital of Rio de Janeiro, Brazil began to build a new and more central capital inland. Constructed over the following two decades according to the design of urban planner Lucío Costa, Brasília, the new capital, became a monument to grand urban ideals. While architects Le Corbusier and Albert Speer had sketched similarly ambitious designs for the reinvention of Paris and Berlin, respectively, but never actually built them, Costa and Brazilian architect Oscar Niemeyer realized every architect's dream with their commission to construct an entire city from scratch. Monumental and sculptural, Brasília is breathtaking in its ambition, with heroic government and public buildings constructed along massive avenues resembling the shape of a bird. UNESCO recognized Brasília's unique contribution to urban architecture by designating it a World Heritage Site in 1987, "a landmark in the history of town planning."

Yet Brasília has been notably less successful as a "machine for living in" than its designers intended. It proved so expensive to construct that it led indirectly to the 1964 military coup and the downfall of the administration that created it. Once constructed, it was hard to populate and generally unpopular, not least because it was perceived to isolate the government in a city of its own far from the people it was meant to serve. Today, climate has taken its toll on Niemeyer's buildings. The city designed around the automobile is now frequently gridlocked, and many poorer people have to live in satellite towns and shanties miles from the center, a situation that was never part of Costa's original vision.

Grand designs are not the only way to make cities into popular, vibrant places for their inhabitants, however. Another Brazilian city, Curitiba, has been held up as a model of how rapidly expanding cities can become more sustainable through the active participation of their citizens. Unlike Brasília, Curitiba has expanded over the last quarter century around an innovative public transportation system featuring "subway buses" that operate like a ground-level subway system (because the city could not afford to excavate an underground subway). Regarded as one of the best models of public transportation in the world, the Curitiba system has reduced fuel consumption by 30 percent and can transport up to 1.8 million passengers per day. One reason for the system's popularity is a government initiative that offered shantytown dwellers travel tokens in exchange for bags of garbage. Another example of the citizen-government partnership involved schemes by which unemployed urban poor can work in exchange for health care, education, or rent. A major expansion of open space was undertaken to make the city a more pleasant place to live, and a cultural center was constructed in the city's abandoned quarries.

Case Study—Indonesia's Kampung Improvement Program

Striving for utopia in a third world megacity is less about realizing some idealized state of urban perfection than about generally improving the lot of the urban poor. One of the most celebrated urban improvement initiatives along these lines is the Kampung Improvement Program (KIP) in Indonesia.

Kampungs are "do-it-yourself" shantytowns on the fringes of Indonesian cities that house a large percentage of the urban population, including 60 percent in Jakarta and 63 percent in Surabaya. More than half of all Kampung dwellings are constructed by their occupants, and unlike squatters, Kampung dwellers have a legal right to occupy their land and construct dwellings of a variety of types and sizes according to their needs. Typically, these settlements also provide employment through their own industrial areas. The Kampungs grew quickly and suffered a variety of problems, such as construction of dwellings on land possibly prone to flooding, large households, open sewage, and poor access to public transportation.

With so many people living in Kampungs, mass relocation was not a practical or affordable option. Therefore, beginning in Jakarta in 1968, KIP was devised to regenerate the Kampungs and improve the lives of their occupants through a systematic program of urban renewal based on a high degree of community participation. With help from the United Nations Development Programme and the World Bank, the program built schools, roads, footpaths, and health care facilities, upgraded water supplies and sanitation, and introduced garbage collection.

KIP is held up as a "best-practice" example of urban improvement for developing countries. The secret of KIP's success can be found in three features of its design. First, it targeted resources through neighborhood organizations, which were able to generate considerable community support for improvements and ensure that projects were truly effective and relevant to the lives of local people. Second, despite limited funds, it managed to improve the lives of an estimated 15 million people and an urban area of around fifty thousand acres in its first thirty years. In Jakarta, the per capita cost of KIP was around $118; in smaller cities, the cost was as low as $23 per person. Building new dwellings or a major new settlement would have helped only a fraction of as many people and probably at a greater overall cost. Third, the program was not conceived as a means of simply improving the urban infrastructure of the Kampungs, but as a way of also improving the lives of their occupants. Separate areas of KIP concentrate on physical development (improving basic facilities, such as roads and sanitation facilities), economic development (supporting community businesses to provide employment), and social development (strengthening local communities and empowering people to improve their own lives).

Since 1969 KIP has been so successful that it has now spread to around five hundred cities and towns in Indonesia. Other countries have modified the program for their needs.

Biographical Sketches

Shigeru Ban is an architect and engineer noted for building structures of low-tech materials, such as cardboard tubes and recycled paper. Fashionable with the architectural avant-garde, Ban's no-nonsense designs have also found an immensely practical application in the form of easily constructed emergency relief shelters for disaster victims and refugees. It takes just six hours to erect one of Ban's four-person emergency houses.

Jaime Lerner pioneered some of the key principles of the late-twentieth-century "sustainable city" during three terms as mayor of Curitiba, Brazil. These principles include expanding cities around well-used public transportation links, ensuring the active participation of citizens, and improving lives through social and cultural activities, as well as improving basic urban infrastructure. Lerner is currently governor of Parana.

Richard Rogers is an architect with a keen interest in developing sustainable cities. He has designed urban master plans for a number of cities, including Berlin, London, and Shanghai. Most recently, he has advised the British government on ways of using urban regeneration to prevent ongoing suburbanization of the countryside.

David Satterthwaite is director of the Human Settlements Program at the International Institute of Environment and Development and has advised numerous organizations on urban environmental issues, including UNCHS, UNICEF, the WCED, and the Intergovernmental Panel on Climate Change. He has written and edited numerous publications on the subject, including *Environmental Problems in an Urbanizing World* (2000) and *The Earthscan Reader on Sustainable Cities* (1999).

Anna Tibaijuka is executive director of the United Nations Centre for Human Settlements and an agricultural economist who has worked with numerous organizations, including the United Nations Conference on Trade and Development (UNCTAD), UNESCO, and UNICEF. She has also worked to encourage educational and local economic development initiatives in Tanzania, her home country.

Directory

International Council for Local Environmental Initiatives, ICLEI World Secretariat, City Hall, West Tower, 16th Floor, Toronto, ONT M5H 2N2, Canada. Telephone: (416) 392-1462, Email: iclei@iclei.org, Web: http://www.iclei.org
Environmental organization linking local governments around the world

International Institute of Environment and Development, 3 Endsleigh Street, London WC1H 0DD, United Kingdom. Telephone: (44) 20 7388 2117, Email: mailbox@iied.org, Web: http://www.iied.org
Organization researching environmental and development policy issues, including those concerning human settlements

Mega-Cities Project, Trinity College, 300 Summit Street, Hartford, CT 06106. Telephone: (860) 297-4035, Web: http://www.megacities.org
International network linking businesses, nongovernmental organizations, and community groups working on urban sustainability

United Nations Human Settlements Programme (UN-HABITAT) formerly the United Nations Centre for Human Settlements (UNHCS), P.O. Box 30030, Nairobi, Kenya. Telephone: (254) 2 621234, Email: habitat@unhabitat.org, Web: http://www.unhabitat.org
Agency concerned with urban sustainability and overseeing the Habitat Agenda

WaterAid, Prince Consort House, 27-29 Albert Embankment, London SE1 7UB, United Kingdom. Telephone: (44) 207 793 4500, Email: information@wateraid.org.uk, Web: http://www.wateraid.org.uk
Organization attempting to relieve problems in developing countries

World Bank, Urban Development Division, 1818 H Street NW, Washington, DC 20433. Telephone: (202) 477-1234, Email: urbanweb@worldbank.org, Web: http://www.worldbank.org/html/fpd/urban
International organization focused on relieving poverty by financing development projects

Further Research

Books

American Association for the Advancement of Science. *AAAS Atlas of Population and the Environment*. Berkeley: University of California Press, 2001.

Ashton, John, ed. *Healthy Cities.* Buckingham, U.K., and Bristol, Pa.: Open University, 1992.

Barton, Hugh. *Sustainable Cities.* London: Earthscan, 2000.

Black, Maggie. *Mega-Slums: The Coming Sanitary Crisis.* London: WaterAid. Also available at http://www.wateraid.org.uk/research/slums.html.

Drakakis-Smith, David. *Third World Cities.* London and New York: Routledge, 2000.

Girardet, Herbert. *The Gaia Atlas of Cities.* New York: Anchor Books, 1993.

Hall, Peter. *Cities of Tomorrow: An Intellectual History of Urban Planning and Design in the Twentieth Century.* Oxford and New York: Blackwell, 1996.

Jacobs, Jane. *The Death and Life of Great American Cities: The Future of Town Planning.* London and New York: Penguin, 1961.

Lynch, Kevin. *The Image of the City.* Cambridge, Mass.: MIT Press, 1968.
Mitchell, William J. *E-topia.* Cambridge, Mass., and London: MIT Press, 1999.
Mumford, Lewis. *The City in History.* New York: Harcourt Brace, 1961.
Rogers, Richard. *Cities for a Small Planet.* London: Faber and Faber, 1997.
Satterthwaite, David, ed. *The Earthscan Reader in Sustainable Cities.* London: Earthscan, 1999.
Sherlock, Harley. *Cities Are Good for Us.* London: Paladin, 1991.

Articles and Reports

"Keep It Simple. Begin It Now. Don't Rush to Have All the Answers: Jaime Lerner's Secrets for Urban Success," http://web.mit.edu/cts/news/current/lerner.html.
Kenworthy, Jeff. "Urban Ecology in Indonesia: The Kampung Improvement Program (KIP)," http://wwwasdev.murdoch.edu.au/cases/kip/kip.pdf.
Report from the Second Global Forum of Parliamentarians on Habitat, Cancun, Quintana Roo, Mexico, 30 January 1998, http://www.sustainabledevelopment.org/BLP/Conferences/What's%20New/Conference%20Reports%20&%20Papers/Turin%20Conference%20/Global%20Parliamentarians-Habitat.
Swerdlow, Joel. "A Tale of Three Cities." *National Geographic,* August 1999, 34.
United Nations, Department of Economic and Social Affairs, Population Division. *World Urbanization Prospects: The 1999 Revision.* New York: United Nations, 2000. Also available at http://www.undp.org/popin/wdtrends/urbanization.pdf.
World Bank. "Enhancing the Quality of Life in Urban Indonesia: The Legacy of Kampung Improvement Programs." Impact Evaluation Report no. 14747, Indonesia Urban Projects, Washington, D.C., 29 June 1995, http://www.worldbank.org/html/oed/14747.htm.
World Bank, Infrastructure Development Group. *Cities in Transition: A Strategic View of Urban and Local Government Issues.* Washington, D.C.: World Bank, 2000. Also available at http://www.worldbank.org/html/fpd/urban.
World Commission on Environment and Development. *Our Common Future.* Oxford and New York: Oxford University Press, 1987

Web Sites

Brasília, City Guide
http://www.civila.com/brasilia

Brasília, UNESCO World Heritage Site
http://www.unesco.org/whc/sites/445.htm

***Global Environment Outlook, 2000* (GEO-2000), Urban Areas**
http://www.grida.no/geo2000/english/0049.htm

The Mega-Cities Project, Global Network, Jakarta, Indonesia
http://www.megacities.org/network/jakarta.asp

United Nations Conference on Human Settlement (Habitat), Best Practices Database
http://www.bestpractices.org

Documents

1. Agenda 21

Declaration on Environment and Development, Rio de Janeiro, 3–14 June 1992

The full text is available at http://www.unep.org/documents/default.asp?documentid=52.

Extracts

Chapter 7: Promoting Sustainable Human Settlement Development

7.1 In industrialized countries, the consumption patterns of cities are severely stressing the global ecosystem while settlements in the developing world need more raw material, energy, and economic development simply to overcome basic economic and social problems. Human settlement conditions in many parts of the world, particularly the developing countries are deteriorating mainly as a result of the low levels of investments in the sector attributable to the overall resource constraints in these countries. . . .

7.4 The overall human settlement objective is to improve the social, economic and environmental quality of human settlements and the living and working environments of all people, in particular the urban and rural poor. Such improvement should be based on technical cooperation activities, partnerships among the public, private and community sectors and participation in the decision making process from community groups and special interest groups such as women, indigenous people, the elderly and the disabled. These approaches should form the core principles of national settlement strategies. In developing these strategies, countries will need to set priorities among the eight programme areas in this document in accordance with their national plans and objectives taking fully into account their social and cultural capabilities. Furthermore, countries should make appropriate provision to monitor the impact of their strategies on marginalized and disenfranchised groups with particular reference to the needs of women.

2. Istanbul Declaration on Human Settlements

Second United Nations Conference on Human Settlements (Habitat II), Istanbul, 3–14 June 1996

The full text is available at http://www.unchs.org/unchs/english/hagenda/ist-dec.htm.

Extracts

1. We, the Heads of State or Government and the official delegations of countries assembled at the United Nations Conference on Human Settlements (Habitat II) in Istanbul, Turkey from 3 to 14 June 1996, take this opportunity to endorse the universal goals of ensuring adequate shelter for all and making human settlements safer, healthier and more liveable, equitable, sustainable and productive.

2. We have considered, with a sense of urgency, the continuing deterioration of conditions of shelter and human settlements. At the same time, we recognize cities and towns as centres of civilization, generating economic development and social, cultural, spiritual and scientific advancement. We must take advantage of the opportunities presented by our settlements and preserve their diversity to promote solidarity among all our peoples. . . .

4. To improve the quality of life within human settlements, we must combat the deterioration of conditions that in most cases, particularly in developing countries, have reached crisis proportions. To this end, we must address comprehensively, *inter alia,* unsustainable consumption and production patterns, particularly in industrialized countries; unsustainable population changes, including changes in structure and distribution, giving priority consideration to the tendency towards excessive population concentration; homelessness; increasing poverty; unemployment; social exclusion; family instability; inadequate resources; lack of basic infrastructure and services; lack of adequate planning; growing insecurity and violence; environmental degradation; and increased vulnerability to disasters.

5. The challenges of human settlements are global, but countries and regions also face specific problems which need specific solutions. We recognize the need to intensify our efforts and cooperation to improve living conditions in the cities, towns and villages throughout the world, particularly in developing countries, where the situation is especially grave, and in countries with economies in transition. In this connection, we acknowledge that globalization of the world economy presents opportunities and challenges for the development process, as well as risks and uncertainties, and that achievement of the goals of the Habitat Agenda would be facilitated by, *inter alia,* positive actions on the issues of financing of development, external debt, international trade and transfer of technology. Our cities must be places where human beings lead fulfilling lives in dignity, good health, safety, happiness and hope.

3. The Habitat Agenda

Second United Nations Conference on Human Settlements (Habitat II), Istanbul, 3–14 June 1996

The full texts is available at http://www.unchs.org/unchs/english/hagenda/haghome.htm.

Extracts

1. We recognize the imperative need to improve the quality of human settlements, which profoundly affects the daily lives and well-being of our peoples. There is a sense of great opportunity and hope that a new world can be built, in which economic development, social development and environmental protection as interdependent and mutually reinforcing components of sustainable development can be realized through solidarity and cooperation within and between countries and through effective partnerships at all levels. International cooperation and universal solidarity, guided by the purposes and principles of the Charter of the United Nations, and in a spirit of partnership, are crucial to improving the quality of life of the peoples of the world. . . .

7. During the course of history, urbanization has been associated with economic and social progress, the promotion of literacy and education, the improvement of the general state of health, greater access to social services, and cultural, political and religious participation. Democratization has enhanced such access and meaningful participation and involvement for civil society actors, for public-private partnerships, and for decentralized, participatory planning and management, which are important features of a successful urban future. Cities and towns have been engines of growth and incubators of civilization and have facilitated the evolution of knowledge, culture and tradition, as well as of industry and commerce. Urban settlements, properly planned and

managed, hold the promise for human development and the protection of the world's natural resources through their ability to support large numbers of people while limiting their impact on the natural environment. The growth of cities and towns causes social, economic and environmental changes that go beyond city boundaries. Habitat II deals with all settlements—large, medium and small—and reaffirms the need for universal improvements in living and working conditions.

8. To overcome current problems and to ensure future progress in the improvement of economic, social and environmental conditions in human settlements, we must begin with recognition of the challenges facing cities and towns. According to current projections, by the turn of the century, more than three billion people—one half of the world's population—will live and work in urban areas. The most serious problems confronting cities and towns and their inhabitants include inadequate financial resources, lack of employment opportunities, spreading homelessness and expansion of squatter settlements, increased poverty and a widening gap between rich and poor, growing insecurity and rising crime rates, inadequate and deteriorating building stock, services and infrastructure, lack of health and educational facilities, improper land use, insecure land tenure, rising traffic congestion, increasing pollution, lack of green spaces, inadequate water supply and sanitation, uncoordinated urban development and an increasing vulnerability to disaster. All of these have seriously challenged the capacities of Governments, particularly those of developing countries, at all levels to realize economic development, social development and environmental protection, which are interdependent and mutually reinforcing components of sustainable development—the framework for our efforts to achieve a higher quality of life for all people. Rapid rates of international and internal migration, as well as population growth in cities and towns, and unsustainable patterns of production and consumption raise these problems in especially acute forms. In these cities and towns, large sections of the world's urban population live in inadequate conditions and are confronted with serious problems, including environmental problems, that are exacerbated by inadequate planning and managerial capacities, lack of investment and technology, and insufficient mobilization and inappropriate allocation of financial resources, as well as by a lack of social and economic opportunities. In the case of international migration, migrants have needs for housing and basic services, education, employment and social integration without a loss of cultural identity, and they are to be given adequate protection and attention within host countries.

WAR CRIMES

Timothy L. H. McCormack

Despite the prevailing view that war is by nature inhumane and uncontrollable, the notion of imposing constraints on the waging of war has existed in every legal, cultural, and religious tradition throughout the history of warfare. With seemingly daily atrocities committed by the armed forces of one side or the other (or both) in ongoing conflicts today, the blatant disregard for the laws of war has become all too familiar. Even though such situations have led many people to believe that law has no place in war, the existence of normative legal standards is a fundamental basis for the objective evaluation of human behavior and for the possibility of future trials of those people responsible for atrocities. Further, the principle of individual criminal liability for violations of international law in times of war has been extended to additional categories of international crime, including crimes against humanity and genocide, committed within or beyond the confines of warfare.

Historical Background and Development

It is sometimes assumed, simplistically, that the origins of contemporary international law of armed conflict date back to medieval codes of chivalry for dueling, which had strict limitations on the circumstances and the manner in which opponents could be struck. Western history does include notions of human dignity and respect for military opposition, and some excellent research by Theodor Meron has analyzed some of these notions in Shakespeare's literature, notably in *Henry V*,—which reflects the ideology and practice of warfare in England at that time. Constraints on the waging of war, however, are not confined to Western culture, and they certainly predate medieval times. The earliest extant writings on the conduct of war are by the Chinese warrior Sun Tzu and date to the sixth century B.C. In *The Art of War,* Sun Tzu exhorts constraint by combatants in, for example, the treatment of civilian populations and prisoners captured by opposing forces. Similarly, the texts of all the major religious traditions and the historical records of all the major civilizations reflect two related concepts: the conduct of war is subject to limitations, and the actions of individuals in excess of those limitations are subject to legal sanction.

By the middle of the nineteenth century a number of countries had developed military codes of conduct. In the United States, for example, President Abraham Lincoln had promulgated the Lieber Code—so-named after its author, the Harvard jurist Francis Lieber—to apply to government forces during the Civil War. The impetus for international agreement on constraints on the waging of war is inextricably linked to the formation of the International Committee of the Red Cross. In 1859 Henri Dunant, a Swiss merchant banker, happened across the aftermath of the Battle of Solferino, part of the French campaign to liberate Italy from the Austro-Hungarian Empire. One day of fighting had left forty thousand men dead and an additional forty thousand to subsequently die from their wounds. Dunant was appalled that so many wounded were left on the battlefield without medical treatment, food, or blankets. After rallying the women of the nearby village of Castiglione to attend to as many of the wounded as possible, Dunant wrote of his observations and experiences in *Un Souvenir de Solferino* and distributed copies throughout Europe to support his call for the establishment of an independent, impartial, humanitarian relief organization to provide assistance to victims of war. His vision was realized with the establishment of the International Committee of the Red Cross (ICRC).

In 1864, the ICRC's inaugural year, the international community of states adopted the first multilateral treaty on the conduct of war—the Convention for the Amelioration of the Condition of the Wounded in Armies in the Field. This convention was followed in 1868 by the St. Petersburg Declaration banning the use of exploding bullets and by a succession of treaties and declarations emanating from the two international peace conferences held at The Hague in 1899 and 1907. By the outbreak of World War I, an identifiable international law of war had been well established (see INTERNATIONAL LAW). Each of the peace treaties imposed upon the defeated Central Powers of World War I contained clauses for the constitution of Allied tribunals for the trial of alleged war criminals. Although these tribunals failed to materialize for political reasons, the principle was established to hold individuals accountable for alleged violations of the international law of war. Germany and Turkey conducted trials of their own nationals under the watchful eye of Allied observers.

Although the international law of war was bolstered during the interwar years—notably by the adoption of the 1925 Geneva Protocol prohibiting chemical and biological warfare and the 1929 Geneva Convention Relative to the Treatment of Prisoners of War—the experiences of World War II proved to be the single most significant catalyst for further development in the field. First, in relation to the development of the law itself, the unprecedented level of civilian casualties and the devastation caused by the war prompted a fundamental review of existing law. The four Geneva Conventions of 1949, which have come to represent the cornerstones of the contemporary international law of war, are the direct result of this review. Secondly, the ruthless attempt by the Nazis to destroy Europe's Jewish population by implementing their so-called Final Solution so shocked the world that international trials for war crimes and crimes against humanity were demanded. The conduct of the trials before the Nuremberg and Tokyo Tribunals established the precedent of individual accountability for violations of international criminal law. The current momentum for international criminal justice would not exist without the precedent of the post-World War II trials for war crimes (see GENOCIDE).

Although the promise of Nuremberg and Tokyo for the establishment of an effective international criminal law regime is as yet unfulfilled, international criminal law has continued to develop and is occasionally enforced. Several states have conducted trials for alleged war crimes and crimes against humanity pursuant to domestic criminal law. With the recent establishment of the ad hoc International Criminal Tribunals for the Former Yugoslavia and for Rwanda, as well as recent efforts to establish the permanent International Criminal Court, the development of international criminal law has experienced a reawakening that is beginning to express itself in an increased commitment to trials at the national level as well as internationally (see map, p. 593).

Current Status

Much of the current research in relation to the law on war crimes either focuses upon the scope of application of the law and the problems associated with the strict legal criteria for applying its rules or upon development of the law itself, such as exposing gaps in it, pushing for new developments, or clarifying the content of specific rules, particularly as they relate to more effective enforcement of the law. Major policies and programs include education and training in the law of armed conflict to increase understanding of and respect for the law. In addition, institution building in international criminal law appears to have inspired some states to take a more proactive approach to the prosecution of international crimes under their domestic legal systems. A number of programs also exist for the collection and preservation of evidence for future trials of alleged war criminals as well as for the identification of war crimes suspects and monitoring of their whereabouts.

Research

The international law of armed conflict, also known as international humanitarian law, regulates conduct in two distinct categories. One category deals with minimum standards of protection for victims of armed conflict—wounded combatants, prisoners of war, and civilians. The principal legal instruments covering this category of rules are the four Geneva Conventions of 1949 (see Document 1) and the bulk of the provisions of the two Additional Protocols of 1977 (see Documents 2 and 3). The other category of the law regulates the so-called means and methods of warfare, including, for example, prohibitions on certain categories of weapons, rules on targeting, the protection of cultural property, the protection of civilian populations, and a prohibition on starvation as a tactic. The principal legal instruments covering this category of rules emanate from the 1899 and 1907 international peace conferences at The Hague as well as from a succession of arms control and disarmament treaties.

It may seem superfluous to state that the existence of war is a necessary precondition for the commission of a war crime, but in a strict legal sense this requirement can prove to be problematic. A substantial amount of research has been done on the issue of how to determine the precise "nature" of a specific conflict. A "state of war" has a strict legal meaning, describing a situation in which there is a formal declaration of war between two or more sovereign nation-states. Since most conflicts do not involve formal declarations of war, the preferred legal approach is to cite the existence of an "armed conflict." The Geneva Conventions of 1949, for example, apply to armed conflicts between two or more states irrespective of a formal declaration of war by any of the parties to the conflict. Although the term *war crime* has remained in use (as a preference over a much clumsier term, such as *armed conflict crime*), the term *law of war* has been replaced by *law of armed conflict* to describe the body of rules that govern the conduct of war, the violation of which constitutes a war crime. The International Committee of the Red Cross and the academic community use the alternative *international humanitarian law* to emphasize the motivation behind the law, which is to alleviate the suffering of people affected by conflict.

The question of the existence of an armed conflict, however, is still not as straightforward as might be expected. International humanitarian law distinguishes between "international armed conflicts" and "noninternational armed conflicts." The bulk of the provisions in the Geneva Conventions only apply to international armed conflicts, which the conventions define as armed conflict between two or more nation-states. Currently, only a small number of armed conflicts in the world fall clearly within this definition. These include the conflict between Ethiopia and Eritrea over their land border, India and Pakistan over Kashmir, and the United States and its allies in Afghanistan after the Taliban government's refusal to hand over Osama Bin Laden. The overwhelming majority of the world's conflicts do not meet this definition of international armed conflict because they are waged within the territory of a single state, sometimes between the government and rebel forces and on other occasions between rival rebel forces. Such conflicts include those in Algeria, Colombia, Liberia, Mozambique, Myanmar, the Philippines, Sierra Leone, the Solomon Islands, Somalia, Sri Lanka, and Sudan.

There is some disparity between the list of acts considered war crimes in international armed conflicts and those that are criminalized in the context of noninternational armed conflicts. The difficulties inherent in characterizing a particular conflict at a particular moment in time can be seen in decisions of the International Criminal Tribunal for the Former Yugoslavia, particularly the tribunal's examination of the Bosnian conflict in determining whether the Serbian government's support for Bosnian Serb militias, who were operating in Bosnia-Herzegovina, rendered the conflict "international" (see INTERNATIONAL CRIMINAL JUSTICE).

A number of scholars have criticized overemphasis on the characterization of conflicts at the expense, on occasion, of punishment for particular conduct. Steven Ratner has exposed many of the inconsistencies and disparities in the distinction between types of conflicts, which he describes as the "schizophrenias of international criminal law." Imagine the perception of injustice when two victims suffer the same atrocity but only one experience is considered a war crime because one victim suffered in the context of an international armed conflict while the other victim suffered the same fate in the context of a noninternational armed conflict. Although the definition of war crimes in Article 8 of the 1998 Rome Statute for an International Criminal Court redresses the disparity of coverage between international and noninternational armed conflicts more extensively than any other international instrument to date, the statute still maintains the distinction and, with it, a lingering unequal level of regulation, between the two types of armed conflict (see INTERNATIONAL CRIMINAL JUSTICE).

The distinction between international and noninternational armed conflicts is not the only sticking point regarding the determination of the existence of an armed conflict. Some situations of internal strife, widespread rioting, and civil disturbance may involve the use of armed force but may not necessarily reach a threshold of violence between rival forces high enough to constitute an armed conflict. The precise threshold for a situation to be considered an armed conflict is not always easy to identify, and there is often some ambiguity in the characterization of the situation for the purposes of identifying applicable international legal standards. For example, despite the volatility and violence in Aceh, Ambon, Kalimantan, Irian Jaya, and on Java, the Indonesian government argues that none of these situations represents an armed conflict. All of them involve armed clashes, rioting, and violence, but are more appropriately regulated by the more general international human rights law—which does not limit itself to armed conflict—than by international humanitarian law (see HUMAN RIGHTS).

In addition to issues about the scope of application of international humanitarian law, extensive recent research has focused on the development of the content of the law. In particular, feminist scholars, such as Kelly Dawn Askin, Christine Chinkin, and Judith Gardam, have exposed the lack of willingness in the past to prosecute sexual offenses as war crimes. Other scholars, including Cherif Bassiouni and Jordan Paust, have argued that rape and sexual violence have been recognized as war crimes for more than a hundred years. The paucity of trials for such offenses, however, despite the longevity of the prohibitions, only reinforces feminist arguments of a tendency to overlook—or at least not take seriously—gender specific atrocities in postconflict trials. Chinkin and Gardam have called for a new protocol to the Geneva Conventions focusing exclusively on increased protection for women in armed conflict. Critics of such a new protocol argue that existing law is adequate to cover these concerns and provides sufficient protection to women; the real problem is a lack of observation of existing law and a lack of systematic enforcement when the law is violated. Irrespective of this debate, the definitions of war crimes and crimes against humanity in the Rome Statute include a more extensive list of sexual offenses than any previous international legal instrument, a development that is directly attributable to the successful efforts of feminist scholars and activists. The brutality of sexual atrocities in the Balkans, particularly the establishment of Serb rape camps for the forcible impregnation of Muslim women to produce ethnic Serb offspring, led to overwhelming support for the arguments of women's groups in the course of negotiations on the Rome Statute.

Arms control and disarmament are aspects of the legal regulation of war that everyone agrees requires the almost constant negotiation of new treaties. Technological developments ensure that international humanitarian law will almost always be engaged in "catching up" because new categories of weapons will require new conventions. The first clear exception to this trend occurred in 1995–1996, with the adoption of an international agreement to ban blinding laser weapons before the technology had been deployed on the battlefield. The conclusion of negotiations for prohibitions on chemical weapons and anti-personnel land mines were much more protracted and followed decades of devastation caused by both categories of weapons. The ICRC is currently promoting a new round of negotiations on responsibility for unexploded ordnance—particularly cluster munitions—many of which remain partially or completely buried, posing grave threats to civilian populations long after hostilities have ceased.

Policies and Programs

The Geneva Conventions of 1949 explicitly acknowledge that if war is to break out, there is a much greater chance of respect for the law of armed conflict if combatants specifically, as well as civilian populations generally, know the law beforehand. Consequently, the International Committee of the Red Cross has a program for disseminating such information. ICRC delegates, many of them former military officers, are currently involved in training programs and seminars with national militaries and representatives from national Red Cross and Red Crescent societies around the world.

Unfortunately, when war does break out international humanitarian law is all too often disregarded. Even though there are uncertainties in the law, the overwhelming majority of atrocities perpetrated in the course of armed conflict represent clear violations of well-established legal rules. Why then are there so few trials of people responsible for war crimes? States cannot claim a lack of legal capacity, or jurisdiction, to explain their failure to prosecute. Under international law, states can try alleged war crimes on any of the following bases:

- territory—the acts occurred on the physical territory of the prosecuting state;
- nationality—the acts were perpetrated outside the prosecuting state's territory but by a national (a citizen or otherwise legal resident) of the prosecuting state;
- passive personality—the acts occurred outside the territory and were perpetrated by a nonnational but the victims of the acts were nationals of the prosecuting state; or
- universality—the acts were committed outside the territory and were perpetrated by a nonnational against nonnationals of the prosecuting state but because the acts constitute crimes against the whole of humanity, any state is free to prosecute them.

Universal jurisdiction, the most extensive of these standards, is the basis on which Spain requested the extradition from the United Kingdom of Augusto Pinochet in 1998 for alleged crimes against humanity committed in Chile and the basis on which the House of Lords twice agreed that the charges against Pinochet constituted "extraditable offences." That is, they were offenses for which Pinochet could be tried in British courts if the charges had been brought against him there. Many people were surprised that Pinochet, as a former head of state, could be tried in foreign courts for acts allegedly committed in his own country against his own nationals, but the reality is that the principle of universal jurisdiction for the prosecution of war crimes has lain largely dormant since the adoption of the Geneva Conventions of 1949. The Pinochet case shows that the failure to try war crimes has nothing to do with a lack of legal capacity, but the lack of political will to investigate and to prosecute.

The experience of the Nuremberg and Tokyo Tribunals raised global expectations that those responsible for initiating World War II and, particularly, for attempting to annihilate the Jews as well as other groups—homosexuals, Jehovah's Witnesses, and the Romany (or Gypsies), for instance—would be brought to justice. Although only twenty-two Germans were tried at Nuremberg, thousands of others were tried either by Allied war crimes tribunals or under the domestic laws of a number of different states (see map, p. 593). The Federal Republic of Germany tried more than ninety thousand defendants for involvement with the Nazis. Many other states tried former Nazis and collaborators on one or another of the four bases of jurisdiction.

Many of these trials were facilitated by the contributions of historians, investigators, and the relentless pursuit of Nazi criminals by international organizations. The Simon Wiesenthal Center is one of the foremost organizations with a dedicated program for the pursuit of Nazi war criminals. A number of governments also maintain war crimes investigation units to minimize the opportunities for former war criminals to conceal their past and enjoy sanctuary in their post-World War II adopted countries. These various entities have made crucial contributions to the identification of witnesses, the preservation of evidence, and the maintenance of pressure on states to initiate proceedings. More than sixty years after the start of World War II, the number of Nazi officials still alive and in good health is steadily dwindling, and trials of them are few. The trials that have been held established important precedents in the countries that conducted them. A number of senior Nazi officials, however, have managed to successfully evade justice because of a lack of political will to institute proceedings against them.

Until recently, the willingness of some states to try former Nazis has not been matched by a commitment to try their own troops for serious breaches of discipline during deployment or to investigate alleged war criminals during conflicts since World War II. Trials of senior officials from discredited political regimes seem to be the only situations, other than alleged atrocities from World War II, that have consistently resulted in national judicial proceedings. The Pinochet case, however, has revolutionized thinking about the possibilities of national trial processes. Suddenly, trials of the people responsible for atrocities wherever they occur seem more attainable than at any other time.

It is naive to suggest that all nations of the world will demonstrate a new willingness to investigate and prosecute those responsible for war crimes, crimes against humanity, and genocide, but pressure is mounting on states to take more seriously their responsibilities for the enforcement of international criminal law. The creation of the two ad hoc International Criminal Tribunals for the Former Yugoslavia and for Rwanda and the prospect of the new International Criminal Court have already raised the stakes for states. The new International Criminal Court will only try individuals if a state with a claim to jurisdiction (on the basis of the nationality of the accused or the territory of the alleged offense) is either "unwilling or genuinely unable" to do so itself. It is likely that the mere possibility that the new court will be able to act will prove a catalyst for states to utilize their own national criminal processes more extensively than in the past. The Pinochet proceedings have sent a clear message to Chile and to other states to take seriously the international crimes committed on their territories or by their nationals. It will become more difficult for states to claim a commitment to the ideals of international criminal justice in the absence of a willingness to investigate and prosecute (or extradite) those suspected of committing war crimes or crimes against humanity in other conflicts.

Regional Summaries

North America

The United States prefers to extradite alleged war criminals from other countries that have settled there rather than try them under U.S. law. In recent years a number of former Nazis have been extradited to face trial elsewhere. The United States has appointed an ambassador-at-large for war crimes and also has an extremely active Office of Special Investigations for War Crimes. All U.S. service personnel alleged to have committed war crimes or crimes against humanity abroad are tried by specially constituted military tribunals under U.S. law.

Canada has passed extensive legislation on war crimes, crimes against humanity, and genocide. On the basis of these laws, Canada has instituted criminal proceedings against former Nazis and, more recently, against Nicholas Ribich, a Canadian national of Serb descent, who fought with the Bosnian Serb militias during NATO air strikes in 1995 in Bosnia-Herzegovina. In the mid-1990s, Canada also tried several members of its military for offenses committed during their deployment to the UN peacekeeping operation in Somalia. It was painful for Canadians to accept the fact that such breaches of military discipline had occurred, and the experience resulted in the disbanding of the Canadian Airborne Regiment, a unit with a previously proud and untarnished history.

Latin America

Much of Latin America has been subject to armed conflicts, military coups, dictatorships, and extensive human rights abuses. The most recent national trials for war crimes or crimes against humanity have occurred in Haiti and in Guatemala. In both states, following a transition from military to democratic civilian rule, trials were instituted in respect of gross human rights violations, including torture, forced disappearances, and mass killings. Other states in the region that have also moved from military to civilian rule have adopted blanket

amnesties for past wrongs as a means of focusing on the future. This was the basic approach in Chile, for example, where Augusto Pinochet was made a senator for life and granted amnesty for the many human rights atrocities committed during his rule in the 1970s. Spain's request for Pinochet's extradition from the United Kingdom to face trial placed a great deal of political pressure on Chile to revisit its commitment to amnesties for past international crimes. Chile thus far has not followed the Guatemalan and Haitian examples. Argentina was, for many years after World War II, a haven for Nazis attempting to avoid justice. In recent years, it has been more willing to extradite these individuals, and a number have faced trial abroad as a consequence.

Selected Trials and Motions for War Crimes or Crimes against Humanity since 1990
1 Canada
Imre Finta, a former Hungarian Nazi, for WWII offenses in Europe.
Nine members of the Canadian Airborne Regiment for offenses during the UN peacekeeping operation in Somalia.
Nicholas Ribich, a Canadian of Serb descent, for war crimes committed while Ribich served as a volunteer with the Bosnian Serb militia during the Balkans conflict.
2 United States
Multiple court-martials of members of U.S. forces for serious breaches of military discipline on overseas deployment.
3 Haiti
Trials for 53 people (37 in absentia) for offenses during military rule in Haiti.
4 Guatemala
Ongoing trials against members of the former military regime for offenses during the civil war.
5 United Kingdom
Andrzej Sawoniuk, a former Nazi, for war crimes committed in Poland in WWII.
Augusto Pinochet for extradition to Spain for offenses committed during military rule in Chile.
6 Belgium
At least 20 Belgian peacekeepers for offenses during the UN peacekeeping operation in Somalia.
7 Denmark
"T" (name suppressed), a Croat, for offenses committed against prisoners in Bosnia-Herzegovina during the Balkans conflict.
8 Germany
Dusko Tadić, a Bosnian Serb, for extradition to the International Criminal Tribunal for the Former Yugoslavia.
Novislav Djajic, Nikola Jorgić, Djuradj Kušljic and Maksim Šokolović, Bosnian Serbs, for war crimes against Bosnian Muslims during the Balkans conflict.
Alfons Götzfried, former Nazi, for war crimes against Jews in Poland during WWII.
9 Austria
Dusko "C", a Bosnian Serb, for offenses in Kucice, a region of Bosnia-Herzegovina.
10 Latvia
Mikhail Farbtukh, former Soviet KGB official, for genocide committed in Latvia during WWII.
11 France
Maurice Papon and Paul Touvier, former Vichy officials, for complicity in Nazi offenses in France during WWII.
12 Switzerland
"G", a Bosnian Serb, for war crimes committed against Bosnian Muslims in the Balkans conflict.
13 Italy
Erich Priebke, former Nazi, for WWII offenses committed in Italy.
14 Lithuania
Aleksandras Likeikis and Gimzauskas Kazys, former officials of the Nazi-sponsored Lithuanian security police, for war crimes against Lithuanian Jews during WWII.
15 Croatia
Dinko Sakic, a former Croatian Nazi, for WWII offenses in Croatia.
Multiple and ongoing trials of Serbs and Croats for offenses in Croatia during the Balkans conflict.
16 Bosnia-Herzegovina
Multiple and ongoing trials of Serbs, Croats, and Muslims for offenses in Bosnia-Herzegovina during the Balkans conflict.
17 Serbia
Multiple and ongoing trials of Muslims and Serbs for offenses in Serbia during the Balkans conflict.
18 Israel
Ivan Demjanjuk, former Nazi, for WWII offenses against European Jews.
19 Ethiopia
More than 2,000 officials of the Mengistu regime awaiting trial for offenses in Ethiopia.
20 Rwanda
More than 120,000 people awaiting trial for alleged involvement in the genocide in Rwanda.
21 Sri Lanka
Multiple and ongoing trials of members of the Sri Lankan armed forces and of Tamil fighters for war crimes and crimes against humanity during the Sri Lankan civil war.
22 Cambodia
Former Khmer Rouge leaders awaiting prosecution pending a decision on a trial format.
23 East Timor
Ongoing UNTAET trials of militia members for offenses after a vote for independence.
24 Australia
Ivan Polyukhovich, Mikael Berezowsky, and Heinrich Wagner, former Nazis, for WWII offenses in Europe.
Source: Timothy L. H. McCormack

Europe

Trials of former Nazis and Nazi collaborators have been held recently in Croatia, France, Germany, and Italy, but it is unlikely that there will be many more such trials arising from the events of World War II. The number of perpetrators of wartime atrocities is dwindling rapidly. Latvia, for example, requested extradition of Konrads Kalejs from Australia to face trial for involvement with the

Nazis, but Kalejs died in Melbourne at the age of eighty-eight before extradition proceedings were completed.

The Balkan states of Bosnia-Herzegovina, Croatia, and Serbia have conducted trials for war crimes and crimes against humanity committed during the conflicts that erupted during the breakup of Yugoslavia. The International Criminal Tribunal for the Former Yugoslavia at The Hague will never be able to prosecute all the atrocities committed in the conflict, so justice is in part dependent on complementary national trial proceedings. Such trials are likely to continue for years.

Other European states have tried suspected war criminals from contemporary conflicts when they have attempted to emigrate without disclosing their wartime involvement in conflicts elsewhere. In addition, Belgium and Italy have tried members of their military forces for offenses committed against civilians while on peacekeeping deployments in Somalia.

Middle East

In the 1960s Israel prosecuted and executed former Nazi Adolph Eichmann (see Case Study—The Trial of Adolph Eichmann). It has also tried John Demjanjuk for alleged atrocities against Jews during WWII. The Demjanjuk trial was difficult for many Israelis, and the outcome controversial because the accused was acquitted for lack of witnesses able to positively identify him. Israel also tried Jewish collaborators—*kapos,* or concentration camp guards—in trials that fueled national feelings of anger and betrayal by those convicted.

One current controversy involves a request in Belgium for the issuance of an arrest warrant against the current Israeli prime minister, Ariel Sharon, for alleged involvement in authorizing Lebanese Christian Phalangist atrocities against Palestinians in the Beirut refugee camps of Sabra and Shatila in 1982 during Israel's occupation of the city. A Belgian court is investigating the request to decide whether to issue the warrant for a trial on the basis of universal jurisdiction.

Sub-Saharan Africa

No other region of the world is as riddled with as many recent and ongoing war crimes and crimes against humanity than sub-Saharan Africa. From Liberia to Somalia and from the Sudan to South Africa, the overwhelming majority of states have suffered atrocious international crimes. Many in the international humanitarian community have expressed profound discouragement at the developed world's demonstrated lack of commitment to assist Africa because it deems the extent and intensity of the conflicts sweeping the continent too overwhelming.

Trials for war crimes and crimes against humanity have been conducted in a number of states, but huge challenges remain. Rwanda currently holds more than 120,000 prisoners awaiting trial for suspected involvement in genocide, and Ethiopia is holding more than 2,000 officials of the deposed Mengistu regime pending trial. In both cases, individual suspects have been imprisoned for years. In South Africa there is ongoing discussion about the extent to which amnesties ought to be granted to perpetrators of apartheid-era atrocities, including those who confessed to their actions before the Truth and Reconciliation Commission that was established in 1995.

Asia and the Pacific

Despite the extensive post-World War II trials of Japanese defendants by the Tokyo Tribunal and by other Allied nations under domestic laws, Japan has never accepted full responsibility for its wartime atrocities. The so-called comfort women—sex slaves for Japanese military officers—want monetary compensation and an apology for the war crimes perpetrated against them, but successive Japanese governments have refused to meet their demands.

After decades of impunity, former Cambodian ruler Pol Pot, just prior to his death, was finally subject to a (limited) trial for crimes against humanity committed by the Khmer Rouge under his leadership in the late 1970s. The Cambodian government has obstructed efforts to establish a hybrid national-international tribunal for the trial of other surviving leaders of the Khmer Rouge. In early 2002 the United Nations announced that it was withdrawing from negotiations with the Cambodian government on this issue because it no longer considered Phnom Phen to be acting in good faith.

Meanwhile, in Indonesia the government wants to avoid an internationalization of trials in regard to military leaders and militia members for atrocities committed in East Timor in 1999 following the announcement of the overwhelming vote of the East Timorese for independence. In East Timor, by contrast, the United Nations Transitional Administration in East Timor established a Serious Crimes Unit that has already conducted some trials of militia members for atrocities committed after the balloting. After unsuccessfully instituting proceedings against three former Nazis in the early 1990s, Australia disbanded its Special Investigations Unit and decided not to pursue other identified war crimes suspects from World War II living there. Successive Australian governments have refused to respond in any meaningful way to allegations that war criminals from more recent conflicts are also living contentedly in Australia free of any fear of prosecution.

Case Study—The Trial of Adolph Eichmann

The Israeli trial of Adolph Eichmann remains one of the most significant war crimes trials of a nonnational under domestic law. Eichmann was a senior Nazi leader who headed up the Jewish Office of the Gestapo and was responsible for implementing the Final Solution. Eichmann had also been intimately involved in the development of the policy of Jewish extermination and was wanted for trial at Nuremberg. After the war, Simon Wiesenthal searched relentlessly for Eichmann and other senior Nazi figures who had fled Europe. In 1960 Wiesenthal discovered Eichmann living in Argentina under an assumed name.

Eichmann was abducted in Argentina and transferred to Jerusalem for trial. His kidnapping caused an international furor, with Argentina complaining to the United Nations Security Council that Israel had violated its sovereignty. The council adopted a resolution acknowledging such a violation and requesting that Israel provide appropriate reparation. Importantly, the Security Council affirmed the desirability of Eichmann facing justice and did not demand his return to Buenos Aires. Eichmann's lawyers attempted to argue that the illegality of the capture tainted Israel's legal capacity, or jurisdiction, and that the trial should be aborted. The District Court of Jerusalem rejected this argument and allowed the trial to proceed. Argentina and Israel ultimately resolved their differences amicably and issued a joint communique to that effect.

The Israeli court trying Eichmann relied upon the principle of universality as well as the fact that his victims were primarily Jewish as the dual bases of jurisdiction in the case. The second basis is intriguing because the state of Israel was created in 1948, and so did not exist during World War II. The argument accepted by the court was that Eichmann's crimes were directed against the Jewish people and that the state of Israel, which grants automatic citizenship to Jews anywhere in the world, had a sufficiently appropriate link with Eichmann's victims to warrant jurisdiction on the basis of nationality—albeit a nationality still in gestation at the time the acts were perpetrated. No state objected to Israel's exercise of jurisdiction and, in the absence of a competent international tribunal, a number of states explicitly approved Israel's willingness to try Eichmann.

The District Court of Jerusalem convicted Eichmann of offenses under Israel's Nazis and Nazi Collaborators (Punishment) Law and sentenced him to death. Eichmann unsuccessfully appealed, and the Israeli High Court upheld his conviction and sentence. Eichmann was executed in June 1962 and, by order of the court, his ashes scattered over the Mediterranean Sea "lest they defile Jewish soil."

Although the Eichmann trial established an important precedent for trying nonnationals for war crimes and crimes against humanity on the basis of universal jurisdiction, the trial was not without its problems and has been subject to sustained criticism. Motivations for the trial became confused, and the judicial process became a forum for the extrajudicial objective of detailing the history of the Holocaust, the evils of the Nazi regime in general, and the subsequent establishment of the state of Israel. Several commentators maintain that the exercise highlights why a trial for Eichmann before an international tribunal, where opportunities for allegations of partiality would be minimized, would have been better. This observation is probably correct, but no competent tribunal existed at the time. For all the weaknesses in the Israeli process, it was preferable, according to many other observers, for Eichmann to face trial than to evade justice and live out a peaceful life in Argentina.

Case Study—The Trial of William Calley

The trial of Lieutenant William Calley for his involvement in the massacre of 504 unarmed civilians in the South Vietnamese hamlet of My Lai is a prime example of the domestic trial of a member of a state's military forces. This particular case attracted intense media scrutiny because, according to Leslie Green, although the United States prosecuted a number of other servicemen for various offenses in the conduct of the Vietnam War, "all the crimes alleged to have been committed in Vietnam pale into insignificance when compared with the extent of the killings perpetrated at My Lai."

On 16 March 1968 a company of U.S. soldiers had been assigned to sweep through the four hamlets of Son My village to rid the area of Viet Cong fighters. Intelligence reports suggested that there was a large concentration of Viet Cong there and that the U.S. soldiers should expect strong armed resistance. Calley was the commanding officer of one of the platoons ordered to go into My Lai. Members of the platoon did not encounter a single armed enemy, but they systematically slaughtered unarmed civilians, including babies and old people. Calley was court-martialed for issuing orders to his troops to herd the villagers into groups and then to kill them. Calley was also court-martialed for summarily executing some of the villagers himself.

Although there was extensive evidence of an attempt by military commanders initially to cover up the incident, too many individuals were involved to successfully suppress what actually happened. Eventually this information reached the media, and extensive coverage of the story exposed much of what had transpired. Calley was convicted in 1972 by court-martial of three counts of premeditated murder and one count of assault with intent to commit murder. He was sentenced to hard labor for the term of his natural life, dismissed from military service, and stripped of all pay and allowances. Calley's sentence was reviewed by the convening authority, the commander of the Third Army, who affirmed the dismissal and forfeitures but reduced the period of incarceration to twenty years' hard labor. Calley's appeal to the U.S. Army Court of Military Review was dismissed and his sentence affirmed.

The secretary of the army later commuted Calley's sentence to ten years, but Calley subsequently only served three and a half years under house arrest; he was paroled after serving one-third of his already reduced sentence. In 1974 Calley instituted civil proceedings in an attempt to have his military conviction overturned. A district court judge found in favor of Calley on the basis that he had been denied a fair trial because of the prejudicial nature of the media circus surrounding the case, to which jury members had been exposed. On appeal to the Fifth Circuit Court of Appeals, a thirteen-judge court reversed the district court ruling and reinstated the verdict of the Court of Military Review. By the time of the Court of Appeals judgment, however, Calley had already been paroled and was not required to serve an additional sentence.

As painful as it was for the U.S. Army to face the reality of the My Lai atrocities perpetrated by its members, the court-martial and appeal process adduced and tested the available evidence, Calley was convicted and sentenced accordingly, the story of the massacre was faithfully recorded in the official reports series of the judgments of the U.S. Army Court of Military Review, and the lessons from the incident can be used repeatedly in the training of soldiers in the United States and elsewhere. The military court proceedings, however, are only part of the story. One of the most perturbing aspects of the affair is the reaction of some Americans to the news of Calley's conviction.

The day after the announcement of Calley's conviction, President Richard Nixon ordered Calley released from military prison to be returned to his apartment and kept under house arrest. Two days later Nixon indicated that he would personally review Calley's case. Nixon's actions prompted a letter of protest from Calley's prosecutor against presidential interference in the case. The scholar Matthew Lippman states that members of Congress publicly condemned the conviction, draft board members resigned in protest, and members of the court-martial were verbally abused. A song entitled "The Battle Hymn of Lt. Calley" sold more than 200,000 copies in the three days after the conviction was announced. The governor of Georgia, Jimmy Carter, organized an American Fighting Men's Day and exhorted the citizens of Georgia to turn their motor vehicle headlights on to "honor the flag as 'Rusty' [Calley's nickname] had done."

While Calley's conviction was greeted with dismay in some corners, one soldier who had intervened in My Lai to save some of the villagers was vilified. Chief Warrant Officer Hugh Thompson was flying a U.S. Army helicopter over the hamlet and saw the carnage below. He landed between advancing U.S. troops and a group of cowering villagers and ordered his gunner to train his weapon on the soldiers. Thompson indicated to Calley that the troops would be shot if they attempted to kill the civilians. He then coaxed the civilians onto his helicopter—seriously overloading it—and flew them to safety. Thompson received abusive mail and phone calls after his testimony against Calley and was questioned by the congressional Armed Services Committee in such a way as to suggest that members of the committee thought he should be court-martialed for his actions. The army finally recognized the heroism of Thompson and his gunner by awarding them Soldier's Medals on the thirtieth anniversary of the massacre at My Lai on 16 March 1998.

Biographical Sketches

Benjamin Ferencz was a member of the U.S. prosecution team at Nuremberg and thereafter dedicated his life to the pursuit of world peace through law. He served in Europe in World War II and had helped liberate a number of concentration camps. Ferencz has published extensively on the concept and desirability of an international criminal court and is still campaigning relentlessly for the realization of this dream.

Raoul Hilberg is a professor of political science at the University of Vermont and widely regarded as the world's leading historian on the Holocaust. His *Destruction of the European Jews* (1961) is considered one of the preeminent scholarly works on the Holocaust. Hilberg has appeared as an expert witness in numerous war crimes trials of former Nazis on the basis of his contribution to the scholarly literature.

Theodor Meron is a judge on the International Criminal Tribunal for the Former Yugoslavia at The Hague and a global authority on the laws of war and on international criminal law. He has worked for the Israeli Foreign Ministry and was for many years Charles Denison Professor of Law at the New York University Law School.

Eli Rosenbaum is the director of the U.S. Office of Special Investigations (OSI), which is charged with identifying and instituting legal proceedings against former Nazis now living in the United States. The OSI is a leading agency for the exposure of alleged war criminals from World War II and under Rosenbaum's leadership has been particularly active.

Simon Wiesenthal is a Holocaust survivor who has devoted his life to exposing Nazi perpetrators of atrocity. Wiesenthal was responsible for tracking Adolph Eichmann to Argentina in the 1960s and, in so doing, facilitating the events that led to Eichmann's trial in Jerusalem.

Directory

Amnesty International, 99-119 Rosebery Avenue, London EC1R 4RE, United Kingdom. Telephone: (44) 207 814 6200, Email: info@amnesty.org.uk, Web: http://www.amnesty.org
Organization committed to individual accountability for the perpetration of international crime, promotes and monitors trials for alleged violations of international criminal law

Asser Instituut, TMC Asser Instituut, 20-22 R J Schimmelpennicklaan, 2517 The Hague, Netherlands. Telephone: (31) 70 342 0300, Email: tmc@asser.nl, Web: www.asser.nl
Organization that publishes the Yearbook of International Humanitarian Law, *the only academic journal attempting to systematically gather information on the practice of states in relation to international humanitarian law*

Crimes of War, American University, 4400 Massachusetts Avenue NW, Washington, DC 20016-8017. Email: infor@crimesofwar.org, Web: www.crimesofwar.org
A collaboration of journalists, lawyers, and scholars that seeks to raise awareness of the laws of war and the human consequences when armed conflict becomes entrenched

Helsinki Foundation for Human Rights, 18 Bracka Street, Apt. 62, 00-028 Warsaw, Poland. Telephone: (48) 22 828 1008, Email: hfhr@hfhrpol.waw.pl, Web: www.hfhrpol.waw.pl/En
Organization promoting education and research in human rights with national committees across Europe, monitors and reports on the human rights situations in countries where it has committees

Human Rights Watch, 350 Fifth Avenue, 34th Floor, New York, NY 10118-3299. Telephone: (212) 290-4700, Email: hrwnyc@hrw.org, Web: http://www.hrw.org
Organization dedicated to protecting the human rights of people around the world, reports on national developments in the pursuit of trials against alleged violators of international criminal law

International Committee of the Red Cross, 19 Avenue de la Paix, 1202 Geneva, Switzerland. Telephone: (41) 22 734 6001, Email: webmaster.gva@icrc.org, Web: www.icrc.org
Organization mandated by governments to provide independent, neutral, and impartial humanitarian assistance to victims of armed conflict wherever it occurs, known as the Guardian of the Geneva Conventions

International Crisis Group, 149 Avenue Louise, Level 16, 1050 Brussels, Belgium. Telephone: (32) 2 502 9038, Email: icgbrussels@crisisweb.org, Web: www.intl-crisis-group.org
Private organization committed to strengthening the capacity of the international community to anticipate, understand, and act to prevent and contain conflict

Simon Wiesenthal Center, 1 Mendele Street, Jerusalem 92147, Israel. Telephone: (972) 2 563 1273, Email: information@wiesenthal.net, Web: www.weisethal.com
Organization dedicated to preserving the history of the Holocaust

Further Research

Books

Angers, Trent. *The Forgotten Hero of My Lai: The Hugh Thompson Story.* Lafayette, La.: Acadian House Publishing, 1999.

Arendt, Hannah. *Eichmann in Jerusalem: A Report on the Banality of Evil.* New York: Viking Press, 1964.

Askin, Kelly Dawn. *War Crimes against Women: Prosecution in International War Crimes Tribunals.* The Hague: Kluwer Law International, 1997.

Bass, Gary Jonathan. *Stay the Hand of Vengeance: The Politics of War Crimes Tribunals.* Princeton, N.J.: Princeton University Press, 2000.

Bassiouni, M. Cherif. *Crimes against Humanity in International Criminal Law.* 2d ed. The Hague: Kluwer Law International, 1999.

Best, Geoffery. *War and Law since 1945.* London: Clarendon Press, 1997.

Denma Translation Group, eds. *Sun Tzu—The Art of War: A New Translation.* Boston: Shambhala Publications, 2001.

Dunant, Henry. *A Memory of Solferino.* Geneva: International Committee of the Red Cross, 1987.

Ferencz, Benjamin B. *An International Criminal Court: A Step toward World Peace. A Documentary History and Analysis.* Vols. 1 and 2. New York: Oceana Publications, 1980.

Gardam, Judith G., and Michelle Jarvis. *Women, Armed Conflict and International Law.* The Hague: Kluwer Law International, 2001.

Goldstein, Joseph, Burke Marshall, and Jack Schwartz, eds. *The My Lai Massacre and Its Cover-Up: Beyond the Reach of Law?* New York: Free Press, 1976.

Green, Leslie C. *The Contemporary Law of Armed Conflict.* Manchester: Manchester University Press, 1993.

Gutman, Roy, and David Rieff, eds. *Crimes of War: What the Public Must Know.* New York: W. W. Norton, 1999.

Hausner, Gideon. *Justice in Jerusalem.* London: Thomas Nelson and Sons, 1967.

Hersh, Seymour M. *My Lai 4: A Report on the Massacre and Its Aftermath.* New York: Random House, 1970.

McCormack, Timothy L. H., and Gerry J. Simpson, eds. *The Law of War Crimes: National and International Approaches.* The Hague: Kluwer Law International, 1997.

Meron, Theodor. *War Crimes Law Comes of Age.* Oxford: Clarendon Press, 1998.

Papadatos, Peter. *The Eichmann Trial.* London: Stevens and Sons, 1964.

Peers, William R. *The My Lai Inquiry.* New York: Norton, 1979.

Pictet, Jean S. *Commentary on the Geneva Conventions of 1949.* Vols. 1–4. Geneva: International Committee of the Red Cross, 1952.

Ratner, Steven R., and Jason S. Abrams. *Accountability for Human Rights Atrocities in International Law: Beyond the Nuremberg Legacy.* 2d ed. Oxford: Oxford University Press, 2001.

Roberts, Adam, and Richard Guelff, eds. *Documents on the Laws of War.* 3d ed. Oxford: Oxford University Press, 2000.

Rogers, A. P. V. *Law on the Battlefield.* Manchester: Manchester University Press, 1996.

Sandoz, Yves, Christophe Swinarski, and Bruno Zimmerman, eds. *Commentary on the Additional Protocols of 8 June 1977 to the Geneva Conventions of 1949.* Geneva: International Committee of the Red Cross and Martinus Nijhoff Publishers, 1987.

Sassòli, Marco, and Antoine A. Bouvier. *How Does Law Protect in War? Cases, Documents and Teaching Materials on Contemporary Practice in International Humanitarian Law.* Geneva: International Committee of the Red Cross, 1999.

Schindler, Deitrich, and Jîři Toman, eds. *The Laws of Armed Conflicts: A Collection of Conventions, Resolutions and Other Documents.* 3d rev. ed. Dordrecht: Martinus Nijhoff Publishers; Geneva: Henry Dunant Institute, 1988.

Taylor, Telford. *Nuremberg and Vietnam: An American Tragedy.* Chicago: Quadrangle Books, 1970.

Woetzel, Robert K. *The Nuremberg Trials in International Law with a Postlude on the Eichmann Case.* New York: Frederick A. Praeger, 1962.

Articles and Reports

Chinkin, Christine. "Women: The Forgotten Victims of Armed Conflict?" In *The Changing Face of Conflict and the Efficacy of International Humanitarian Law,* edited by Helen Durham and Timothy L. H. McCormack. The Hague: Kluwer Law International, 1999.

Gardam, Judith. "Women and the Law of Armed Conflict: Why the Silence?" *International and Comparative Law Quarterly* 46 (1997): 55.

Greenwood, Christopher. "Historical Development and Legal Basis." In *The Handbook of Humanitarian Law in Armed Conflicts,* edited by Dieter Fleck. Oxford: Oxford University Press, 1995.

———. "International Humanitarian Law and the Laws of War: Report for the Centennial Commemoration of the First Hague Peace Conference 1899." In *The Centennial of the First International Peace Conference: Reports and Conclusions,* edited by Frits Kalshoven. The Hague: Kluwer Law International, 2000.

Lippman, Matthew. "War Crimes: The My Lai Massacre and the Vietnam War." *San Diego Justice Journal* 1 (1999): 309.

Meron, Theodor. "Shakespeare's *Henry V* and the Law of War." *American Journal of International Law* 86, no. 1 (1992).

Ratner, Steven. "The Schizophrenias of International Criminal Law." *Texas International Law Journal* 3 (1998): 237.

Schwarzenberger, Georg. "The Eichmann Judgment: An Essay in Censorial Jurisprudence." *Current Legal Problems* 15 (1962): 248.

Documents

1. The Geneva Conventions of 1949

Negotiated under the auspices of the International Committee of the Red Cross and opened for signature in Geneva on 12 August 1949

The full text of the four conventions is available at www.icrc.org/ihl.nsf/WebCONVFULL.

Extract

Article 2 [common to all four conventions: Geneva Convention (I) for the Amelioration of the Condition of the Wounded and Sick in Armed Forces in the Field; Geneva Convention (II) for the Amelioration of the Condition of Wounded, Sick and Shipwrecked Members of Armed Forces at Sea; Geneva Convention (III) Relative to the Treatment of Prisoners of War; and Geneva Convention (IV) Relative to the Protection of Civilian Persons in Time of War]:

In addition to the provisions which shall be implemented in peacetime, the present Convention shall apply to all cases of declared war or of any other armed conflict which may arise between two or more of the High Contracting Parties, even if the state of war is not recognized by one of them.

The Convention shall also apply to all cases of partial or total occupation of the territory of a High Contracting Party, even if the said occupation meets with no armed resistance. . . .

Article 3 [common to all four conventions]:

In the case of armed conflict not of an international character occurring in the territory of one of the High Contracting Parties, each party to the conflict shall be bound to apply, as a minimum, the following provisions:

Persons taking no active part in the hostilities, including members of armed forces who have laid down their arms and those placed *hors de combat* by sickness, wounds, detention or any other cause, shall in all circumstances be treated humanely without any adverse distinction founded on race, colour, religion or faith, sex, birth or wealth, or any similar criteria.

To this end, the following acts are and shall remain prohibited at any time and in any place whatsoever with respect to the above-mentioned persons:

(a) violence to life and person, in particular murder of all kinds, mutilation, cruel treatment and torture;

(b) taking of hostages;

(c) outrages upon personal dignity, in particular, humiliating and degrading treatment;

(d) the passing of sentences and the carrying out of executions without previous judgment pronounced by a regularly constituted court affording all the judicial guarantees which are recognized as indispensable by civilized peoples.

The wounded and sick shall be collected and cared for.

2. Protocol Additional to the Geneva Conventions of 12 August 1949 and Relating to the Protection of Victims of International Armed Conflict (Protocol I)

Negotiated under the auspices of the International Committee of the Red Cross and opened for signature in Geneva on 8 June 1977

The full text is available at www.icrc.org/ihl.nsf/WebCONVFULL.

Extract

Article 1 General Principles and Scope of Application

1. The High Contracting Parties undertake to respect and to ensure respect for this Protocol in all circumstances.

2. In cases not covered by this Protocol or by other international agreements, civilians and combatants remain under the protection and authority of the principles of international law derived from established custom, from the principles of humanity and from dictates of public conscience.

3. This Protocol, which supplements the Geneva Conventions of 12 August 1949 for the protection of war victims, shall apply in the situations referred to in Article 2 common to those Conventions.

4. The situations referred to in the preceding paragraph include armed conflicts which peoples are fighting against colonial domination and alien occupation and against racist regimes in the exercise of their right of self-determination, as enshrined in the Charter of the United Nations and the Declaration on Principles of International Law concerning Friendly Relations and Co-operation among States in accordance with the Charter of the United Nations.

3. Protocol Additional to the Geneva Conventions of 12 August 1949 and Relating to the Victims of Non-International Armed Conflicts (Protocol II)

Negotiated under the auspices of the International Committee of the Red Cross and opened for signature in Geneva on 8 June 1977

The full text is available at www.icrc.org/ihl.nsf/WebCONVFULL.

Extract

Article 1 General Principles and Scope of Application

This Protocol, which develops and supplements Article 3 common to the Geneva Conventions of 12 August 1949 without modifying its existing conditions of application, shall apply to all armed conflicts which are not covered by Article I of the Protocol Additional to the Geneva Conventions of 12 August 1949, and relating to the Protection of Victims of International Armed Conflicts (Protocol I) and which take place in the territory of a High Contracting Party between its armed forces and dissident armed forces or other organized armed groups which, under responsible command, exercise such control over a part of its territory as to enable them to carry out sustained and concerted military operations and to implement this Protocol.

This Protocol shall not apply to situations of internal disturbances and tensions, such as riots, isolated acts of violence and other acts of a similar nature, as not being armed conflicts.

WOMEN

Aili Tripp

Since the United Nations held the first international conference on women in Mexico City in 1975, important steps have been taken toward furthering gender equality, with women making gains in education, health care, employment, and other areas. The international community has gradually come to accept women's rights as human rights, but in spite of the strides taken, many challenges remain. In the area of political participation, for instance, women still are underrepresented in nearly all national legislative bodies, holding an average of 14 percent of parliamentary seats worldwide. In education, particularly in developing countries, women continue to lag behind men in access to educational opportunities. About two-thirds of the world's 960 million illiterates are women. Such inequalities are being addressed slowly by policymakers.

Historical Background and Development

The first advocates of women's rights in Europe, especially in the area of education, emerged in the seventeenth century. Women generally were not the beneficiaries of the social, political, and economic rights that accompanied the eighteenth-century Enlightenment, despite its democratic ideals and emphasis on individual rights. Thus, women like Mary Wollstonecraft, author of *A Vindication of the Rights of Woman* (1792), began advocating for educational and political equality with men.

The first major international struggle in defense of women's rights was over the right to vote, which started in Europe and spread around the world, in part as a consequence of colonization. New Zealand was the first country to grant women the right to vote, in 1893. Finland was the first country in Europe to grant voting rights to women (1906); Canada was the first in North America (1918), Ecuador the first in Latin America (1928), Sri Lanka the first in Asia (1931), and Senegal the first in Africa (1945). Women in the United States gained the right to vote in 1920. During the period of decolonization following World War II, a large number of newly independent nations institutionalized universal suffrage.

As increasing numbers of women joined the workforce in the industrially developed countries, they confronted new forms of discrimination. In the United States and parts of Europe, the changing labor market, the phenomenon of more women attaining higher levels of education, changes in expectations regarding marriage, and the introduction of birth control pills were all driving forces in the 1960s and 1970s in what became known as the women's liberation movement. The movement quickly took on international dimensions as women began to resist discrimination and demand equality in political, economic, social, religious, educational, and other institutions. National, regional, and international women's organizations focused on such issues as abortion, sexual harassment, violence against women, political representation, migration, sex trafficking and coerced prostitution, access to credit, land and property rights, legal rights, and many other concerns that had not been on the agenda prior to the 1970s. In international fora, women leaders sought to frame women's rights as human rights, bringing greater recognition to women's demands for equality and opposition to discrimination. Women's organizations worked through the United Nations to encourage governments to commit to advancing women's status with international conventions and agreements such as the Convention on the Elimination of All Forms of Discrimination against Women (see Document 1).

Current Status

Women's status is influenced by a combination of factors, including cultural and religious beliefs, access to education, as well as economic and political opportunities and conditions. Women's movements, both local and global, have played important roles in advancing women's position in society. By examining current research along with the current policies and programs, it is apparent that progress as well as setbacks have been made in improving the lives of women worldwide.

Research

During the last decade, considerable progress was made in improving women's status, but not surprisingly current research tends to focus on the enormous hurdles that still must be jumped, especially in low income countries, which usually rank low on the Human Development Index (HDI) and the Gender-Related Development Index (GDI) (see Table 1 and map, p. 611). The HDI is based on a combination of three indicators: life expectancy at birth, education, and standard of living, as measured by real per capita gross domestic product (GDP). The Gender-Related Development Index measures the same elements as the HDI but accounts for disparities between men and women. Another tool for evaluating women's status is the Gender Empowerment Measure, which examines whether women and men are able to actively participate in economic and political life and take part in decision making. Women's status is reflected in the effect of various societal factors on their lives, including politics, economic activity, health and reproductive rights, violence and other forms of abuse, and education.

Politics. One of the most telling indicators of women's status is their representation in positions of political decision making. Female representation in national legislatures provides a useful glimpse into how countries compare in their commitment and openness to women in prominent law-making positions. Since the 1960s there has been a gradual increase worldwide in the level of female representation in national legislatures, with a jump, according to Inter-Parliamentary Union data, from roughly 5 percent in 1960 to 14 percent in 2001 (see Table 2). The biggest gains have been in Africa, where the increase was almost tenfold during the last four decades, whereas Eastern European countries and those of the former Soviet Union experienced sharp decreases with the demise of communism at the end of the 1980s and into the 1990s. Only the Nordic countries have been able to consistently maintain female representation rates above 30 percent, which is considered the "critical mass" that allows a group with a particular set of interests to potentially have a significant impact. Only 9 out of 178 countries have more than one-third female representation. Sweden has the highest levels of female representation, with women constituting 43 percent of the parliament.

Economic Activity. There has been a growing awareness among policymakers that such key economic indicators as GDP, which measures the value of economic output produced within a country, do not account for women's unpaid labor in the home and in their communities (see LABOR AND EMPLOYMENT). This includes taking care of the family, volunteer work, subsistence agricultural labor, and self-employment or contracted labor in informal markets, which involve small or microscale enterprises that tend to be untaxed and unlicensed and are prevalent in many developing countries. Were such labor to be accounted for, economic reform and welfare and labor policies would be structured to respond not only to the demands of the market, but also to the needs and priorities of those people involved in unpaid labor, informal labor markets, and other forms of "hidden" labor. In India, for example, 94 percent of working women belong to the informal sector, working in their homes rolling cigarettes and producing foodstuffs, garments, lace, and footwear, according to the Self-Employed Women's Association. Also included among this group are weavers, potters, patch workers, incense makers, and spinners. Waste paper collectors recycle and sell their finds. Some are service workers, others are agricultural workers.

New understandings of women's labor are reconfiguring the way many policymakers think of the market as well as notions of value, efficiency, and productivity. Debates focus on how best to account for women's labor in the home. Some would like to adopt a market cost, output-based evaluation scheme to measure how much it would cost if all the services performed inside the home were sold on the market. A second approach, similar to the first, suggests measuring women's work by replacement, that is, determining how much it would cost to have someone come in to perform household jobs. A third approach involves opportunity cost. Here one determines how much a person could earn in a job outside the home if he or she were not doing housework full time. Still others argue that community work and household work have an intrinsic value of their own that cannot and should not be captured by value for exchange because the very act of quantification diminishes its value; one cannot put a price tag on nurturing and loving one's children.

Globalization has opened opportunities for some women, but it has also posed new challenges as financial crises in several regions, caused in part by the increasing global nature of economic activity, have forced women to serve as the primary safety net for their households. In Tanzania, for example, when government policies and economic crisis undermined the real wages of workers and prices of crops in the 1980s, women were the most aggressive in seeking informal sector sources of income and engaging in subsistence activities, such as farming produce. Without their pragmatic and creative solutions to economic hardship, the formal economy would have collapsed, as male workers who dominate the formal workforce would have had no choice but to leave their jobs in pursuit of informal income, which in some cases would mean the loss of health and retirement benefits, transportation, housing, and access to phones. Globalization has increased women's share of paid employment in industries and services since the mid-1980s in most parts of the world, resulting in the phenomenon called the feminization of labor. According to Guy Standing of the International Labour Organization, in 74 percent of developing countries women's share of work in these sectors rose, while in 66 percent of developing countries the male rate fell, and in industrialized countries male participation fell in 95 percent of all countries. Despite this trend, the terms and conditions of employment remain generally poorer for women when compared with men. In part because of these contradictory consequences of globalization, scholars have adopted competing interpretations of globalization. One group touts the benefits of transnational capital flows and the expansion of global markets for women, while another group criticizes the inequality and job insecurity for women created by the new world order.

Health and Reproductive Rights. Women worldwide are healthier than ever as demonstrated by the rise in their life expectancy rates (see HEALTH). Drinking water is safer; sanitation is better; many infectious diseases have been virtually eradicated; nutrition has improved; and medical care and family planning services are more accessible. Nevertheless, according to the United Nations Development Programme's *Human Development Report, 2001,* the average life expectancy of women in twenty-one of the world's poorest nations remains below age 50. The World Health Organization and the United Nations Children's Fund (UNICEF) have estimated that a woman's risk of dying from maternal causes is 1 in 16 in least developed countries, while a woman's risk is 1 in 4,085 in industrialized countries. Infections, blood loss, and unsafe abortions account for the majority of maternal deaths, many of which would be preventable with proper prenatal care and skilled health personnel attending births.

An overwhelming 70 percent of all HIV/AIDS cases are in Africa. According to the Joint United Nations Programme on HIV/AIDS (UNAIDS), in countries worldwide where HIV is transmitted primarily through heterosexual relations, women are two to four times more likely than men to become infected. This is in part for physiological reasons, but also because social and cultural factors can make it difficult for women to insist on safe sex practices. Women also may have less access to public health information and services.

Fertility rates are decreasing worldwide, contributing to slower population growth rates (see POPULATION). Sub-Saharan Africa has not, however, experienced this decline, and in some African countries fertility rates have actually risen. Africa also leads the world in births by teenagers. According to the *Human Development Report, 2001,* in highly developed countries the average fertility rate is 1.7 children per woman, while in least developed countries the average fertility rate is 5.6 children. The decline in fertility rates is the result of successful family planning programs, female education, and expanded job opportunities. Family planning allows women to space or limit the number of children they have, improving the health of the mother and of the children. It is difficult to obtain accurate statistics on abortion, but according to Population Action International, the average number of abortions annually is roughly 50 million, 40 percent of which are illegal and most likely unsafe.

Violence and Other Forms of Abuse. Although violence against women has increasingly been acknowledged in legislative measures prohibiting it, violence against wives and marital rape are still acceptable in many if not most countries. In the United States, it was not until 1994 that the Violence Against Women Act declared domestic violence a federal crime. Generally, in a global context, few rapes are reported, even fewer are prosecuted and the perpetrators convicted, and sentences remain light. Mass rape and torture of women and girls have also been used as weapons of war in international and civil conflict, as witnessed in the former Yugoslavia in the 1990s. The trafficking of women and girls for purposes of forced labor, prostitution, and slavery continues unabated. The U.S. State Department estimates that more than 1 million women and children are trafficked internationally each year, and about fifty thousand women and children are brought into the United States under false pretenses or voluntarily, only to find themselves working in sweatshops or in the sex industry.

Education. Literacy rates are rising worldwide, and they are rising faster for women than men (see LITERACY AND EDUCATION). Girls' enrollment in primary school is increasing, as the gap between girls' and boys' enrollments has been cut in half between 1975 and 1995. More women than ever are attaining a university education. Educating women has multiple benefits: It helps women in their pursuit of a livelihood and has implications for the nutrition, health, and well-being of the entire household. It improves women's bargaining power in the home by giving them more knowledge, confidence, and leverage to defend their interests vis-à-vis husbands and other family members concerning decisions affecting the family's future, including child birth.

Policies and Programs

In 1975 the United Nations held the First World Conference on Women (in Mexico City), and the UN Commission on the Status of Women declared 1975 International Women's Year, followed by the UN Decade of Women (1976–1985), which culminated in the Third World Conference on Women in 1985 (in Nairobi). In 1995 the Fourth World Conference on Women was held (in Beijing). These conferences helped galvanize the international women's movement and assisted women throughout the world in making strides toward gender parity. Several international conventions, treaties, and platforms of action are testaments of these gains and of ongoing challenges as their implementation, monitoring, and enforcement remain problematic.

Convention on the Elimination of All Forms of Discrimination against Women (CEDAW). After thirty years of work by the UN Commission on the Status of Women, CEDAW was adopted by the General Assembly in 1979 and entered into force on 3 September 1981. As of May 2001, more than two-thirds of all UN members—or 168 countries—had ratified the treaty, which commits them to take steps to end discrimination against women and incorporate the principle of gender equality into their legal systems. The convention also commits governments to establishing public institutions and adopting other measures to protect women against discrimination, exploitation, and trafficking. The convention guarantees women equal opportunities in public life, politics, education, health, and economic activities. CEDAW also addresses the influences of culture and tradition in shaping family roles and women's opportunities more generally. It is the only human rights treaty to affirm the reproductive rights of women: Women's role in procreation should not be used against them as a basis for discrimination. Moreover, states are obligated to include family planning advice through their education systems, to provide women with the information to make informed decisions regarding family planning, and to allow women the right to decide freely on the number and spacing of their children. CEDAW also allows women the right to choose their nationality and that of their children.

Protocol to Prevent, Suppress and Punish Trafficking in Persons, Especially Women and Children. This protocol, opened for signature in December 2000, supplements the UN Convention against Transnational Organized Crime. Trafficking includes the recruitment, transportation, transfer, holding, and receipt of people through coercion, abduction, fraud, or deception. It also applies to the abuse of power to exploit someone through prostitution, sexual exploitation, forced labor, slavery, servitude, or other such means. The protocol contains strong law enforcement provisions against the trafficking of individuals, but much to the dismay of women's and human rights organizations it does not contain equally strong protections for the people trafficked. This means that governments are not obligated to pay for any services (for example, health care) rendered the victim although they may do so voluntarily.

The Inter-Parliamentary Union Plan of Action. The Inter-Parliamentary Union (IPU) is the organization of national parliaments, and prior to the 1995 UN Beijing conference it determined that because men dominate political and parliamentary life in all countries, it would advocate temporary affirmative action measures, under the assumption that when parity is reached the measures will be abolished. Quota systems, the IPU's 1994 Plan of Action states, should promote a situation in which neither sex occupies a disproportionate number of seats relative to its percentage in the population. In the 1990s new efforts to introduce quotas to improve women's legislative representation were especially notable in Latin America and Africa.

The Beijing Declaration and Platform for Action that emerged out of the Fourth World Conference on Women obligated governments to work toward gender parity, fight discrimination, and enhance the status of women in the following areas: poverty, education, health, the economy, human rights, media, armed conflict, environment, political representation, violence against women, and the welfare of girls (see Document 2). It also discussed institutional mechanisms for the advancement of women, such as legislative quotas, changes in laws, policies to address gender imbalances. The Beijing Declaration helped step up ways to promote "gender mainstreaming," eliminating gender discrimination and establishing gender equality at all stages of policy making. Gender mainstreaming has been increasingly implemented in not only national government bodies, such as ministries, but also into the practices of international bodies like the United Nations Development Programme, the World Bank, and the European Union.

UN Security Council Resolution 1325. This resolution, passed on 31 October 2000, calls for states to include women in peace negotiations and give them roles in peacekeeping missions around the world. It also requires protection for women and girls against sexual assault in civil conflicts and heightened efforts to place women in decision-making positions in international institutions. Prior to the passage of this resolution, women had been active in informal peace initiatives in civil conflicts in Bosnia, Burundi, Colombia, Guatemala, Israel, Northern Ireland, and Rwanda. In these countries they had formed coalitions of women's organizations "across enemy lines" that focused on practical concerns, such as education and housing. Since the resolution was passed, however, women generally have been left out of formal peacekeeping and peacebuilding efforts as evident in the aftermath of the U.S. bombing of Afghanistan.

Gender Budgets. After the 1995 women's conference in Beijing, many countries adopted women's budgets patterned along the lines of South Africa's 1994 budget exercise and the budgets of federal and state governments in Australia. By 2000 gender-sensitive budget initiatives had been adopted in eighteen countries in four regions. Gender budget initiatives are generally coordinated by the finance ministries and involve collaboration among nongovernmental organizations and legislatures. They involve analysis of existing budgets to determine the differential gender impact on women, men, girls, and boys, with the intention of making recommendations for future budgets to improve the way in which funds are allocated. Such initiatives have thus far been adopted in Barbados, Botswana, Malawi, Mozambique, Namibia, Sri Lanka, Tanzania, Uganda, and Zimbabwe, among others.

Many of the instruments discussed above and the policies flowing from them represent a shift in accepted norms and goals regarding gender equity. In spite of some gains, gender-related policies have not always translated into major transformations if success is judged by the continuing absence of women in key leadership positions within economic, political, military and peacekeeping, religious, and other powerful societal institutions. At the same time, some of the most important changes are being advanced through women's national and local grass-roots organizations that are addressing problems of literacy, access to credit, legal aid, violence against women, and many other such concerns.

Regional Summaries

North America

In the United States, women's status has slowly been improving through the passage of legislation at the federal and state level. The Equal Pay Act of 1963,

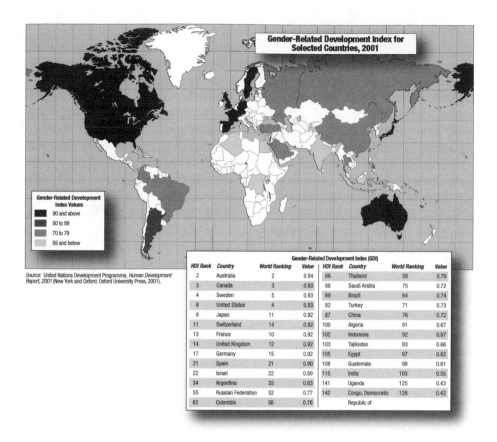

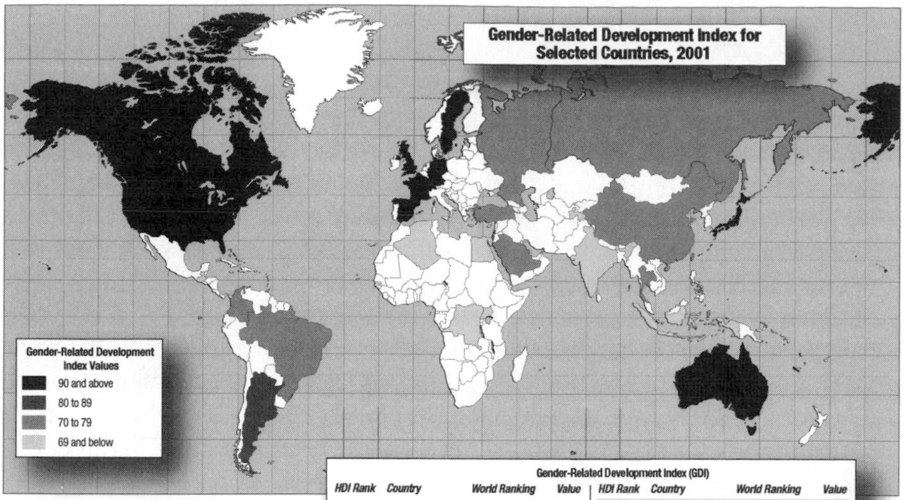

Source: United Nations Development Programme, *Human Development Report, 2001* (New York and Oxford: Oxford University Press, 2001).

Gender-Related Development Index (GDI)

HDI Rank	*Country*	*World Ranking*	*Value*	*HDI Rank*	*Country*	*World Ranking*	*Value*
2	Australia	2	0.94	66	Thailand	58	0.76
3	Canada	3	0.93	68	Saudi Arabia	75	0.72
4	Sweden	5	0.93	69	Brazil	64	0.74
6	United States	4	0.93	82	Turkey	71	0.73
9	Japan	11	0.92	87	China	76	0.72
11	Switzerland	14	0.92	100	Algeria	91	0.67
13	France	10	0.92	102	Indonesia	92	0.67
14	United Kingdom	12	0.92	103	Tajikistan	93	0.66
17	Germany	15	0.92	105	Egypt	97	0.62
21	Spain	21	0.90	108	Guatemala	98	0.61
22	Israel	22	0.89	115	India	105	0.55
34	Argentina	33	0.83	141	Uganda	125	0.43
55	Russian Federation	52	0.77	142	Congo, Democratic Republic of	128	0.42
62	Colombia	56	0.76				

Title VII of the Civil Rights Act of 1964, and Title IX, the Educational Amendments of 1972, are examples of landmark legislation affecting women's status. More recently, in the 1990s, the Family and Medical Leave Act, which was signed into law in 1993, permits any employee who has worked for at least one year to take up to twelve weeks of unpaid leave a year to look after a newborn, adopted child, or other family members in need of care. By 1993 almost twenty-seven states had legislation barring an abusive spouse or partner from the home. In 1994 the Violence Against Women Act declared domestic violence a federal crime. Many states have begun adopting legislation that would lift the privilege of spousal immunity, which permits one spouse to forego testifying against the other. Such new laws would allow prosecutors to call on abused wives to testify against their husbands.

Nevertheless, major obstacles to women's full equality remain. The Equal Rights Amendment (ERA) has not been ratified. Critics feared that the ERA would lead to unisex bathrooms and women being drafted into the military. Proponents argued that many of the victories that women had won with respect to civil rights protections and gender equity in education and pay could be erased through legislative action in Congress. Without the amendment, women have had to fight lengthy and expensive political and judicial battles on individual issues to ensure that they are not discriminated against on the basis of sex and in order to gain rights automatically granted men.

Women still are not close to parity with men in key areas of political and economic life. According to 2001 Inter-Parliamentary Union statistic, women account for only 13 percent of the seats in Congress. In 1999 women made up 46 percent of the workforce, according to the U.S. Bureau of Labor Statistics' *Employment and Earnings* reports, but in traditionally male-dominated fields they lagged far behind. For instance, only 15 percent of architects were women, as were 10 percent of engineers. Further, according to the U.S. Census Bureau's *Current Population Reports,* the median income of U.S. families with women as the sole breadwinner was slightly more than $22,000 in 1998, but households with men as the sole breadwinner fared much better, at more than $35,000.

Women in Canada have had a slight edge over women in the United States in terms of political representation. Canadians elected their first female prime minister in 1993, and today women constitute 32 percent of the Senate and 21 percent of the House of Commons. Yet Canada's labor market is highly segregated by gender, and women's earnings are on average about 61 percent of men's, according to the *Human Development Report, 2001.* Canadian women are among the healthiest in the world, with a life expectancy of 81 years. Naomi Neft and Ann Levine report that in terms of social welfare provisions, Canadian women fare better, with seventeen weeks of maternity leave for full-time workers, and 60 percent of the mother's salary paid by unemployment insurance for up to fifteen weeks.

Latin America

In Latin America, women constitute one-third of the labor force, make up more than half of the university students in many countries, and hold roughly 13 percent of legislative seats, a large increase from an average of 2 percent in 1970, based on Inter-Parliamentary Union data. Many of the changes in female representation are the result of pressure from women's movements for the adoption of national laws requiring parties to increase female candidacies. Women's movements also succeeded in having governments create state agencies that address women's concerns, change discriminatory laws, and adopt policies to improve women's lives in general. Brazil, for example, passed a legal code in August 2001 that makes women equal to men. It abolishes the concept of "paternal power," which had allowed Brazilian fathers to unilaterally make all decisions on behalf of their families. The new code requires husbands and wives to divide authority, and single mothers can be regarded as heads of households. In spite of such progressive legislation, frequently these laws are poorly implemented due to lack of funding and weak enforcement mechanisms.

Women are still often prohibited from certain categories of employment. In some countries, sex crimes can only be committed against a woman deemed "honest." Abortion is considered a crime in all Latin American countries, with the exception of Cuba. This has led to millions of women seeking clandestine abortions at enormous risk to their health and lives. Domestic violence remains one of the largest problems, with approximately 50 percent of women admitting to suffering from violence in the home. By the late 1990s twelve Latin American countries had passed laws declaring domestic violence a crime and implementing policy measures for enforcement. Hundreds of police stations staffed by women and for women in need of assistance were formed throughout the region following Brazil's adoption of them in 1985. They have been important in dealing with cases of rape and domestic violence.

Europe and the Former Soviet Union

The biggest changes in women's status in the 1990s were experienced by women in Eastern Europe and the former Soviet republics as a result of economic and political reforms. The fall of communist governments left women without the safety net of social security provisions, low-cost child care, job security, and relatively high levels of political representation. According to UNICEF's *Women in Transition,* by the end of the 1990s Russia had one of the largest gender gaps in wages, with women earning about 40 percent of what men earned. In Ukraine women earned one-third the wages that men did. Prior to the 1990s Soviet women enjoyed job security and one of the highest rates of labor force participation in the world. By the end of the 1990s female unemployment was on the rise in all the former Soviet republics. In Russia, Ukraine, and many of the other former Soviet republics, women constituted more than 70 percent of the unemployed.

A consequence of women's unemployment and lack of job security in the former Soviet Union and Eastern Europe is the growing problem of sex trafficking. Criminal groups lure young women with the promise of working as waitresses and barmaids overseas and then confiscate their passports, sometimes raping and beating them into submission, and forcing them to work as prostitutes. The number of women trafficked from Ukraine, Russia, and other former Soviet republics were among the highest in the world, matching or even surpassing the number of Asian and Latin American women being trafficked.

Economic uncertainty has also contributed to precipitous drops in birth and marriage rates throughout the former Soviet Union. In Estonia, Latvia, and Lithuania, for example, fertility rates dropped by 40 percent between 1989 and 1997, and marriage rates similarly dropped by 52 percent during the same period. Changes in women's political status were also stark. In the 1990s Eastern Europe and the former republics of the Soviet Union experienced the sharpest drops in female legislative representation in the world as quotas that had guaranteed women seats in parliament were eliminated. According to Inter-Parliamentary Union statistics, the percentage of seats occupied by women in the legislature dropped in the region from a high of 31 percent in 1980 to 9 percent in 1990, before rising slightly to 11 percent by 2000. In contrast, the Nordic countries experienced an increase in women's representation from 32 percent in 1990 to 38 percent in 2000, reflecting the overall improvement of the status of women in this part of Europe. Rates of female representation for the rest of Europe rose as women increased their number of seats from 11 percent in 1990 to 18 percent in 2000.

North Africa and the Middle East

There is considerable variation in the rights enjoyed by women in the Middle East. Tunisian women, for example, have made great strides in key areas. According to Tunisian government statistics, school enrollment of 6-year-old girls reached more than 99 percent in 2001. The percentage of young women attending universities rose to 52 percent in 2000 compared with 26 percent in 1975. Women constitute more than one-fourth of magistrates, one-fifth of lawyers, one-third of journalists, and one-third of professors. Tunisia has outlawed polygamy, and women can retain custody of their children in divorce. Women can obtain abortion on request and have access to medical services and contraception, which accounts in part for Tunisia's low fertility rate.

Similar gains for women are evident in other parts of North Africa and the Middle East. For example, while almost all other regions reported declines in female enrollment at the secondary level, North Africa was the only region that had no decline. Maternity leave benefits in many Middle Eastern countries are comparable to those in Europe and superior to those in the United States, where women get twelve weeks with no pay. Most women in the Middle East enjoy paid maternity leave. Women in Algeria have fourteen weeks leave, fourteen weeks in Mauritania, and twelve weeks in Morocco—with 100 percent of their wages paid by social security. According to the UN Statistics Division, maternal mortality rates in Kuwait, Qatar, and the United Arab Emirates are comparable to European rates, and in Iran and Jordan they are much lower than the average rates of states in Africa, Asia, and Latin America.

Many of the gains of the women's and feminists movements in the Middle East, especially in the areas of education and employment, came increasingly under threat in the 1990s as a result of the rise of Islamic fundamentalism. In some countries Islamists colluded with or succeeded in pressuring the state to curtail women's rights. National and international women's organizations, including, for example, Women Living Under Muslim Laws, have been calling for reforms in marriage, family, and personal conduct codes and have resisted limits on women's employment and opposed domestic violence and female genital cutting.

Women's organizations have also targeted the practice of honor killings, in which a woman, who is seen as the property of her husband, can be murdered by a family member with impunity if she "dishonors" the family by disobeying her husband or is thought to have committed a number of other acts considered dishonorable. Women can be murdered for being seen with a male nonfamily member without the permission of a male of the family or for marrying outside her faith. If a girl is sexually molested by a family member and becomes pregnant, she can be killed by the family. Young women who are raped may be killed.

Honor killings are also practiced in countries outside the region, including in Bangladesh, Brazil, Ecuador, India, and Pakistan, among others. The United Nations Population Fund estimates that as many as five thousand women and girls are murdered each year in honor killings around the world. Such killings are legally sanctioned in Jordan, Morocco, and Syria, and there is evidence of the practice in Egypt and Israel. Women's organizations have been especially active in resisting honor killings in Jordan and are working to have them outlawed.

Sub-Saharan Africa

The new generation of women's organizations that emerged and grew exponentially after the mid-1980s in Africa is significantly different from earlier associations in their goals, mobilization, and relation to the state. Women are taking their claims to land and inheritance to court on a scale not seen in the past and are challenging laws and constitutions that do not uphold gender equality. In addition, they are moving into government, legislative, party, and other leadership positions that previously were the almost exclusive domain of men. In Mozambique, Namibia, South Africa, and Uganda women have won provisions that guarantee them a greater number of seats in parliament. In the 1990s women sought presidential nominations throughout Africa and ran for the presidency in Kenya and Liberia.

Women have taken advantage of the new democratic openings of the 1990s, even when these opportunities were limited and precarious. The expansion of women's organizations and associational life more generally accompanied moves away from the single-party systems common in the 1980s in sub-Saharan Africa and toward multiparty politics and the abandonment of military regimes in favor of civilian rule. The expansion of freedom of speech and of association, although usually still constrained, also increased possibilities for new forms of organization in associations independent of the government and ruling party. The international women's movement and shifting international aid strategies gave added impetus to women's mobilization, especially in the areas of income generation and political participation. The spread of cell phones, email, and the Internet in the late 1990s, although primarily in the cities, enhanced networking exponentially Africa-wide, internationally, and domestically. These new connections, coupled with a significant increase in women with secondary and university educations, set the stage for new forms of mobilization and political action.

Central and South Asia

In South Asia the women's movement has focused, among other things, on issues such as economic empowerment through organizations like the Self-Employed Women's Association in India and the Grameen Bank in Bangladesh (see DEVELOPMENT AID). Such organizations successfully have linked economic empowerment to social empowerment issues, including access to health care, literacy, housing, opposing domestic violence, and other concerns. Women's organizations have also focused on rising prices, the link between alcohol and greater incidence of domestic violence, unfair housing practices, discrimination in employment, violence against women in general, and inadequate health care.

Female infanticide has been a major concern of the women's movement. In countries where sons are generally preferred to daughters—such as Bangladesh, India, and Pakistan (as well as Brunei and China)—the sex ratio is skewed, with men outnumbering women. This is related to the nutritional and medical neglect of girls and in some cases female infanticide and feticide (abortion after the sex of the fetus has been determined). According to a report by Naomi Neft and Ann Levine, female infanticide, through starvation, abandonment, or other more active means accounts for at least ten thousand infant deaths a year in India alone. Honor killings are also sanctioned in some parts of this region. More than a thousand women were victims of honor killings in 1999, based on figures of the Human Rights Commission in Pakistan. In India, women's organizations have also worked to eradicate so-called dowry deaths, the murder of young brides whose husbands or in-laws have not delivered adequate dowries. *Sati,* which has been outlawed since 1829, is the old custom in which a widow is burned alive on her husband's funeral pyre as a sign of devotion. Although widow immolation is rare—there have been about forty cases since independence in 1947—with the rise of Hindu fundamentalism in the 1980s the practice has changed in one significant respect. Women who have carried it out are now glorified, with countless people visiting shrines for them. Roop Kanwar's self-immolation in 1987, the most recent case, is particularly glorified.

The most severe setbacks for women in South Asia were experienced in Afghanistan after the Taliban came to power in 1996. Women and girls in Afghanistan become essentially "invisible," as their personal freedoms were eliminated. Women were forbidden to work outside the home and were forced to veil from head to toe. They were not permitted to move outside the home without being accompanied by a male family member, and restrictions were placed on girls' education and access to medical services. Hardest hit were the more than thirty thousand widows who were the sole providers for their families.

East and Southeast Asia

The women's movement in East Asia and Southeast Asia has focused on issues ranging from the low wages and working conditions of women in factories to prostitution, sex tourism, and sex trafficking. Another issue of concern has been the migration of women to the Middle East and other parts of Asia and Europe primarily as domestic and sex workers. There are more than 2 million Filipino workers overseas, half of whom are women. These women often suffer poor working conditions, sexual harassment, and physical abuse.

Although women have benefited monetarily from new employment generated by globalization, they receive lower wages than men, are discriminated against when trying to access higher paying jobs, suffer greater job insecurity, and have found that they can be indispensable when pregnant. They may not enjoy the privilege of being able to organize laborers or have proper representation in the workplace. Cheap labor by women has often been used as an excuse for not providing adequate social services in many countries, as their wages are seen as a source of compensation.

Women represent 70 percent of the growing part-time labor market in Japan, according to that country's Health and Welfare Ministry. Part-time workers make up more than one-fifth of the labor force. Women working part-time are paid only 51 percent of the wages earned by men despite doing similar jobs and putting in long hours of work. As women grow older, the gap in pay increases. Moreover, part-time workers do not have benefits, paid vacation, or bonuses.

Data

Table 1 Gender-Related Development Index

HDI Rank		Ratio of Estimated Female to Male Earned Income	Percentage of Adult Literacy, 1999 (age 15 and above)		Life Expectancy at Birth, 1999 (years)	
			Female	Male	Female	Male
2	Australia	0.67	99	99	82	76
3	Canada	0.61	99	99	81	76
4	Sweden	0.68	99	99	82	77
6	United States	0.61	99	99	80	74
9	Japan	0.43	99	99	84	77
11	Switzerland	0.49	99	99	82	76
13	France		99	99	82	75
14	United Kingdom	0.61	99	99	80	75
17	Germany	0.50	99	99	81	74
21	Spain	0.42	97	99	82	75
22	Israel	0.50	94	98	80	77
34	Argentina		97	97	77	70
55	Russian Federation	0.63	99	99	73	60
62	Colombia	0.45	92	92	75	68
66	Thailand		94	97	73	67
68	Saudi Arabia		66	84	73	70
69	Brazil		85	85	72	64
76	Georgia				77	69
82	Turkey	0.45	76	93	72	67
87	China		76	91	73	68
100	Algeria		56	77	71	68
102	Indonesia		81	92	68	64
103	Tajikistan		99	99	70	65
105	Egypt	0.37	43	66	69	65
108	Guatemala		61	76	68	62
115	India		45	68	63	62
141	Uganda		56	77	44	43
142	Congo, Democratic Republic of		49	72	52	50

Source: United Nations Development Programme, *Human Development Report, 2001* (New York and Oxford: Oxford University Press, 2001).

Table 2 Percentage of Women in National Legislatures of Selected Countries as of 1 March 2002

Country	Lower or Single House	Upper House or Senate
Algeria	3	6
Argentina	31	33
Australia	25	29
Brazil	7	6
Canada	21	32
China	22	—
Colombia	12	13
Congo	12	—
Egypt	2	—
France	11	11
Georgia	7	—
Germany	31	25
Guatemala	9	—
India	9	9
Indonesia	8	—
Israel	16	—
Japan	7	5
Jordan	1	8
Russian Federation	8	3
Spain	28	24
Sweden	43	—
Switzerland	23	20
Tajikistan	13	12
Thailand	9	11
Turkey	4	—
Uganda	25	—
United Kingdom	18	16
United States	14	13

Source: Inter-Parliamentary Union, "Women in National Parliaments," http://www.ipu.org/wmn-e/world.htm.

Case Study—Opposing Female Genital Cutting in Kapchorwa, Uganda

The struggle to eradicate female genital cutting has been taken up by women's organizations in parts of Africa where it is practiced and elsewhere. Ugandan efforts to abolish the practice are typical of such initiatives. Female genital cutting was only practiced in Uganda among a small group of Sebei in the eastern Kapchorwa District. Until the 1990s, the Sebei sincerely believed that their identity, culture, and values would be undermined by the abolition of female genital cutting, which was part of the initiation ceremony into womanhood. In the ritual, the clitoris and labia minora of girls and women aged 15 to 25 are removed. Strong social pressure and intimidation by older women kept girls submitting to the practice, which was considered an act of purification and a status symbol. Community by-laws forbade women from milking a cow, fetching water, or grinding corn in front of uncut women. Moreover, uncut girls and women were treated like children and so could not attend clan meetings or speak in public.

In the 1990s the Kapchorwa Council of Women petitioned the government to take measures to end female genital cutting after it found that many young women wanted to resist the practice. Meanwhile, the *cheyoshetap-tum,* the elderly women who performed the cuttings and profited from them, campaigned to promote the practice. Powerful local male elders felt their authority and leadership threatened and got the District Council to pass a law in 1988 making female cutting compulsory, threatening to cut women by force if they refused.

National and local Ugandan women's groups, linking the practice to issues of women's equality, lobbied the government to pressure the Sebei into ending female genital cutting. One of the leading forces behind the campaign was Jane Kuka, a Kapchorwa teacher who later became a parliamentarian and a government minister. Nongovernmental organizations provided funds for the female elders as an alternate source of income. They also successfully worked to transform the initiation ceremony so that the spirit of the practice was maintained, but without the actual cutting. Moreover, they did not criticize the Sebeis' culture and values or call them into question. They incorporated education on cutting, AIDS, family planning, and income-generating strategies into the initiation process. In the span of a decade, the practice of female genital cutting had diminished considerably and was on its way out, as the Sebei elders joined efforts to eradicate it. In 1998 the Sabiny Elders Association was awarded the United Nations Population Award for its work in combating genital cutting. Political pressure, health education, and the modification of the initiation ceremony combined with economic incentives for the women who carried out the cutting produced a cultural transformation that protected the integrity of the Sebei as a people.

Biographical Sketches

Flora Brovina is a pediatrician, journalist, and leading activist for the human rights of ethnic Albanian women in Kosovo. As the founder and president of the Albanian Women's League of Kosovo, she became known for her efforts to promote interethnic tolerance and understanding between ethnic groups in Kosovo. During the war between Serbia and Kosovo in 1998, Brovina established the Center for the Rehabilitation of Women and Children to provide assistance to those who had fled war-torn areas of Kosovo. Brovina was arrested by Serbian authorities in 1999 and charged with committing acts of terrorism against Yugoslavia. As a result of an international campaign and a change of government in Yugoslavia, her twelve-year prison sentence was commuted in 2000.

Asma Jahangir has been a leading advocate for women's rights and human rights in Pakistan for more than two decades. Jahangir and her sister, Hina Jilani, established the first all-women's law firm in Pakistan. They were founding members of the Women's Action Forum, an interest group for women's rights, and in 1986 they set up AGHS Legal Aid, the first free legal aid center in Pakistan. That same year, Jahangir became a founding member of the Human Rights Commission of Pakistan. As a lawyer before the supreme court of Pakistan, Jahangir has drawn attention to victims of domestic and fundamentalist violence and female victims of so-called honor killings. As a result of these and other efforts, Jahangir has faced attempts on her life, been arrested, and experienced intimidation and public abuse.

Mary Robinson was the first woman elected president of Ireland, a position that she relinquished to head the Office of the United Nations High Commissioner for Human Rights. As president, Robinson used her position to promote women's rights and to draw attention to human rights abuses from Northern Ireland to Rwanda. As a Labour Party senator for twenty years, she was a vocal supporter of women's rights in the areas of contraception, divorce, and abortion.

Nawal el Saadawi is a novelist, psychiatrist, and women's rights activist. The groundbreaking *Hidden Face of Eve* (1977) is her best-known work, exploring violence against women and girls, female genital cutting, prostitution, sexual relationships, marriage, divorce, and Islamic fundamentalism. Saadawi's protestations against Egyptian president Anwar Sadat's policies toward women landed her in prison in 1980. Upon her release in 1982, she formed the Arab Women's Solidarity Association, the first legal, independent feminist group in Egypt. The organization was banned by the Egyptian government in 1991. Saadawi's life has been constantly threatened by Islamists, who have also tried to intimidate her through court action.

Benedita da Silva rose from the slums of Rio de Janeiro to become the first Afro-Brazilian senator in Congress. She had been a leader of a grass-roots movement, organizing her neighborhood around issues of water, sewage, electricity, and keeping drug dealers away. In the 1980s she helped found the Brazilian Worker's Party and won a seat on the city council. Later, as a congresswoman, she gained acclaim for her work on the rights of women, blacks, street children, and indigenous peoples.

Directory

Association of Women in Development, 10 Sandy Hall c/o Virginia Polytechnic University, Blacksburg, VA 24061. Telephone: (703) 231-3765, Email: awid@awid.org, Web: http://www.awid.org
International membership organization connecting, informing, and mobilizing for gender equality, sustainable development, and women's human rights

Development Alternatives with Women for a New Era, Extra Mural Department, University of West Indies, Pinelands, St. Michael, Barbados. Telephone: (809) 436-6312, Email: admin@dawn.org.fj, Web: http://www.dawn.org.fj
Network of women scholars and activists from the third world who conduct feminist research and analysis of the global environment and work for economic justice, gender justice, and democracy

Global Alliance Against Traffic in Women, International Coordination Office, P.O. Box 36, Bangkok Noi Office, Bangkok 10700, Thailand. Telephone: (662) 864 1427 8, Email: gaatw@mozart.inet.co.th, Web: http://www.inet.co.th/org/gaatw
Coalition that coordinates, organizes, and facilitates work on issues related to trafficking in persons and women's labor migration

Global Fund for Women, 425 Sherman Avenue, Suite 300, Palo Alto, CA 94306. Telephone: (415) 853-8305, Email: gfw@globalfundforwomen.org, Web: http://www.globalfundforwomen.org
Grant-making foundation supporting women's human rights organizations in the areas of economic independence, increasing girls' access to education, and stopping violence against women

International Center for Research on Women, 1717 Massachusetts Avenue NW, Suite 501, Washington, DC 20036. Telephone: (202) 797-0007, Email: info@icrw.org, Web: http://www.icrw.org
Organization working in the areas of poverty reduction and economic growth, HIV/AIDS, reproductive health and nutrition, social conflict, population and social transition, and policy and communications

International Research and Training Institute for the Advancement of Women, P.O. Box 21747, Santo Domingo, Dominican Republic. Telephone: (809) 685-1222, New York (212) 963-5684, Email: instraw.hq.sd@codetel.net.do, Web: http://www.un-instraw.org
UN institution devoted to research and training for the advancement of women

International Women's Tribune Centre, 777 United Nations Plaza, New York, NY 10017. Telephone: (212) 687-8633, Email: iwtc@iwtc.org, Web: http://iwtc.org
Group dedicated to achieving women's full participation in shaping the development process through information dissemination, education, communication, networking, technical assistance, and training resources for women worldwide

Isis International Women's Information and Communication Service, Casilla 2067, Correo Central, Santiago, Chile. Telephone: (56) 2 633 4582 or 638-2219, Email: isis@isis.cl, Web: http://www.isis.cl
Feminist organization dedicated to women's information and communication needs

United Nations Development Fund for Women (UNIFEM), 304 East 45th Street, 6th Floor, New York, NY 10017. Telephone: (212) 906-6400, Email: unifem@undp.org, Web: http://www.unifem.undp.org
UN organization promoting women's empowerment and gender equality by ensuring the participation of women at all levels of development planning and practice, supporting efforts that link the needs and concerns of women to all critical issues on the national, regional, and global agendas

Women, Law and Development International, 1350 Connecticut Avenue NW, Suite 1100, Washington, DC 20036. Telephone: (202) 463-7477, Email: wld@wld.org, Web: http://www.wld.org
Human rights organization that holds forums for women leaders from around the world to articulate strategies for promoting and defending women's rights, initiates and carries out research, and assists in the launching of independent regional women's rights organizations

Women Living Under Muslim Laws, International Coordination Office, P.O. Box 28445, London N19 5NZ, United Kingdom. E-mail: run@gn.apc.org, Web: http://www.wluml.org/english/about.htm
International network that provides information, solidarity, and support for women whose lives are shaped, conditioned, or governed by laws and customs said to derive from Islam

Women'sNet, SANGONeT, P.O. Box 31. Johannesburg 2000, South Africa. Telephone: (27) 11 838 6943/4, Email: women@wn.apc.org, Web: http://womensnet.org.za
Networking support program enabling South African women to use the Internet to find the people, issues, resources, and tools for promoting women's social activism

Women's World Banking, 104 East 40th Street, Suite 607, New York, NY 10016. Telephone: (212) 953-2300, Email: wwb@swwb.org, Web: http://www.womensworldbanking.org
Organization that helps affiliates provide responsive, efficient, and sustainable microfinance services

World Association of Women Entrepreneurs, 25 Avenue de l'Orée, Bte 1, 1050 Brussels, Belgium. Telephone: (322) 648 18 42, Email: wpresd.fcem@planet.tn, Web: http://www.fcem.org
Association of women business owners from more than thirty-five countries

Further Research

Books

Basu, Amrita, ed. *The Challenge of Local Feminisms: Women's Movements in Global Perspective.* Boulder: Westview Press, 1995.

Burns, Nancy, Kay Lehman Schlozman, and Sidney Verba. *The Private Roots of Public Action: Gender, Equality, and Political Participation.* Cambridge, Mass.: Harvard University Press, 2001.

Cook, Rebecca J. *Human Rights of Women: National and International Perspectives.* Philadelphia: University of Pennsylvania Press, 1994.

James, Stanlie M., and Claire Robertson, eds. *Genital Cutting and Transnational Sisterhood: Disputing U.S. Polemics.* Champaign: University of Illinois Press, 2002.

Kabeer, Naila. *Reversed Realities: Gender Hierarchies in Development Thought.* London and New York: Verso, 1994.

Neft, Naomi, and Ann D. Levine. *Where Women Stand: An International Report on the Status of Women in 140 Countries, 1997–1998.* New York: Random House, 1997.

Nelson, Barbara J., and Najma Chowdhury. *Women and Politics Worldwide.* New Haven: Yale University Press, 1994.

Rahman, Anika, and Nahid Toubia, eds. *Female Genital Mutilation: A Guide to Laws and Policies Worldwide.* London and Atlantic Highlands, N.J.: Zed Books, 2000.

Razavi, Shahra. *Gendered Poverty and Well-Being.* Oxford and Malden, Mass.: Blackwell Publishers, 2000.

Seager, Joni, Angela Wilson, and Joan Jarrett. *The State of Women in the World Atlas.* New rev. 2d ed. London and New York: Penguin, 1997.

Stephen, Lynn. *Women and Social Movements in Latin America: Power from Below.* Austin: University of Texas Press, 1997.

United Nations Children's Fund. *Women in Transition.* The Monee Project, CEE/CIS/Baltics, Regional Monitoring Report, no. 6. Florence, Italy: UNICEF, International Child Development Centre, 1999.

United Nations Development Fund for Women. *Progress of the World's Women, 2000: A New Biennial Report.* 2001, http://www.undp.org/unifem/progressww/index.html.

Articles and Reports

Bergeron, Suzanne. "Political Economy Discourses of Globalization and Feminist Politics." *Signs* 21, no. 4 (2001): 983–1006.

Budlender, Debbie. "The Political Economy of Women's Budgets in the South." *World Development* 28, no. 7 (2000): 1365–1378.

Bunch, Charlotte. "Women's Rights as Human Rights: Toward a Revision of Human Rights." *Human Rights Quarterly* 12 (1990): 476–498.

Chen, Martha, Jennefer Sebstad, and Lesley O'Connell. "Counting the Invisible Workforce: The Case of Homebased Workers." *World Development* 27, no. 3 (1999): 603–610.

Gunning, Isabelle. "Arrogant Perception, World Travelling and Multicultural Feminism: The Case of Female Genital Surgeries," *Columbia Human Rights Law Review* 23, no. 2 (1992): 189–248.

James, Stanlie M. "Shades of Othering: Reflections on Female Circumcision/Genital Mutilation." *Signs* 23, no. 4 (1998): 1031–1048.

Jaquette, Jane. "Women in Power: From Tokenism to Critical Mass." *Foreign Policy* (fall 1997): 23–27.

———. "Regional Differences and Contrasting Views." *Journal of Democracy* 12, no. 3 (2001): 111–125.

Htun, Mala. "Women in Latin America: Unequal Progress toward Equality." *Current History,* March 1999, 133–139.

Reynolds, Andrew. "Women in the Legislatures and Executives of the World: Knocking at the Highest Glass Ceiling." *World Politics* 51 (July 1999): 547–572.

Standing, Guy. "Global Feminization through Flexible Labor: A Theme Revisited." *World Development* 27, no. 3 (1999): 583–602.

Tripp, Aili Mari. "The New Political Activism in Africa." *Journal of Democracy* 12, no. 3 (2001): 141–155.

Web Sites

Beijing +5
http://www.undp.org/gender/beijing5
http://www.unifem.undp.org/beijing+5

Convention on the Elimination of All Forms of Discrimination against Women
http://www.un.org/womenwatch/daw/cedaw

Fourth World Conference on Women, Platform for Action, Beijing, 1995
http://www.un.org/womenwatch/daw/beijing/platform/plat1.htm

Human Development Report, 2001
http://www.undp.org/hdr2001

Inter-Parliamentary Union, Women in National Parliaments
http://www.ipu.org/wmn-e/world.htm

Progress of the World's Women, 2000
http://www.unifem.undp.org/progressww/index.html

Women Watch
http://www.un.org/womenwatch

Women's Human Rights Net
http://www.whrnet.org

World Bank Gender Statistics
http://genderstats.worldbank.org

The World's Women, 2000: Trends and Statistics
http://www.un.org/Depts/unsd/ww2000/index.htm

Documents

1. Convention on the Elimination of All Forms of Discrimination against Women (CEDAW)

United Nations General Assembly, 3 September 1981; as of May 2001 ratified by 168 countries

The full text is available at gopher://gopher.un.org:70/00/ga/cedaw/convention.

Extract

The States Parties to the present Convention . . . have agreed on the following:

PART I

Article 1

For the purposes of the present Convention, the term "discrimination against women" shall mean any distinction, exclusion or restriction made on the basis of sex which has the effect or purpose of impairing or nullifying the recognition, enjoyment or exercise by women irrespective of their marital status, on a basis of equality of men and women, of human rights and fundamental freedoms in the political, economic, social, cultural, civil or any other field.

Article 2

States Parties condemn discrimination against women in all its forms, agree to pursue by all appropriate means and without delay a policy of eliminating discrimination against women and, to this end, undertake:

(a) To embody the principle of the equality of men and women in their national constitutions or other appropriate legislation if not yet incorporated therein and to ensure, through law and other appropriate means, the practical realization of this principle;

(b) To adopt appropriate legislative and other measures, including sanctions where appropriate, prohibiting all discrimination against women;

(c) To establish legal protection of the rights of women on an equal basis with men and to ensure through competent national tribunals and other public institutions the effective protection of women against any act of discrimination;

(d) To refrain from engaging in any act or practice of discrimination against women and to ensure that public authorities and institutions shall act in conformity with this obligation;

(e) To take all appropriate measures to eliminate discrimination against women by any person, organization or enterprise;

(f) To take all appropriate measures, including legislation, to modify or abolish existing laws, regulations, customs and practices which constitute discrimination against women;

(g) To repeal all national penal provisions which constitute discrimination against women.

Article 3

States Parties shall take in all fields, in particular in the political, social, economic and cultural fields, all appropriate measures, including legislation, to ensure the full development and advancement of women, for the purpose of guaranteeing them the exercise and enjoyment of human rights and fundamental freedoms on a basis of equality with men.

Article 4

1. Adoption by States Parties of temporary special measures aimed at accelerating de facto equality between men and women shall not be considered discrimination as defined in the present Convention, but shall in no way entail as a consequence the maintenance of unequal or separate standards; these measures shall be discontinued when the objectives of equality of opportunity and treatment have been achieved.

2. Adoption by States Parties of special measures, including those measures contained in the present Convention, aimed at protecting maternity shall not be considered discriminatory.

Article 5

States Parties shall take all appropriate measures:

(a) To modify the social and cultural patterns of conduct of men and women, with a view to achieving the elimination of prejudices and customary and all other practices which are based on the idea of the inferiority or the superiority of either of the sexes or on stereotyped roles for men and women;

(b) To ensure that family education includes a proper understanding of maternity as a social function and the recognition of the common responsibility of men and women in the upbringing and development of their children, it being understood that the interest of the children is the primordial consideration in all cases.

Article 6

States Parties shall take all appropriate measures, including legislation, to suppress all forms of traffic in women and exploitation of prostitution of women.

IN WITNESS WHEREOF the undersigned, duly authorized, have signed the present Convention.

2. Platform of Action Mission Statement

Fourth World Conference on Women, Beijing, 1995

The full text is available at http://www.un.org/womenwatch/daw/beijing/platform/plat1.htm.

Extract

Mission Statement

1. The Platform for Action is an agenda for women's empowerment. It aims at accelerating the implementation of the Nairobi Forward-looking Strategies for the Advancement of Women and at removing all the obstacles to women's active participation in all spheres of public and private life through a full and equal share in economic, social, cultural and political decision-making. This means that the principle of shared power and responsibility should be established between women and men at home, in the workplace and in the wider national and international communities.

Equality between women and men is a matter of human rights and a condition for social justice and is also a necessary and fundamental prerequisite for equality, development and peace. A transformed partnership based on equality between women and men is a condition for people-centred sustainable development. A sustained and long-term commitment is essential, so that women and men can work together for themselves, for their children and for society to meet the challenges of the twenty-first century.

2. The Platform of Action Mission Statement reaffirms the fundamental principle set forth in the Vienna Declaration and Programme of Action, adopted by the World Conference on Human Rights, that the human rights of women and of the girl child are an inalienable, integral and indivisible part of universal human rights. As an agenda for action, the Platform seeks to promote and protect the full enjoyment of all human rights and the fundamental freedoms of all women throughout their life cycle.

3. The Platform of Action Mission Statement emphasizes that women share common concerns that can be addressed only by working together and in partnership with men towards the common goal of gender equality around the world. It respects and values the full diversity of women's situations and conditions and recognizes that some women face particular barriers to their empowerment.

4. The Platform for Action requires immediate and concerted action by all to create a peaceful, just and humane world based on human rights and fundamental freedoms, including the principle of equality for all people of all ages and from all walks of life, and to this end, recognizes that broad-based and sustained economic growth in the context of sustainable development is necessary to sustain social development and social justice.

5. The success of the Platform of Action Mission Statement will require a strong commitment on the part of Governments, international organizations and institutions at all levels. It will also require adequate mobilization of resources at the national and international levels as well as new and additional resources to the developing countries from all available funding mechanisms, including multilateral, bilateral and private sources for the advancement of women; financial resources to strengthen the capacity of national, subregional, regional and international institutions; a commitment to equal rights, equal responsibilities and equal opportunities and to the equal participation of women and men in all national, regional and international bodies and policy-making processes; and the establishment or strengthening of mechanisms at all levels for accountability to the world's women.

WORLD TRADE

Kar-yiu Wong

World trade has experienced impressive growth since World War II, drawing countries closer and making them more interdependent. With large amounts of products crossing national borders daily, various economic sectors have come under constant pressure to adjust, causing substantial changes in income distribution, resource allocation, economic welfare, and economic growth, which affect countries' social, political, and cultural characteristics (see CULTURAL PRESERVATION and INCOME EQUALITY). In view of the uncertain consequences of such changes, government planners and economists have long speculated whether it makes sense for a country or, indeed, the world, to actively promote international trade.

Historical Background and Development

Mercantilism, which was loosely advocated in various writings between 1500 and 1750, was one of the earliest theories of international trade. It suggests that governments increase their wealth by discouraging imports and encouraging the production of exports, through which they can accumulate gold and silver. This outlook implies that one country's gain is another country's loss. If all countries were to follow the mercantilists' advice and deter imports, however, there would be no exports.

Adam Smith, one of the founders of the classical school of economics, strongly criticized mercantilist ideas. In *An Inquiry into the Nature and Causes of the Wealth of Nations,* often referred to simply as *The Wealth of Nations,* Smith applies the labor theory of value to demonstrate the nature and effects of foreign trade. Using simple, hypothetical examples, he shows that free trade can benefit all trading countries. According to Smith, a country gains from trade not because it has accumulated additional precious metal through the selling of exports, but because it is able to consume a basket of goods not feasible before the trading relationship. He also introduces the concept of absolute advantage. According to this theory, a country has an absolute advantage in a good if, as compared with another country, it requires fewer inputs (units of labor in the original theory) to produce one unit of the good, and as two countries trade according to their absolute advantages, both of them gain (or at least do not lose).

David Ricardo, another classical economist, extended Smith's theory with the concept of comparative advantage. Based on Ricardo's theory, a country has a comparative advantage in a good if it can produce the product with fewer inputs (labor inputs in the original theory) compared to producing another good. If countries trade according to their comparative advantages, both countries gain (or at least do not lose). Ricardo's theory is considered to be more robust than Smith's because there are cases in which no country has an absolute advantage or in which one country has absolute advantage in all goods. In these cases, Smith's theory is not applicable but Ricardo's is.

The work of Smith and Ricardo was enormously influential in work on trade theory and policy formulation. In the early twentieth century, Eli F. Heckscher and Bertil Ohlin proposed that the patterns of trade between countries (as determined by which goods are exported and which are imported) could be explained in terms of their labor endowment and capital. Their work is summarized by the so-called Heckscher-Ohlin theorem. They introduced a new way of looking at world trade and formulating trade theory. It also led to the development of the neoclassical framework for trade.

The neoclassical framework extended some aspects of classical economics. For example, such contemporary economists as Avinash Dixit, Murray Kemp, and Paul Samuelson have shown that free trade is good for a country. The neoclassical framework is also useful in analyzing how trade might affect income distribution, which, in turn, can be used to explain why trade liberalization might elicit different responses and different degrees of support from different groups of people in a country (see INCOME INEQUALITY). The neoclassical framework was later modified by various economists to reflect real world situations. For example, the assumption of perfect competition was eliminated in the face of such phenomena as monopoly and oligopoly. Once some of the assumptions of the framework are dropped, however, it is no longer certain that free trade will benefit a country. It is usually said that an economy is distorted if some of the neoclassical assumptions are not satisfied.

Trade theorists also focus on international trade orders, examining methods for allowing countries to conduct international trade in more harmonious and beneficial ways. After World War II, for instance, a number of international trade agreements and organizations were instituted. Over the past five decades, these trade organizations have implemented procedures and systems to promote the freer movement of products across borders.

More recently, the idea of "fair trade" has been suggested as an alternative to, or for use in addition to, free trade. While the meaning of fair trade may vary from one occasion to another, the movement attempts to look beyond market forces. According to the Fair Trade Federation, fair trade criteria are as follow:

- paying a fair wage in the local context;
- offering employees opportunities for advancement;
- providing equal employment opportunities for all people, particularly the most disadvantaged;

- engaging in environmentally sustainable practices;
- being open to public accountability;
- building long-term trade relationships;
- providing healthy and safe working conditions within the local context; and
- providing financial and technical assistance to producers whenever possible.

Currently, fair trade principles are being applied primarily in regard to the production of specific agricultural products, such as coffee and tea, and handcrafted products and clothing. Fair trade sales total $400 million annually, which is roughly 0.01 percent of the $3.6 trillion of all products exchanged internationally. These figures should rise as the fair trade movement spreads.

Current Status

Examining the welfare effects of international trade—that is, how international trade affects the aggregate economic welfare of an economy or the world—is fundamental to any analysis of trade policy. The welfare effects of trade come in many forms, including increased production capacity, general economic growth, and expanded employment. So, too, foreign trade takes many forms: trade in goods or services, movement of capital or labor, and movement of financial assets, to name a few. Since trade in goods, the so-called merchandise trade, is undoubtedly the most important form of trade and has received the most attention from government planners, economists, and the media, this chapter focuses mainly on merchandise trade.

Research

The current literature on international trade addresses three major propositions concerning the impact of free trade on the economic welfare of countries: free trade is better than no trade for an economy; free trade is the best policy for the world economy; free trade is the best policy for a small, open economy.

It is easy to understand the intuition behind these propositions and their implications: When a country trades with other countries, it exports products that are produced relatively less expensively at home; conversely, it imports products that are produced more expensively at home. Consequently, foreign trade encourages countries to make more of the commodities they are good at producing and discourages them from making the commodities that they are relatively poor at producing. Through imports and exports, consumers are able to share the fruits of specialization. Herein, lies the benefit of free trade.

According to the second proposition, however, free trade is not just good policy for individual countries, it is the best policy for the world. This means that impediments to the flow of commodities hurt the welfare of some and possibly all countries. The logic behind this is simple: The world as a whole is a closed economy. If it does not make sense for a single government to restrict the movement of products within an economy, it does not make sense to have restrictions on the movement of products within the world. The third proposition states that free trade is the best policy for a small economy, that is, one that has no power to affect prices in the world markets. The best thing such economies can do is take world prices as a given, allowing the free movement of goods and factors of production through its borders.

Given the seeming logic and intuition behind these three proposals, policy-imposed trade restrictions are more common than what one might expect. Why are governments and policymakers not acting in ways consistent with the spirit of these propositions? The validity of these propositions is based on assumptions of the neoclassical framework, but the real world is far more complicated than these assumptions take into consideration. Among these assumptions are perfect competition and no externality.

Perfect competition assumes that none of a large number of economic agents in a market has the power to manipulate market price, but this is not always the case. Two conditions stand in opposition to perfect competition: monopoly, when there is only one supplier of a product, such as a local electric utility, and a monopsony, when there is only one purchaser of a product, such as a government that purchases military equipment. An intermediate condition is an oligopoly, when there are a limited number of firms producing a particular product but none of them controls the market. Externality exists if the action of an economic agent affects other agents and such effects are not fully compensated for or penalized.

If these two conditions are satisfied, the economy is said to be free of distortion. If one of these conditions is violated, it creates distortion. In reality, distortions are common. In particular, it is recognized that the assumptions of perfect competition and no externality do not hold for many industries and countries. To illustrate the implication of these distortions, the cases of externality and oligopoly are discussed below.

Externality can occur in production or consumption, although production externality is more common. For example, a firm may spend money on the research and development (R&D) that results in the development of a new technology. This technology, or part of it, might spread to other firms, which do not share the cost of R&D. Such a transfer is called technology spillover and is considered a positive externality, because other firms benefit from it. Pollution is another example of externality, although a negative one, because pollution caused by one company can affect negatively the productive capacity of other companies.

In the presence of externality, the production levels chosen by a firm might diverge from the levels that government policymakers consider optimum given the needs of the economy and society. Consider first pollution and other types of negative externality. The government might want companies to decrease production and thus pollute less if there is a direct link between production levels and pollution levels. The divergence exists because the company will not care much about the negative effects of pollution on other firms, but the government will. This is why it is sometimes said that in the presence of negative externality without government intervention, a company will overproduce. Thus, regulation might be in order. In the case of a positive externality, such as R&D and technology spillover, the opposite occurs. A company ignores the benefits other companies gain through spillover and chooses an R&D level lower than what the government would prefer. From the government's point of view, the company underproduces. Thus, subsidies on R&D might be suggested.

Suppose now that an economy characterized by externality trades freely with another economy. Would their economies necessarily benefit? First it must be noted that free trade creates two effects—comparative advantage and externality—and they may produce opposite results. Comparative advantage is positive and is due to the fact that with free trade a country produces more of the goods that it is relatively better at producing; conversely, a country will produce fewer of the goods that it is relatively not good at producing. This effect leads to the first proposition discussed above—free trade is good for an economy. As noted, in the absence of government intervention, positive externality is linked to underproduction and negative externality is linked to overproduction. If trade appropriately encourages the output level of the industry subject to positive externality, the externality effect is positive. The combination of comparative advantage and externality effects produces the total impact of free trade on the economic welfare of an economy. If the externality effect is negative and significant in magnitude, then free trade can bring harm to an economy.

Oligopoly, a market with a limited number of producers, is common. For example, the car, computer, airplane, motion picture, and petroleum industries are oligopolistic. Oligopolies tend to develop naturally in industries that require a large investment in R&D or in capital expenditures, and oligopolistic firms behave quite differently from competitive firms. First, each firm has the ability to affect market price through a change in output level, an ability called monopoly power. Consider Boeing, the aircraft manufacturing giant. If Boeing substantially boosts its production, prices would fall, as manufactures will have to drop their prices to sell the extra airplanes on the market. Firms with monopoly power, however, tend to supply fewer products and charge a higher price than would a competitive firm. So, food and drinks sold inside a theater, where only an authorized supplier is allowed to sell these products, are more expensive than they are outside the theater, where competition exists. Second, since there are a small number of suppliers in the market, the production decisions of each firm will greatly affect what other firms decide to produce. Thus Boeing is extremely sensitive to the production decisions of Airbus, and vice versa.

When free trade is allowed, world prices and trade volumes depend not only on market conditions and technology, but also on how firms compete. In general, all these factors interact, so it is difficult to predict outcomes. It is more or less like forecasting the weather. Given the level of difficulty in determining all these factors, the effects of trade on the economy are in general ambiguous, and there is no guarantee that free trade will be beneficial to an economy.

Policies and Programs

In the real world, free trade is less common than traditional theory suggests it should be. This is in part due to direct trade interventions, such as import and export taxes and subsidies, and quantitative restrictions, such as quotas. Other domestic policies also can have significant impacts on foreign trade. For example, health requirements or environmental regulations can affect trade levels by, for instance, increasing costs of production.

National governments use various arguments to justify trade restrictions and other interventions. Some are found in trade theory, as it is recognized that the real world diverges from the theoretical model that neoclassical assumptions describe. Some arguments, however, are based on nontrade or noneconomic objectives, such as employment, environment, labor standards, and health concerns (see ENERGY, GLOBAL WARMING, HEALTH, LABOR AND EMPLOYMENT, and POLLUTION). While trade theorists are careful when talking about the benefits of free trade, given the divergence between theory and reality, they are still generally skeptical of trade-impediment or trade-promotion arguments. Some of the issues in this area concern external monopoly power, trade war, political economy, strategic trade policies, and noneconomic objectives.

External Monopoly Power. In world markets, size does matter. Large economies, which can influence world prices by changing their trade volume, have significant incentives for imposing trade restrictions. In world markets, large economies can act like monopolists (big suppliers of its products) *and* monopsonists (big buyers of foreign products). For example, Boeing could supply less and charge more, and governments could buy less and pay less. Since individual consumers and producers within the markets of these large economies are too small and too numerous to regulate monopoly and monopsony power, the government can intervene with policies, such as tariffs, to meet this goal. In other words, for a large open economy, a tariff of an optimal rate can push the welfare of the economy to the maximum, even though free trade is beneficial.

Trade War. Trade restrictions for the purpose of exercising monopoly and monopsony power may not, however, work as expected. In some cases, such policies could bring harm instead of benefits. The external monopoly power argument is based on the assumption that, in the face of tariffs imposed by one government, other governments will allow free trade or remain passive in policy setting. There are, however, two reasons why other governments will not remain passive. First, while a tariff may improve the economic welfare of one country, it will hurt other countries by reducing the potential market and, consequently, decreasing the economic viability of the affected industry. Second, these additional countries, being large and open, have reasons to exploit their monopoly or monopsony power with tariffs of their own. When all large economies impose tariffs on imports, a trade war results.

A trade war is usually a lose-lose situation. When a country imposes a tariff with the purpose of trying to improve its welfare, it shrinks the trade opportunities available to other countries. When these countries retaliate with their own tariffs, they also limit the trading opportunities available to the country that imposed the initial tariff. As a result, in a trade war all countries risk contracted trade, and all of them therefore could be hurt.

Political Economy. In some cases, foreign trade is restricted not necessarily because of economic factors, but because of interactions between political forces within the economy. In Western democratic societies, individuals and groups of individuals have the right to express opinions about government policies and to exert pressure on the government for or against a particular policy. Individuals can pool resources to lobby for or against a particular measure. In many cases, such activities can determine the outcome of a political debate. Sometimes a policy is adopted not because it best improves the economic welfare of individuals, but because it is backed by politically strong lobbying groups.

Western democratic societies have built-in structures that tend toward more trade restrictive policies than what economic theory would determine. The reason is that people who would benefit from trade restrictions are usually more concentrated, smaller in number, and more devoted to their cause. For example, workers in a domestic import-competing industry, one that goes up against imports from foreign producers, (such as the automotive industry in the United States), might be faced with the threat of being laid off. Given the size of the workforce, however, they can organize and pool the resources necessary to lobby for trade protection (see LABOR AND EMPLOYMENT).

On the other hand, consumers of foreign products benefit from free trade, but they are more difficult to organize into lobbying groups. These consumers are larger in number but less devoted to organizing than workers in the industries affected, because the benefit to each individual is small (although the gain as a group might be significant if tallied). This was evident in the debate over the North American Free Trade Agreement (NAFTA) (see Document 1). Even though most economists thought that NAFTA would benefit the economies of Canada, Mexico, and the United States, especially from the perspective of lower prices for consumers, other vocal groups, such as labor unions whose workers were threatened by lower-cost labor in Mexico, organized and stood against the agreement.

Strategic Trade Policies. Strategic trade policies refer to measures that governments take when markets are less than perfectly competitive. This would be the case regarding aircraft production, where for example, Boeing and Airbus, the latter of which is operated by a consortium of European companies, are competing in a market characterized as oligopolistic. The presence of oligopoly, which is widespread in most economies, requires a unique set of policies in order to render benefits to the economy. One approach is for government not to restrict trade, as in the traditional framework of perfect competition, but instead to promote it, using for example export subsidies that support the R&D needs of a firm or industry or their production. The rationale is that, when a government promotes a local firm's production and export capacity, the firm's rivals in other countries will respond by lowering output to avoid flooding the marketplace, which helps the subsidized firms capture a larger share of the market, usually at the expense of its rivals. The export promotion policies adopted by many countries, such as Japan, can be regarded as strategic trade policies, so named because they help to position a firm or industry within the world marketplace. A recent dispute between Boeing and Airbus can be explained in terms of this type of policy, with Boeing and the U.S. government accusing the Europeans of unfair trade practices for subsidizing the production and export of airplanes by Airbus to place it at an advantage.

Trade theorists, however, are skeptical about the usefulness of strategic trade policies for several reasons. First, the success of a strategic trade policy depends on a range of factors and conditions. If the right conditions are not met, the optimal policy could turn out to be a trade restriction, rather than an export subsidy, which could have a devastating effect on economic welfare. Second, the appropriate use of a strategic export subsidy requires a lot of information. The difficulty for a local government is that much of the information, such as firms' cost structures and technology, is firm specific. Firms hardly have incentive to reveal this information to the government, and if they know how the information will be used to determine the amount of the subsidy, they will likely give misleading information in order to obtain a larger subsidy. Third, firms in oligopolistic markets are large entities, likely already taking in big profits. Politically it is difficult to ask the rest of the economy to subsidize these firms, making their profits even greater. Fourth, subsidy expenditures have to be raised from the economy or taken from the government's budget. This can be politically costly. Furthermore, with limited budgets, the government may have to target only select industries for promotion. To target the right industries may require information that the government does not have or is costly to obtain. Fifth, when firms believe that the government is thinking of subsidizing exports, they will have incentives to lobby for subsidies in their own industry, thus wasting finite resources on lobbying. The policy outcome may, therefore, depend more on the political power of various firms than on the economic merits of different plans for subsidization.

Noneconomic Objectives. Some arguments for trade restrictions are based on noneconomic objectives, which can be domestic or foreign. Domestic noneconomic objectives include employment improvement and protection of an infant industry that has the potential to expand significantly, and foreign noneconomic objectives include a variety of internationally accepted standards, such as protection of the environment, prohibitions on child labor, and improvement in human rights records (see GLOBAL WARMING, HUMAN RIGHTS, and POLLUTION).

Trade restrictions often are used to achieve these objectives. For example, if an industry is faced with layoffs in an import-competing industry, a tariff could limit competition from abroad. If a new industry is developing, tariffs might be recommended to protect it during it's the early stages of development. Trade sanctions or restrictions can also be used to put pressure on countries or foreign firms to improve their environmental protection practices, press for restrictions on child labor, or improve conditions for other workers.

Trade theorists usually are cautious about the use of trade policies to achieve noneconomic goals and argue that trade restrictions are not the best policy for achieving such objectives. For example, if a government's objective is to improve the employment level in an industry under import competition, a production subsidy, which the government would pay to firms for boosting production, is better than a tariff because a production subsidy does not negatively affect consumer price. An even better policy is an employment subsidy, which a firm receives for each worker it employs, because it helps workers directly without unintended effects.

Sometimes trade restrictions may not achieve the desired objective. For example, a trade sanction might be used to pressure a country into adopting a particular policy, such as environmental protection. The sanction will not, however, work if the targeted country does not feel the potential damage is high enough. An example of trade sanctions that have not achieved their desired objectives are those against Iraq following the Gulf War.

Regional Summaries

Although practically every country has an open economy, not every one of them is equally trade oriented. Some countries are able to generate larger volumes of trade while others are less capable (see Tables 1 and 2 and map, p. 636). Trade volume is affected by a number of factors: technologies, resources, government policies, distances between borders, and noneconomic factors, such as political, historical, social, cultural, and legal institutions and traditions. The data in the following summaries of trade are taken from the International Monetary Fund's *Directions of Trade Statistics.*

North America

Although geographically Mexico is often considered part of Central America, it is treated here as a North American country because it signed the North American Free Trade Agreement with the United States and Canada. The United States not only has the biggest economy in the world, it also is the biggest trader in terms of exports and imports. In 2000 it sold products worth $836 billion to the rest of the world and purchased foreign goods worth $1,190 billion, much more than any other country. Canada and Mexico are also big traders, selling $274 billion and $163 billion of products while buying $248 billion and $143 billion of goods, respectively. They are the United States' major trading partners.

The United States has huge trade deficits, meaning that it imports more than it exports. For example, in 2000 it recorded a merchandise trade deficit of $354 billion, which was bigger than the level of export or import of nearly all other countries (except for the exports and imports of Germany and the exports of Japan and China). U.S. trade deficits, which worry many policymakers and have been used as an argument for protectionist measures, were mainly financed by the surpluses of other trade accounts: trade in services, current account (including the income earned by U.S. firms invested abroad), and capital account (net inflow of foreign capital). Other countries' willingness to hold U.S. dollars also helped finance part of the deficit.

Latin America

Brazil is the largest country and the biggest trader in Latin America. In 2000 its trade volume, the sum of the value of its imports and exports, of $120.6 billion was more than twice that of the second-ranked country in the region, Argentina, whose trade volume totaled $51.2 billion. Venezuela and Chile also had high trade volumes, selling and buying goods worth $44.2 billion and

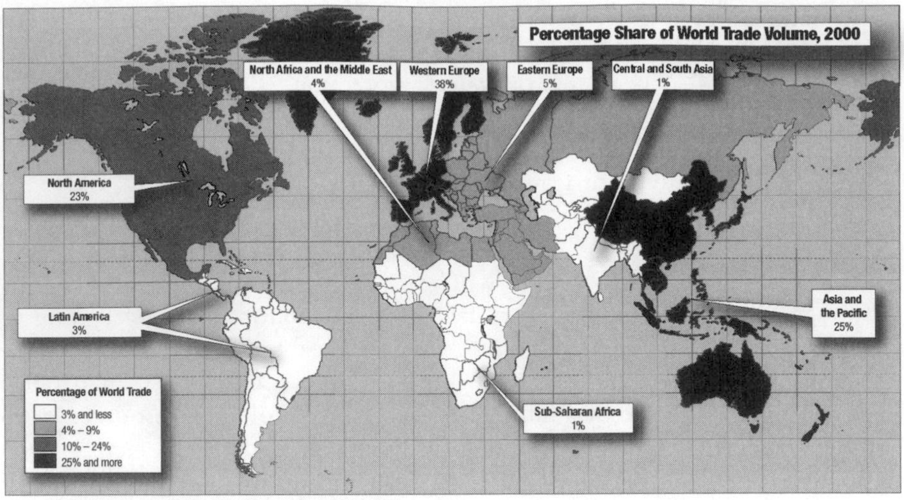

Source: International Monetary Fund, *Directions of Trade Statistics* (Washington, D.C.: IMF, 2001).
Note: Volume of trade equals sum of values of exports and imports.

$37.0 billion, respectively. In general, however, South American countries have small trade volumes. This is due, in part, to their location relatively far away from other countries, and because most of them traditionally have adopted import substitution policies geared toward development of domestic industries. Additionally, the countries of Central America are small, and their trade volumes are commensurate.

Western Europe

In 2001 Western Europe had the biggest share of the world's trade, accounting for 38.1 percent of all trade. This is due mainly to the formation of the European Union, within which products, capital, and workers are given freedom of movement among member countries. The three countries in this region with the highest trade volume were Germany ($1,031.5 billion), France ($635.9 billion), and the United Kingdom ($625.2 billion). It is interesting to note that most of the countries in this region are trade dependent. That is, they rely heavily on trade with other countries. Eleven out of twenty of them had a foreign trade volume greater than $100 billion in 2000.

Even though Western European countries have large foreign trade volumes and more or less similar trade policies, they differ greatly in trade balances. For example, Germany had a trade surplus of $91.2 billion, while the United Kingdom experienced a trade deficit of $52.2 billion. Such a difference in performance shows that Western European countries are far from being homogeneous. They have a wide range of tastes, technologies, and human and natural resources available for production, and government fiscal and monetary policies, which also affect capital accounts.

Eastern Europe

Eastern Europe consists mainly of the former socialist countries of Europe, including Russia. They are called transition economies because they are moving from an economic system characterized by government command and control to economies more dependent on market forces. Turkey is also included here due to its geographic location. The economies of these countries are less developed, and they do not trade significantly with the rest of the world. Despite the size of this region and the number of countries, it generated only about 5 percent of world trade in 2000. Russia, no doubt, is first in terms of production and is also the biggest trader in this region. Its trade volume in 2000 was $155.2 billion, more than twice that of the second biggest trading nation in the region, Poland ($77.4 billion). Turkey followed at $76.9 billion, Hungary at $60.5 billion, and the Czech Republic at $60.1 billion. None of the other countries in this region had a trade volume of more than $30 billion.

Russia experienced a financial crisis and a sharp devaluation of its currency in 1998. The near collapse of its economy and the lack of foreign currency reserves greatly diminished Russia's ability to purchase foreign products. In 2000 Russia still faced serious domestic economic problems. Other transition economies had their share of problems related to moving toward free markets. One positive factor regarding foreign trade is that these nations are privatizing state-run enterprises, which allows for more flexibility in production and trade with other countries.

North Africa and the Middle East

The biggest traders in this region in 2000 were Saudi Arabia ($109.8 billion) and the United Arab Emirates ($71.4 billion), both of which are important petroleum exporting countries. The next biggest trading country was Israel, with a trade volume of $63.5 billion. Israel, which is not a petroleum exporter, is the most advanced country in this region in terms of trade diversity and viability. Other countries have much smaller trade volumes. For example, in 2000 the combined trade volume of the next three biggest traders was less than that of Saudi Arabia: Iran at $36.7 billion; Algeria at $31.5 billion; and Egypt at $25.7 billion.

Algeria, Iran, Iraq, Kuwait, Libya, Qatar, Saudi Arabia, and the United Arab Emirates are members of the Organization of Petroleum Exporting Countries (OPEC). (The other members are Indonesia, Nigeria, and Venezuela.) Petroleum is the most important export of these countries, and thus their ability to earn foreign reserves depends largely on demand for oil, which in turn is linked to economic conditions (see ENERGY). For example, the Asian economic crisis in 1997 caused a substantial drop in Asian oil imports.

Sub-Saharan Africa

With the exception of Nigeria and South Africa, countries in sub-Saharan Africa are not big foreign traders. In 2000 South Africa's trade volume was $57.9 billion and Nigeria's was $30.1 billion. All other sub-Saharan countries had a combined trade volume of less than $10 billion. South Africa is the most economically developed nation in this region, while Nigeria is a member of OPEC and depends on petroleum exports for foreign reserves. All the other countries in the region are less developed and smaller. Furthermore, these sub-Saharan nations are not well positioned to trade with other countries because of domestic, economic, and political problems and a severe lack of efficient financial systems and transportation infrastructure.

Central and South Asia

Like Sub-Saharan Africa, Central and South Asia are relatively isolated economically from the rest of the world. For most countries in this region, foreign trade is not important. Bhutan, Mongolia, and Nepal are geographically isolated and other countries—such as Afghanistan—have such severe domestic problems that their ability to focus on economic development, let alone international trade, is nearly nonexistent. They also lack the transportation infrastructure and financial systems necessary to support large-scale trade activities.

India and Pakistan have the biggest economies and are major trading nations. In 2000 India, the second most populous country in the world, had a trade volume of $92.9 billion, which was more than that of all the other countries in this region combined. Yet India's trade volume was a mere 0.7 percent of the world total. Pakistan's trade volume came in a distant second, at $19.6 billion.

East Asia and the Pacific

The economies in this region share an important feature: Most, if not all, trade heavily with other countries. The biggest trader is Japan, which had a trade volume of $860.9 billion in 2000. With the competitive edge of many of its products and continuous technological improvements, Japan is the second biggest exporter in the world and has maintained trade surpluses for years. China is the second largest trader in this region, with a trade volume of $604.5 billion, a surprisingly small figure given that its population is much larger than Japan's. It should be noted, however, that China only opened its doors to foreign trade and foreign investment around 1979. Its economy and foreign trade have since been rising rapidly and steadily.

Hong Kong, Singapore, South Korea, and Taiwan, four newly industrialized economies, are well known for their high rates of growth and aggressiveness in promoting exports. Other Asian economies, including those of Indonesia, Malaysia, the Philippines, and Thailand have been following similar paths in promoting trade and growth. Australia, the big economy in the Southern Hemisphere, is more self-reliant, with a relatively small trade volume, and is an important trading partner of New Zealand.

Most countries in this region are members of the Asia-Pacific Economic Cooperation forum, or APEC, of which Canada, Chile, Mexico, Peru, Russia, and the United States are also members. APEC was established in 1989 to promote trade opportunities and economic cooperation among its members. It is expected that foreign trade will continue to be important factor to the growth of these economies.

Data

Table 1 Trade of Selected Countries in Billions of Dollars, 2000

Country	Exports	Imports	Trade Balance	Trade Volume
Algeria	21.93	9.58	12.35	31.51
Argentina	27.86	23.30	4.56	51.16
Australia	66.48	67.25	–0.77	133.73
Austria	62.94	67.49	–4.55	130.43
Belgium	157.84	160.91	–3.07	318.75
Brazil	62.27	58.28	3.99	120.55
Canada	274.26	247.50	26.76	521.76
Chile	20.58	16.39	4.19	36.97
China	392.32	212.17	180.15	604.49
Colombia	14.67	10.15	4.52	24.82
Congo, Democratic Republic of	1.37	0.71	0.66	2.08
Czech Republic	28.91	31.22	–2.31	60.13
Denmark	44.95	42.29	2.66	87.24
Egypt	5.99	19.70	–13.71	25.69
Finland	46.51	34.48	12.03	80.99
France	321.72	314.20	7.52	635.92
Georgia	0.54	0.99	–0.45	1.53
Germany	561.35	470.12	91.23	1,031.47
Guatemala	4.75	5.30	–0.55	10.05
Hong Kong	116.65	187.87	–71.22	304.52
Hungary	29.18	31.28	–2.10	60.46
India	47.52	45.33	2.19	92.85
Indonesia	66.78	31.87	34.91	98.65
Iran	24.01	12.69	11.32	36.70
Ireland	79.78	46.68	33.10	126.46
Israel	30.83	32.62	–1.79	63.45
Italy	236.00	227.04	8.96	463.04
Japan	517.87	343.00	174.87	860.87
Korea	178.50	136.52	41.98	315.02
Malaysia	118.80	82.97	35.83	201.77
Mexico	163.05	143.36	19.69	306.41
Netherlands	216.55	213.32	3.23	429.87
Nigeria	22.35	7.77	14.58	30.12
Norway	59.93	28.77	31.16	88.70
Philippines	45.71	44.98	0.73	90.69
Poland	29.63	47.73	–18.10	77.36
Portugal	25.26	39.77	–14.51	65.03
Russia	116.98	38.25	78.73	155.23
Saudi Arabia	75.33	34.46	40.87	109.79
Singapore	123.74	128.62	–4.88	252.36
South Africa	32.12	25.81	6.31	57.93
Spain	112.18	149.94	–37.76	262.12
Sweden	89.01	70.40	18.61	159.41
Switzerland	99.83	95.29	4.54	195.12
Tajikistan	1.28	0.66	0.62	1.94
Thailand	72.59	52.91	19.68	125.50

Table 1 Trade of Selected Countries in Billions of Dollars, 2000 (*continued*)

Country	Exports	Imports	Trade Balance	Trade Volume
Turkey	28.08	48.80	–20.72	76.88
Uganda	0.39	0.85	–0.46	1.24
United Arab Emirates	36.16	35.20	0.96	71.36
United Kingdom	286.48	338.69	–52.21	625.17
United States	835.82	1,189.64	–353.82	2,025.46
Venezuela	29.57	14.65	14.92	44.22

Source: International Monetary Fund, *Directions of Trade Statistics* (Washington, D.C.: IMF, 2001).

Table 2 Trade of Various Regions in Billions of Dollars, 2000

Region	Export	Import	Balance	Volume	Percentage of Volume
North America	1,273.13	1,580.50	–307.37	2,853.63	22.75
Latin America	212.91	202.58	10.33	415.49	3.31
Western Europe	2,425.24	2,351.07	74.17	4,776.31	38.08
Eastern Europe	314.31	299.03	15.28	613.34	4.89
Middle East and North Africa	278.96	194.39	84.57	473.35	3.77
Sub-Saharan Africa	94.84	80.08	14.76	166.30	1.33
Central and South Asia	86.08	87.25	–1.17	173.33	1.38
Pacific	1,742.08	1,328.55	413.53	3,070.63	24.48
World	6,427.55	6,123.45	304.10	12,542.38	100.00

Source: International Monetary Fund, *Directions of Trade Statistics* (Washington, D.C.: IMF, 2001).

Case Study—GATT and WTO

In 1947 twenty-three countries formed the General Agreement on Tariffs and Trade (GATT). The agreement called for member countries to engage in multilateral negotiations on reducing trade restrictions. Since that time, GATT has conducted eight rounds of trade talks. The two most successful rounds were the Kennedy Round (1962–1967), after which member states' tariffs on manufactured products were reduced by an average of 35 percent, and the Tokyo Round (1974–1979), after which the average tariff on manufacturing products in the United States dropped to 4.3 percent, in Canada to 5.2 percent, in France to 6.0 percent, in Japan to 2.9 percent, in the United Kingdom to 5.2 percent, and in West Germany to 6.3 percent.

In 1986 GATT initiated the Uruguay Round of talks with the primary objective of easing restrictions on trade in services and agricultural products. The negotiations quickly ran into resistance, especially from European countries, over subsidy reductions for agricultural products. An agreement was finally reached by 117 countries on 15 December 1993. It took effect on 1

January 1995. One of the provisions of the Uruguay Round was to replace GATT with a new trade group, the World Trade Organization (WTO). The WTO was charged with supervising implementation of the Uruguay Round agreement and conducting new multilateral trade liberalization talks covering more goods and services than GATT did.

In structuring multilateral trade liberalization, GATT and the WTO play a unique role that no single country is capable of doing (see Document 2). If countries were to follow a host of independent policies, they would be inclined toward trade wars. An international organization such as GATT or WTO can provide coordination, enforce trade liberalization mechanisms, and supervise trade agreements. The WTO and its efforts to strengthen its global reach, however, have come under a great deal of criticism in recent years. As large companies have gained access to more markets through increased trade liberalization, their power has increased. These corporations can make noneconomic objectives recognized by many nations and worldwide institutions, such as environmental protection and fair labor standards, harder to implement. Since noneconomic goals often have a negative impact on profits, companies often resist incorporating them into their strategies.

Perhaps the most controversial feature of the WTO is its ability to settle trade disputes between member countries. Critics argue that nations lose part of their sovereignty by allowing the WTO to evaluate and adjudicate the validity of their trade policies and sometimes even domestic policies. This potential loss of sovereignty is complicated by the perception that the WTO is not a truly fair and representative organization, but one ruled by the few large economies of the world. The most extreme criticism, perhaps, is that due to the political pressure that large corporations often exert on their governments' trade representatives through lobbying efforts, the decisions of the WTO are in danger of being made not by objective economic judges, but by parties interested in promoting their own economic welfare over the welfare of the world.

Biographical Sketches

Jagdish Bhagwati of Columbia University is one of most influential trade theorists. He has made important contributions to the theory of distortion, trade policy analysis, economic welfare, immigration, and relations between political economy and trade policy. In 1971 he founded the *Journal of International Economics,* the preeminent journal in the field. Bhagwati later founded another journal, *Economics and Politics,* with a focus on the relationship between economics and political science. He has served as economic policy adviser to the director-general of GATT and is currently special adviser to the United Nations on globalization and an external adviser to the WTO.

Elhanan Helpman has made significant contributions to the so-called new theory of international trade, which emphasizes imperfect competition and certain types of technologies. In 1981 he demonstrated how intraindustry trade (the simultaneous export and import of similar products) and interindustry trade (the export and import of different products) can be analyzed in a single framework. In 1984 he published an authoritative survey on the theory of international trade with imperfect competition.

Ronald Winthrop Jones has published numerous papers analyzing issues of international trade within the neoclassical and related frameworks. He has also made important contributions to the theory of externality, international factor movement, and more recently fragmentation of production and trade.

Murray C. Kemp has made considerable contributions to trade theory, welfare economics, the theory of externality, and international capital movement. One of his 1962 papers, published in *Economic Journal,* along with work by Paul Samuelson, ignited interest in issues related to the welfare effects of foreign trade. In 1996 he published what is considered one of the first works to extend the traditional framework of international trade to international capital movement.

Paul Krugman is an important figure in the new theory of international trade. In 1979 in the *Journal of International Economics* he highlighted some of the important features of monopolistic competition and intraindustry trade in differentiated products. His other contributions include work on exchange rates and target zones, currency crises, and economic geography. In 1991 the American Economic Association awarded him the John Bates Clark medal, which is given once every two years to "that American economist under forty who is adjudged to have made a significant contribution to economic thought and knowledge."

Paul Anthony Samuelson is a member of the economics faculty at the Massachusetts Institute of Technology and an influential writer in many fields, including international trade, consumer theory, welfare economics, capital theory, dynamics, mathematical economics, public finance, and macroeconomics. His contributions to the theory of international trade include factor price equalization, social welfare, and social utility, gains from trade, and the Stolper-Samuelson theorem. He was awarded the Nobel Prize in Economics in 1970.

Directory

Asia-Pacific Economic Cooperation, 438 Alexandra Road, Suite 14-00, Alexandra Point, Singapore 119958. Telephone: (65) 276 1880, Email: info@mail.apecsec.org.sg, Web: http://www.apecsec.org.sg
Primary regional vehicle for promoting open trade and practical economic cooperation with the goal of advancing Asia-Pacific economic growth and community

Association of Southeast Asian Nations, 70A Jalan Sisingamangaraja, Jakarta 12110, Indonesia. Fax: (62) 21 7398234, 7243504, Web: http://www.aseansec.org
Regional organization promoting economic growth, social progress, and cultural development and collaboration on matters of common interest to Southeast Asian states

Fair Trade Federation, 1612 K Street NW, Suite 600, Washington, DC 20006. Telephone: (202) 872-5329, Web: http://www.fairtradefederation.com
Association of fair trade wholesalers, retailers, and producers committed to providing fair wages and employment opportunities to economically disadvantaged artisans and farmers worldwide

International Monetary Fund, 700 19th Street NW, Washington, DC 20431. Telephone: (202) 623-7000, Web: http://www.imf.org
Organization established to promote international monetary cooperation, foster economic growth and high levels of employment, and provide temporary financial assistance to countries to ease balance of payment adjustments

Organization for Economic Cooperation and Development, 2 Rue André Pascal, 75775 Paris Cedex 16, France. Telephone: (33) 1 45 24 8200, Web: http://www.oecd.org
Thirty-member organization promoting economic cooperation and development, plays a prominent role in fostering good governance in public service and corporate activity

Organization of Petroleum Exporting Countries, 93 Obere Donaustrasse, 1020 Vienna, Austria. Telephone: (43) 1 21112 279, Web: http://www.opec.org
Cartel of eleven developing countries heavily reliant on oil revenues as a source of income

World Trade Organization, 154 Rue de Lausanne, 1211 Geneva 21, Switzerland. Telephone: (41) 22 739 5111, Email: enquiries@wto.org, Web: http://www.wto.org
Organization dealing with the rules of trade between nations, helps producers of goods and services, exporters, and importers conduct business

Further Research

Books

Appleyard, Dennis R., and Alfred J. Field. *International Economics.* Boston: Irwin/McGraw-Hill, 2001.

Bhagwati, Jagdish N. *Protectionism.* Cambridge, Mass.: MIT Press, 1988.

———. *A Stream of Windows.* Cambridge, Mass.: MIT Press, 1998.

Bhagwati, Jagdish N., Arvind Panagariya, and T. N. Srinivasan. *Lectures on International Trade.* Cambridge, Mass.: MIT Press, 1998.

Caves, Richard E., Jeffrey A. Frankel, and Ronald W. Jones. *World Trade and Payments: An Introduction.* New York: Harper Collins College Publishers, 1993.

Ethier, Wilfred J. *Modern International Economics.* New York: W. W. Norton, 1995.

Krueger, Anne O., ed. *The WTO as an International Organization.* Chicago: University of Chicago Press, 1998.

Krugman, Paul. *Pop Internationalism.* Cambridge, Mass.: MIT Press, 1998.

Krugman Paul, and Maurice Obstfeld. *International Economics: Theory and Policy.* Reading, Mass.: Addison-Wesley, 2000.

Roberts, Russell. *The Choice: A Fable of Free Trade and Protectionism.* Upper Saddle River, N.J.: Prentice Hall, 2001.

Rodrik, Dani. *Has Globalization Gone Too Far?* Washington, D.C.: Institute for International Economics, 1997.

Schott, Jeffrey J. ed. *The Uruguay Round: An Assessment.* Washington, D.C.: Institute for International Economics, 1994.

———, ed. *The World Trading System: Challenges Ahead.* Washington, D.C.: Institute for International Economics, 1996.

Whalley, John, and Colleen Hamilton. *The Trading System after the Uruguay Round.* Washington, D.C.: Institute for International Economics, 1996.

Wong, Kar-yiu. *International Trade in Goods and Factor Mobility.* Cambridge, Mass.: MIT Press, 1995.

Articles and Reports

Bhagwati, Jagdish N. "The Generalized Theory of Distortions and Welfare." In *Trade, Balance of Payments, and Growth: Papers in International Economics in Honor of Charles P. Kindleberger,* edited by Jagdish N. Bhagwati et al., 69–90. Amsterdam: North Holland Company, 1971.

Bhagwati, Jagdish N., and T. N. Srinivasan. "Optimal Intervention to Achieve Non-Economic Objectives." *Review of Economic Studies* 36 (1969): 27–38.

Brander, James A., and Paul R. Krugman. "A 'Reciprocal Dumping' Model of International Trade." *Journal of International Economics* 15 (1983): 313–323.

Brander, James A., and Barbara J. Spencer. "Export Subsidies and International Market Share Rivalry." *Journal of International Economics* 18 (1985): 83–100.

Eaton, Jonathan, and Gene M. Grossman. "Optimal Trade and Industrial Policy under Oligopoly." *Quarterly Journal of Economics* 101 (1986): 383–406.

Grossman, Gene M. "Strategic Export Promotion: A Critique." In *Strategic Trade Policy and the New International Economics,* edited by Paul R. Krugman, 47–68. Cambridge, Mass.: MIT Press, 1986.

International Monetary Fund. *Directions of Trade Statistics.* Washington, D.C.: IMF, 2001.

Kemp, Murray C., and Henry Y. Wan, Jr. "An Elementary Proposition concerning the Formation of Customs Unions." *Journal of International Economics* 6 (1976): 95–97.

Samuelson, Paul A. "The Gains from International Trade Once Again." *Economic Journal* 72 (1962): 820–829.

U.S. International Trade Commission. "Assessment of the Economic Effects on the United States of China's Accession to the WTO," 1999, ftp://ftp.usitc.gov/pub/reports/studies/pub3229.pdf.

Wong, Kar-yiu. "Welfare Comparison of Trade Situations." *Journal of International Economics* 30 (1991): 49–68.

Web Site

Asian Recovery Information Center
http://aric.adb.org

Documents

1. North American Free Trade Agreement

Passed by the governments of Canada, Mexico, and the United States, 1993; entered into force, 1994

The full text is available at http://www.nafta-sec-alena.org/english/index.htm.

Extract

Article 102

1. The objectives of this Agreement, as elaborated more specifically through its principles and rules, including national treatment, most-favored-nation treatment and transparency, are to:

a) eliminate barriers to trade in, and facilitate the cross-border movement of, goods and services between the territories of the Parties;

b) promote conditions of fair competition in the free trade area;

c) increase substantially investment opportunities in the territories of the Parties;

d) provide adequate and effective protection and enforcement of intellectual property rights in each Party's territory;

e) create effective procedures for the implementation and application of this Agreement, for its joint administration and for the resolution of disputes; and

f) establish a framework for further trilateral, regional and multilateral cooperation to expand and enhance the benefits of this Agreement.

2. Trading into the Future

World Trade Organization, 1999

The full text is available at http://www.wto.org/english/res_e/doload_e/tif.pdf.

Extract

The World Trade Organization (WTO) is the only international body dealing with the rules of trade between nations. At its heart are the WTO agreements, negotiated and signed by the bulk of the world's trading nations. These documents provide the legal ground-rules for international commerce. They are essentially contracts, binding governments to keep their trade policies within agreed limits. Although negotiated and signed by governments, the goal is to help producers of goods and services, exporters, and importers conduct their business.

The system's overriding purpose is to help trade flow as freely as possible—so long as there are no undesirable side effects. That partly means removing obstacles. It also means ensuring that individuals, companies and governments know what the trade rules are around the world, and giving them the confidence that there will be no sudden changes of policy. In other words, the rules have to be "transparent" and predictable. Because the agreements are drafted and signed by the community of trading nations, often after considerable debate and controversy, one of the WTO's most important functions is to serve as a forum for trade negotiations. A third important side to the WTO's work is dispute settlement. Trade relations often involve conflicting interests. Contracts and agreements, including those painstakingly negotiated in the WTO system, often need interpreting. The most harmonious way to settle these differences is through some neutral procedure based on an agreed legal foundation. That is the purpose behind the dispute settlement process written into the WTO agreements.

INDEX